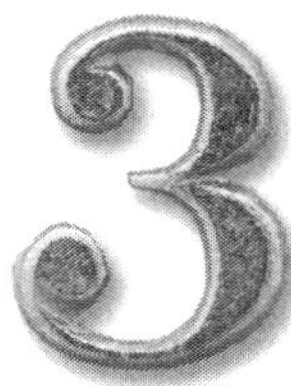

1095 Days of Drawings By Scott B. Jones

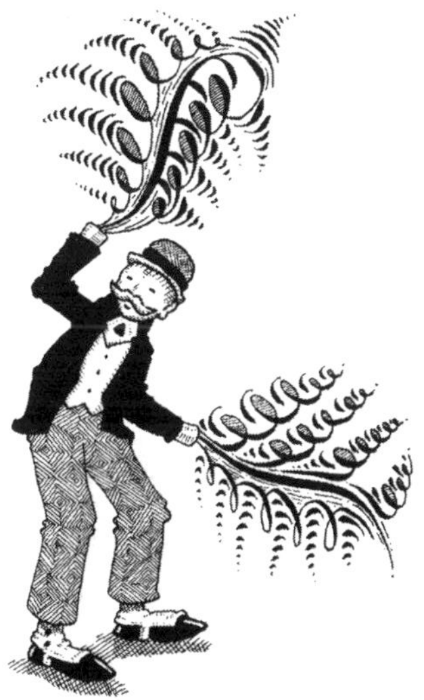

Dedicated to Susan E. Walker

That's the story, Harry!

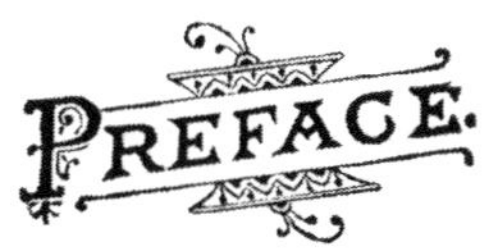

Greetings and welcome to my third book of illustrations. This volume contains 1095 days of drawings from 2017 followed by two earlier years of consecutive daily drawings from 2012 and 2013.

The first volume of this series, *Scott B. Jones: 365 Days of Drawings Plus One Comic Book* and the second volume, *2016. 2014.: 731 Days of Drawings From The Fountain Pen of Scott B. Jones* comprise the layers of content from the years 2014 through 2016.

Publishing the first book in 2015 without the forethought that I might want to continue publishing hard copies of a project consisting of daily drawings since January 1st, 2012 is the reason for the odd chronology of what should be consecutive years.

The summer of 2013 is when I began to use fountain pens to illustrate these books. Vintage (1920's and earlier) fountain pens are almost exclusively used in my work. They have proven to be an interesting tool to use. With no two nibs being exactly the same, they inspire and complement daily creativity on a mechanical level.

And that is that. Enjoy the book!

All the best,

Scott B. Jones

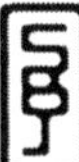

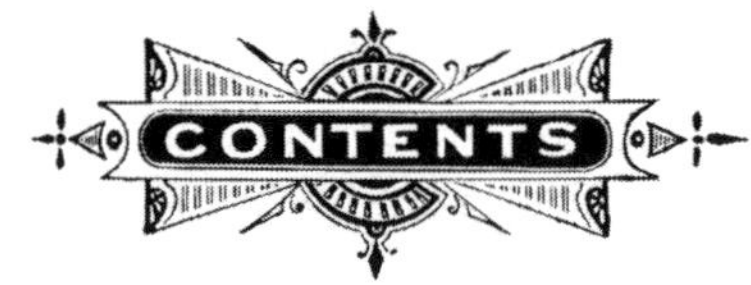
CONTENTS

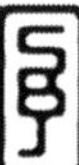

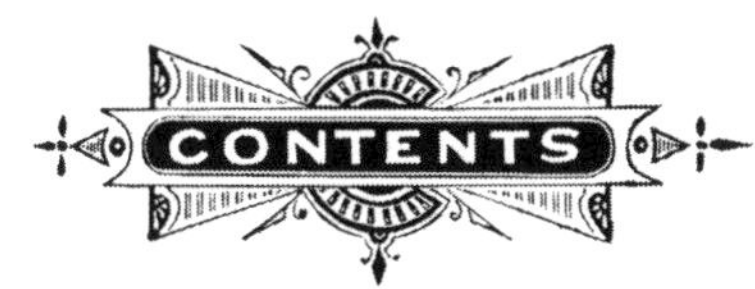

2013

JANUARY

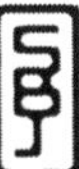

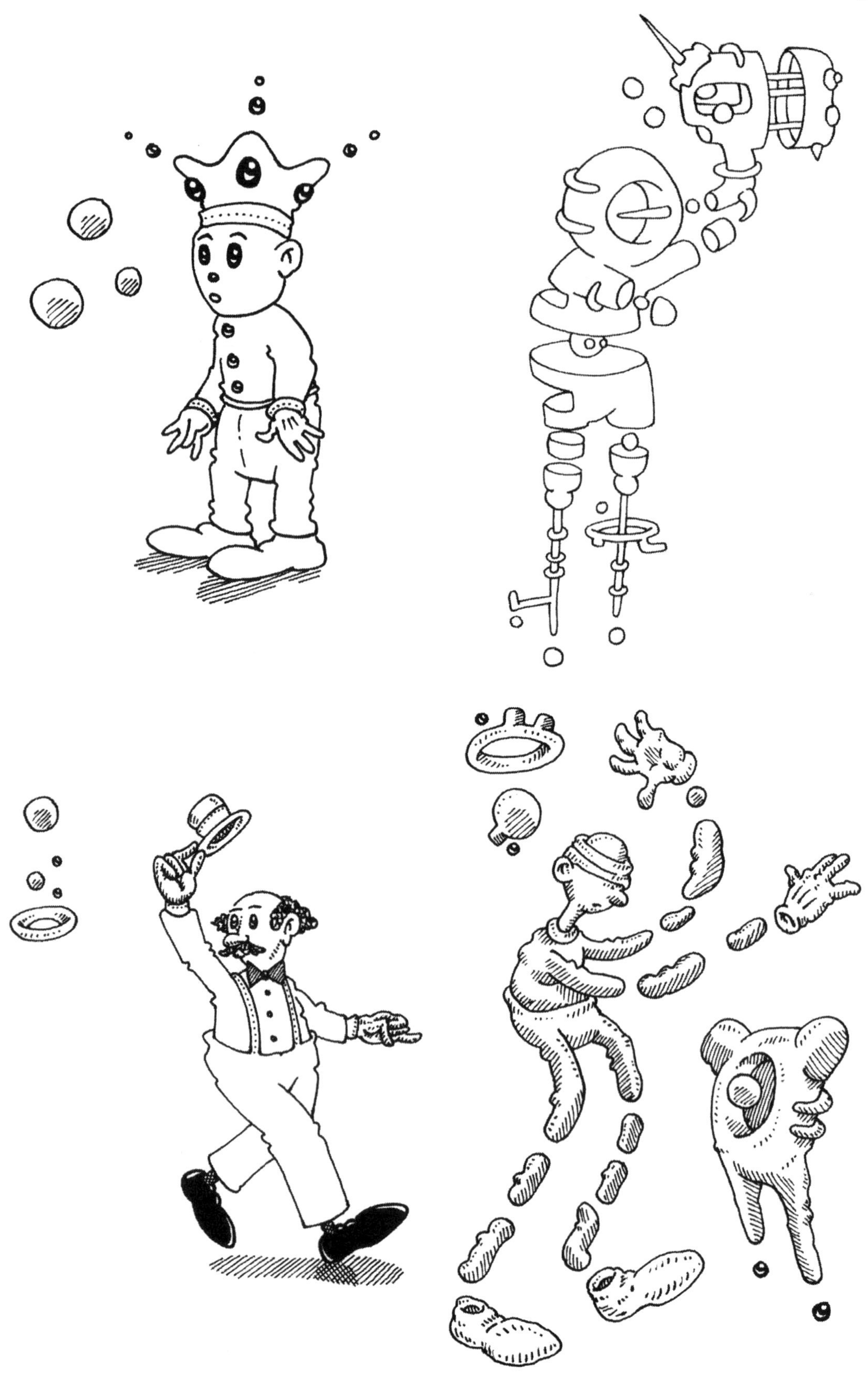

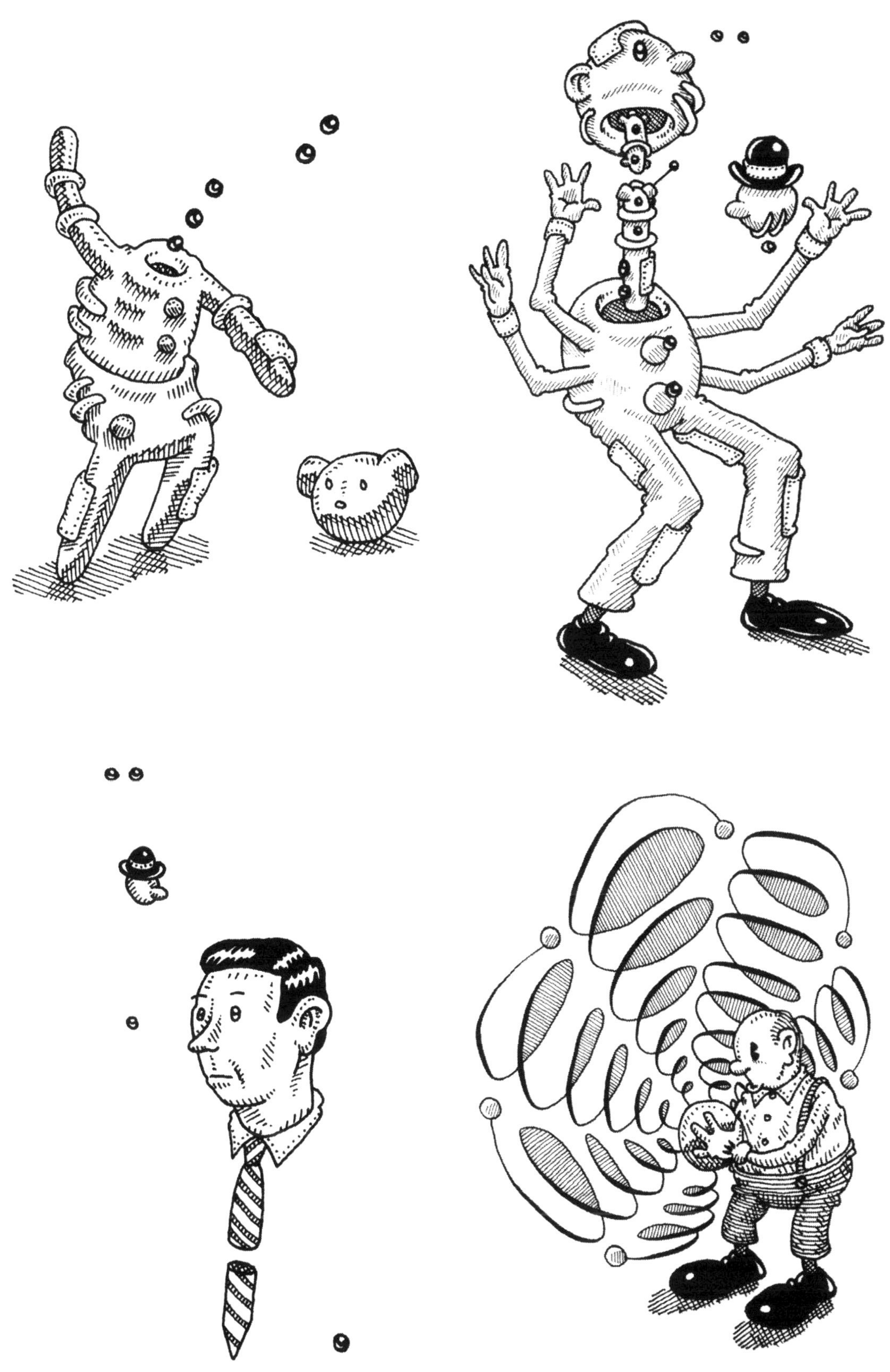

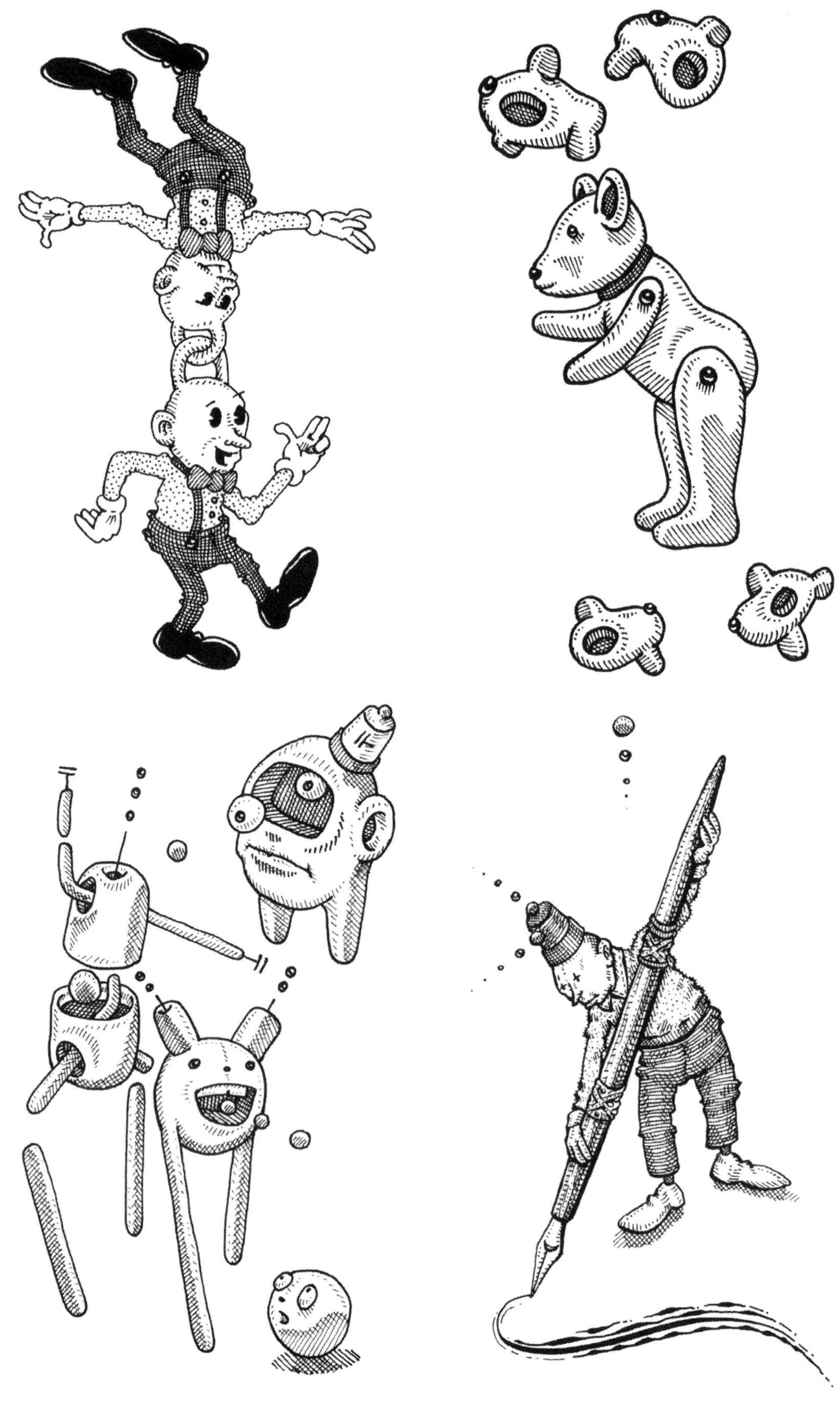

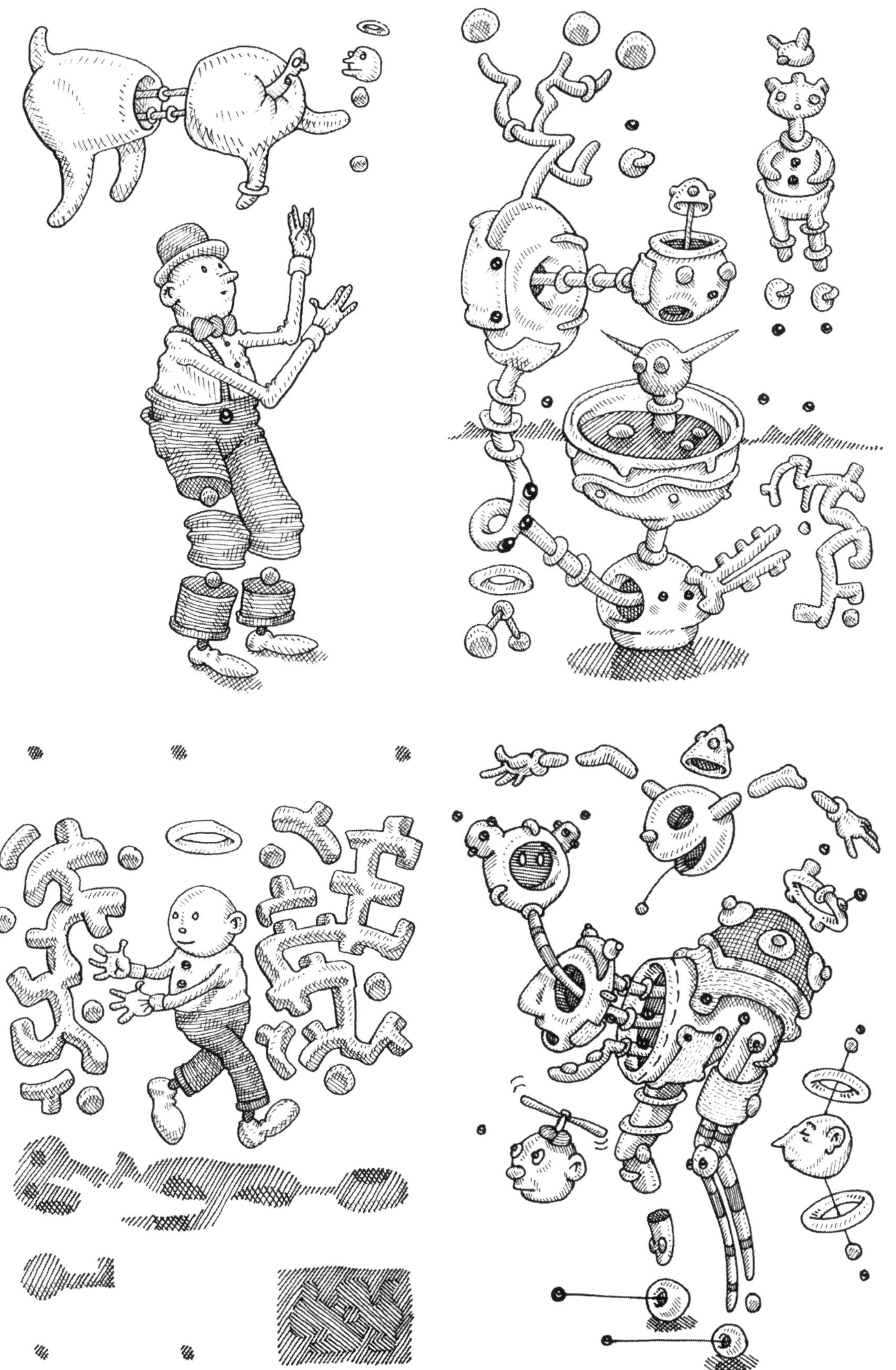

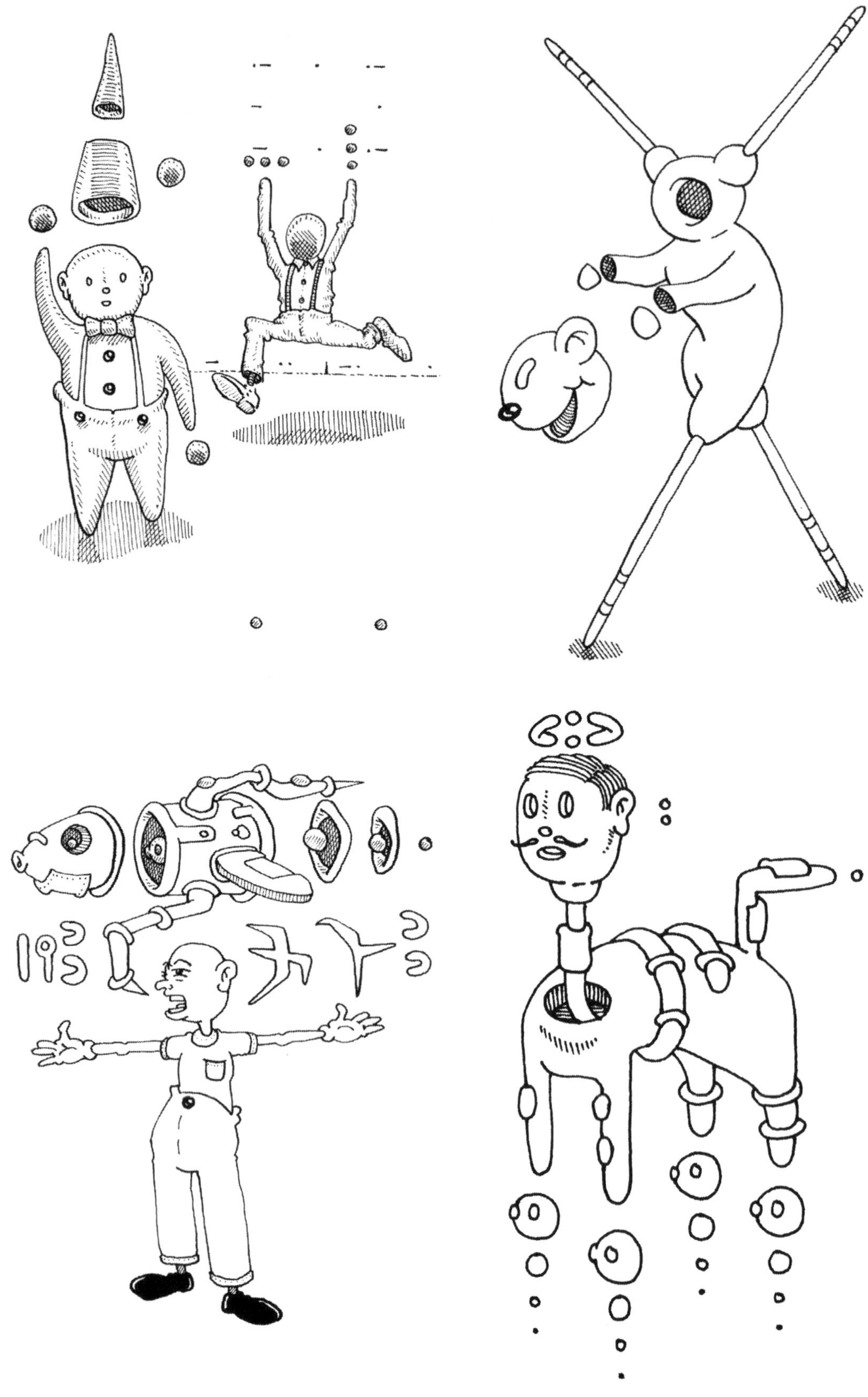

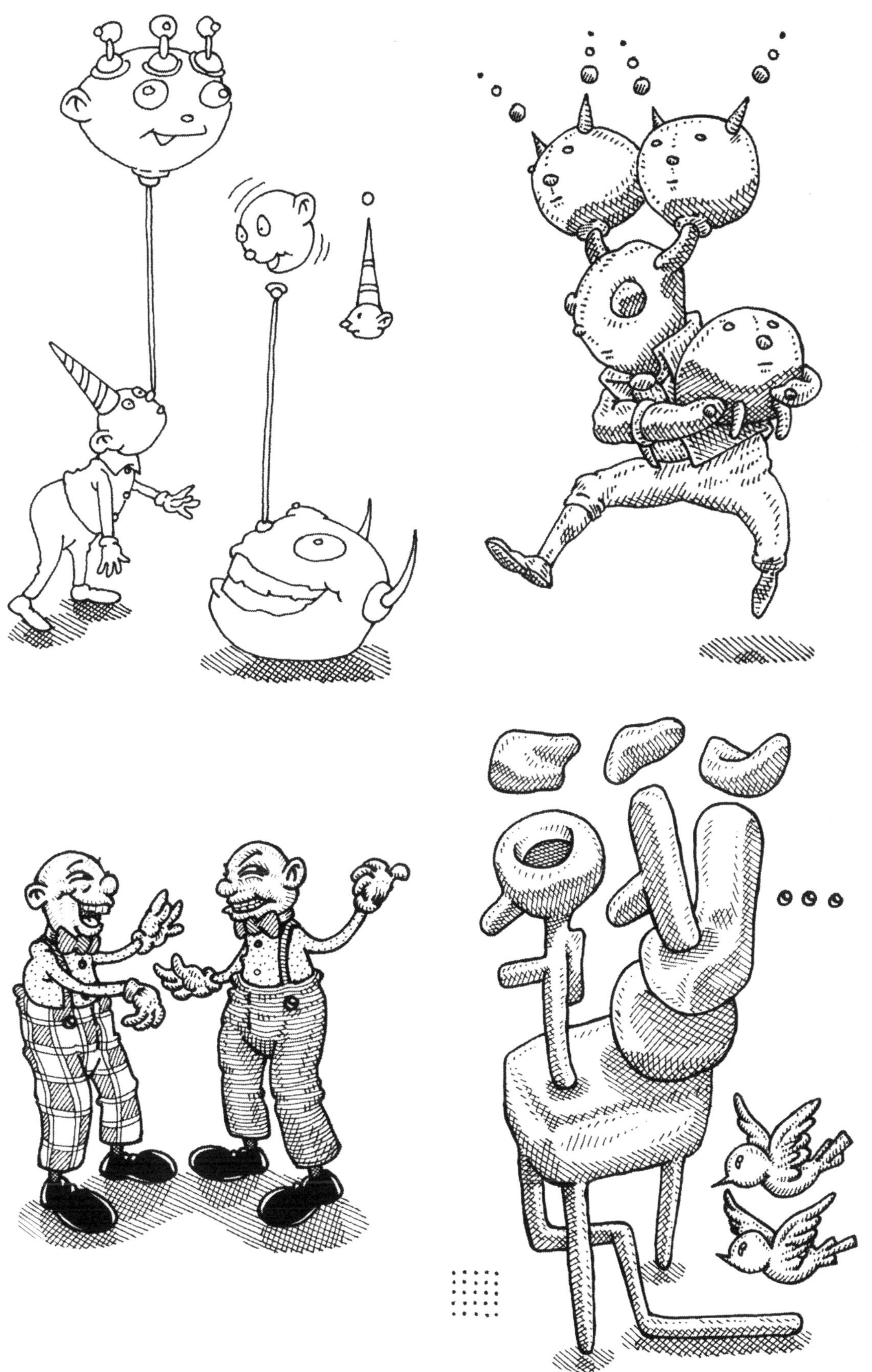

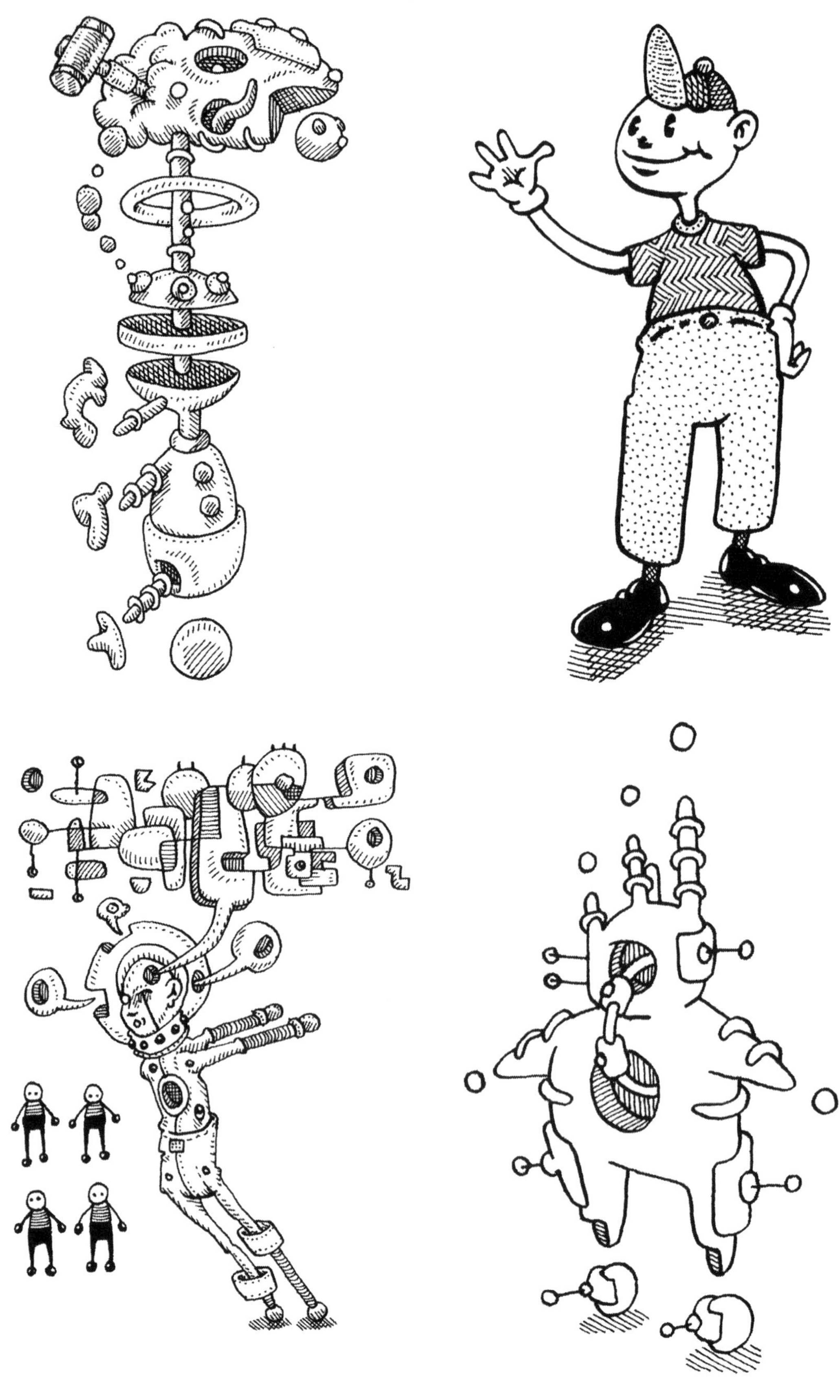

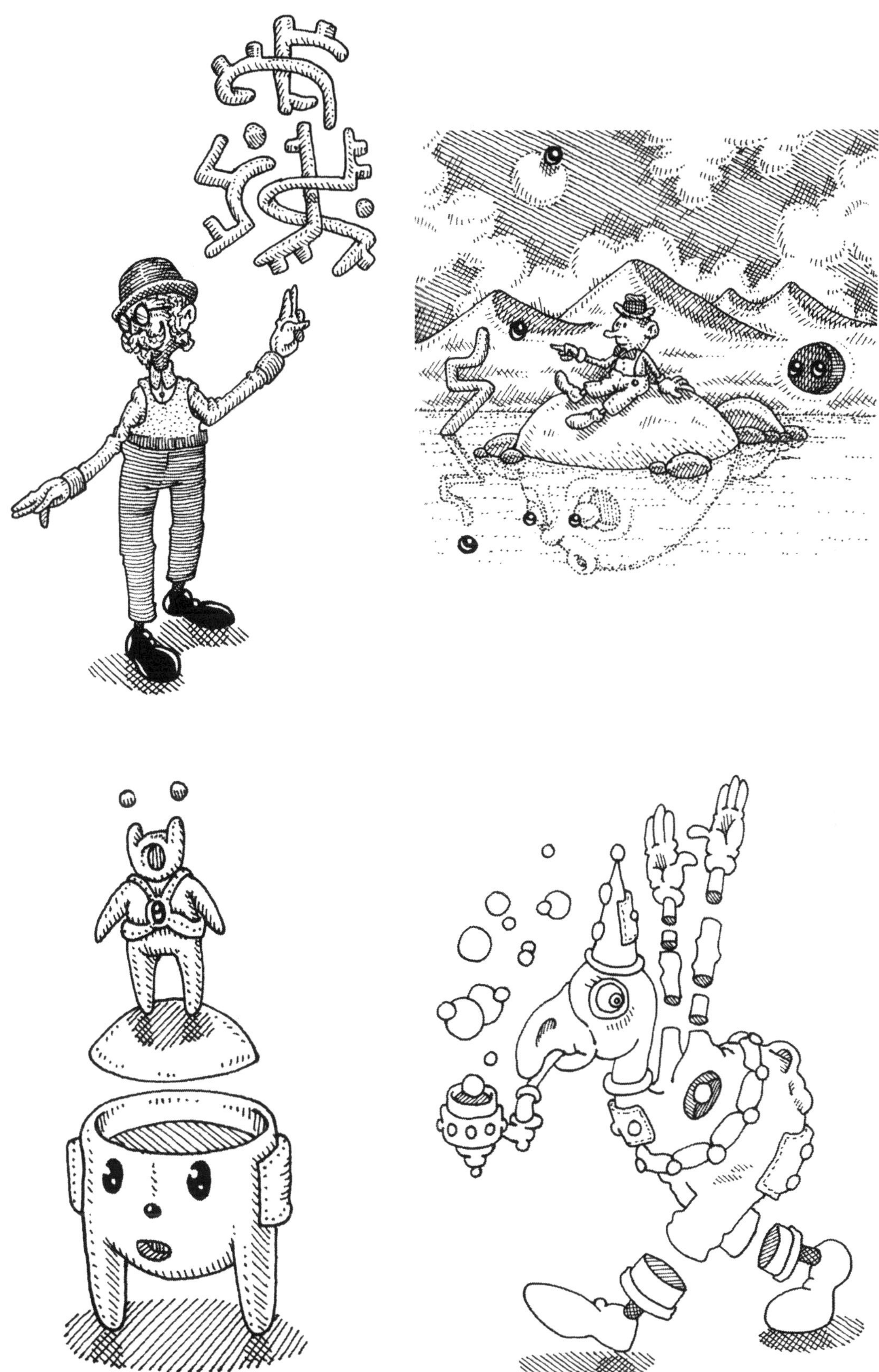

2017

February

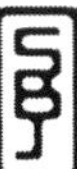

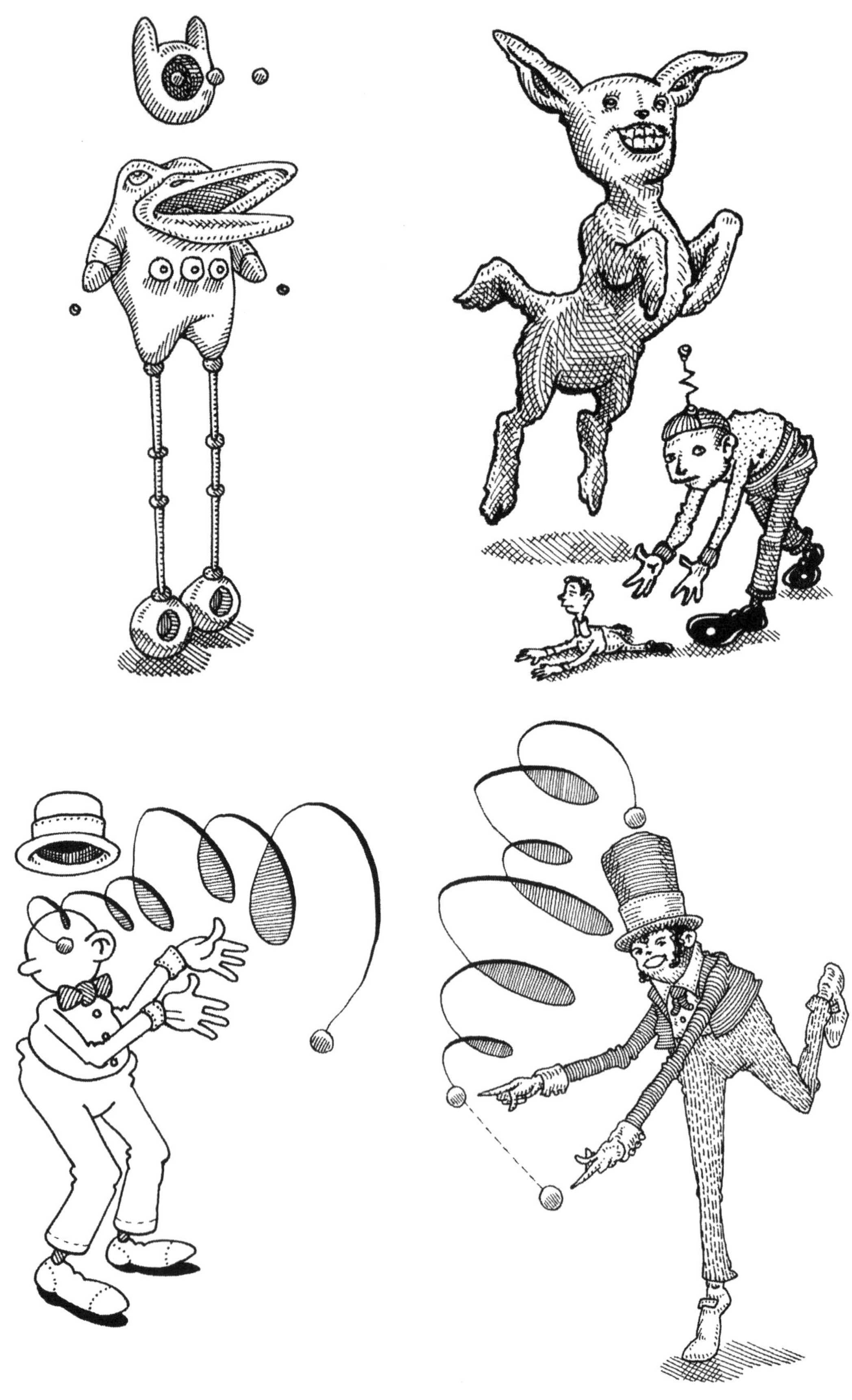

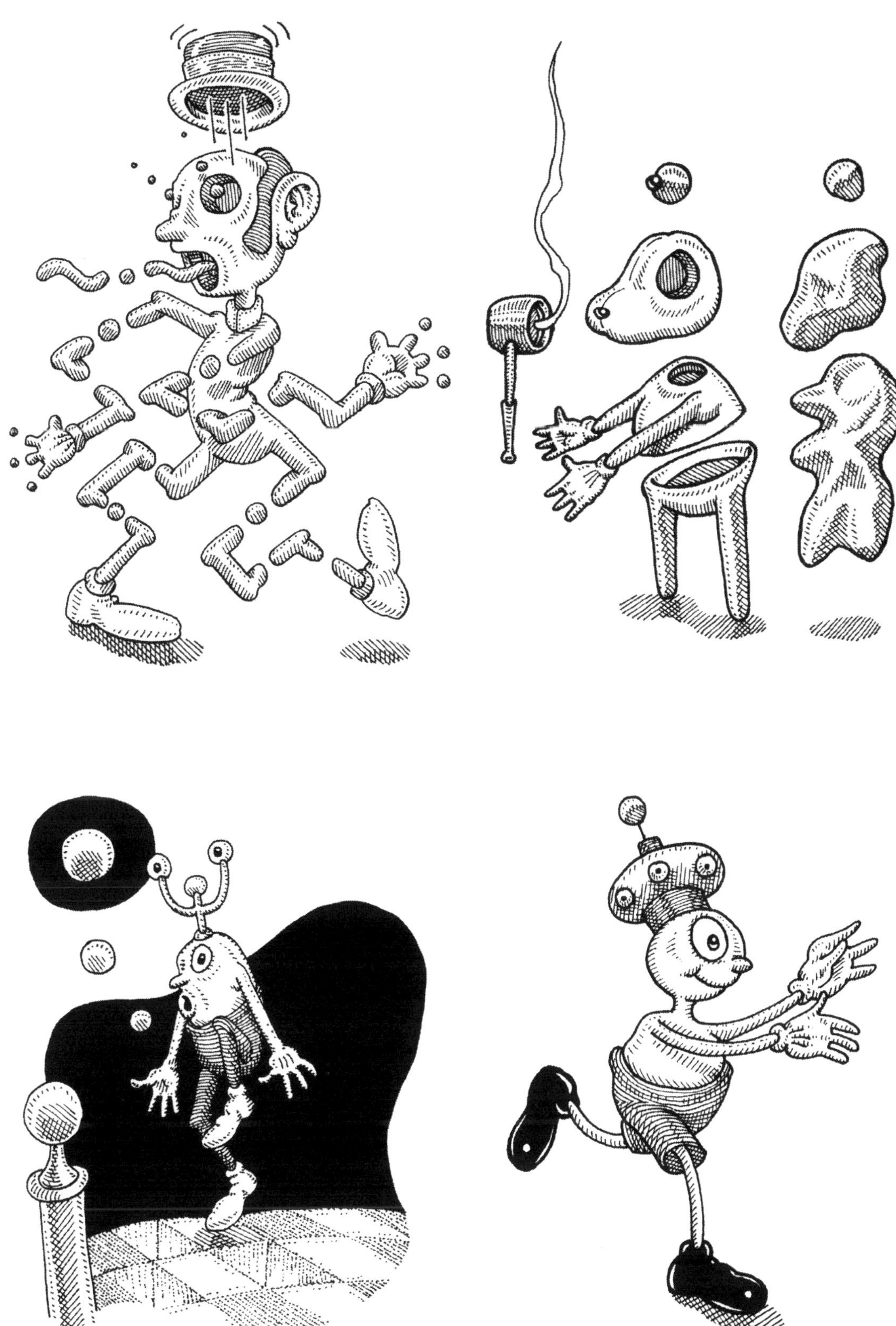

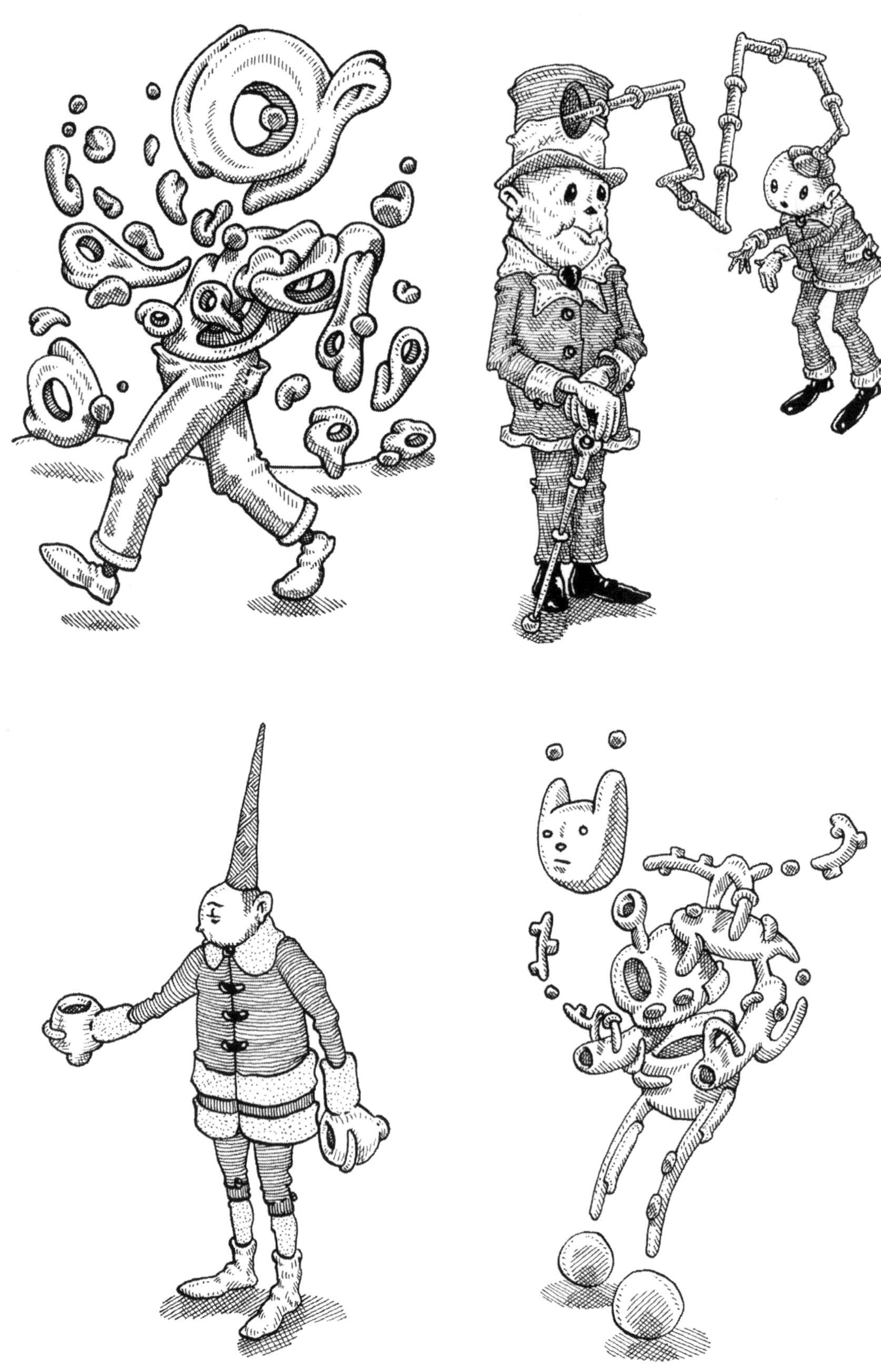

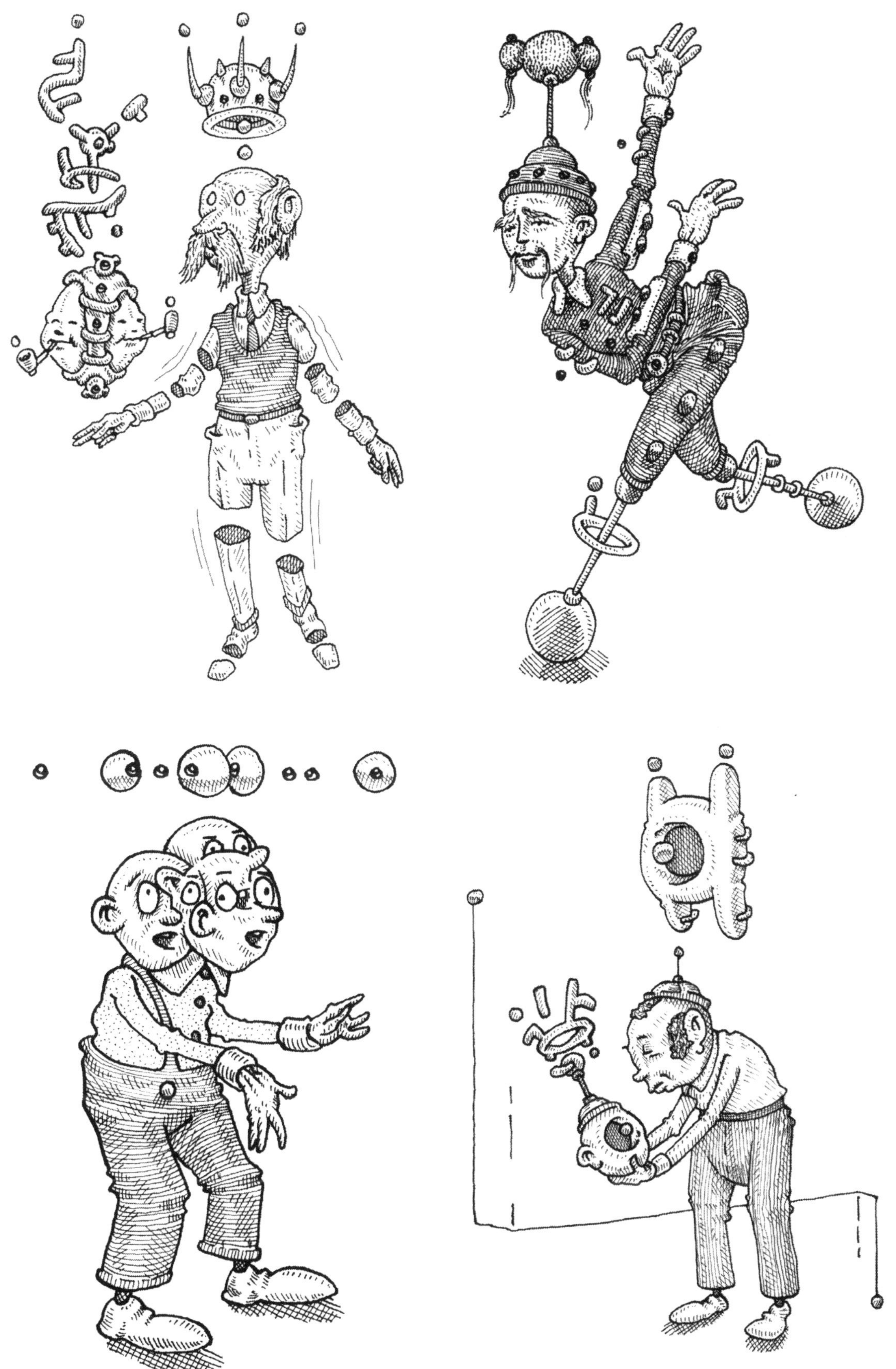

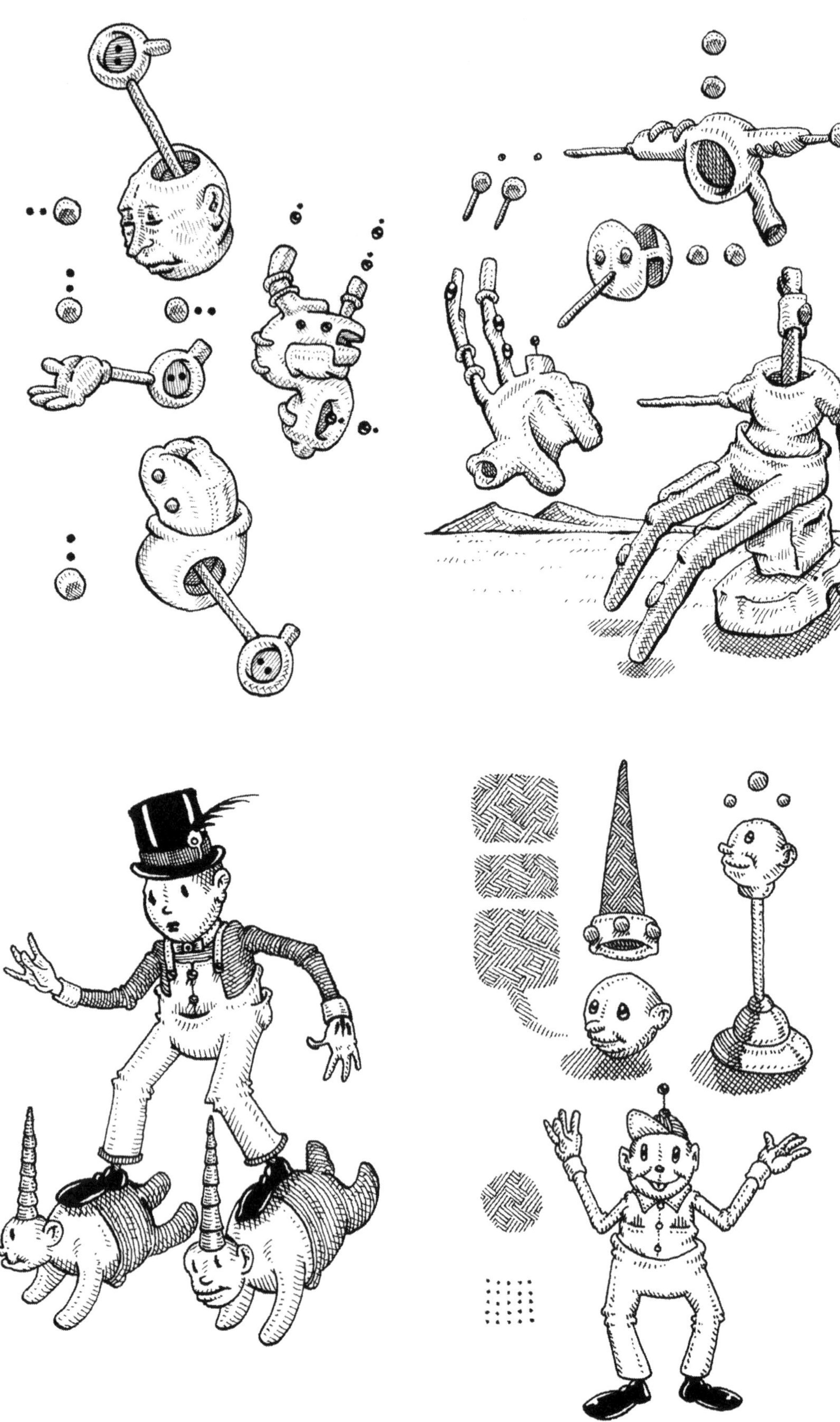

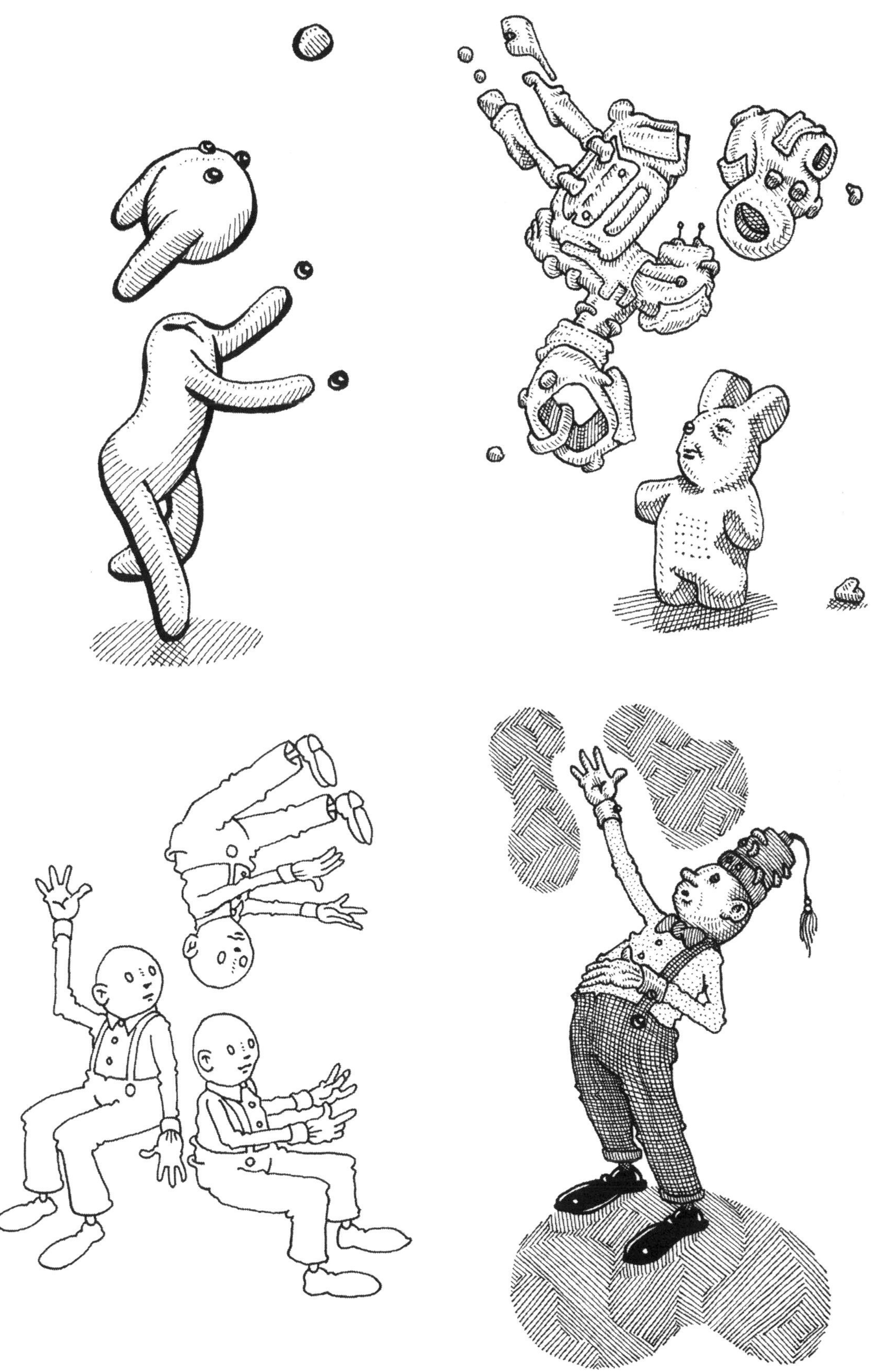

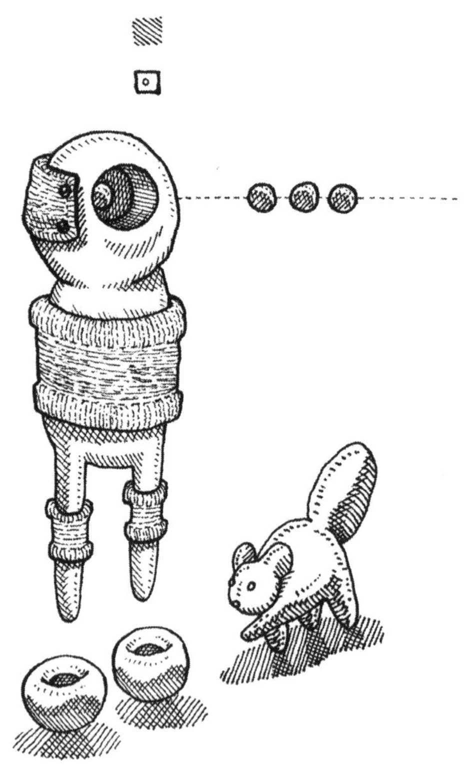

2017

March

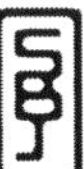

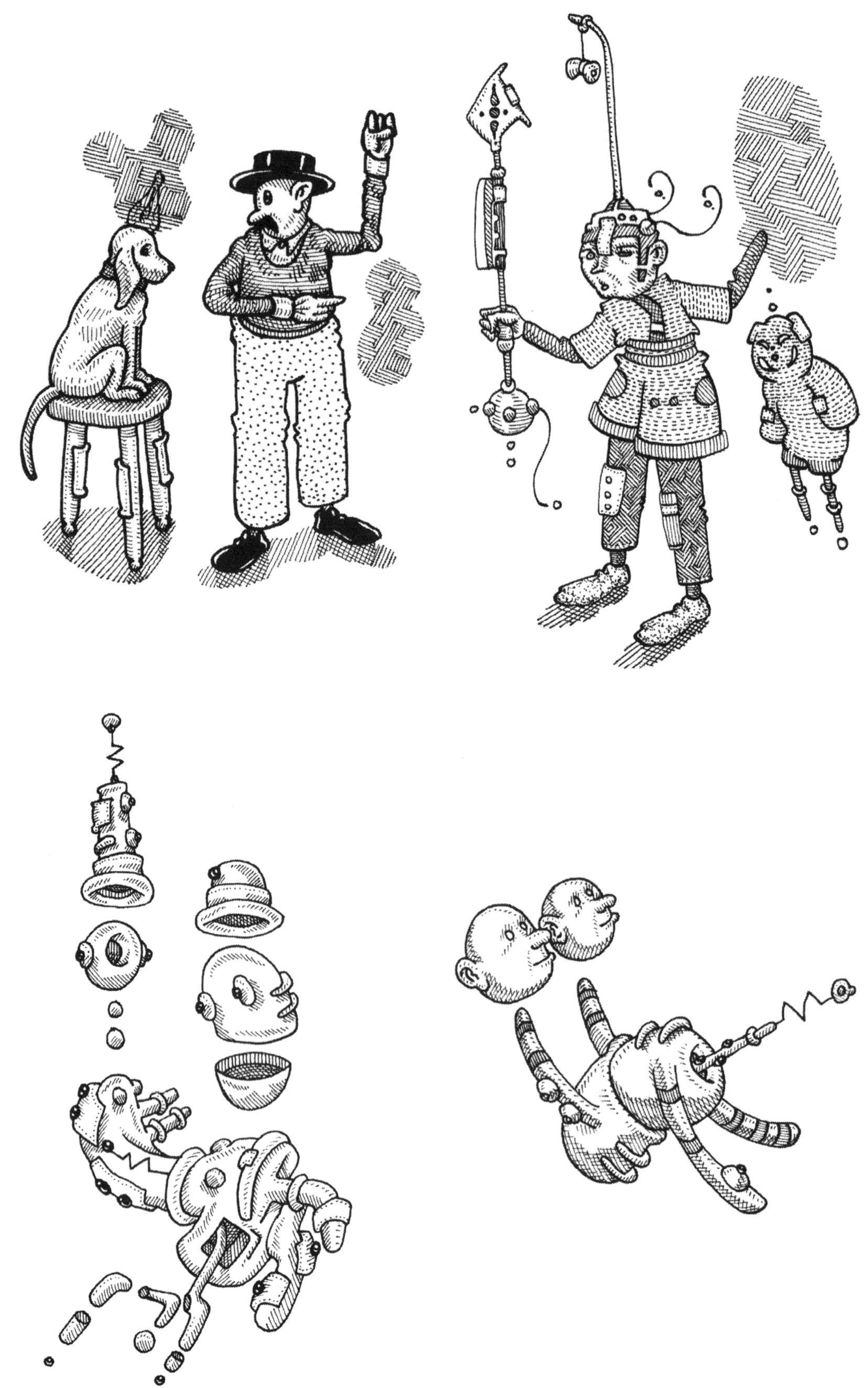

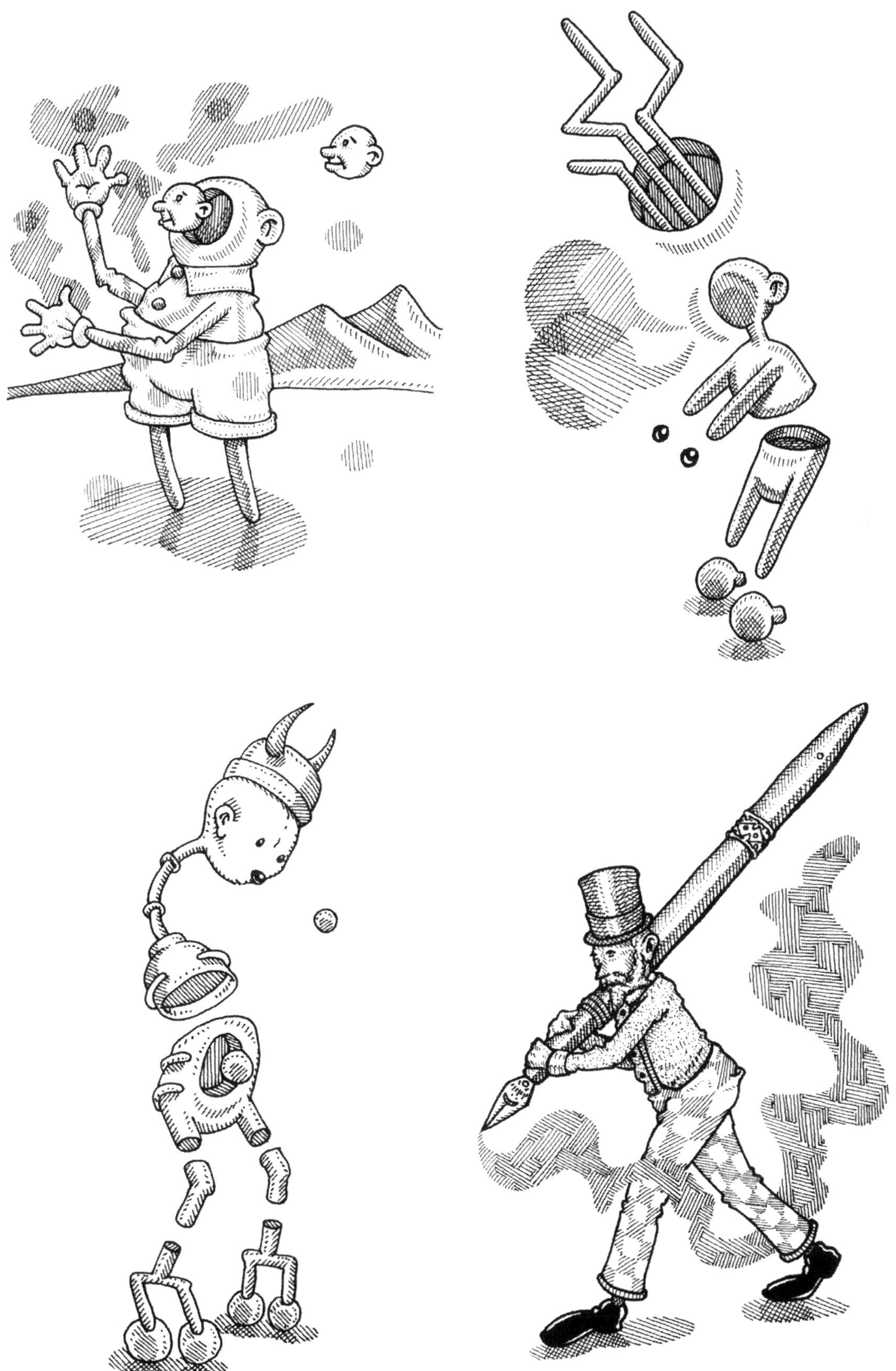

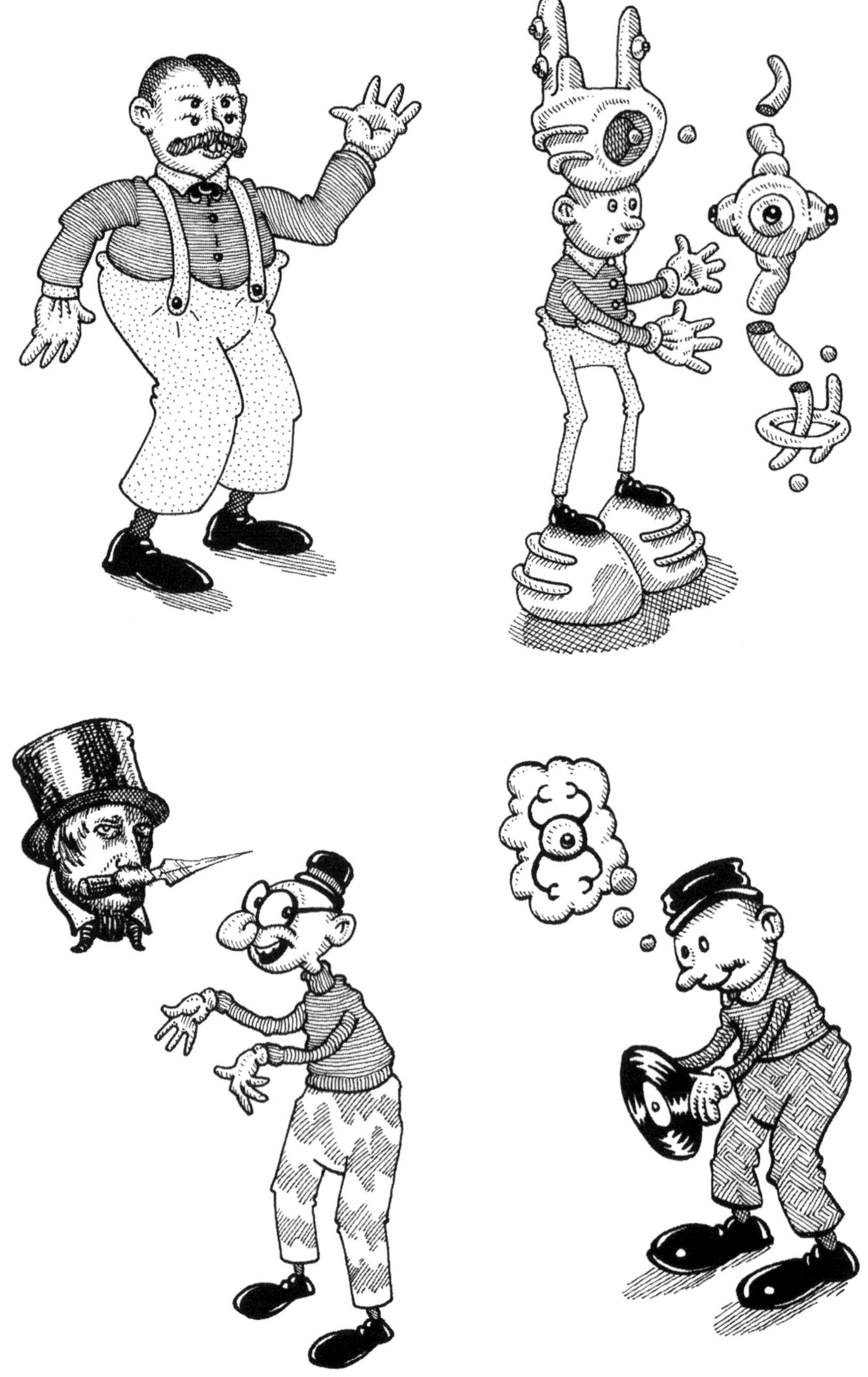

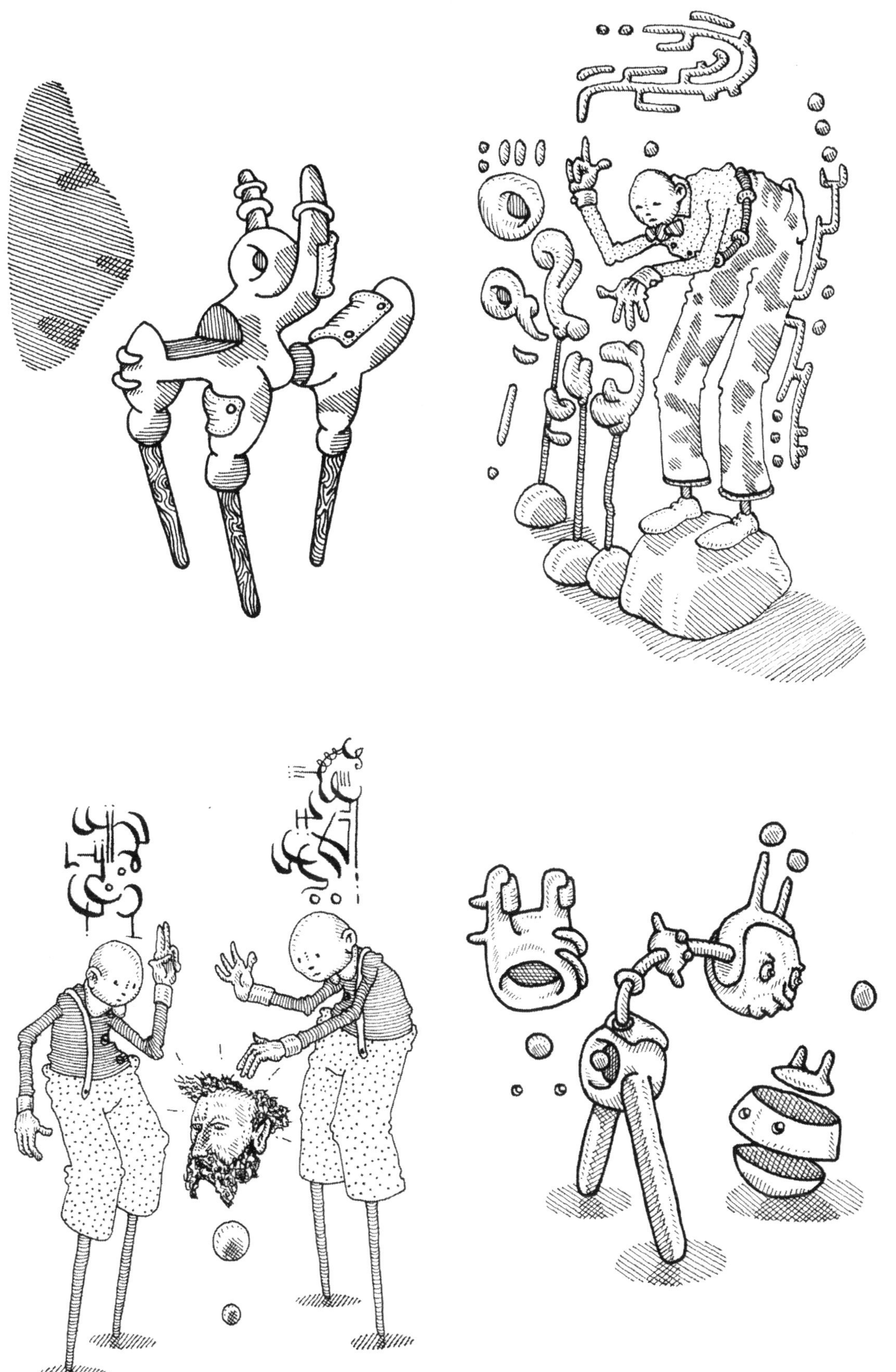

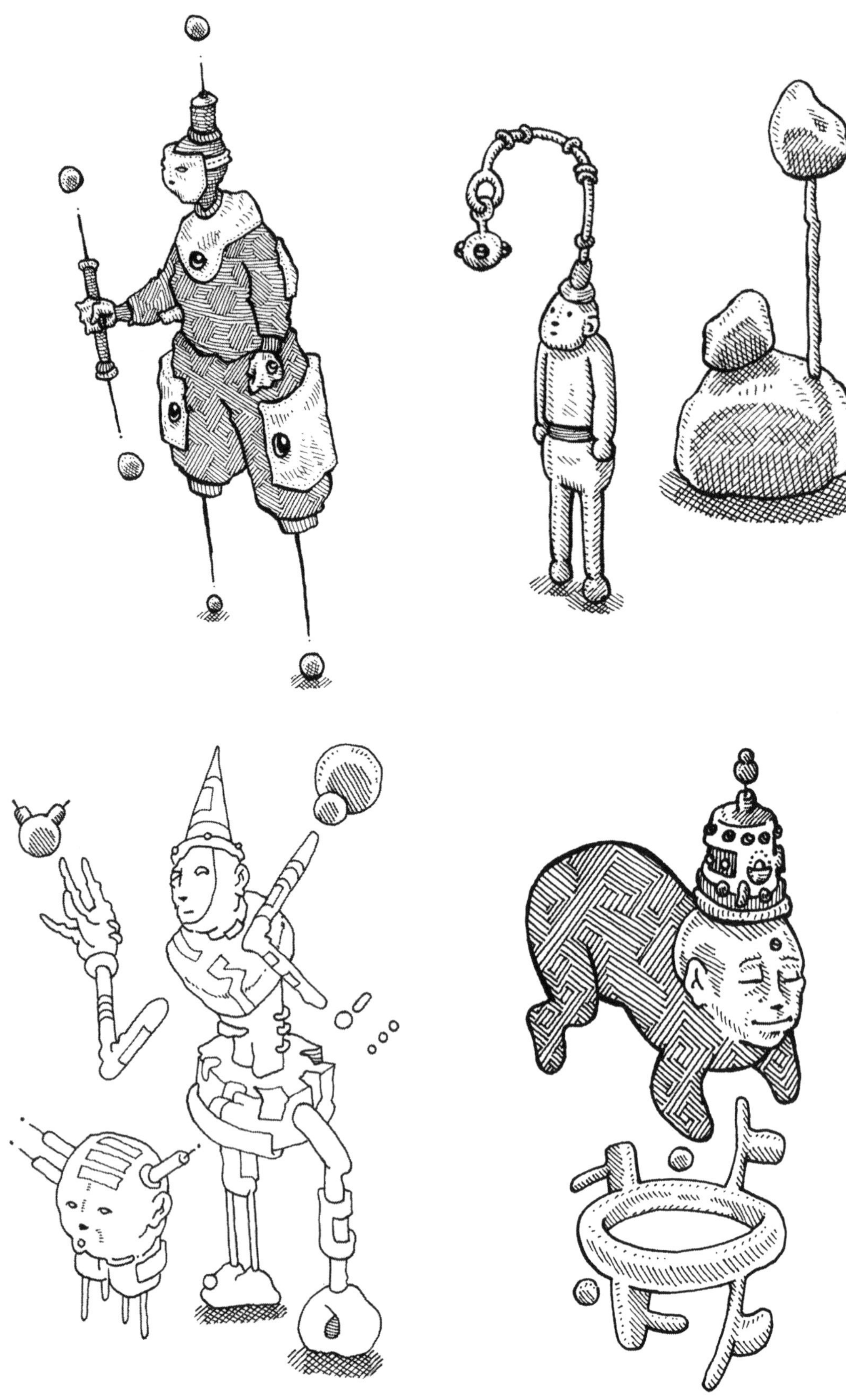

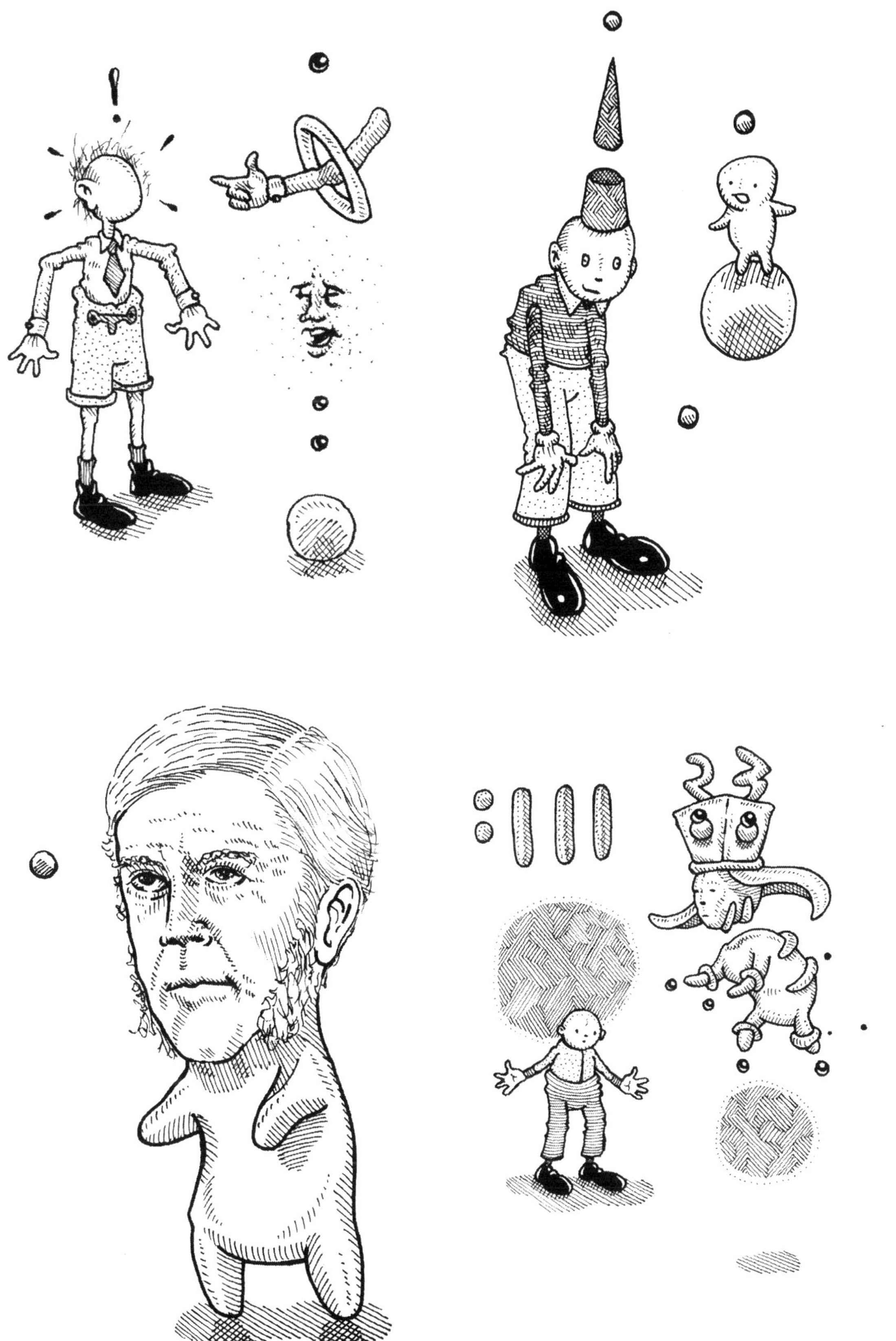

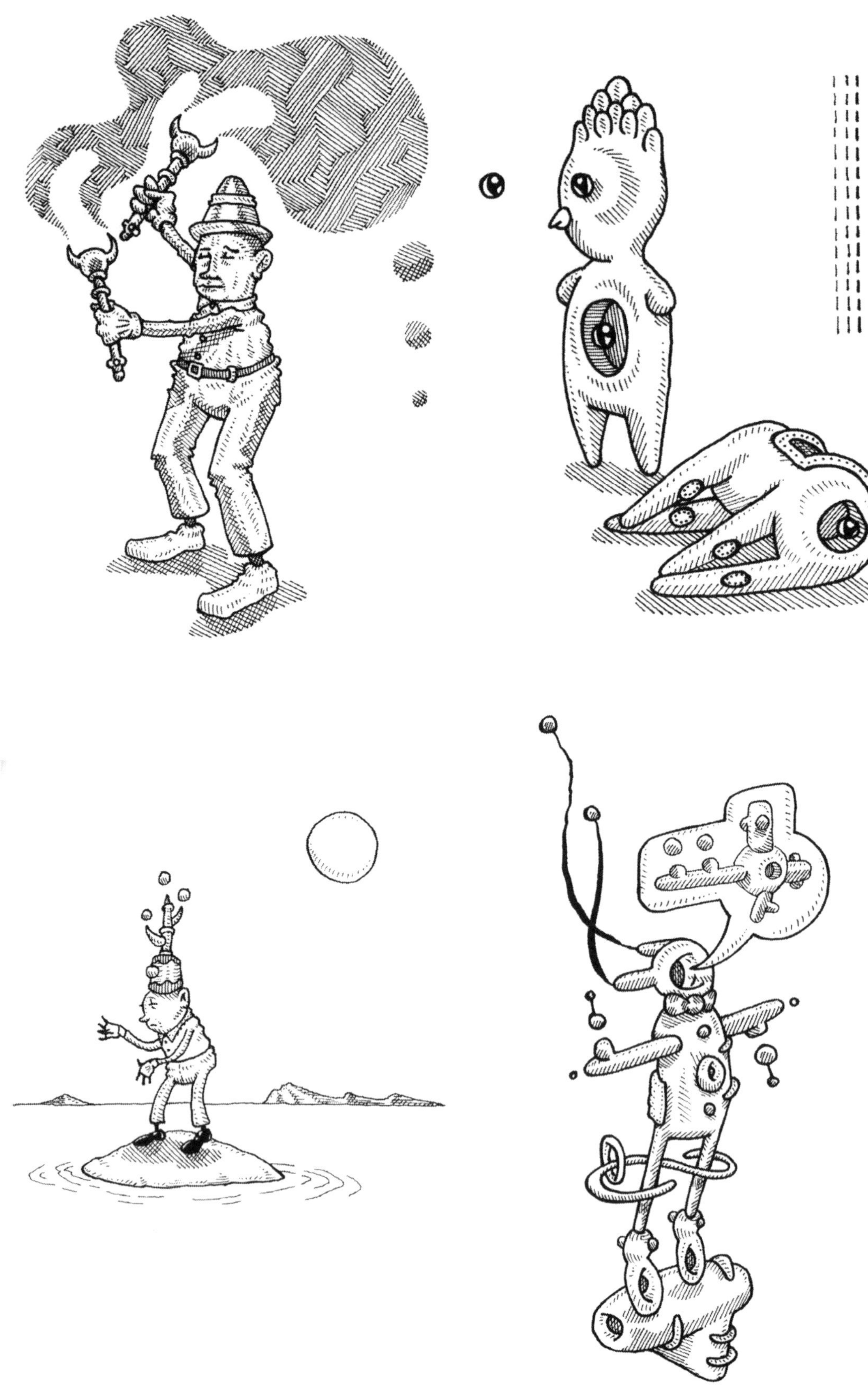

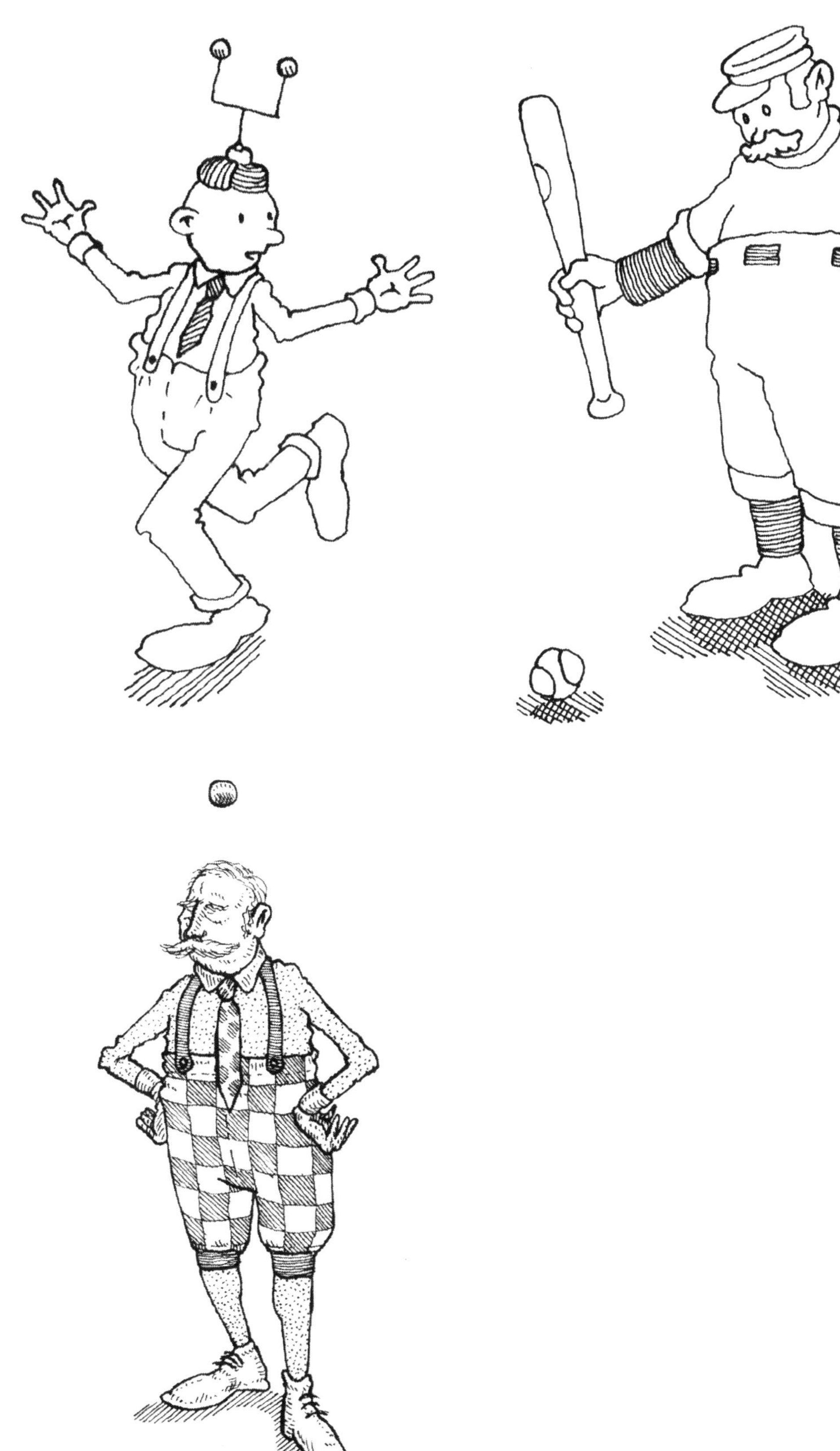

2017

April

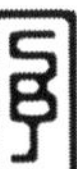

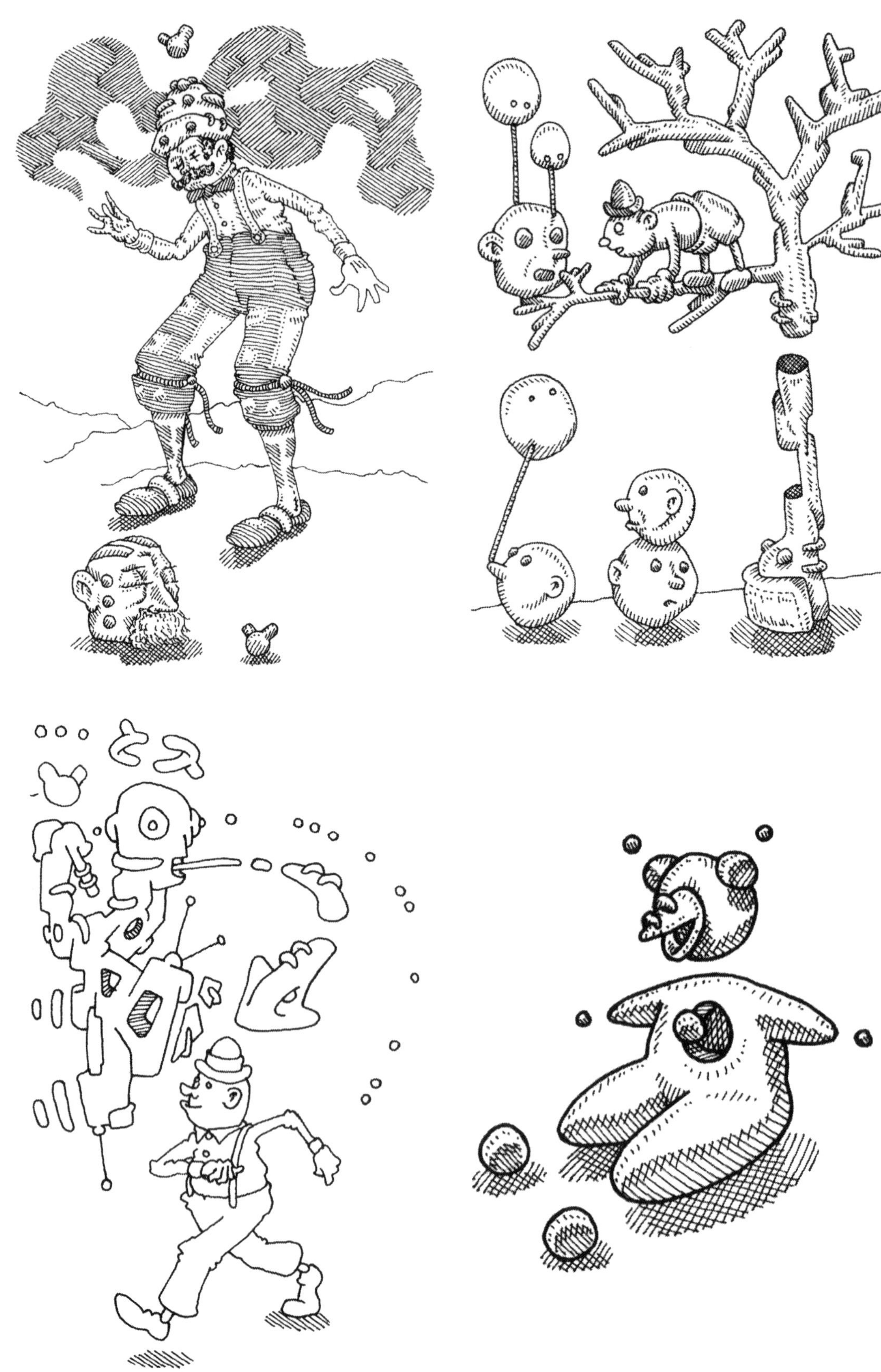

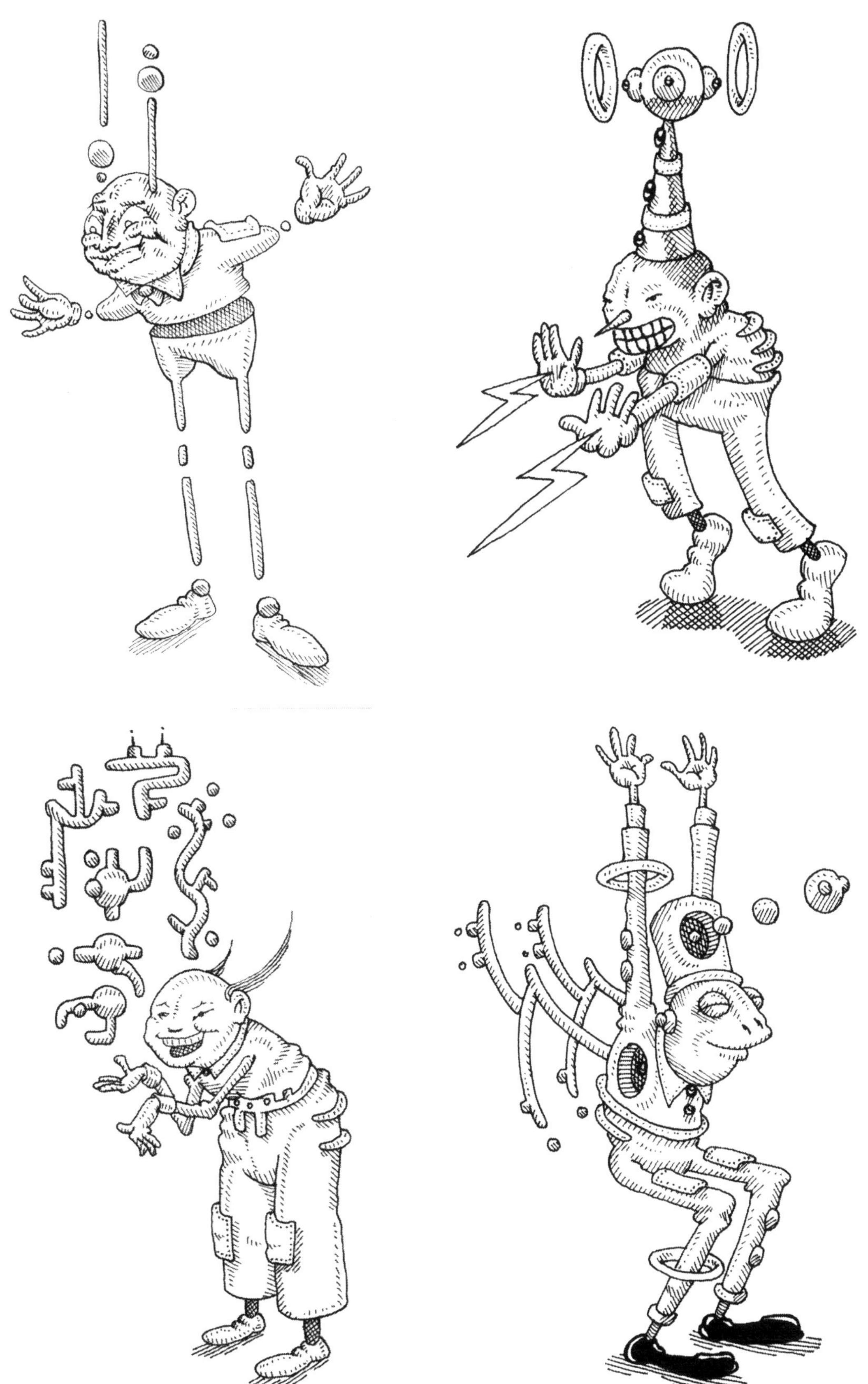

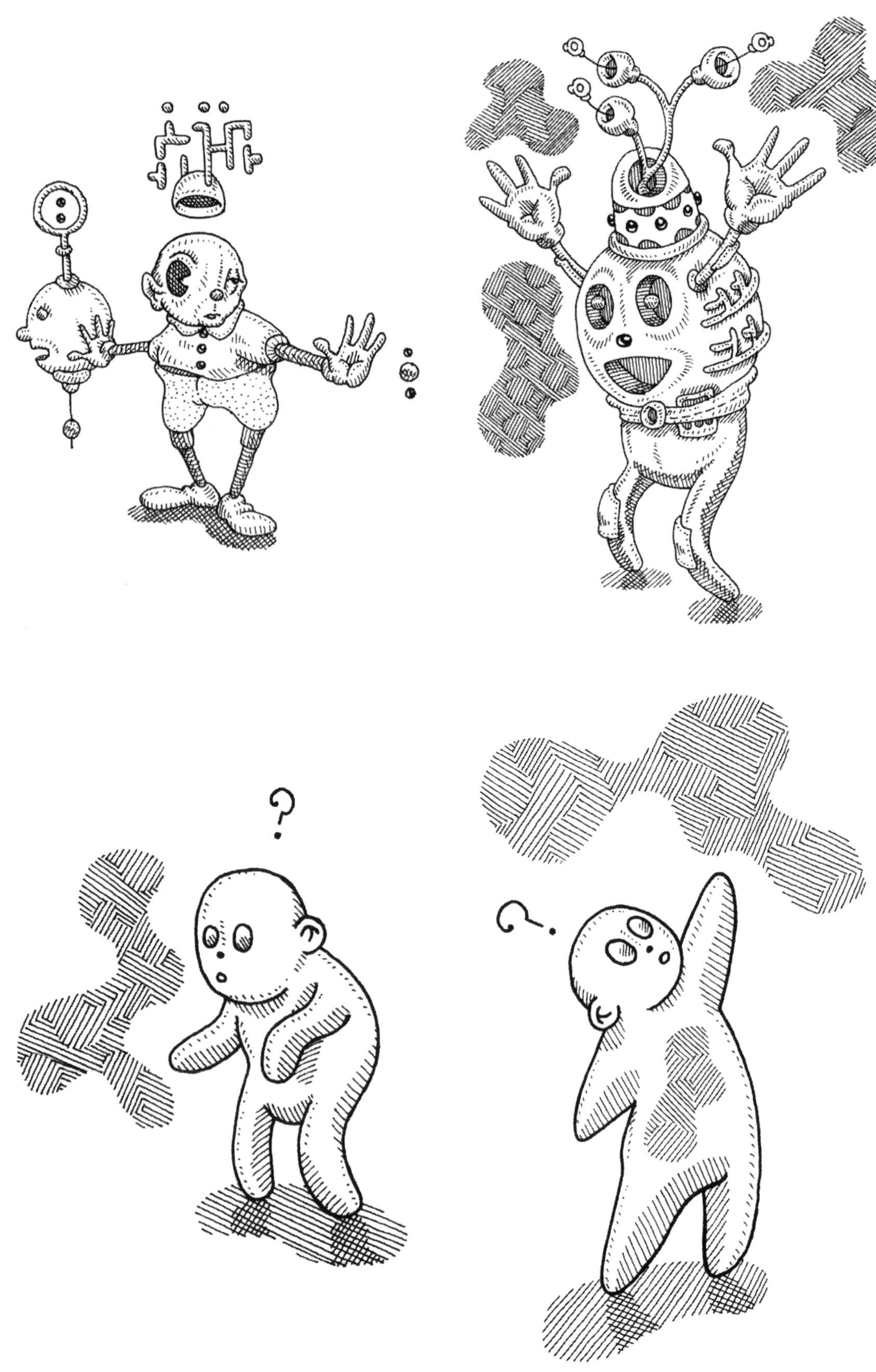

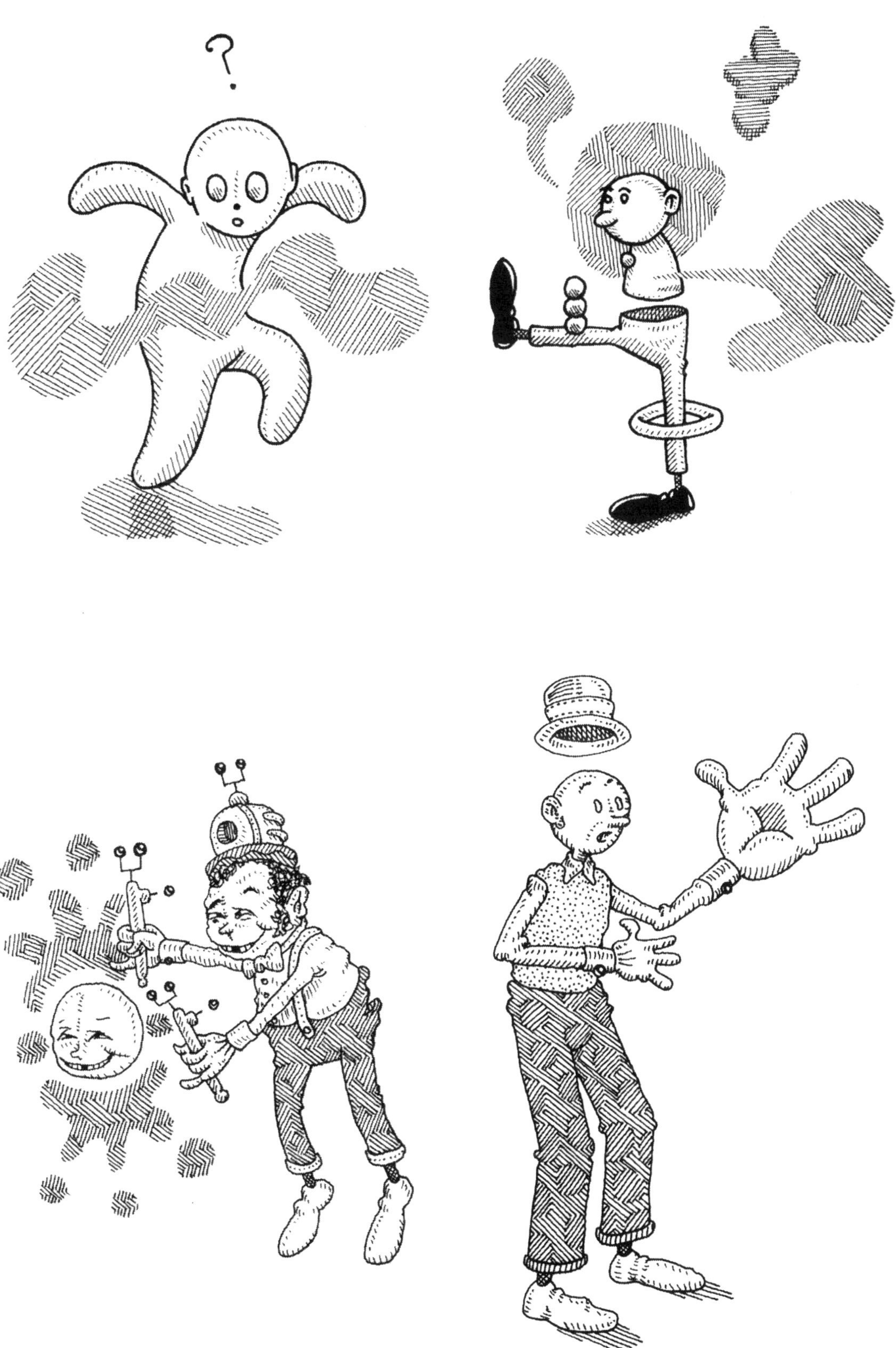

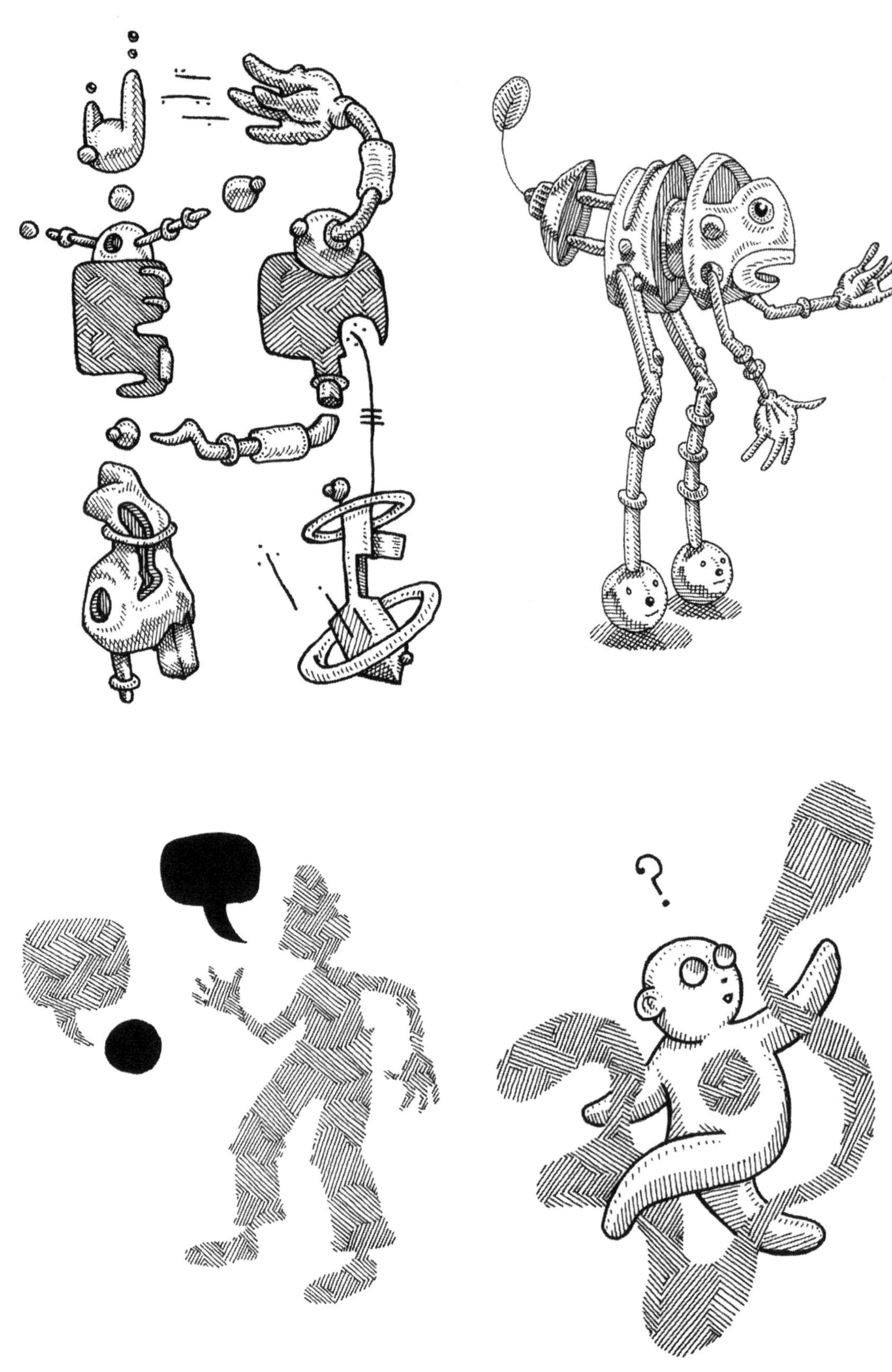

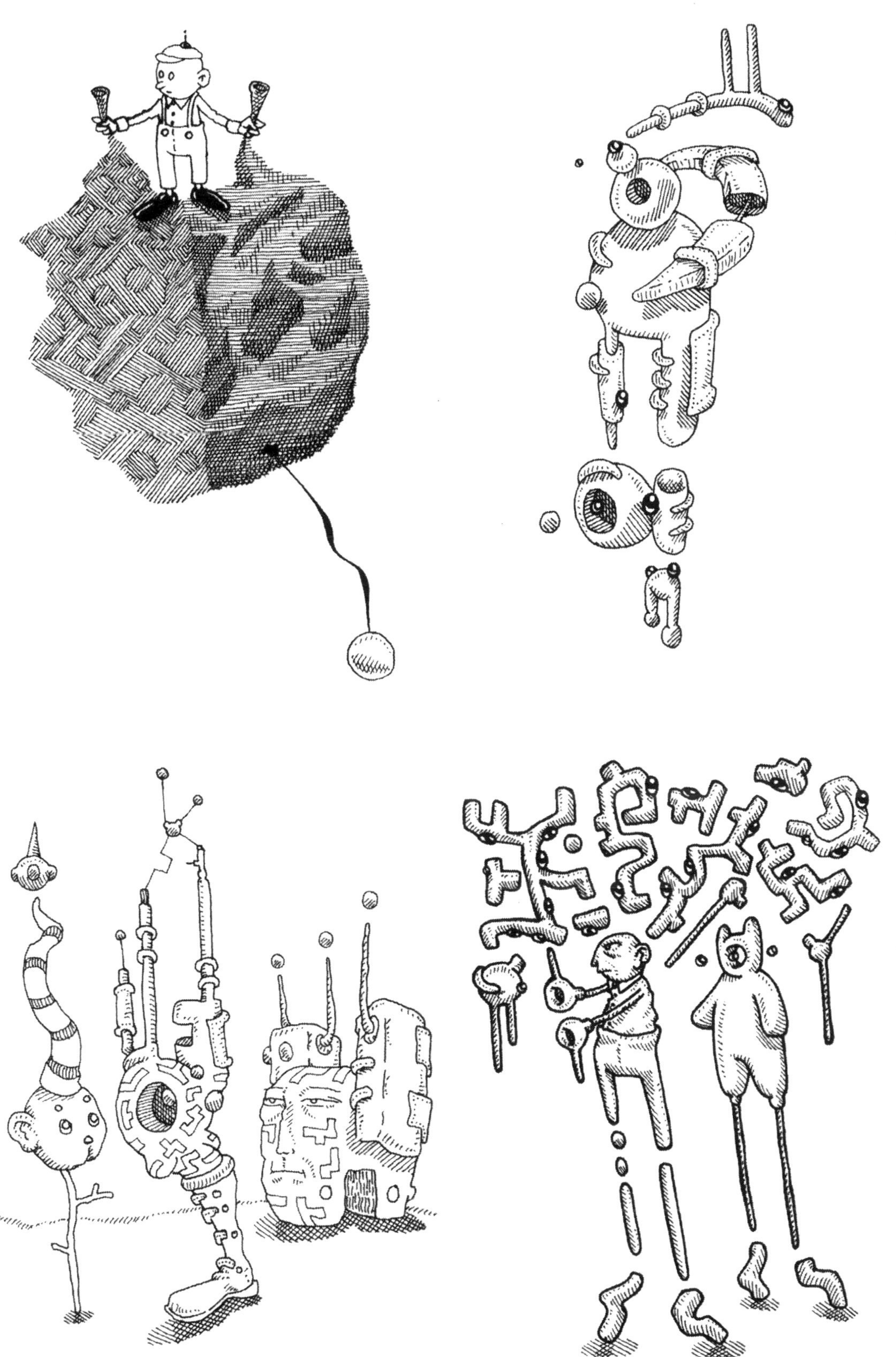

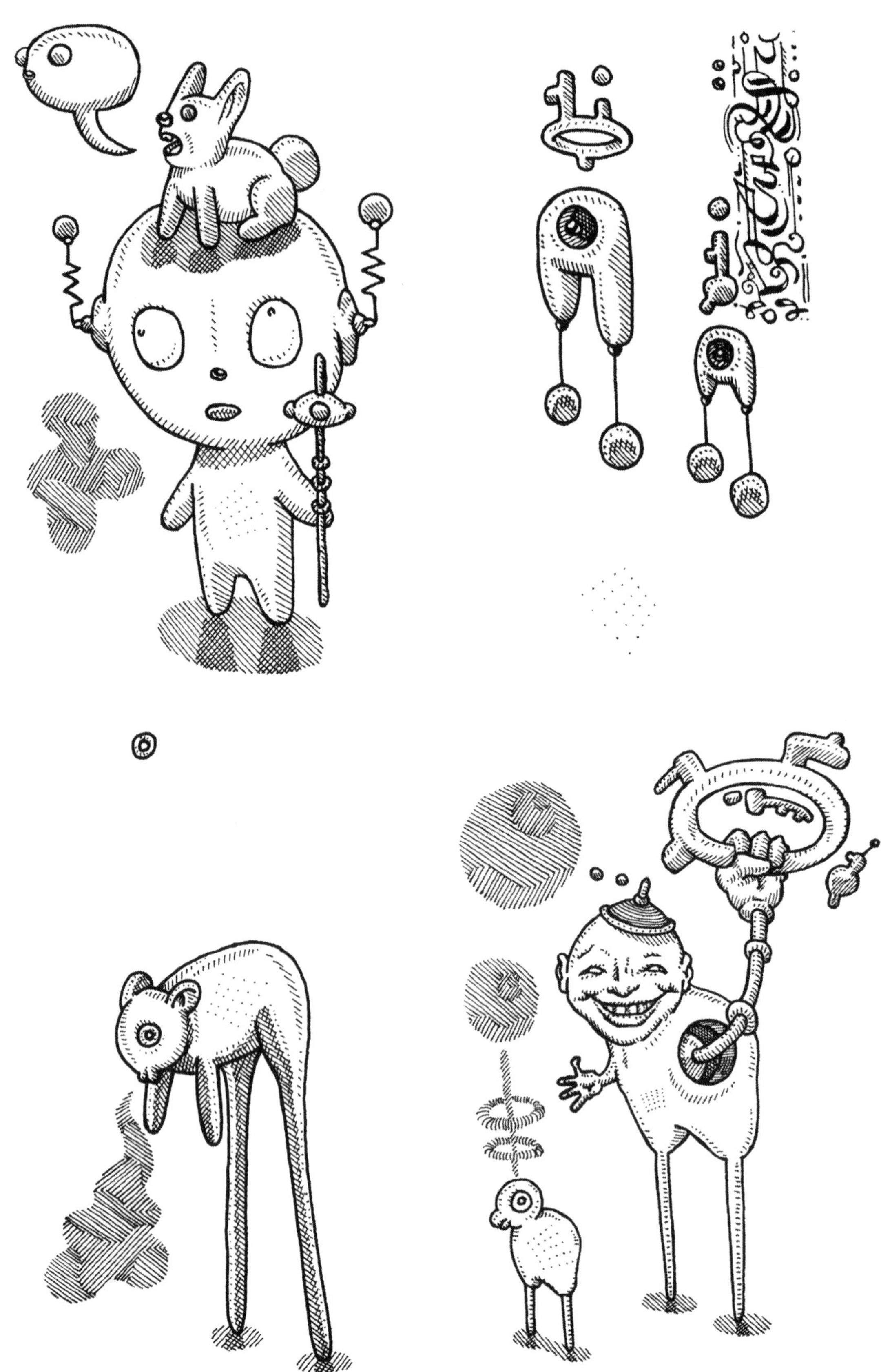

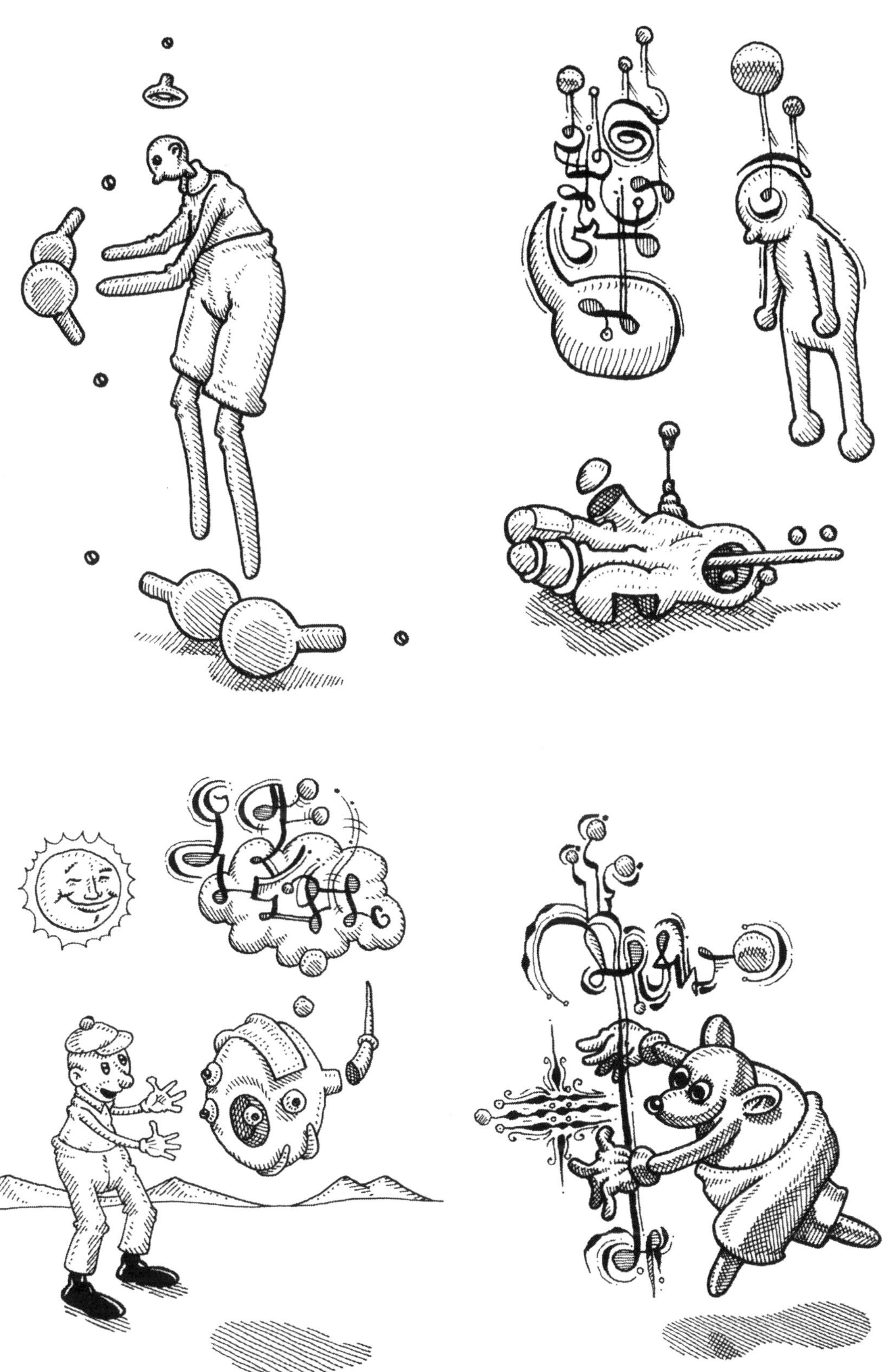

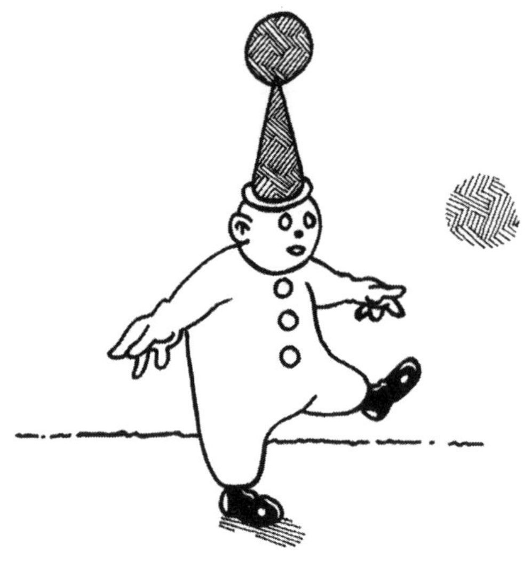

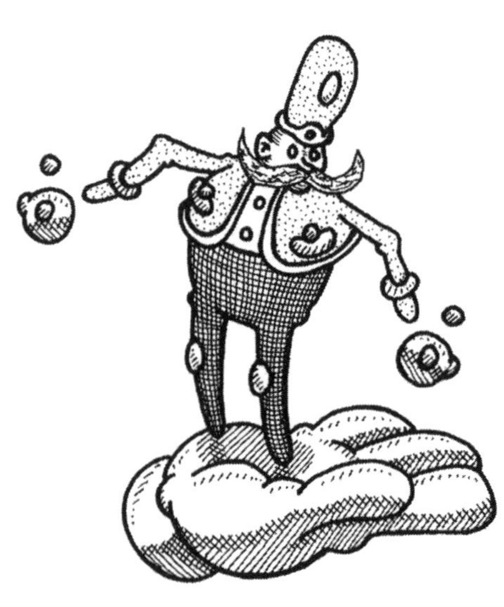

2017

May

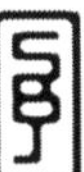

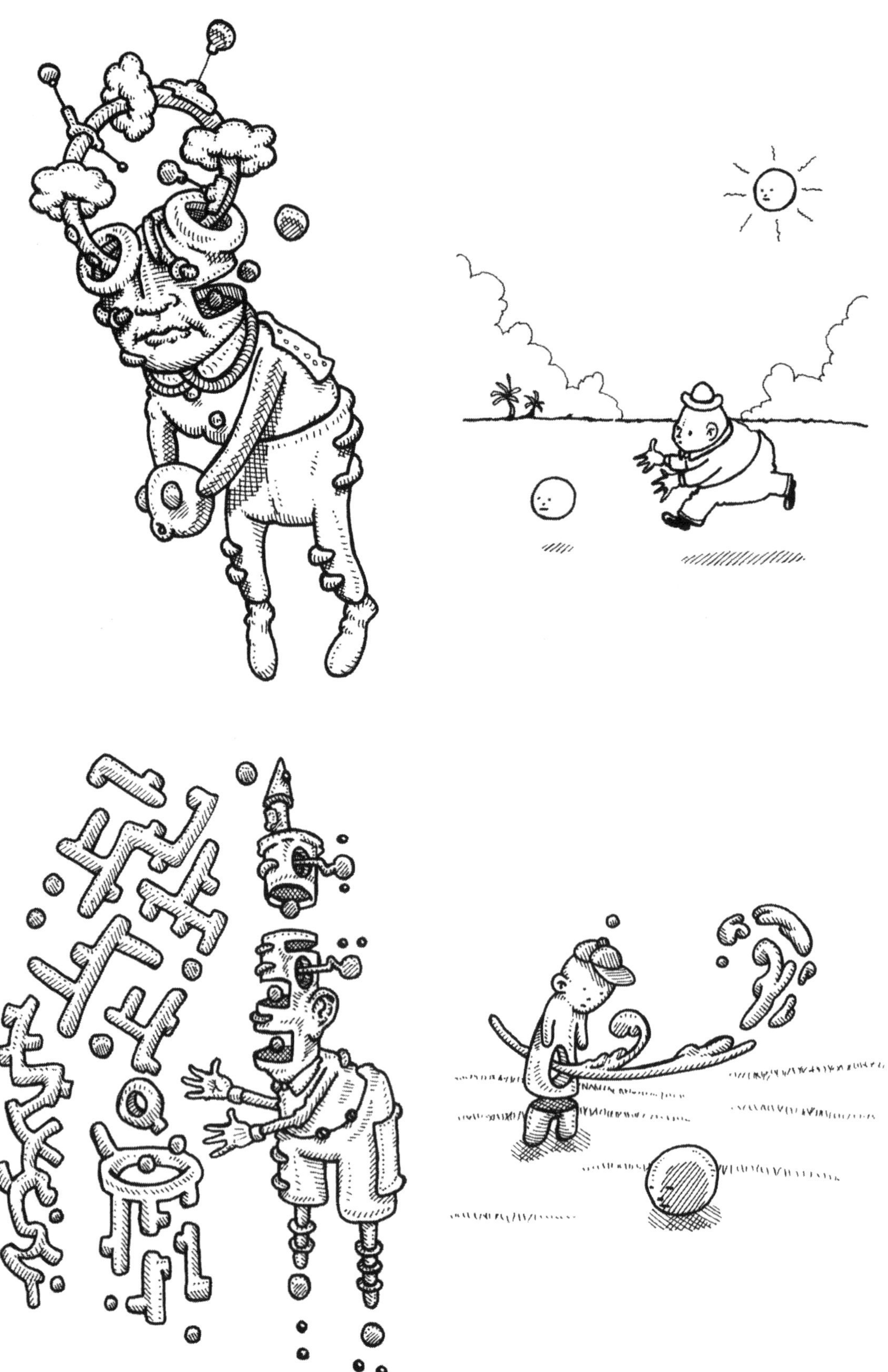

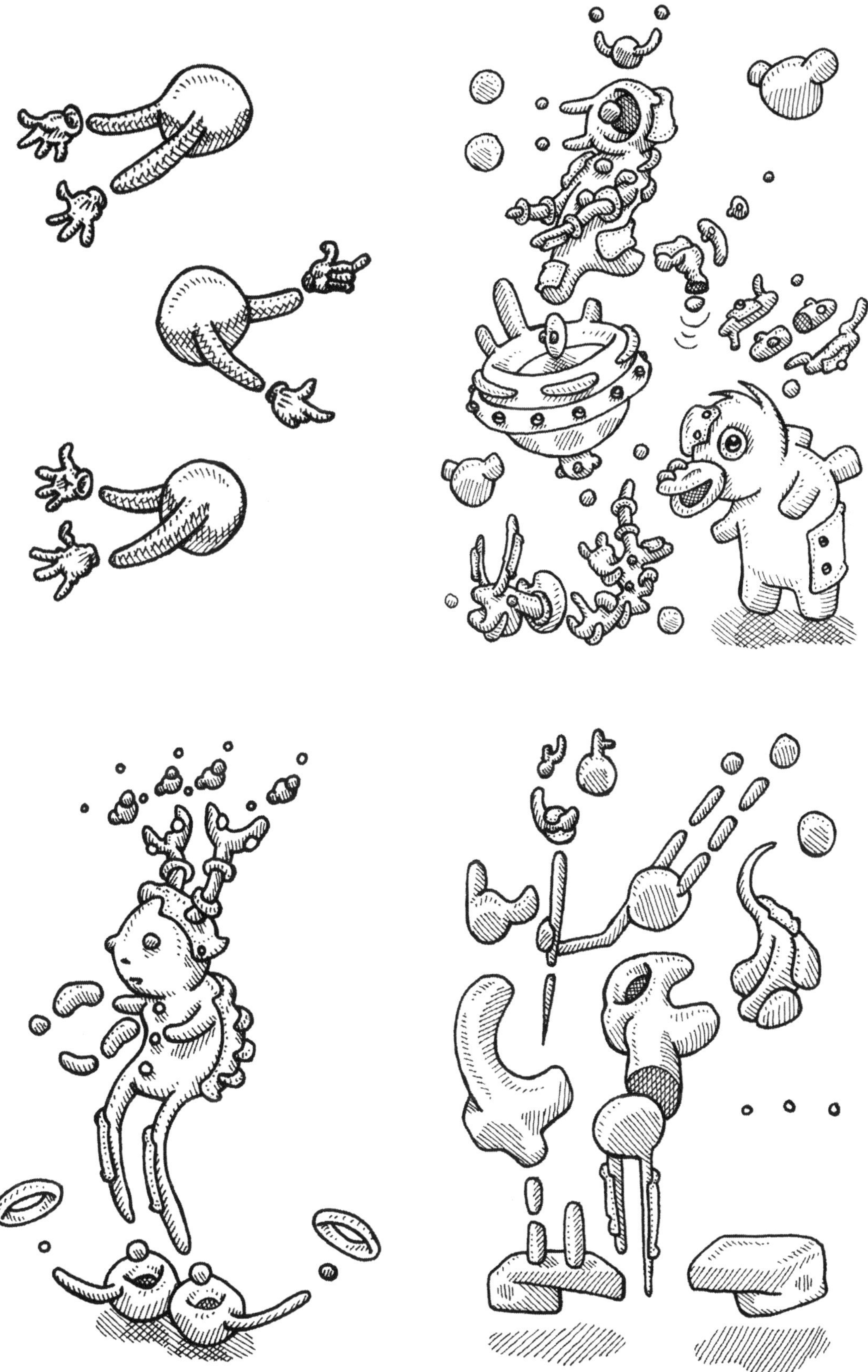

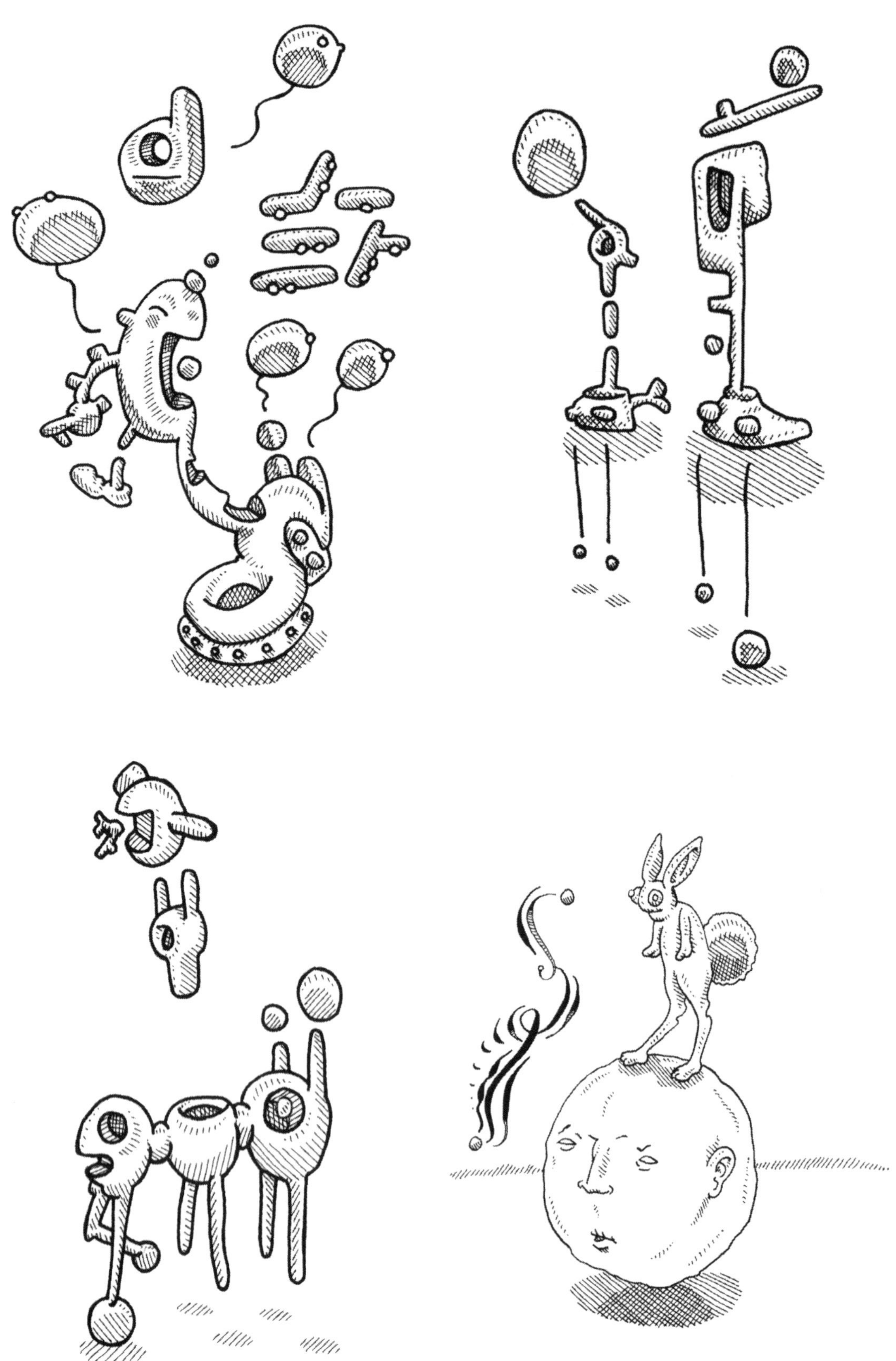

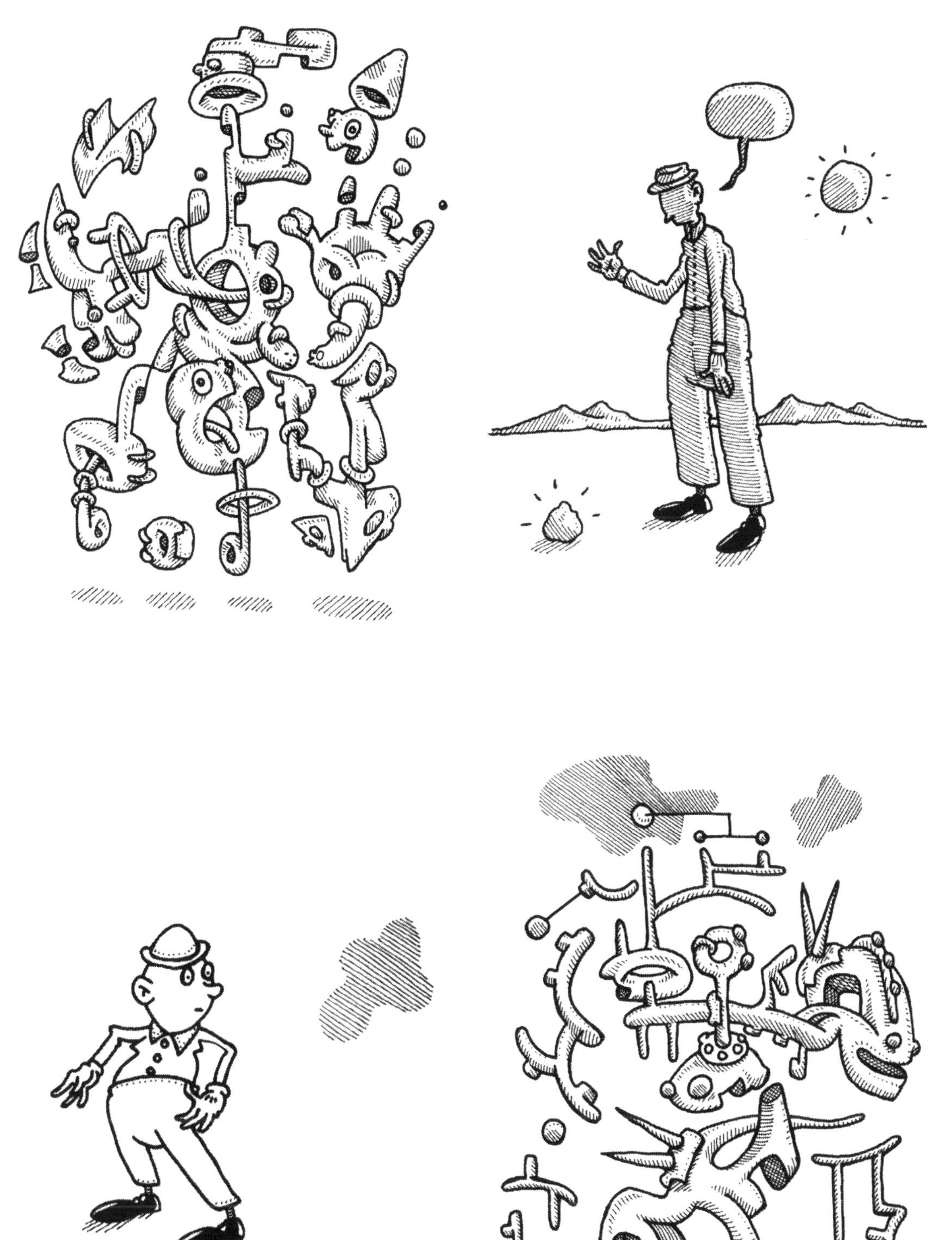

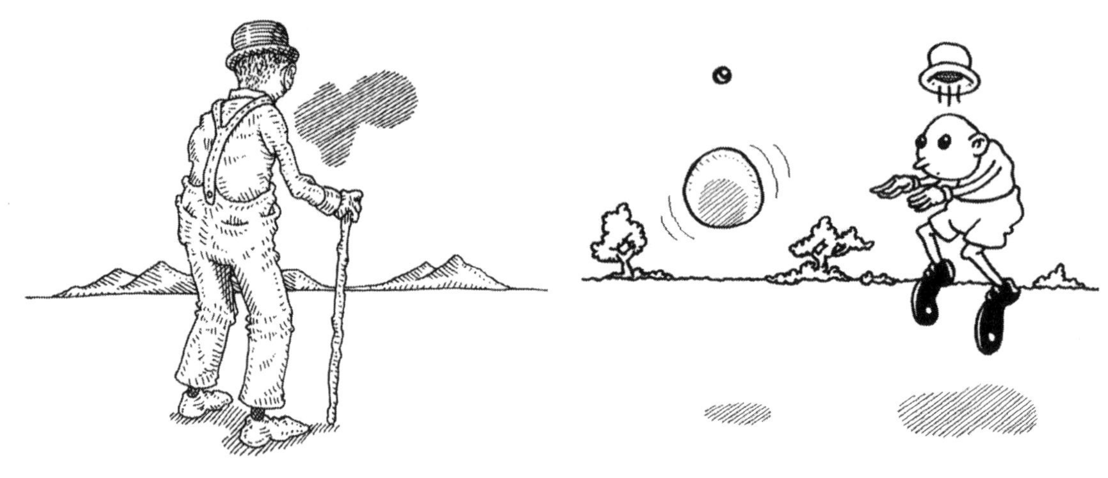

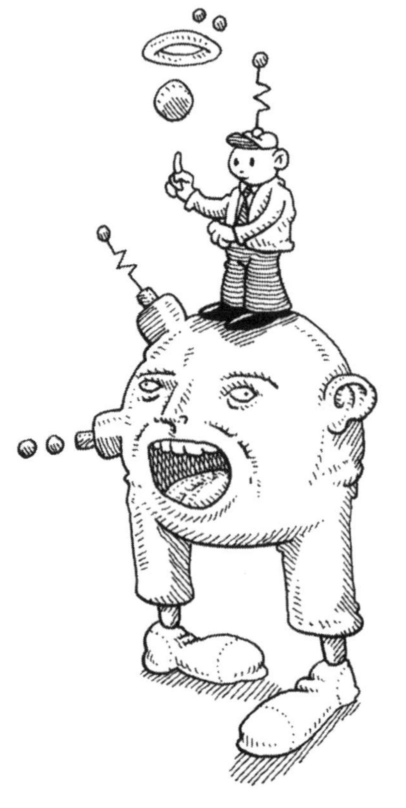

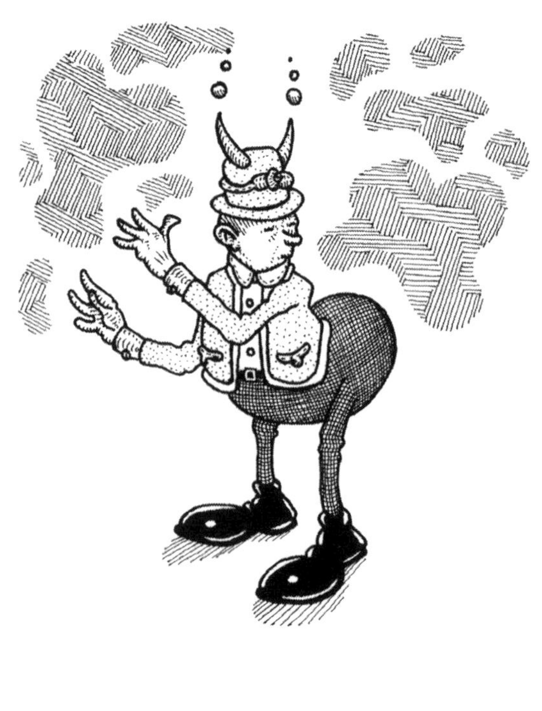

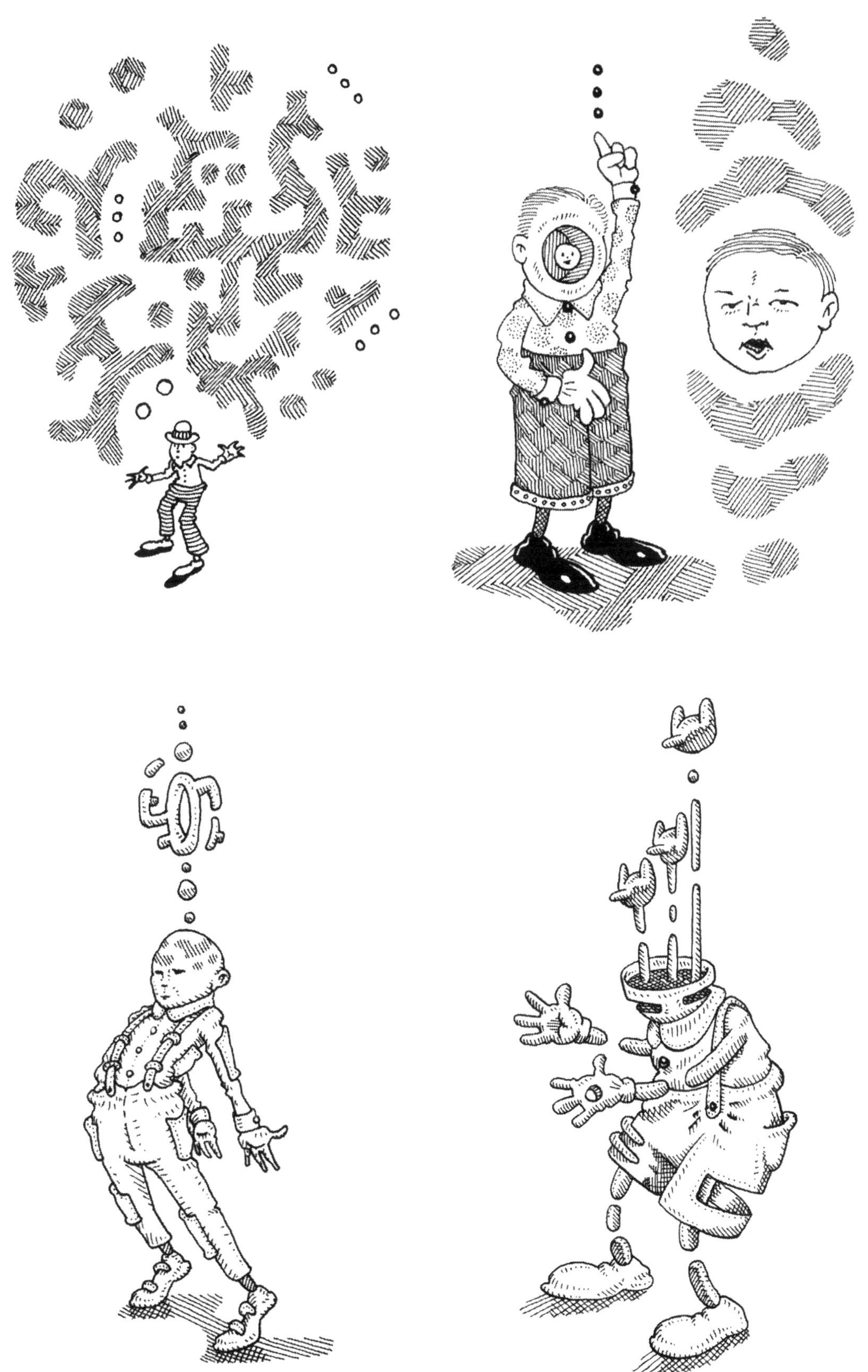

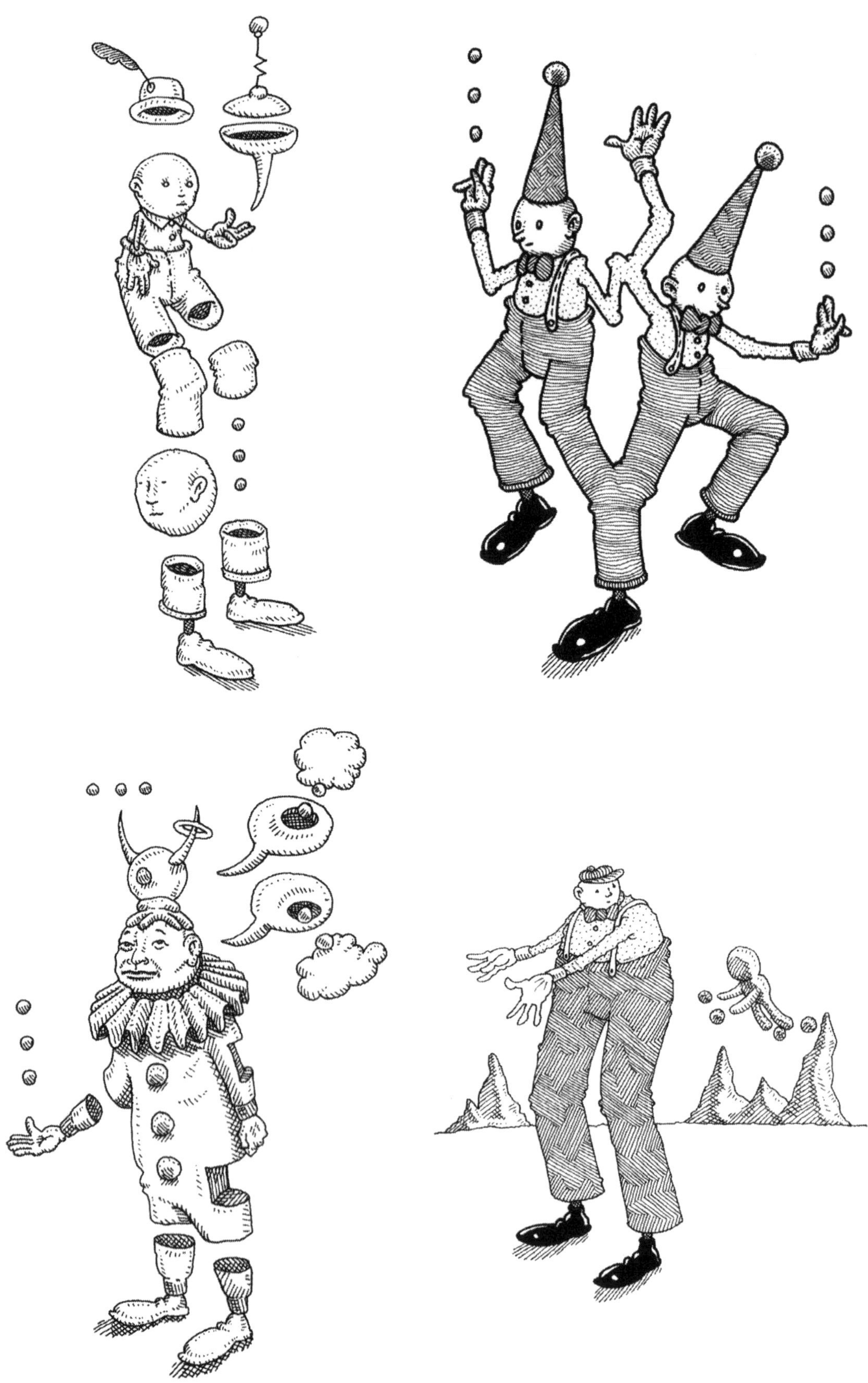

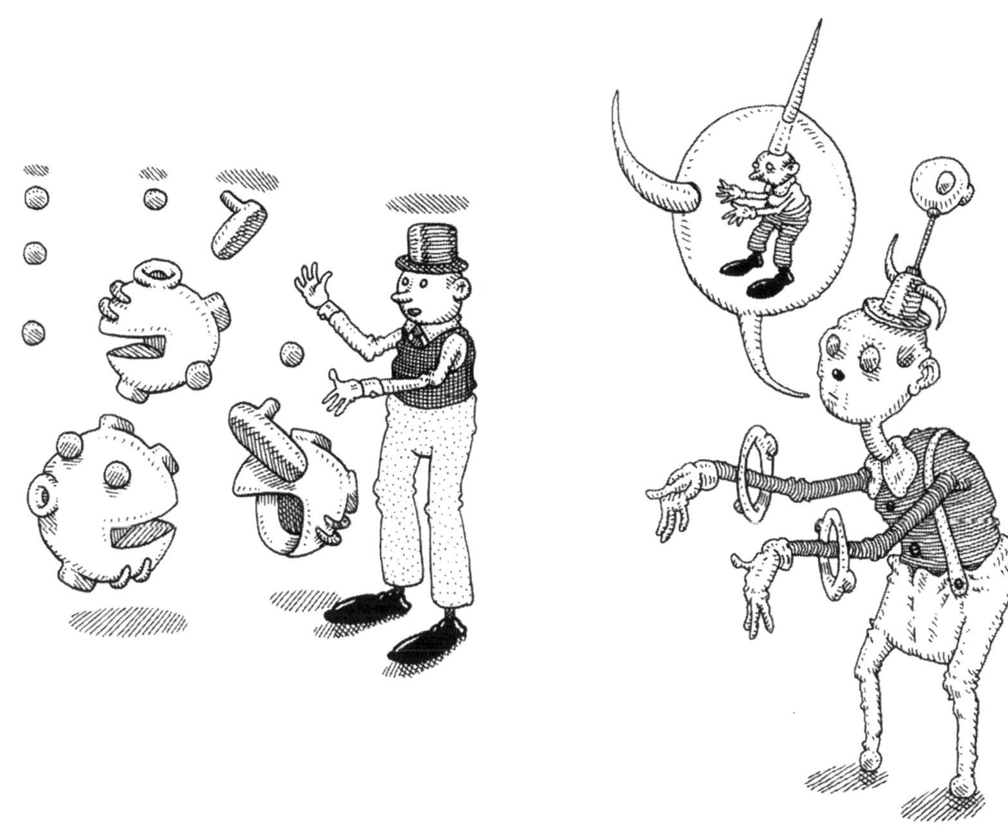

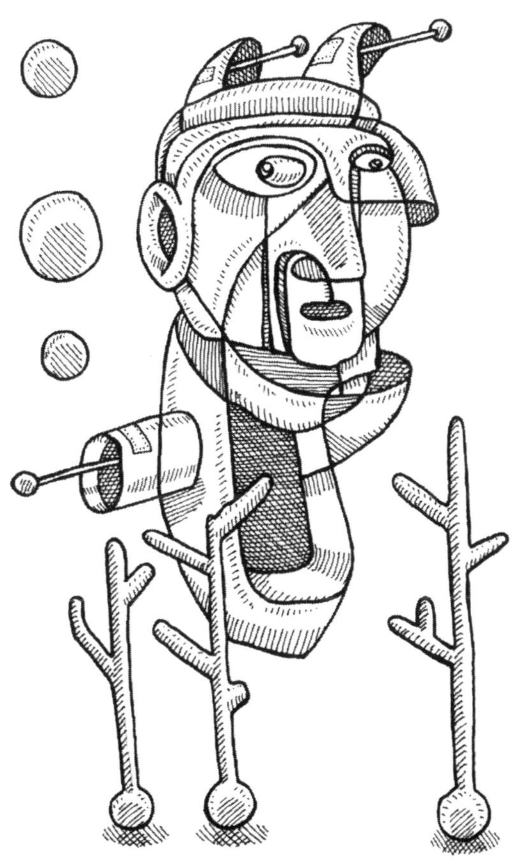

2017

June

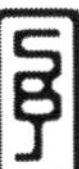

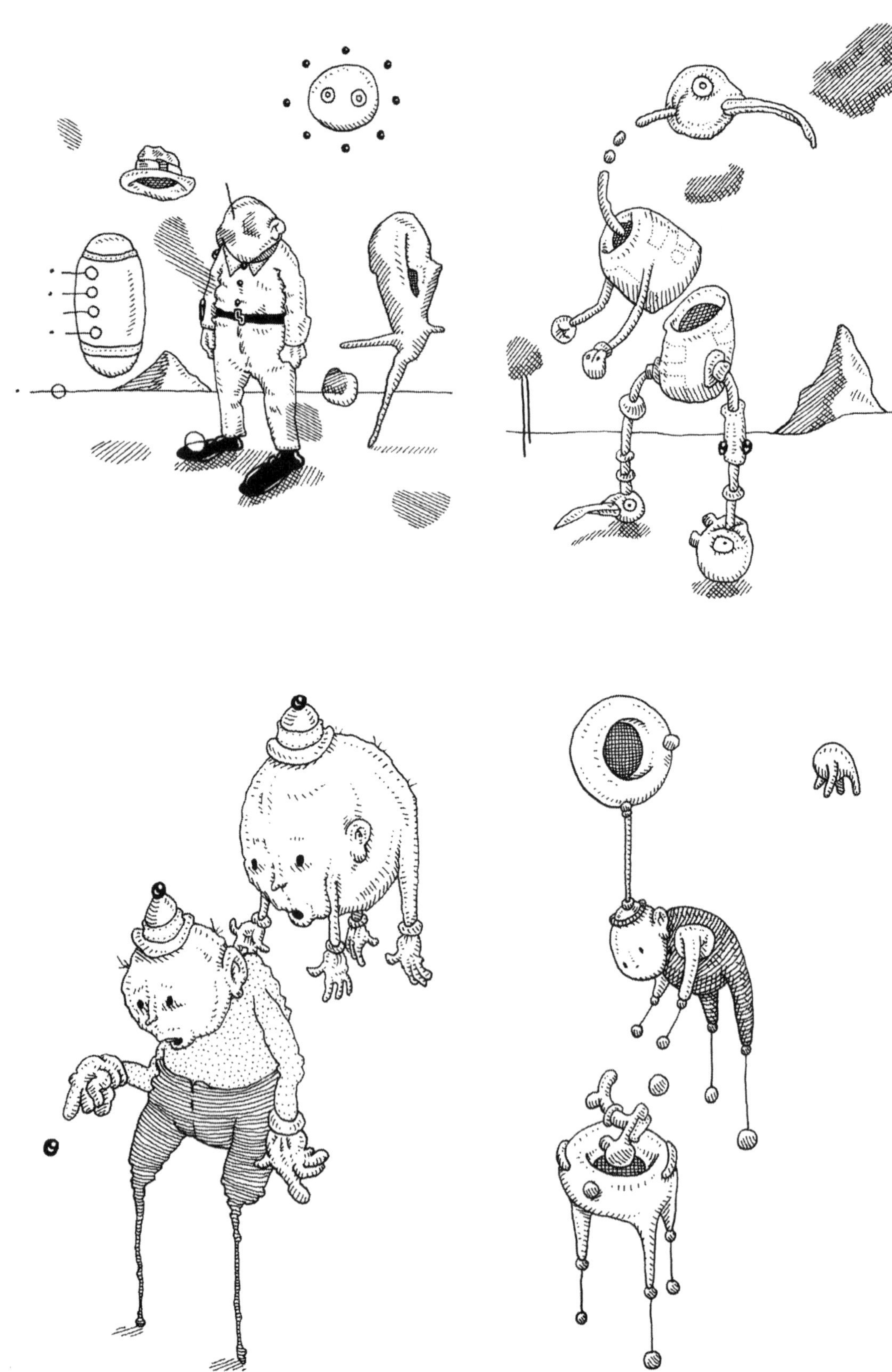

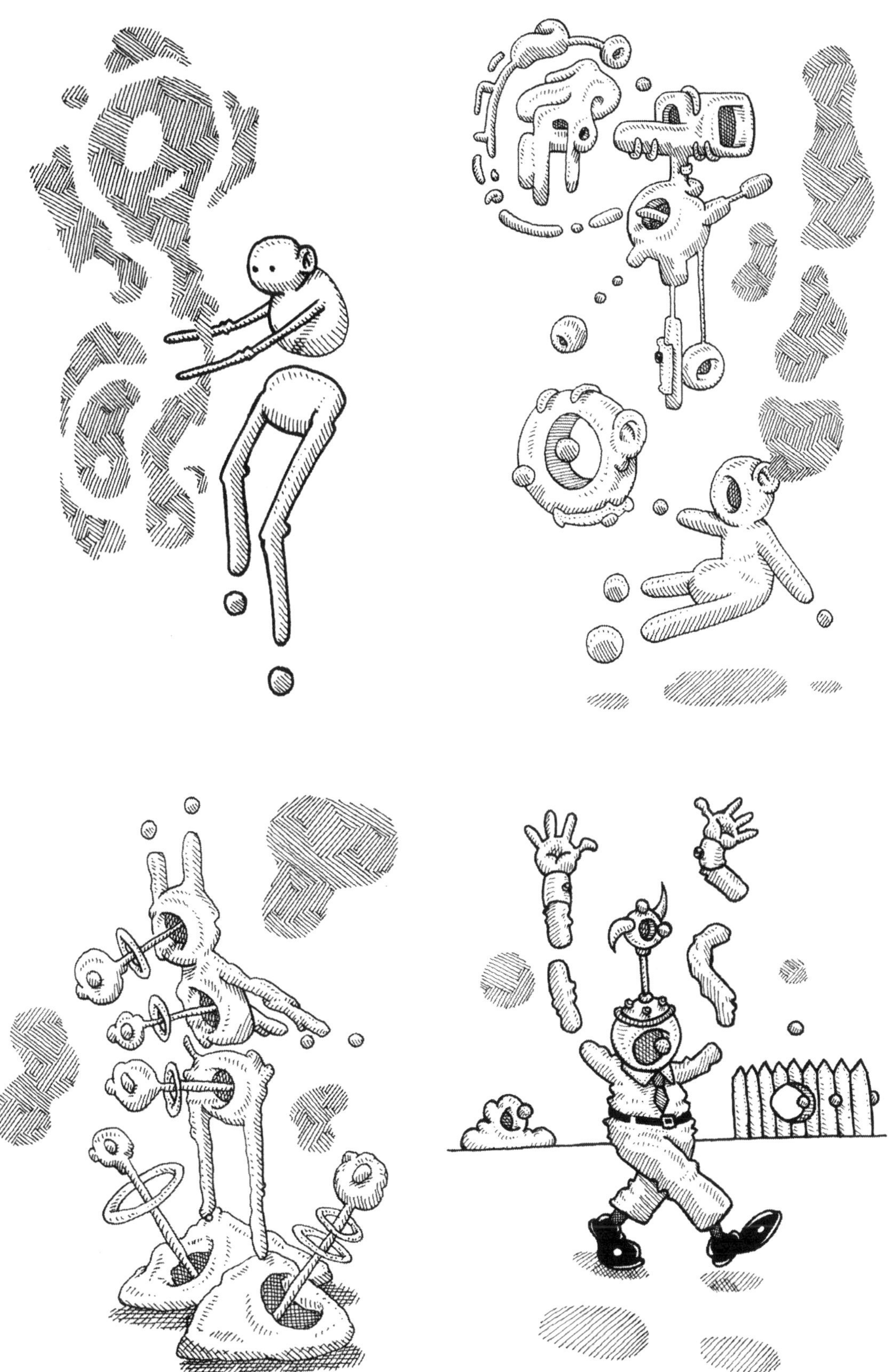

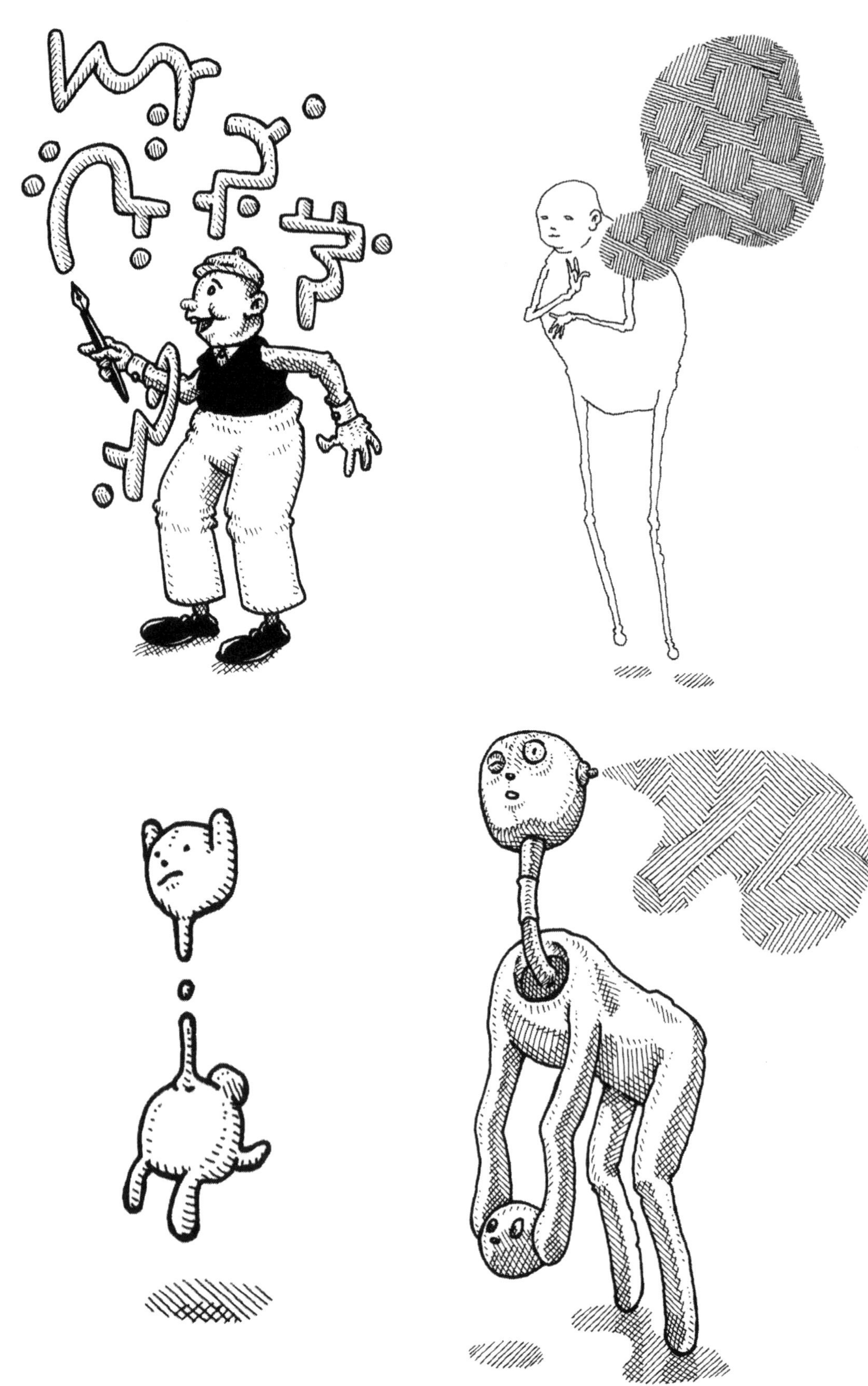

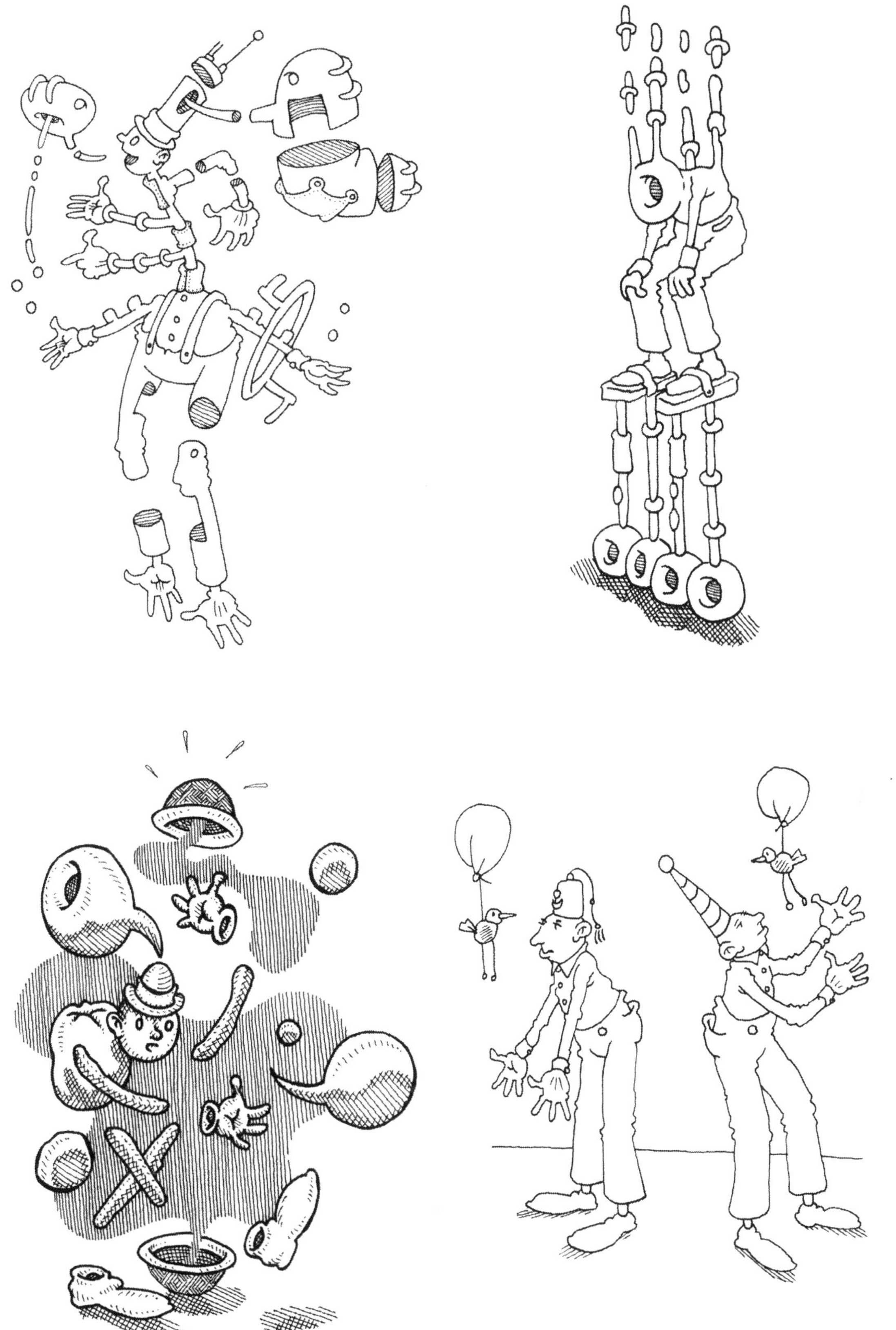

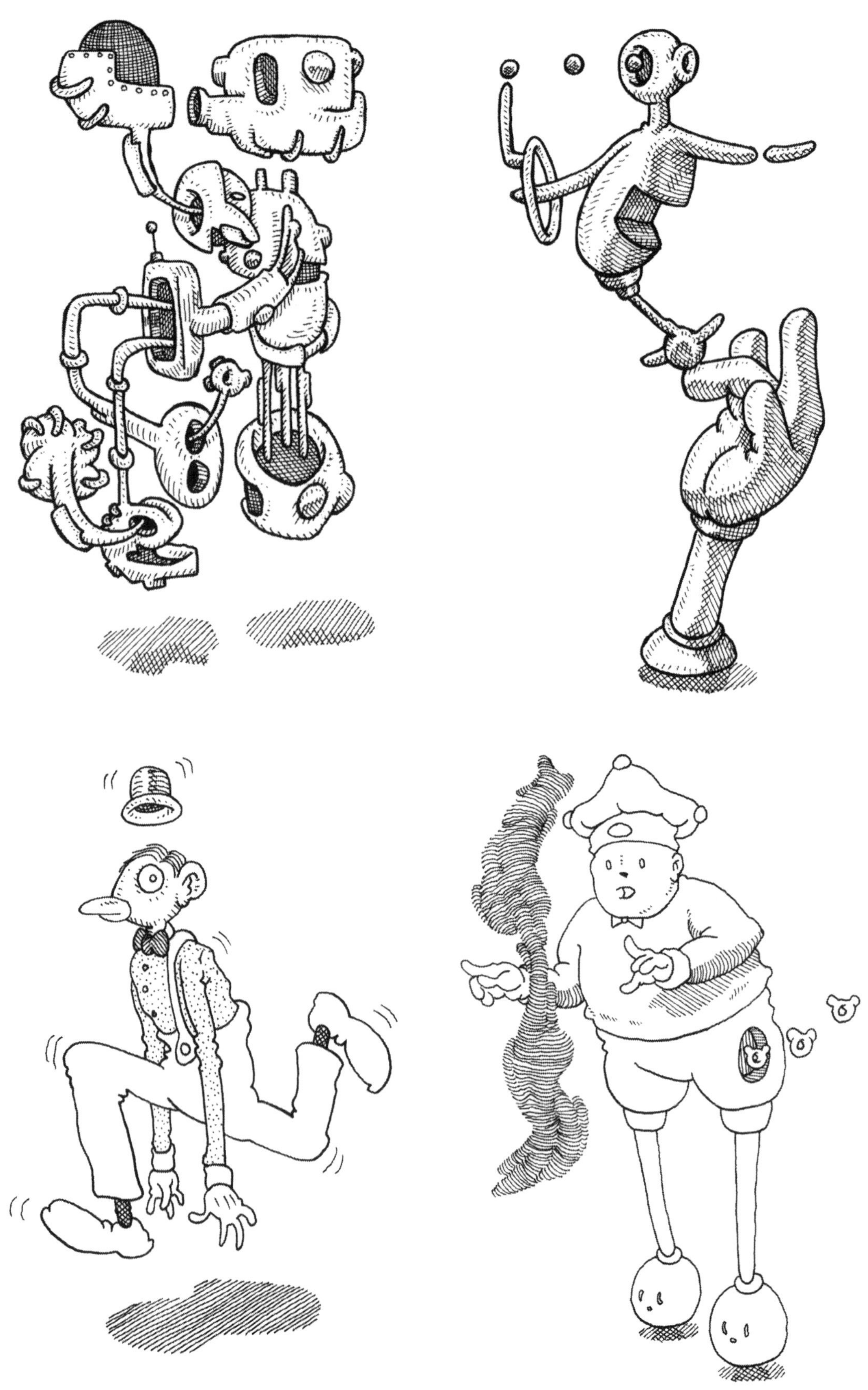

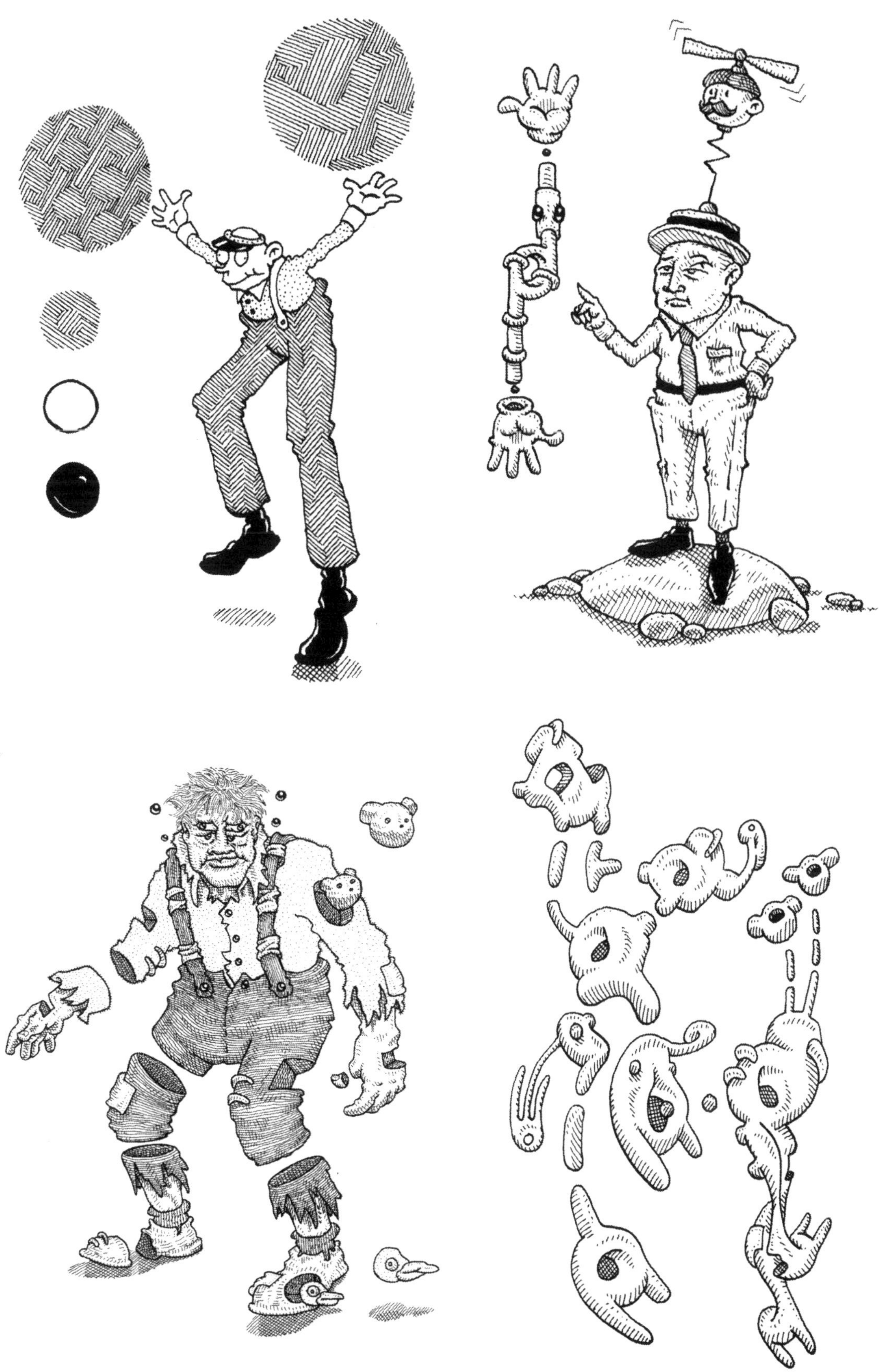

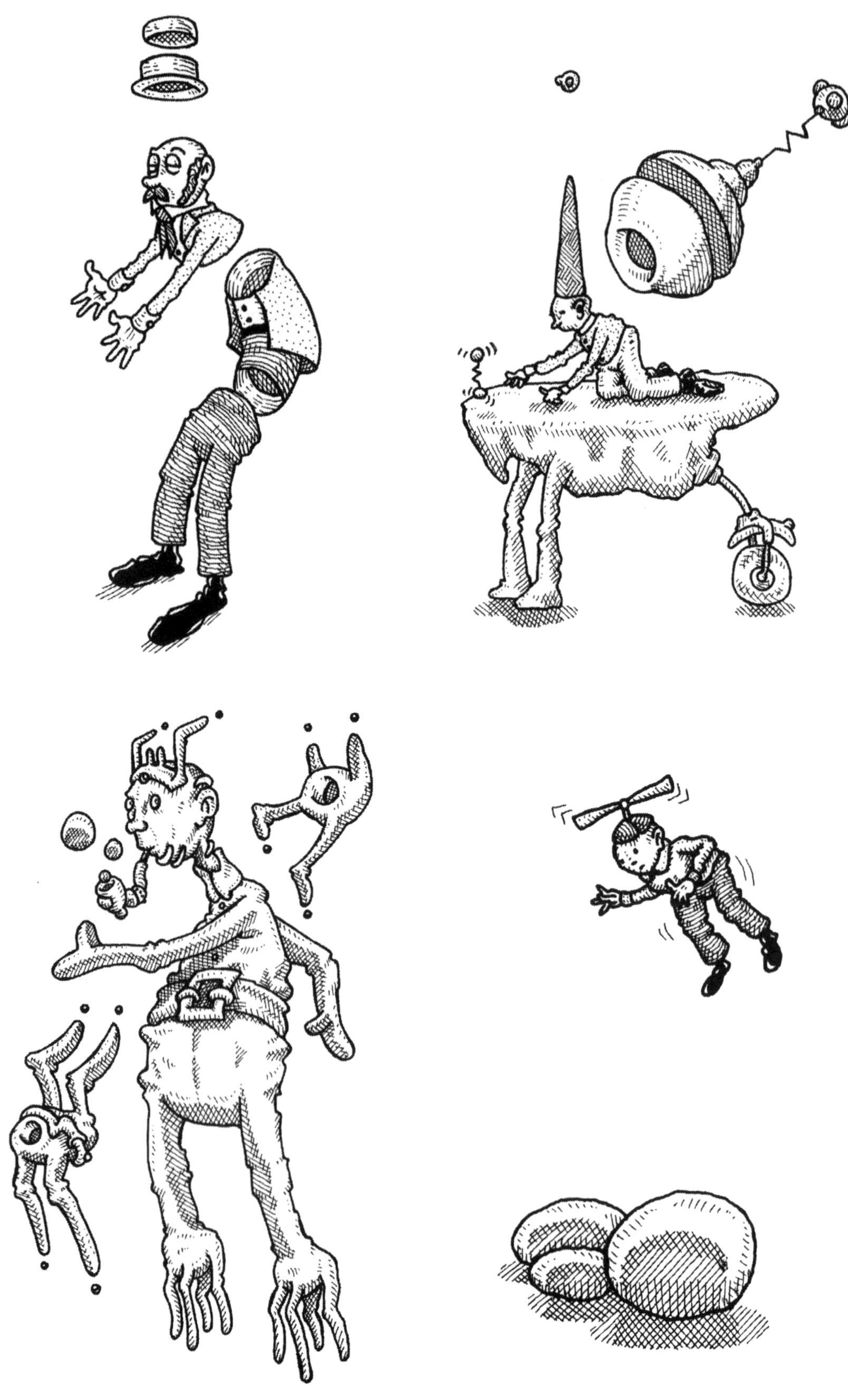

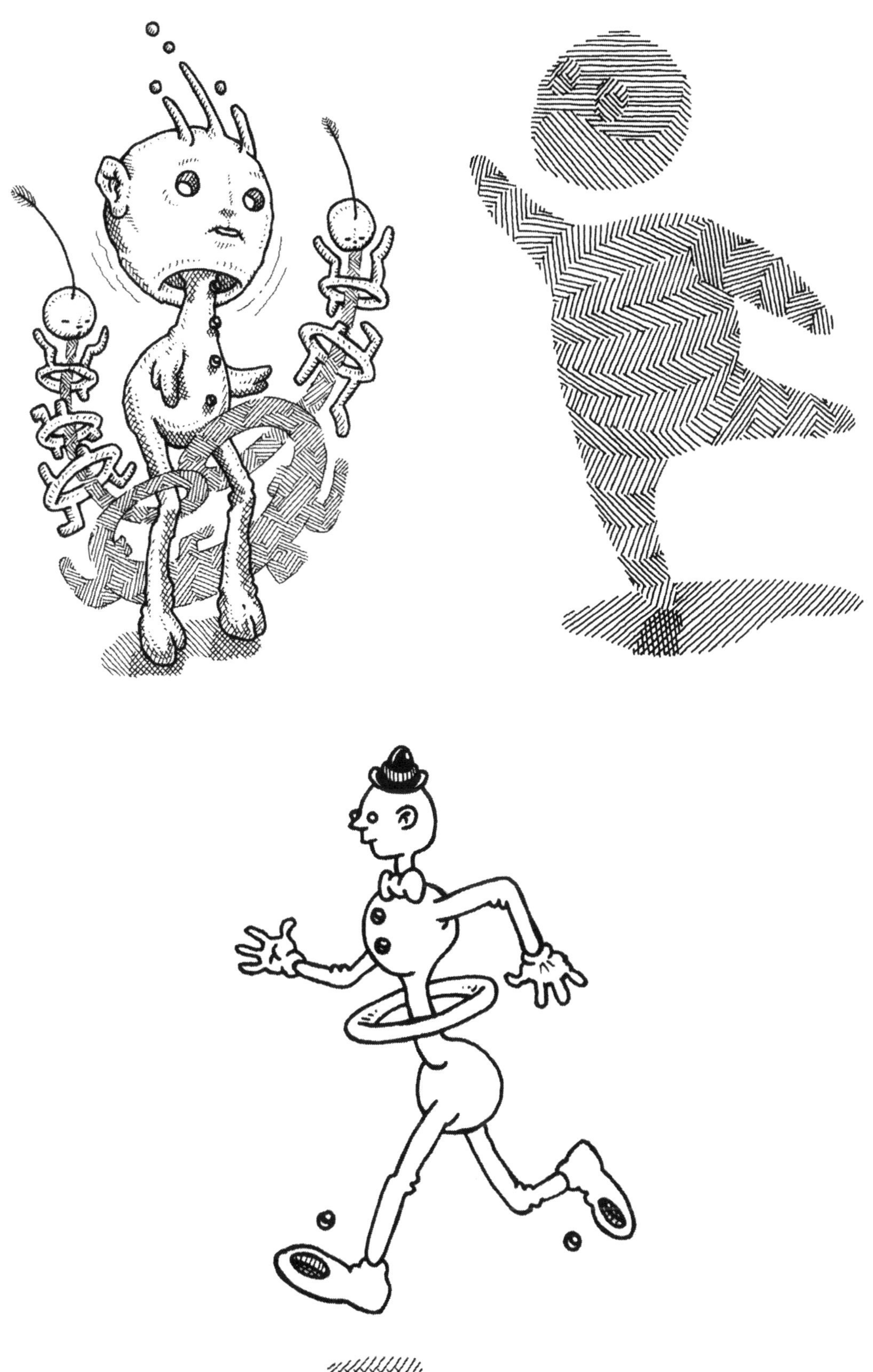

2017

July

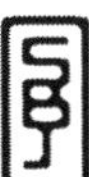

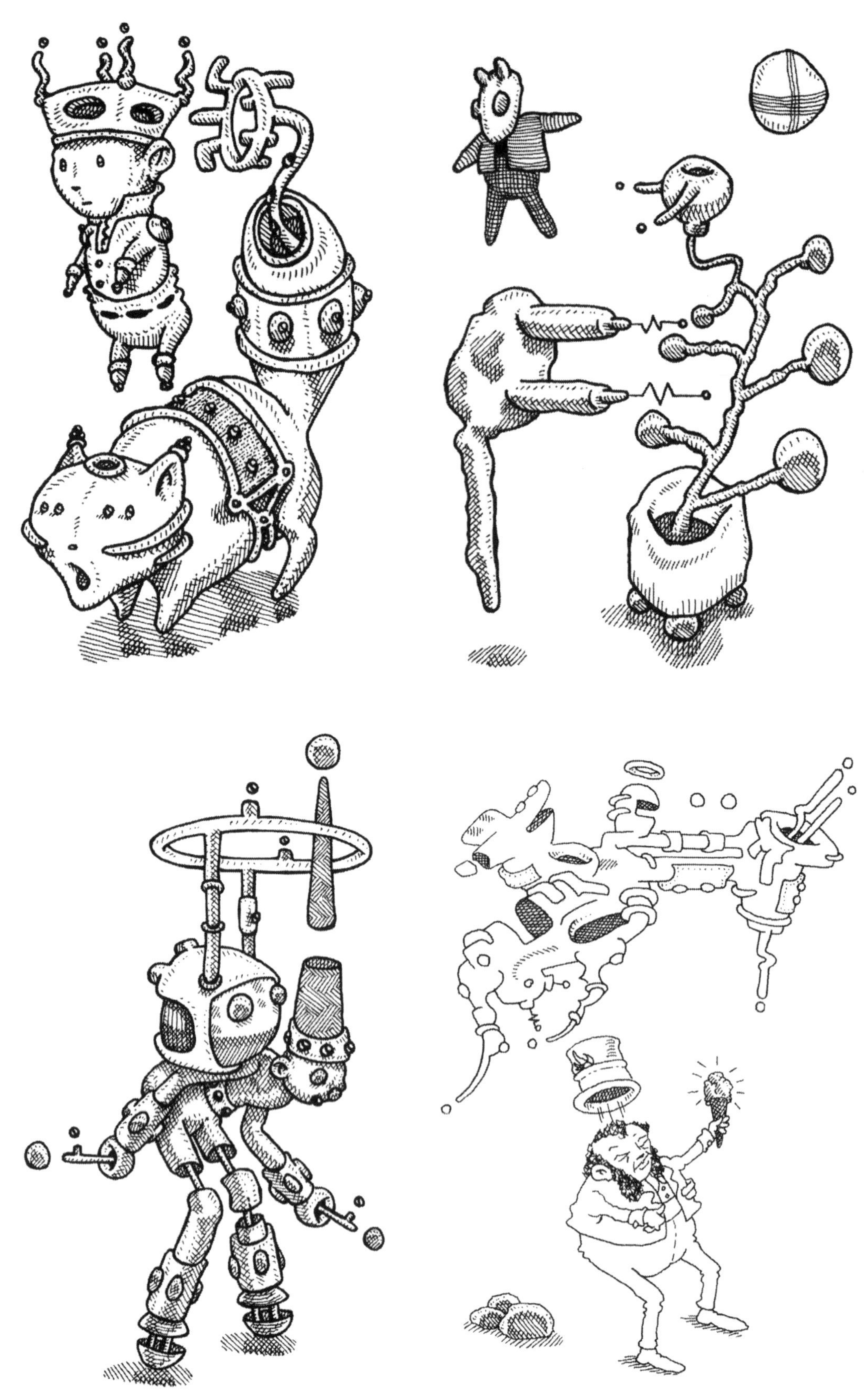

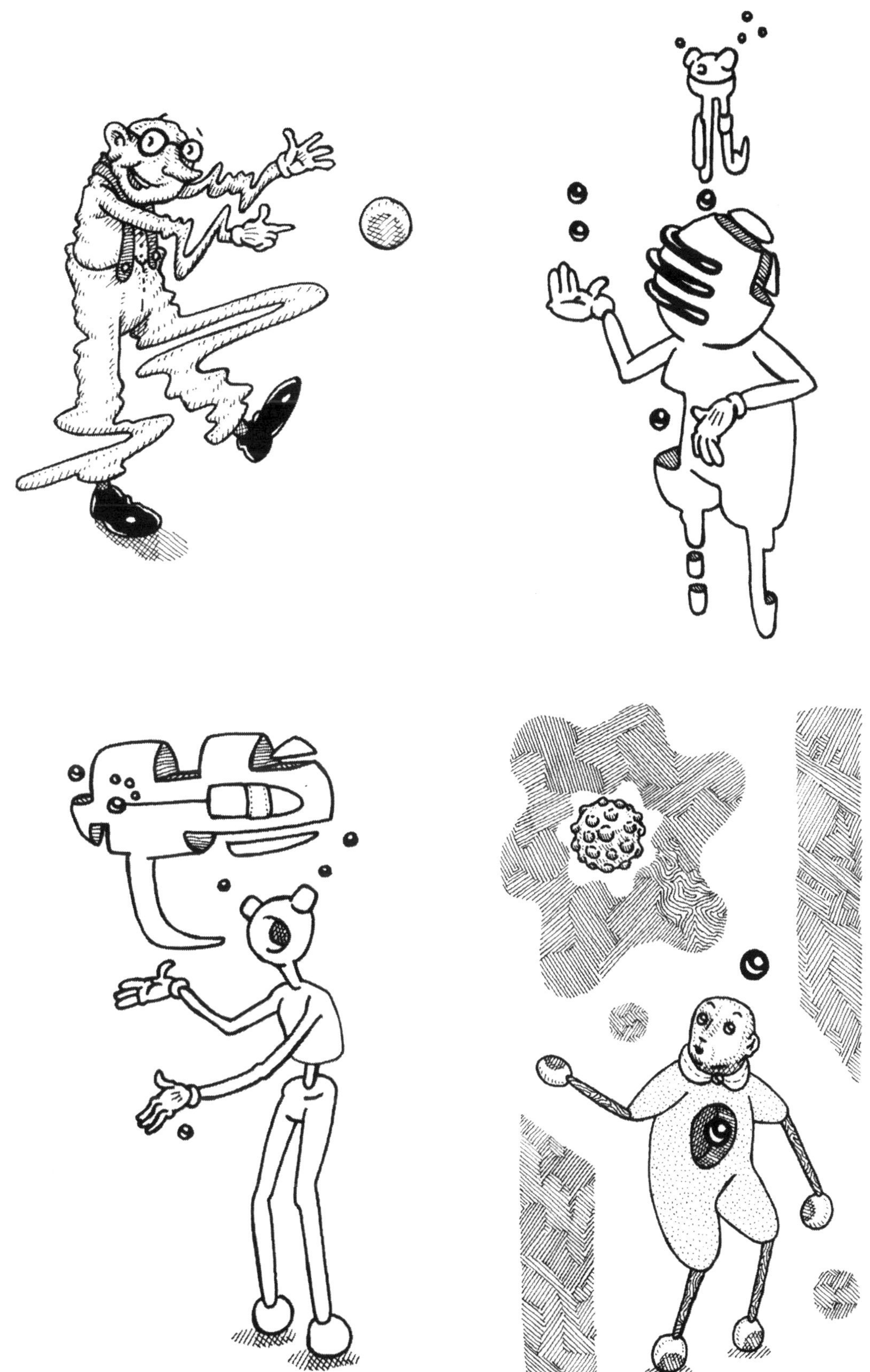

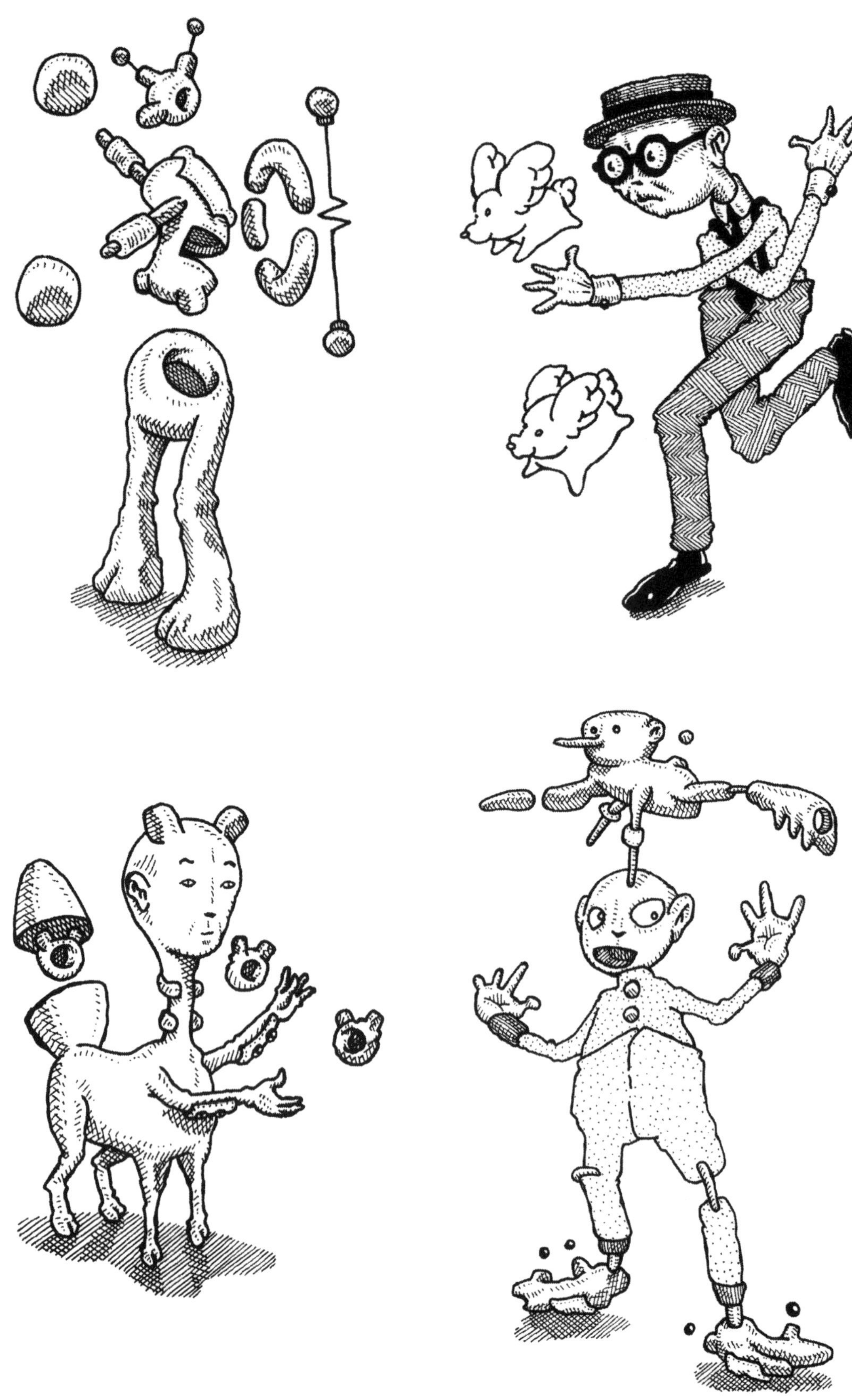

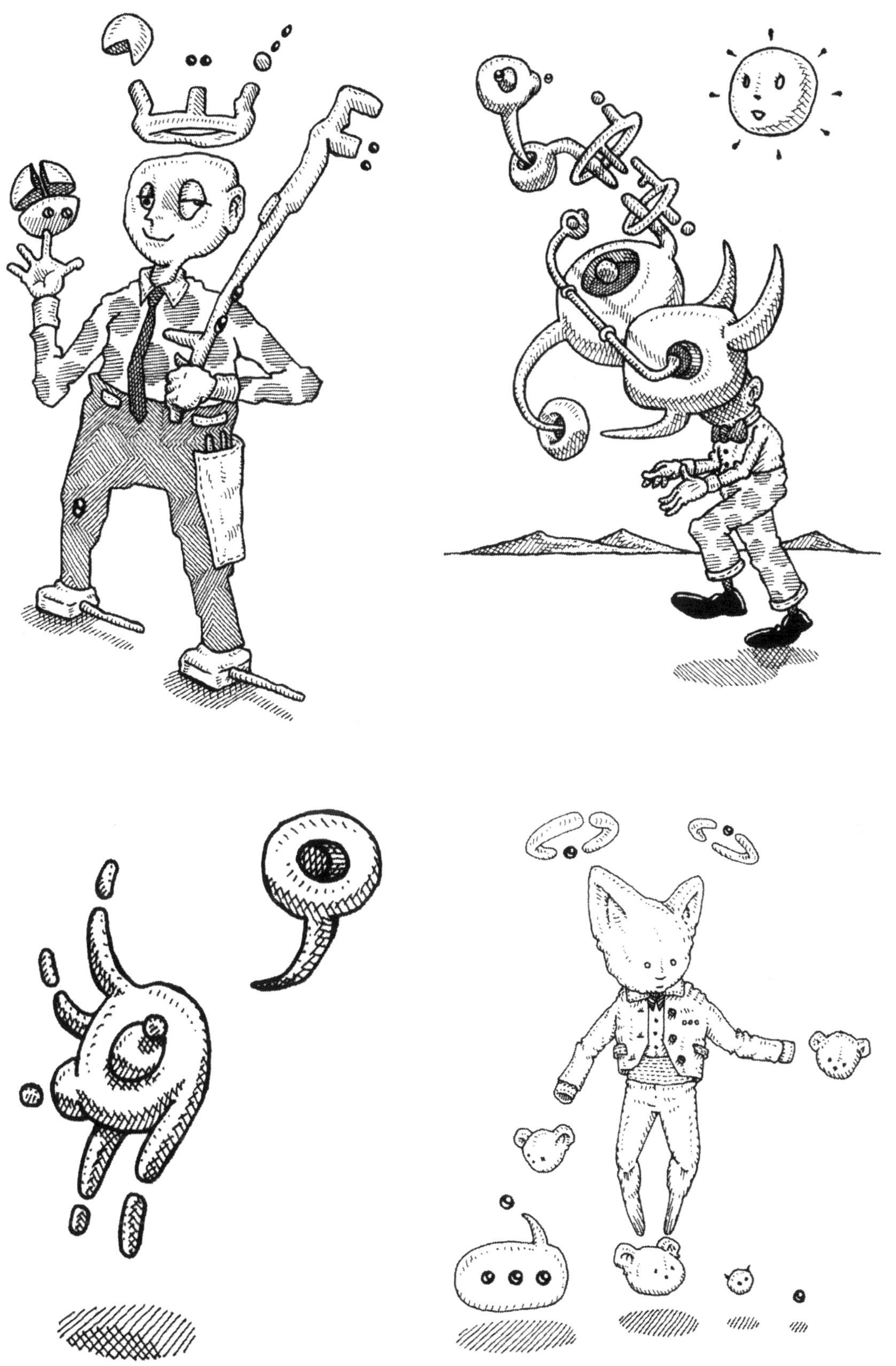

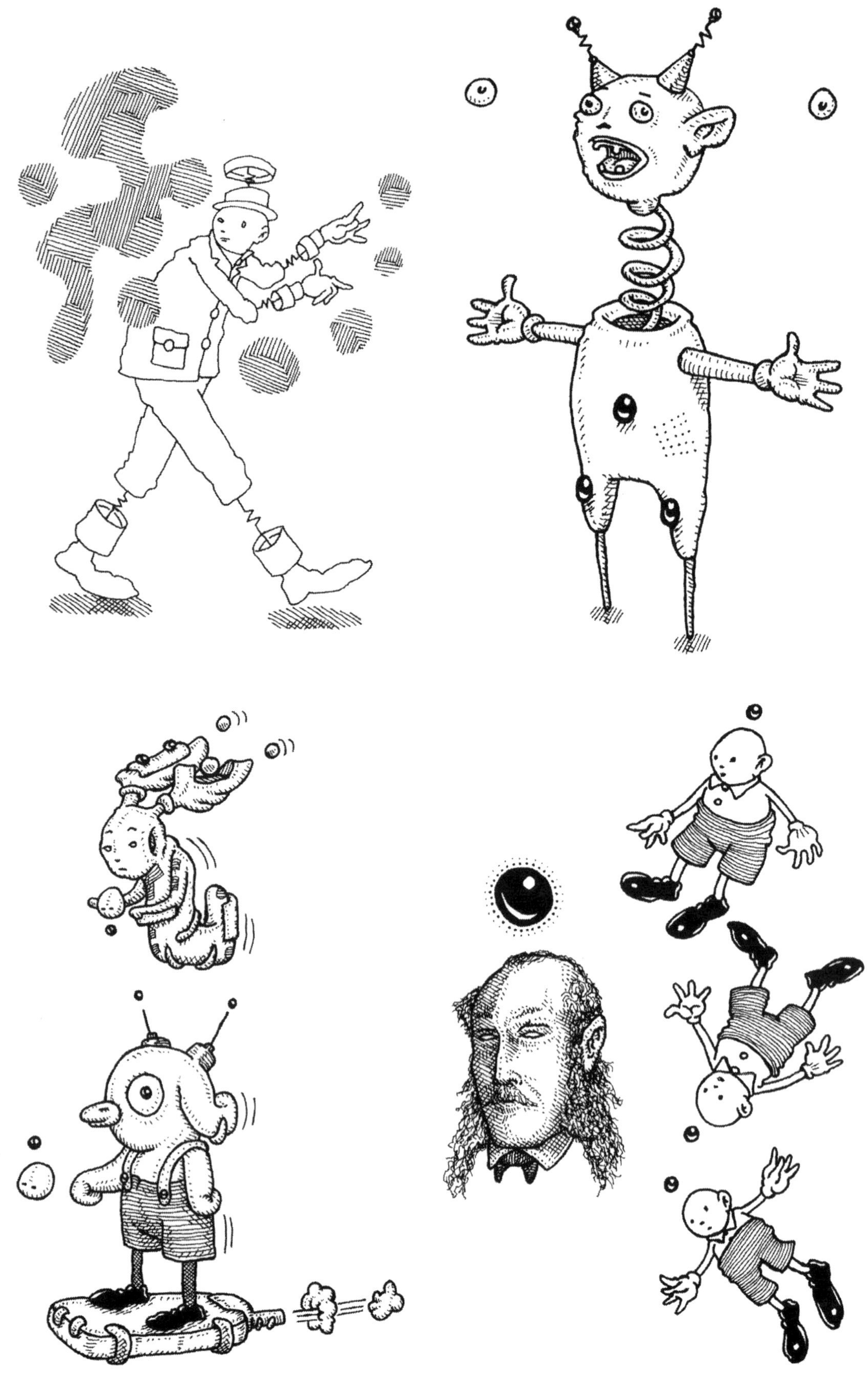

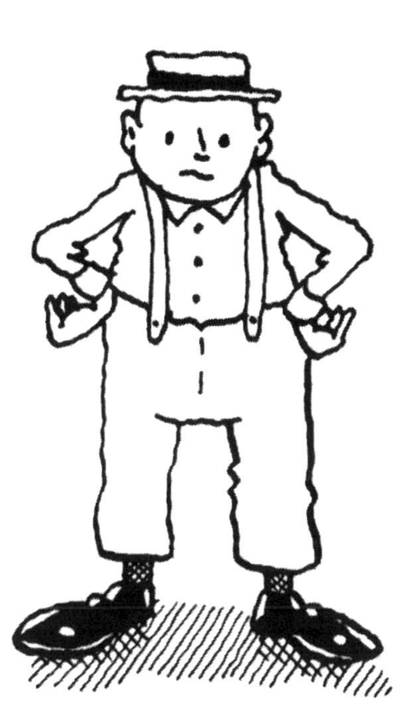

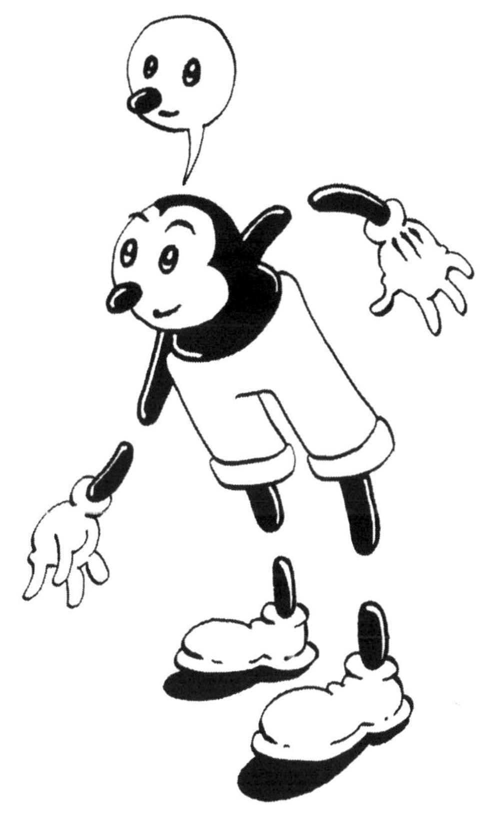

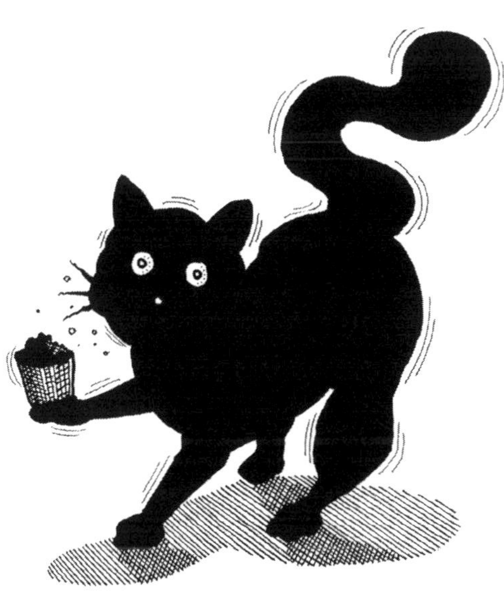

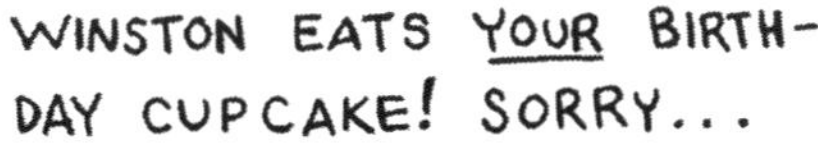
WINSTON EATS YOUR BIRTH-
DAY CUPCAKE! SORRY...

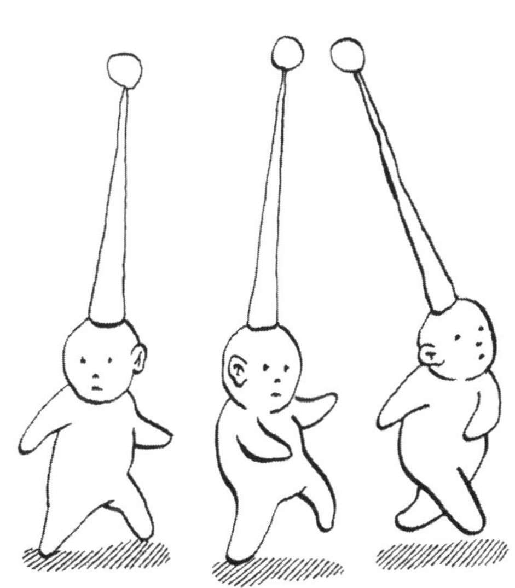

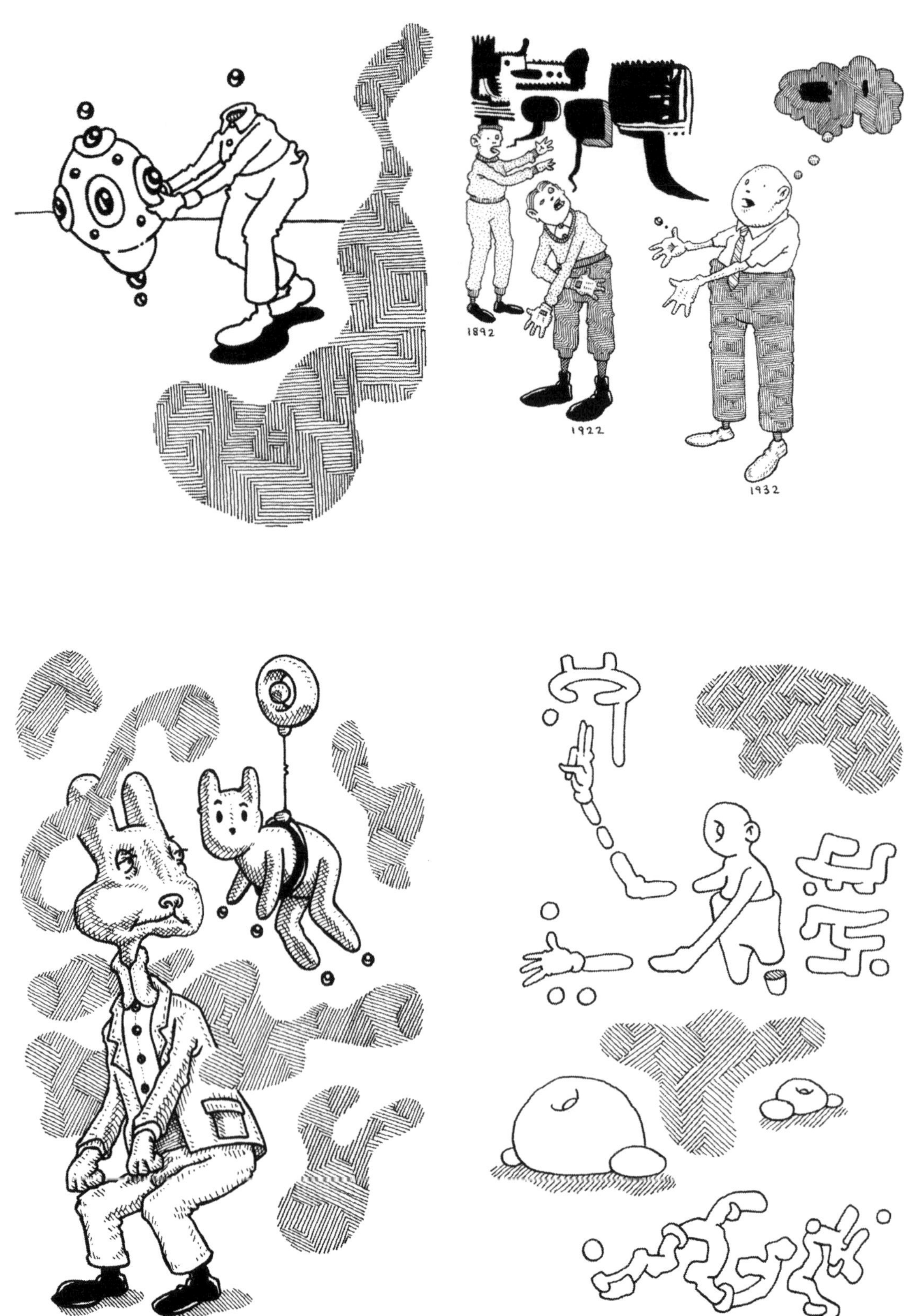
1892
1922
1932

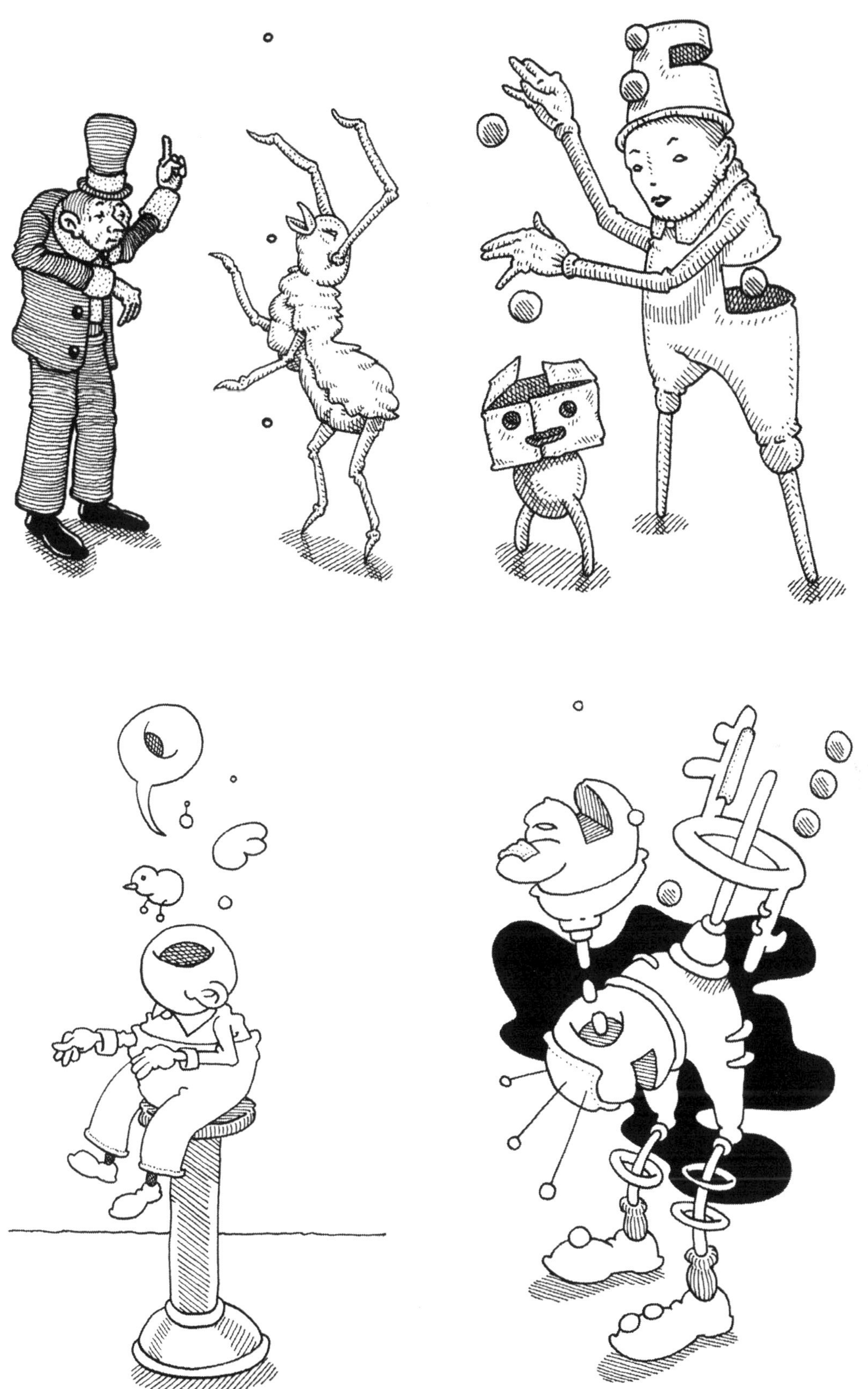

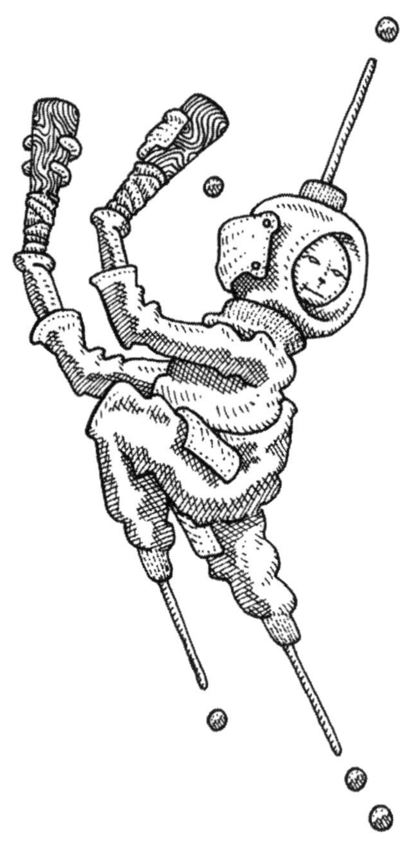

2017

AUGUST

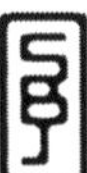

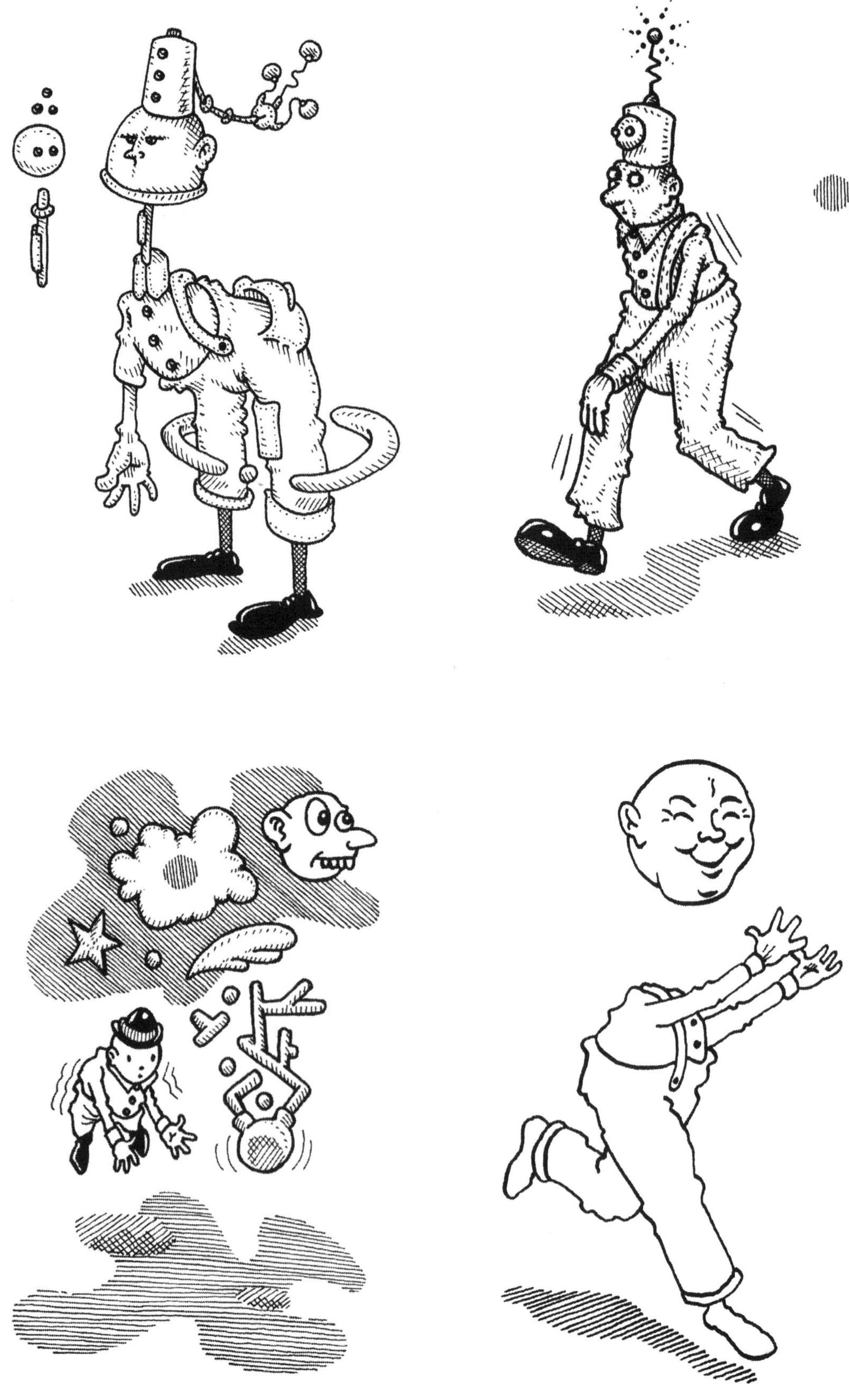

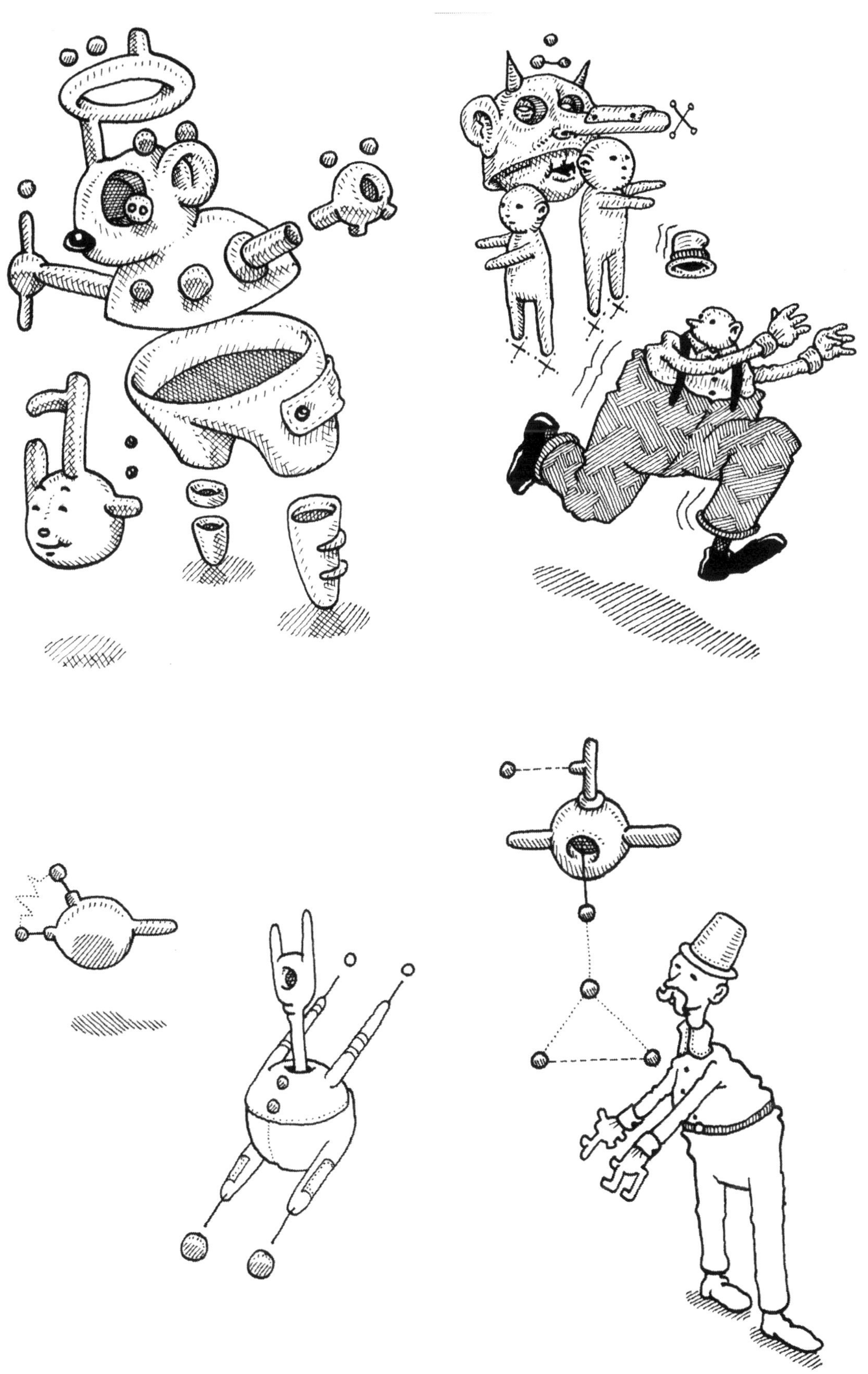

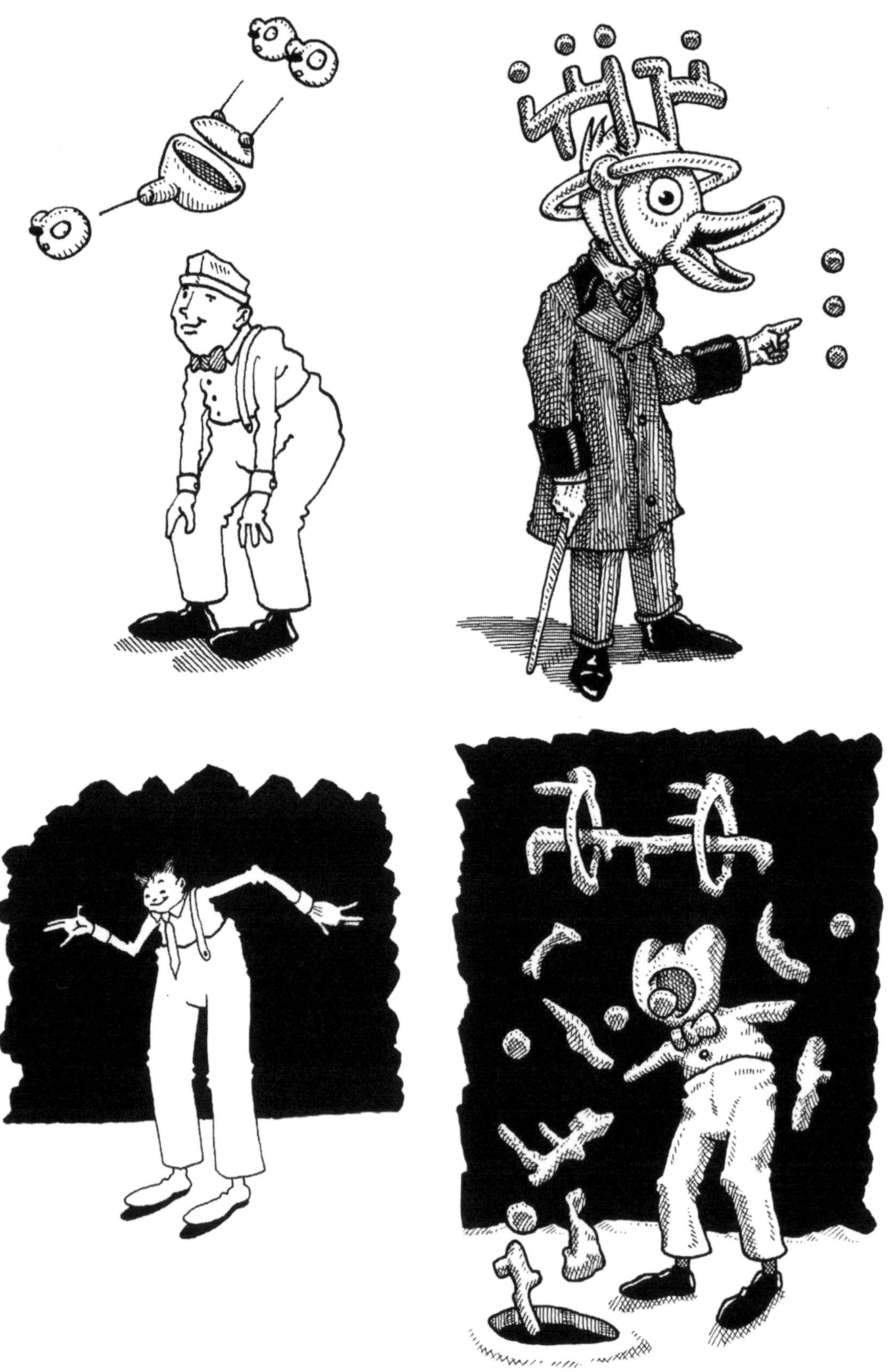

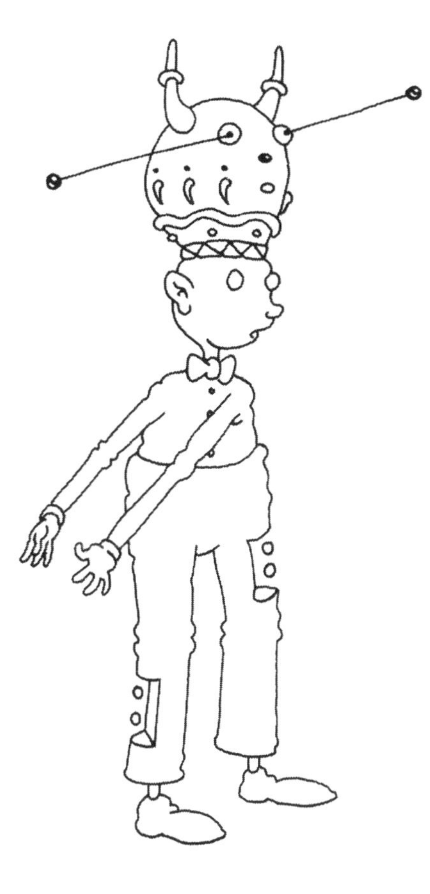

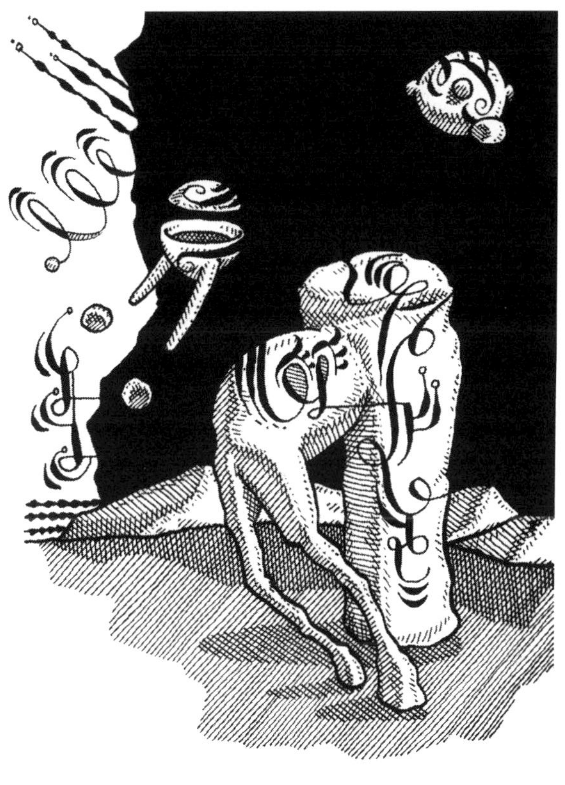

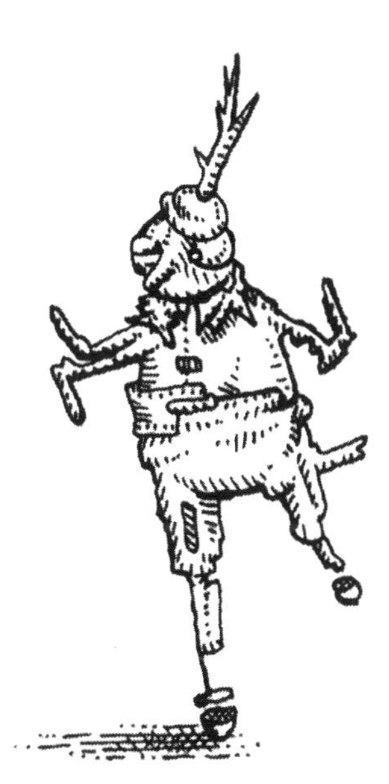

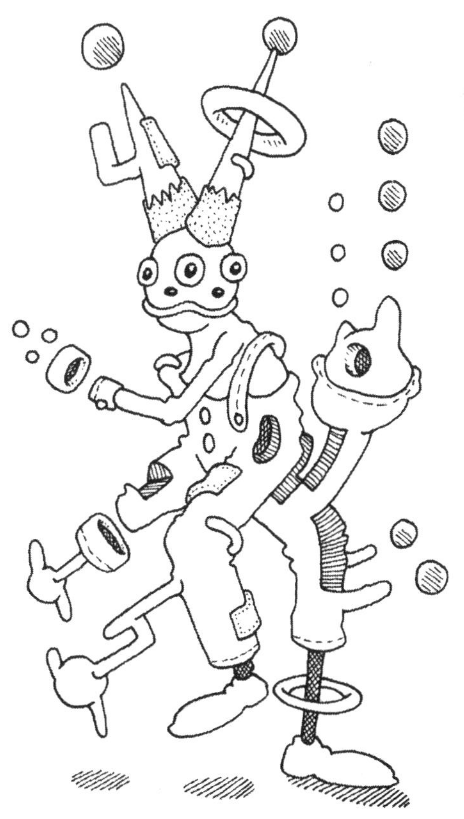

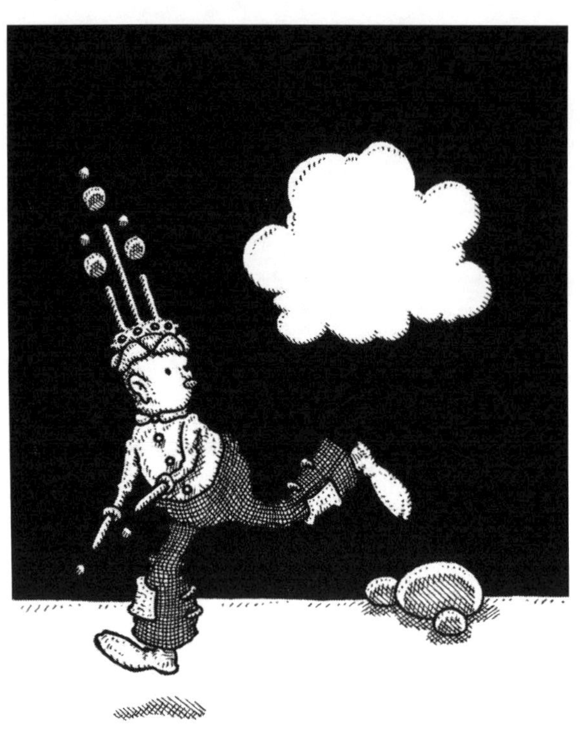

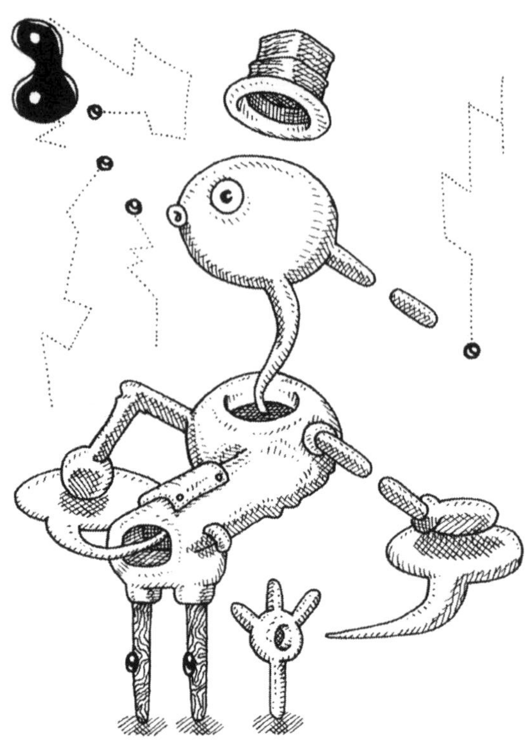

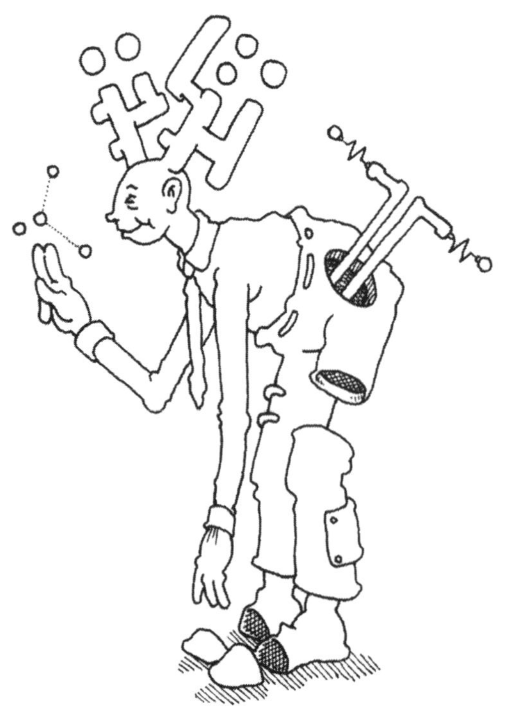

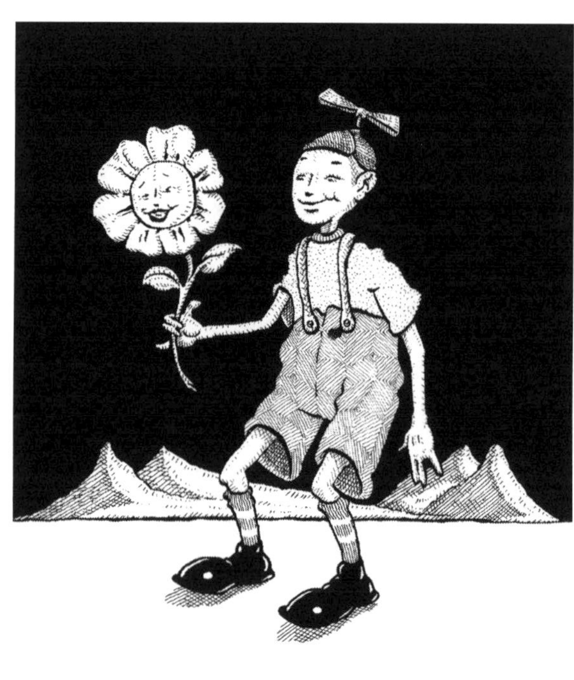

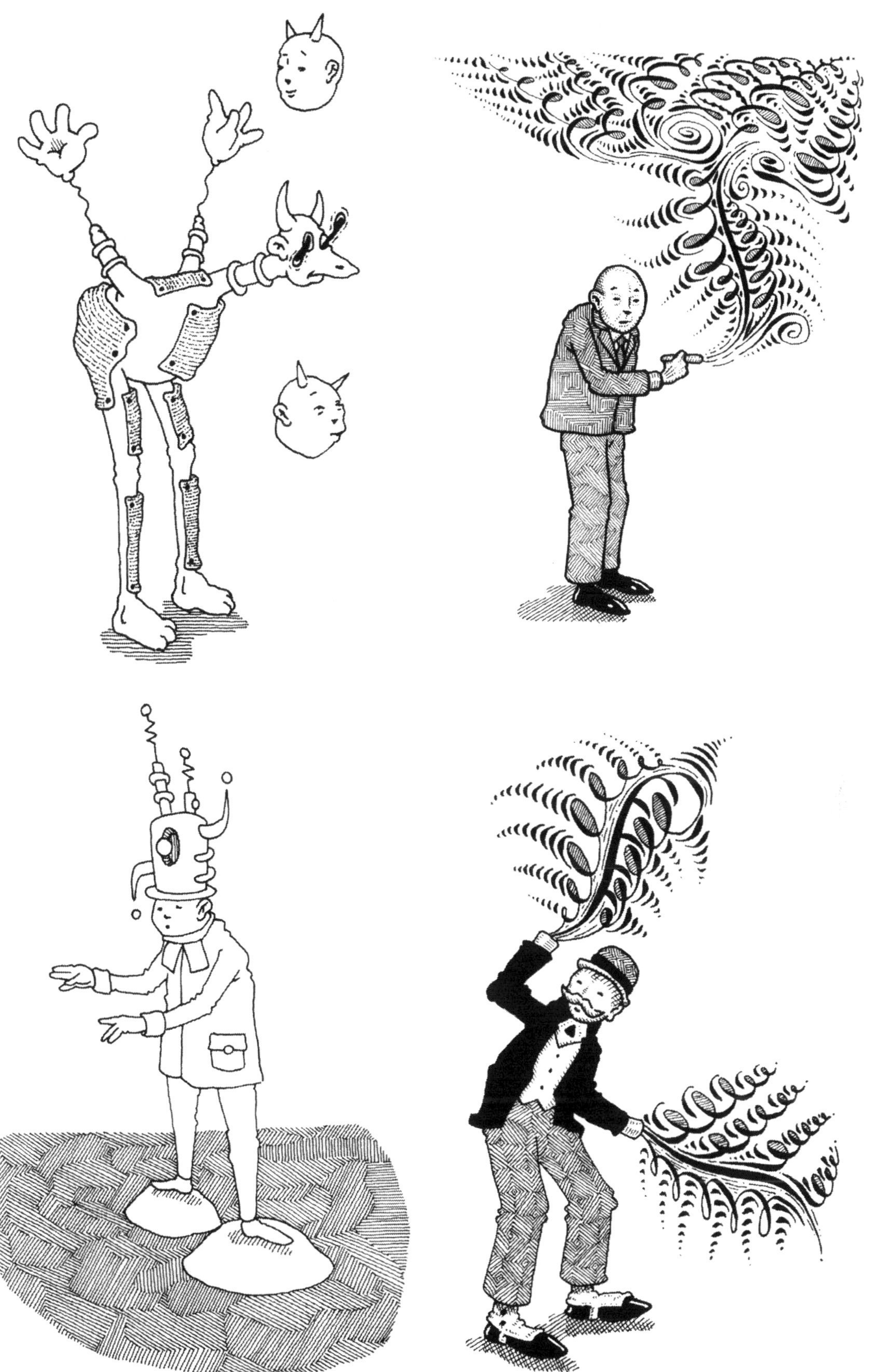

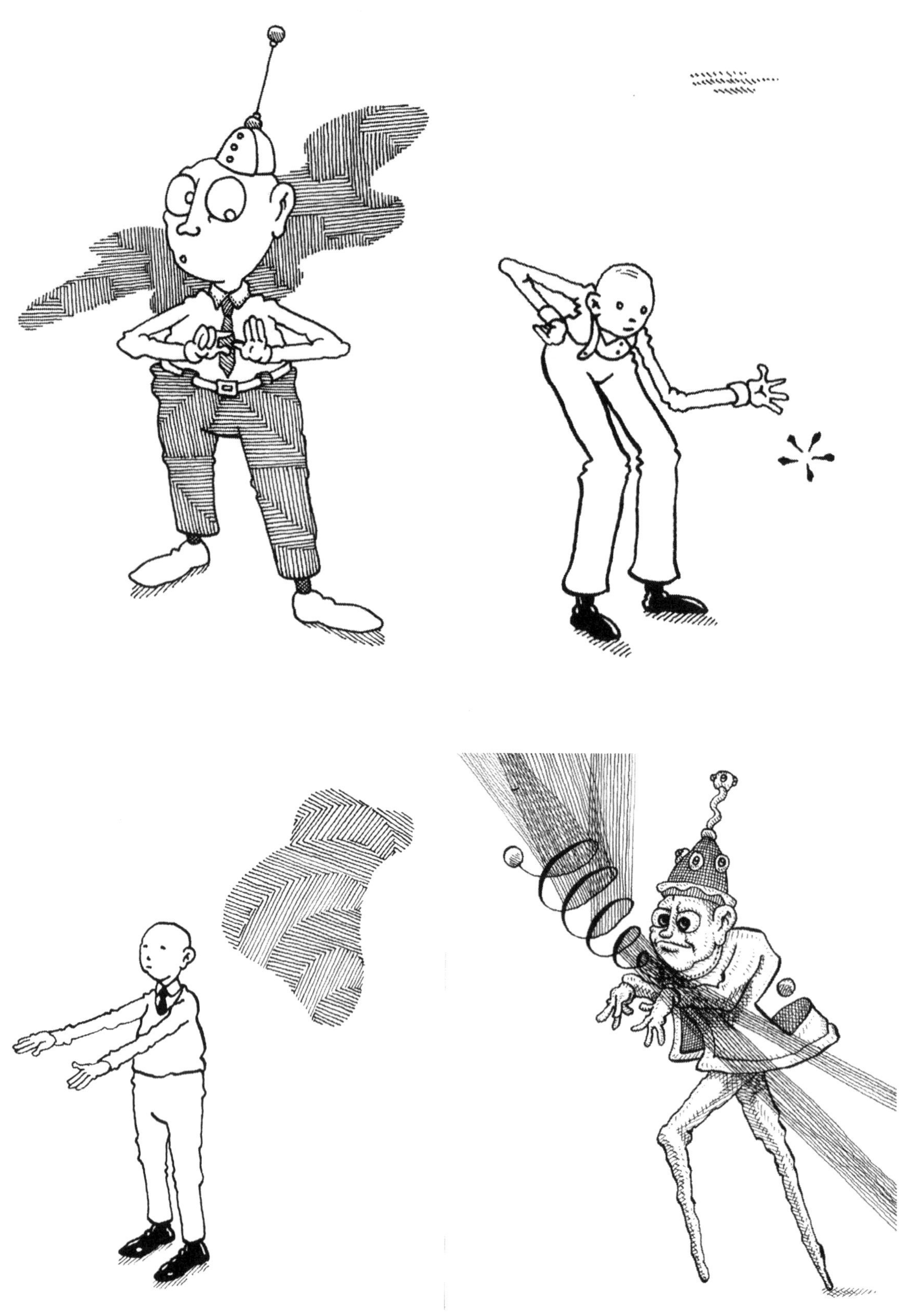

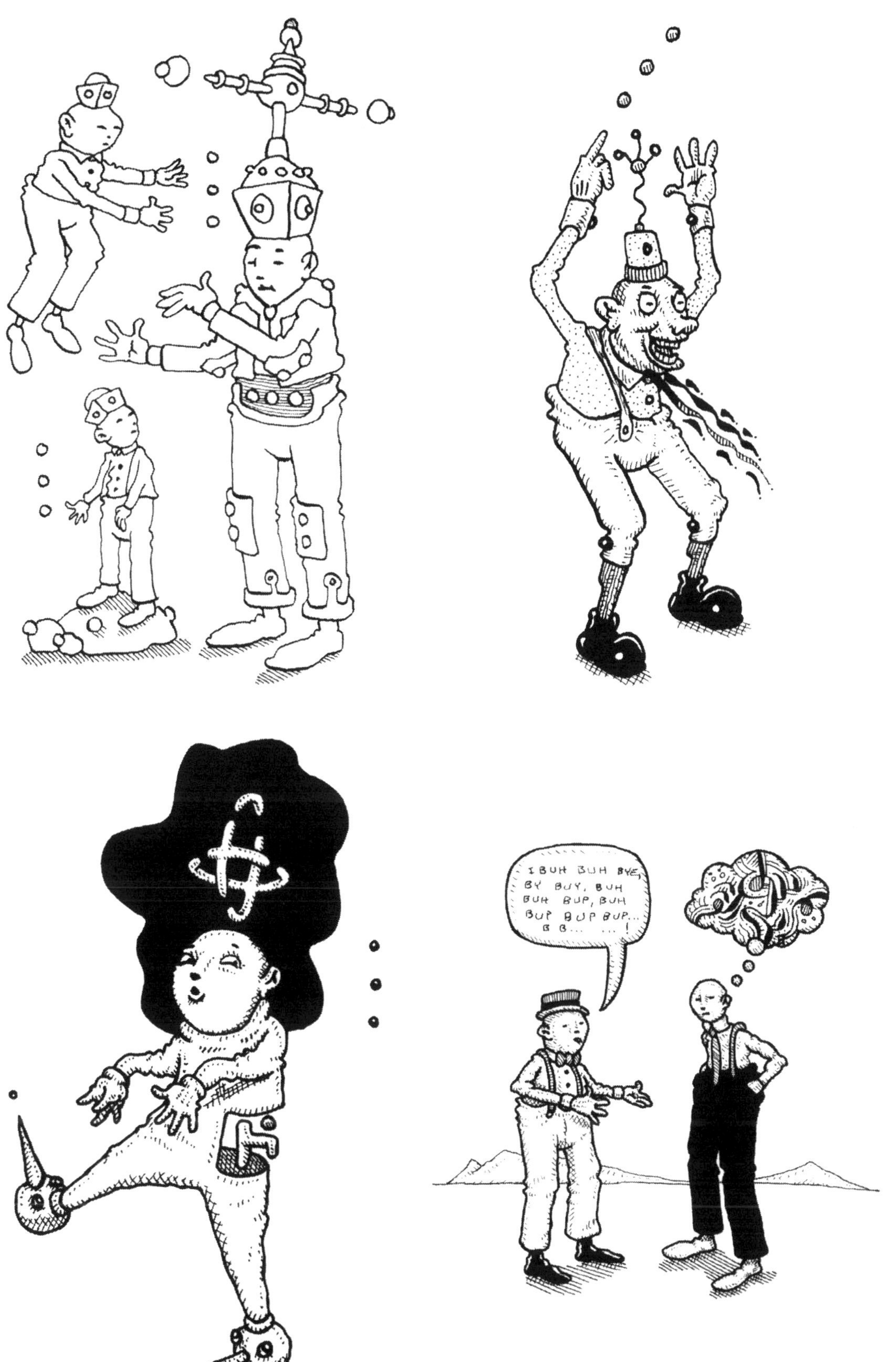
I BUH BUH BYE, BY BUY, BUH BUH BUP, BUH BUP BUP BUP... B B... ...!

2017

SEPTEMBER

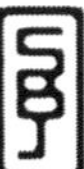

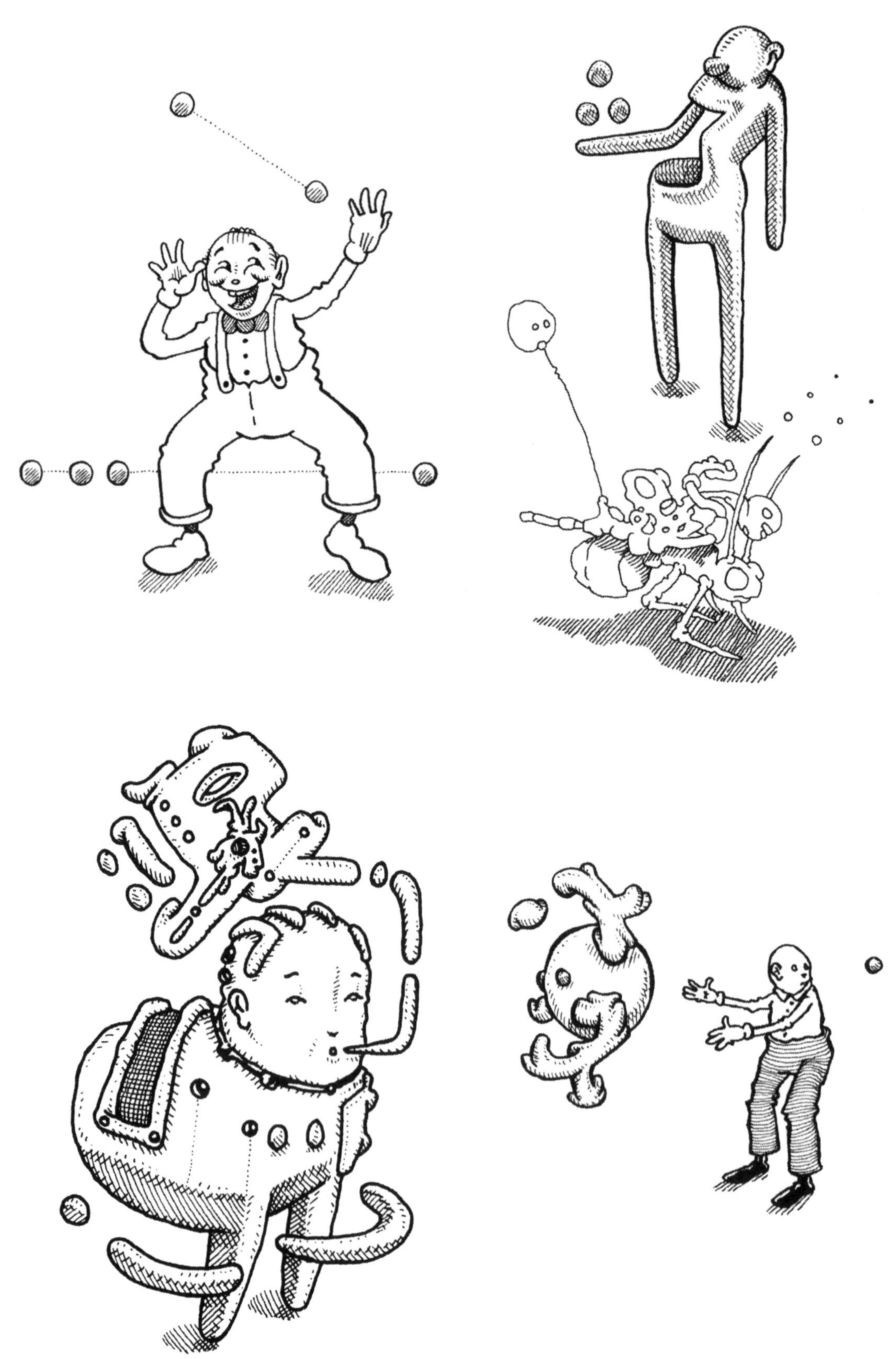

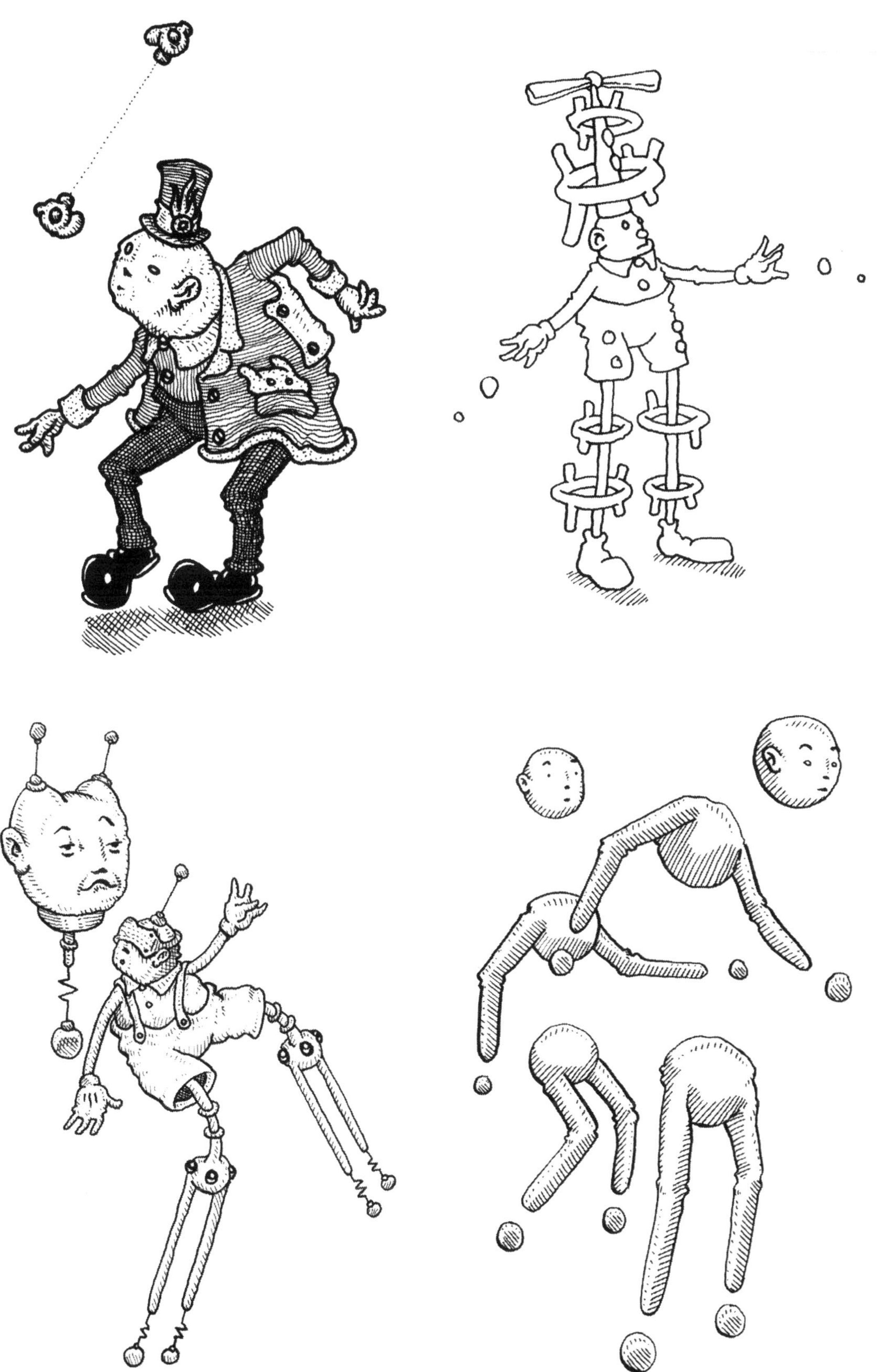

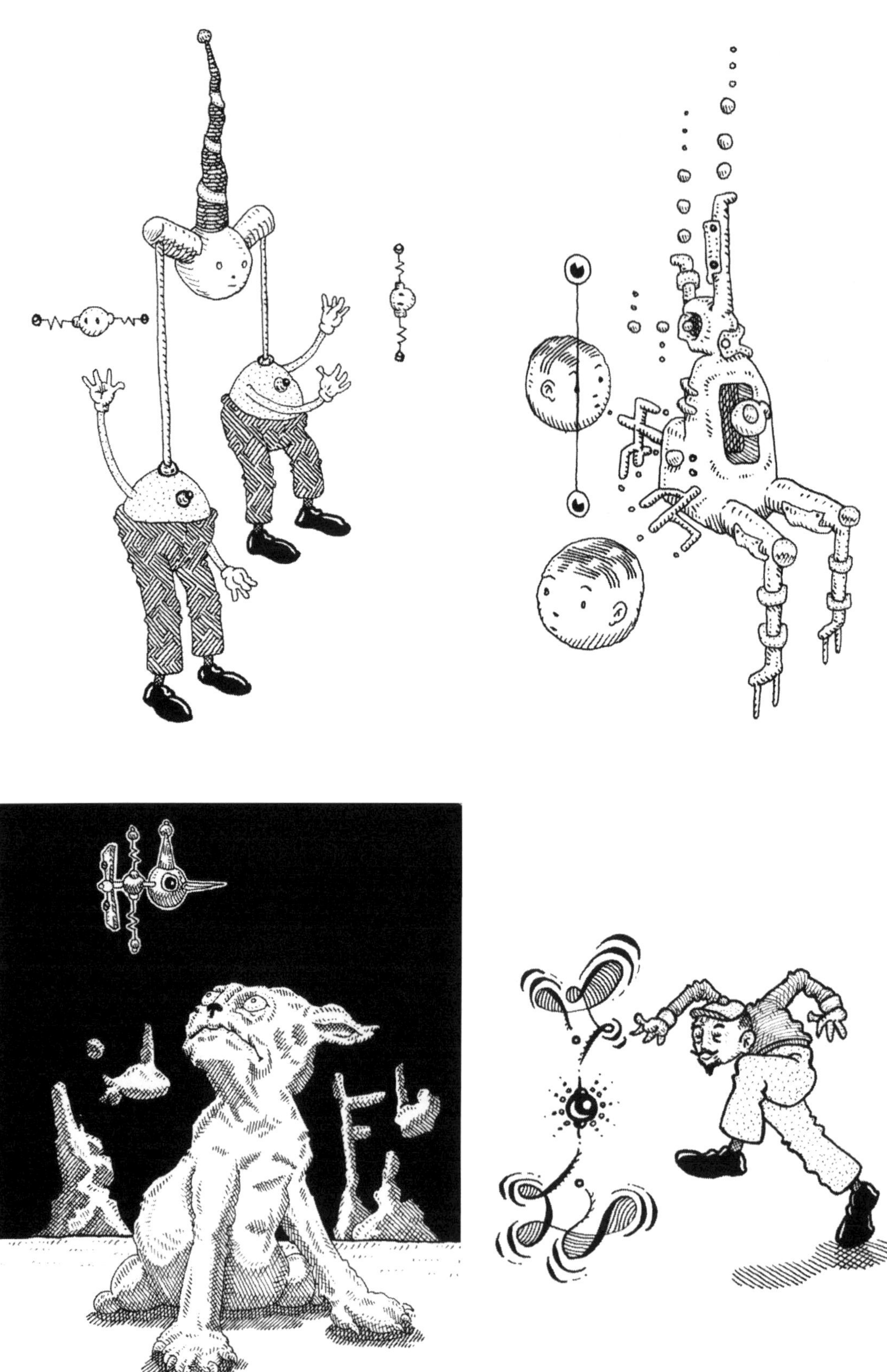

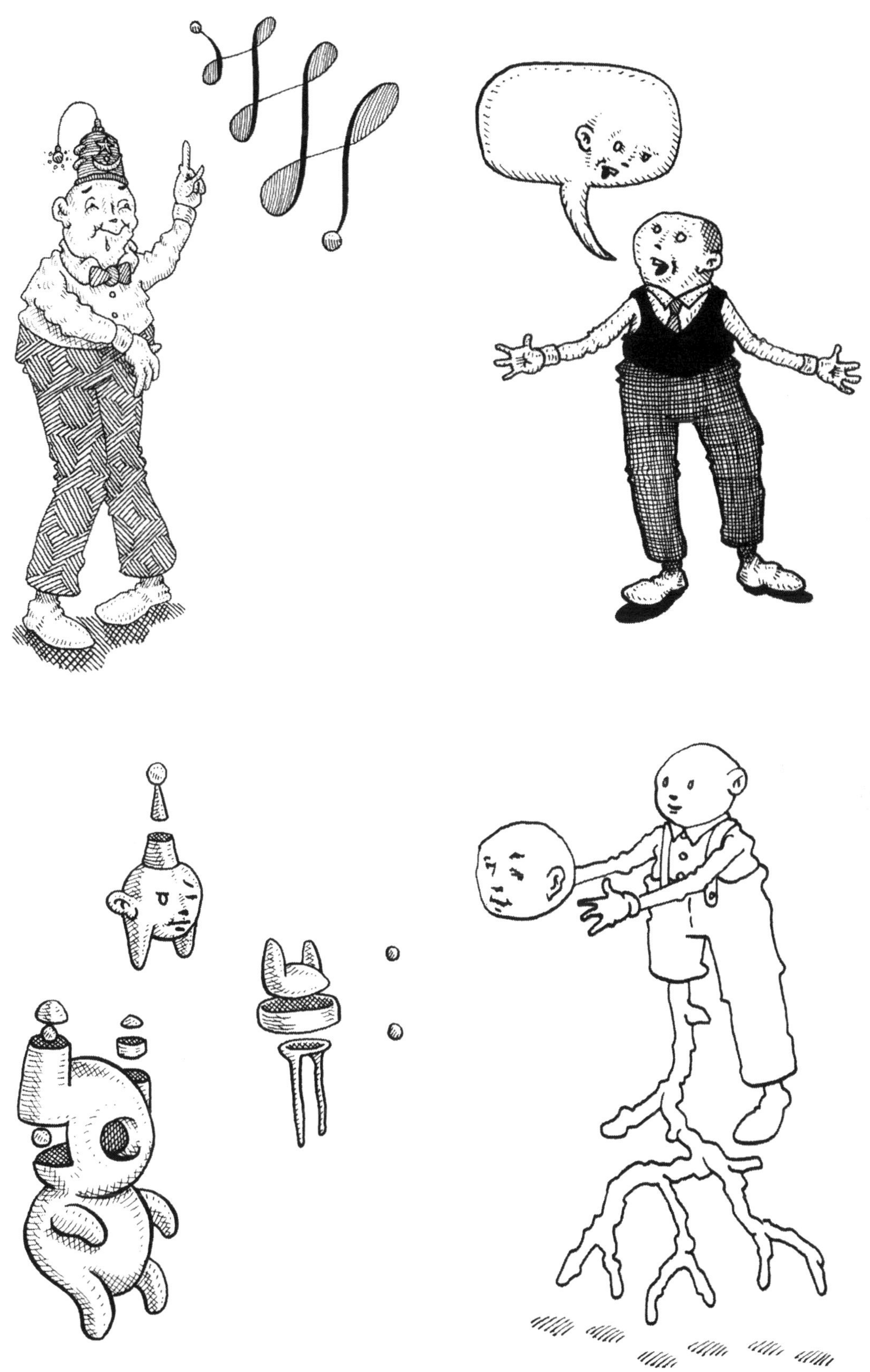

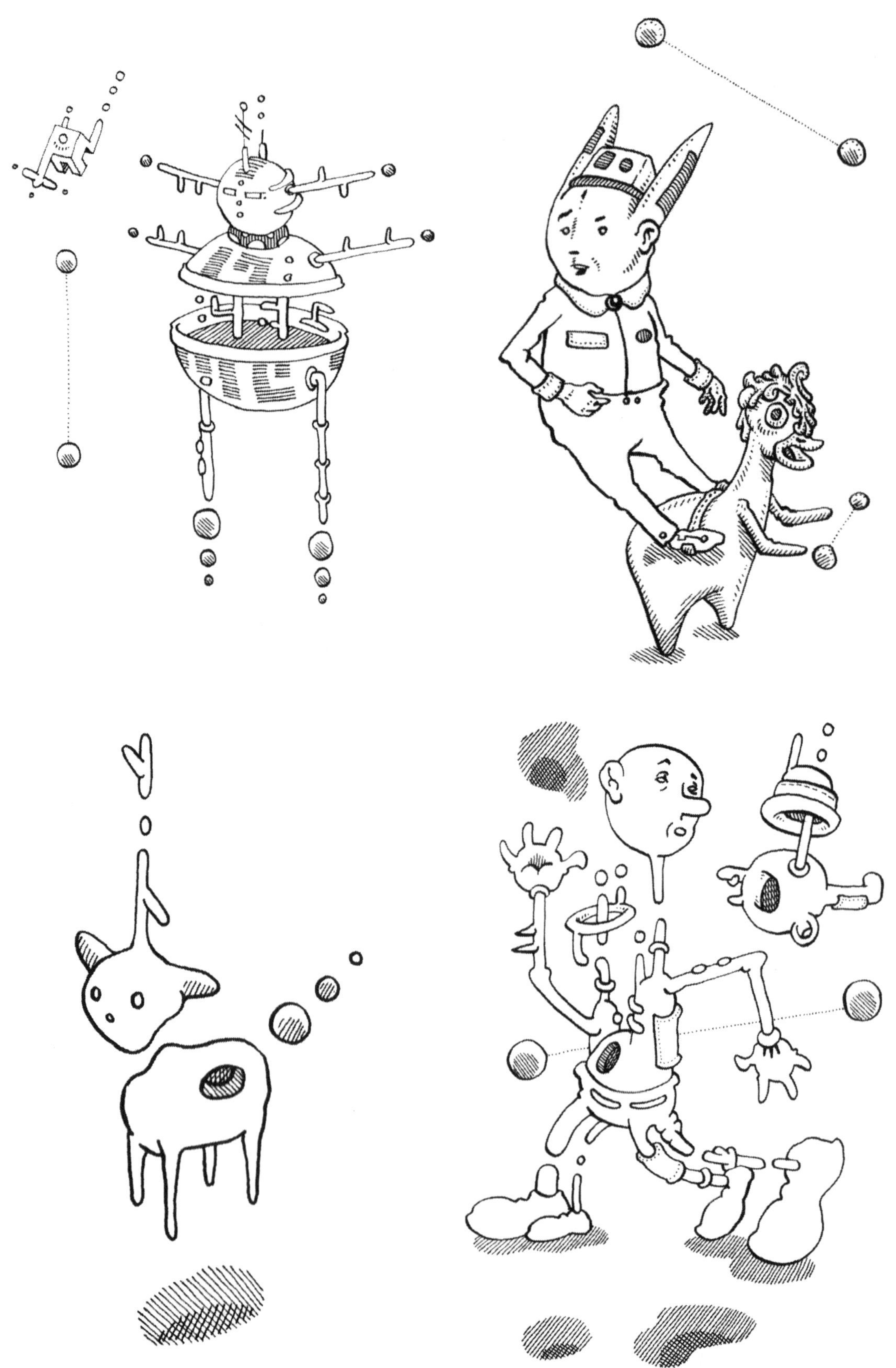

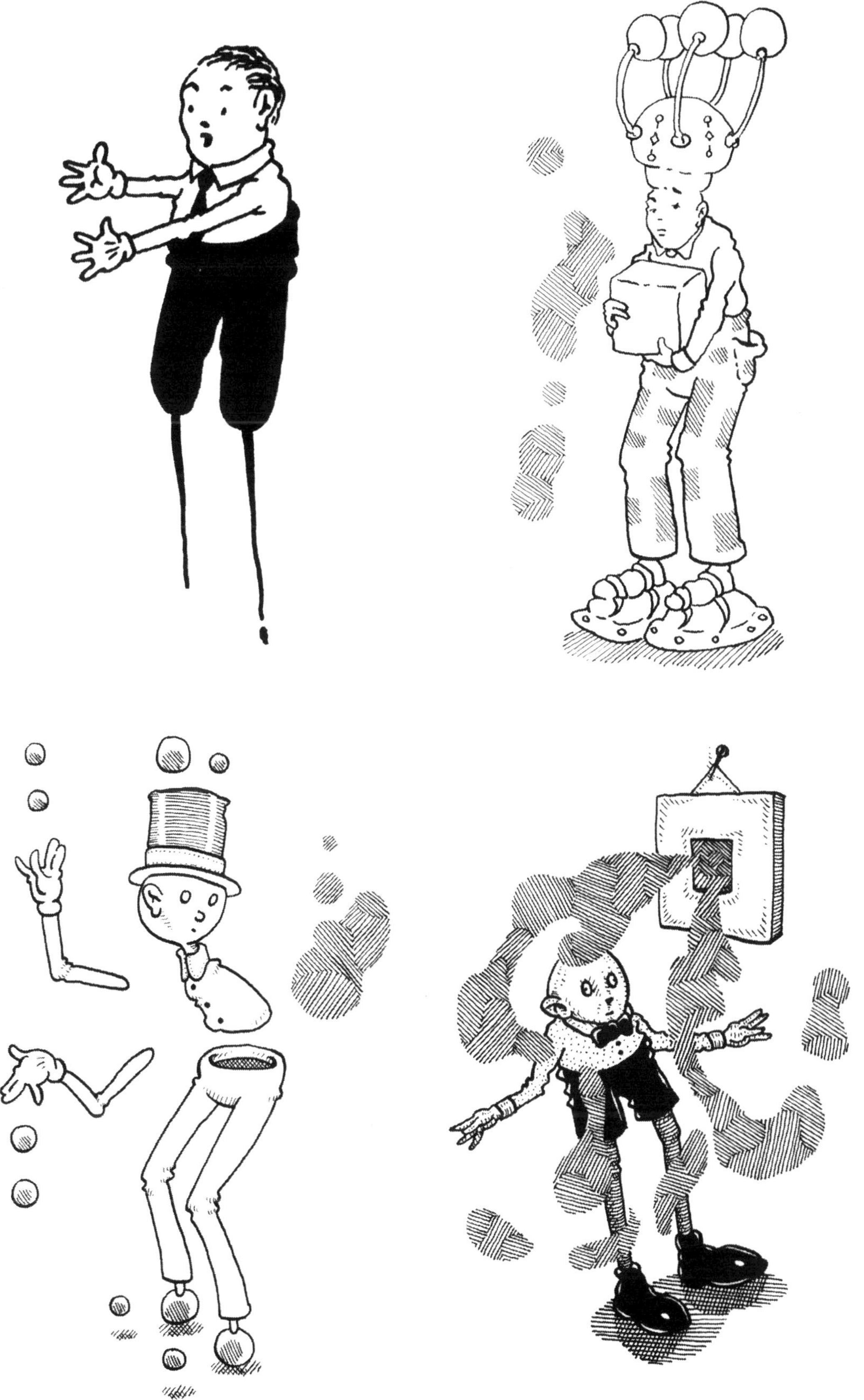

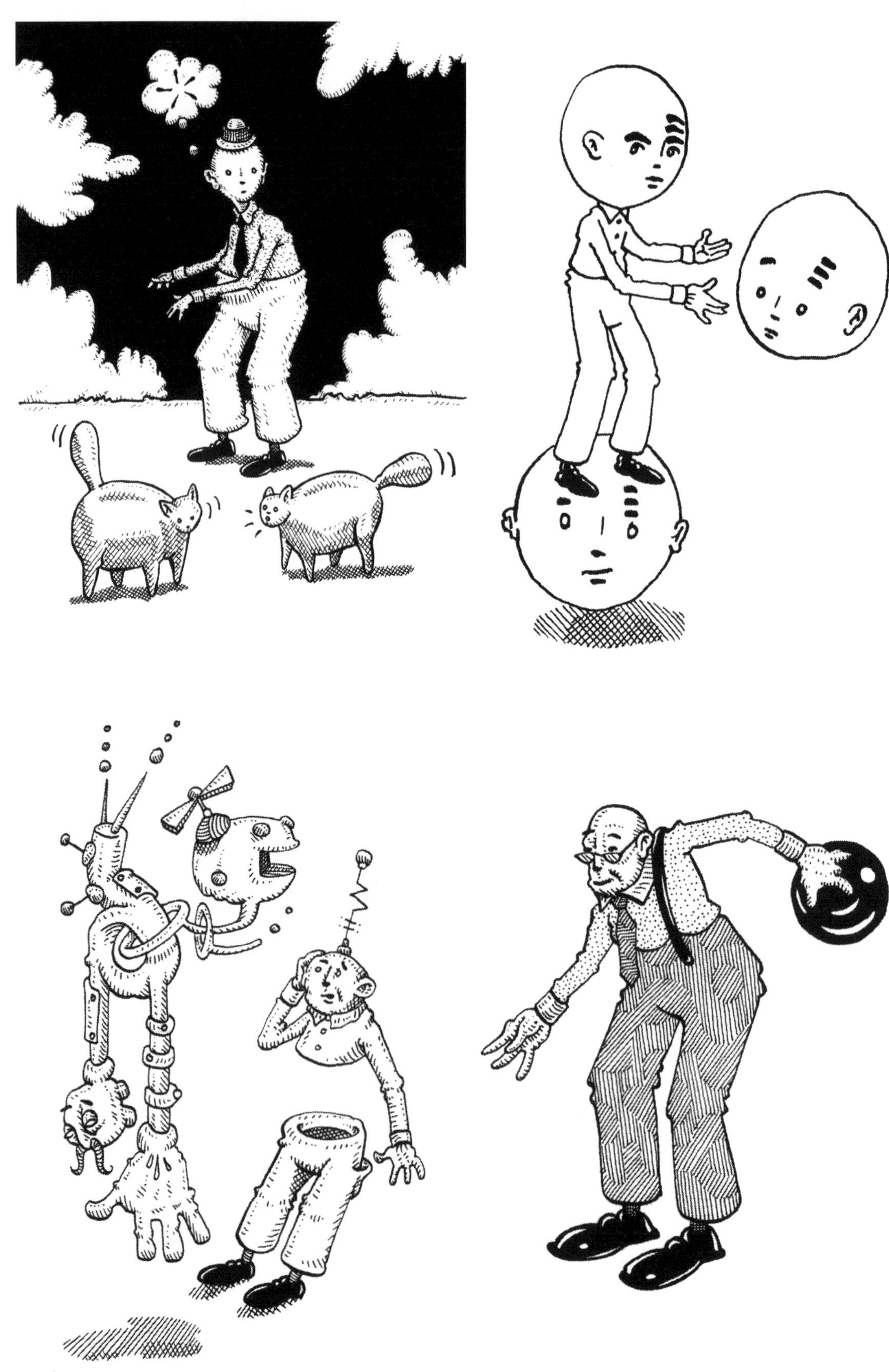

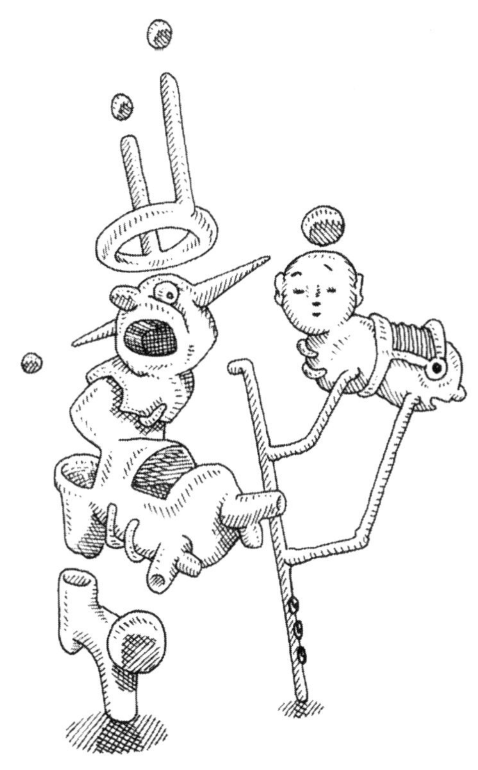

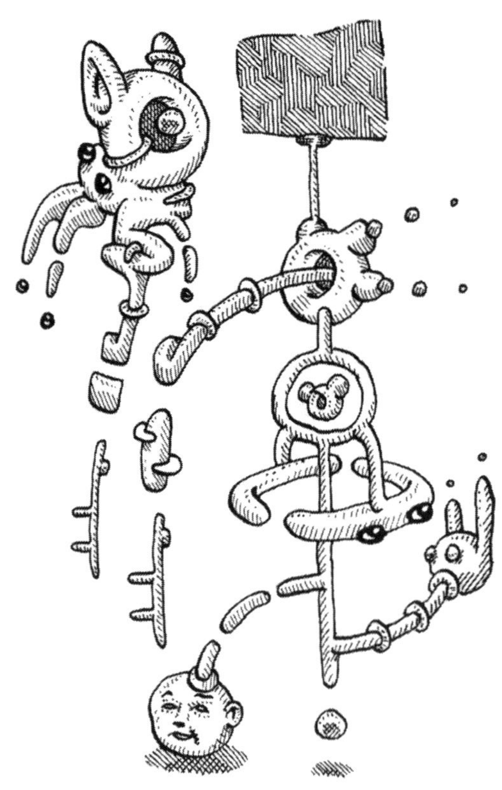

2017

October

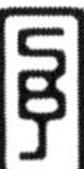

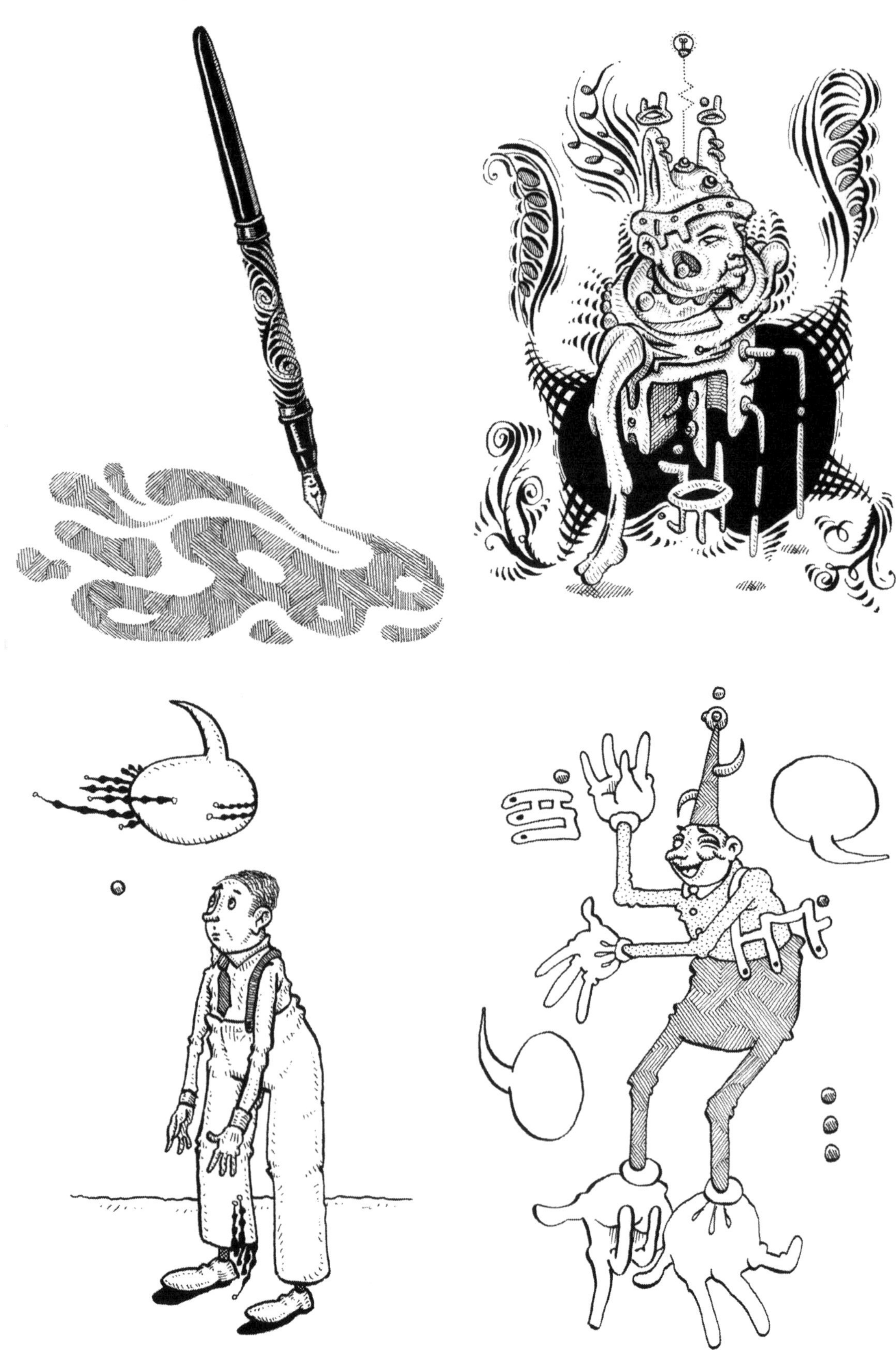

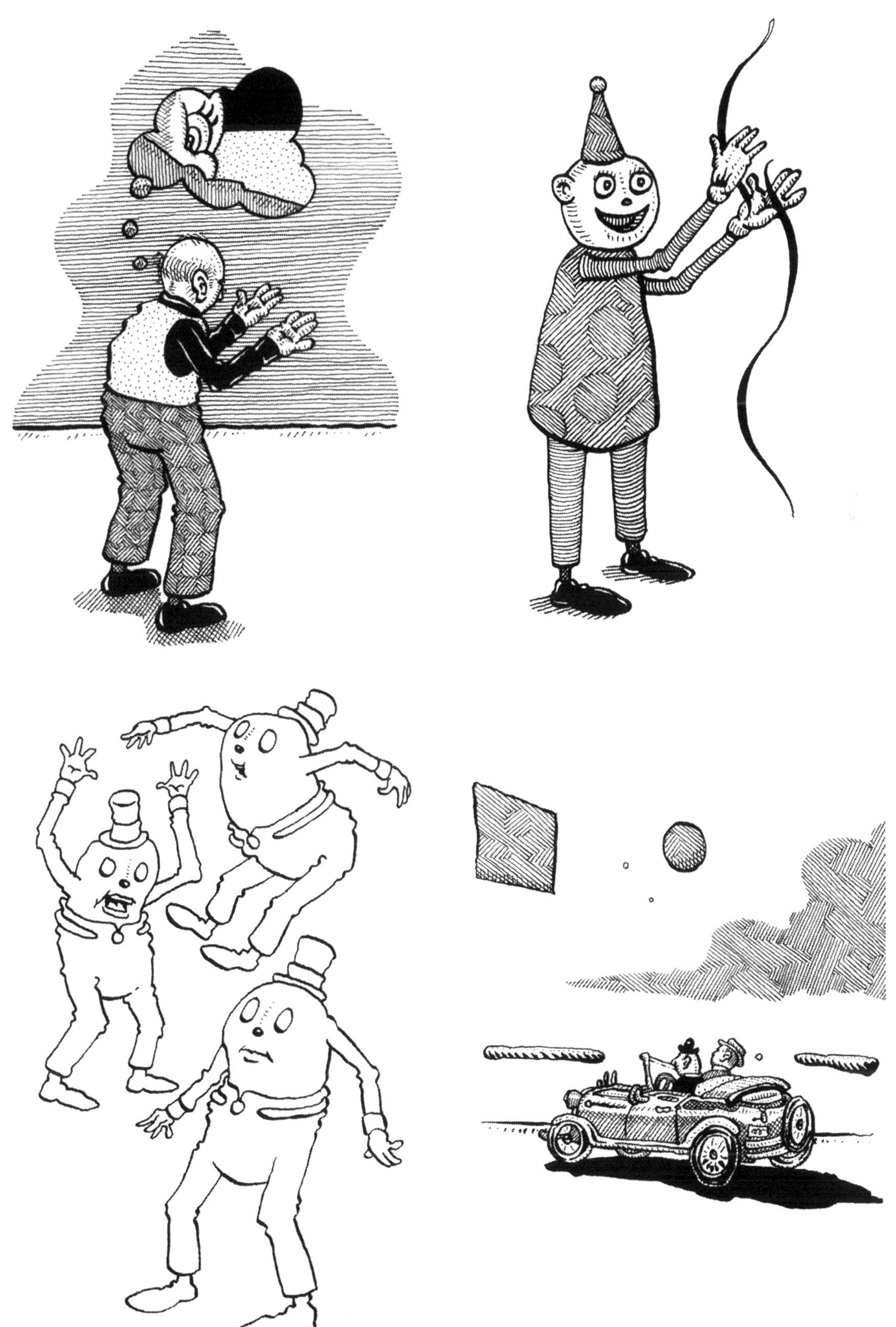

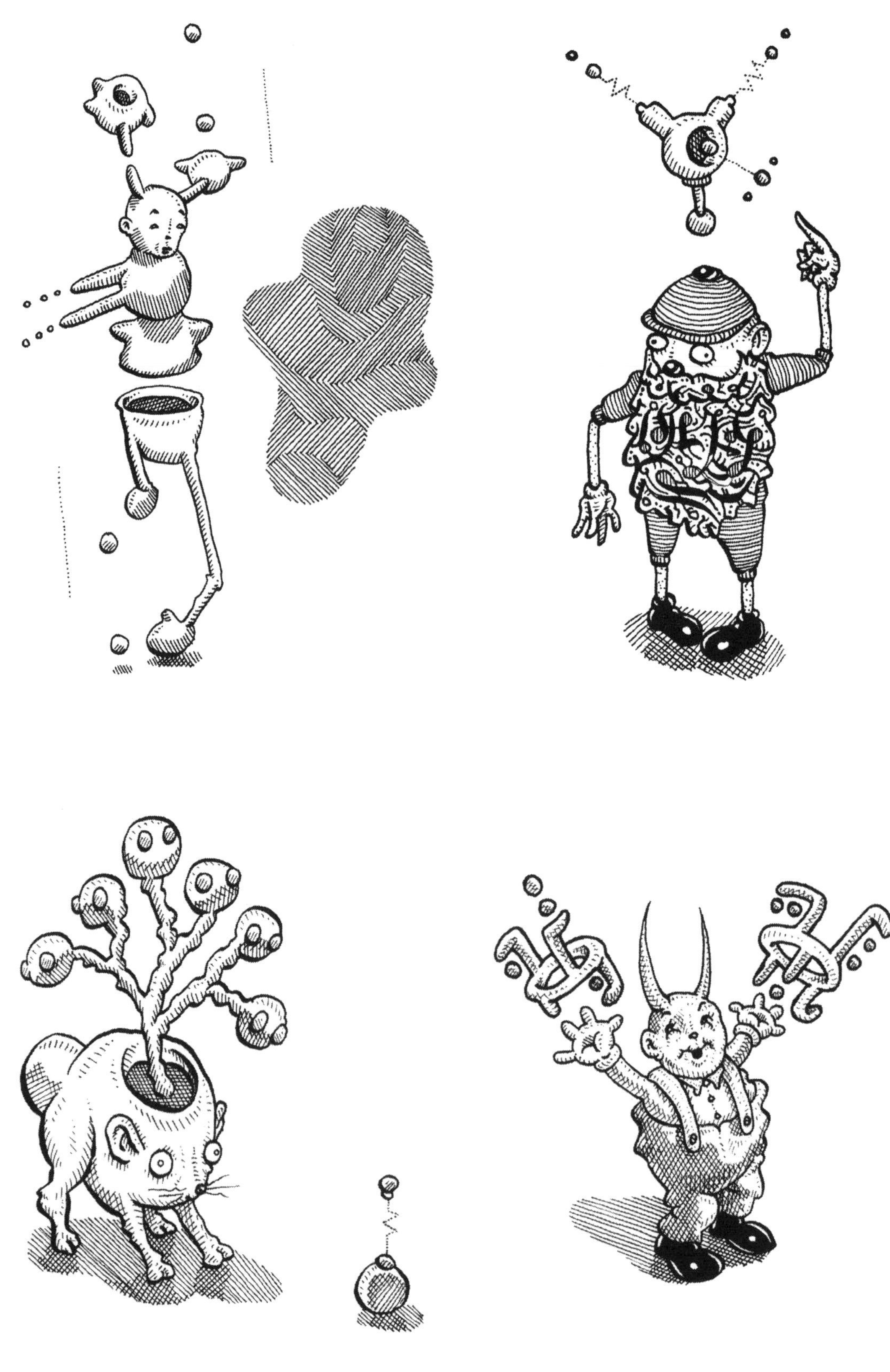

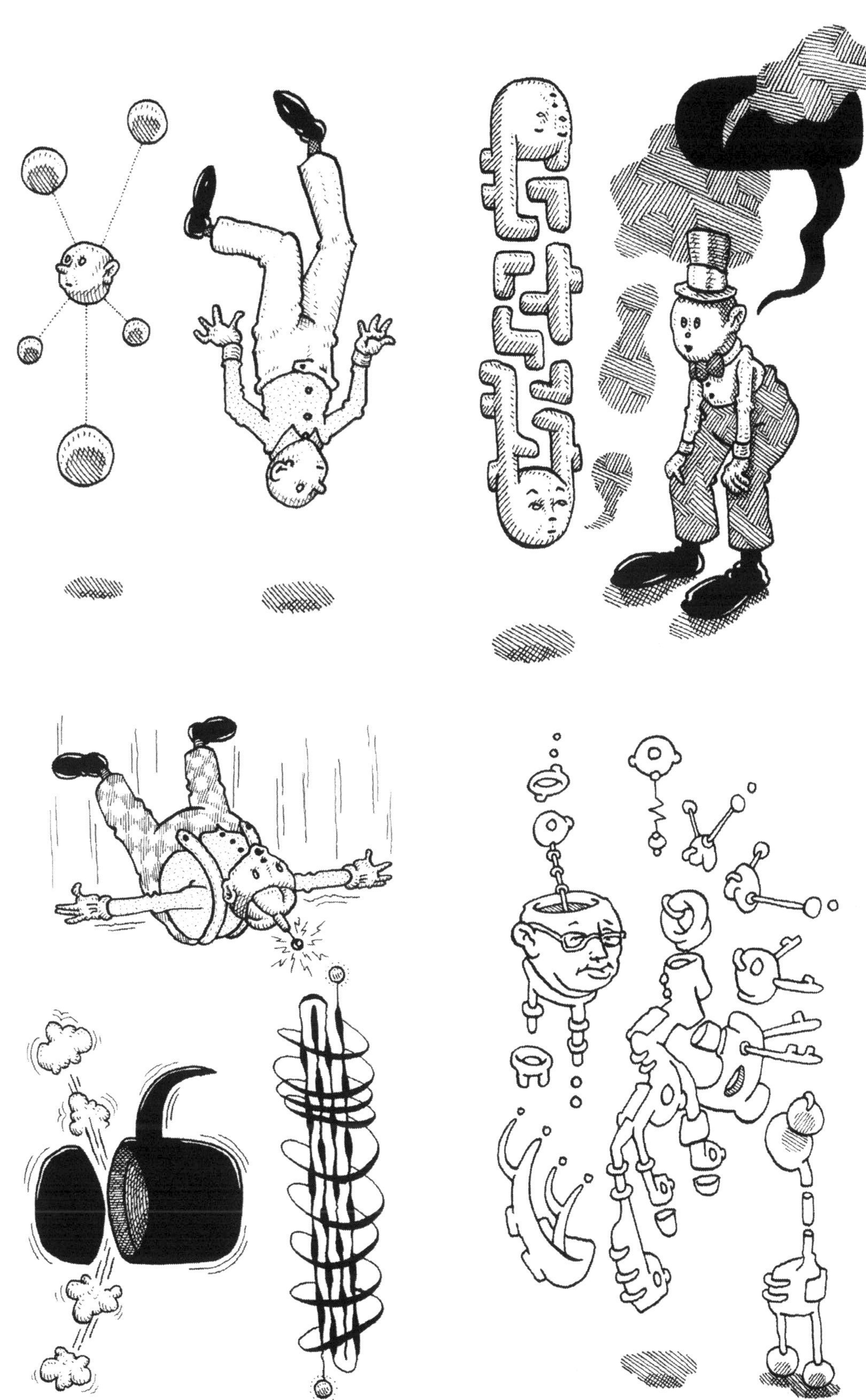

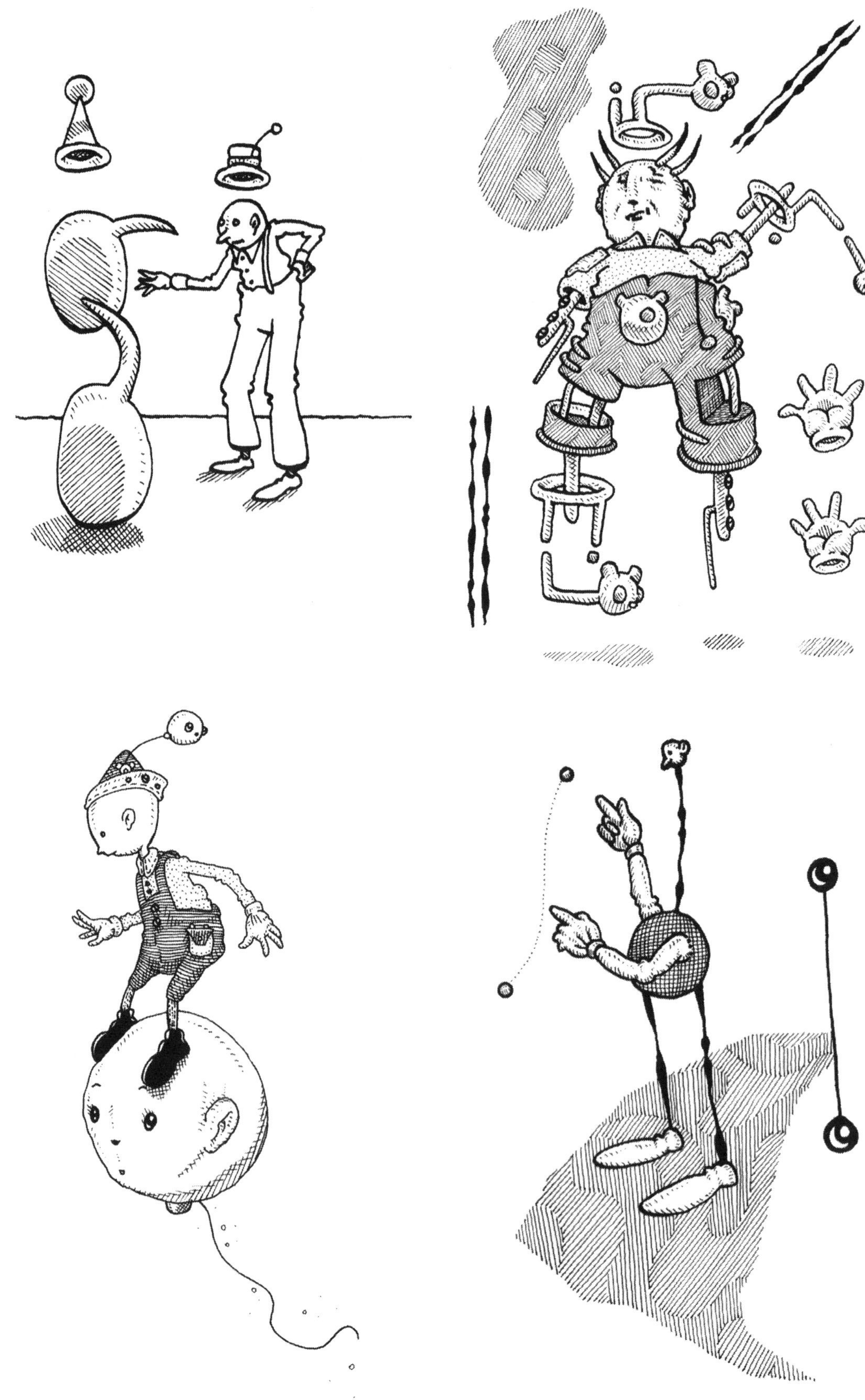

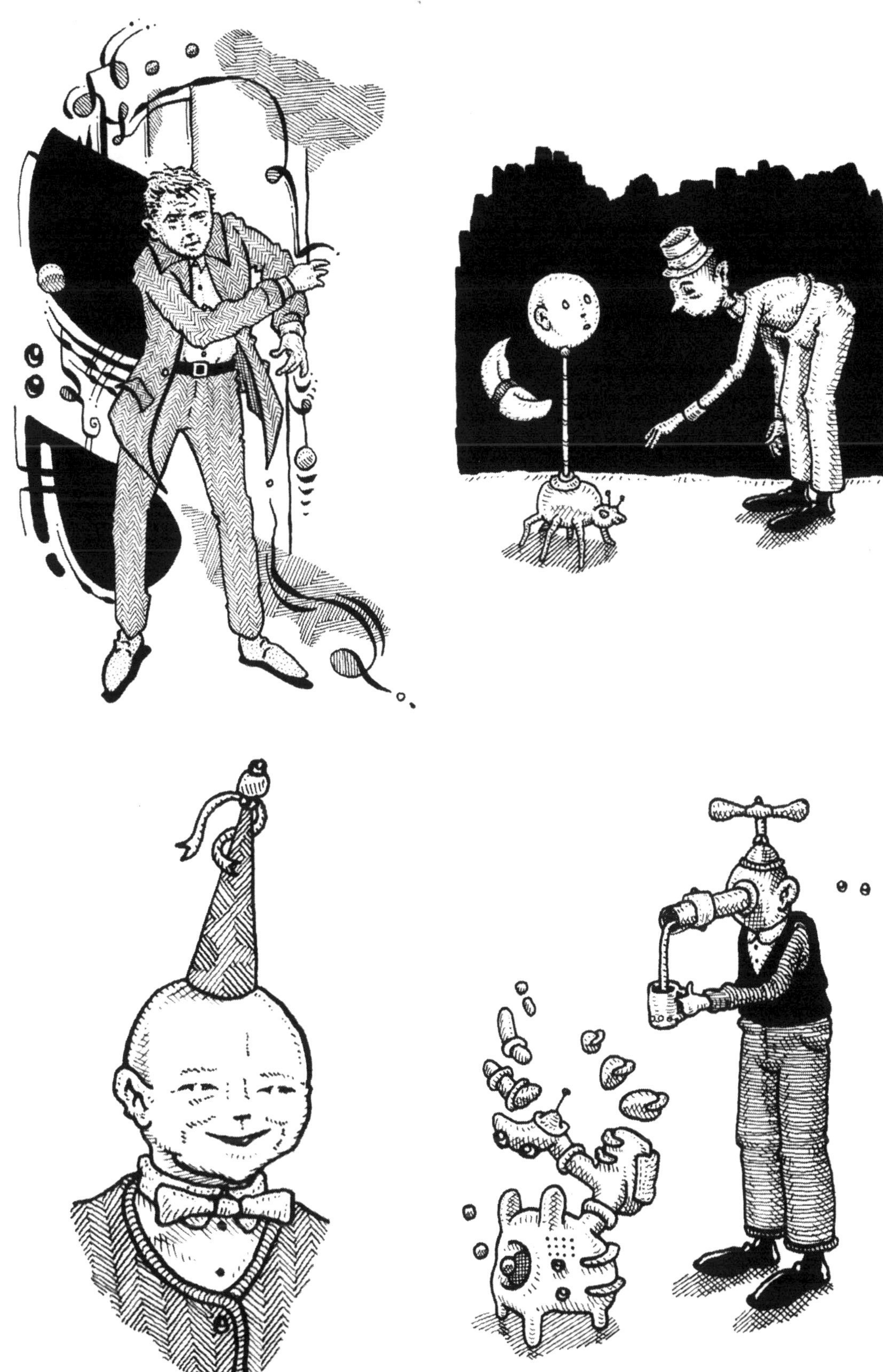

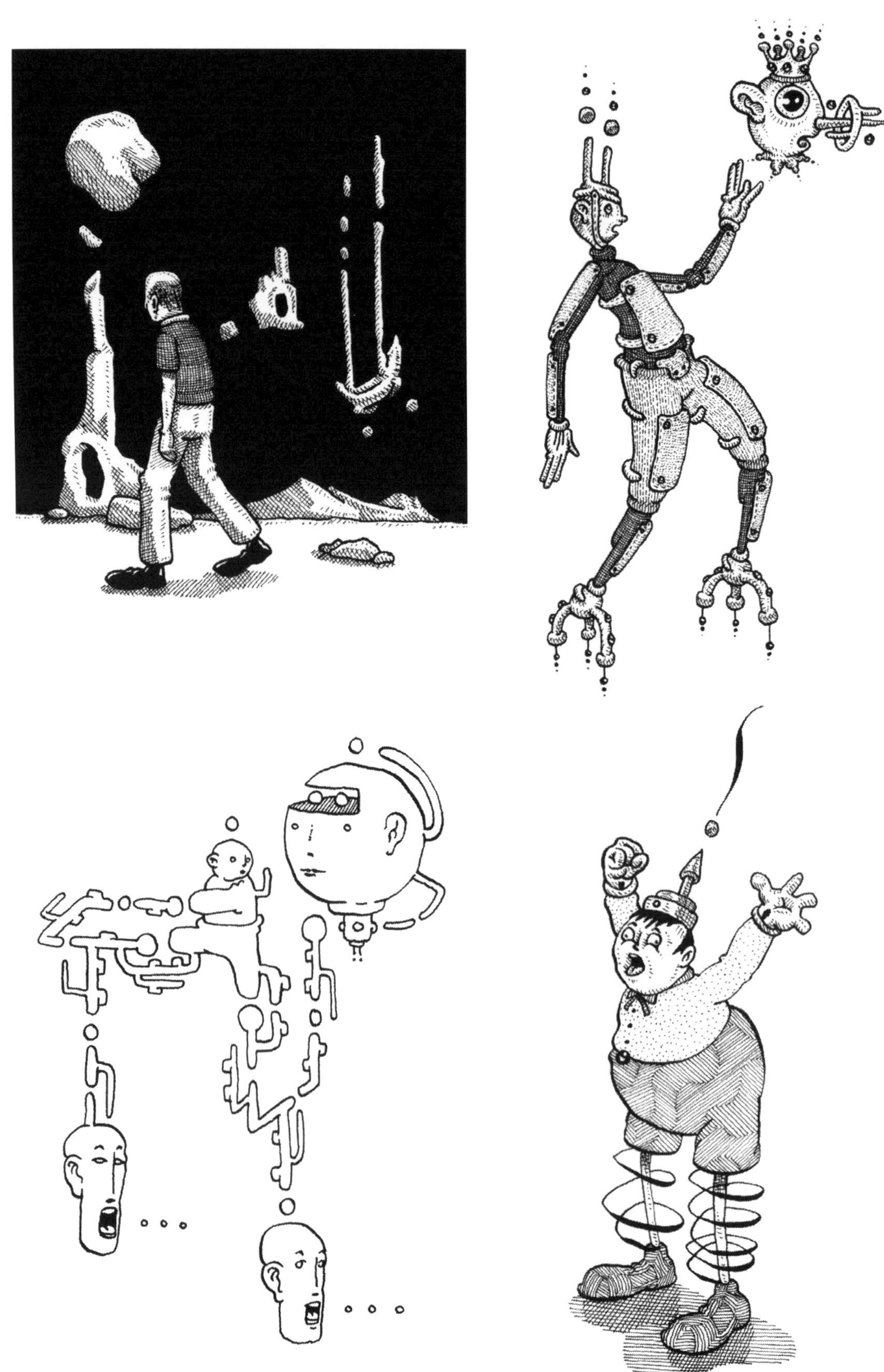

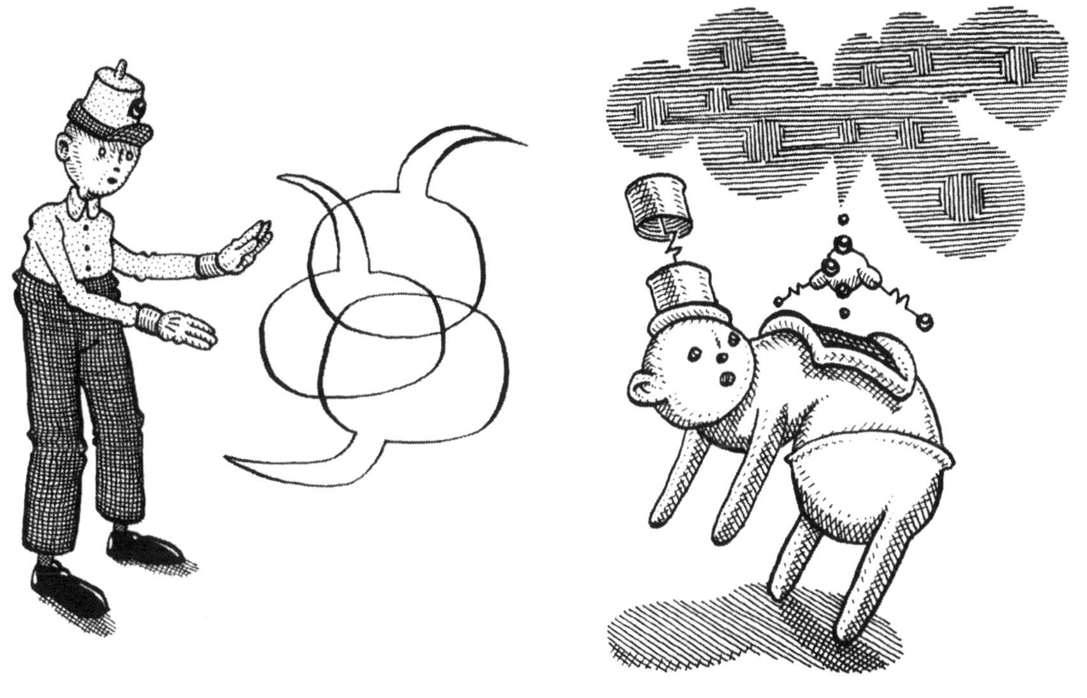

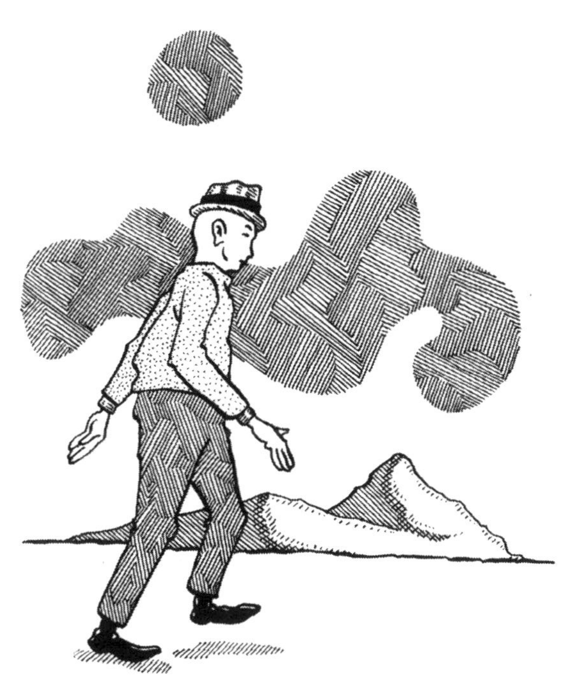

2017

November

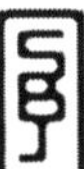

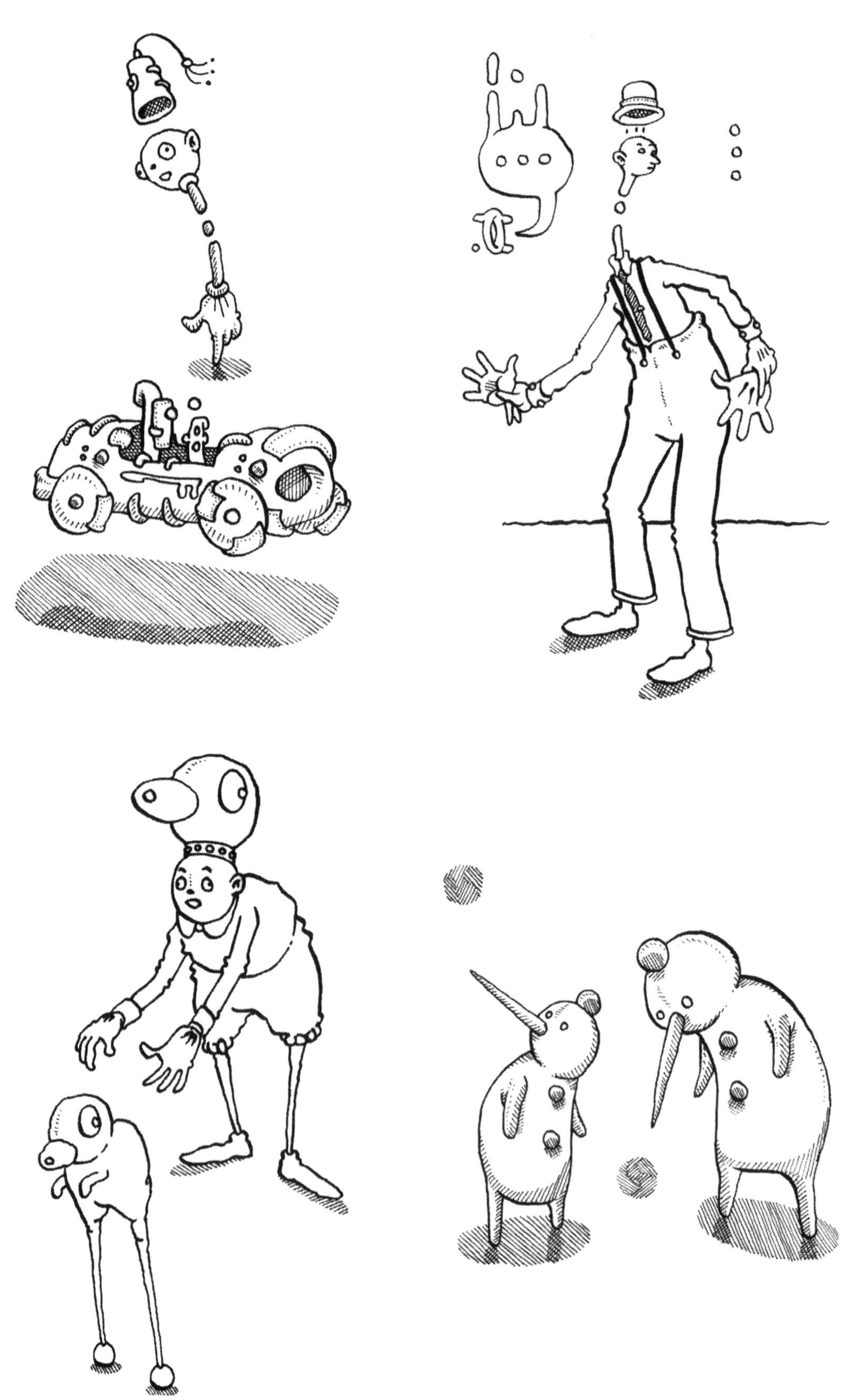

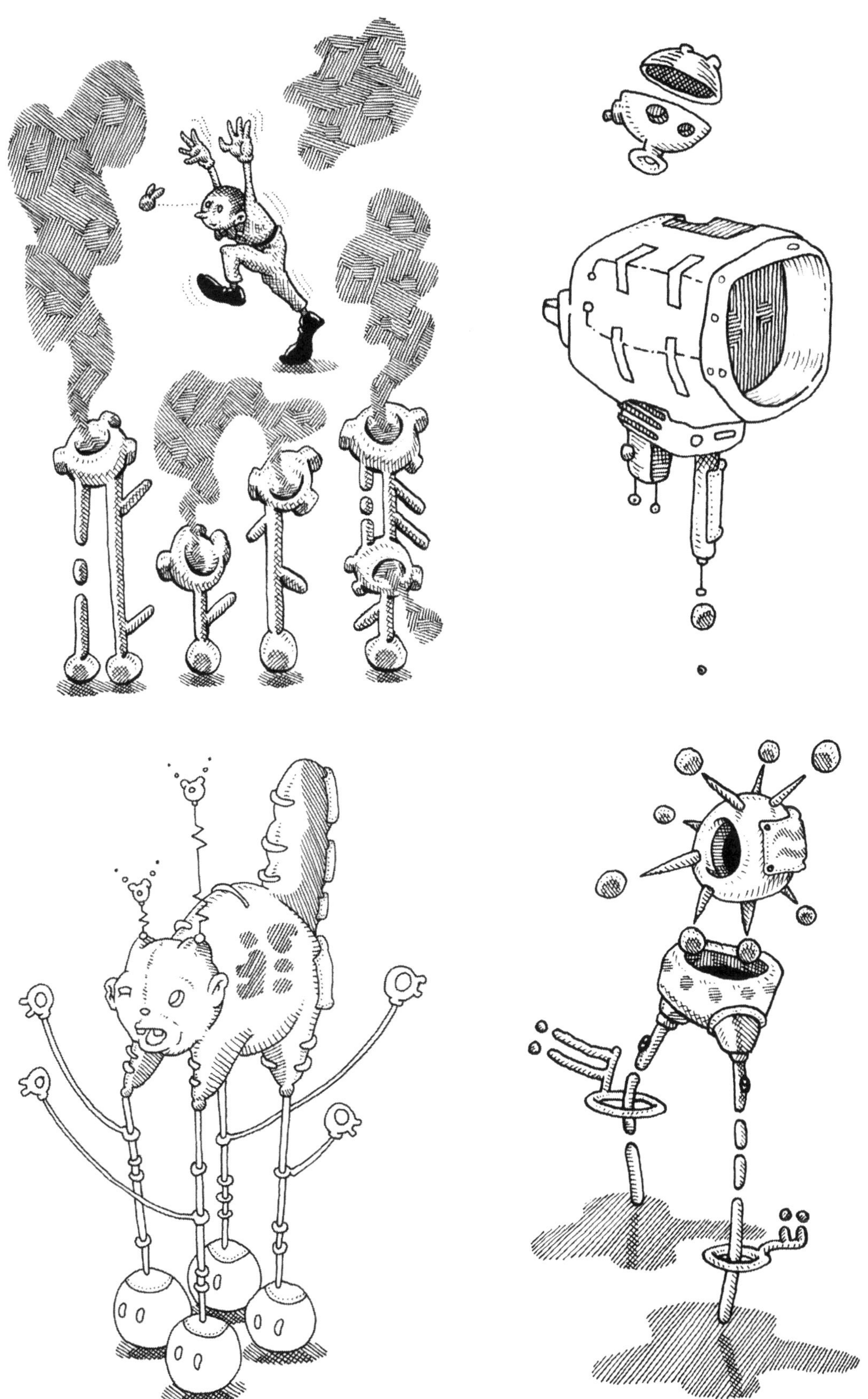

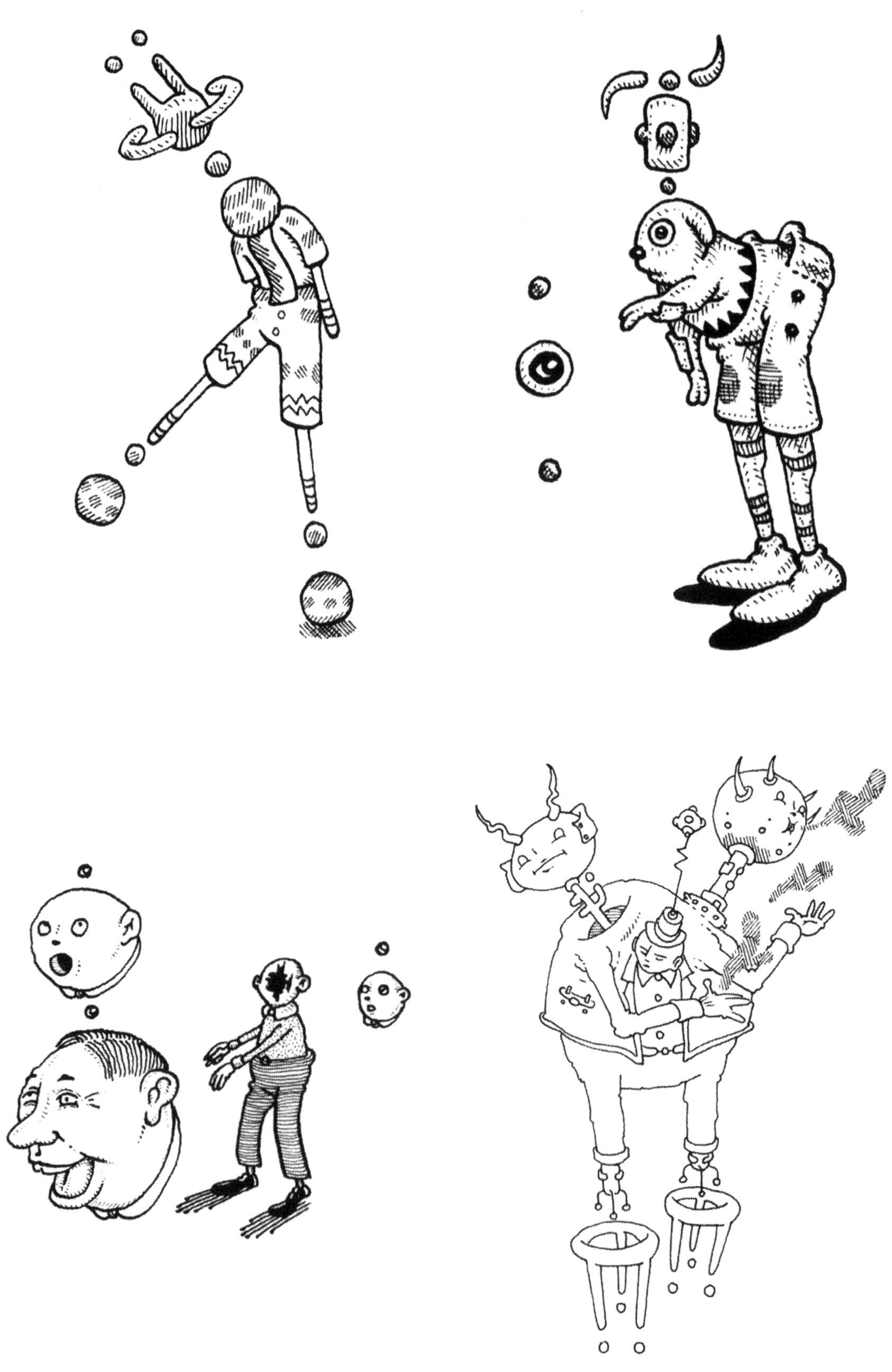

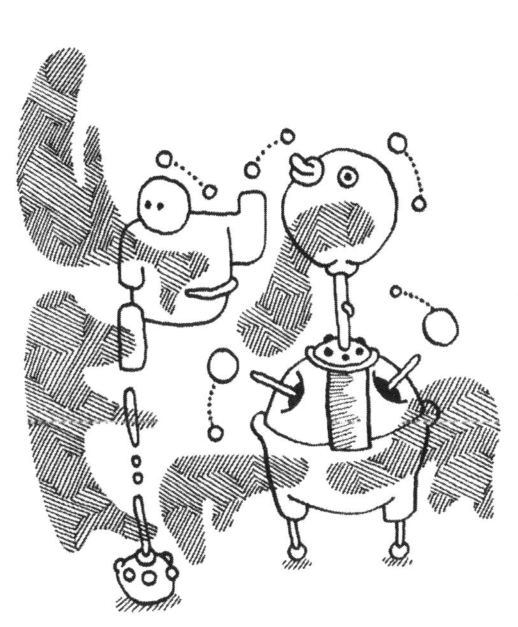

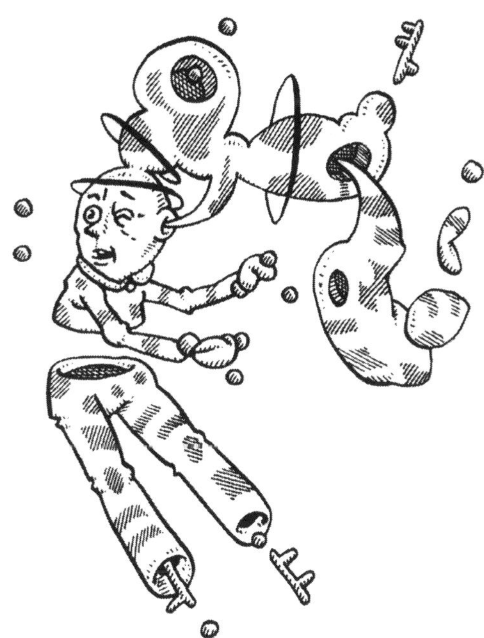

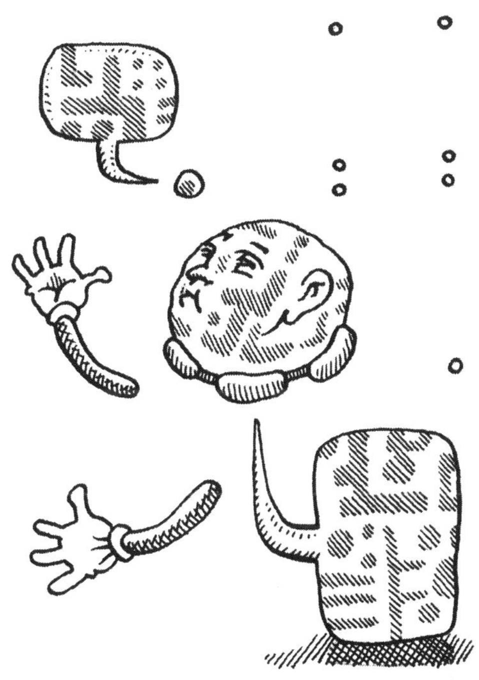

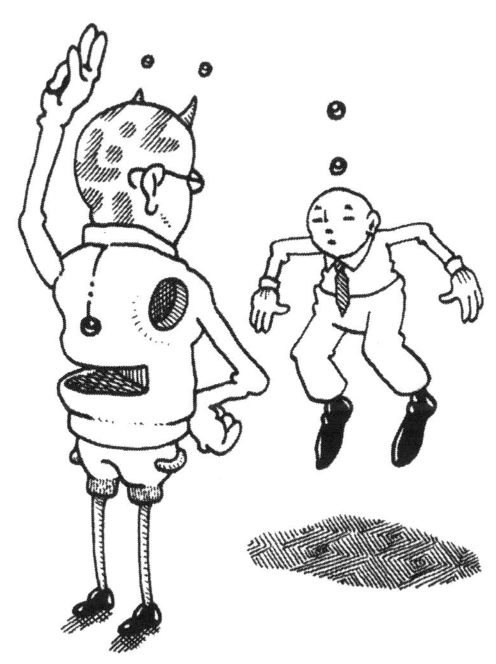

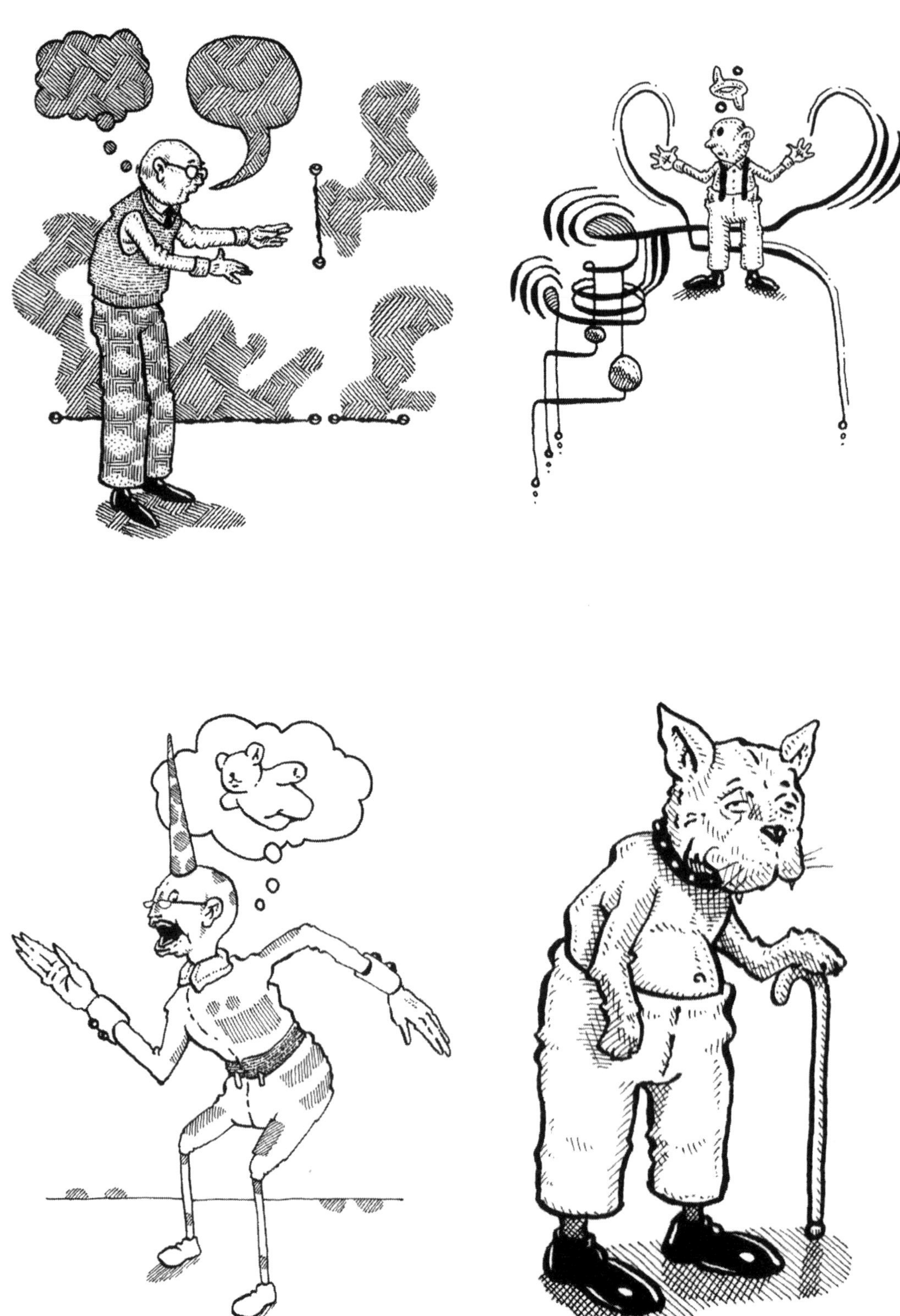

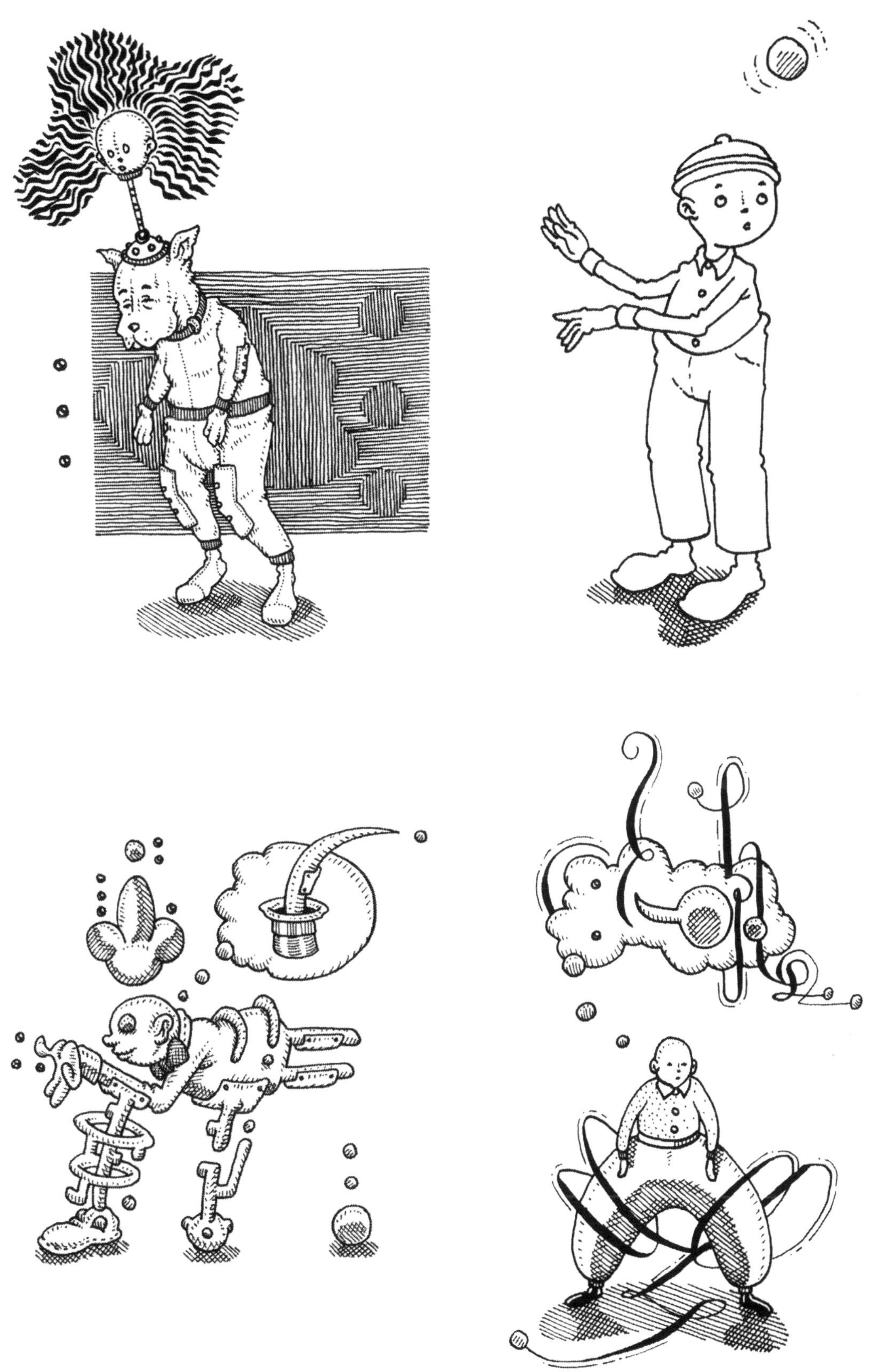

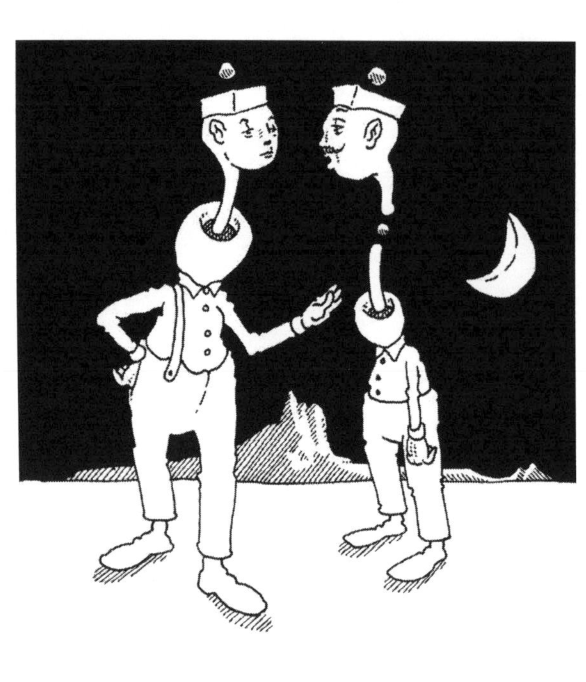

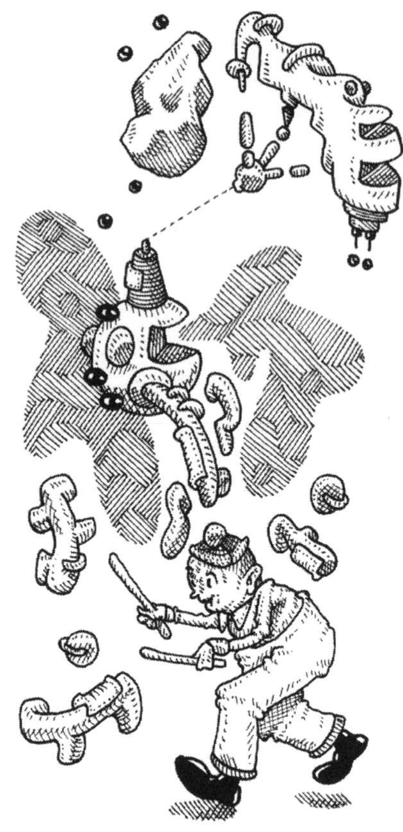

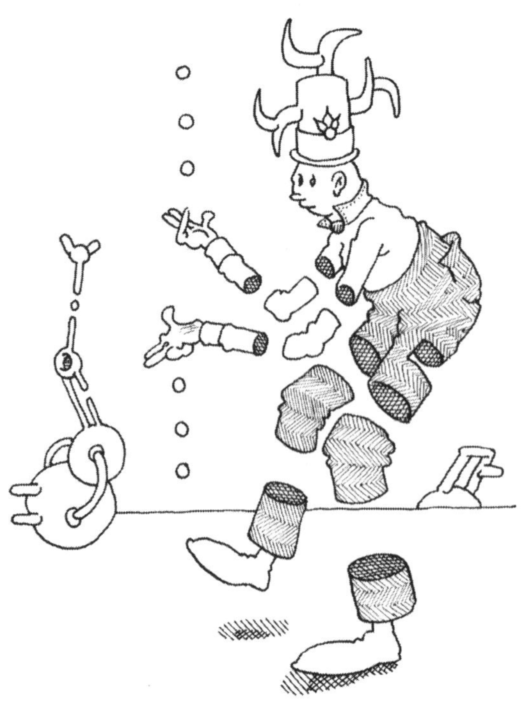

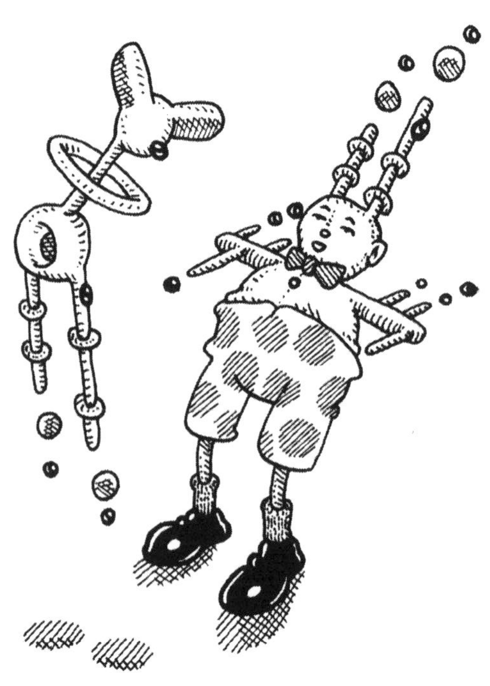

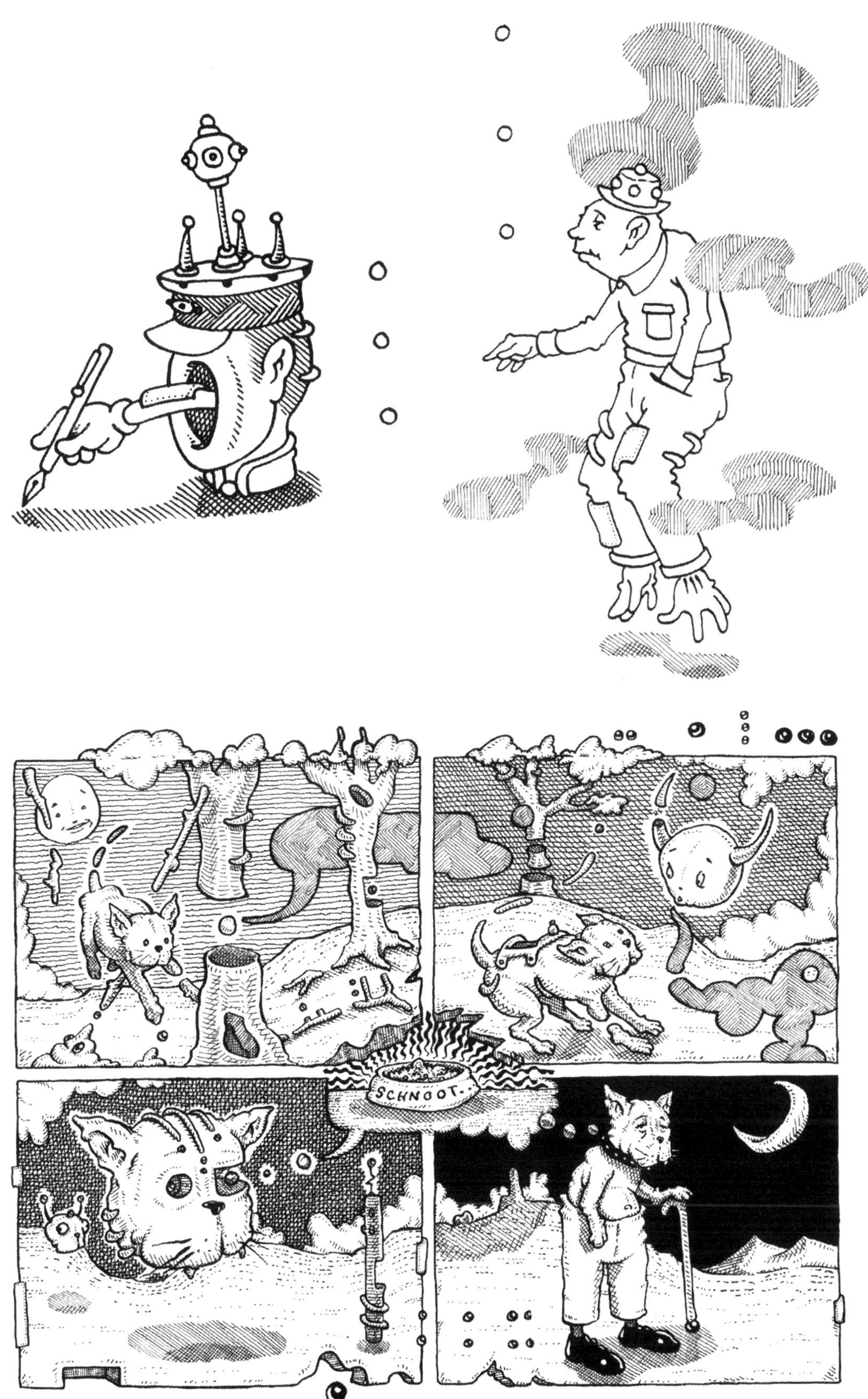
SCHNOOT..

2017

DECEMBER

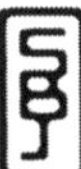

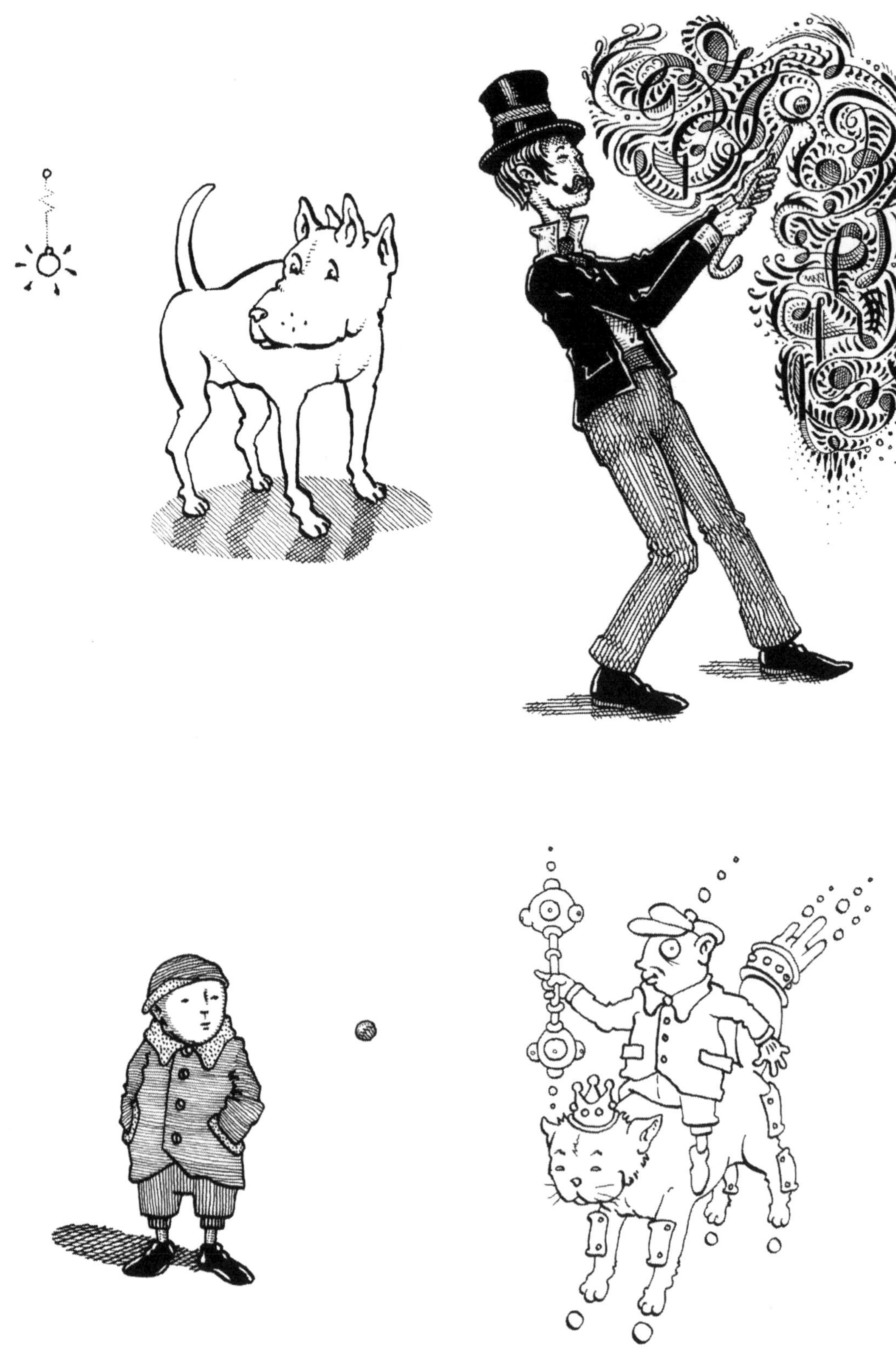

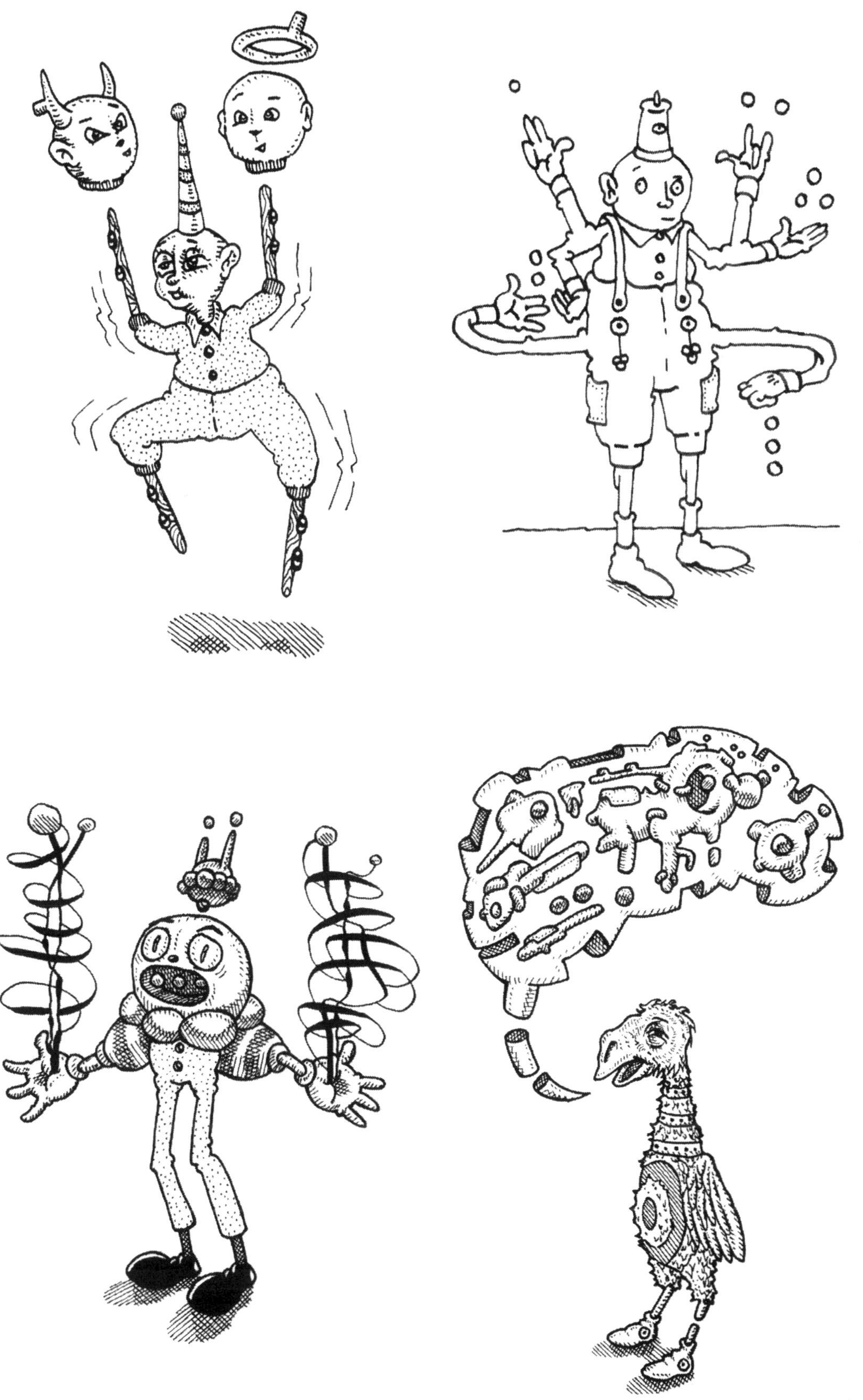

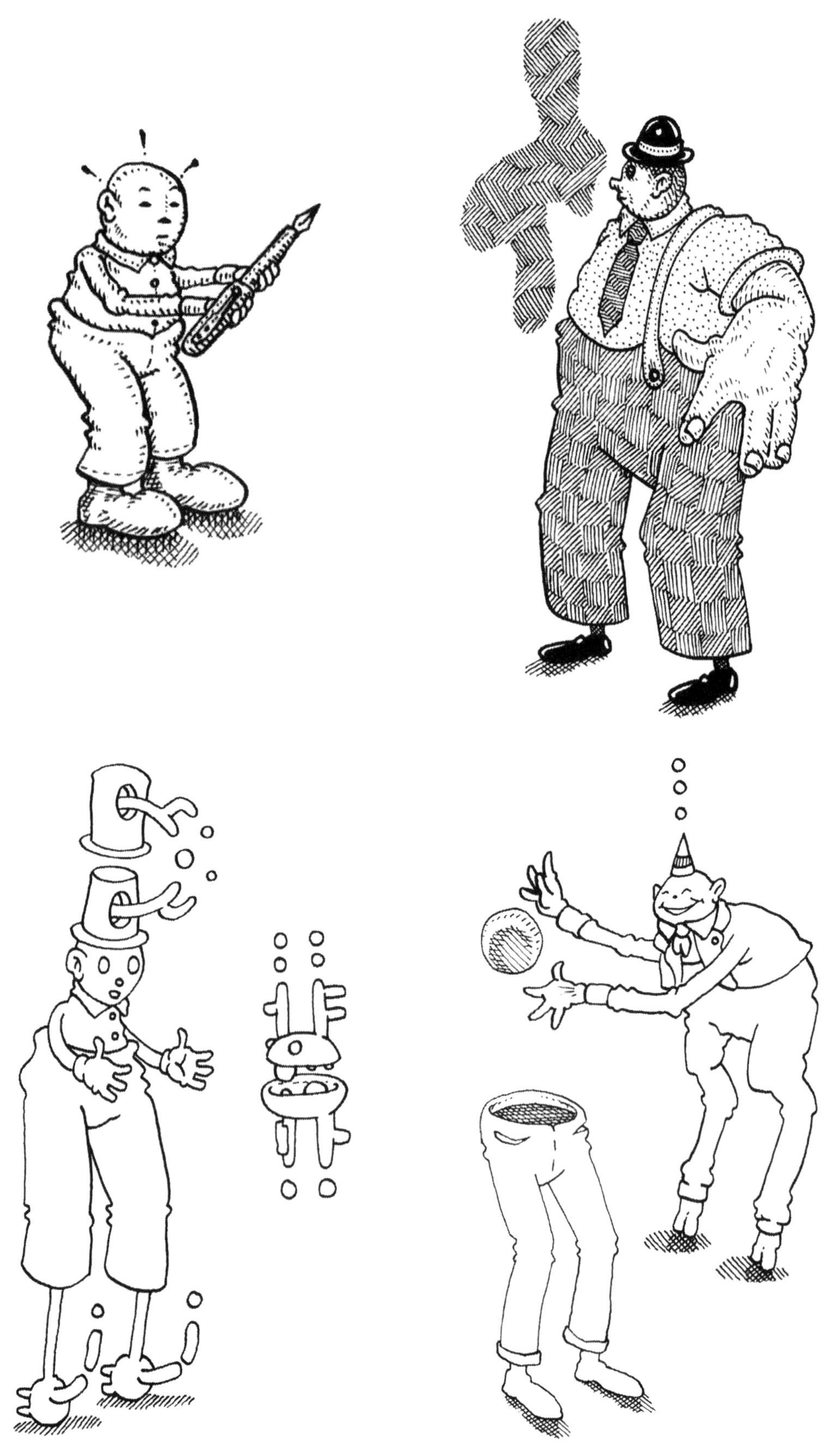

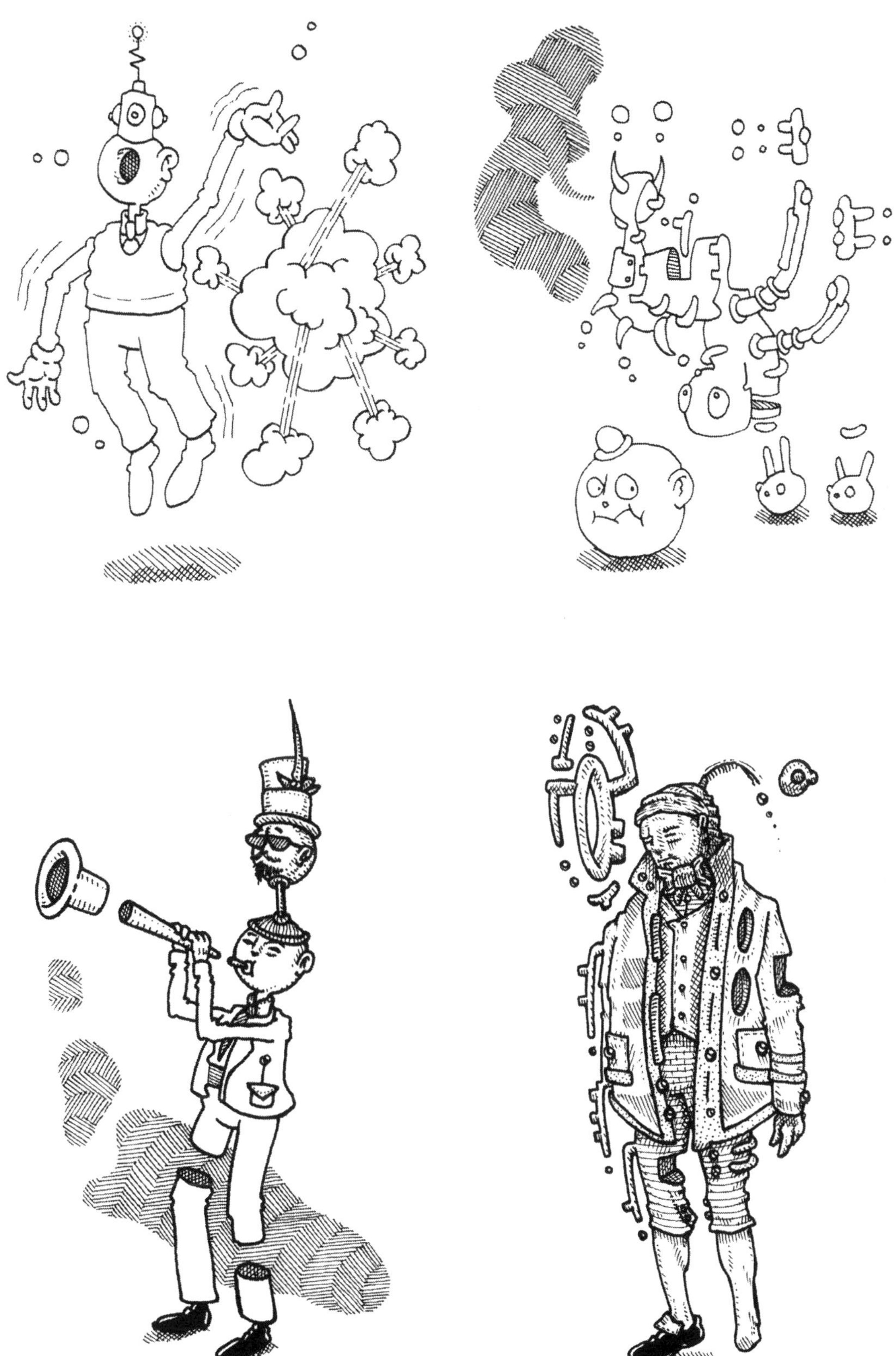

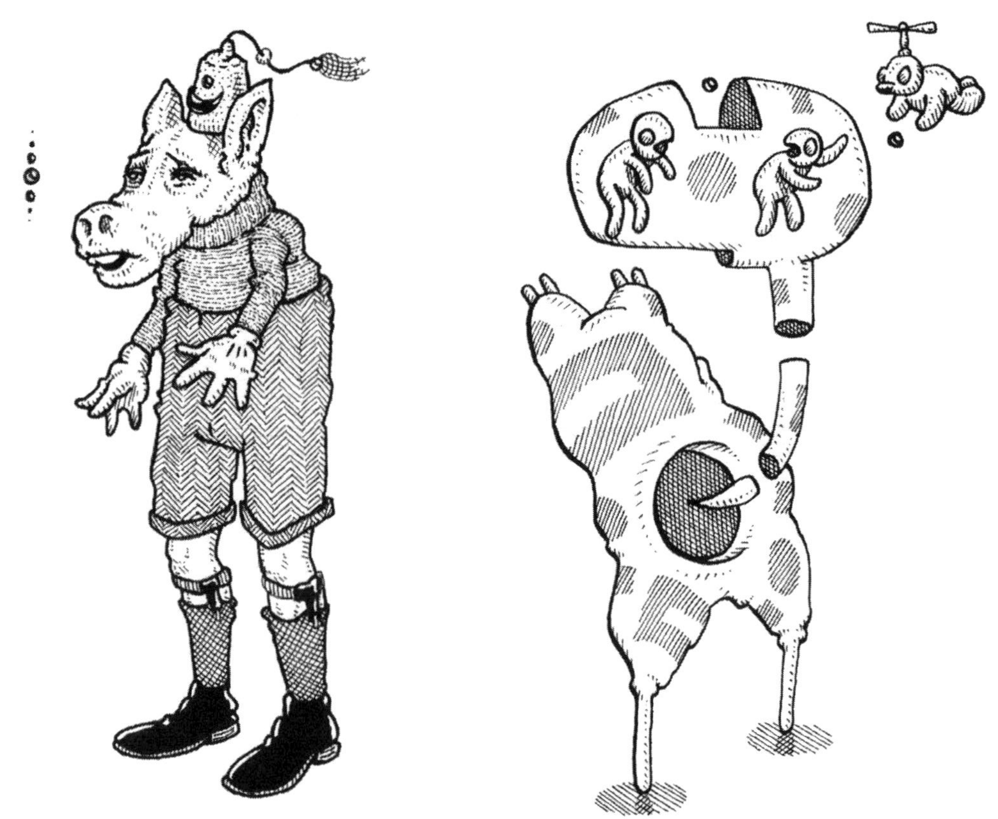

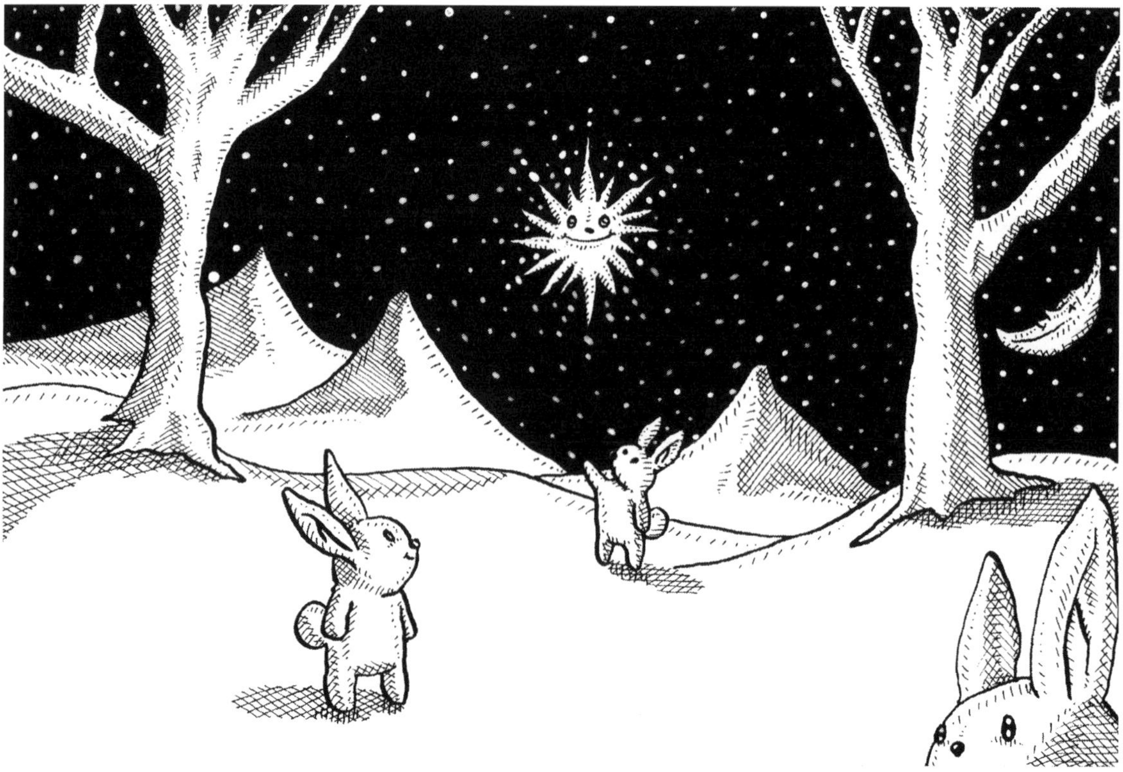

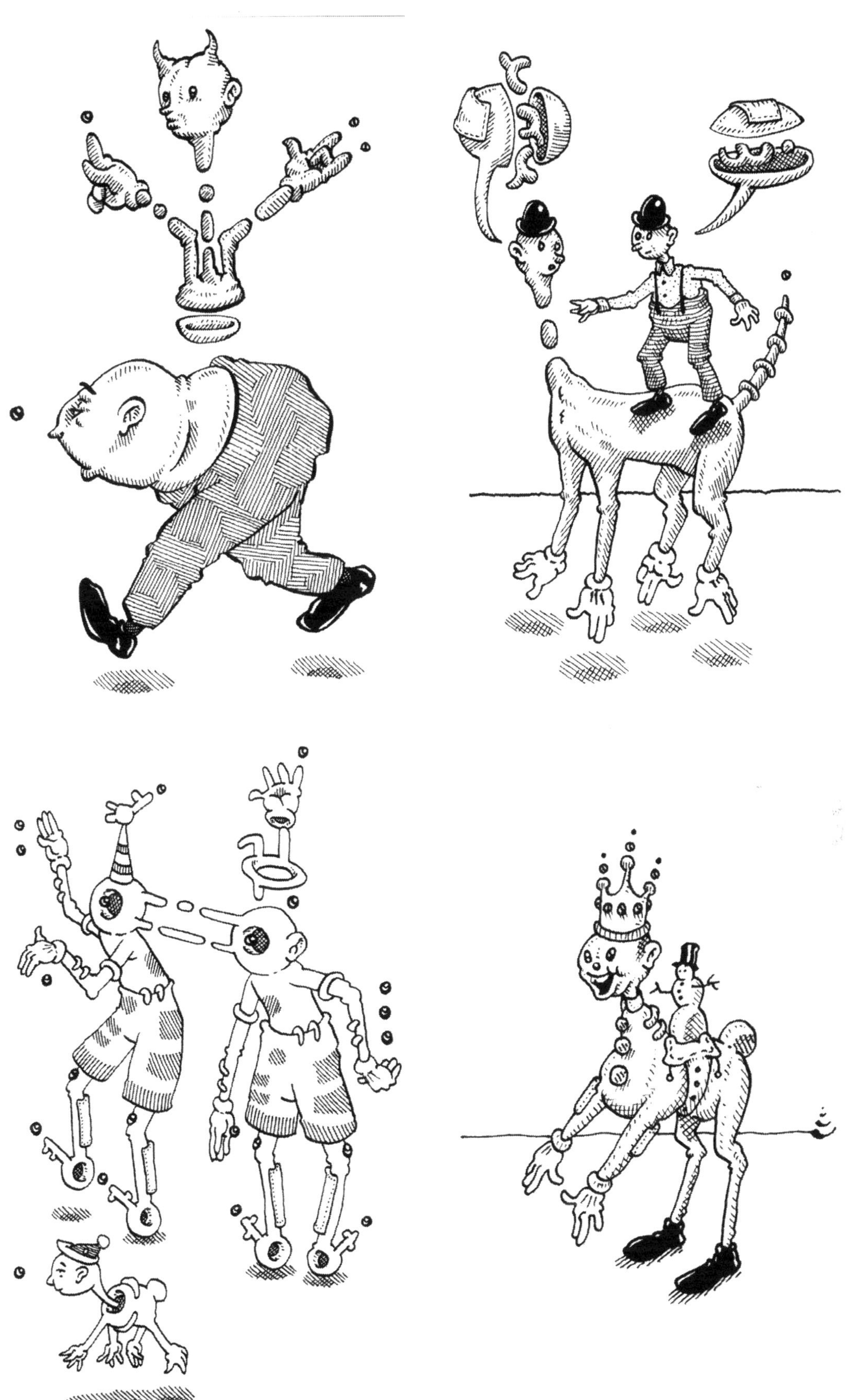

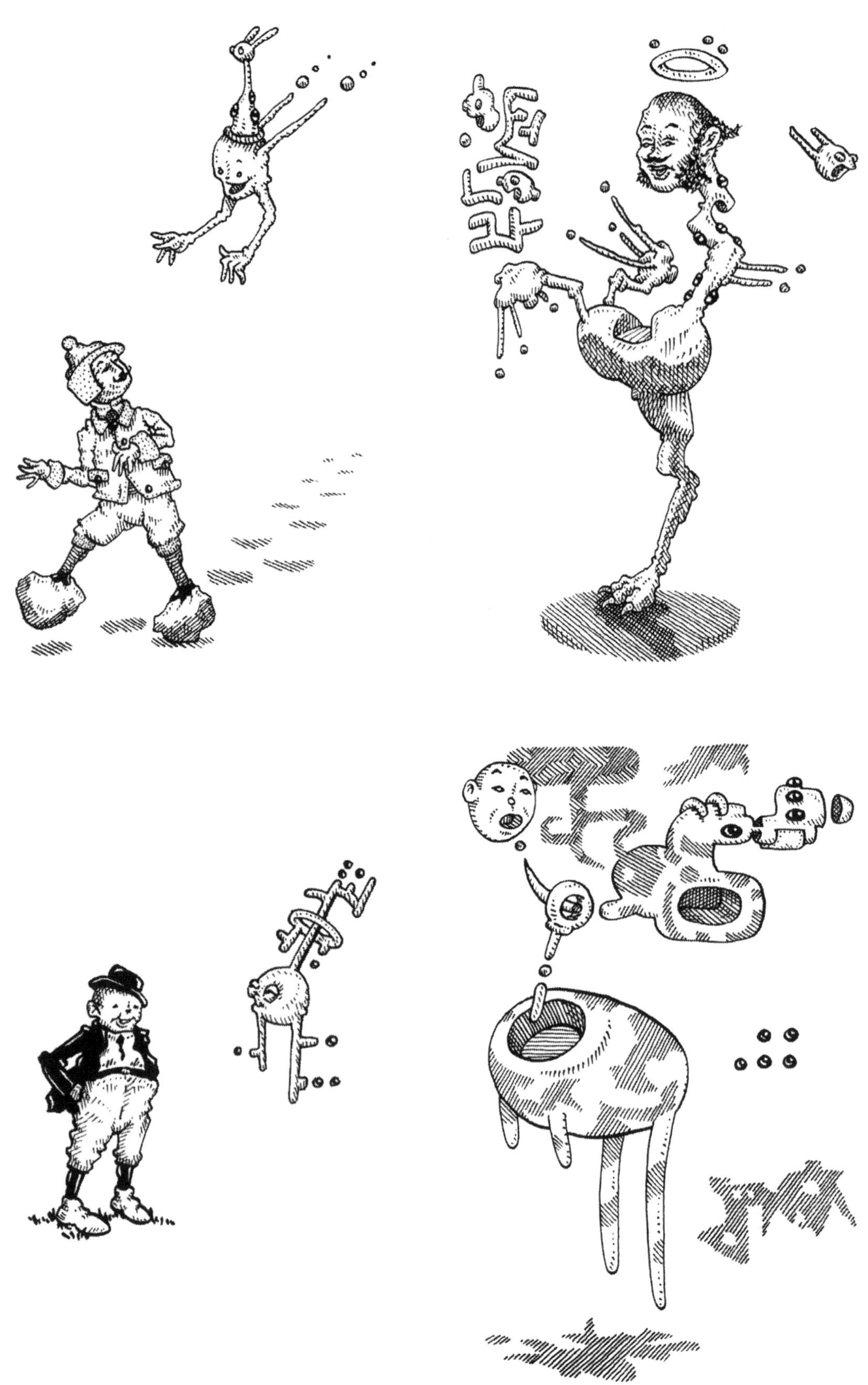

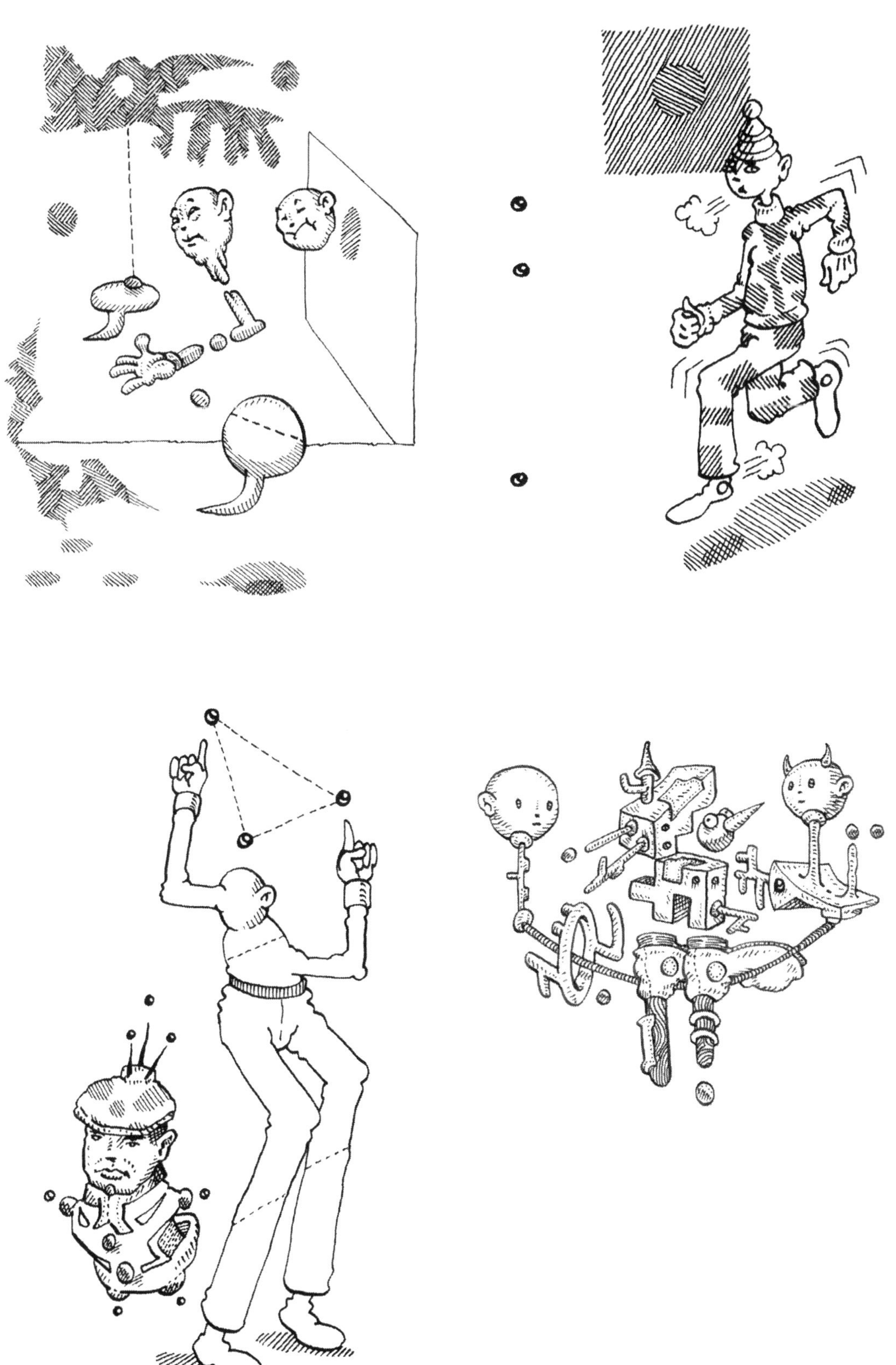

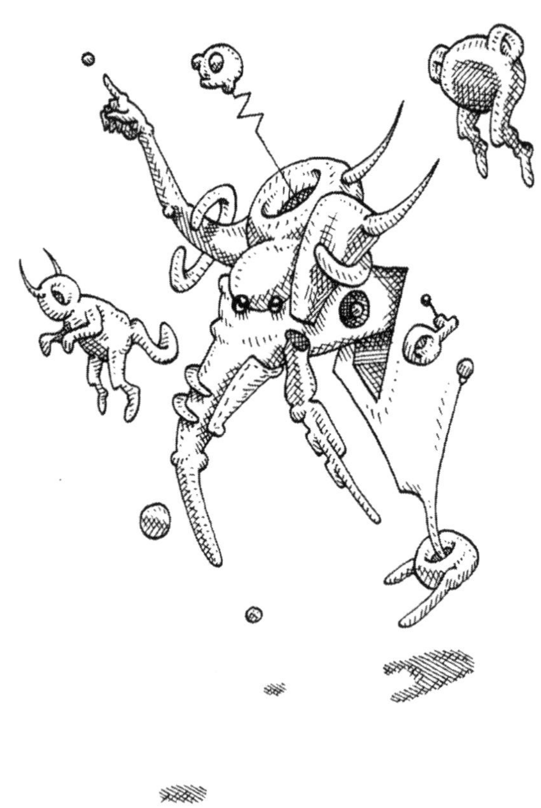

2012

JANUARY

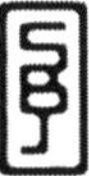

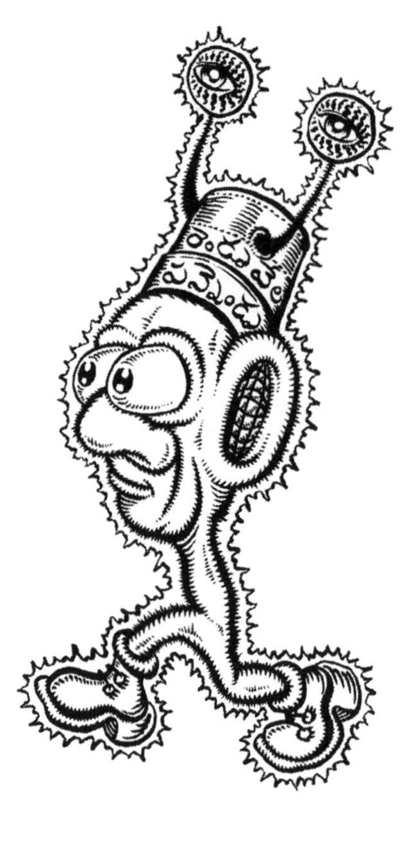

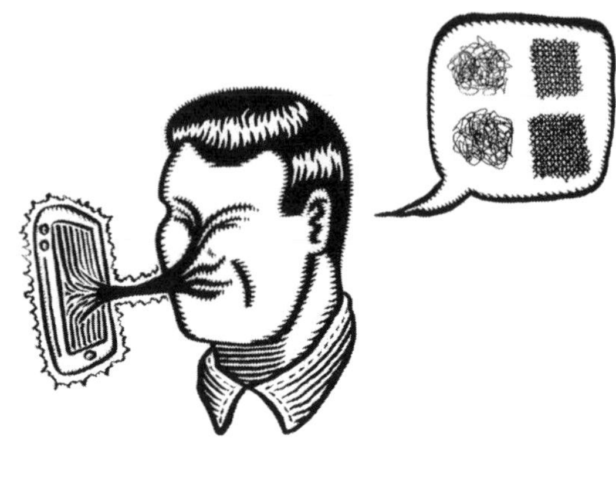

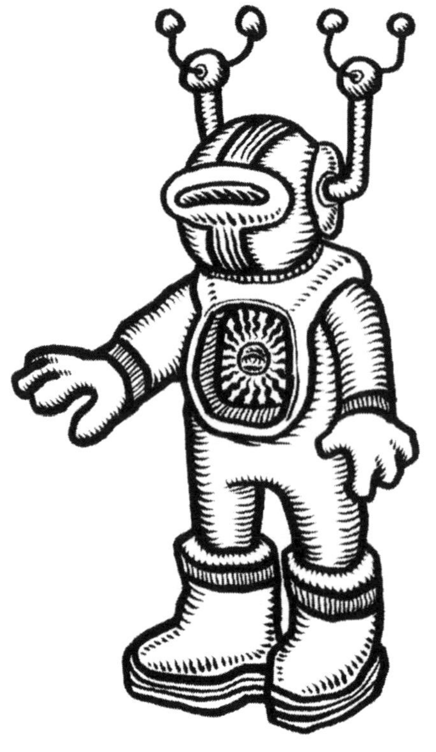

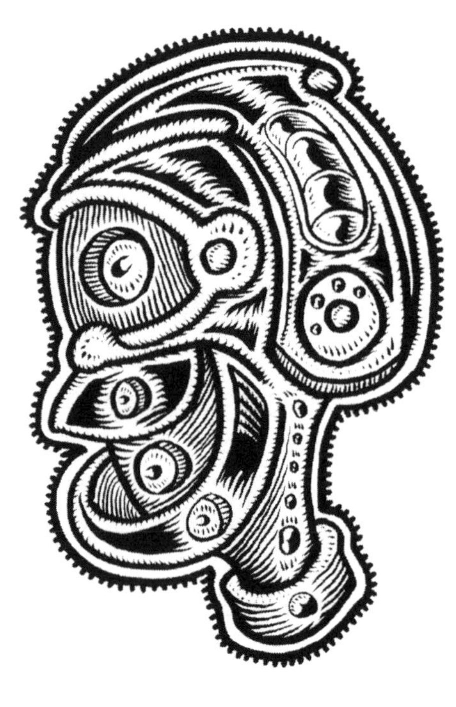

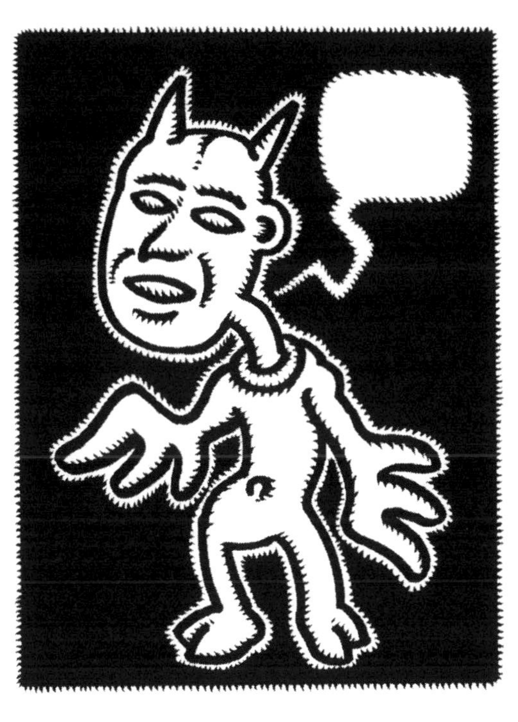

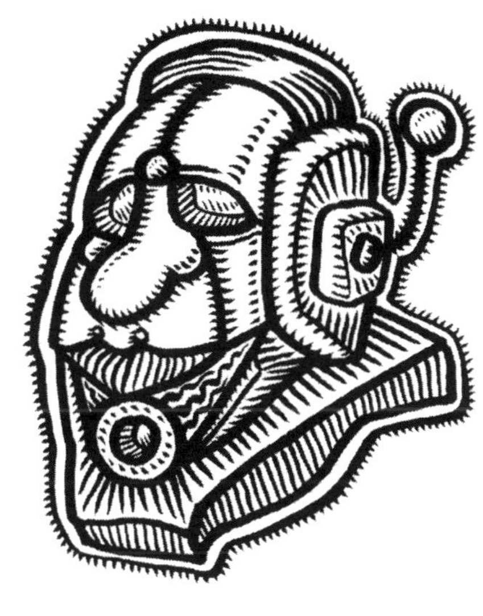

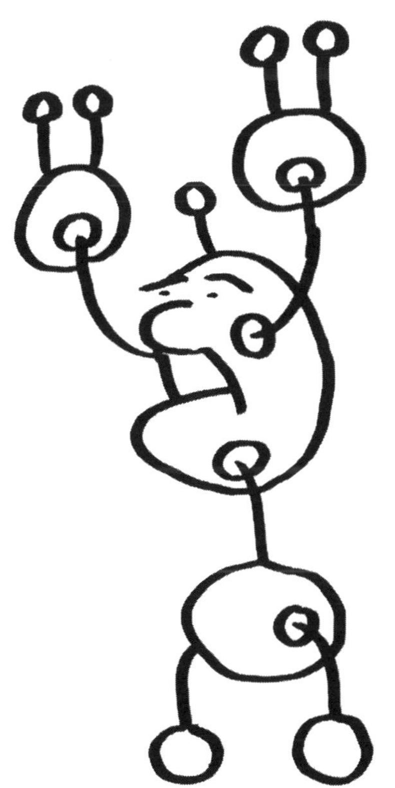

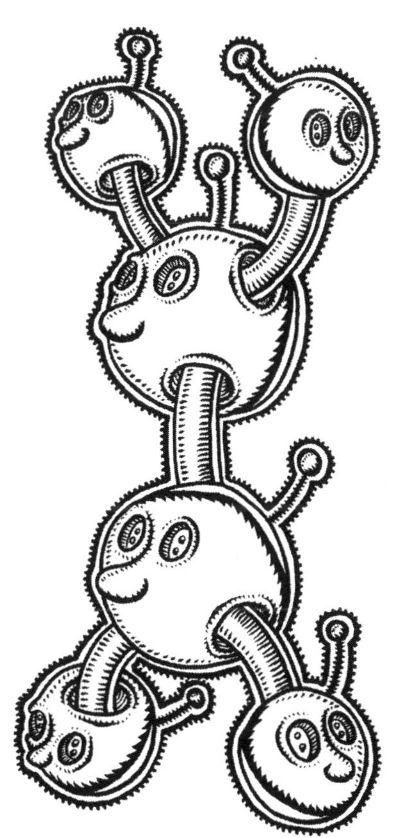

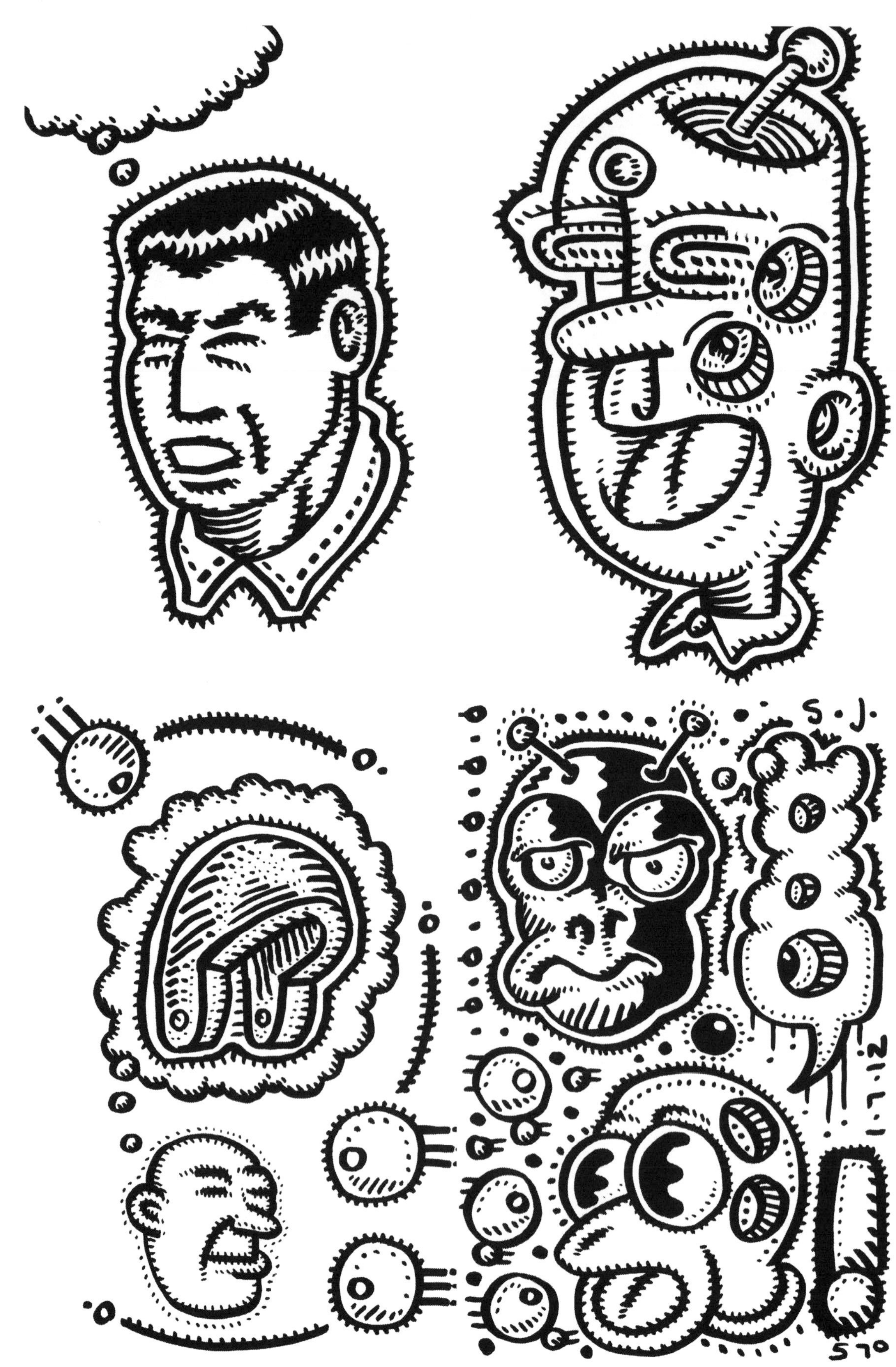
S.J.

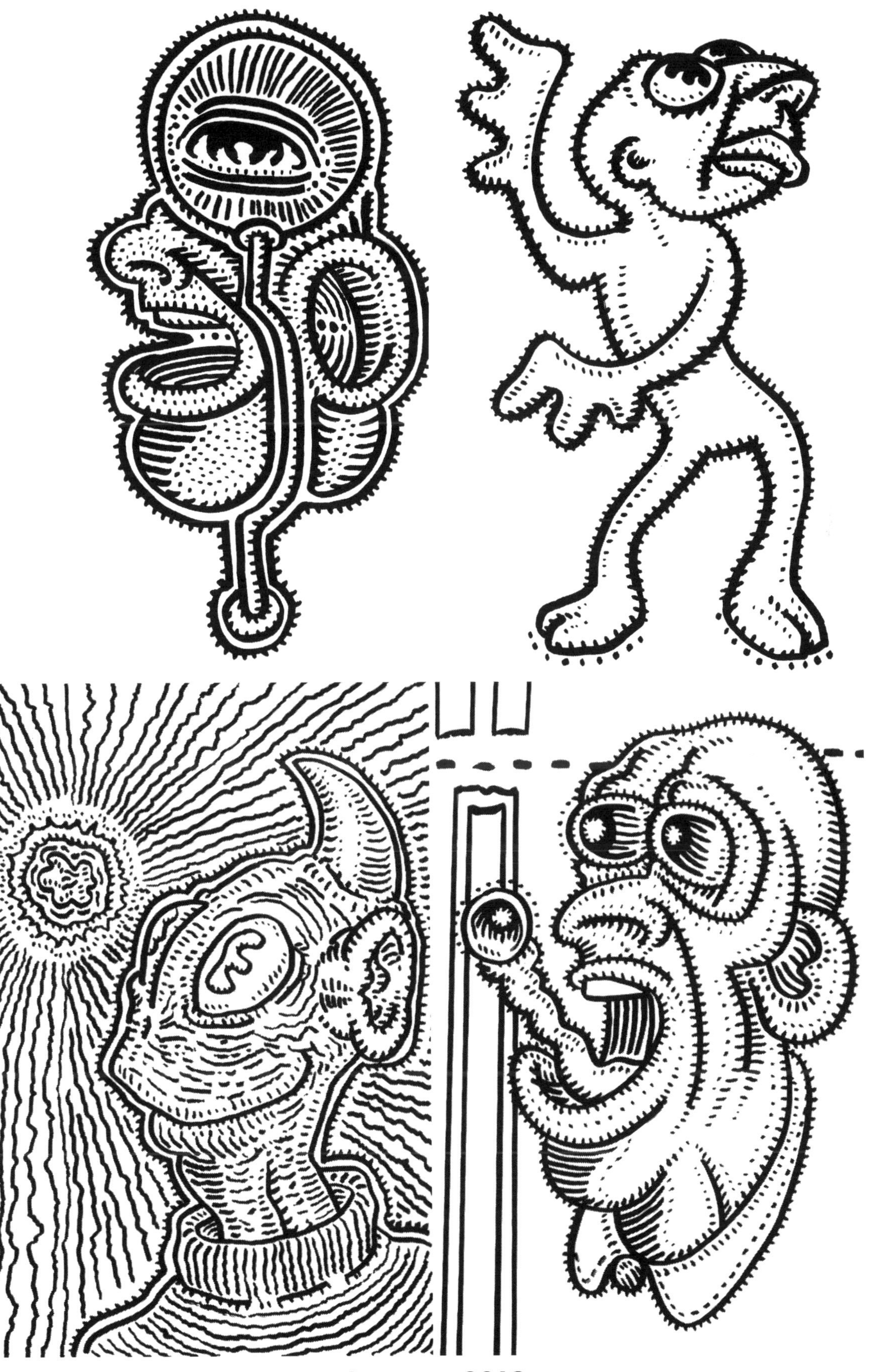

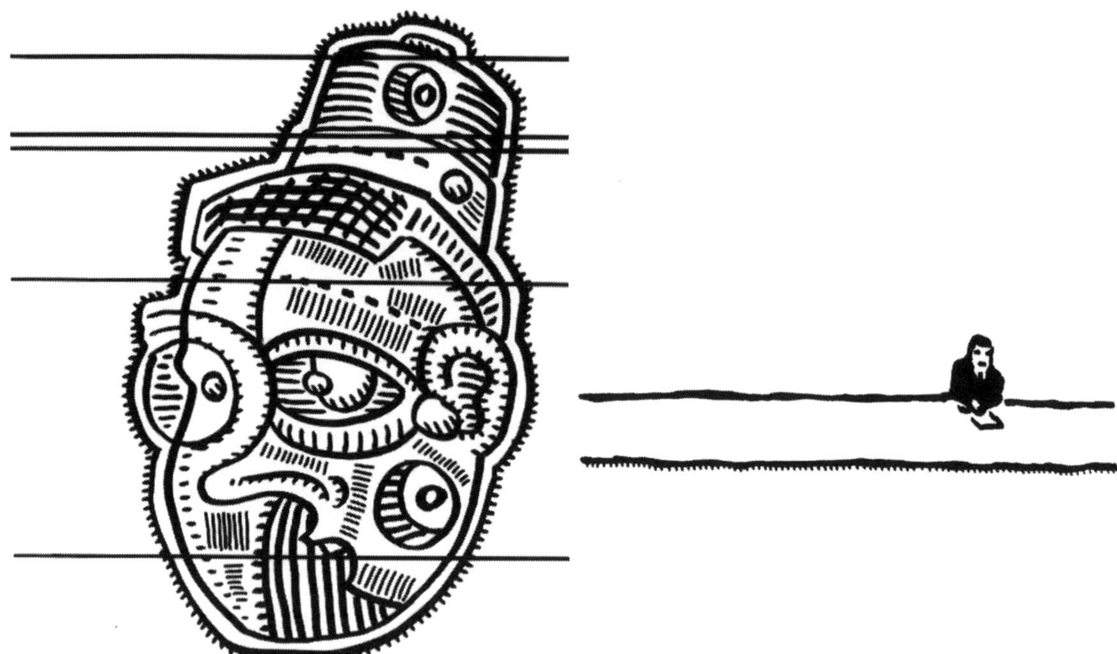
it's a NO-NO

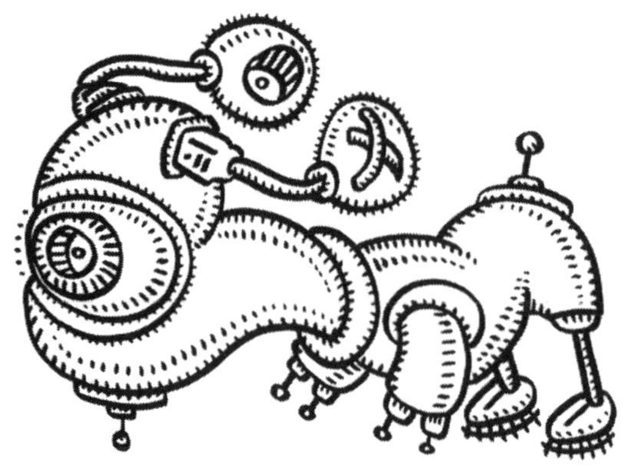

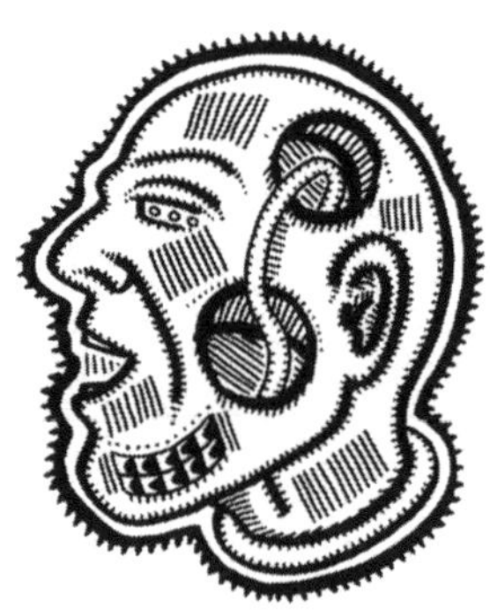

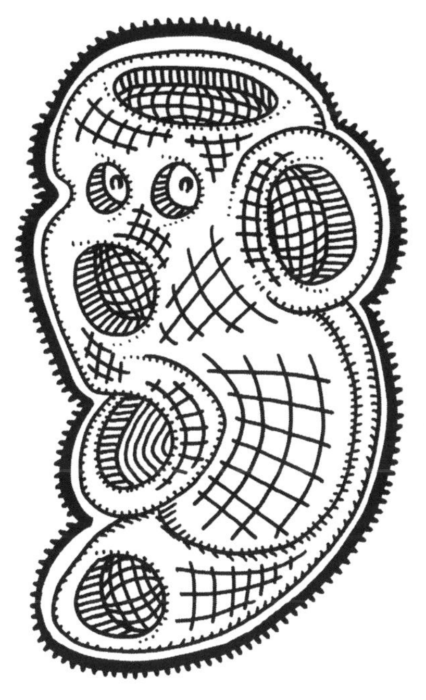

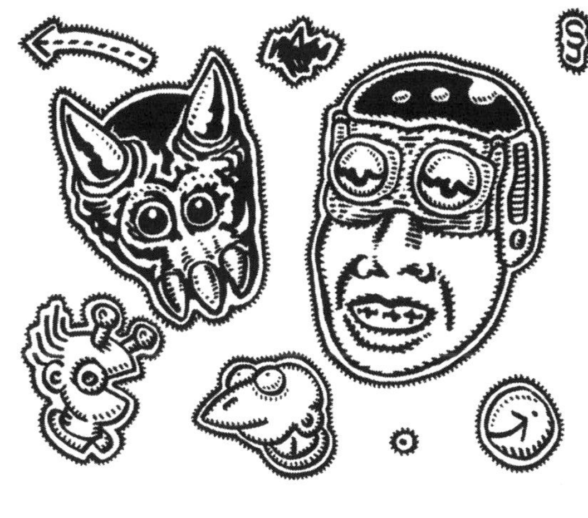

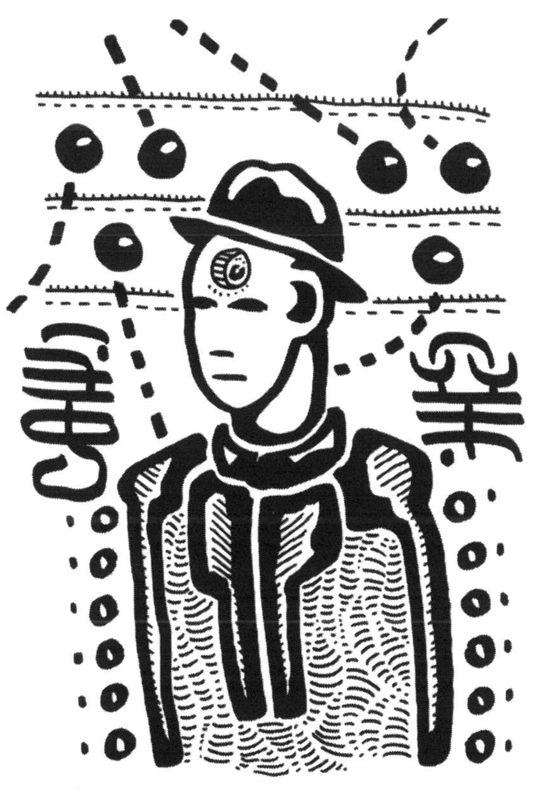

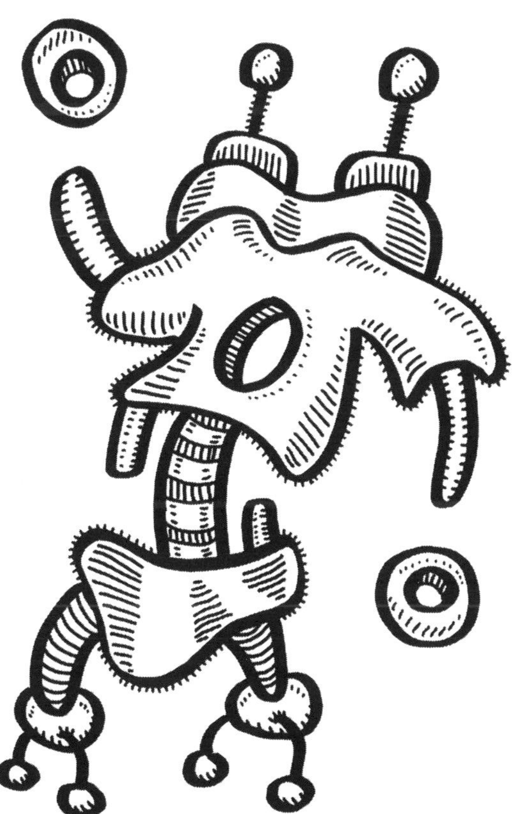

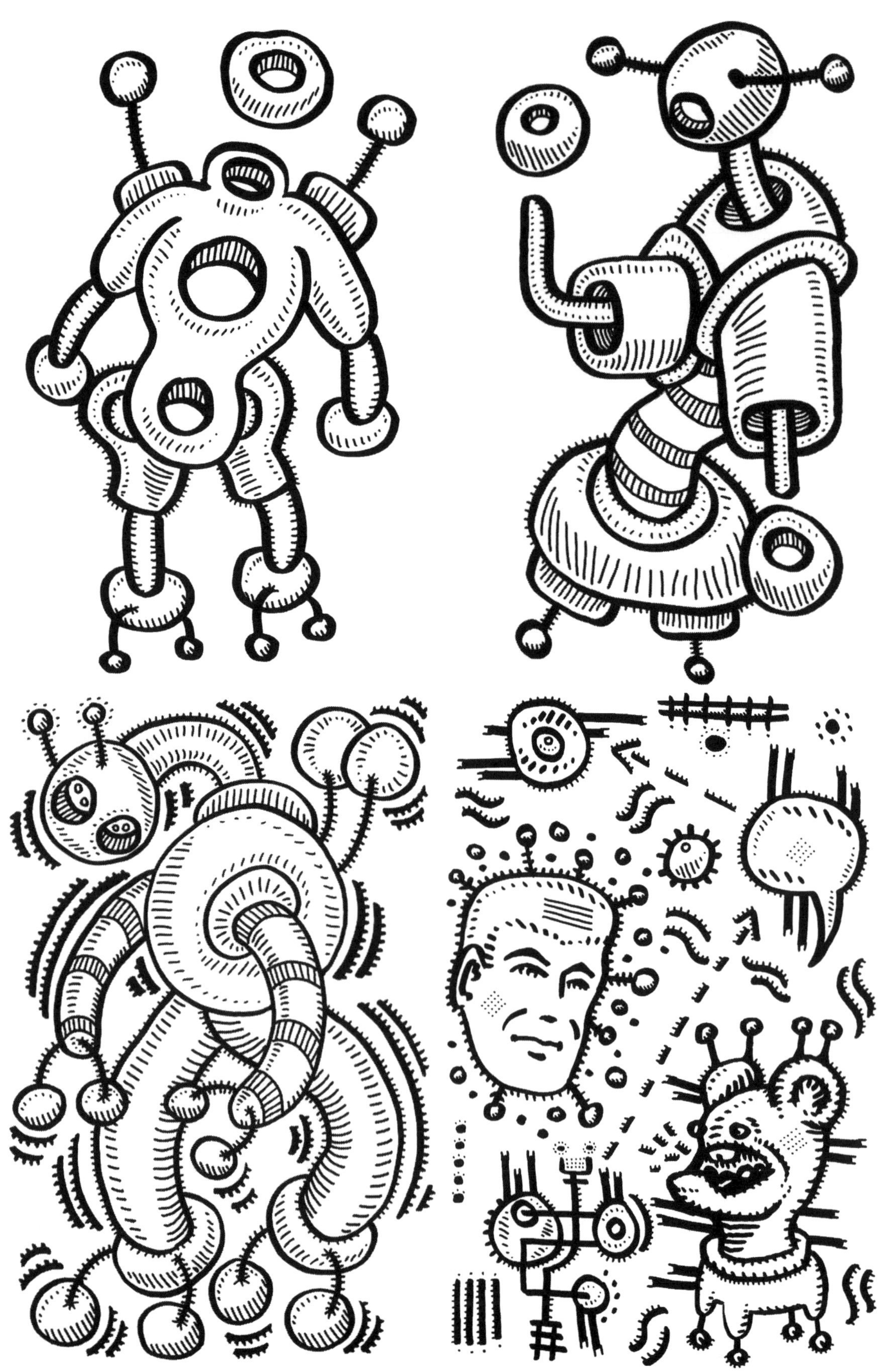

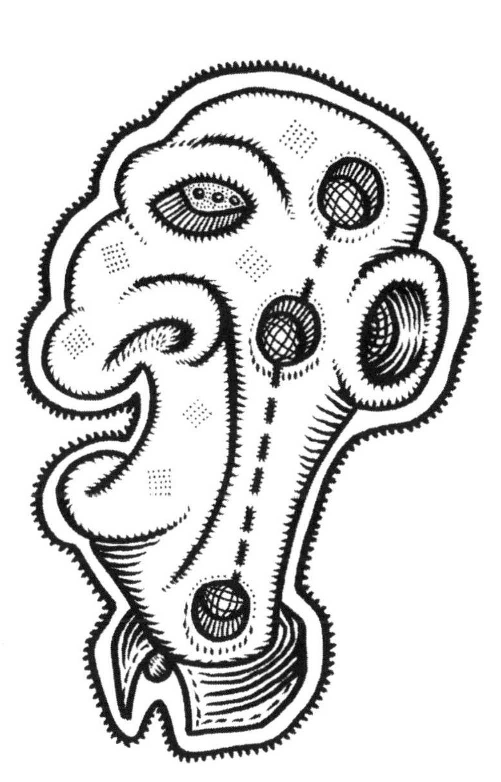

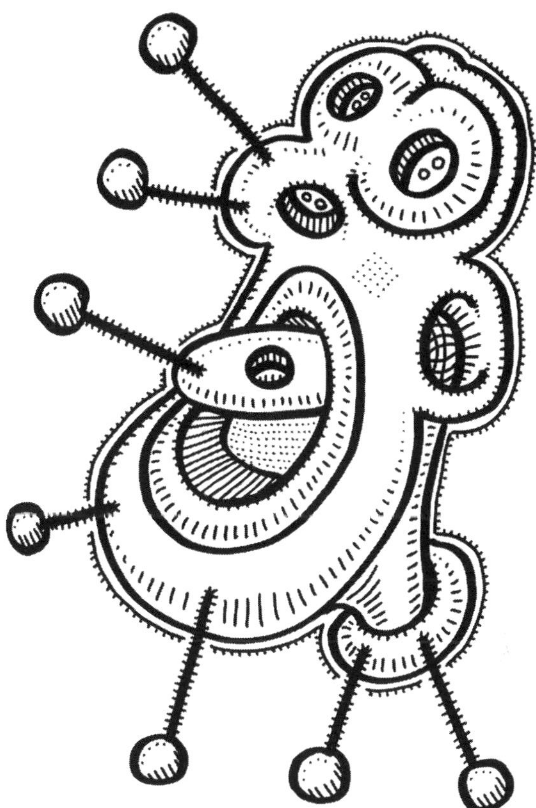

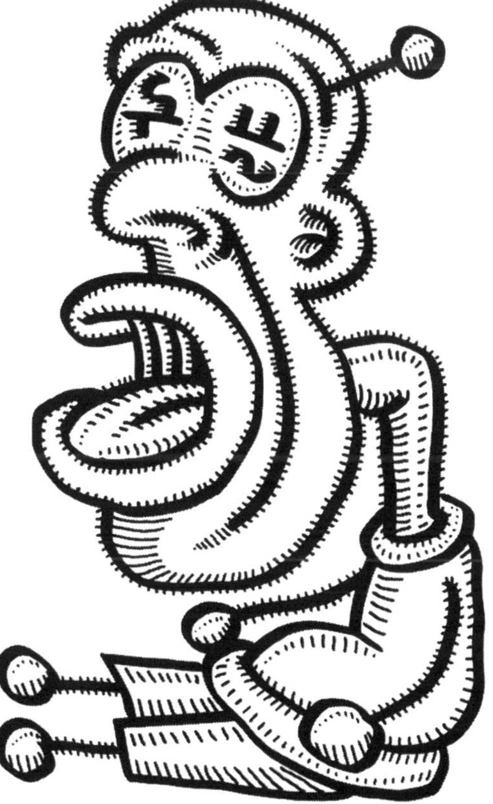

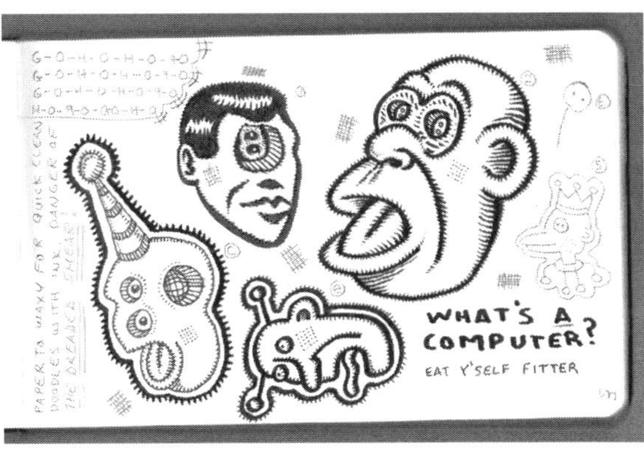
WHAT'S A COMPUTER?
EAT Y'SELF FITTER

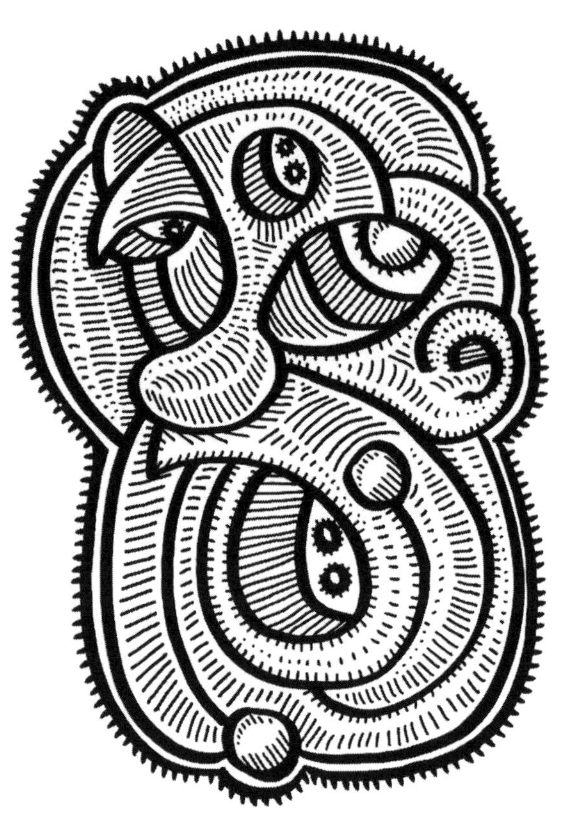

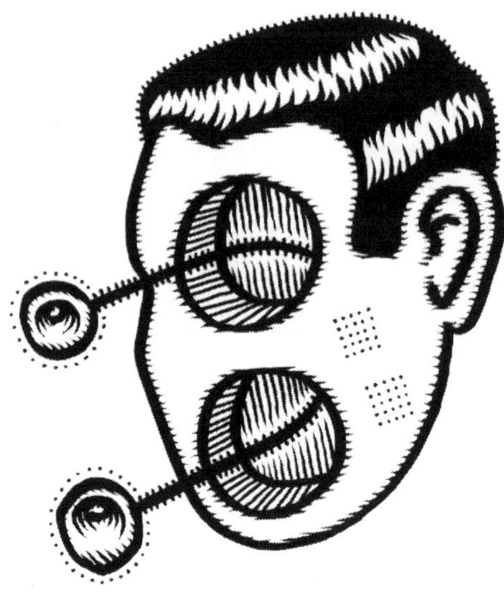

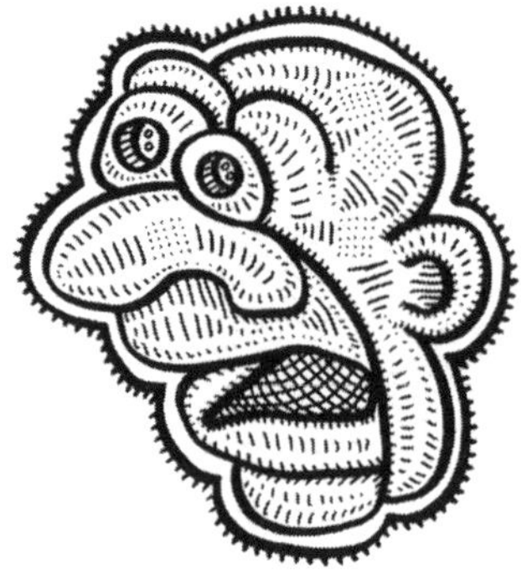

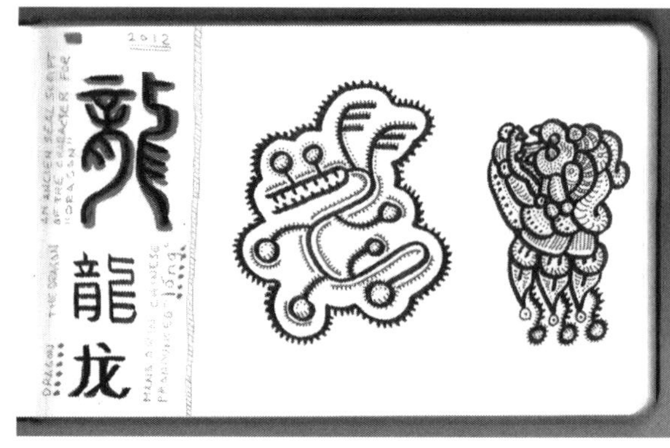
2012
龍
龙

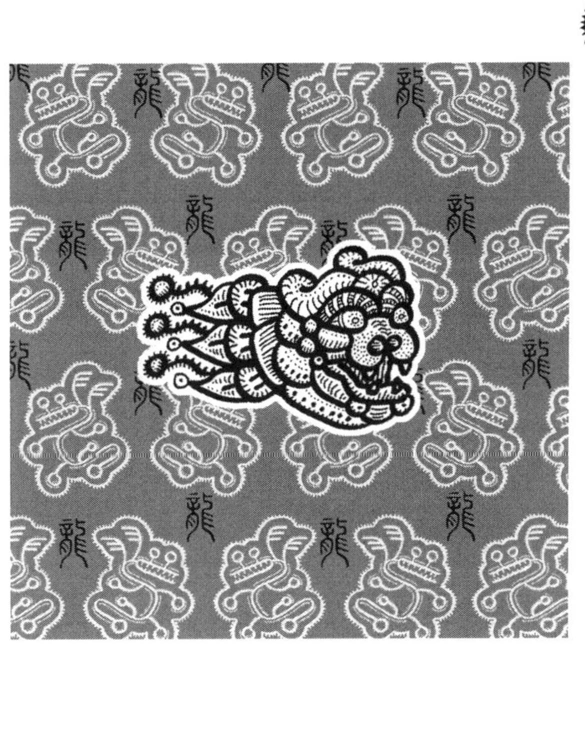

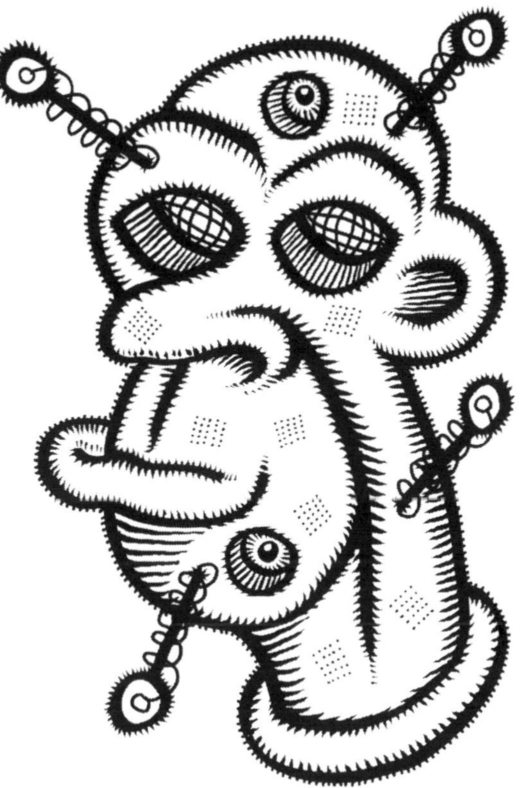

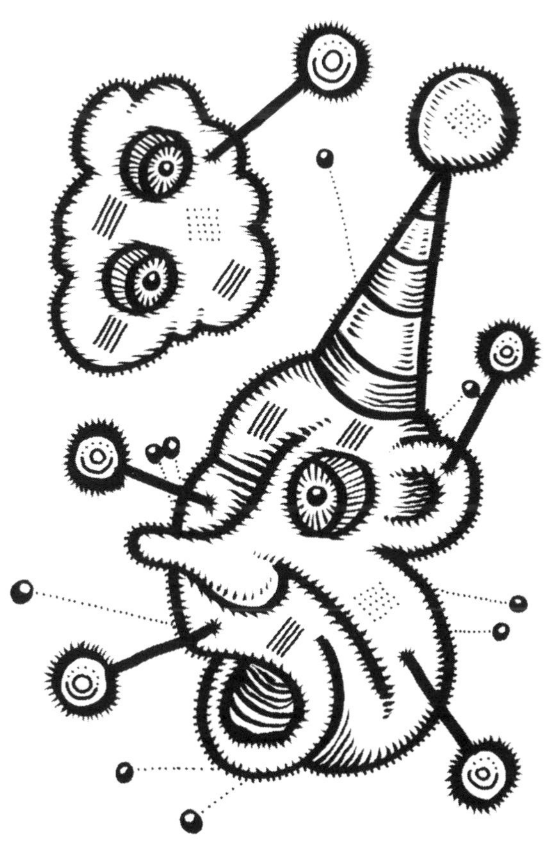

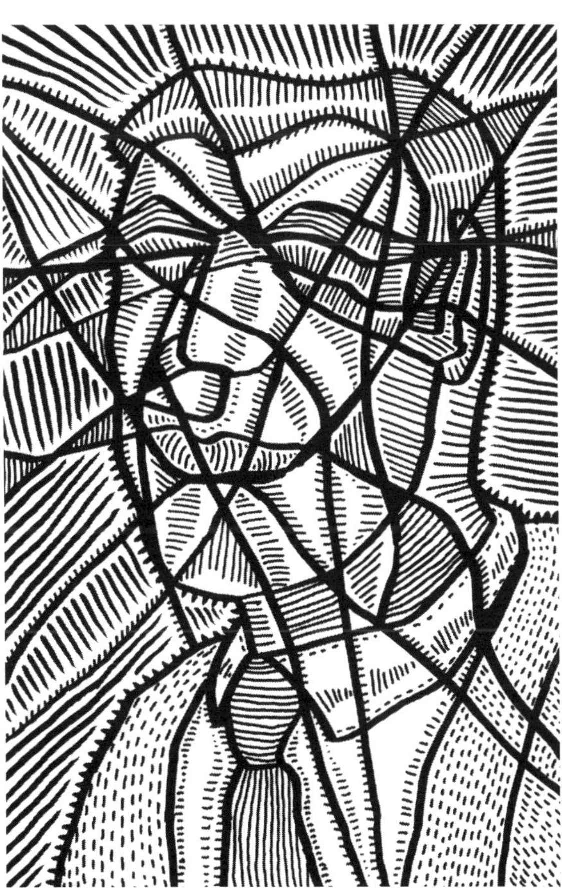

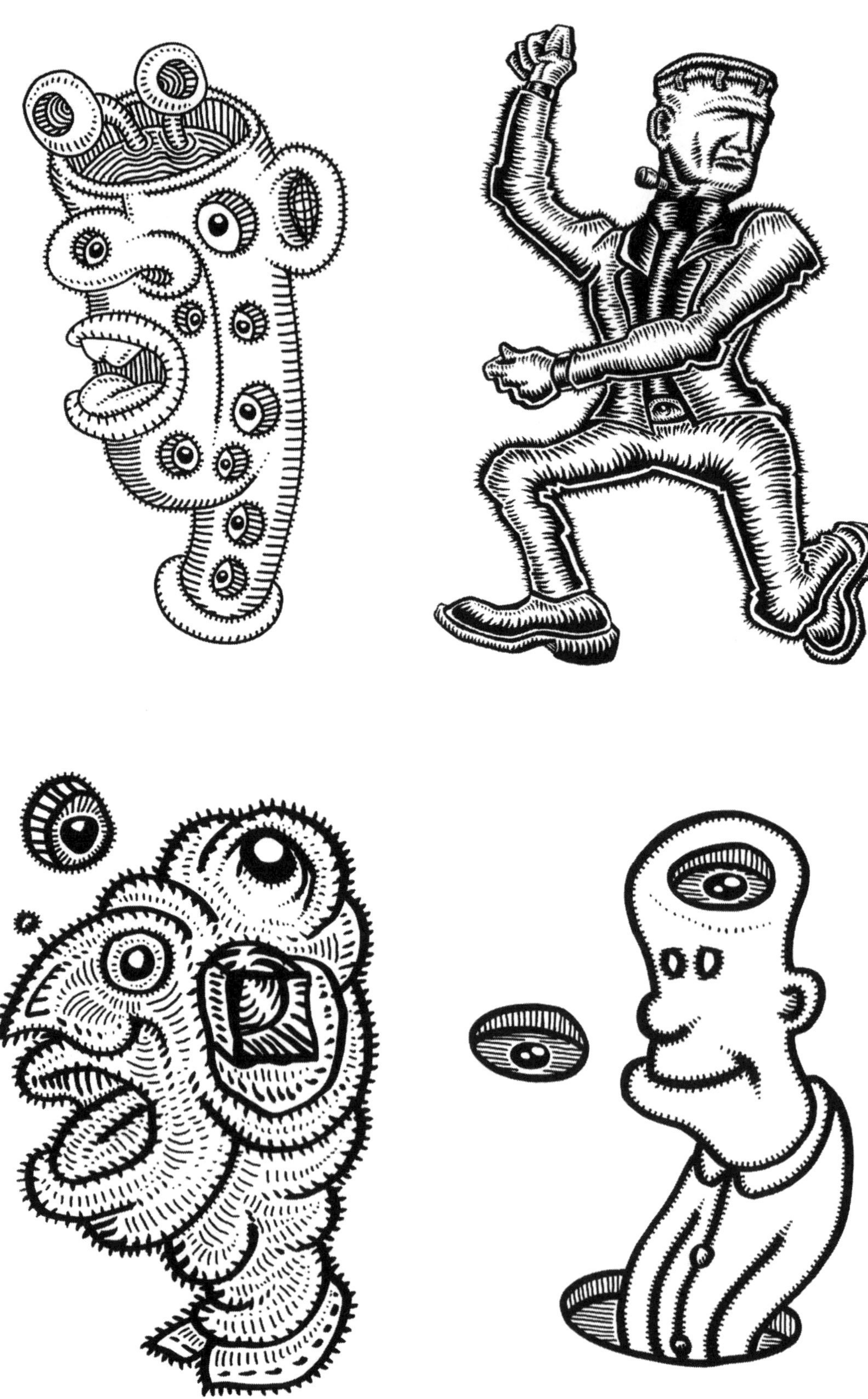

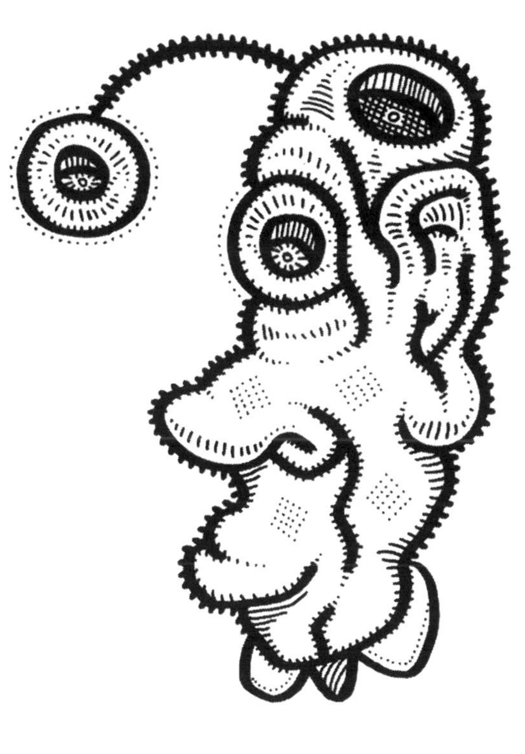

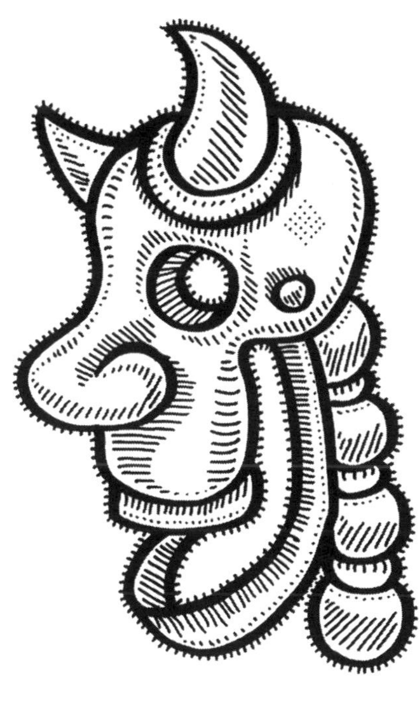

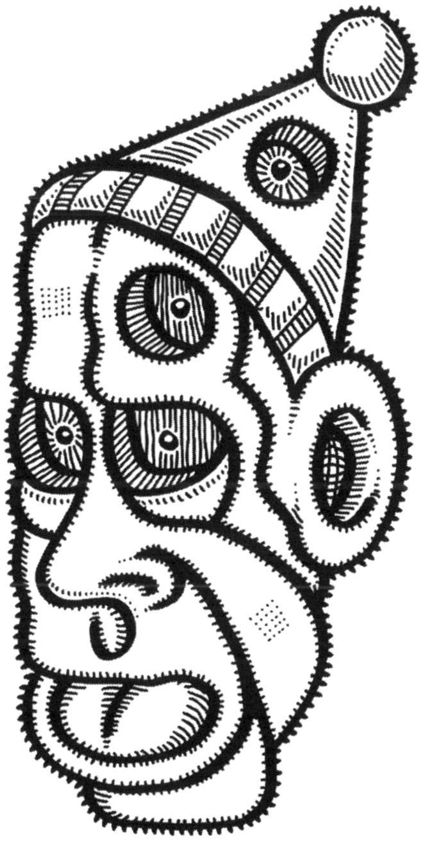

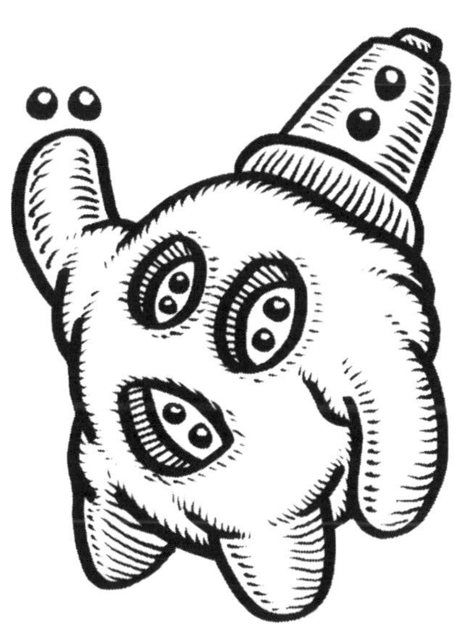

2012

February

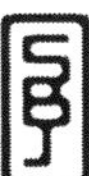

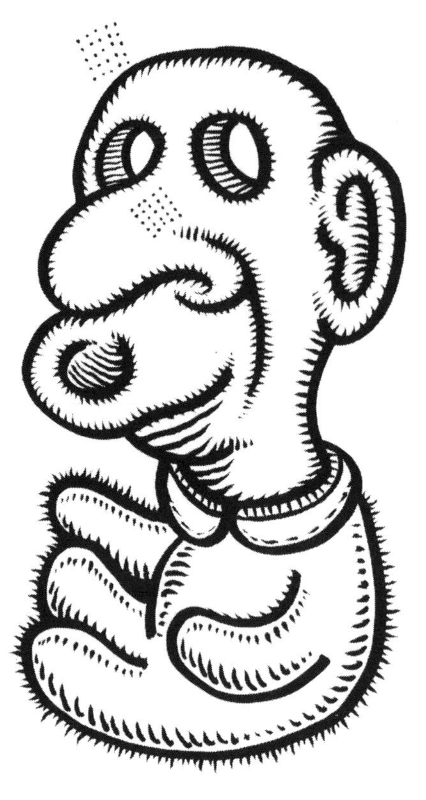

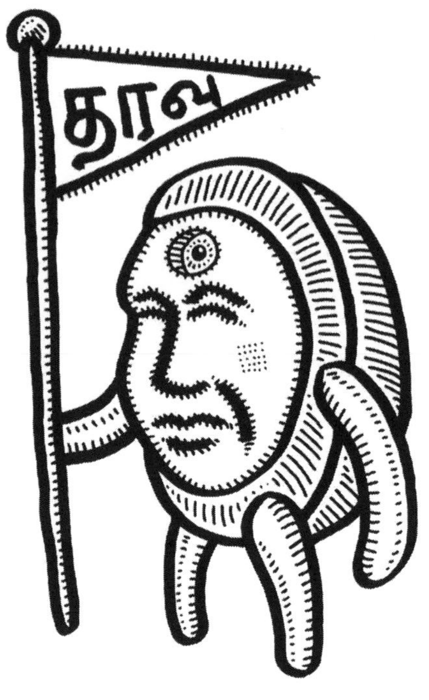
தரவு

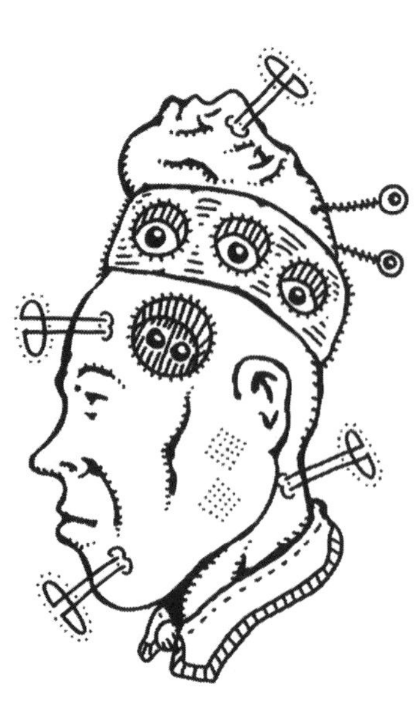

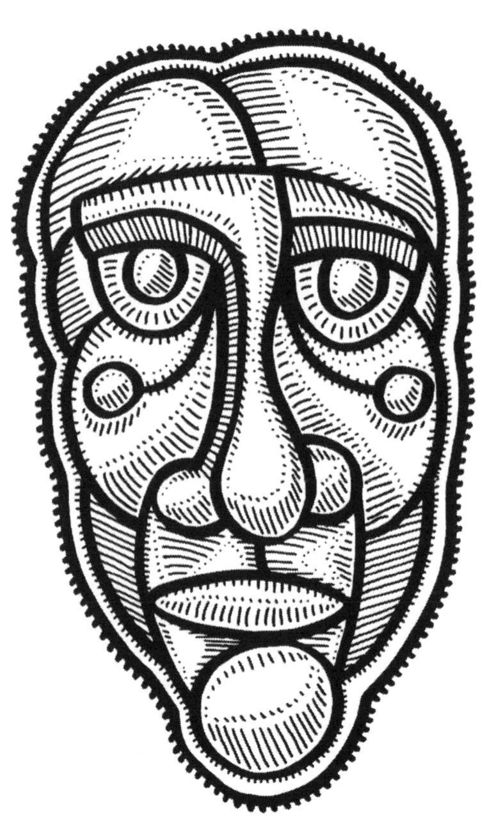

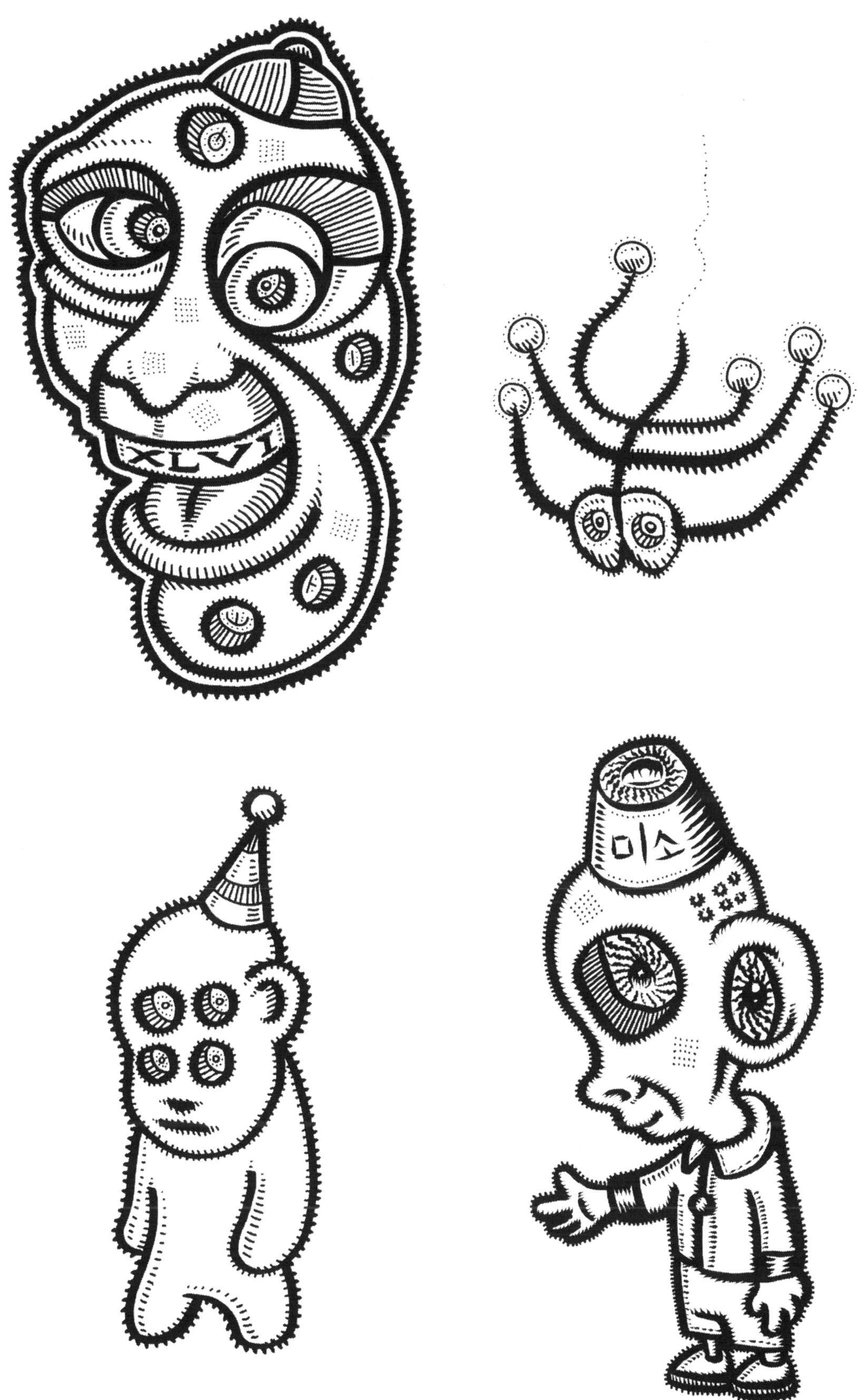
XLVI
미소

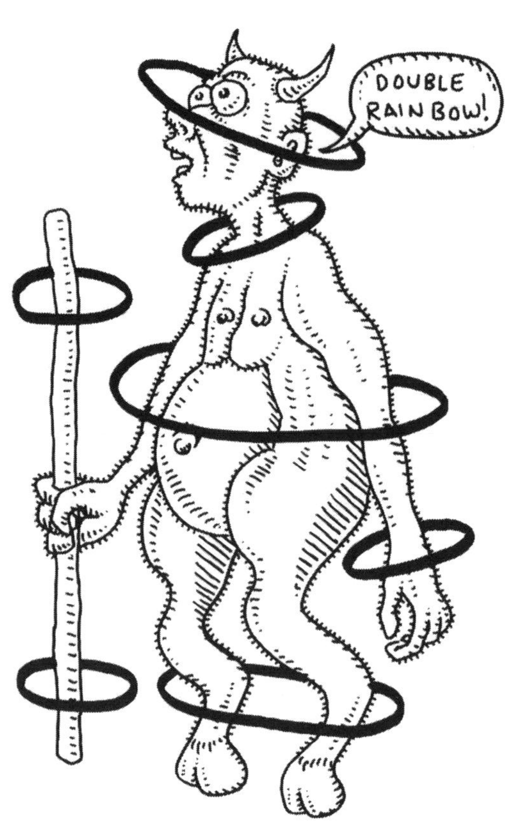
DOUBLE RAIN BOW!

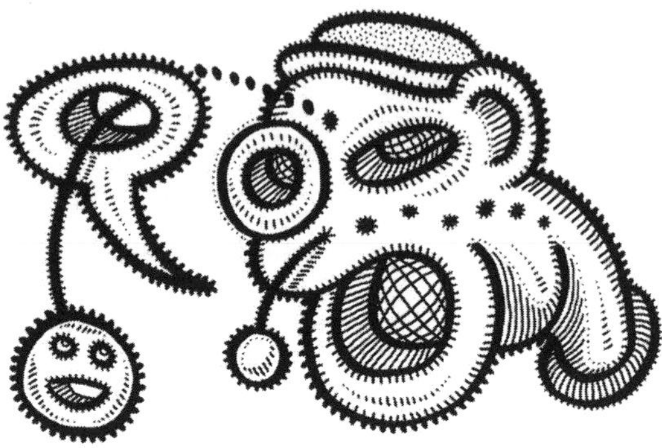

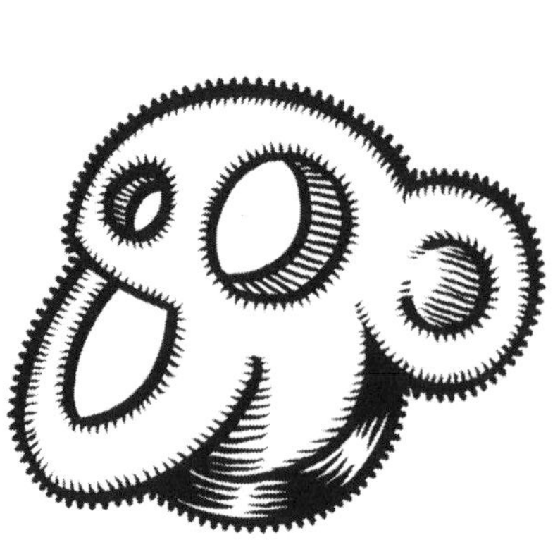

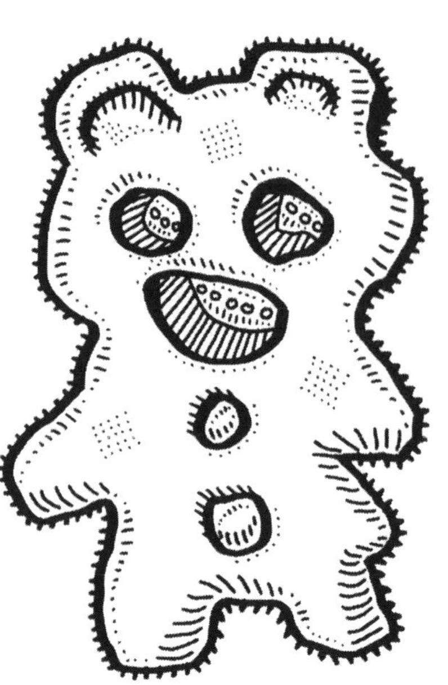

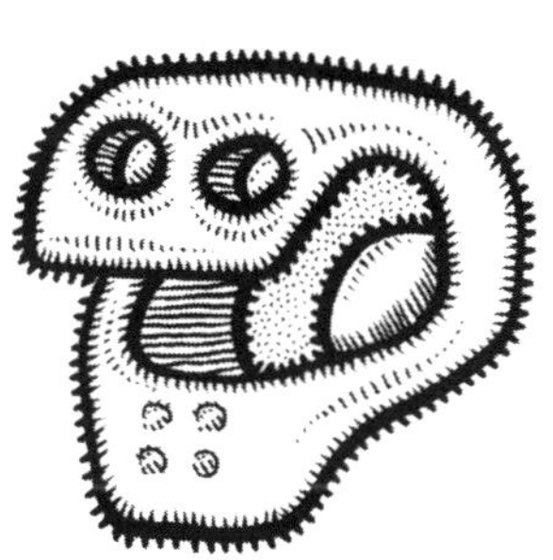

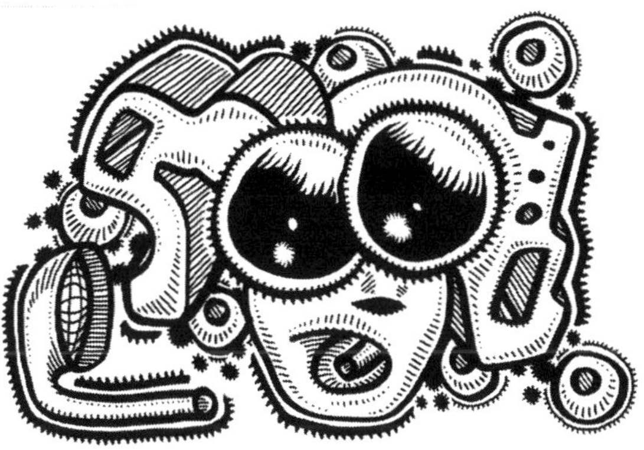

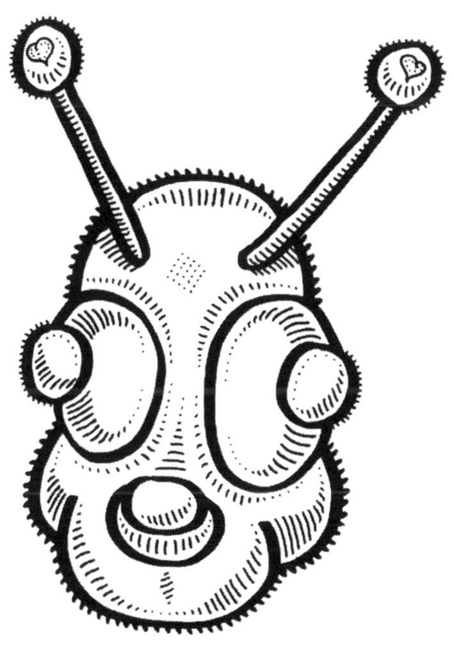

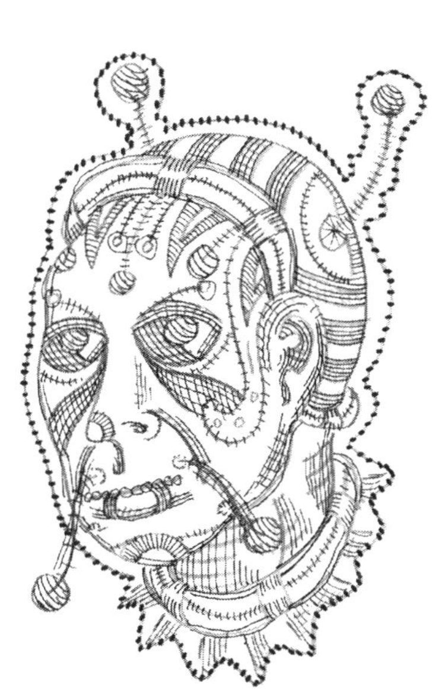

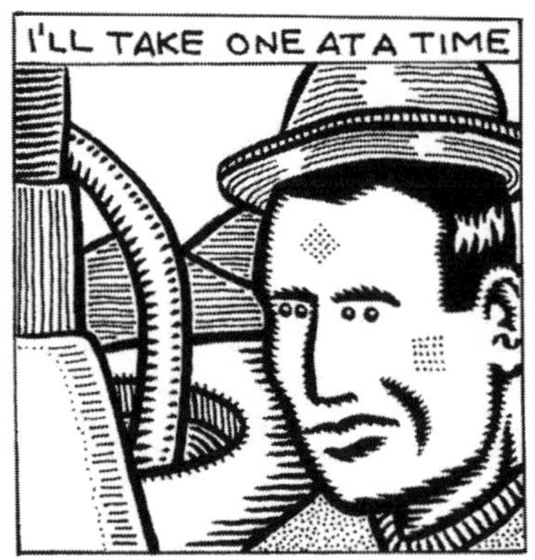
I'LL TAKE ONE AT A TIME

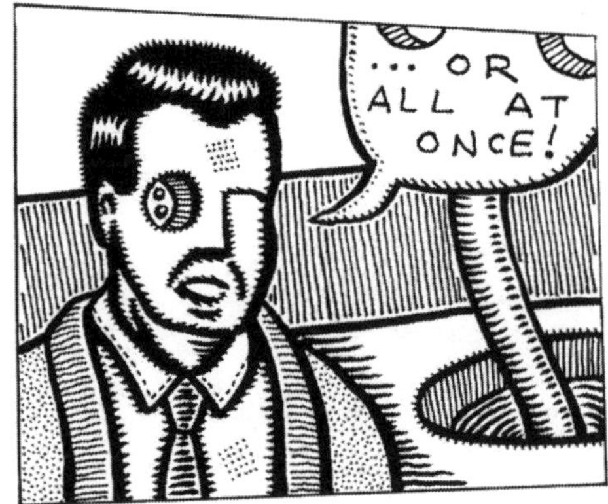
... OR ALL AT ONCE!

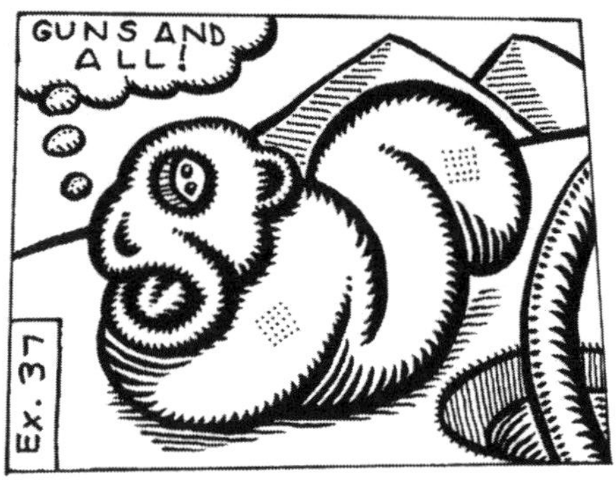
GUNS AND ALL!
Ex. 37

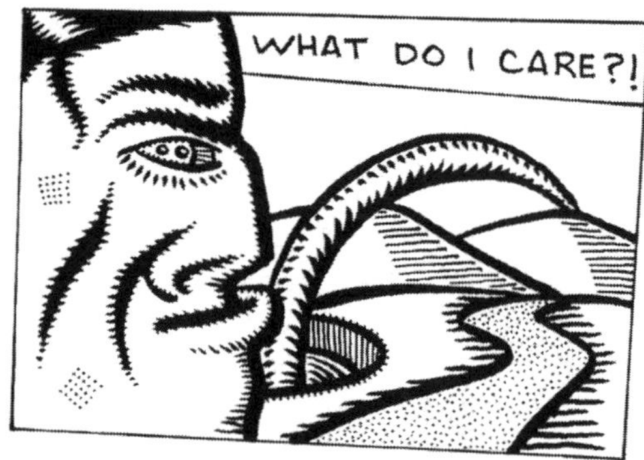
WHAT DO I CARE?!

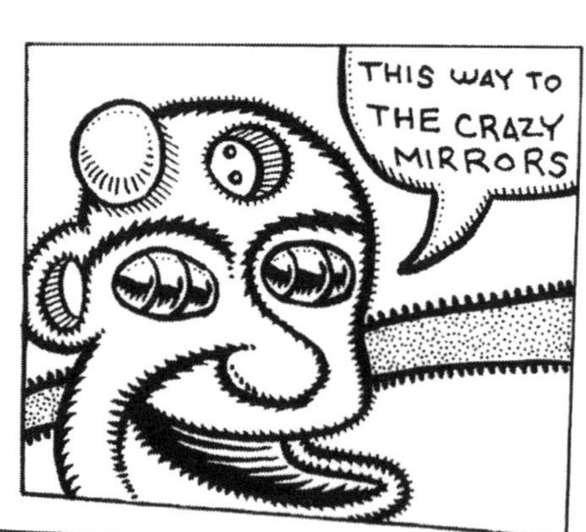
THIS WAY TO THE CRAZY MIRRORS

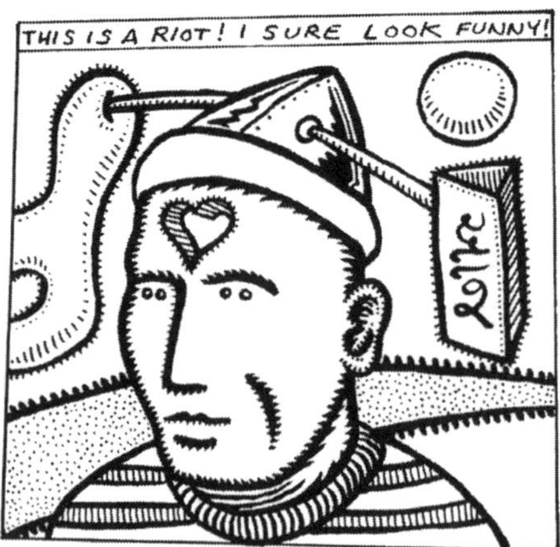
THIS IS A RIOT! I SURE LOOK FUNNY!

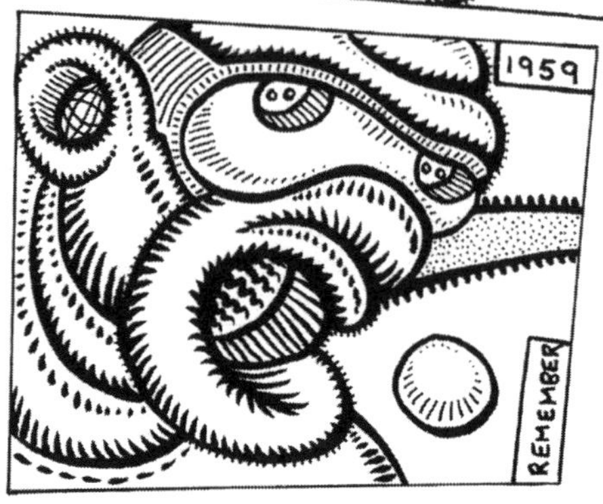
1959
REMEMBER

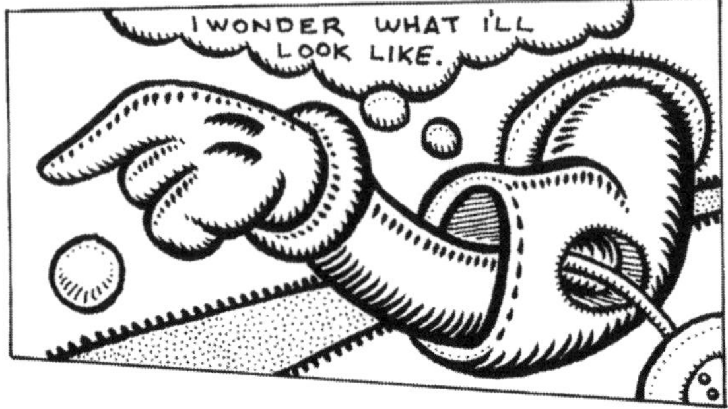
I WONDER WHAT I'LL LOOK LIKE.

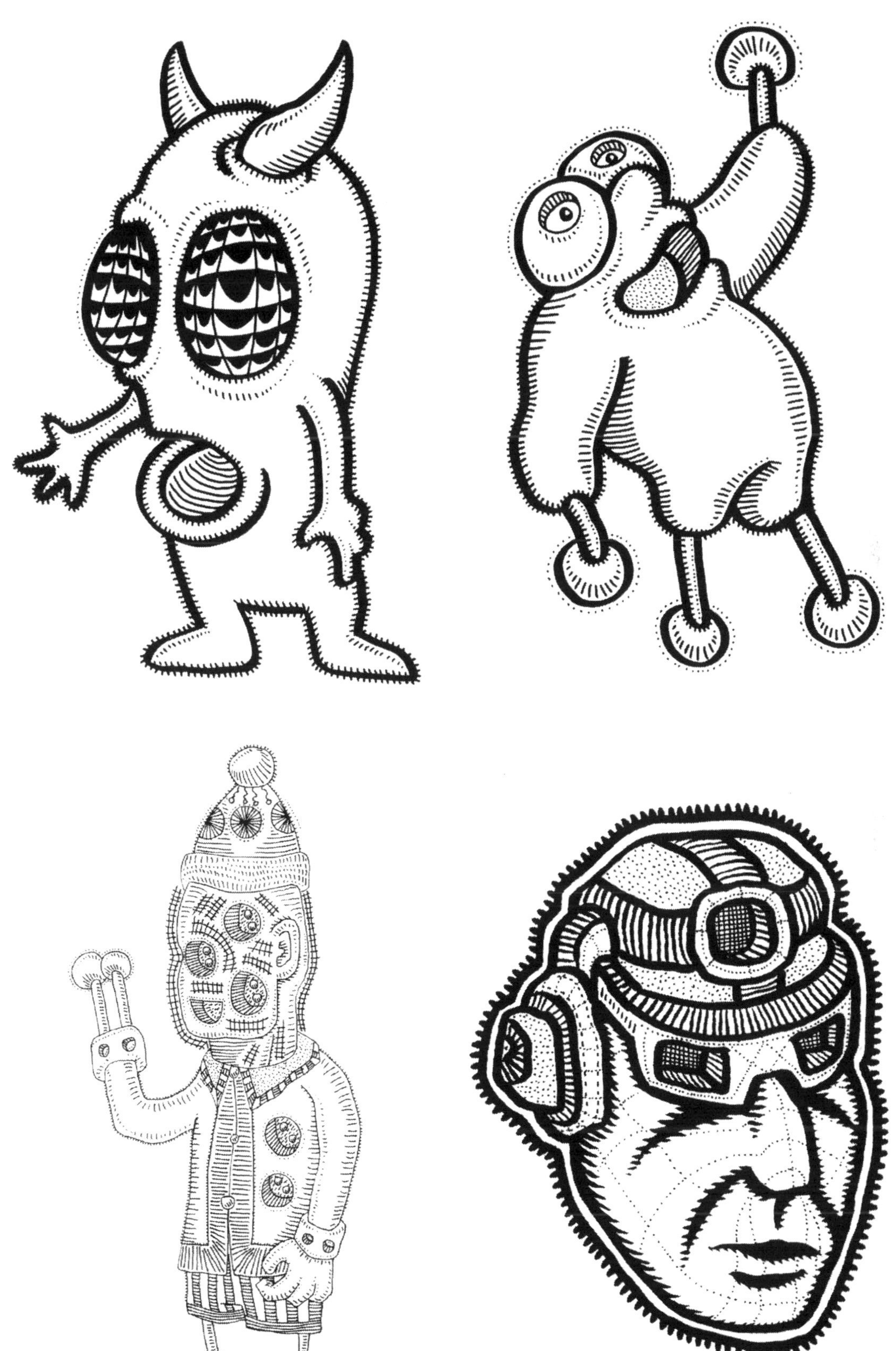

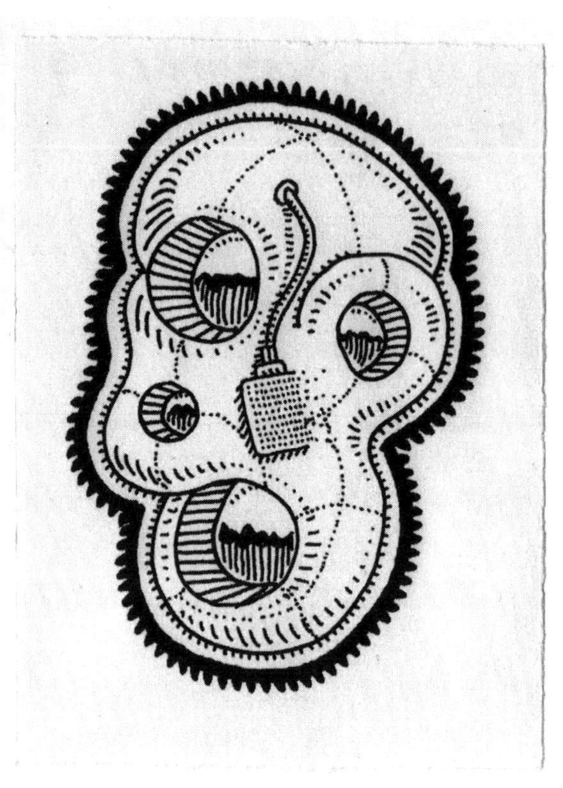

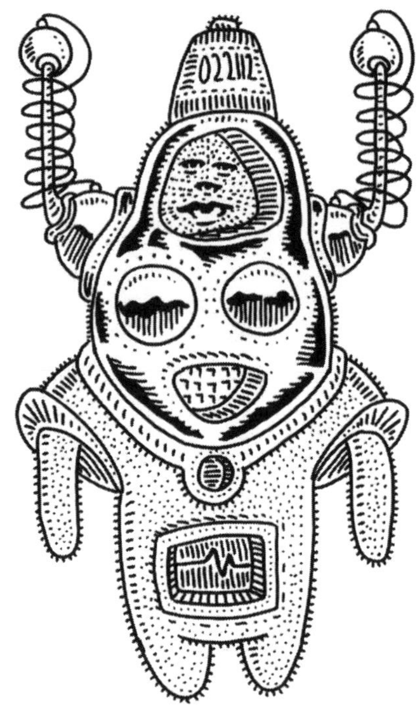
022112

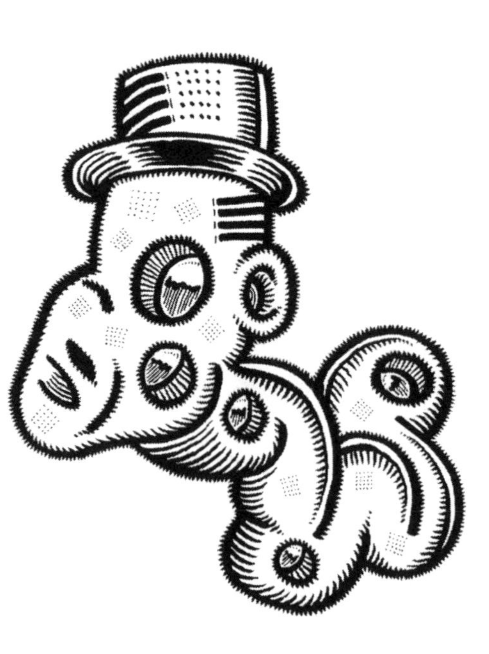

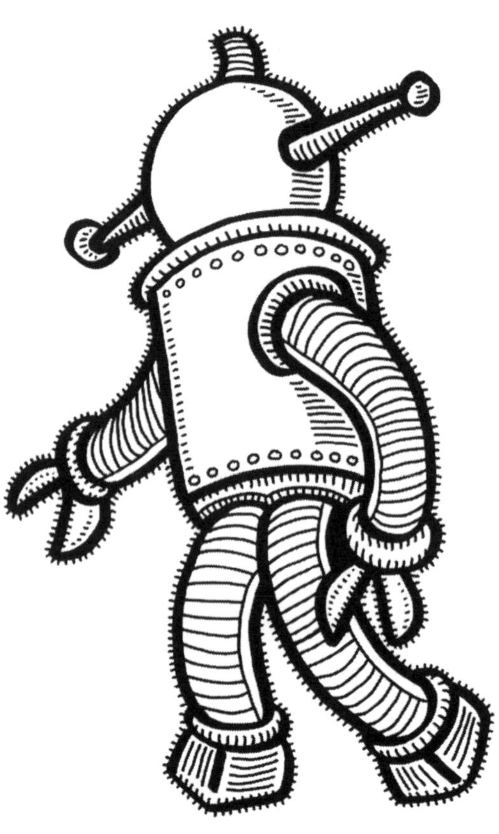

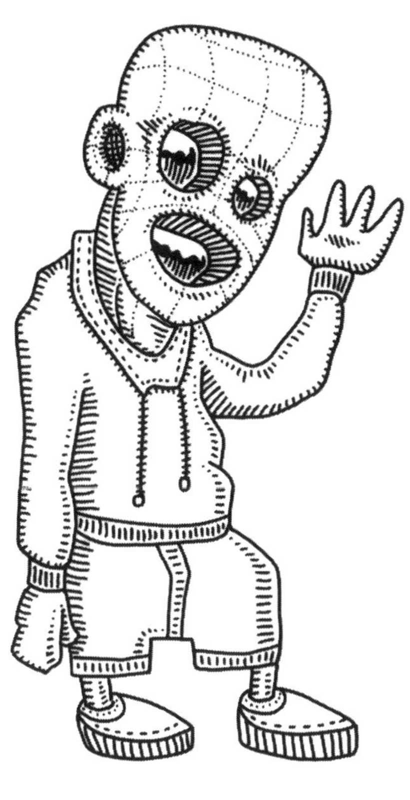

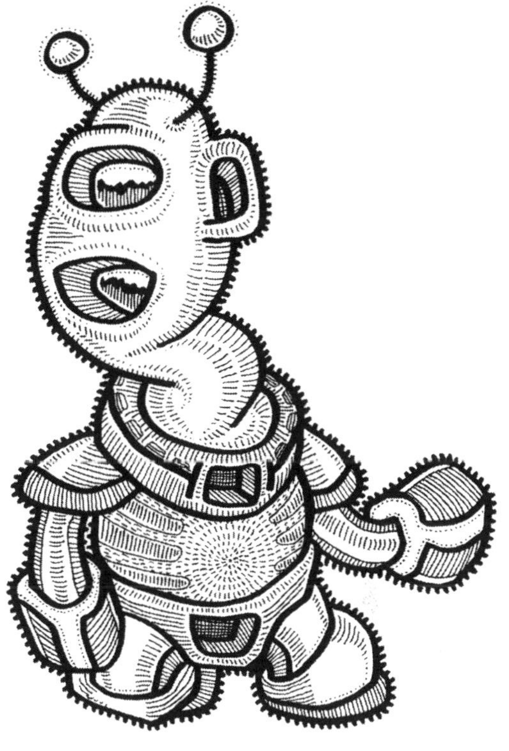

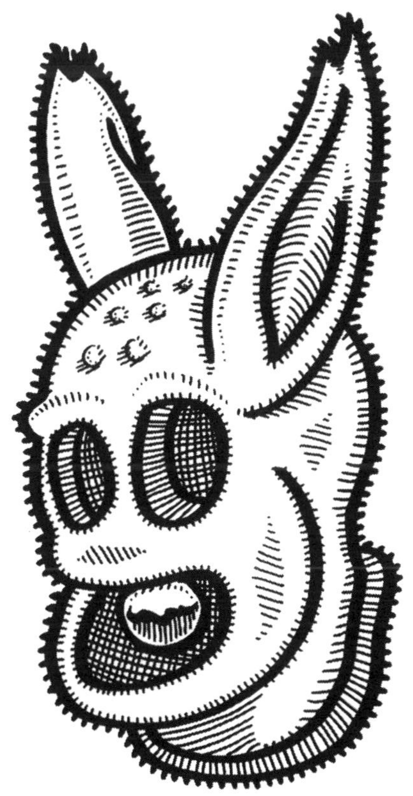

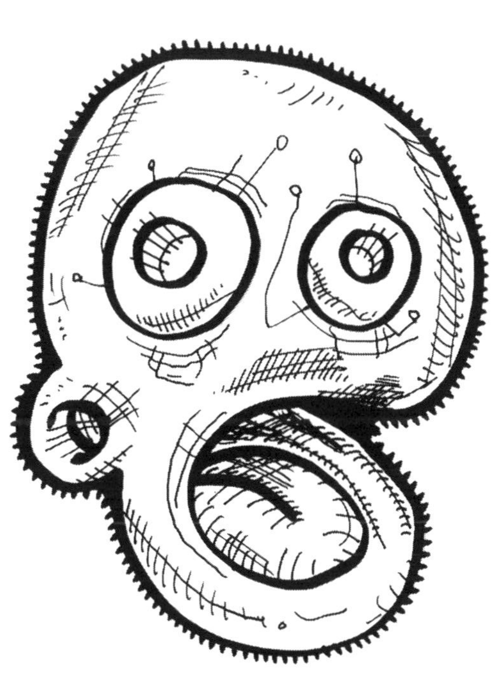

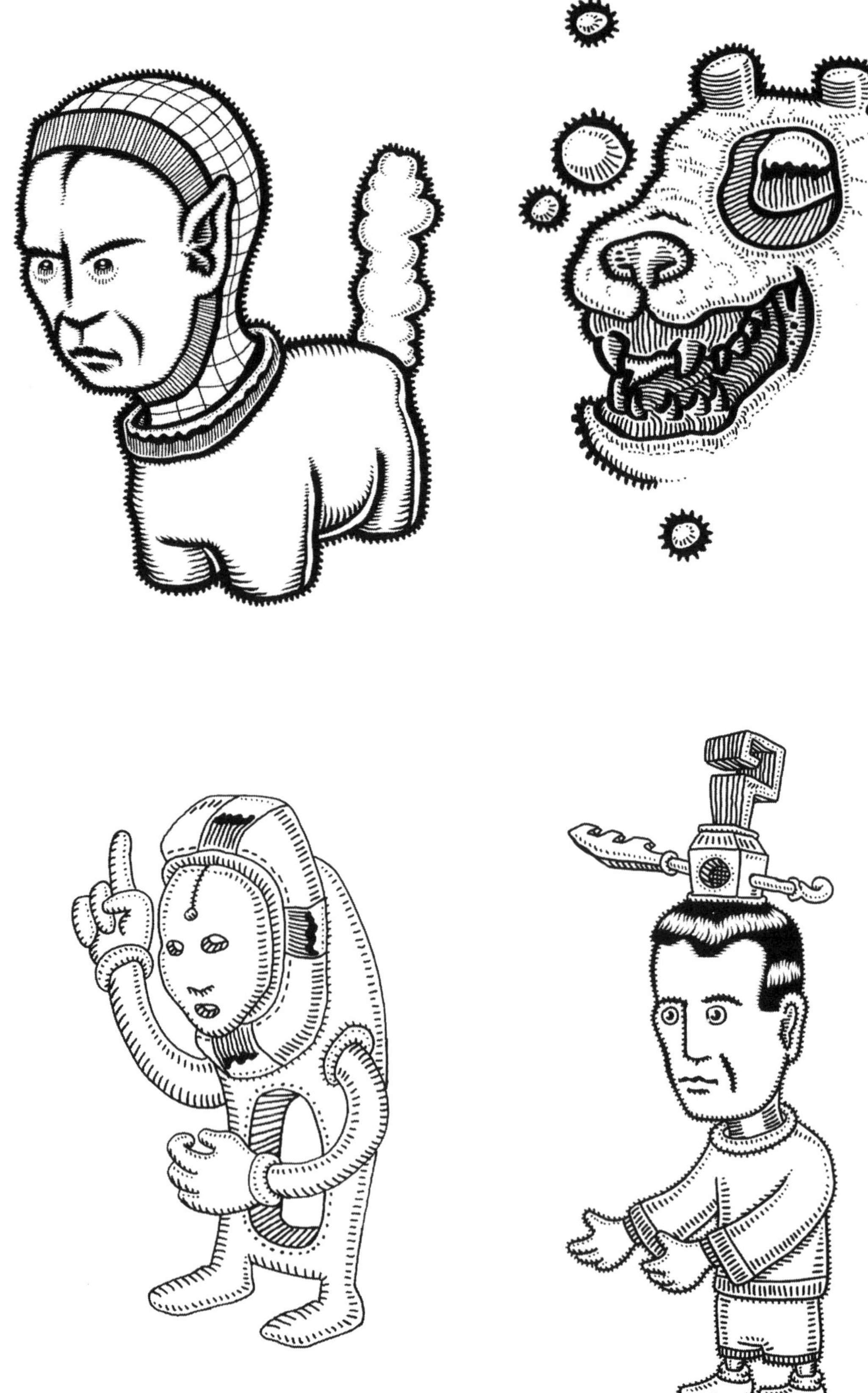

2012

MARCH

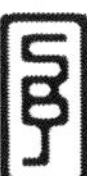

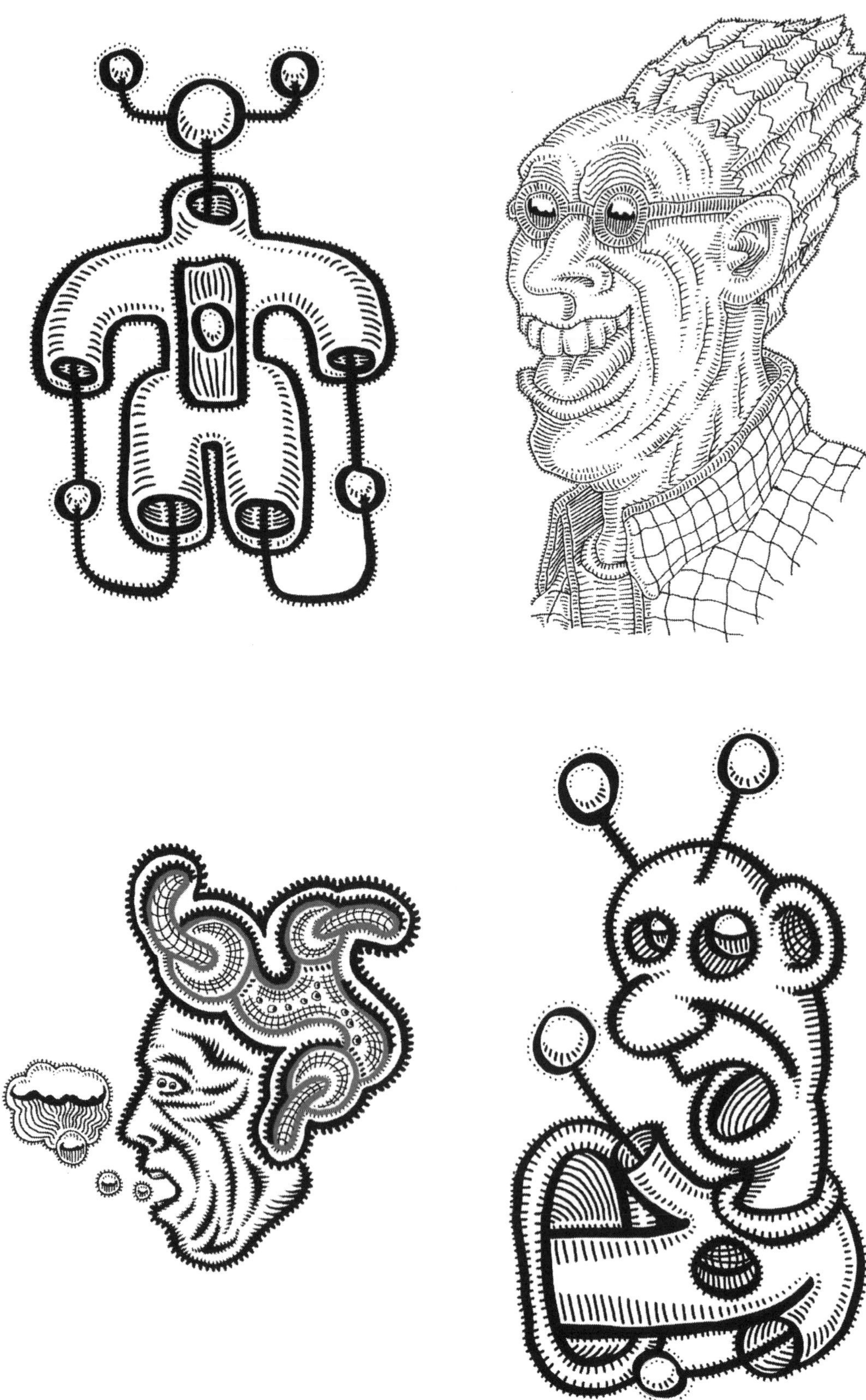

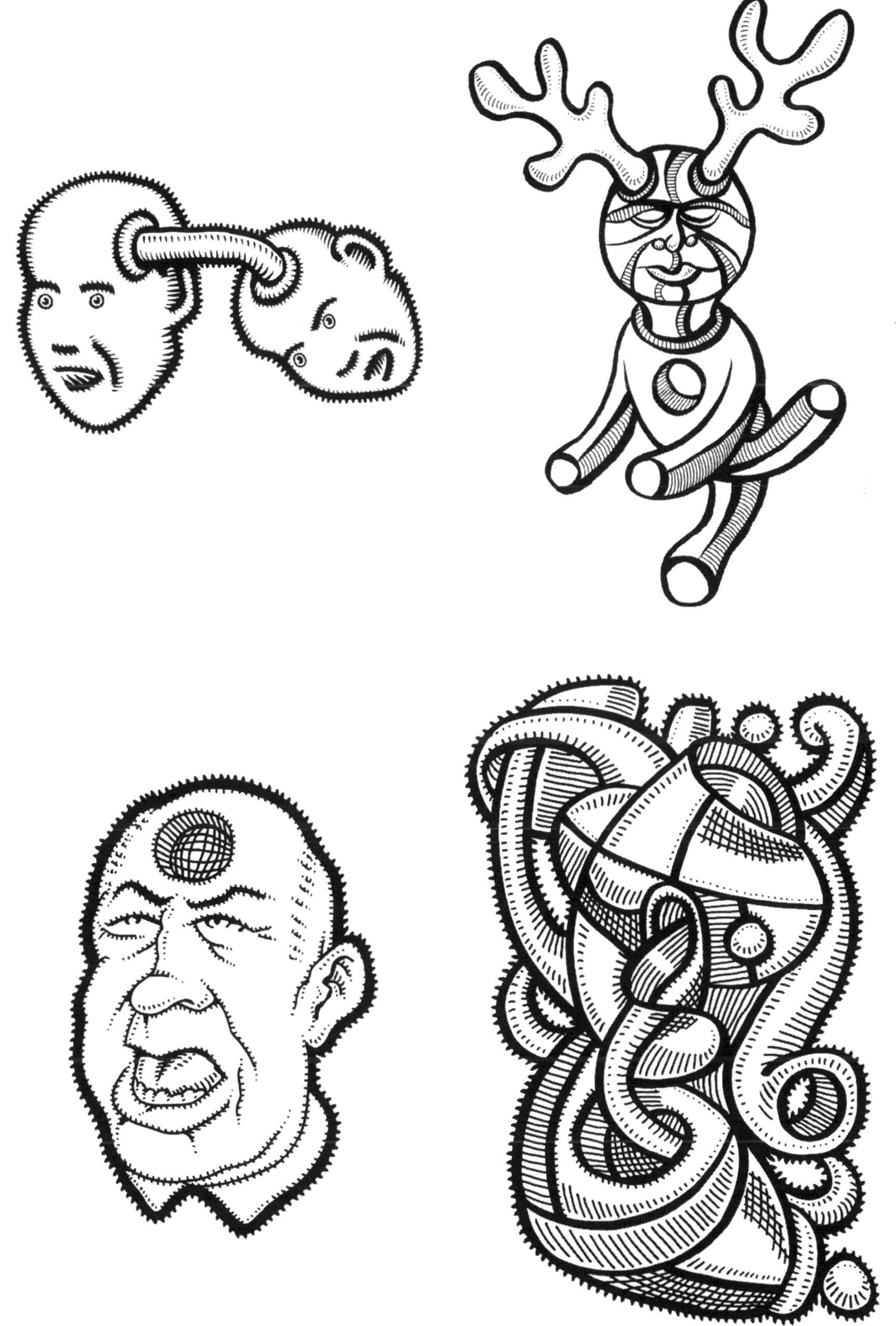

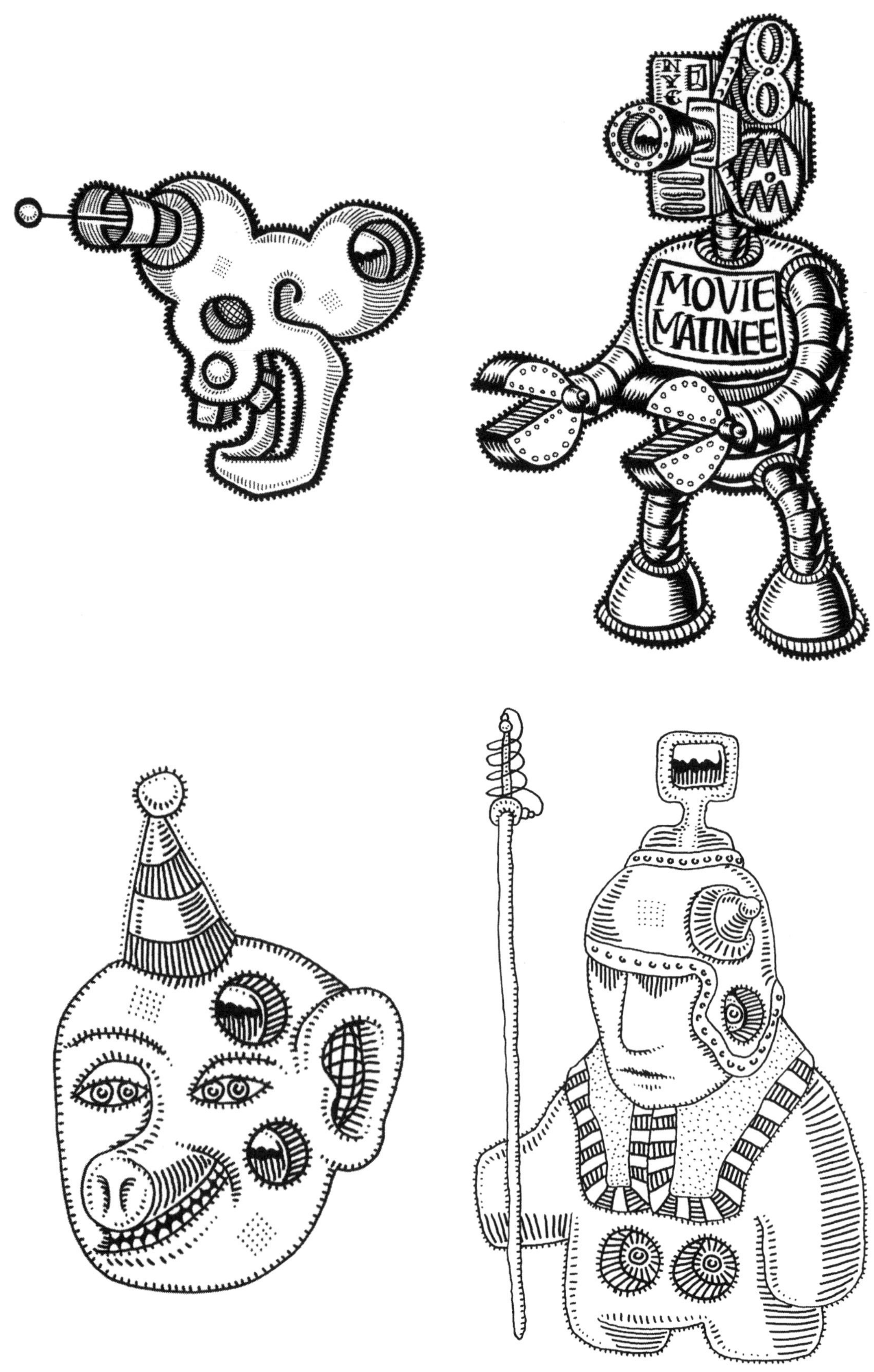
NYC
8
MM
MOVIE
MATINEE

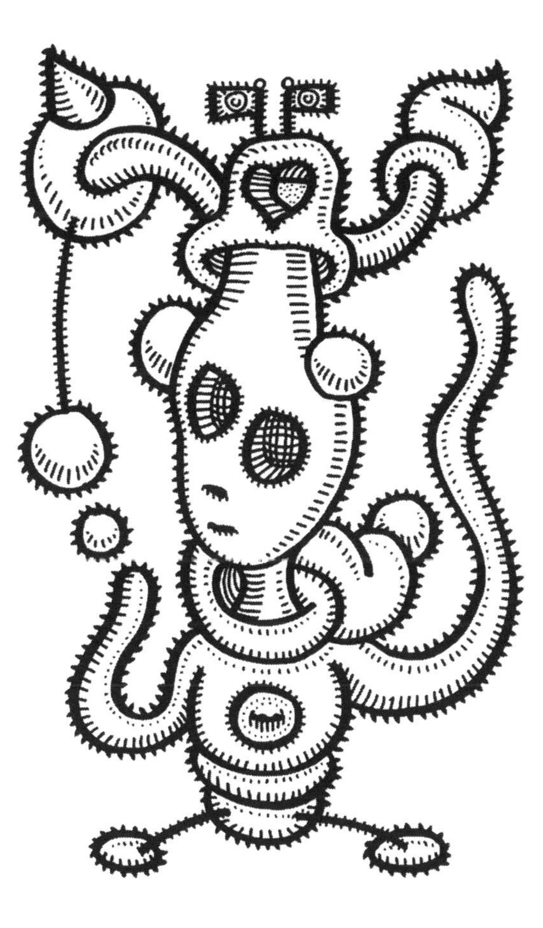

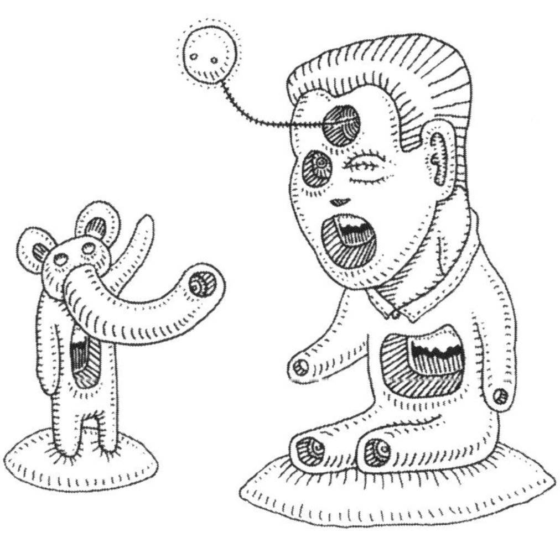

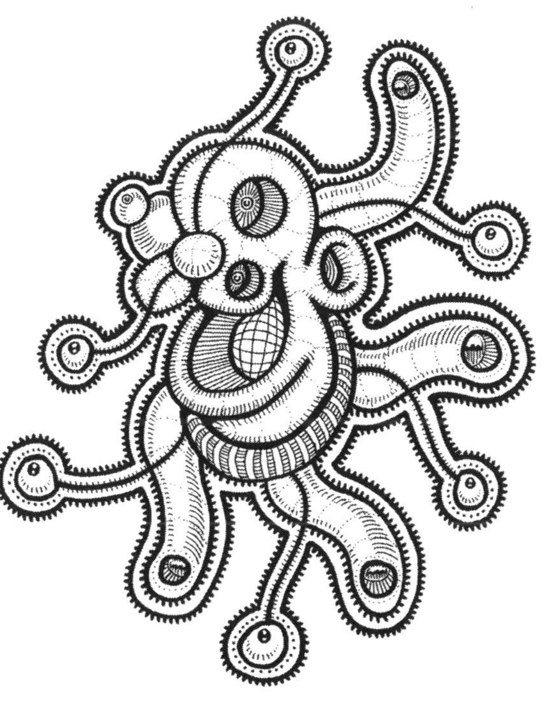

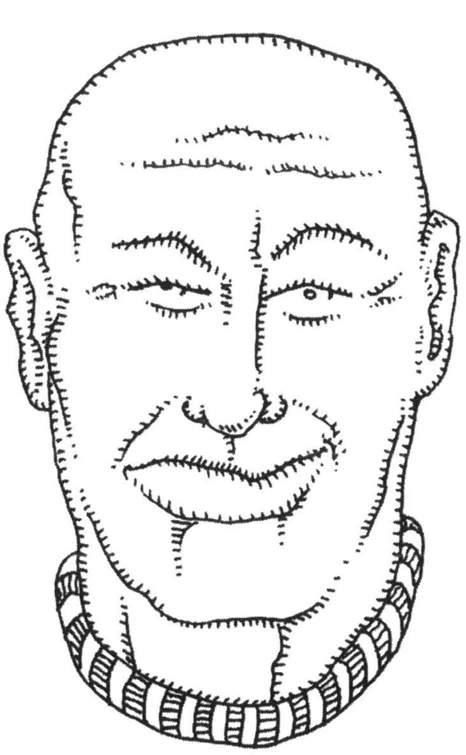

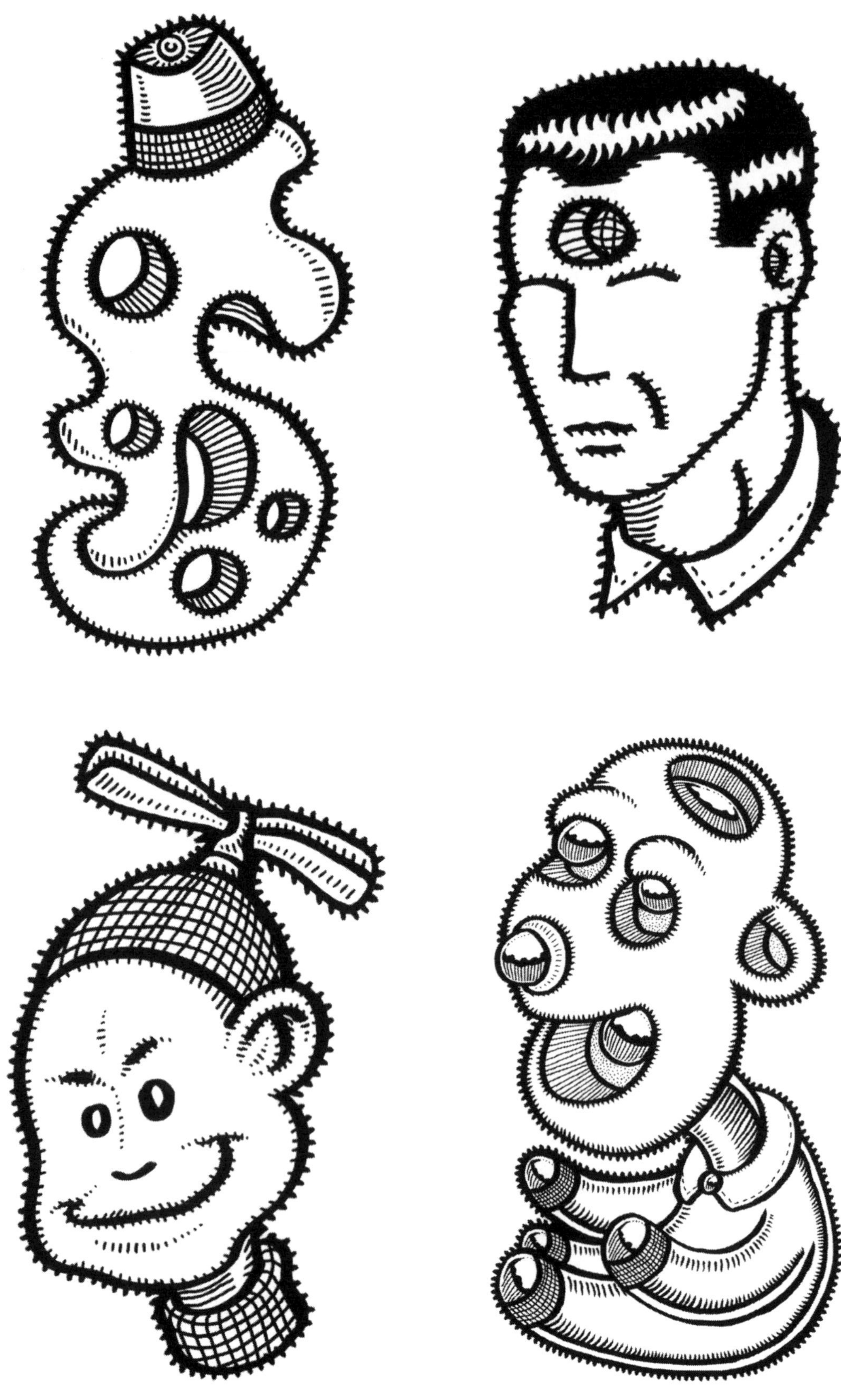

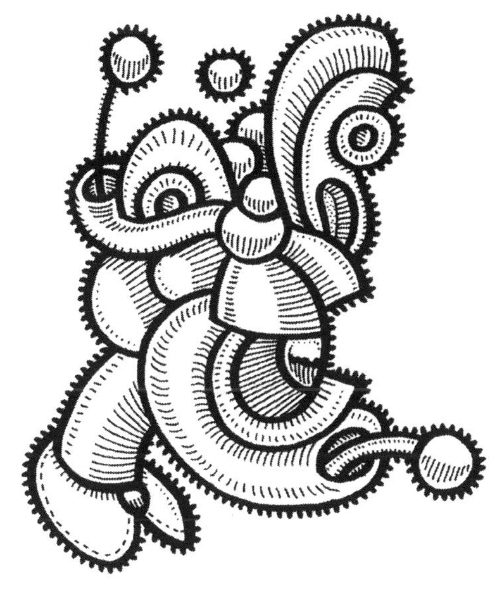

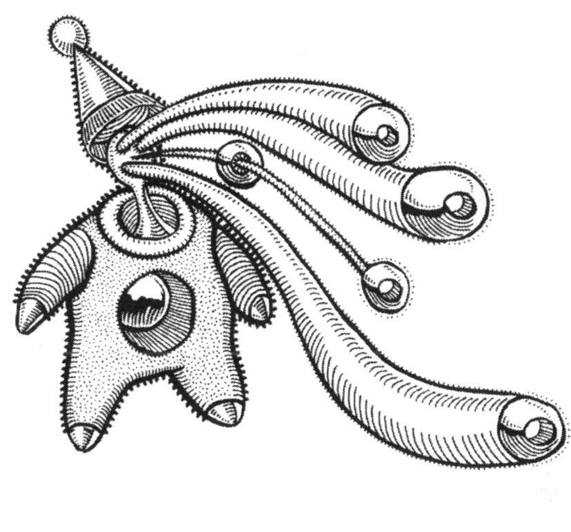

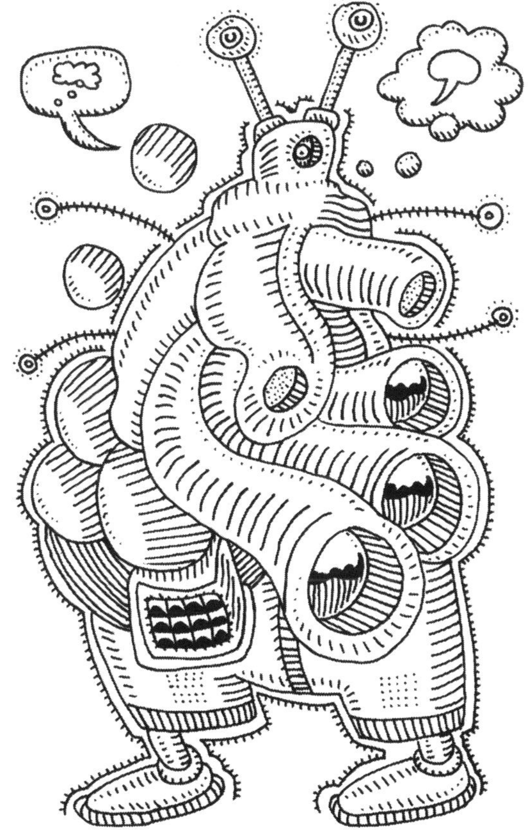

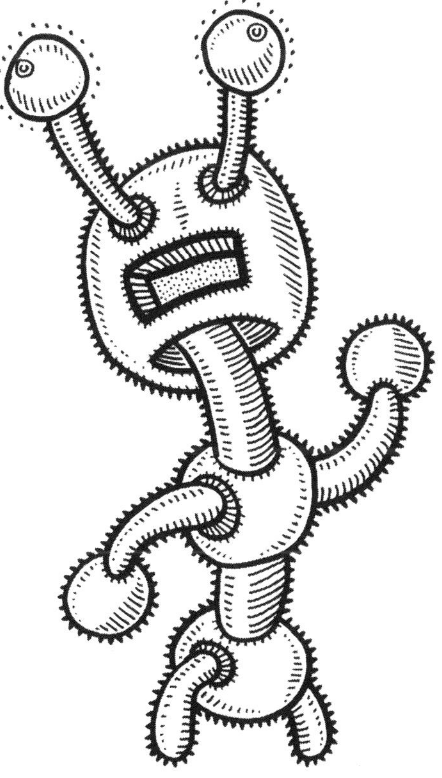

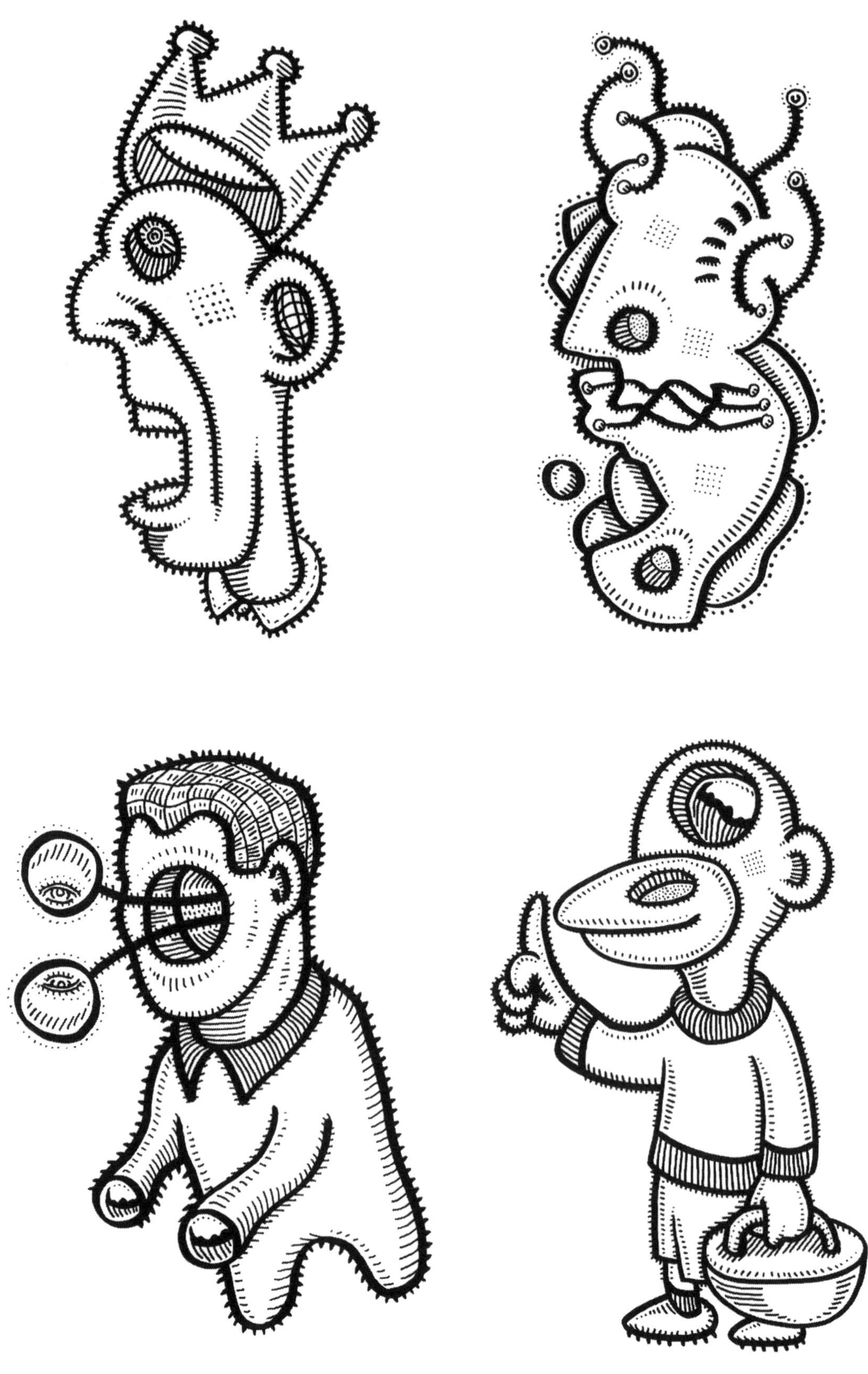

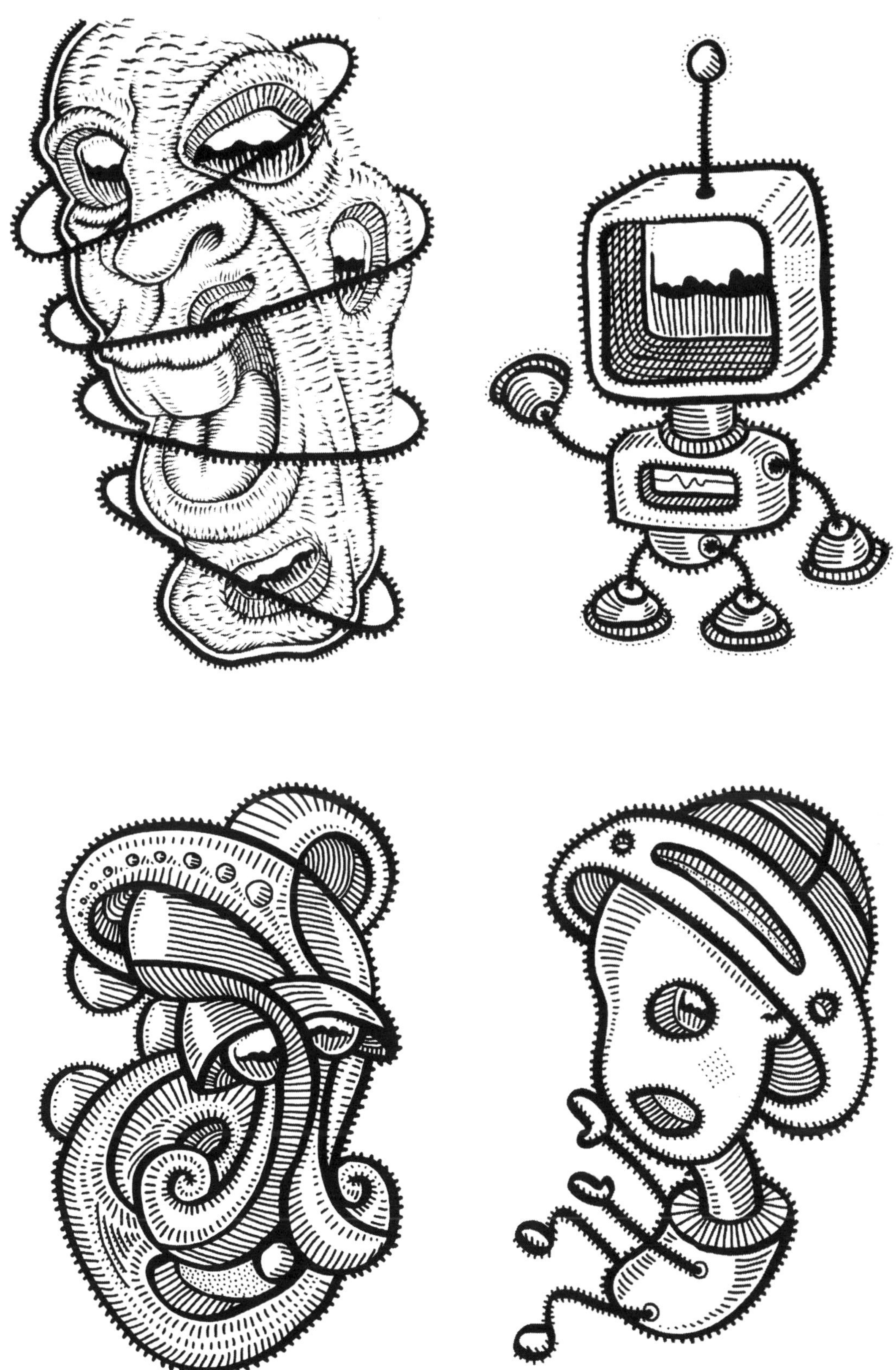

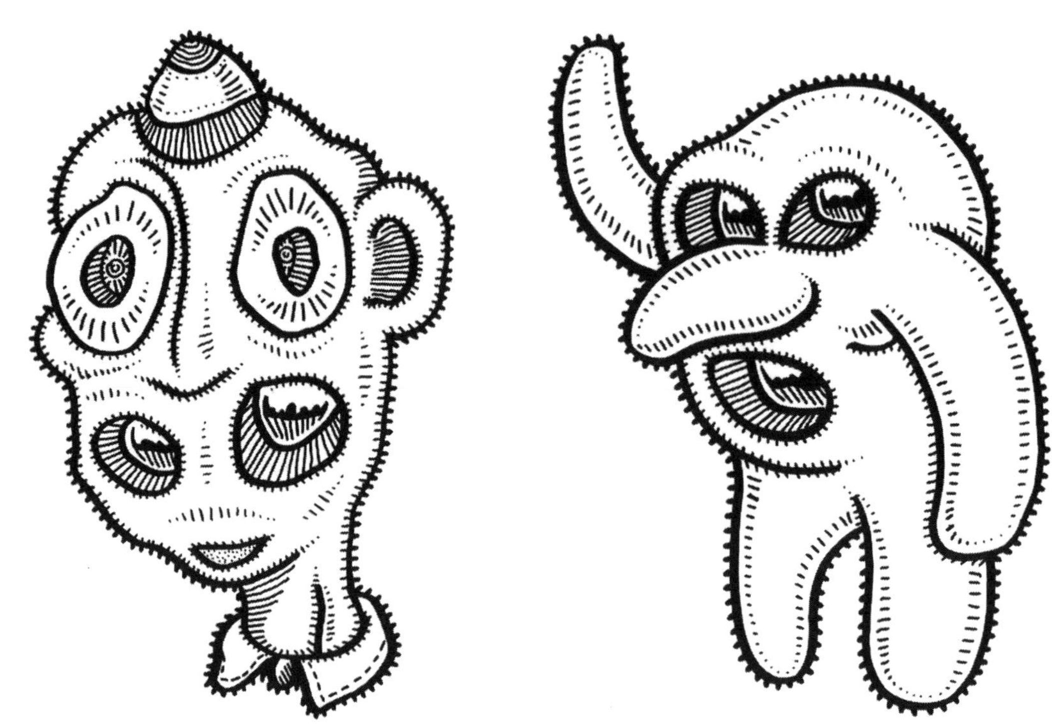

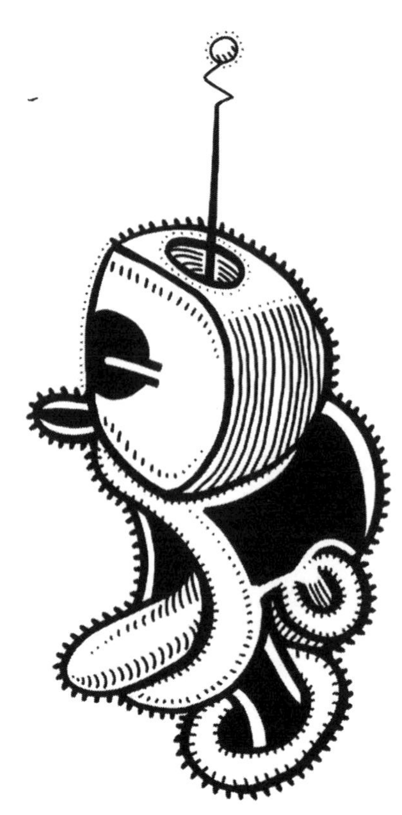

2012

APRIL

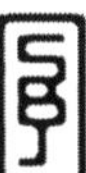

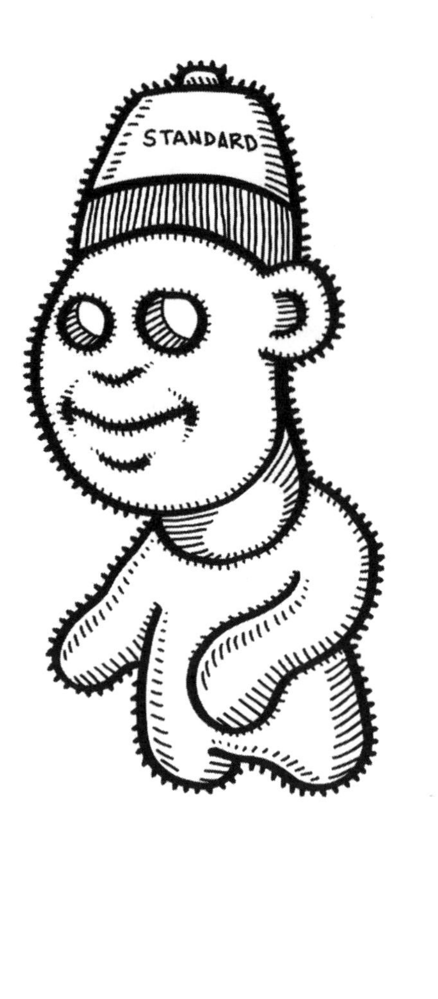
STANDARD

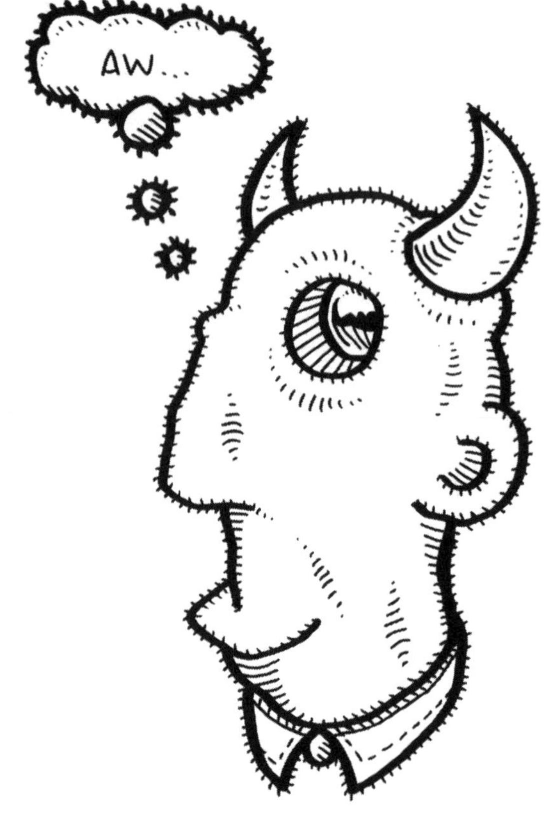
AW...

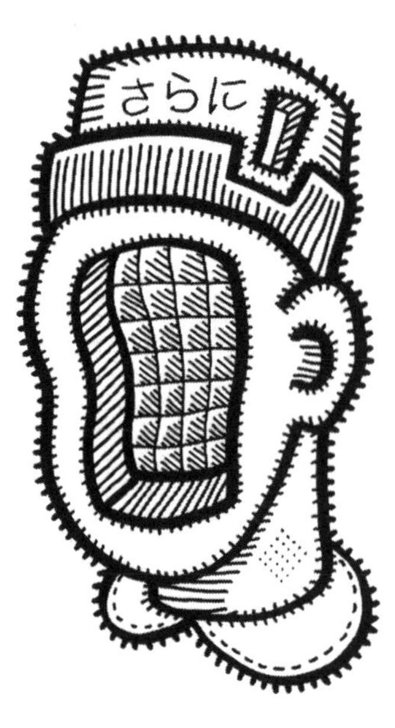
さらに!

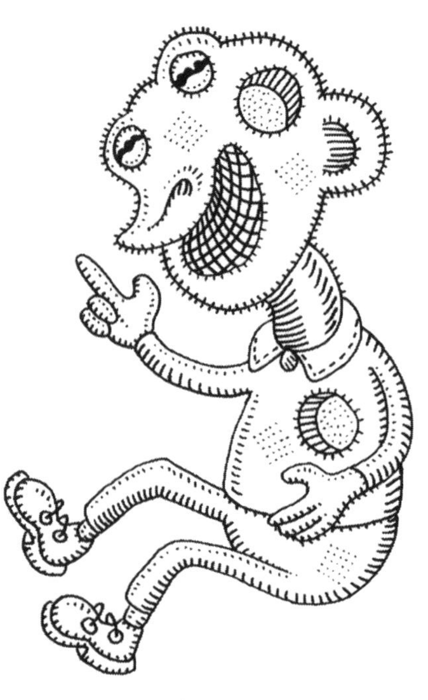

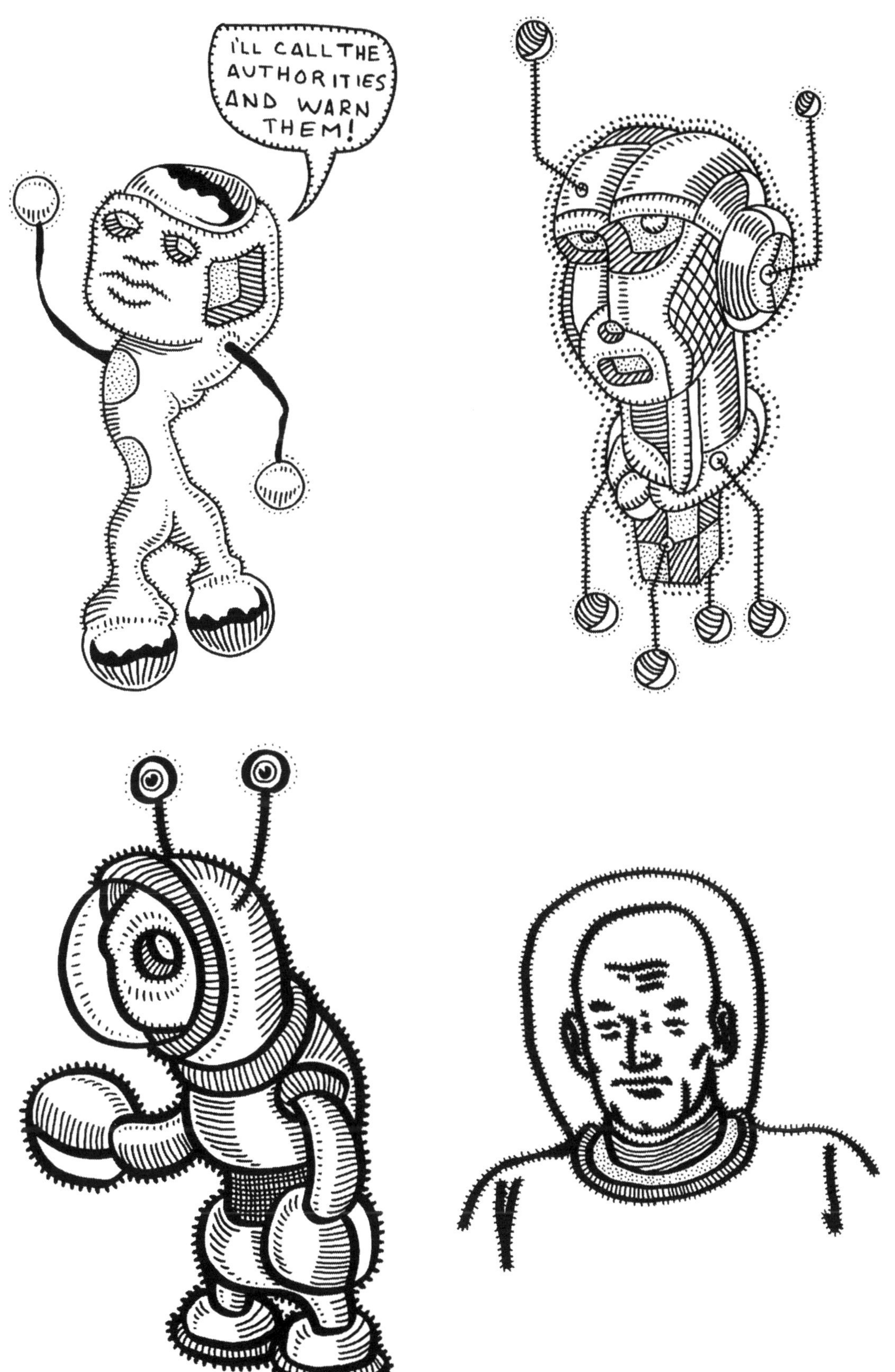
I'LL CALL THE AUTHORITIES AND WARN THEM!

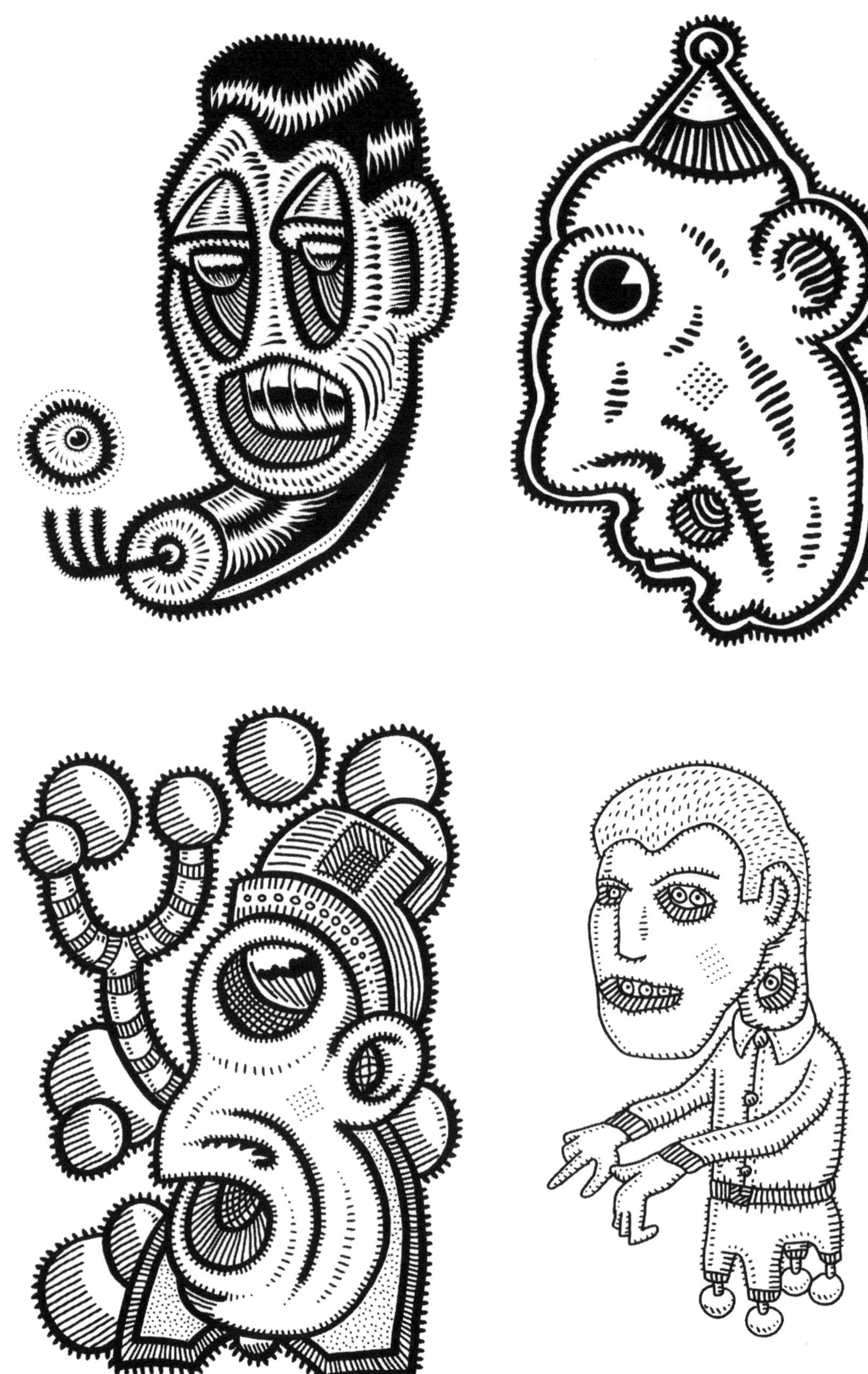

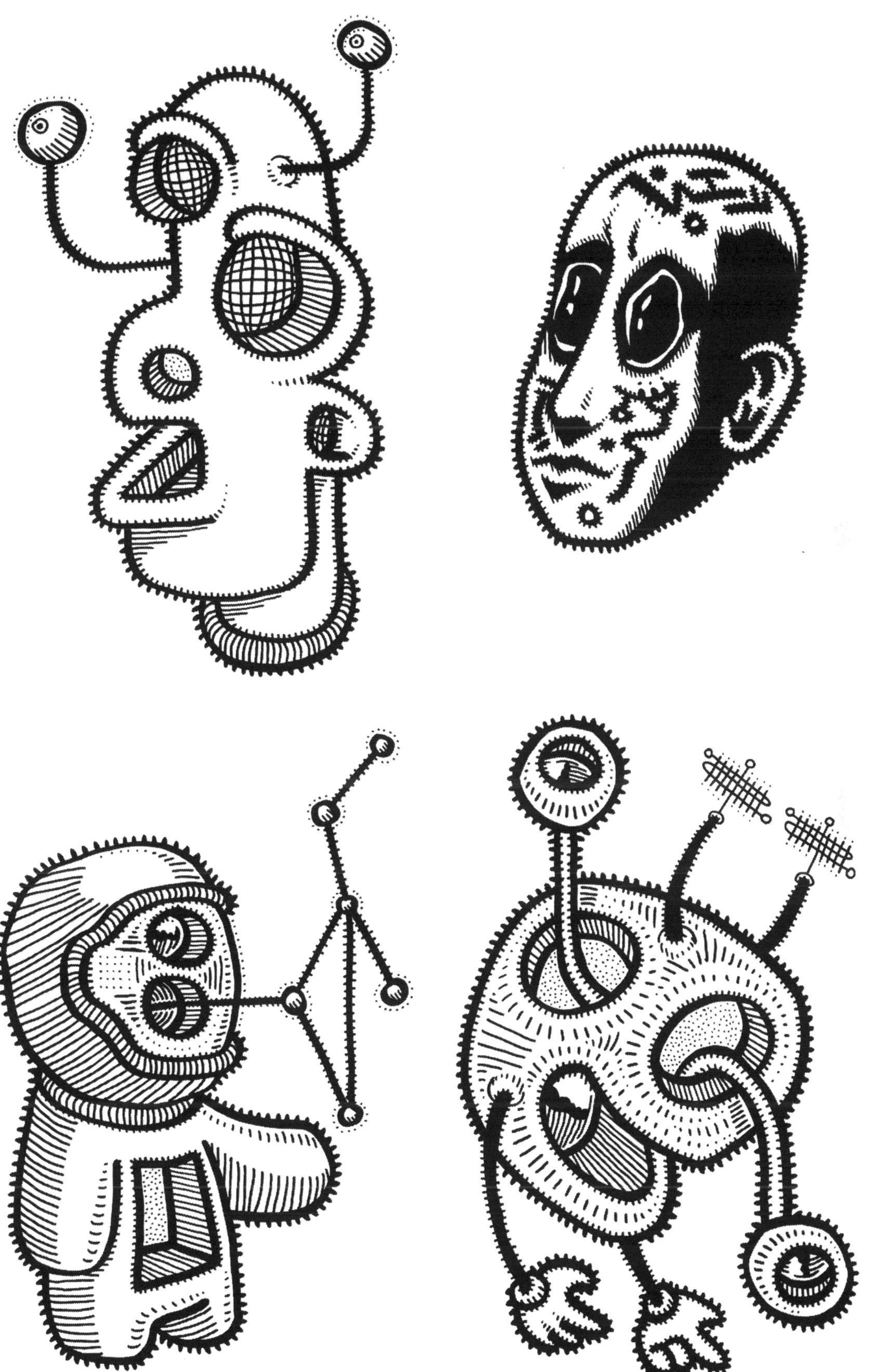

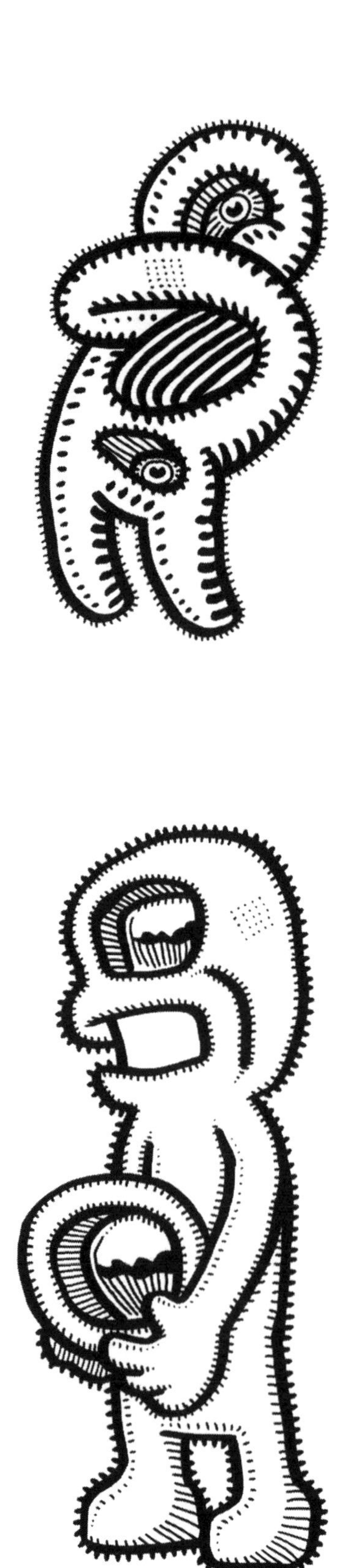
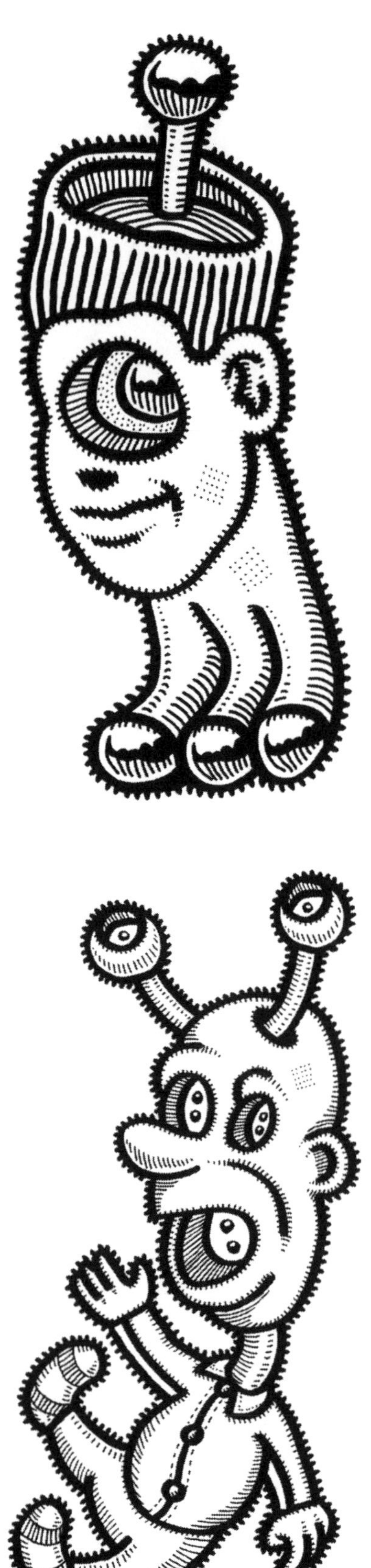

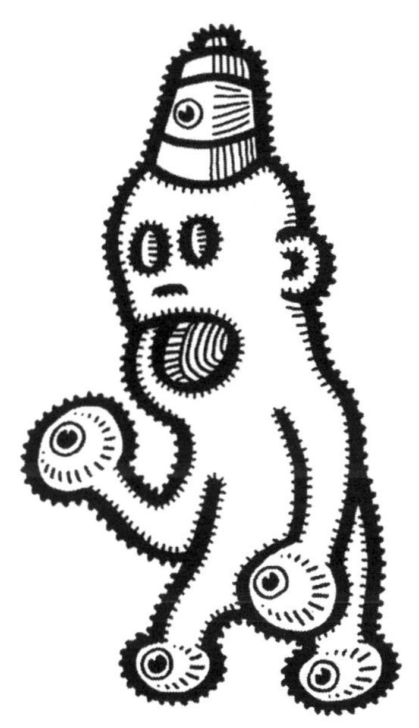

2012

MAY

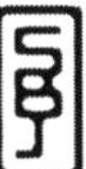

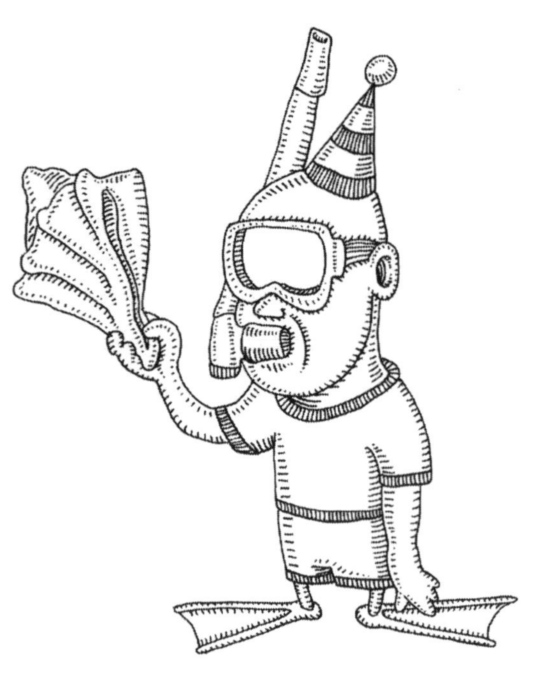

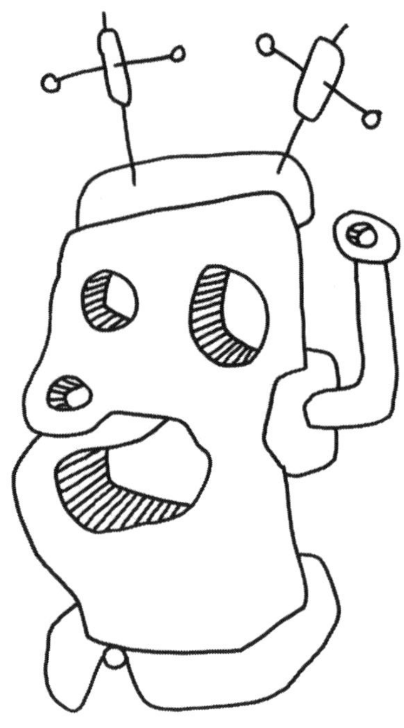

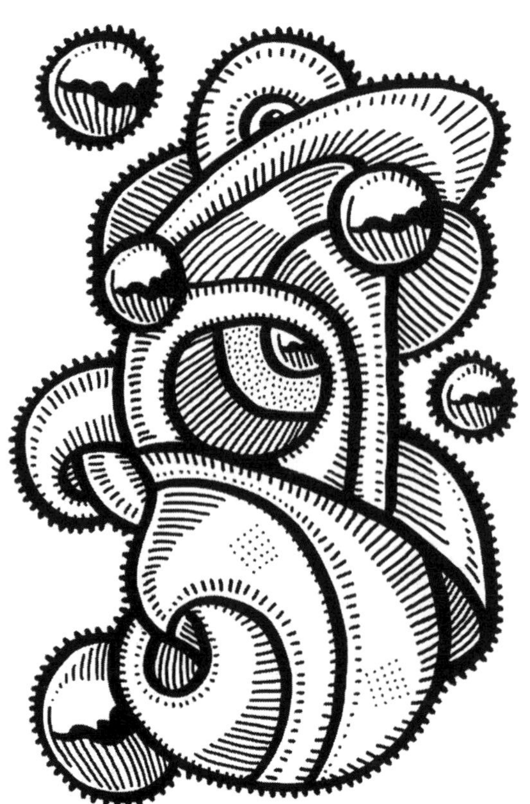

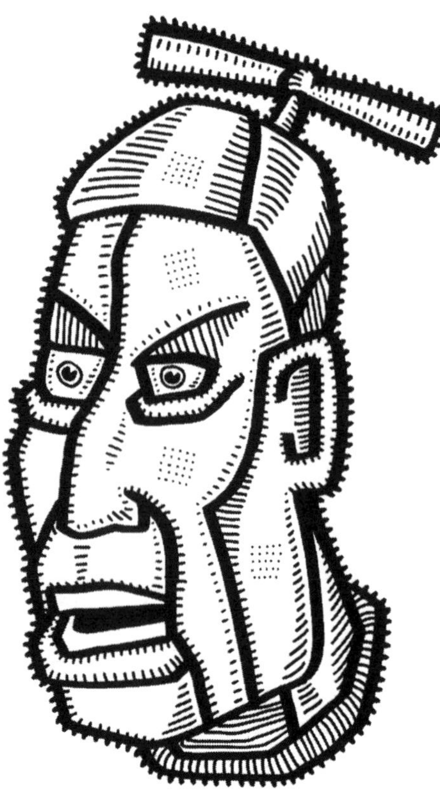

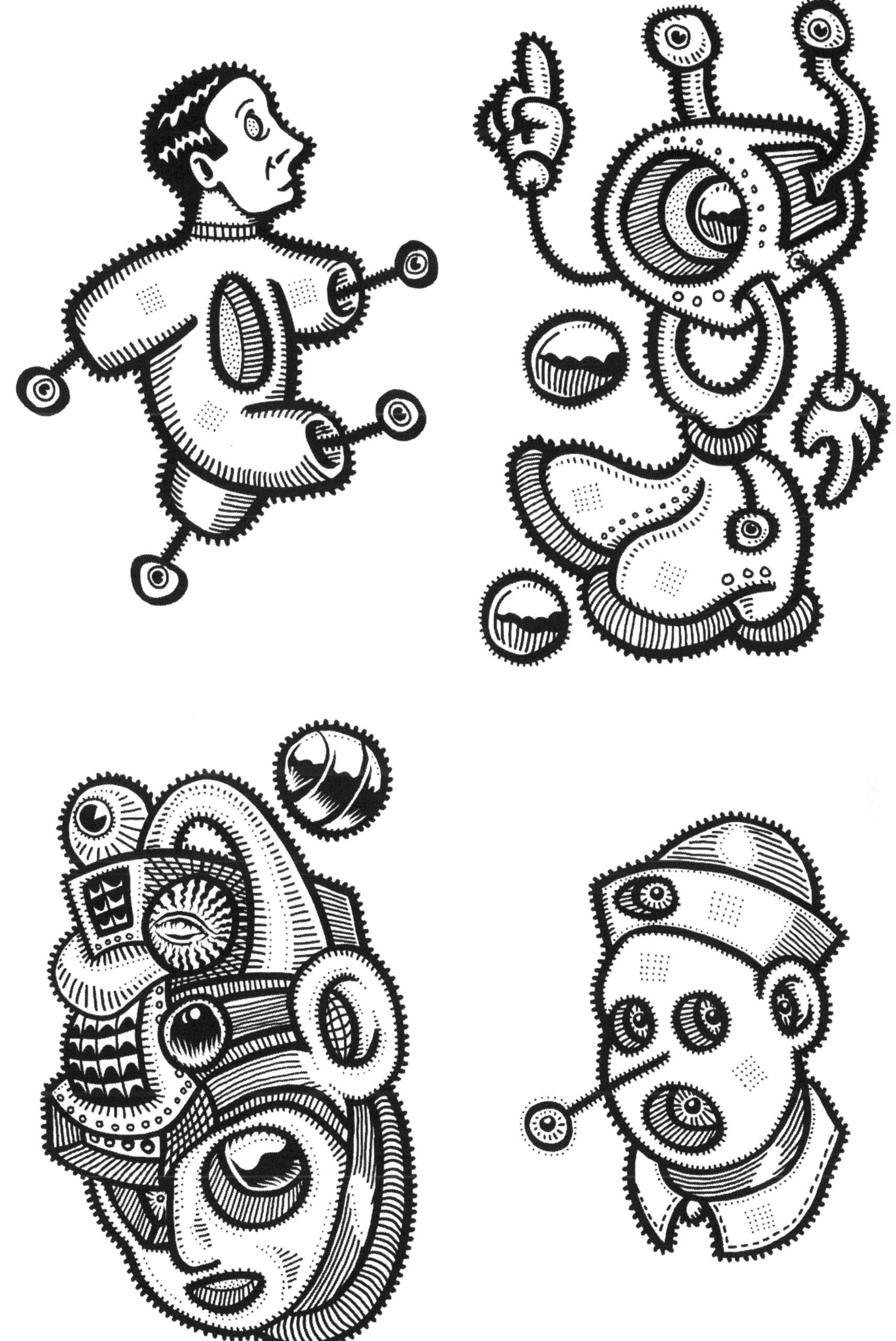

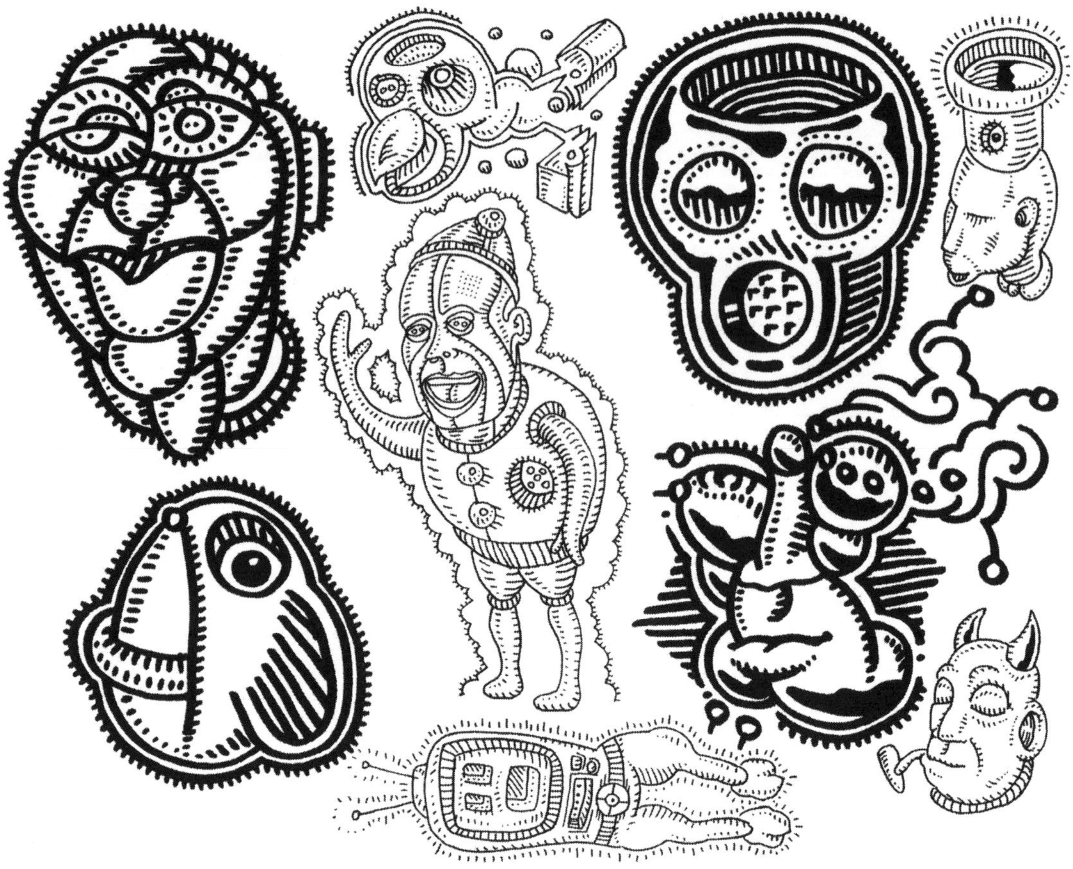

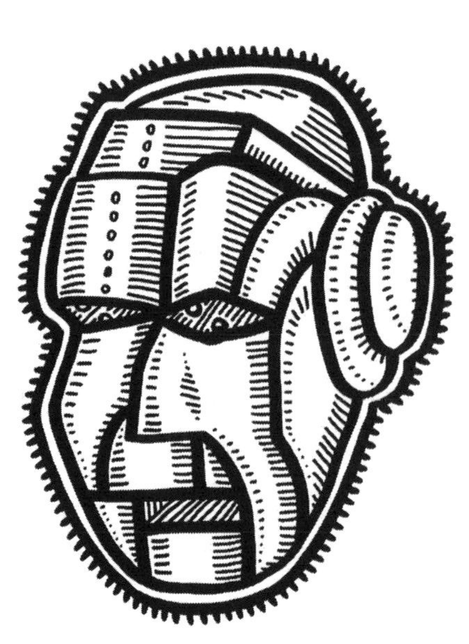

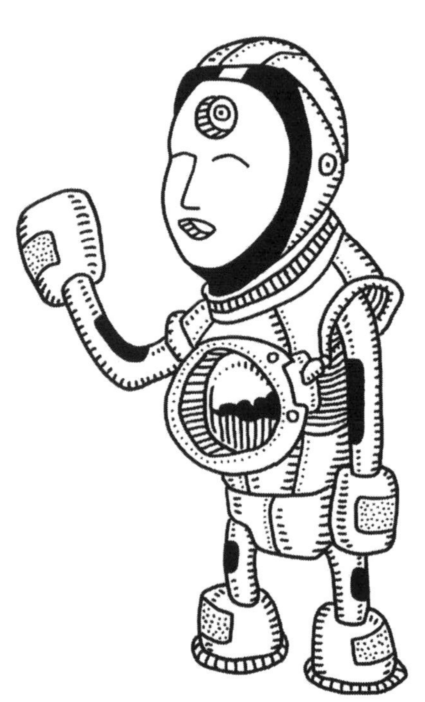

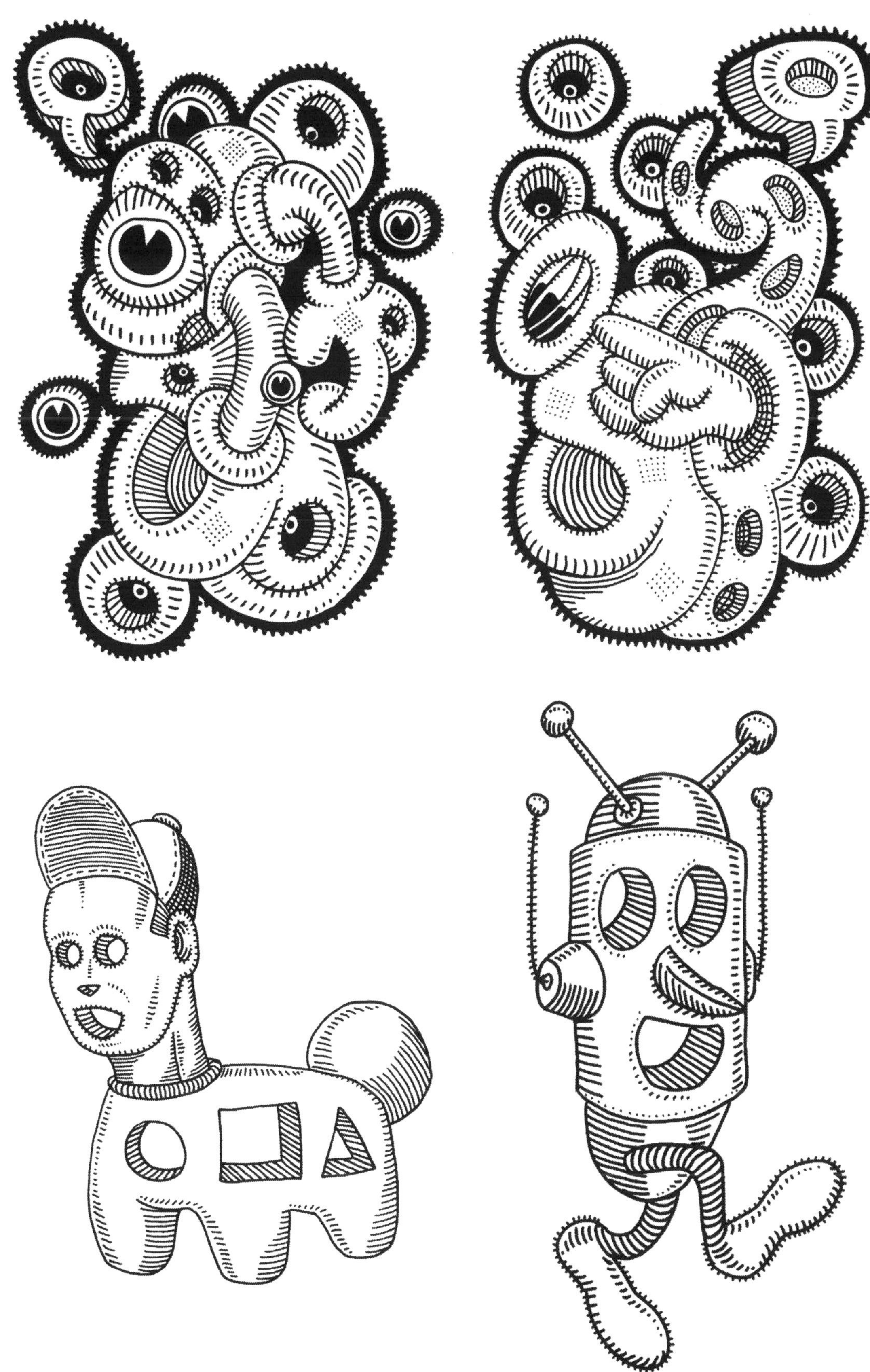

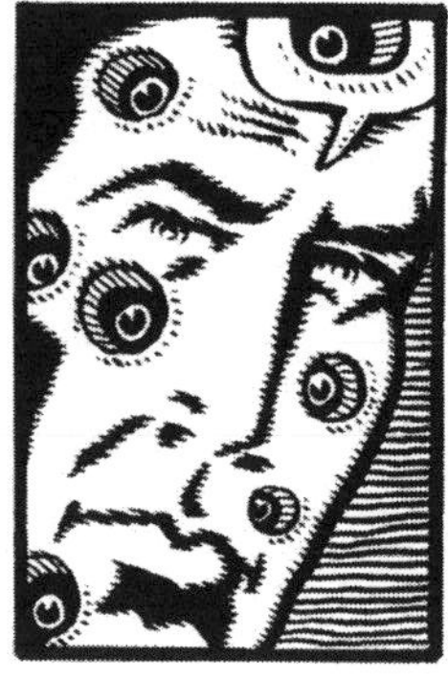

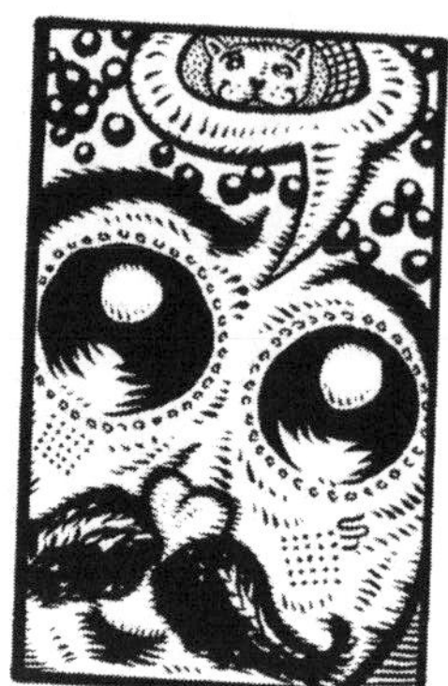

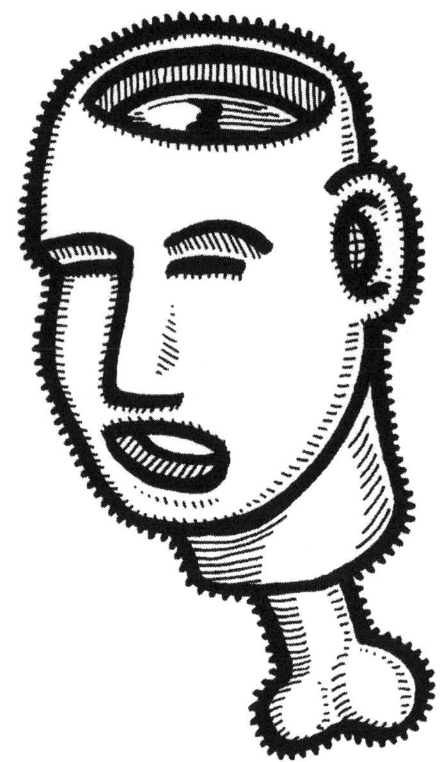

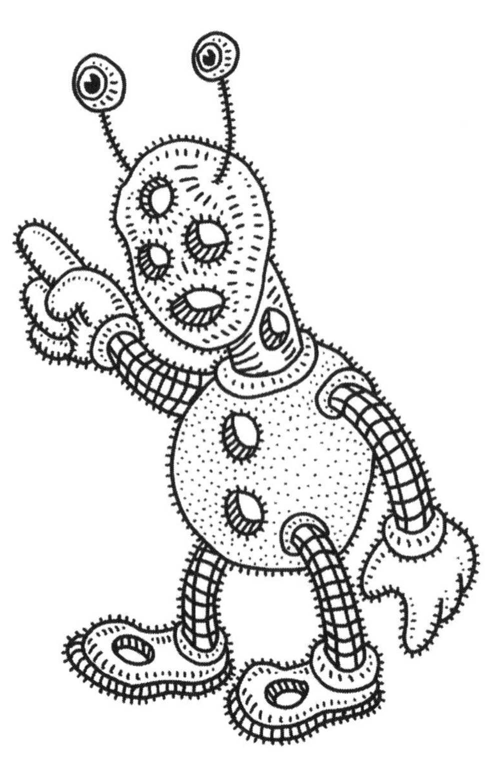

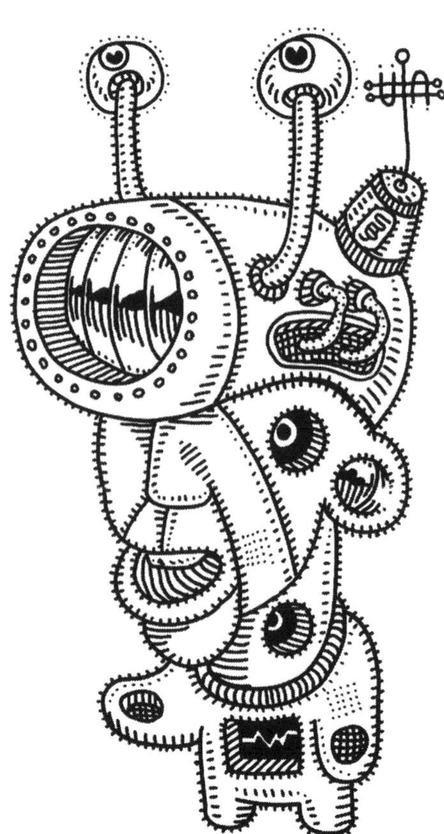

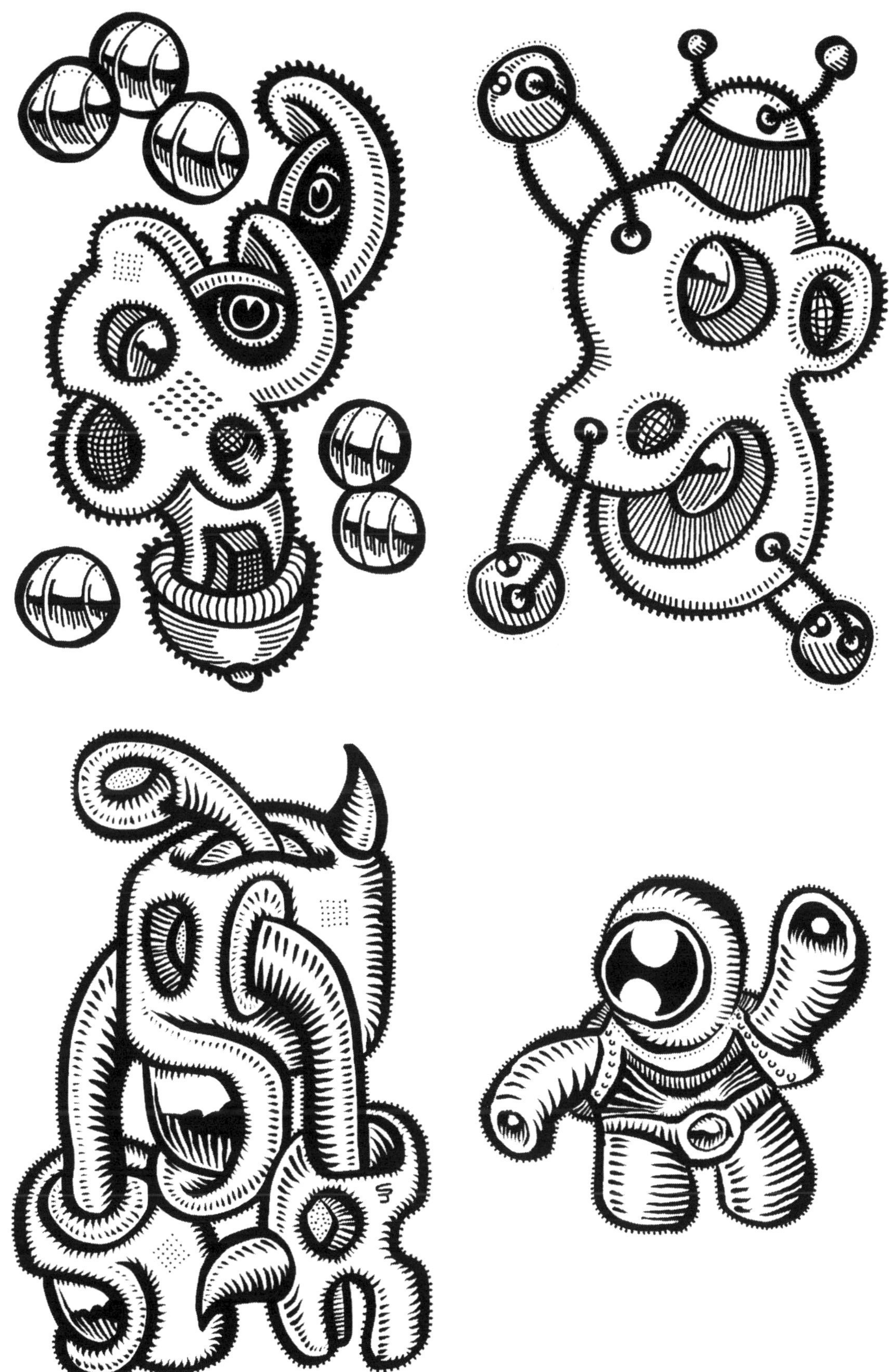

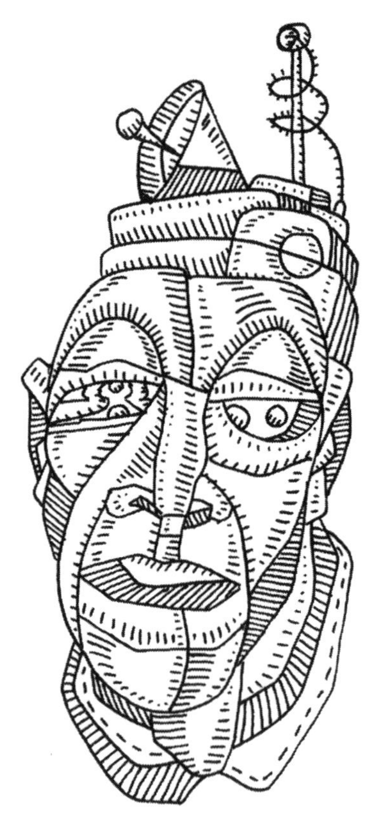

2012

JUNE

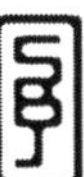

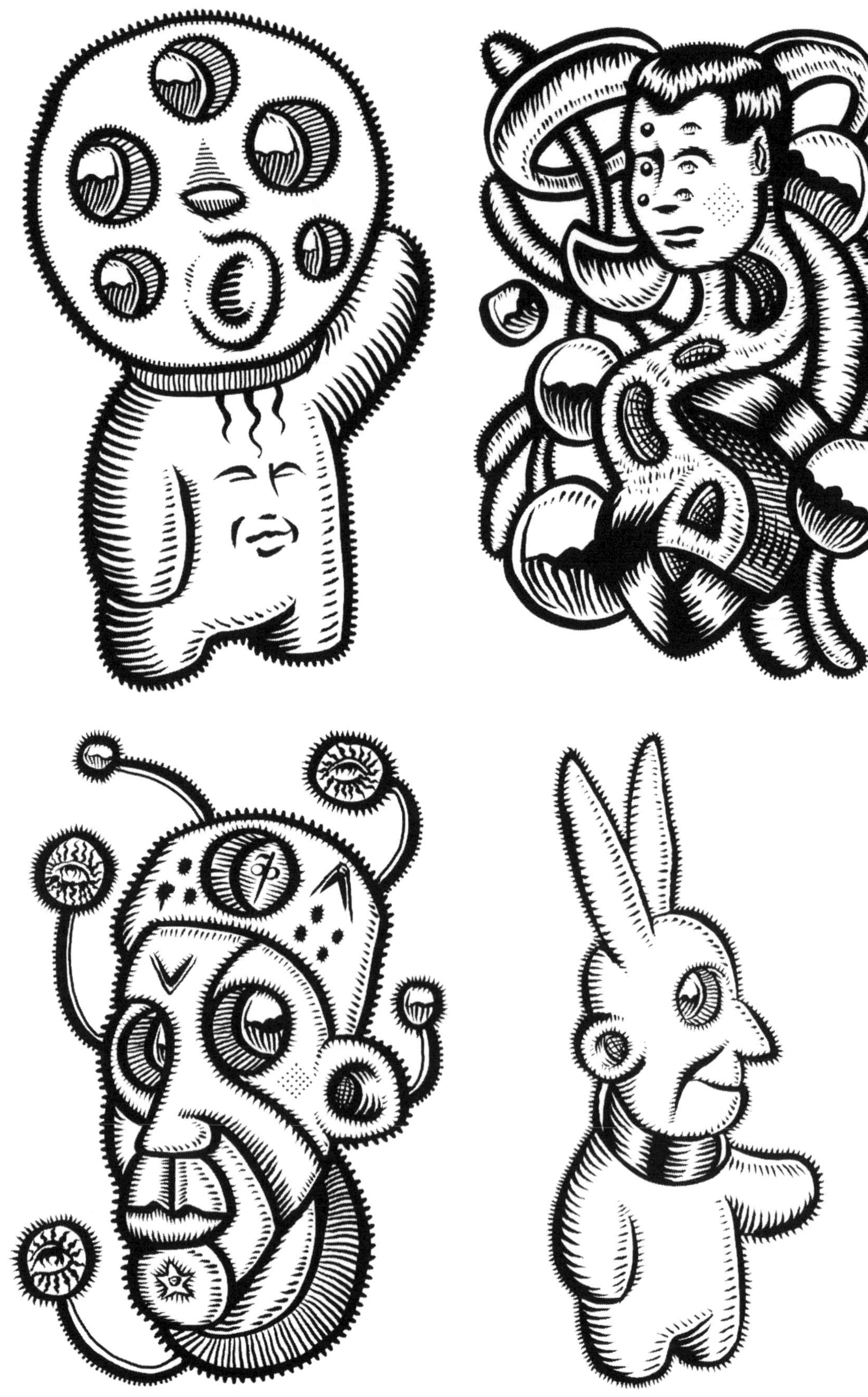

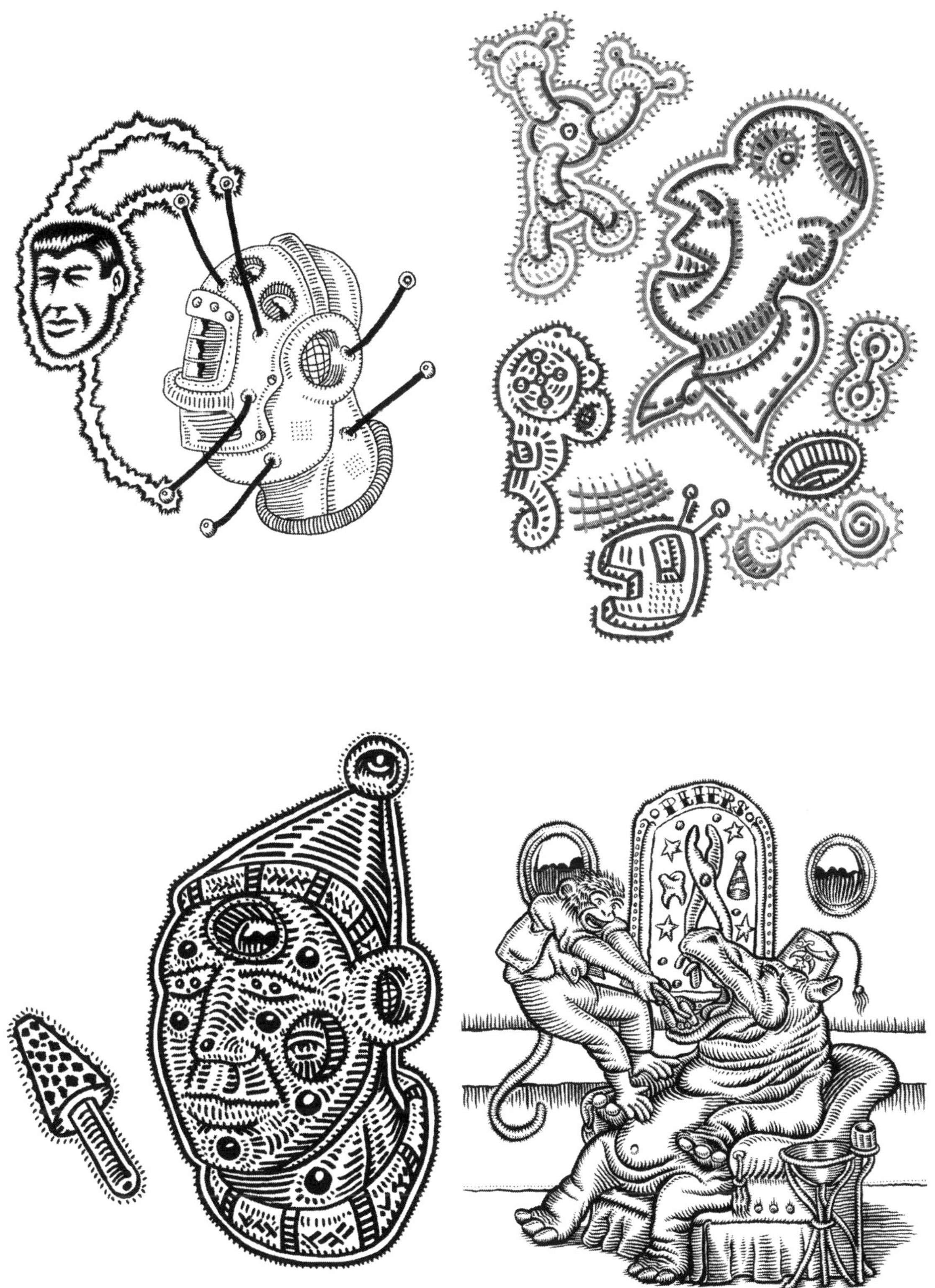
PLIERS
CONICAL RASP

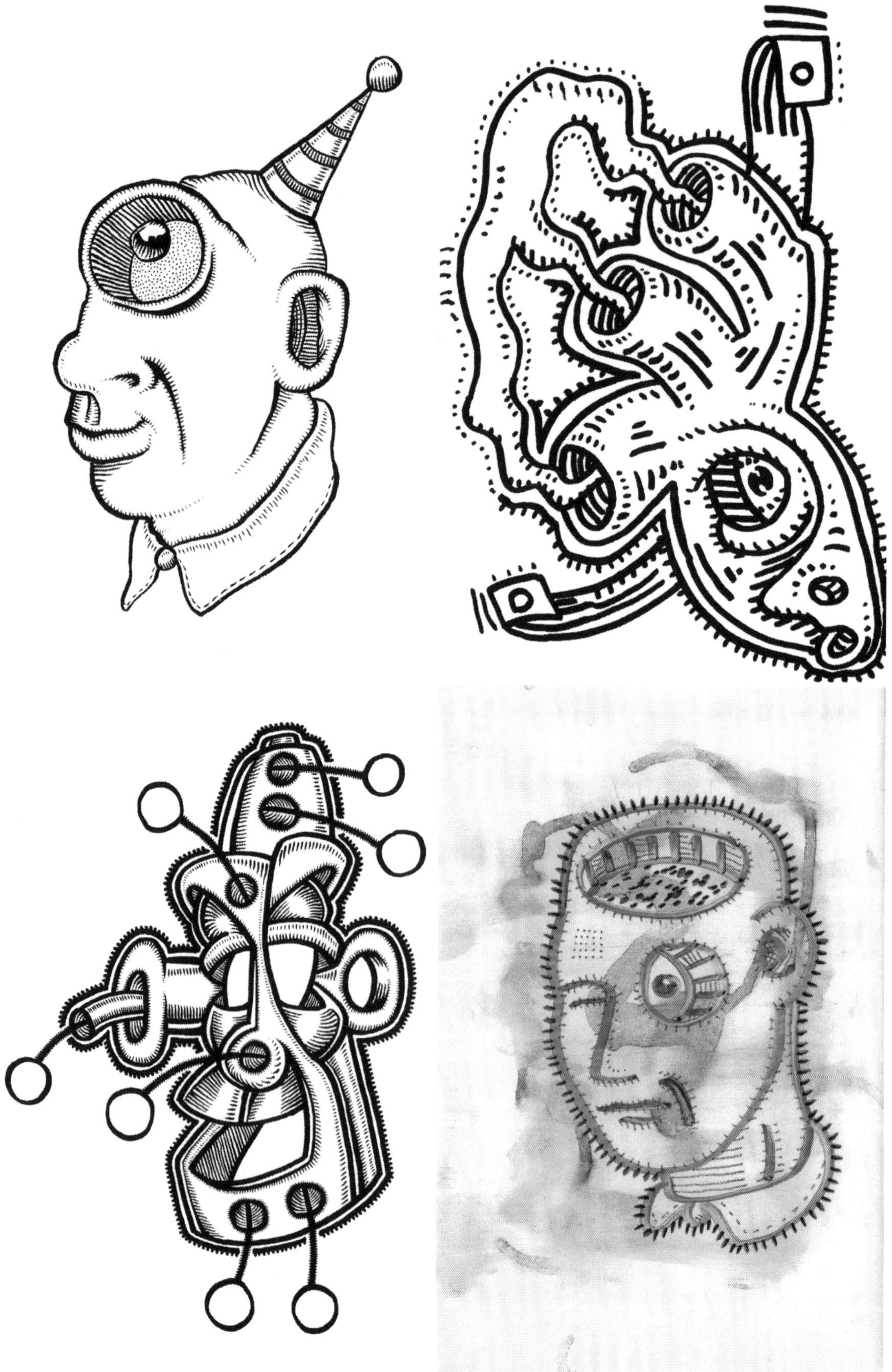

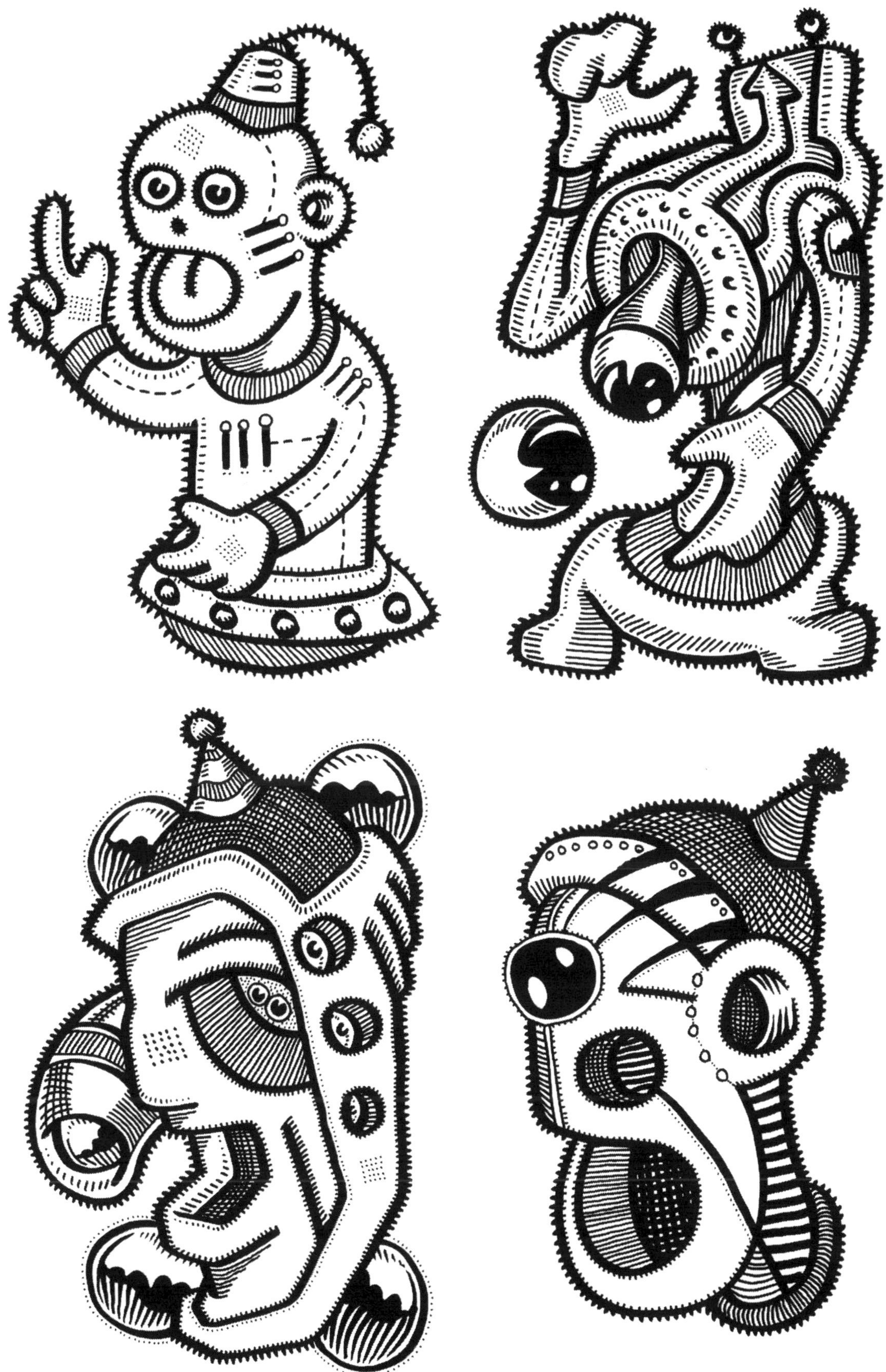

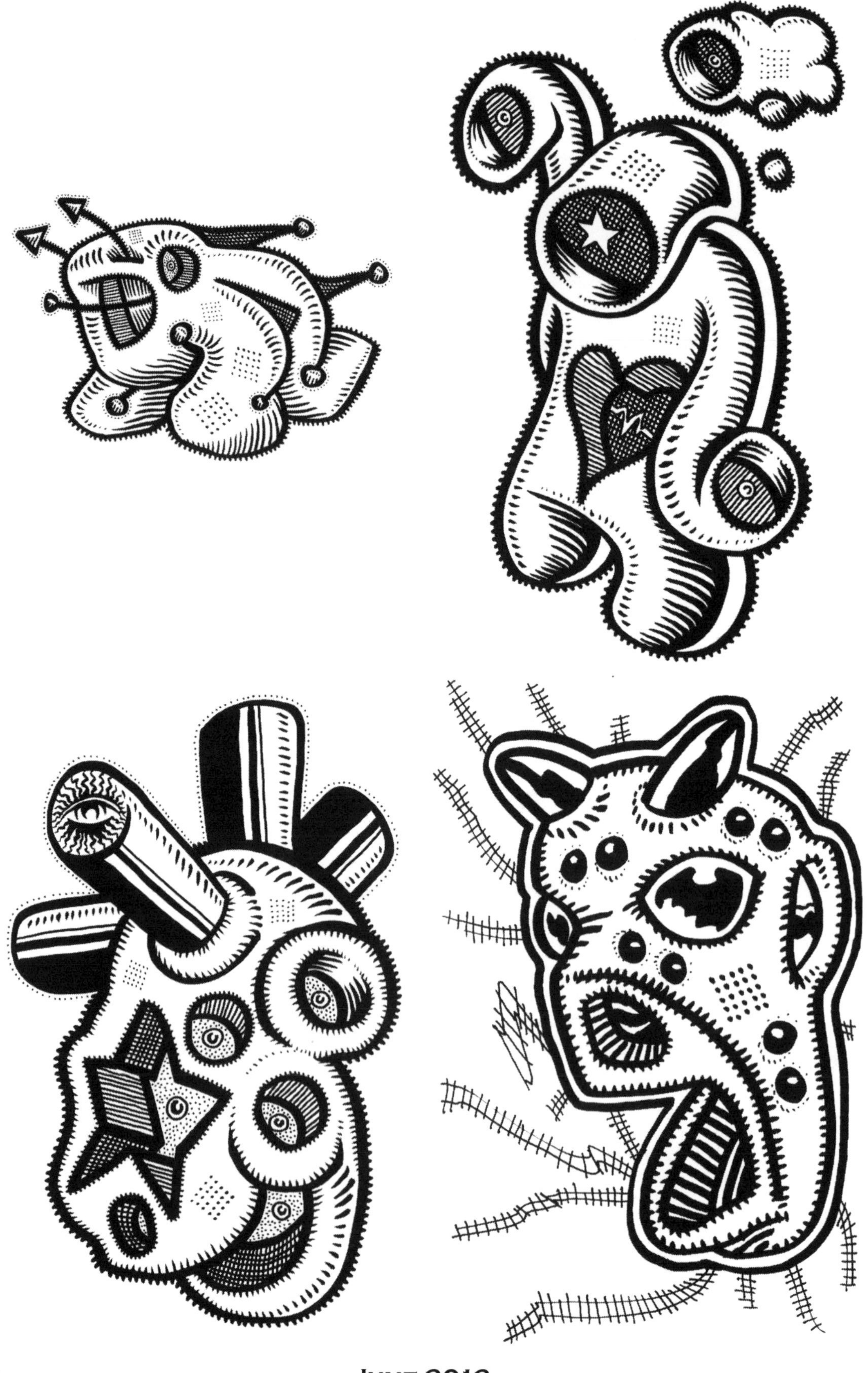

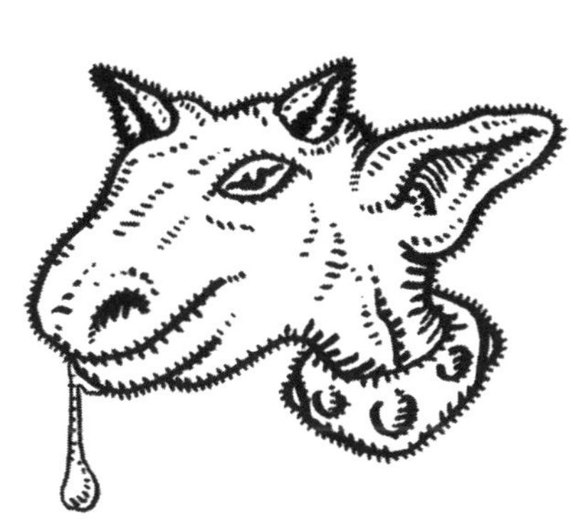

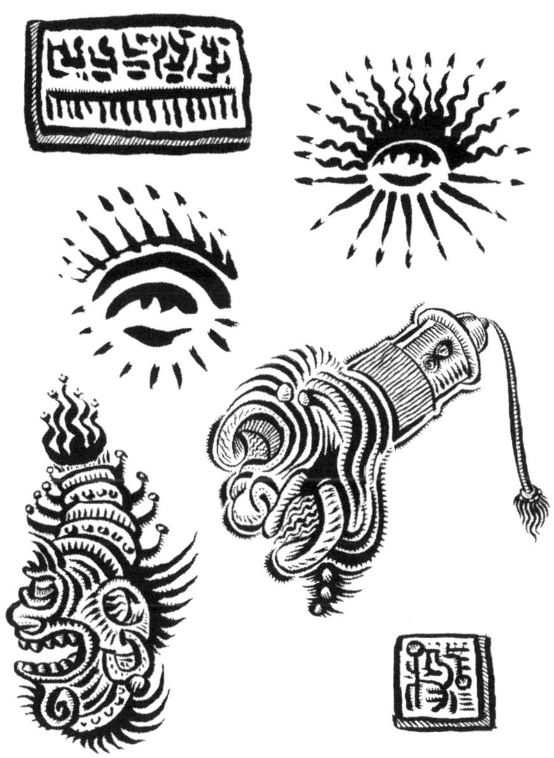

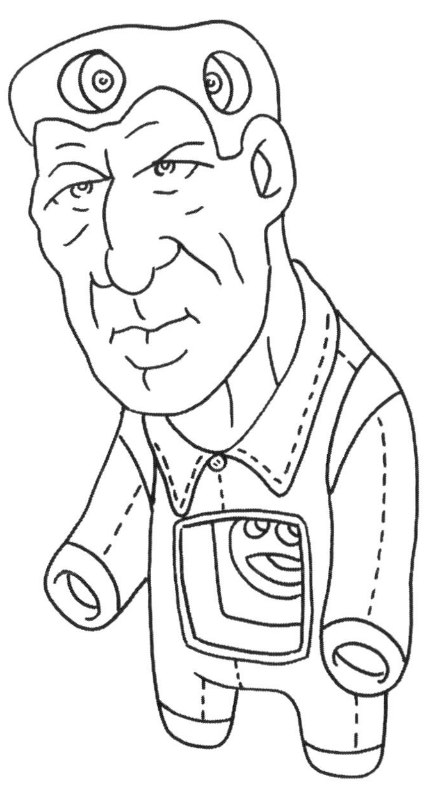

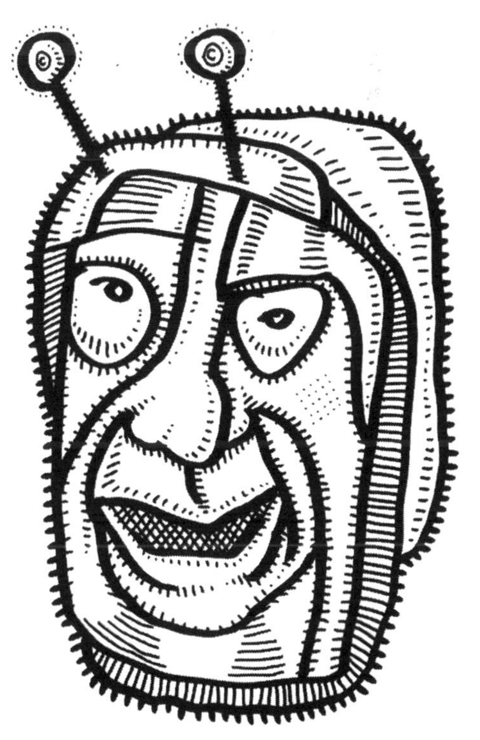

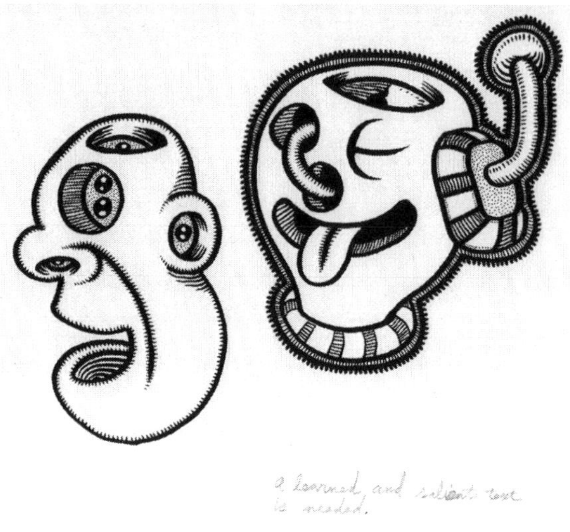

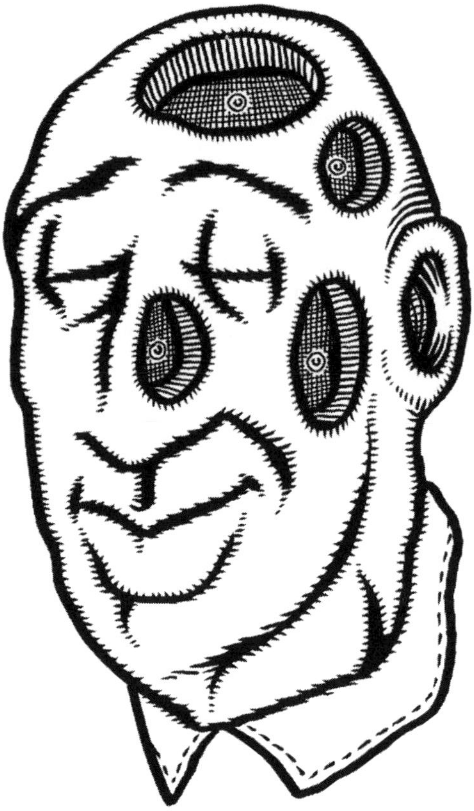

a learned and salient tone
is needed.

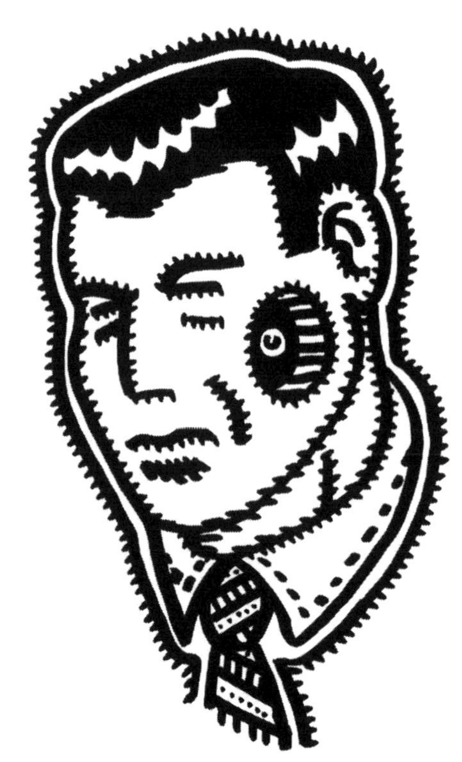

2012

JULY

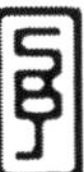

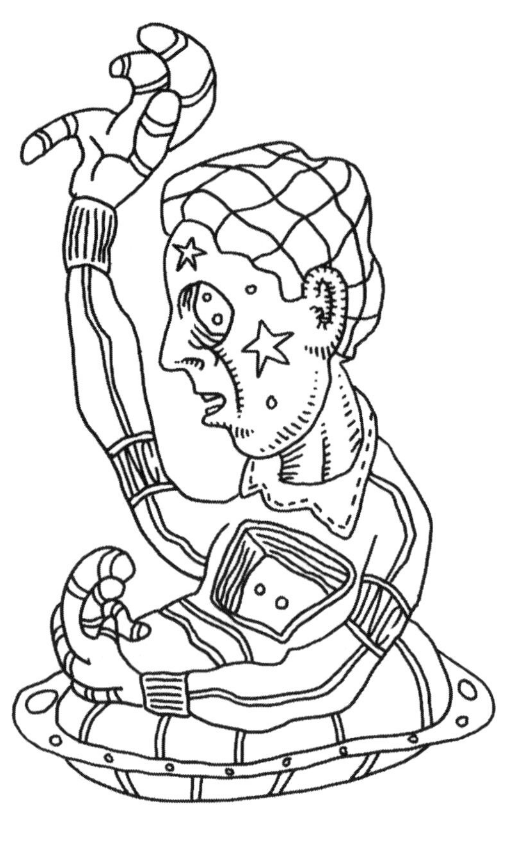
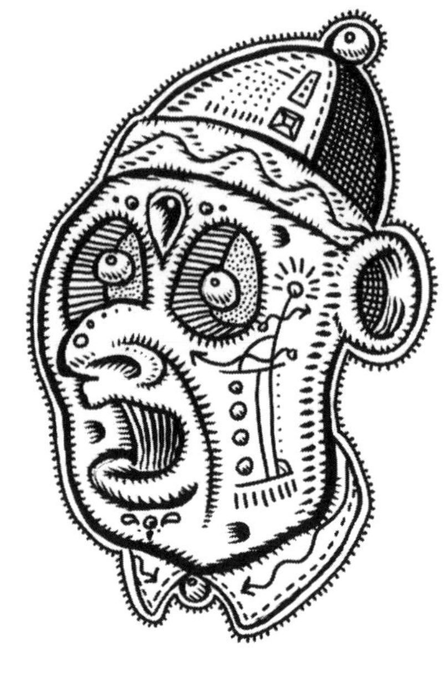
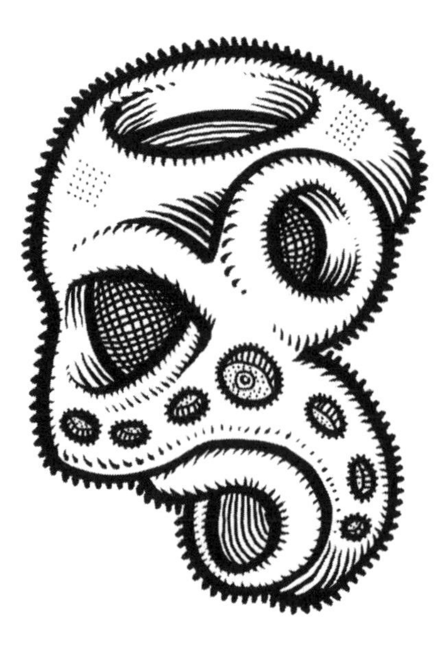
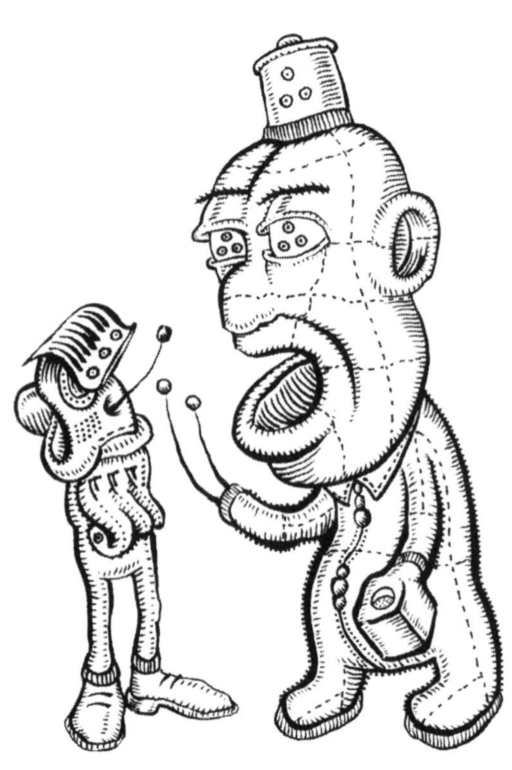

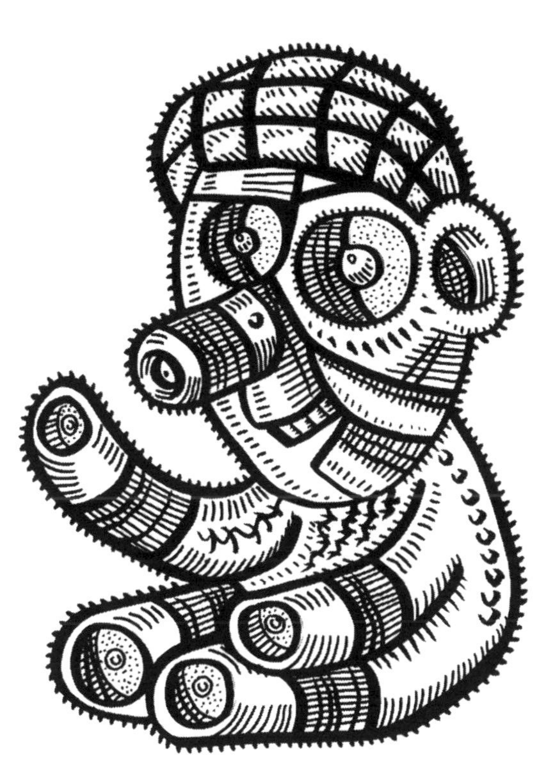
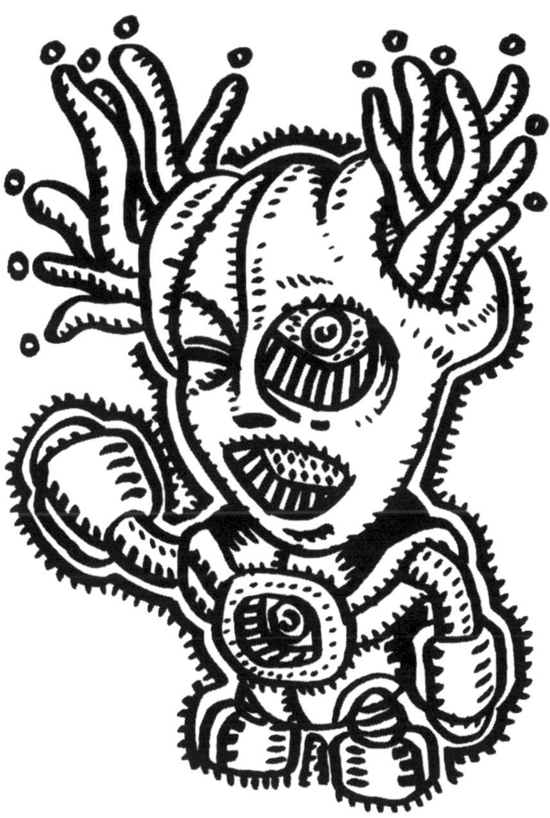
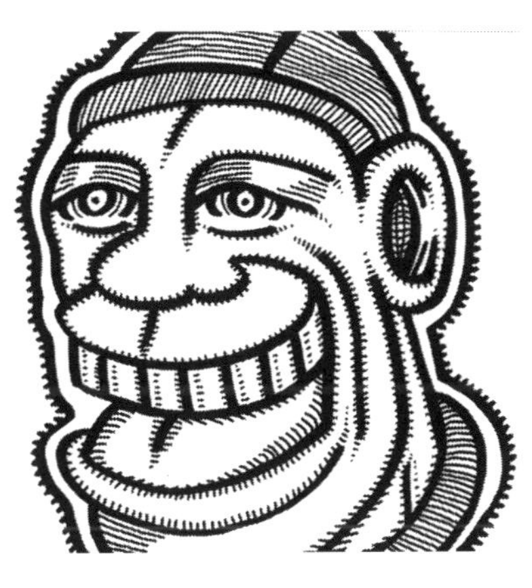
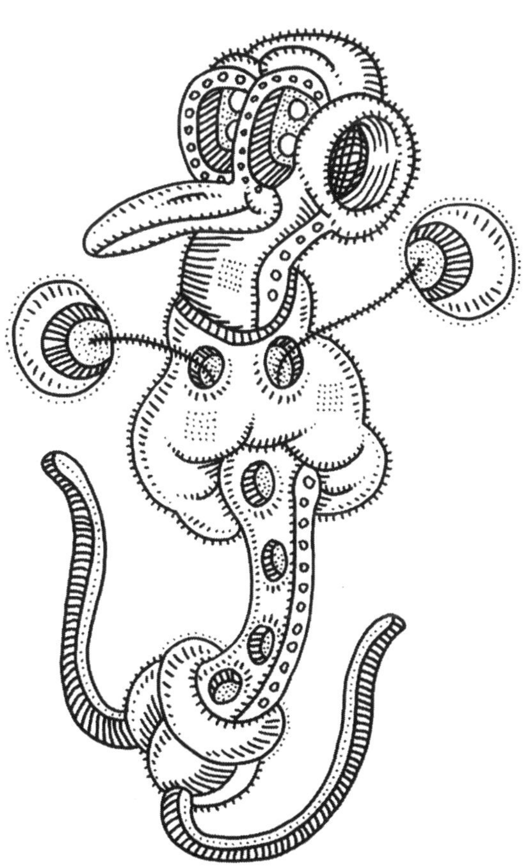

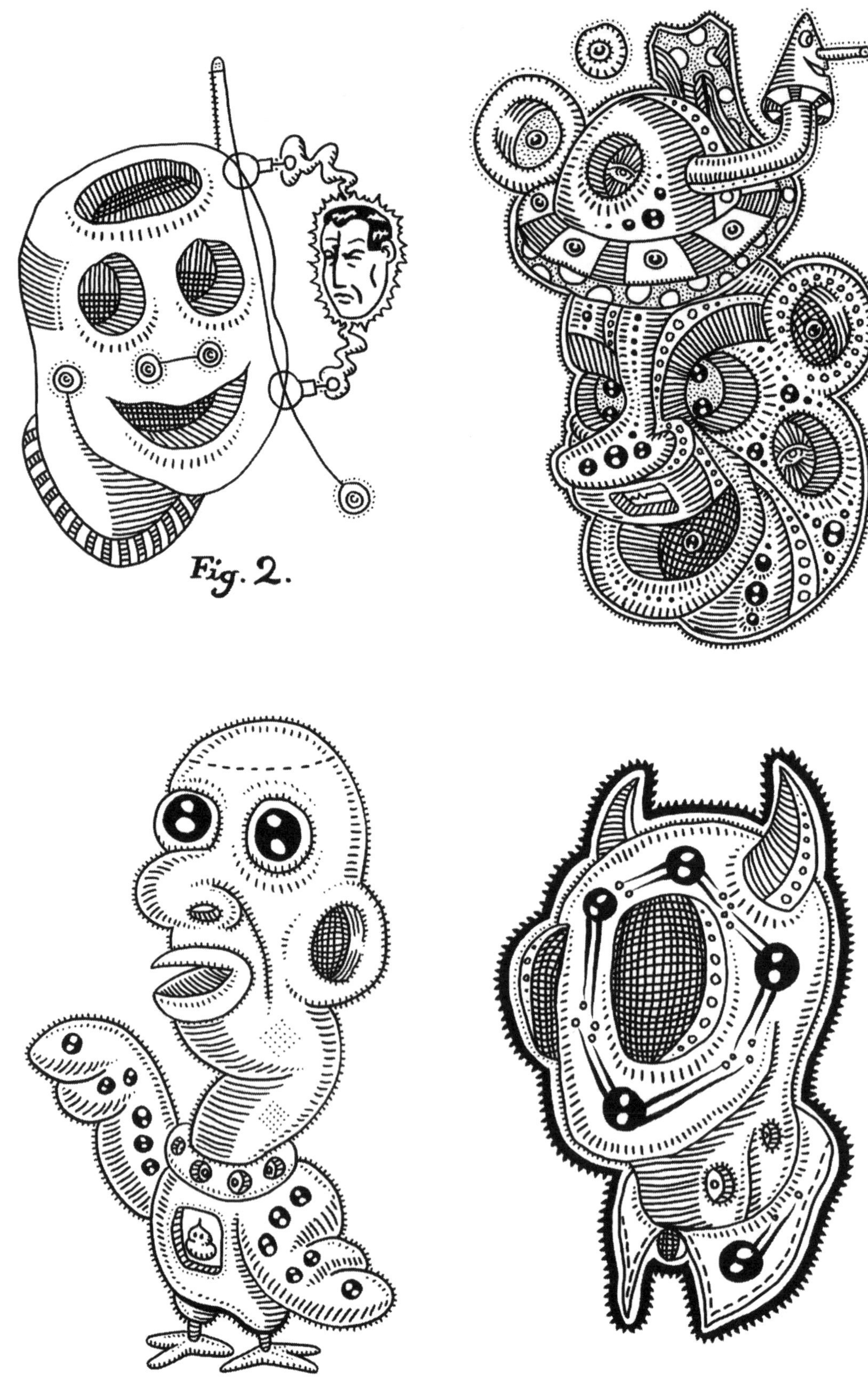
Fig. 2.

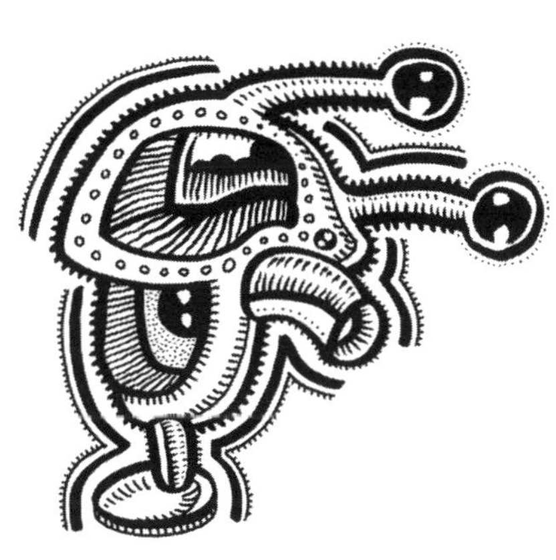
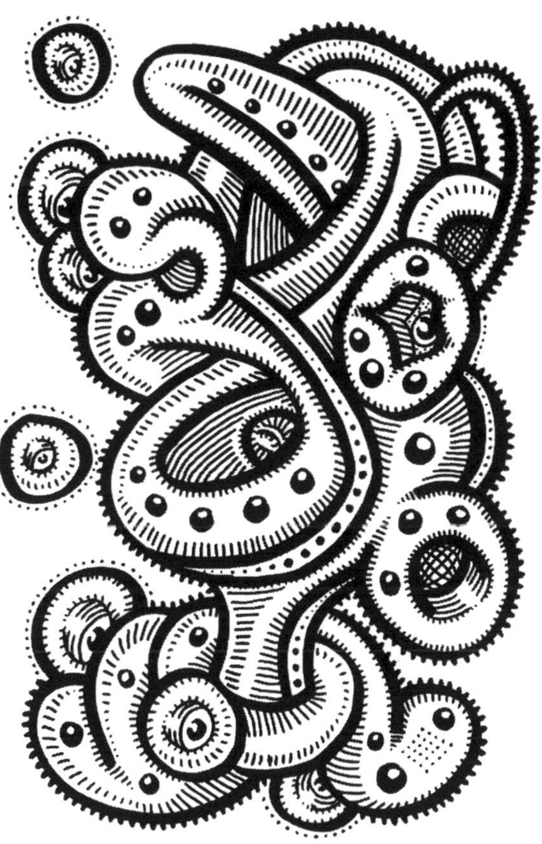
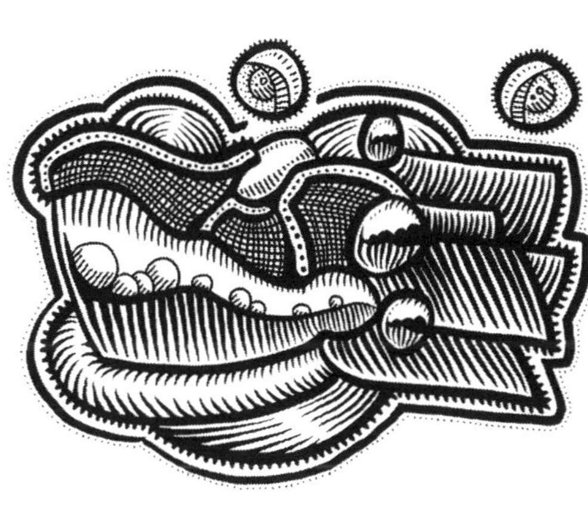
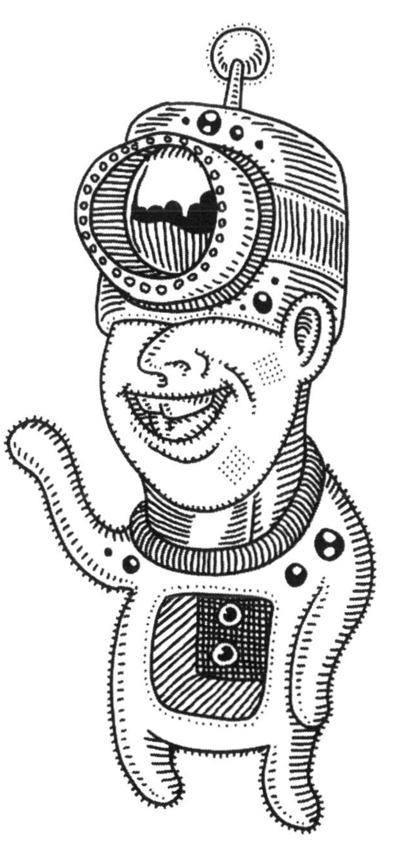

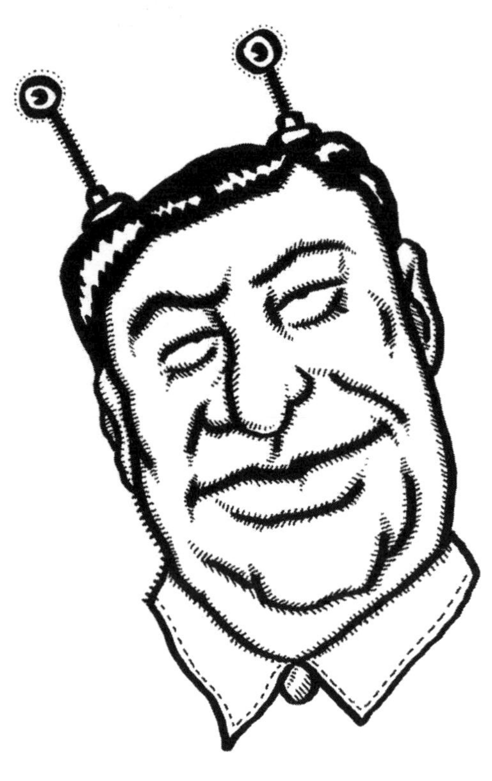

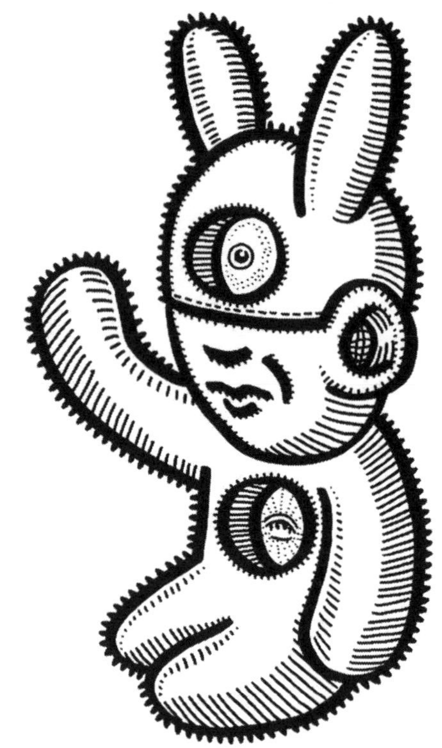

Jake

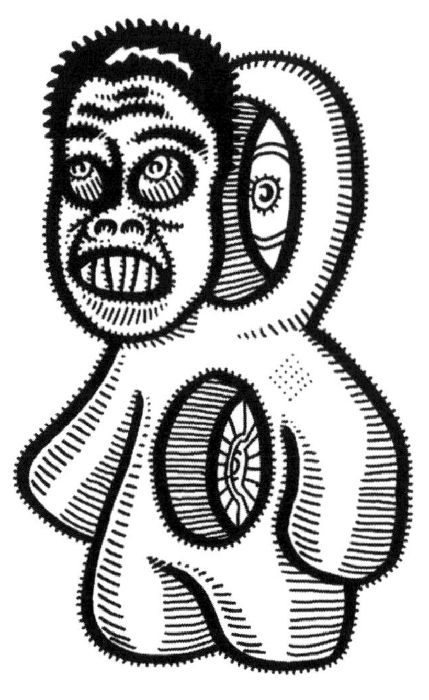

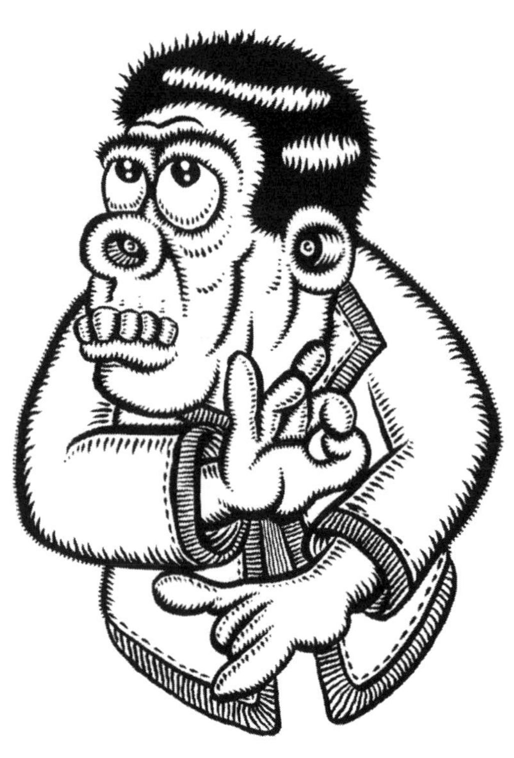

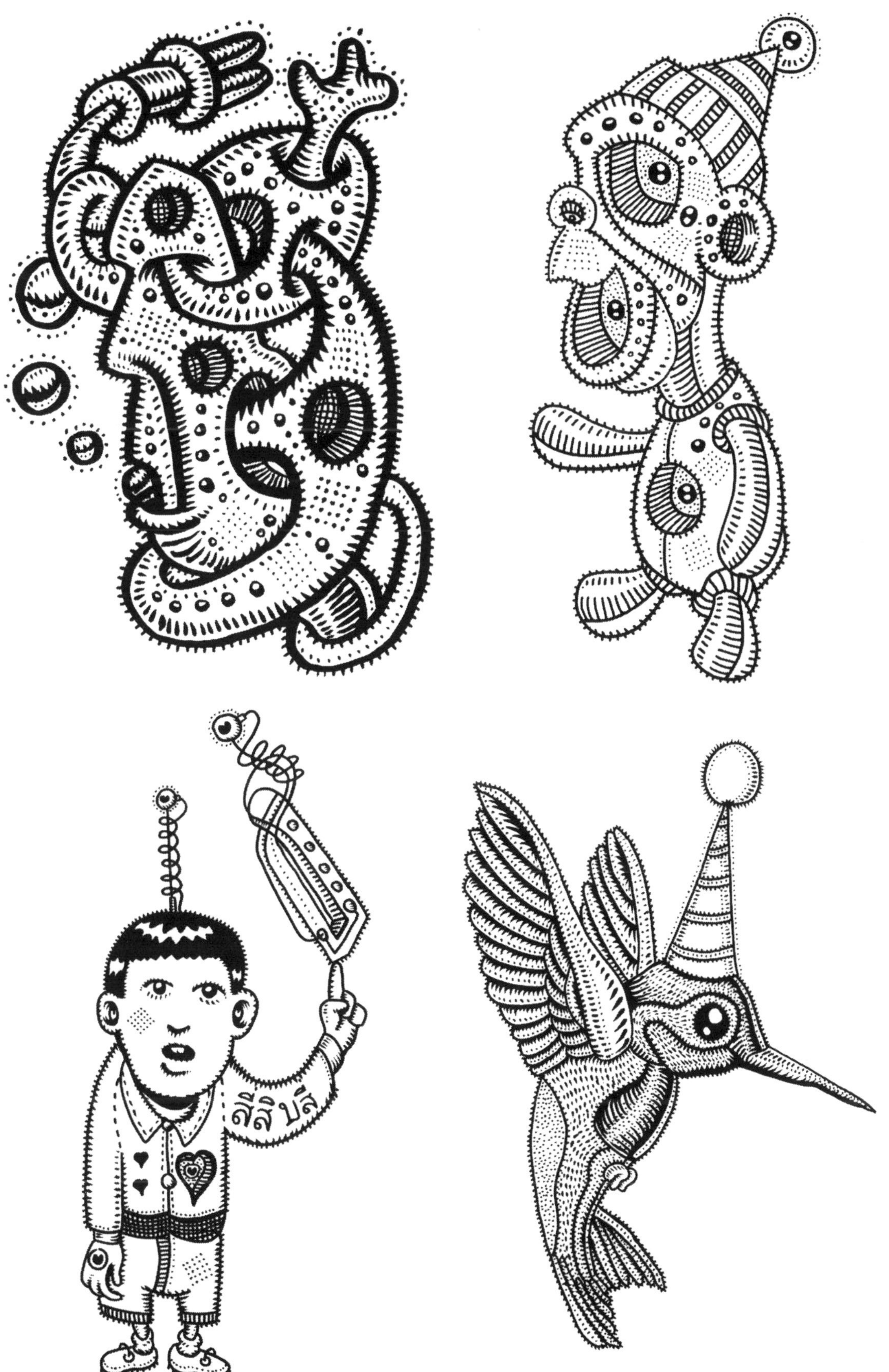
ลีลิ บีล

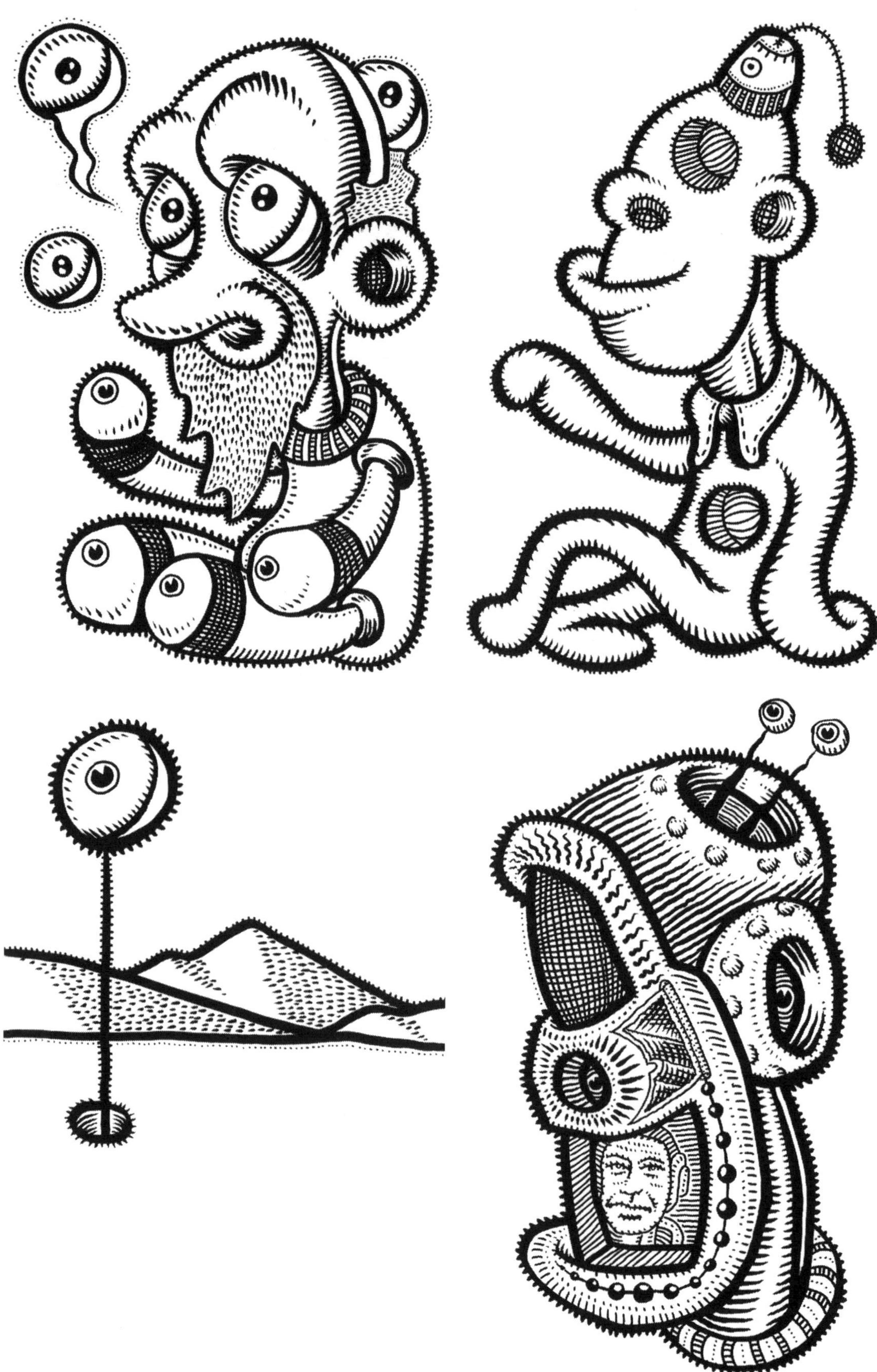

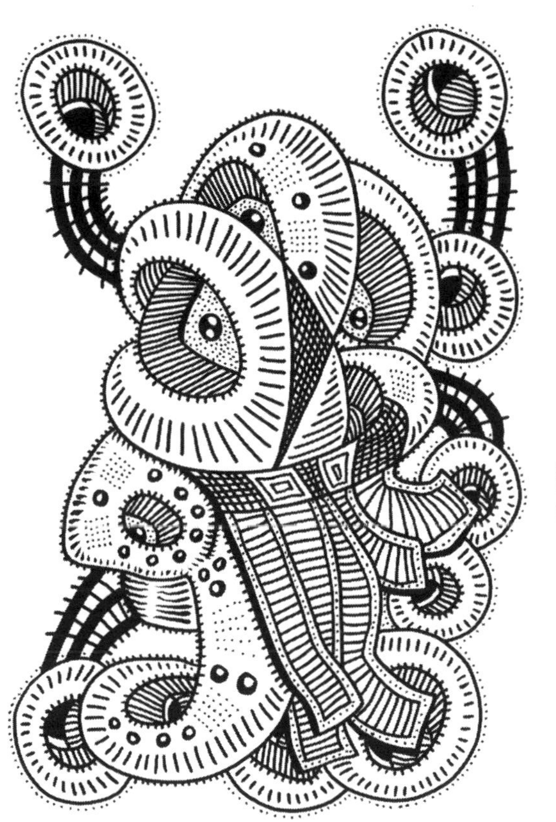

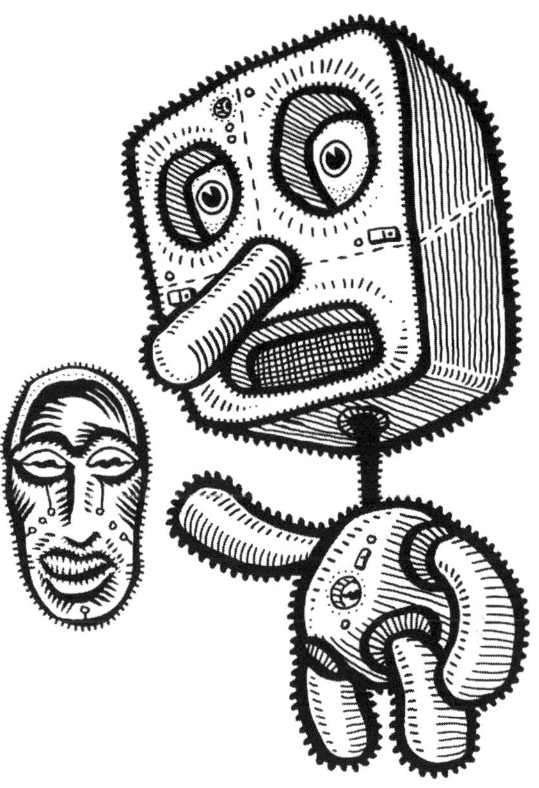

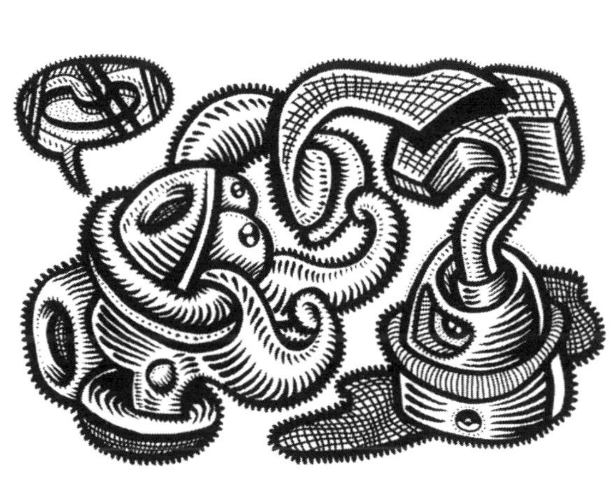

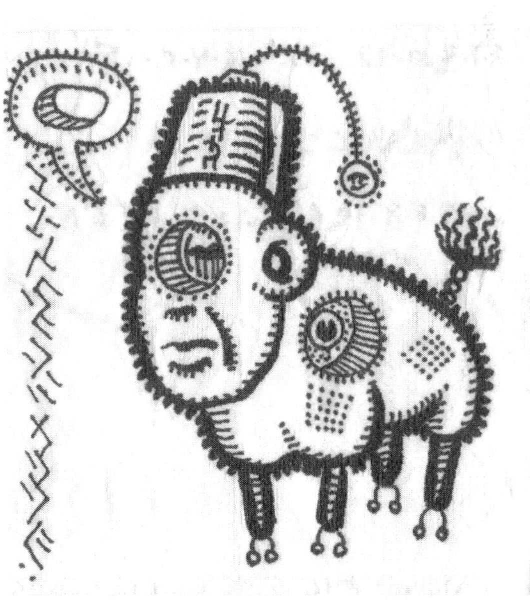

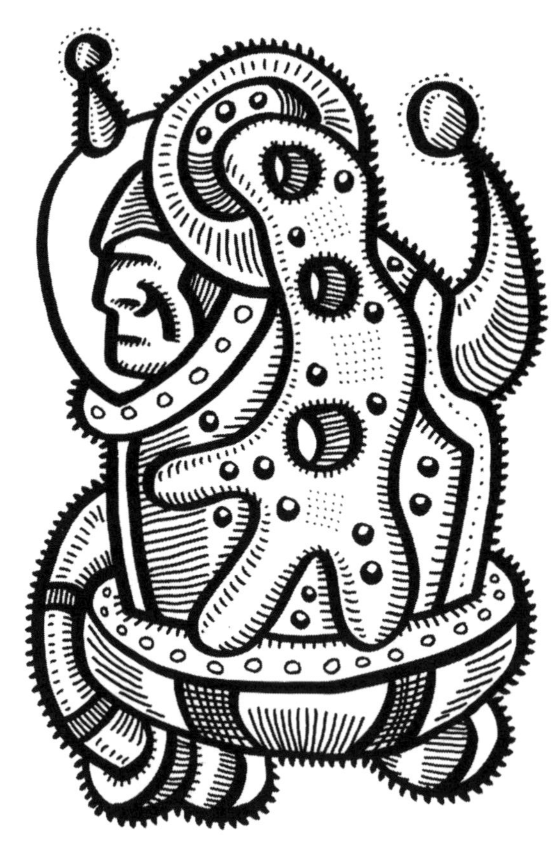

2012

August

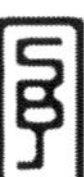

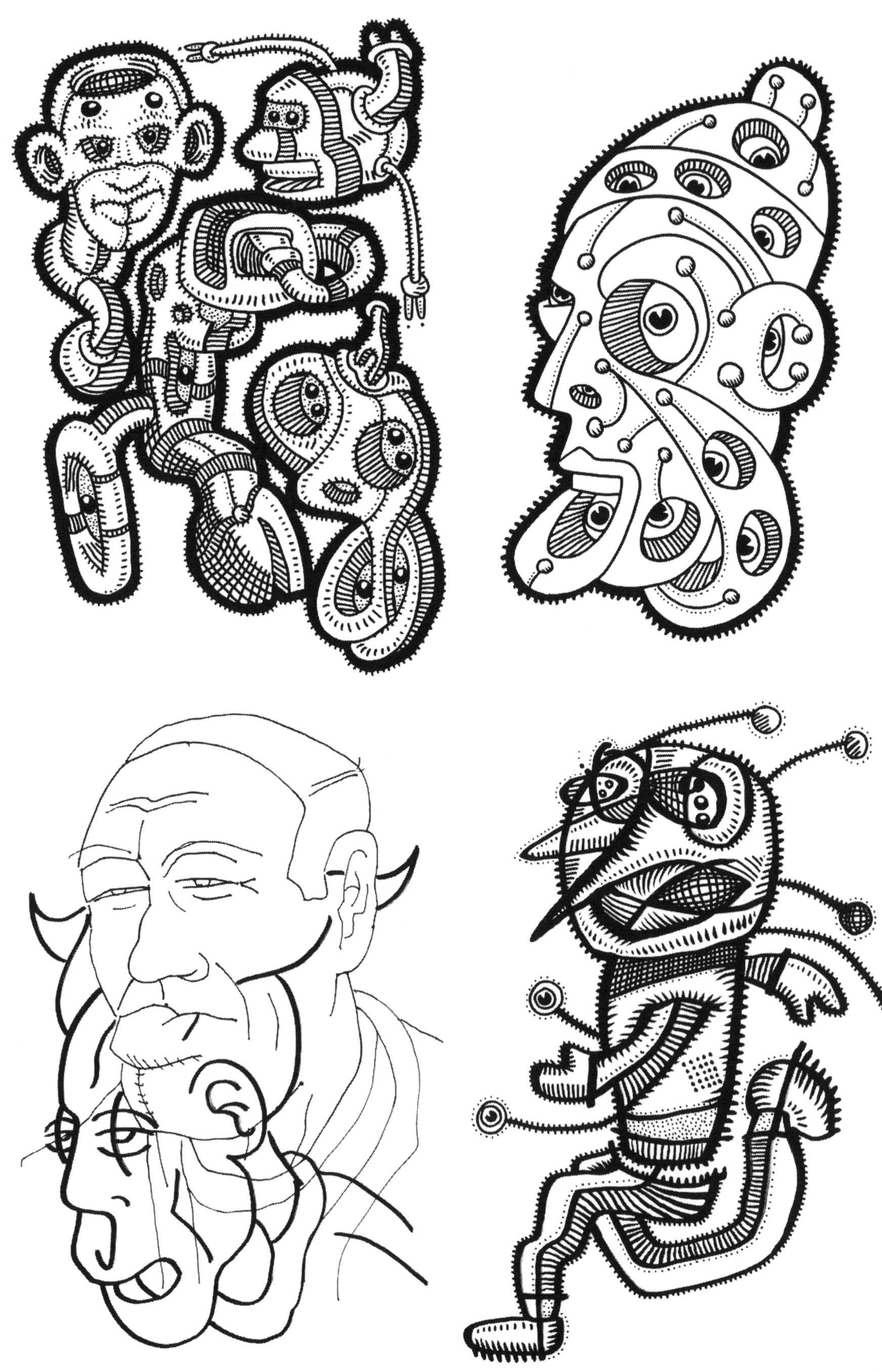

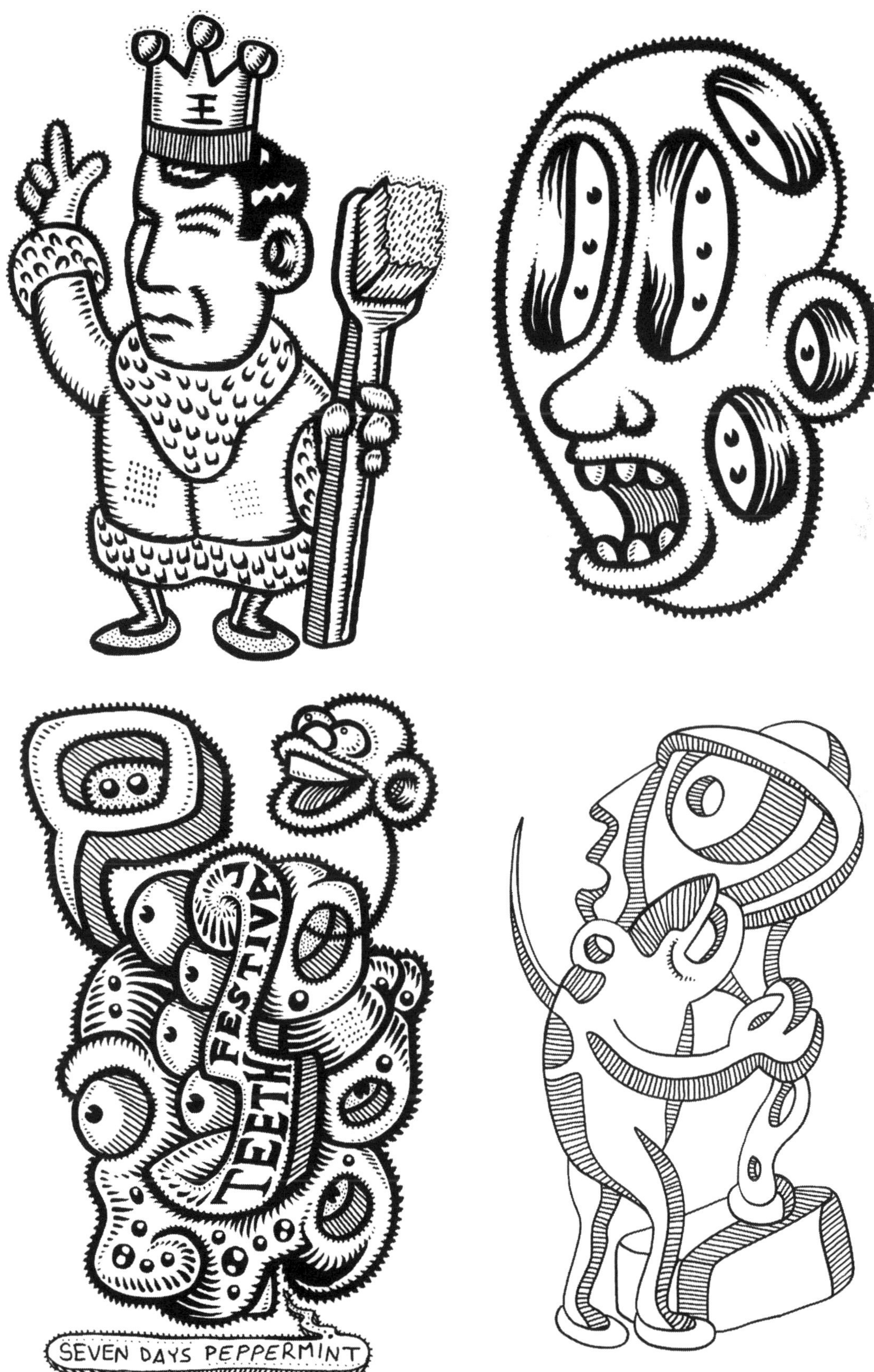
TEETH FESTIVAL
SEVEN DAYS PEPPERMINT

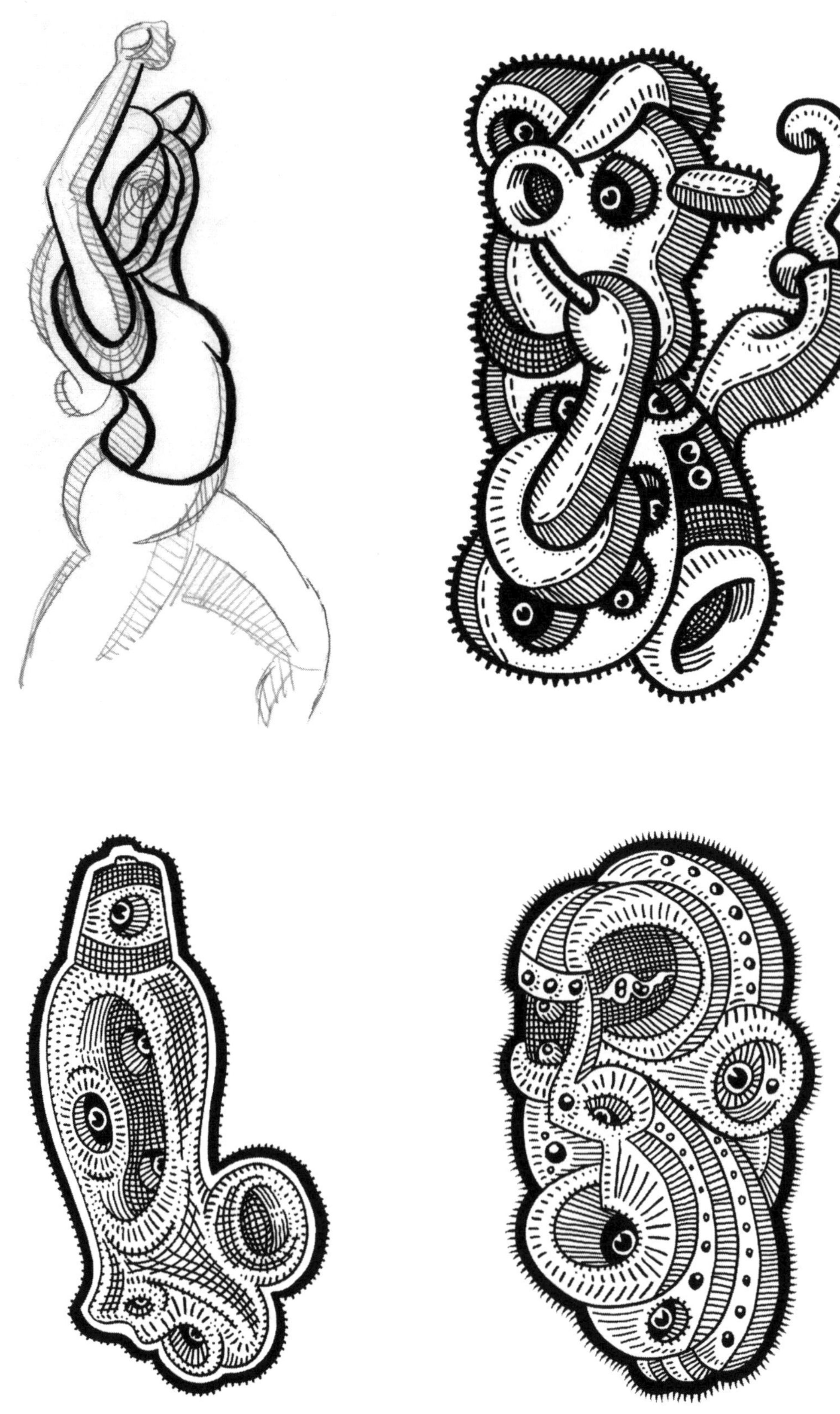

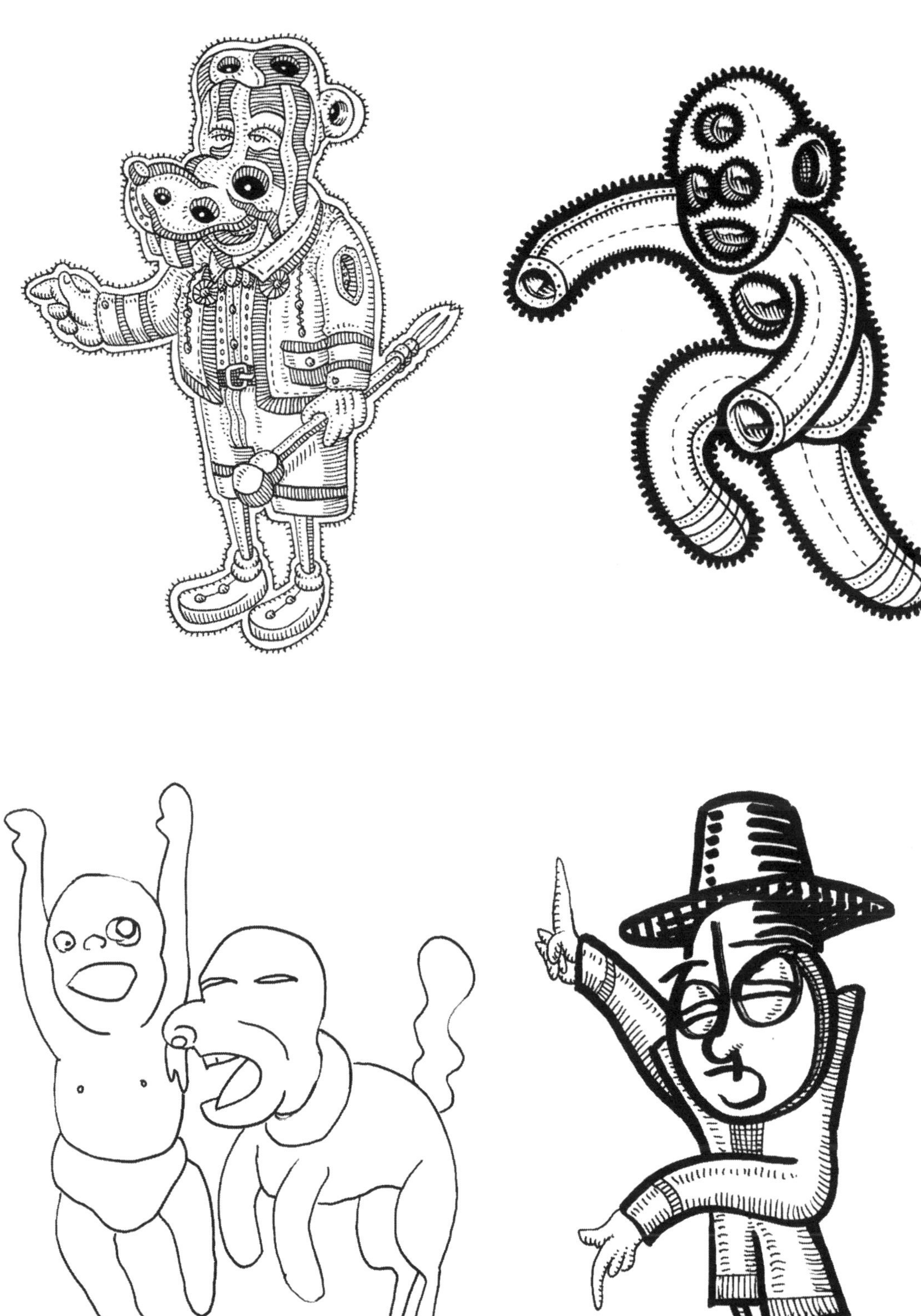

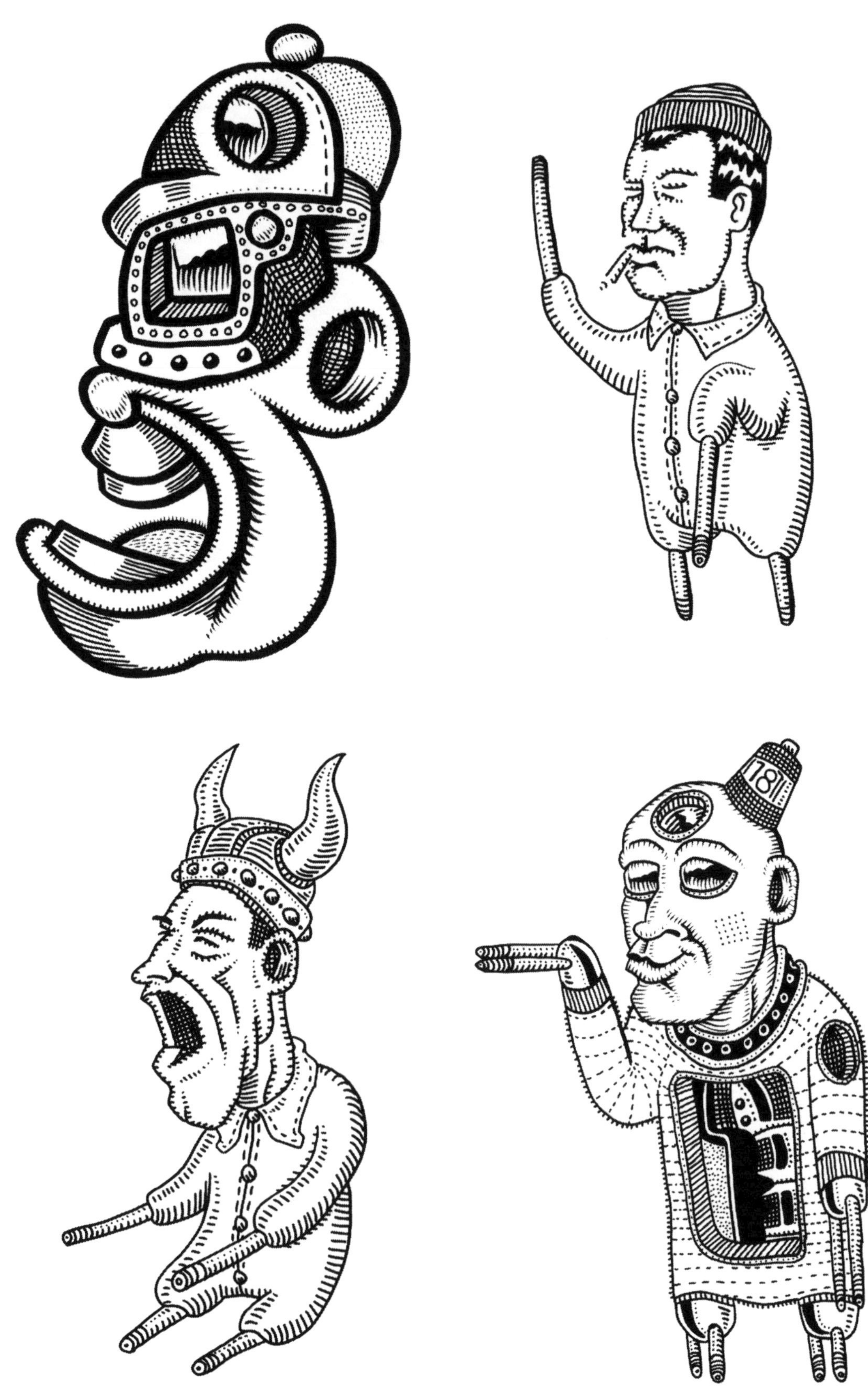
78

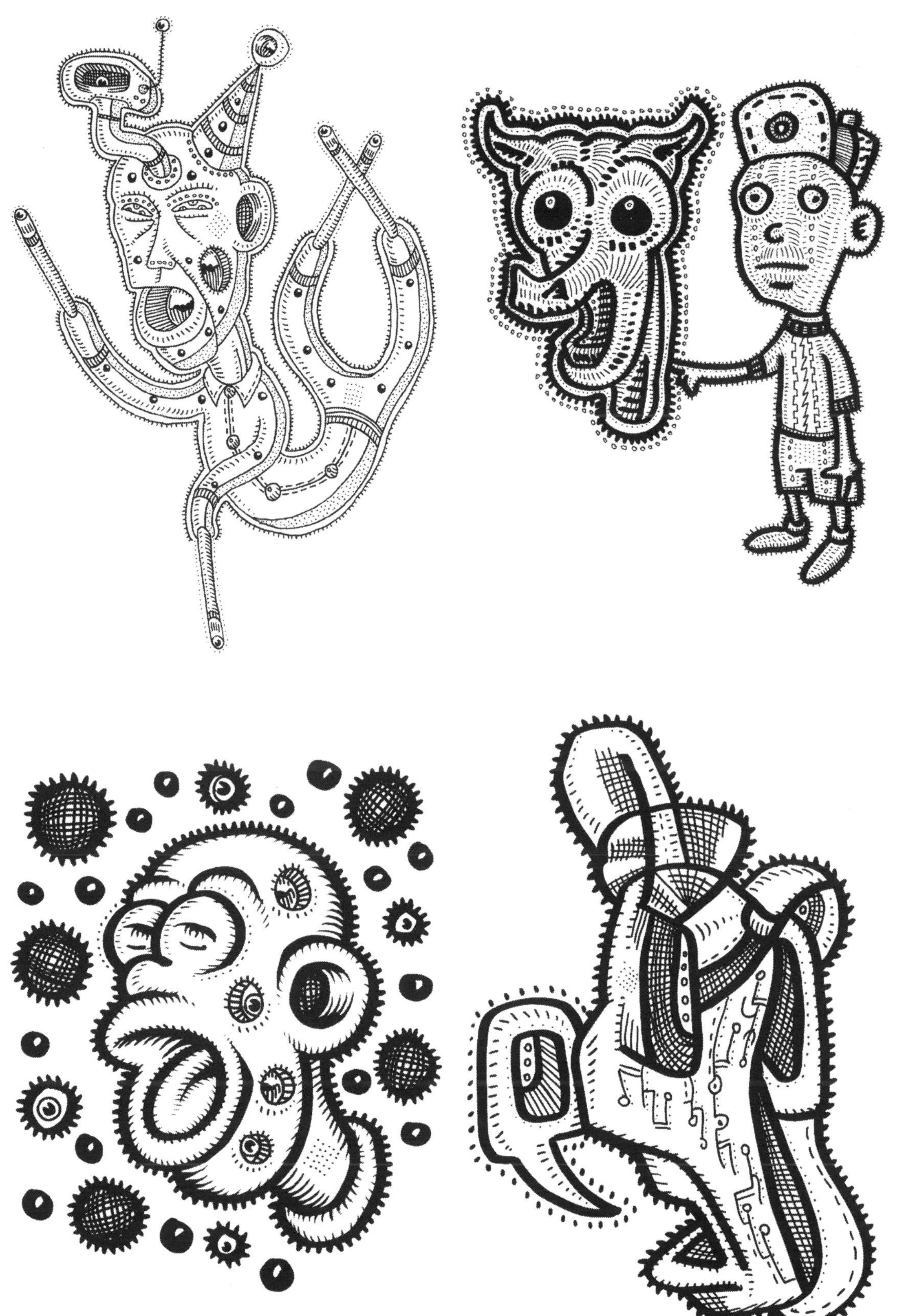

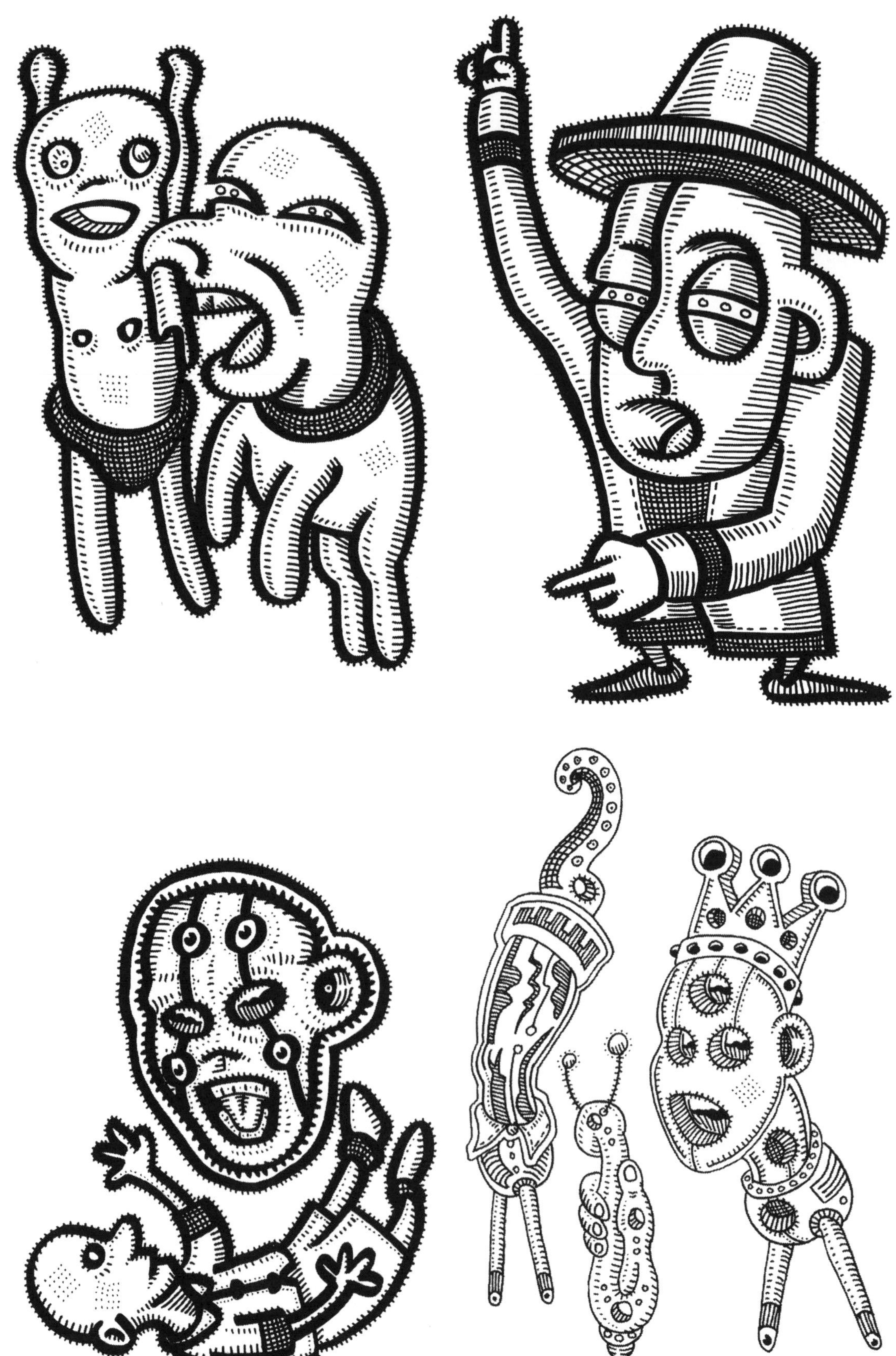

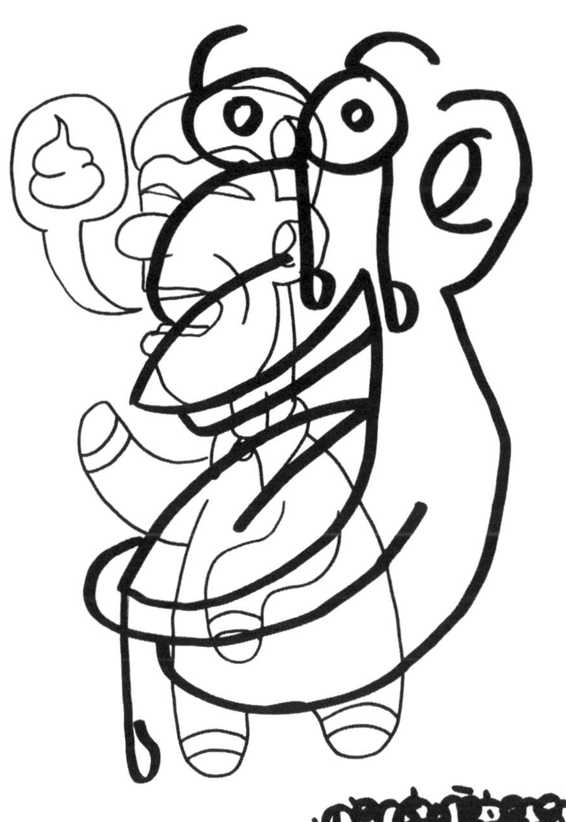

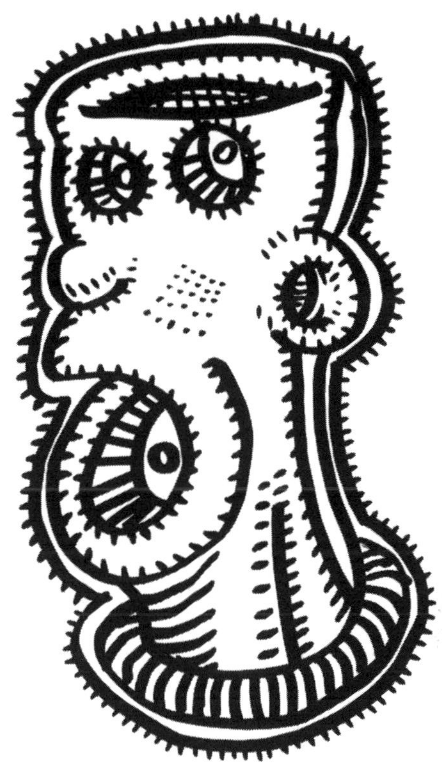

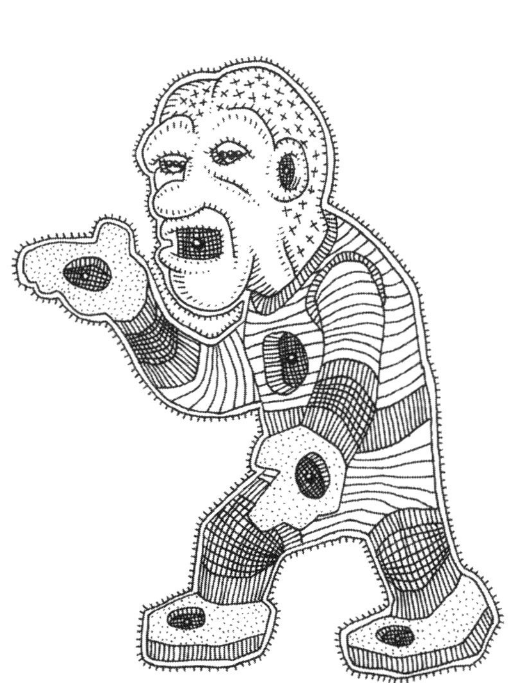

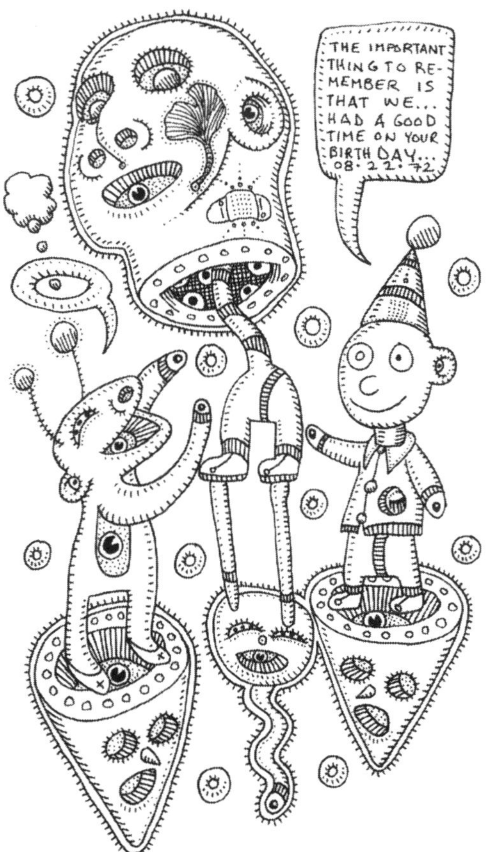
THE IMPORTANT THING TO RE-MEMBER IS THAT WE... HAD A GOOD TIME ON YOUR BIRTH DAY... 08.22.72

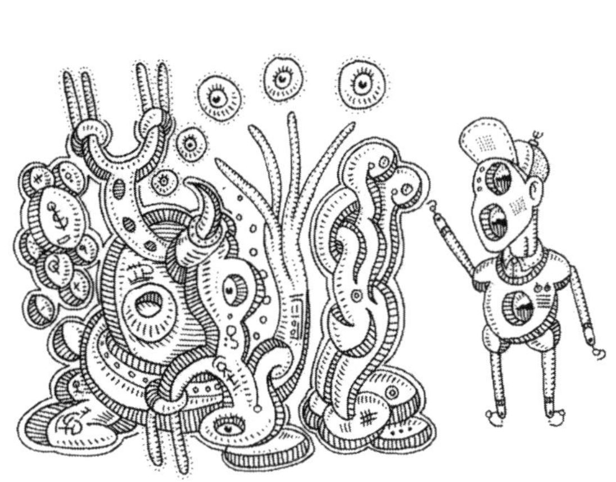
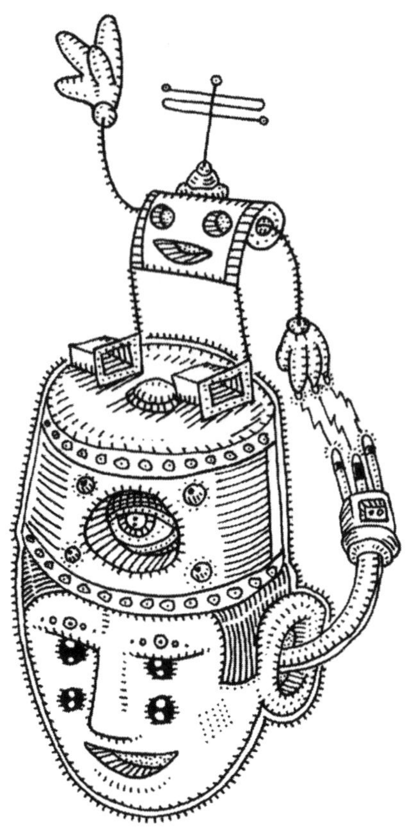
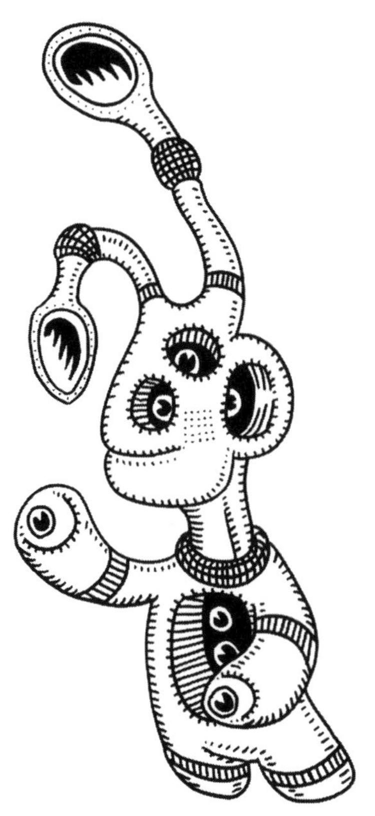
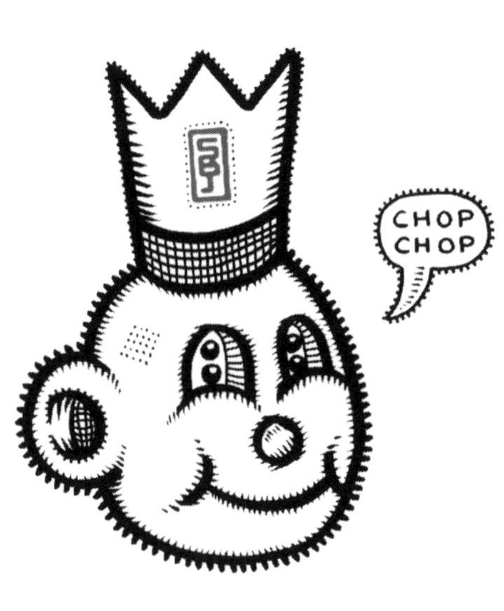
SBJ
CHOP CHOP

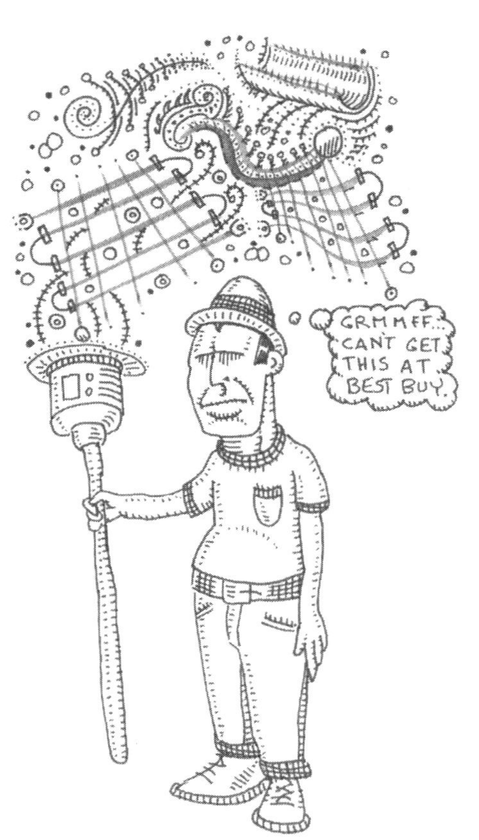
GRMMFF...
CAN'T GET
THIS AT
BEST BUY.

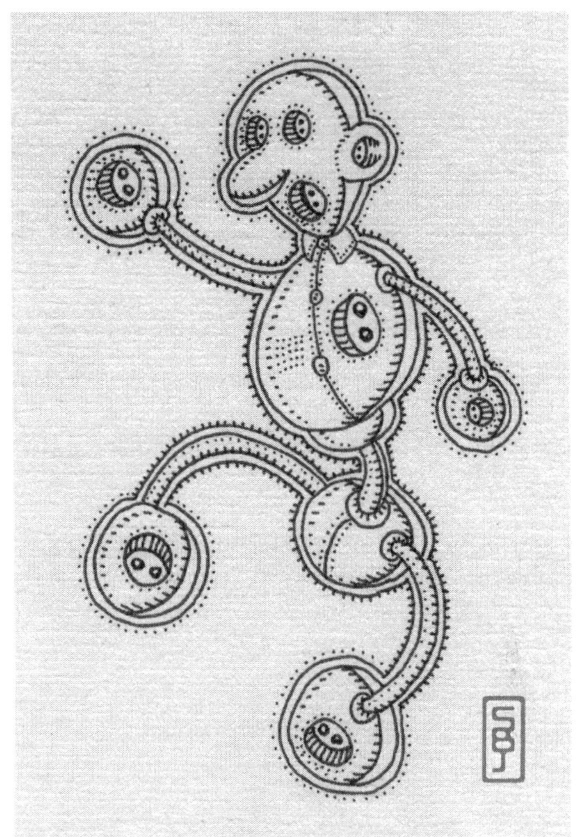

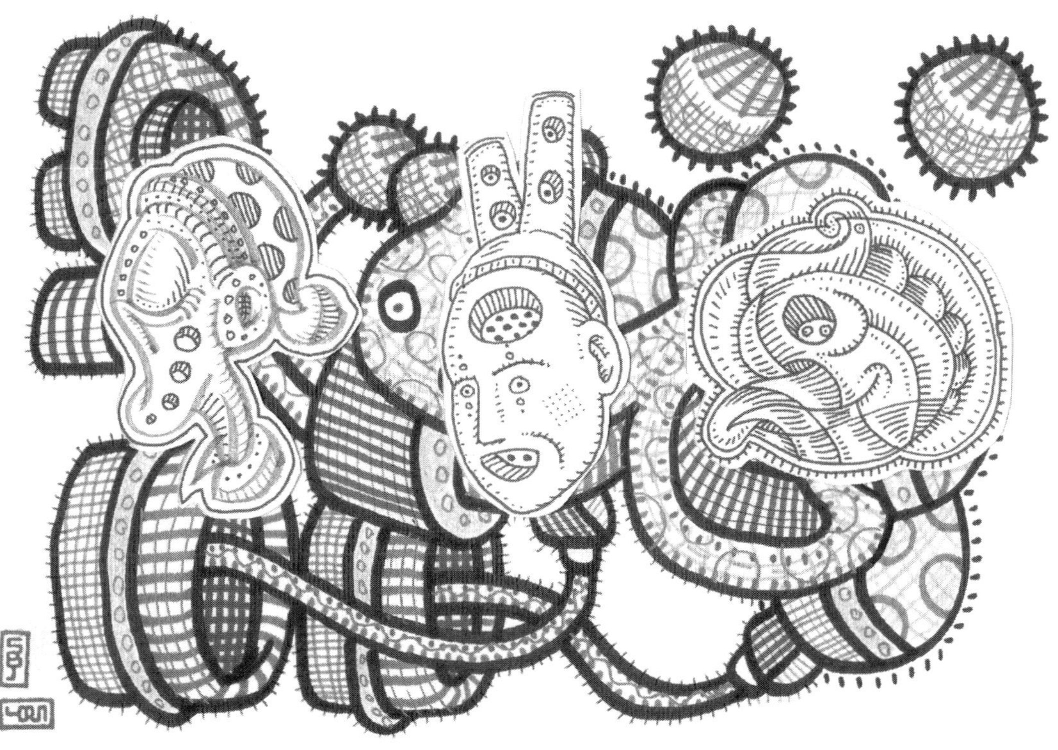

2012

SEPTEMBER

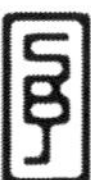

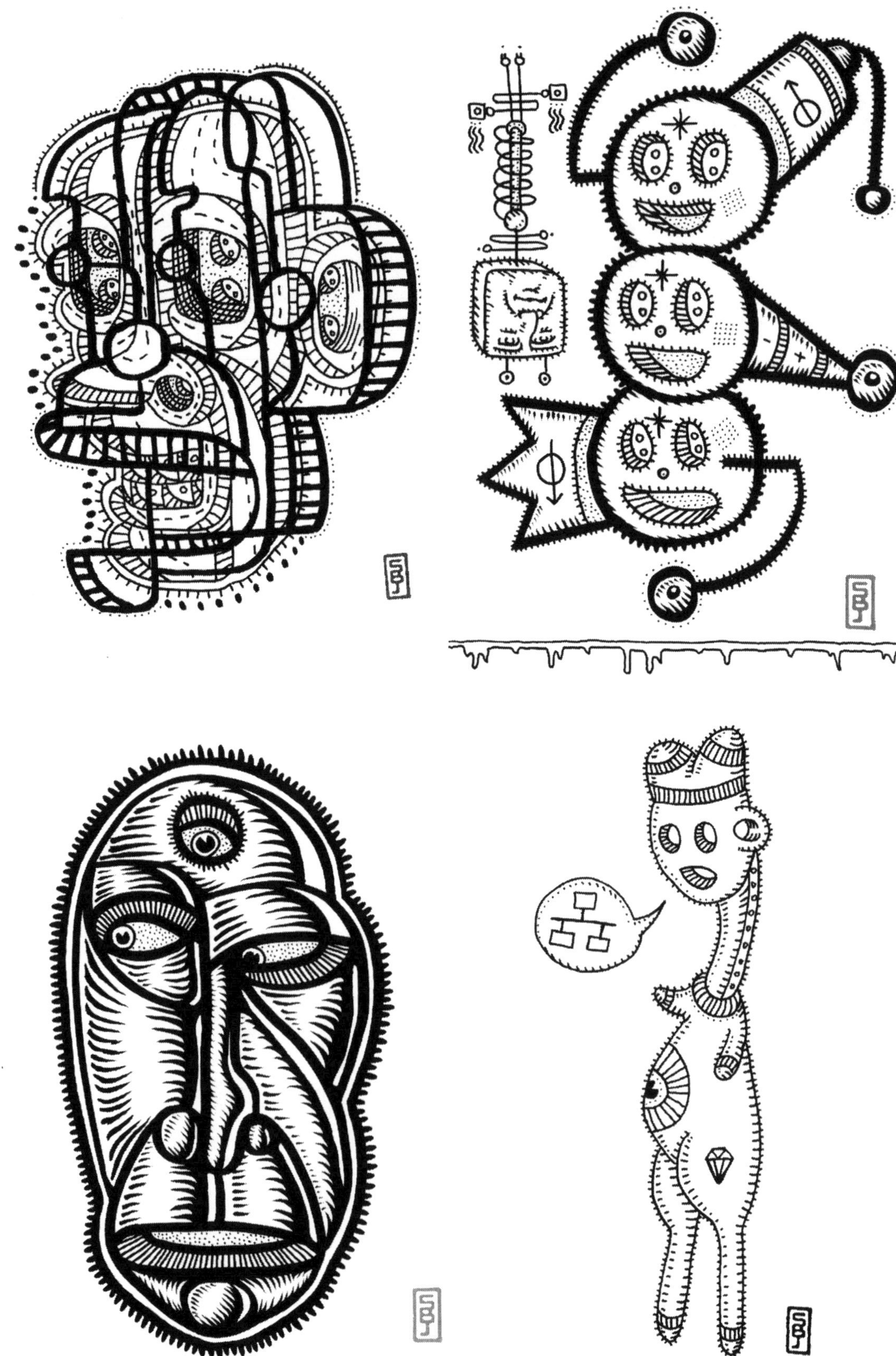

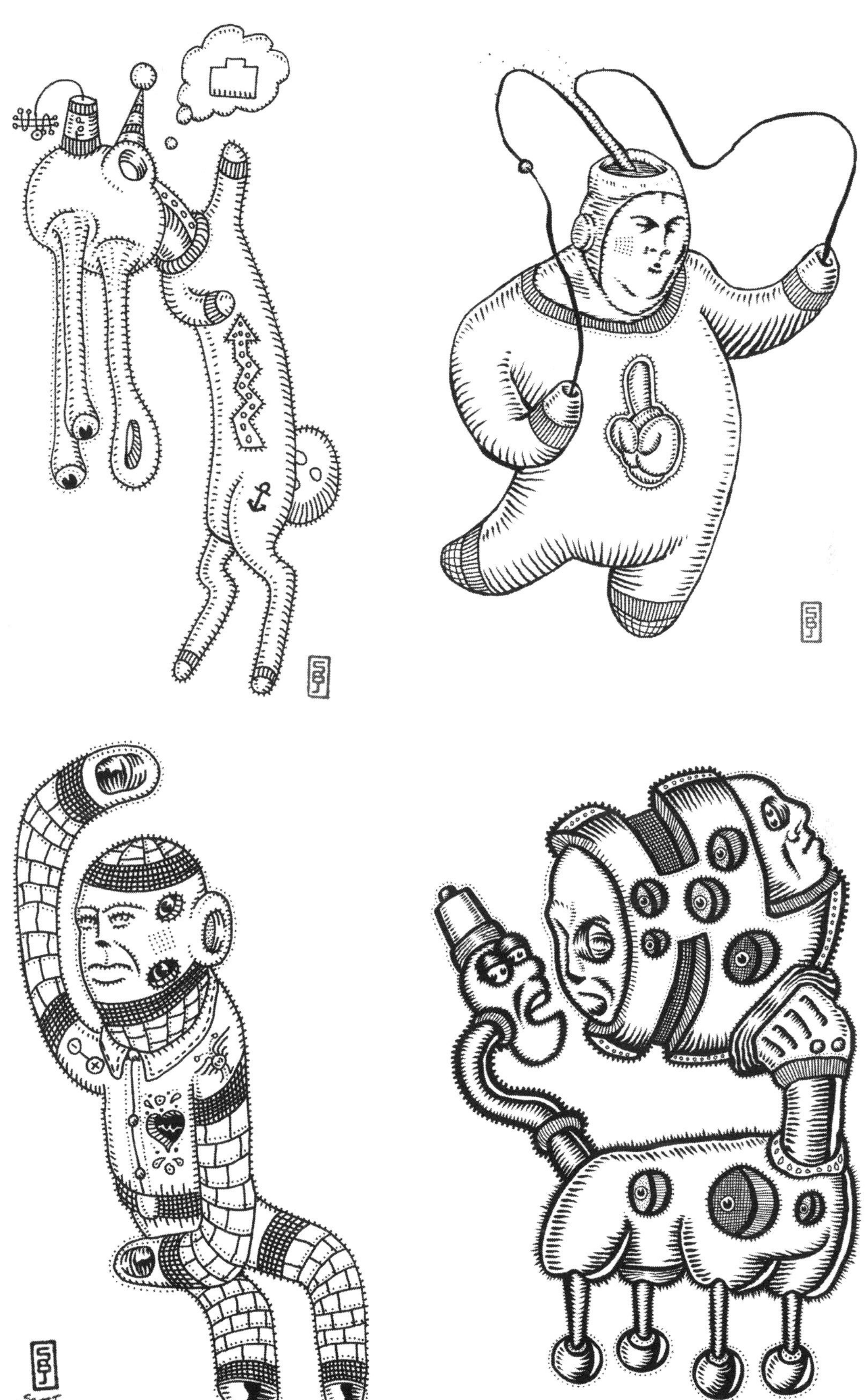
SBJ
SBJ
SBJ
SCOTT JONES

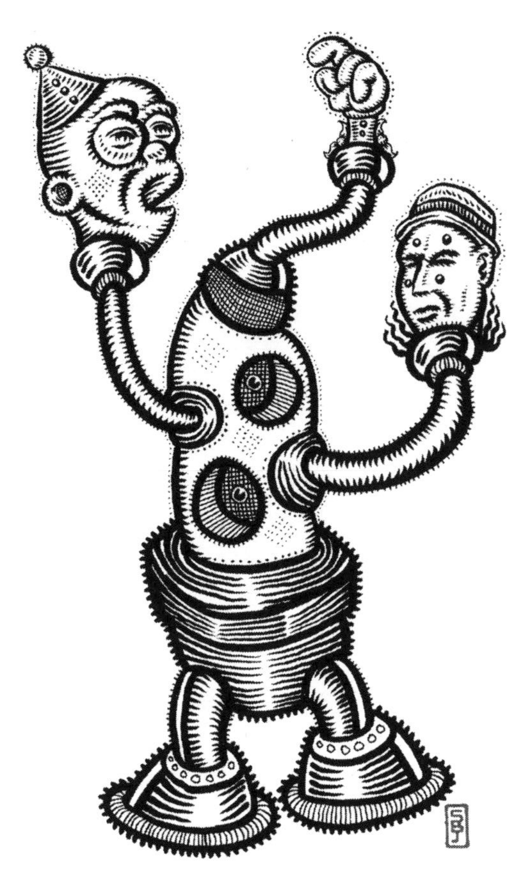

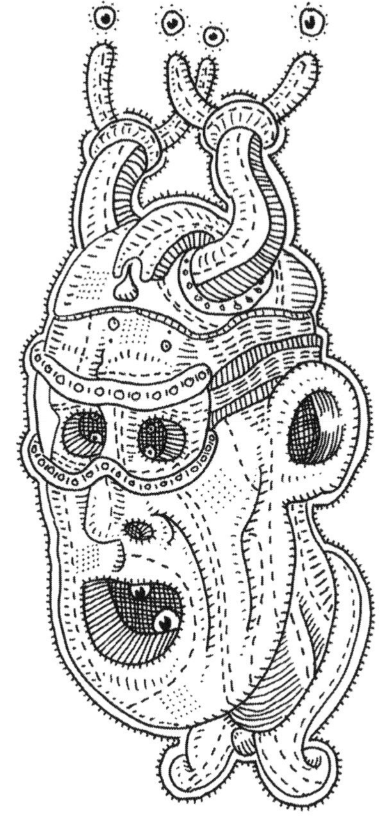

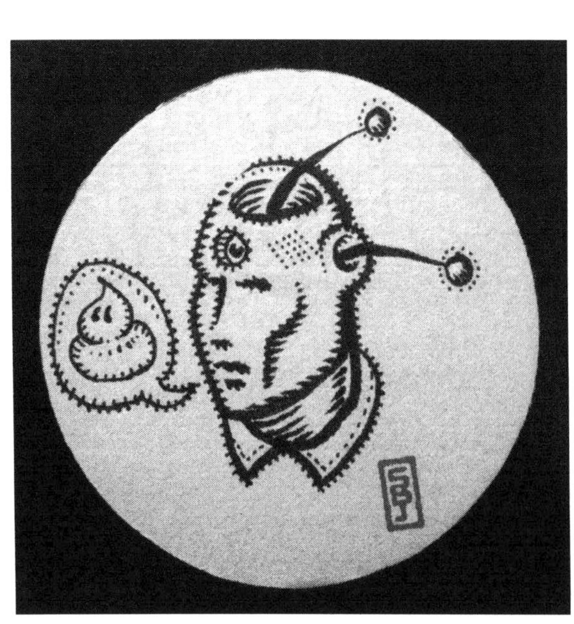

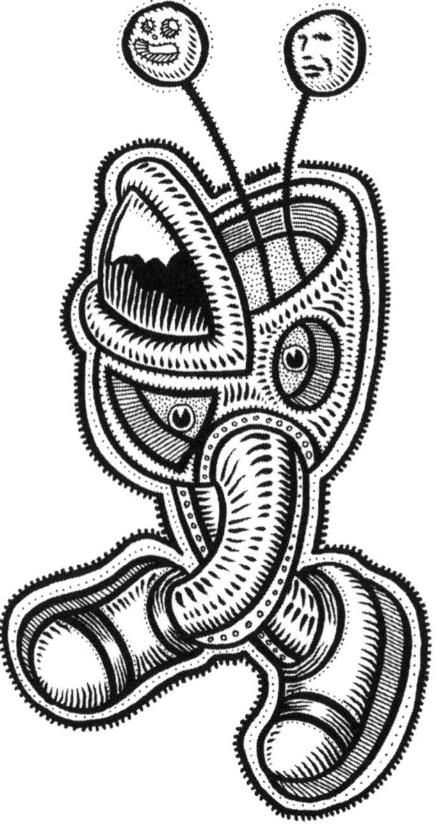

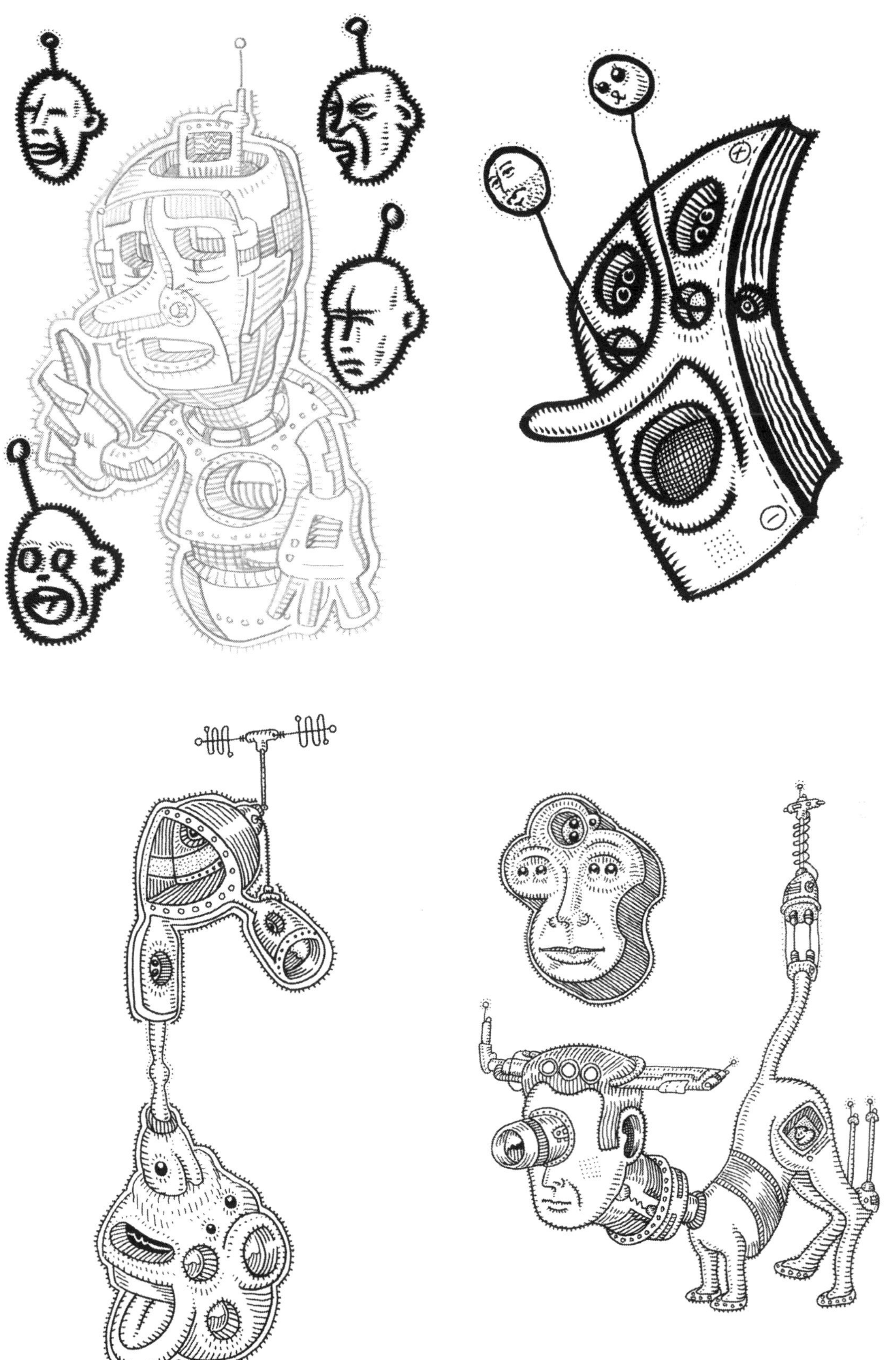

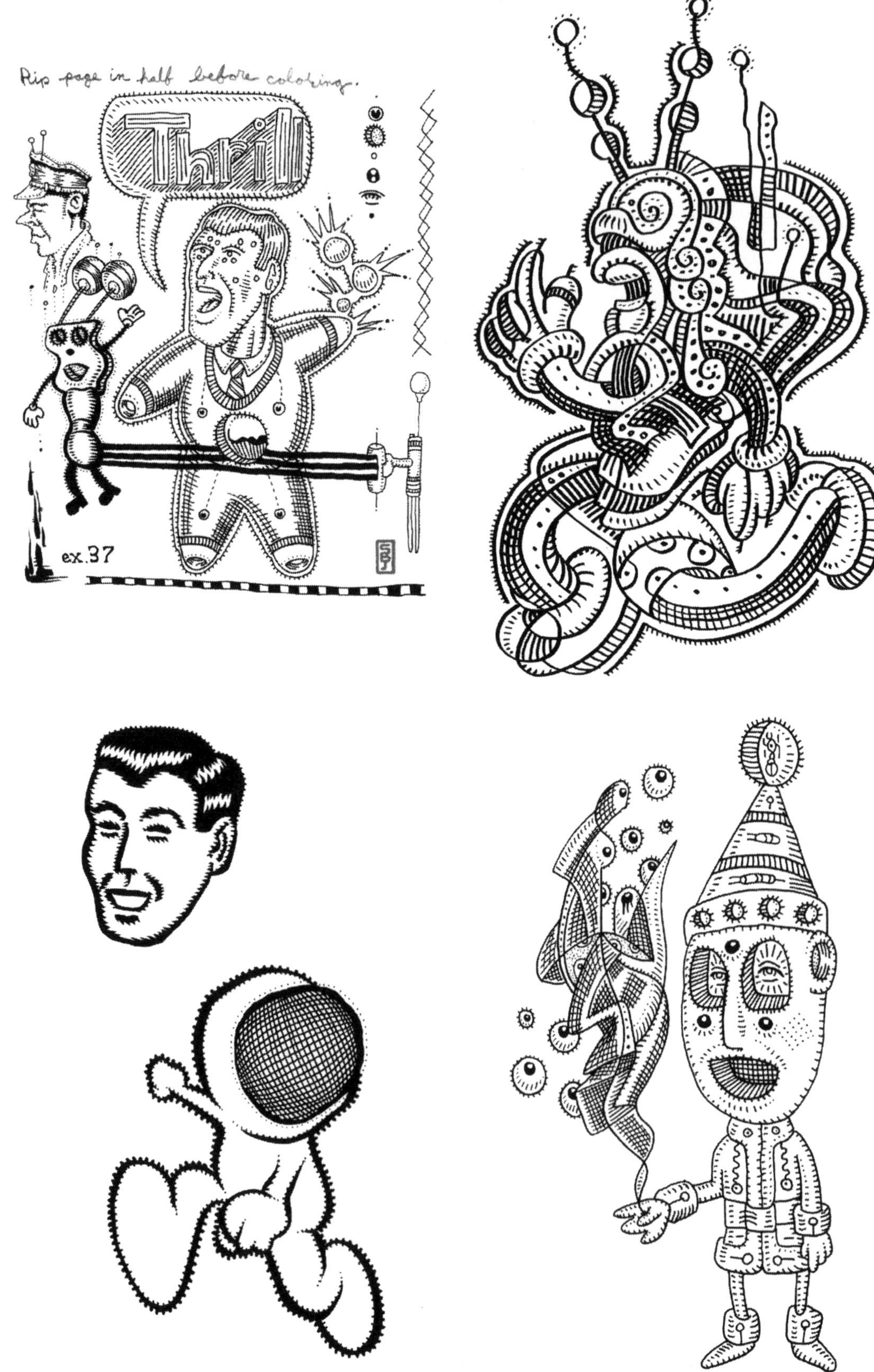
Rip page in half before coloring.
Thrill
ex.37

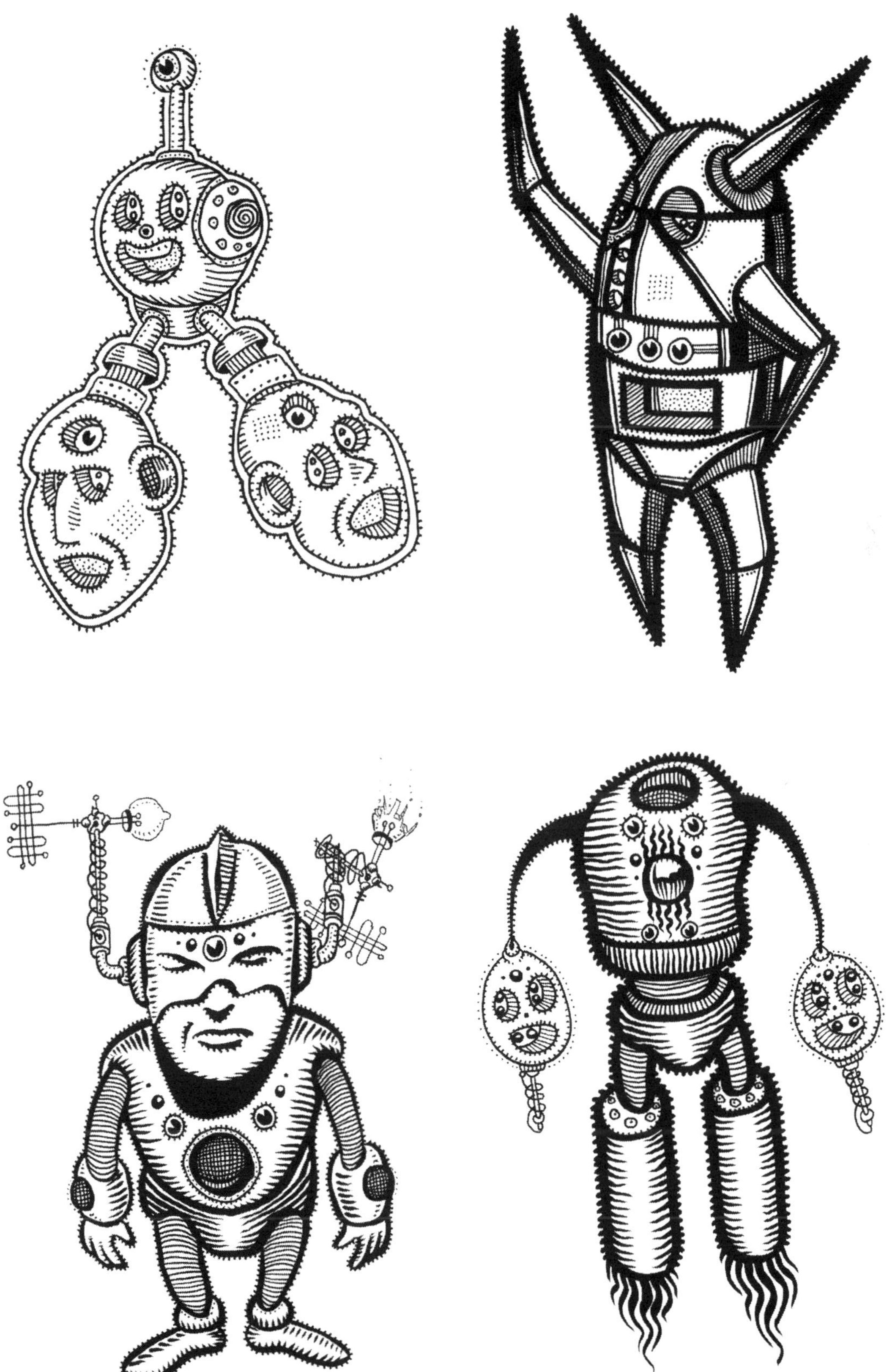

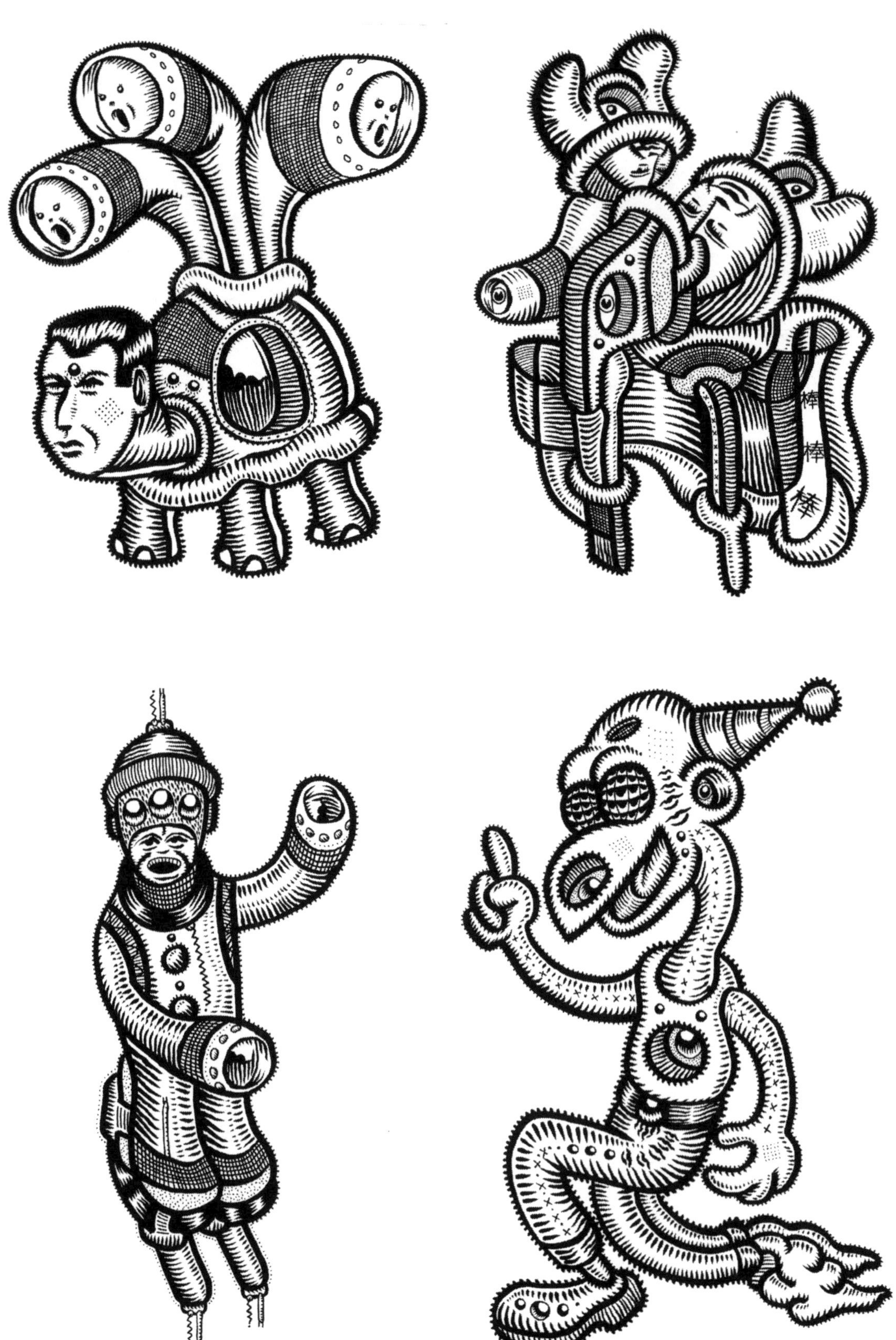
棒
棒
棒

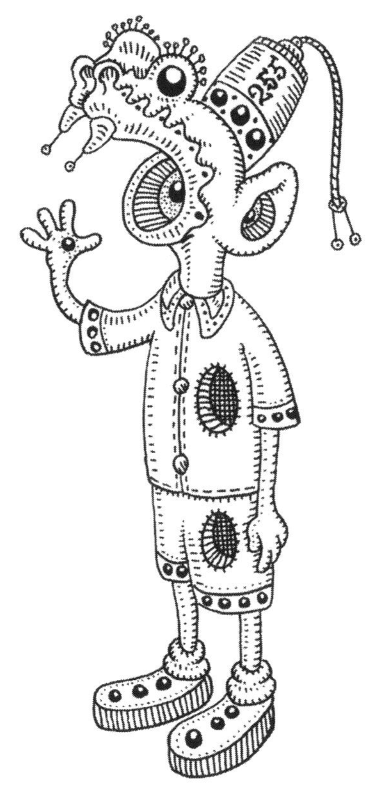
255

2012

OCTOBER

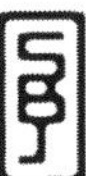

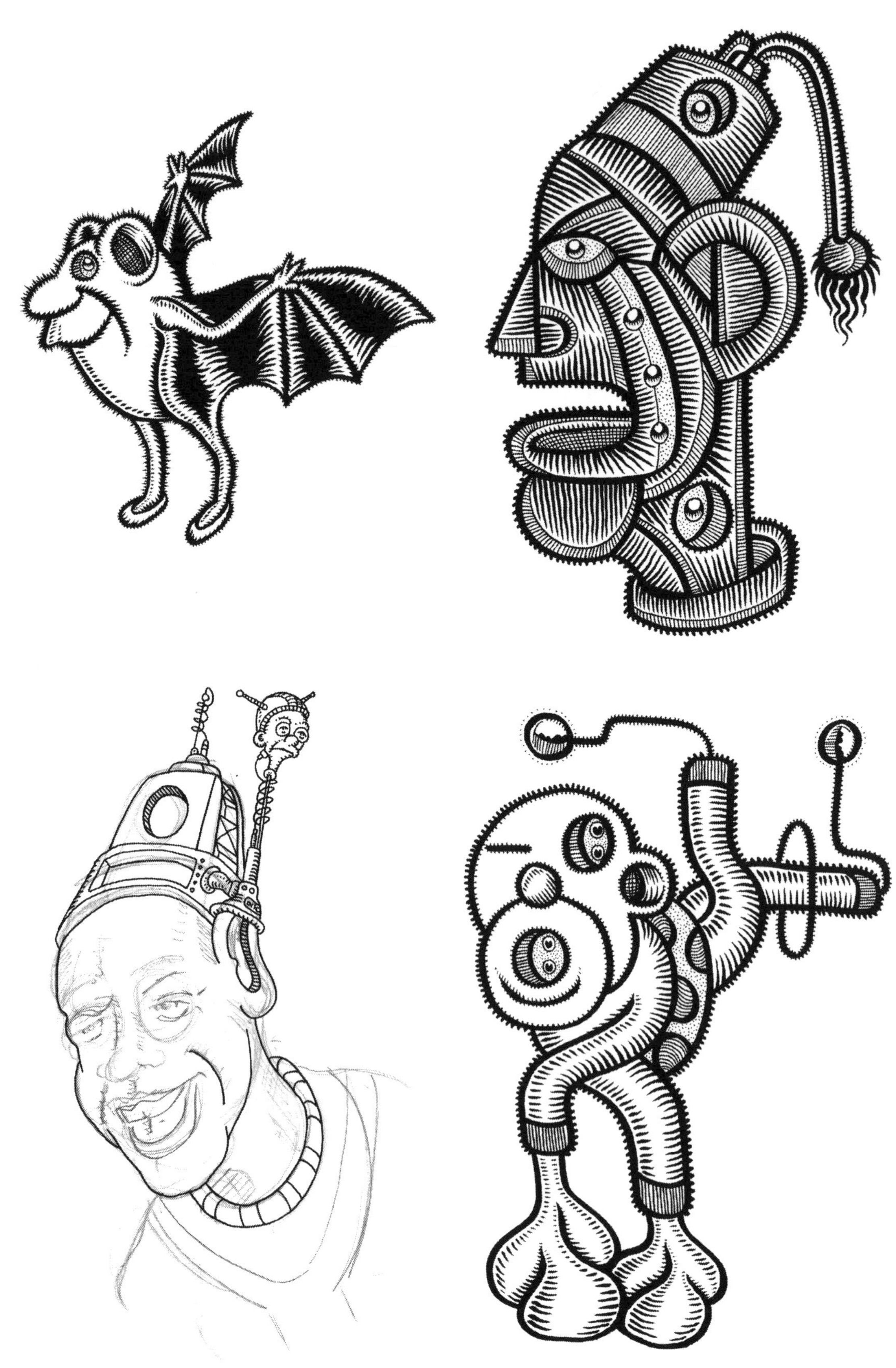

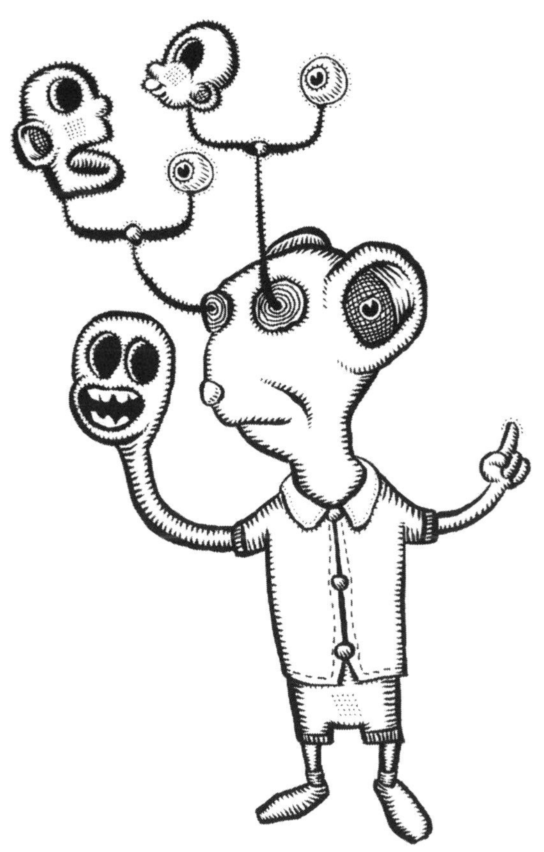

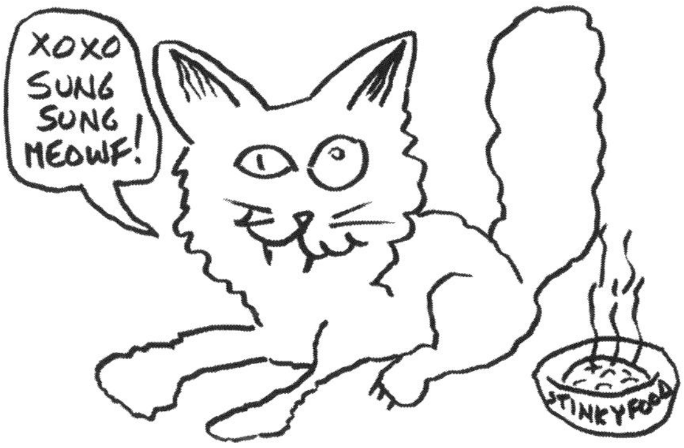

XOXO
SUNG
SUNG
MEOWF!

STINKYFOOD

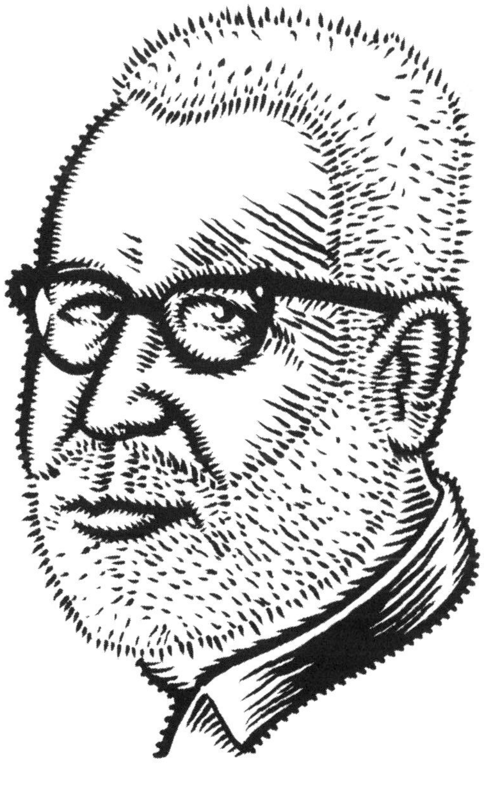

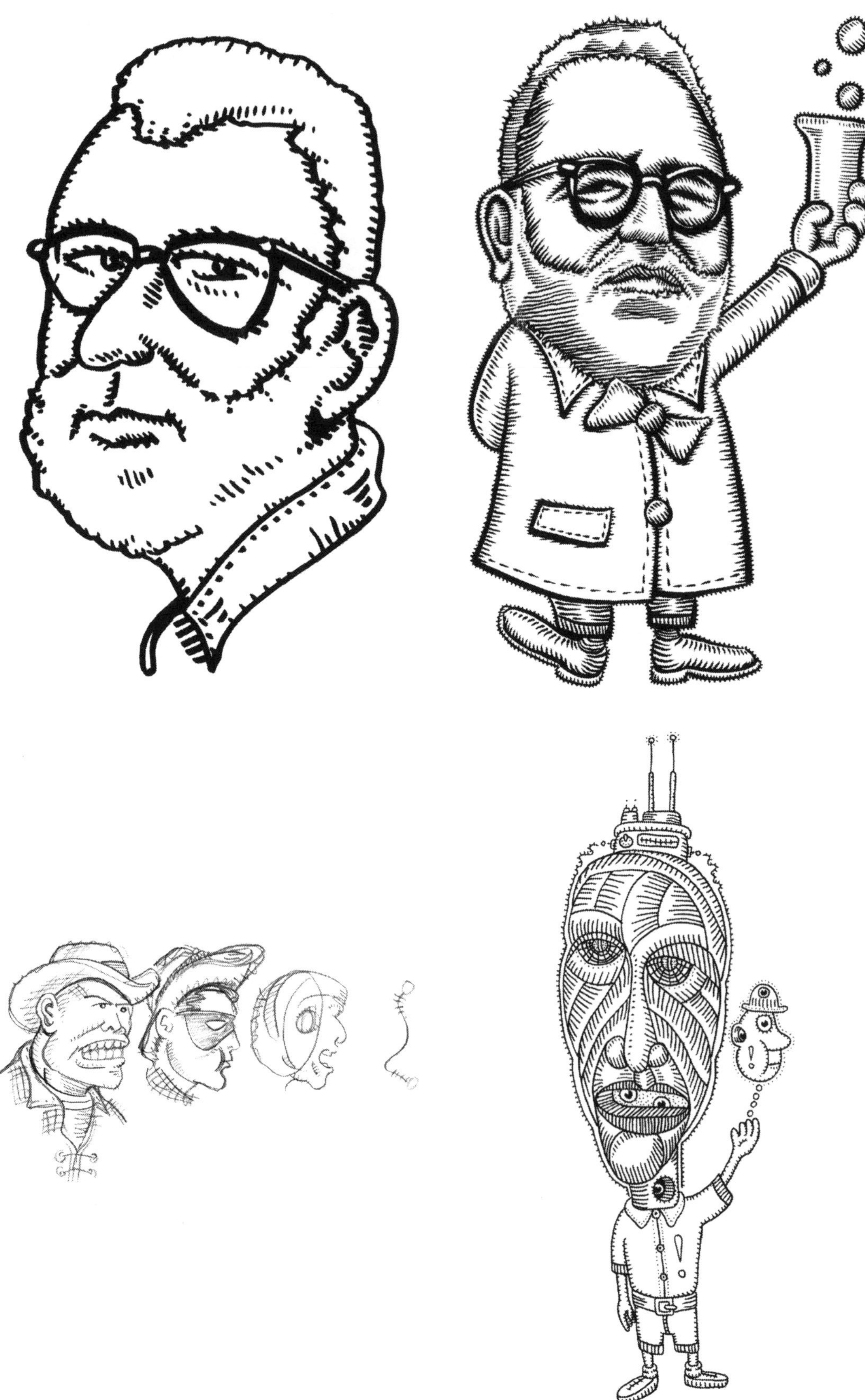

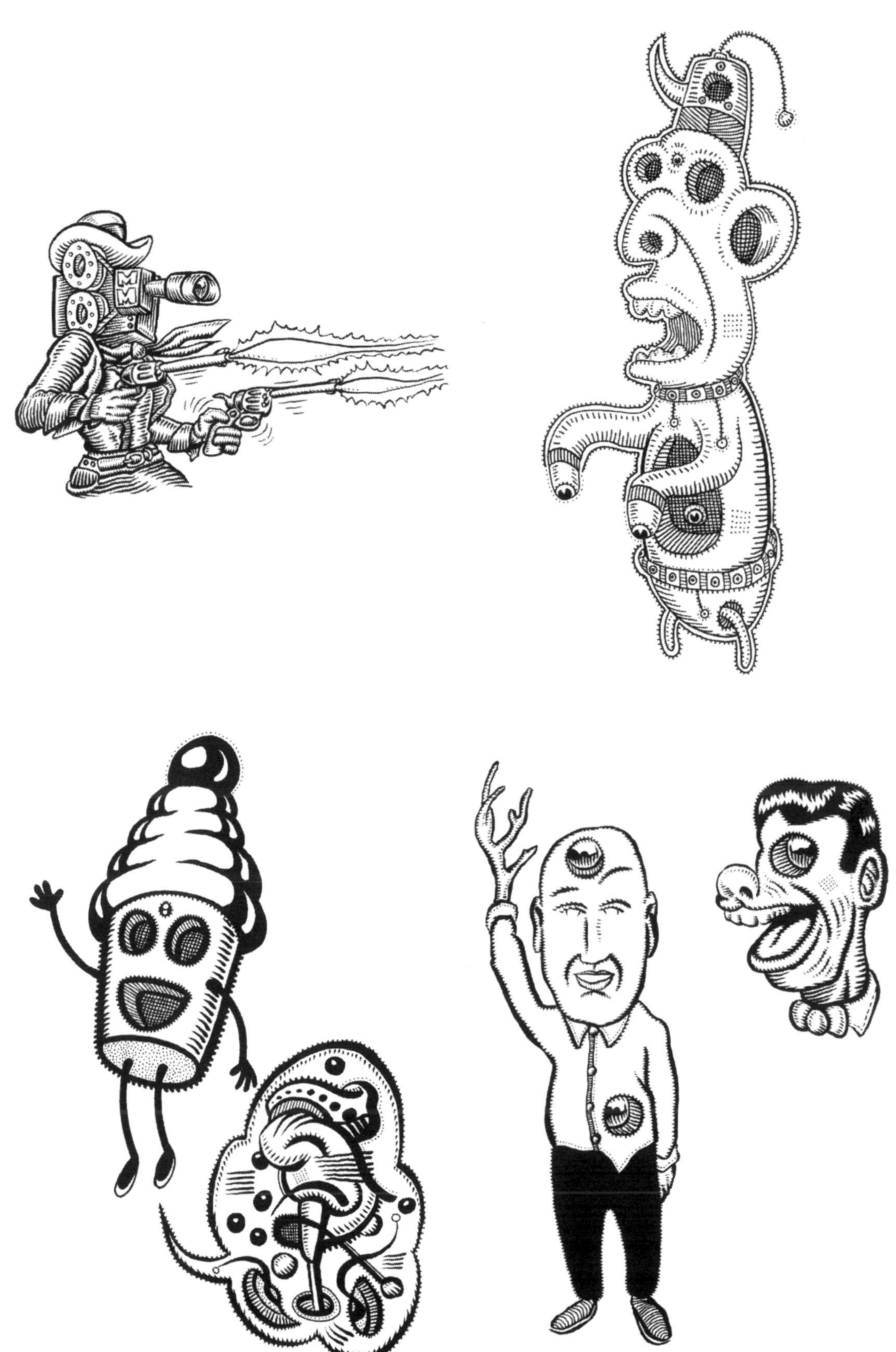

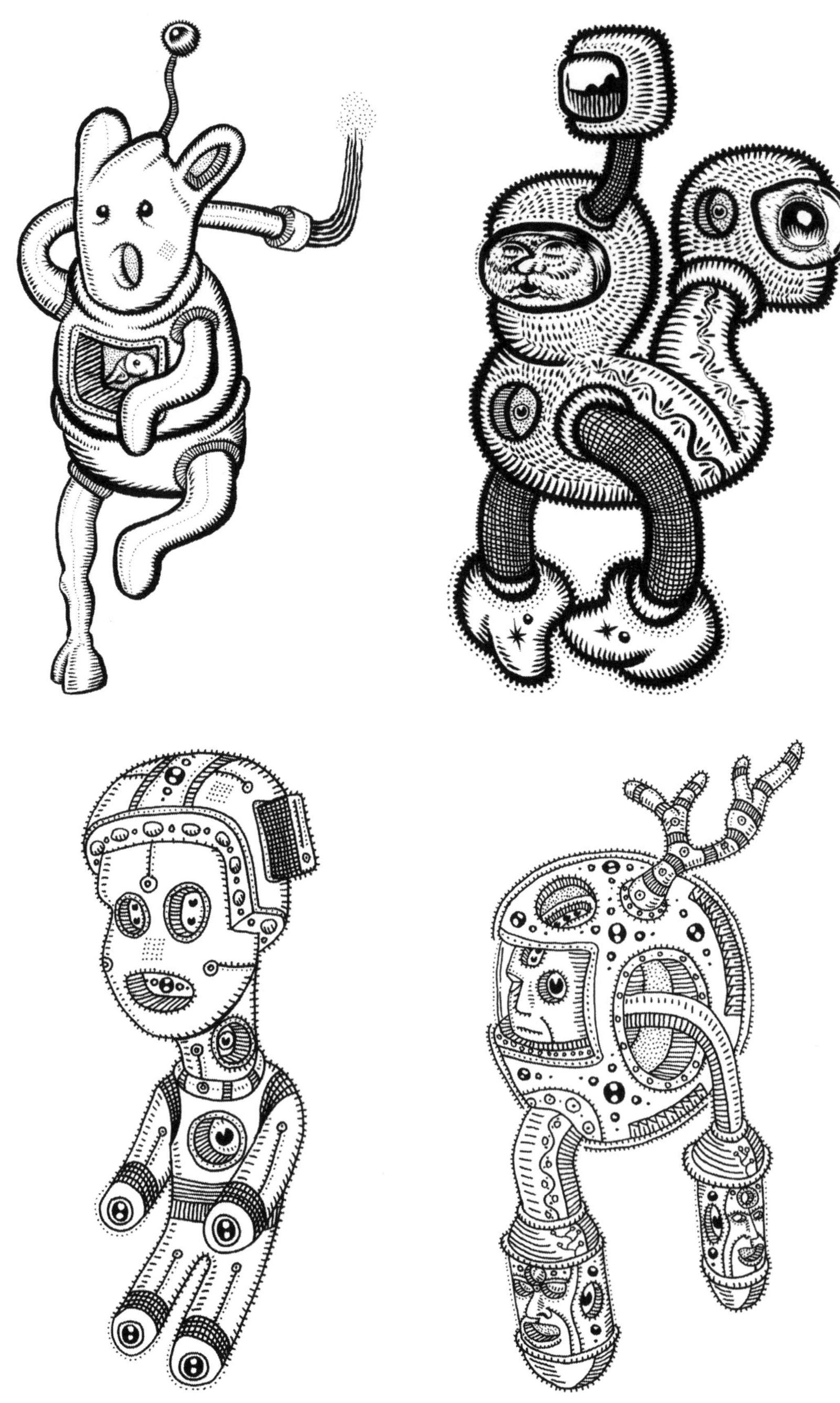

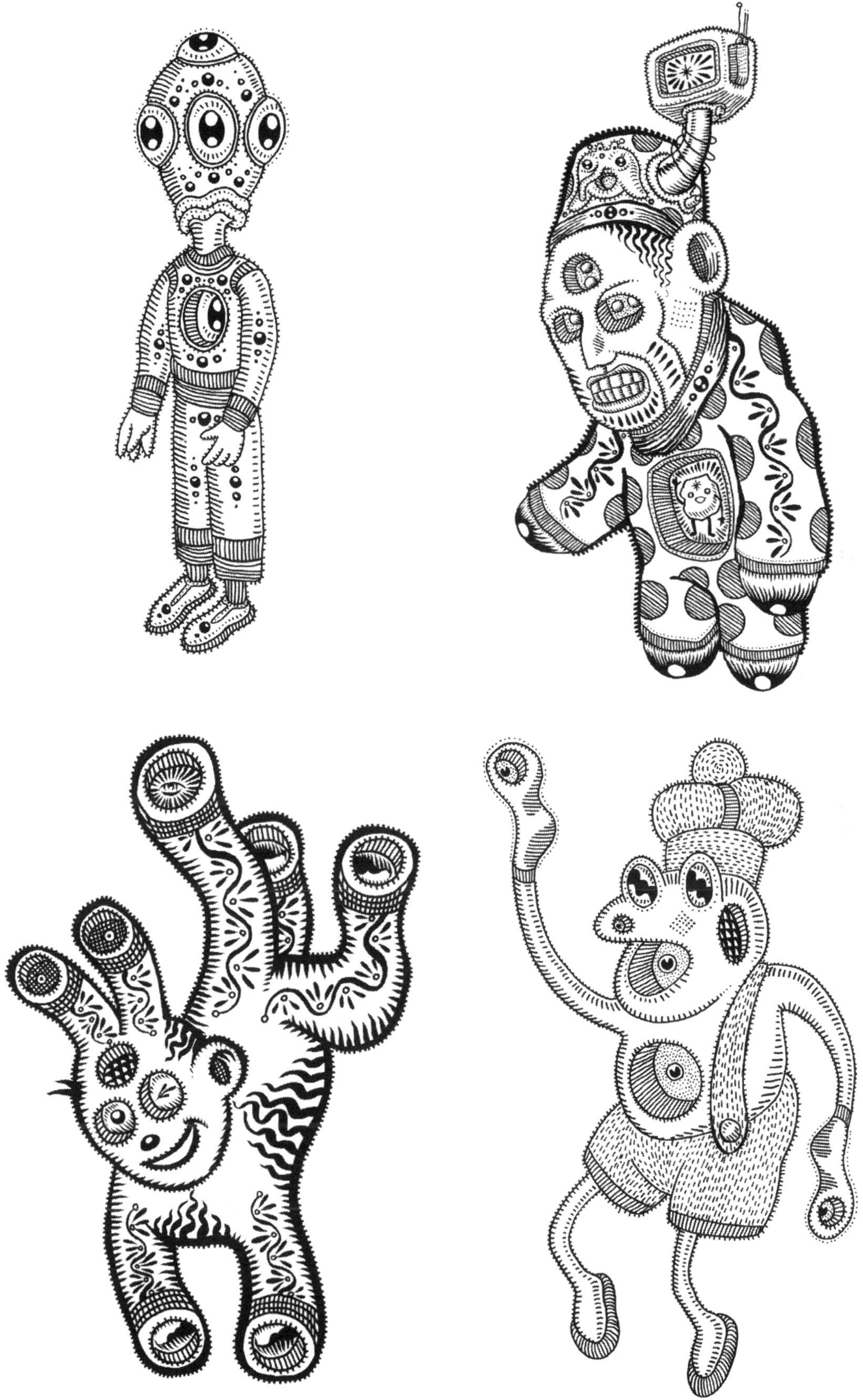

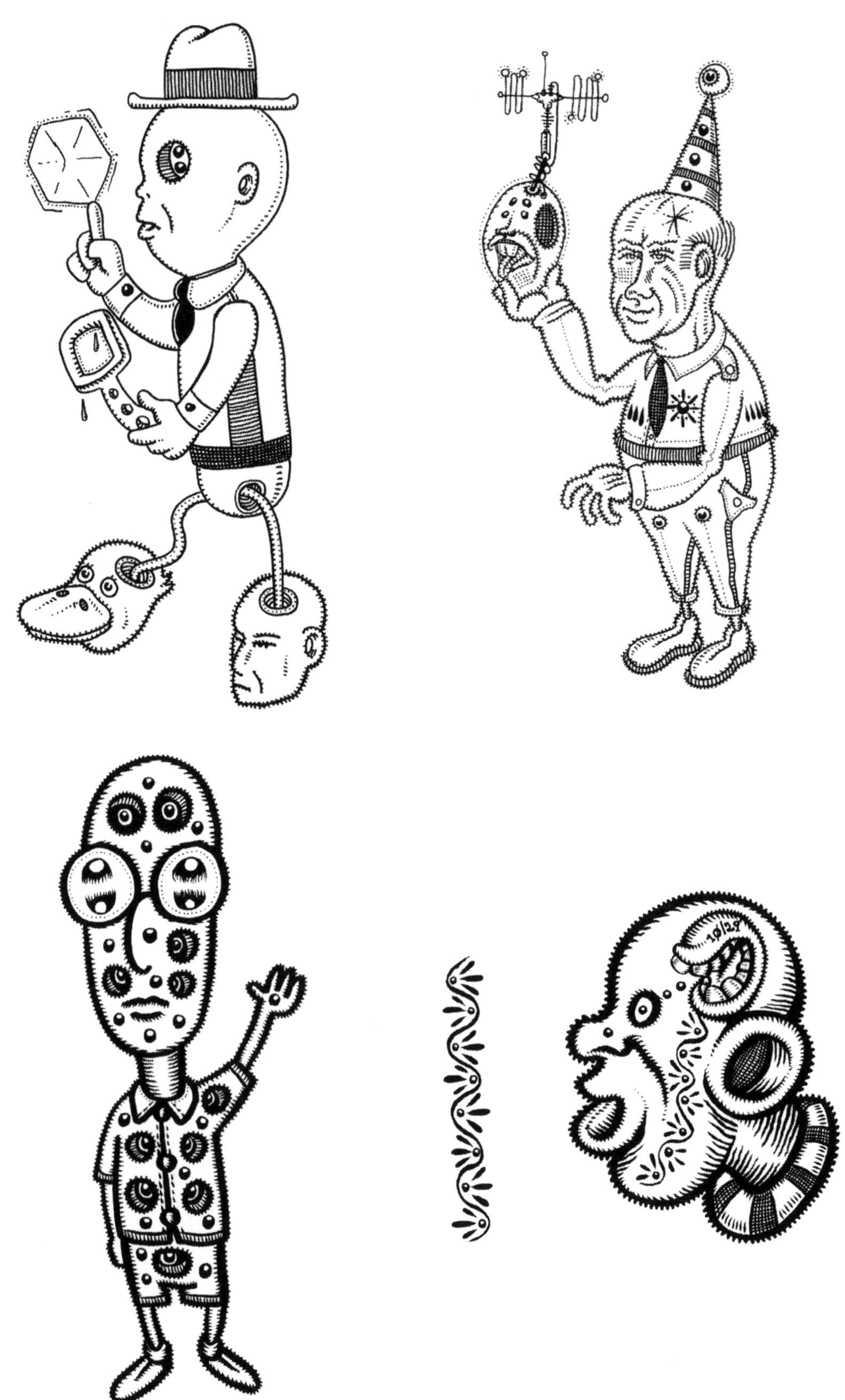

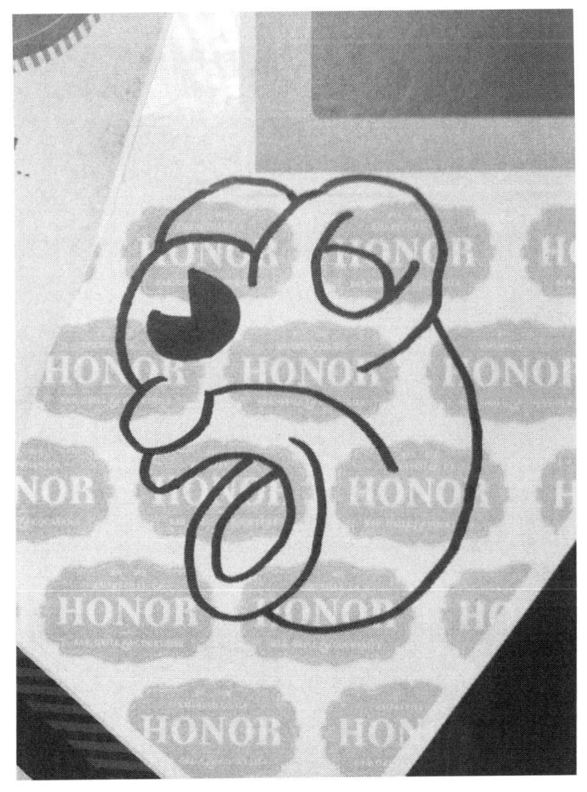
HONOR
HONOR
HONOR

2012

November

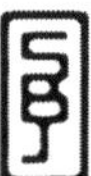

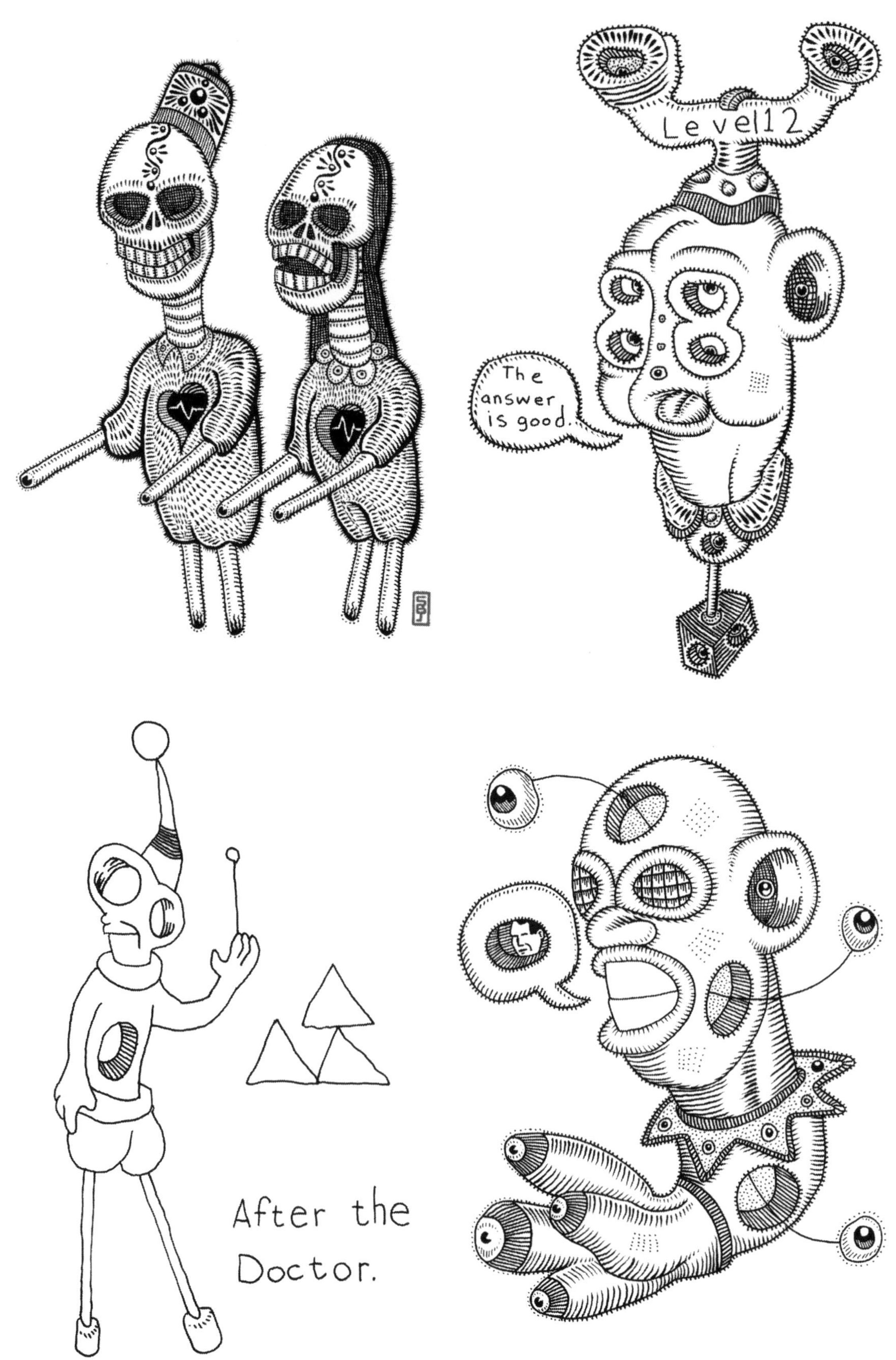
Level2
The answer is good.
After the Doctor.

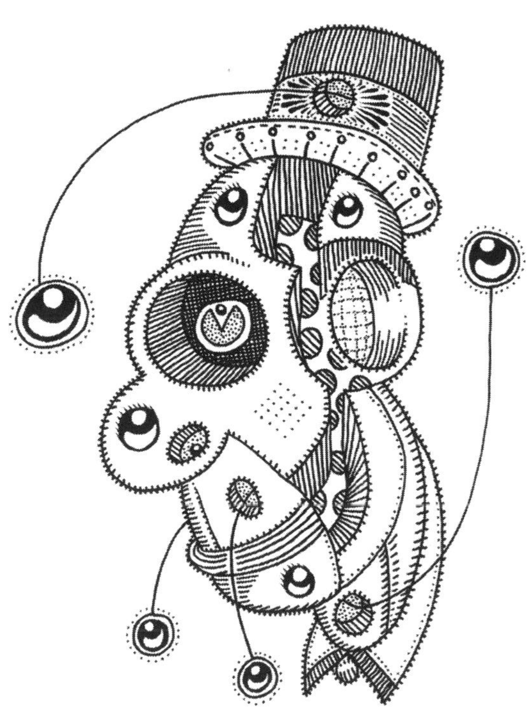

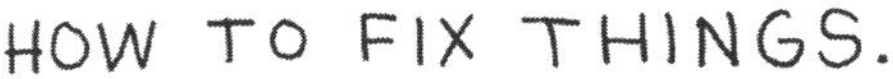

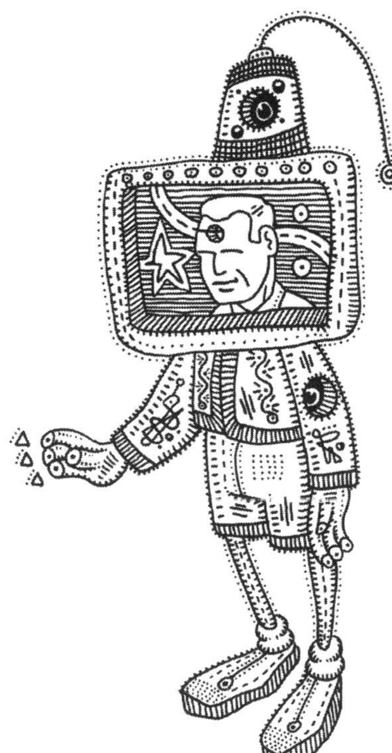

ROYAL FOOTMAN NAMED GPS.

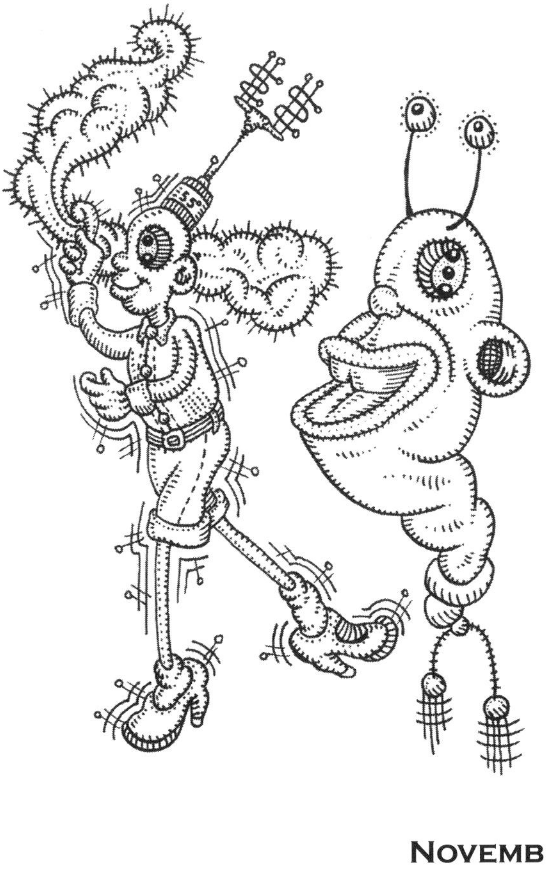

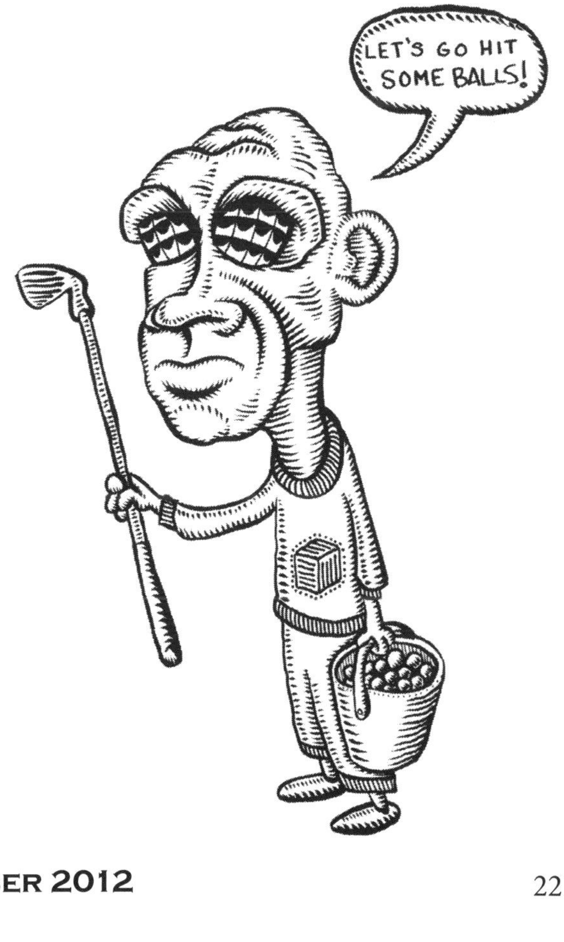

LET'S GO HIT SOME BALLS!

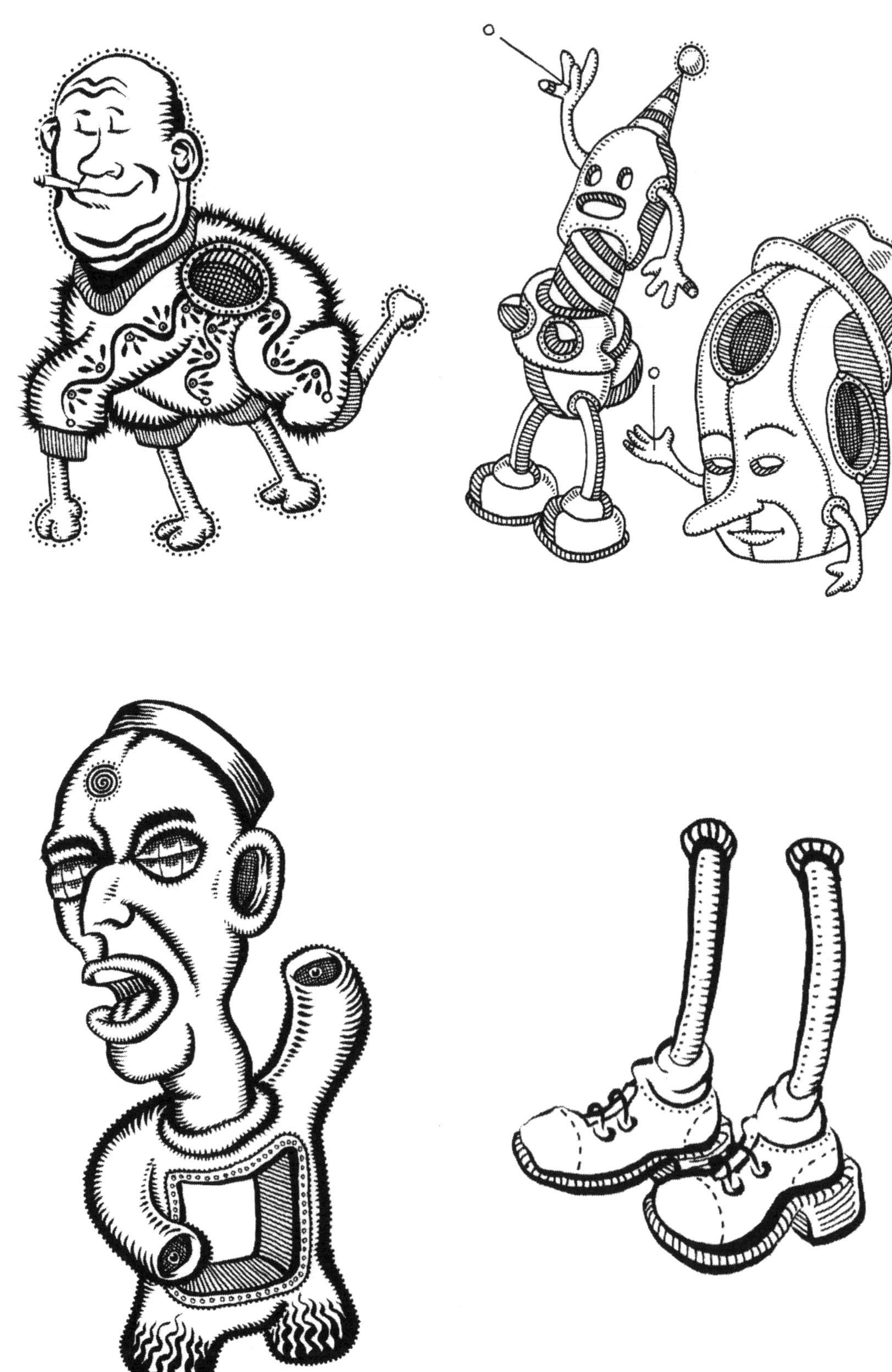

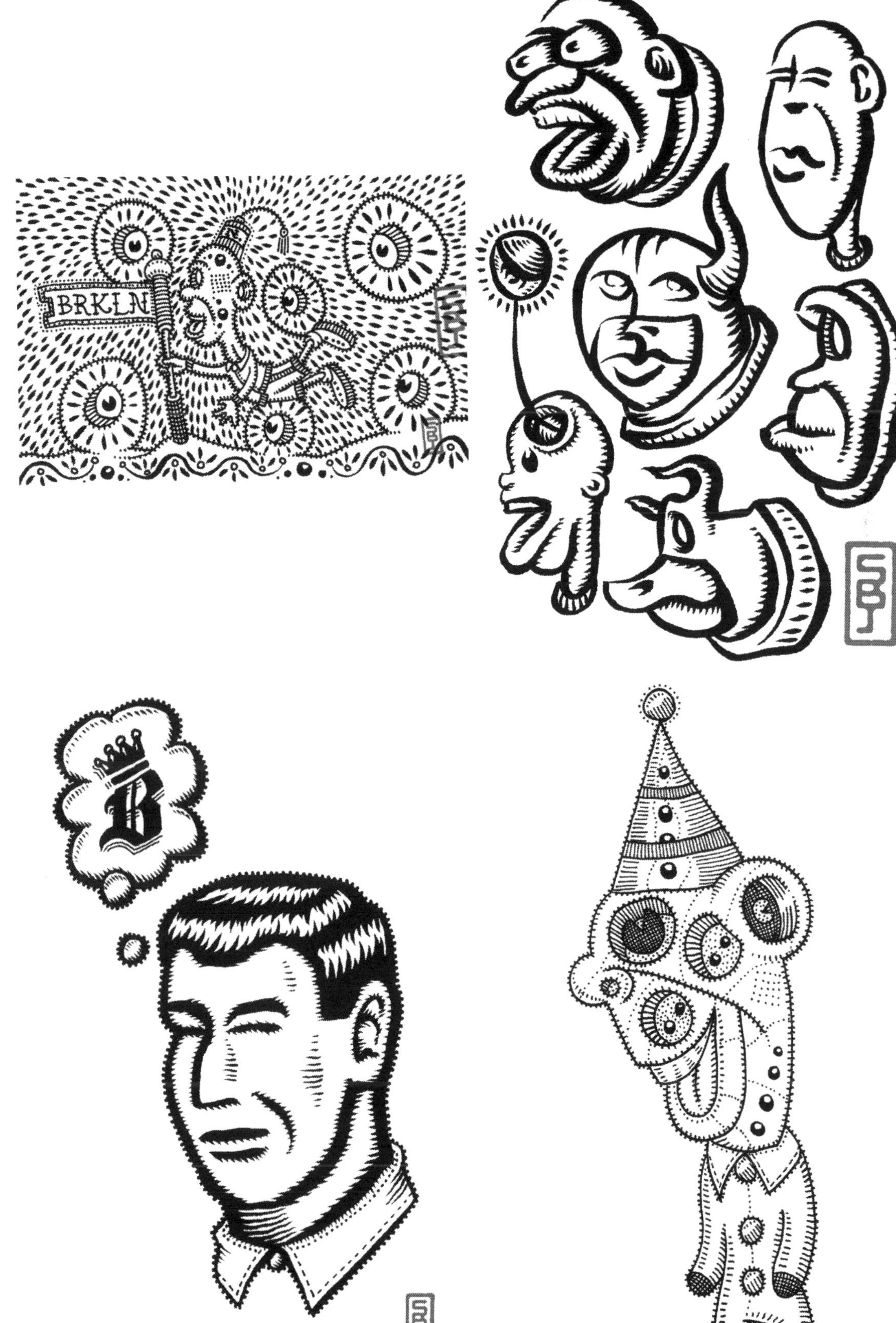
BRKLN

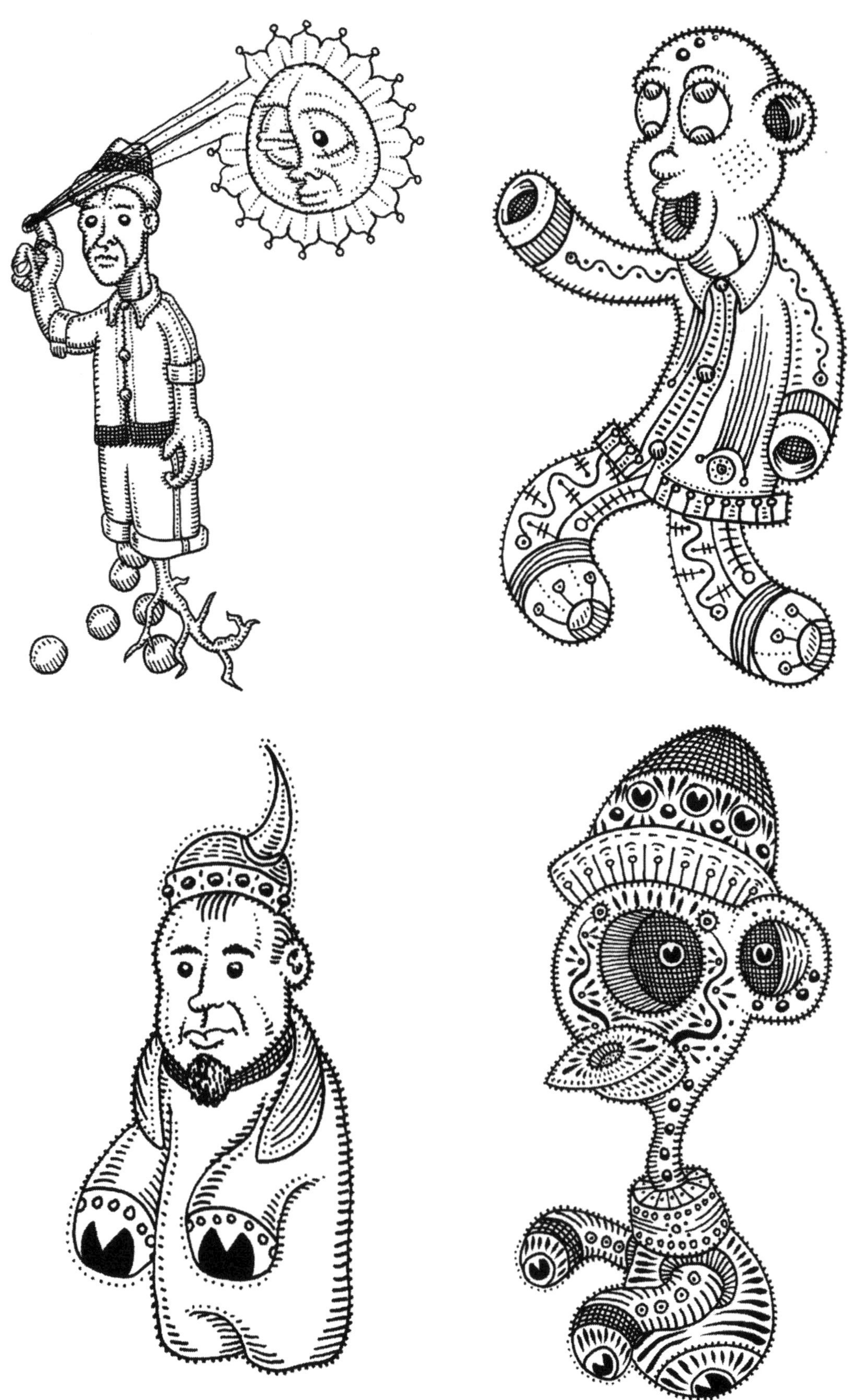

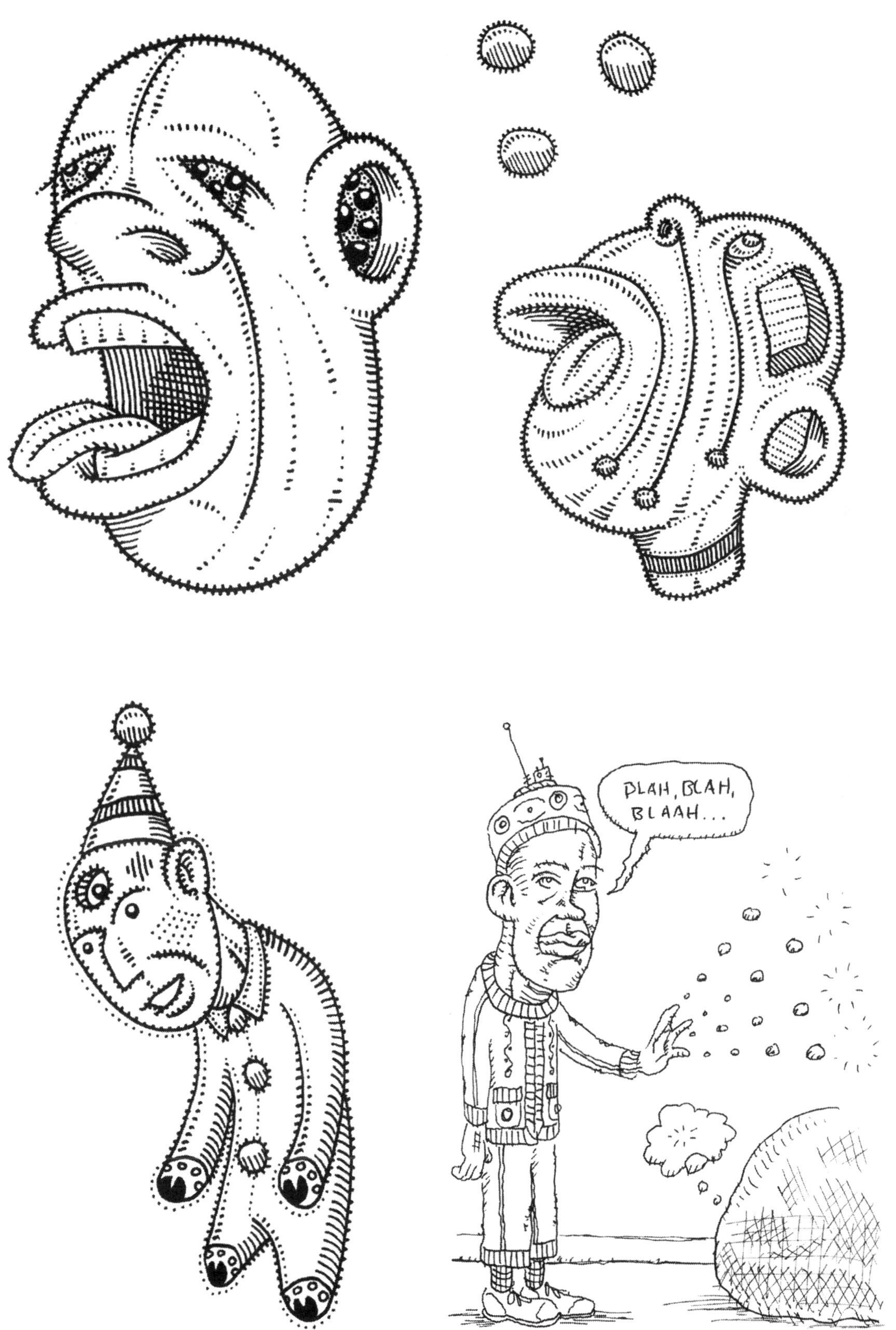
BLAH, BLAH,
BLAAH...

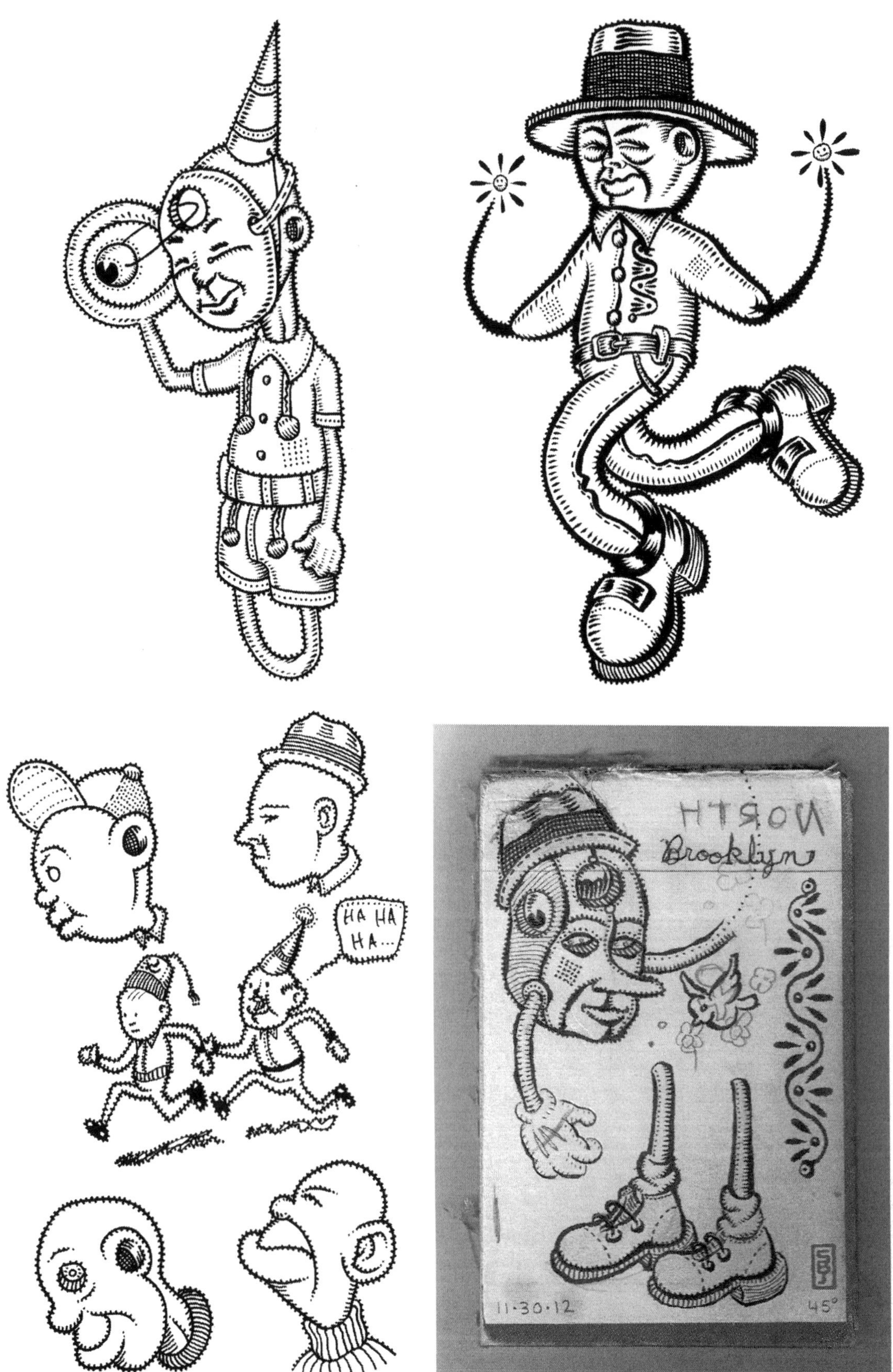
HA HA
HA...
NORTH
Brooklyn
SBJ
11-30-12
45°

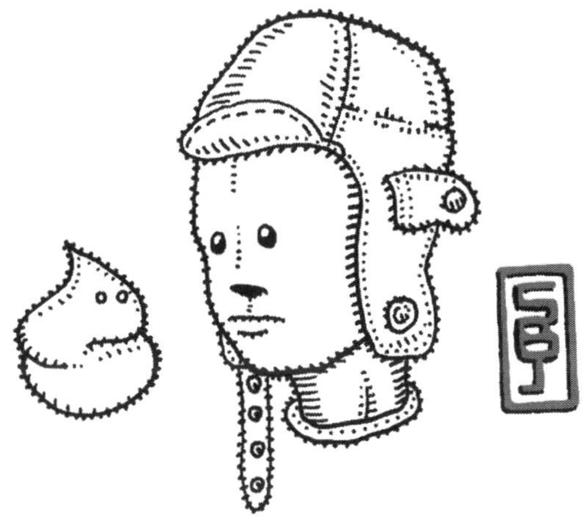

2012

December

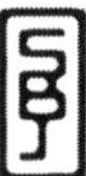

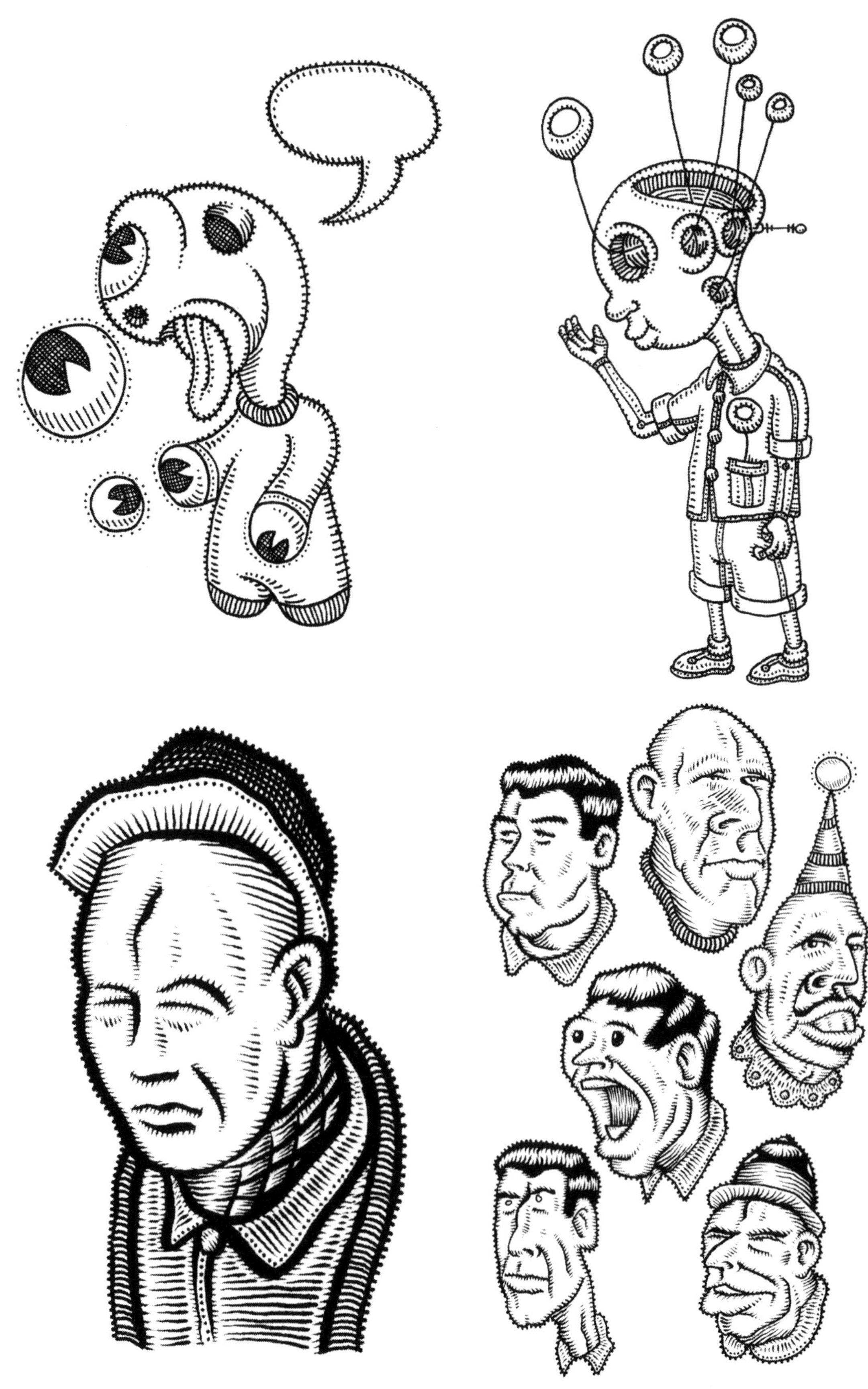

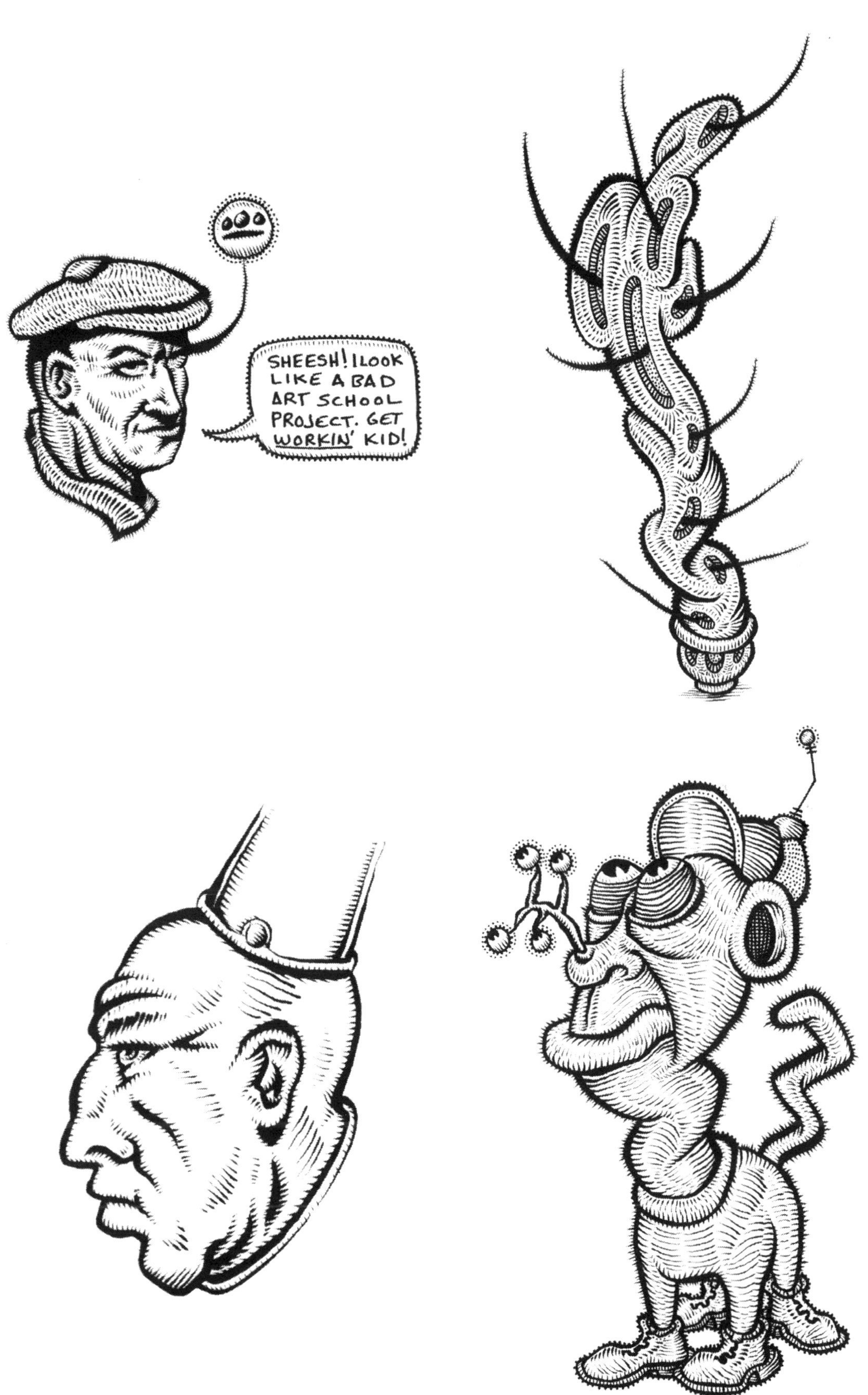
SHEESH! I LOOK LIKE A BAD ART SCHOOL PROJECT. GET WORKIN' KID!

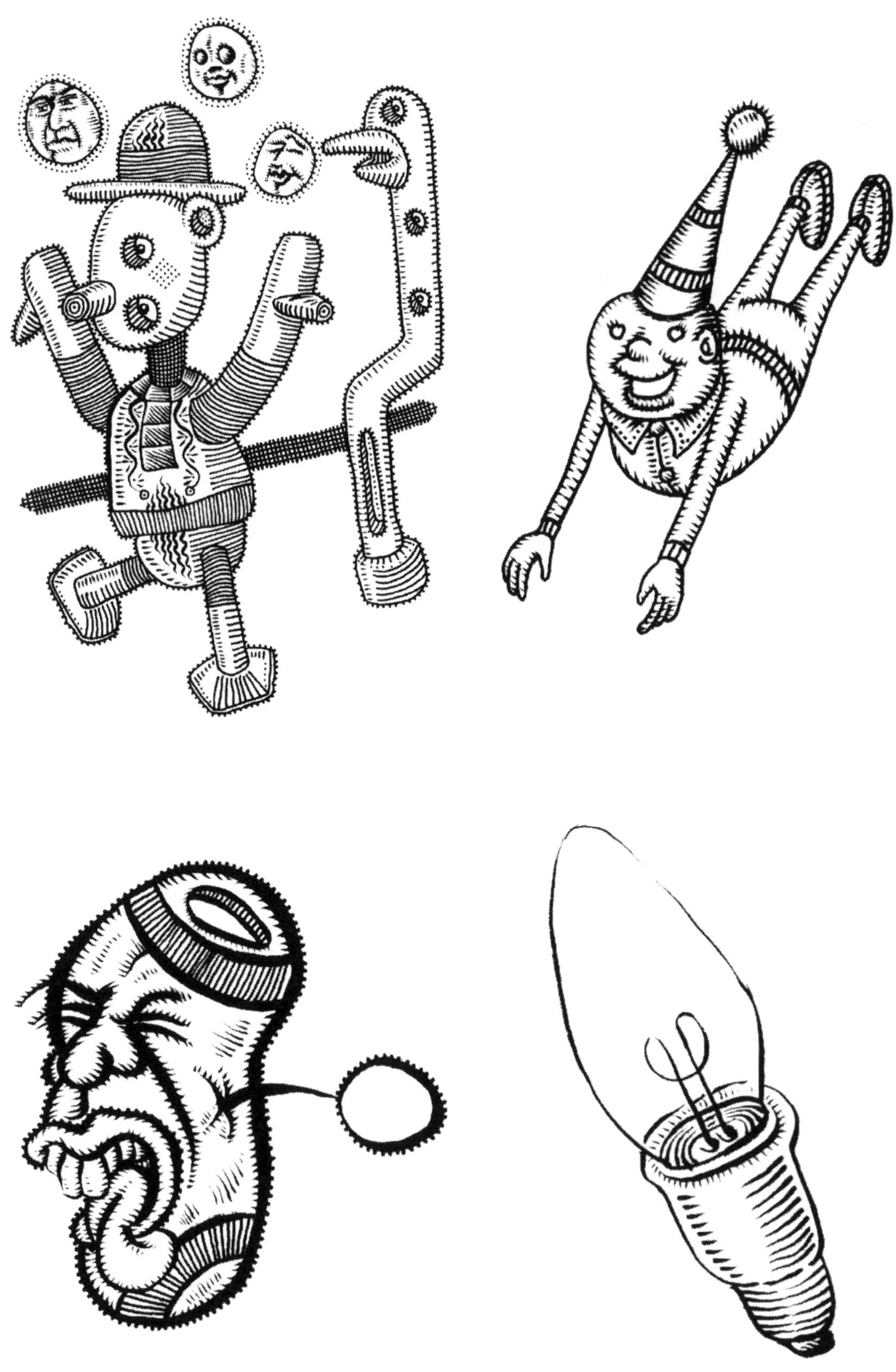

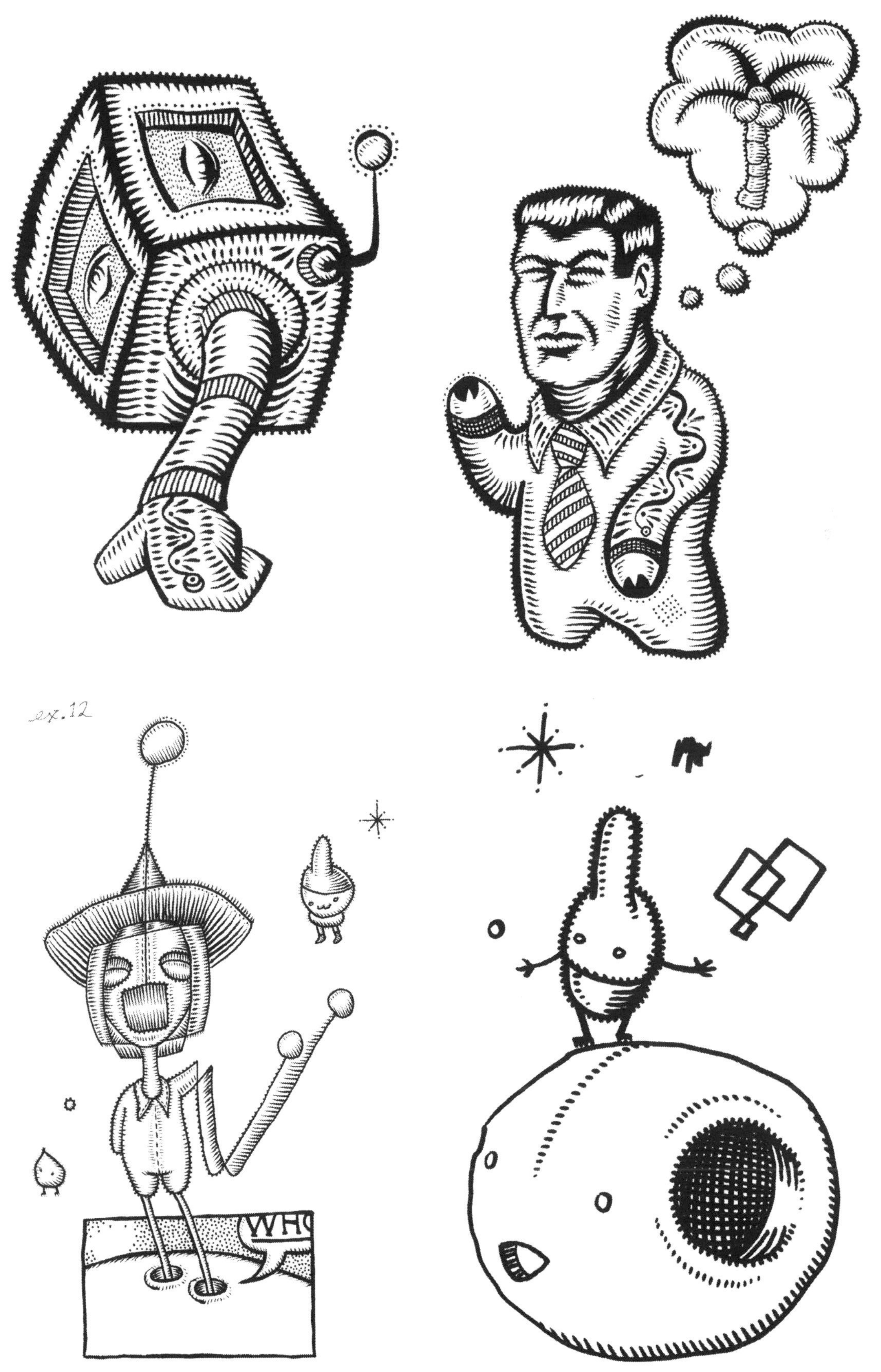
ex.12
WH

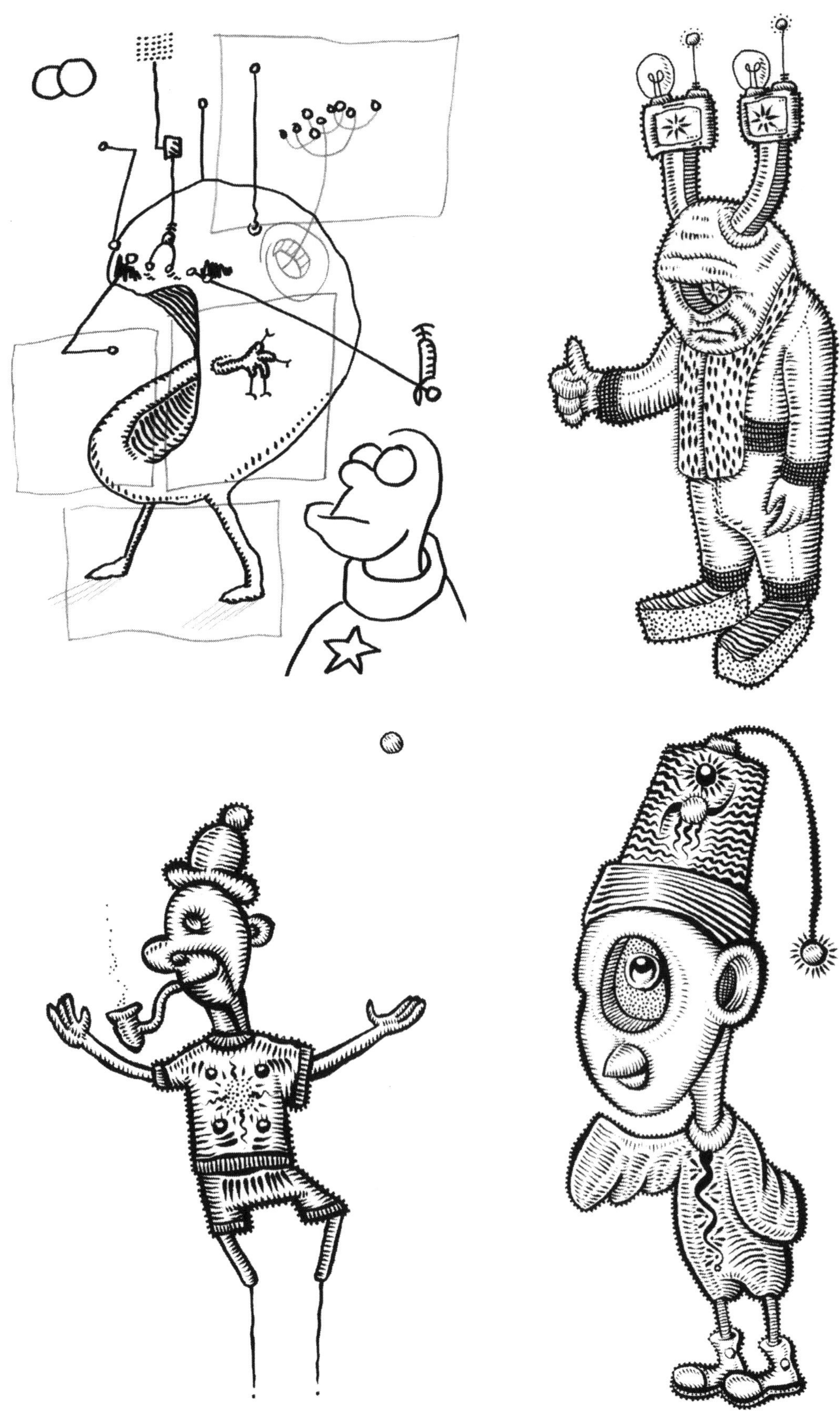

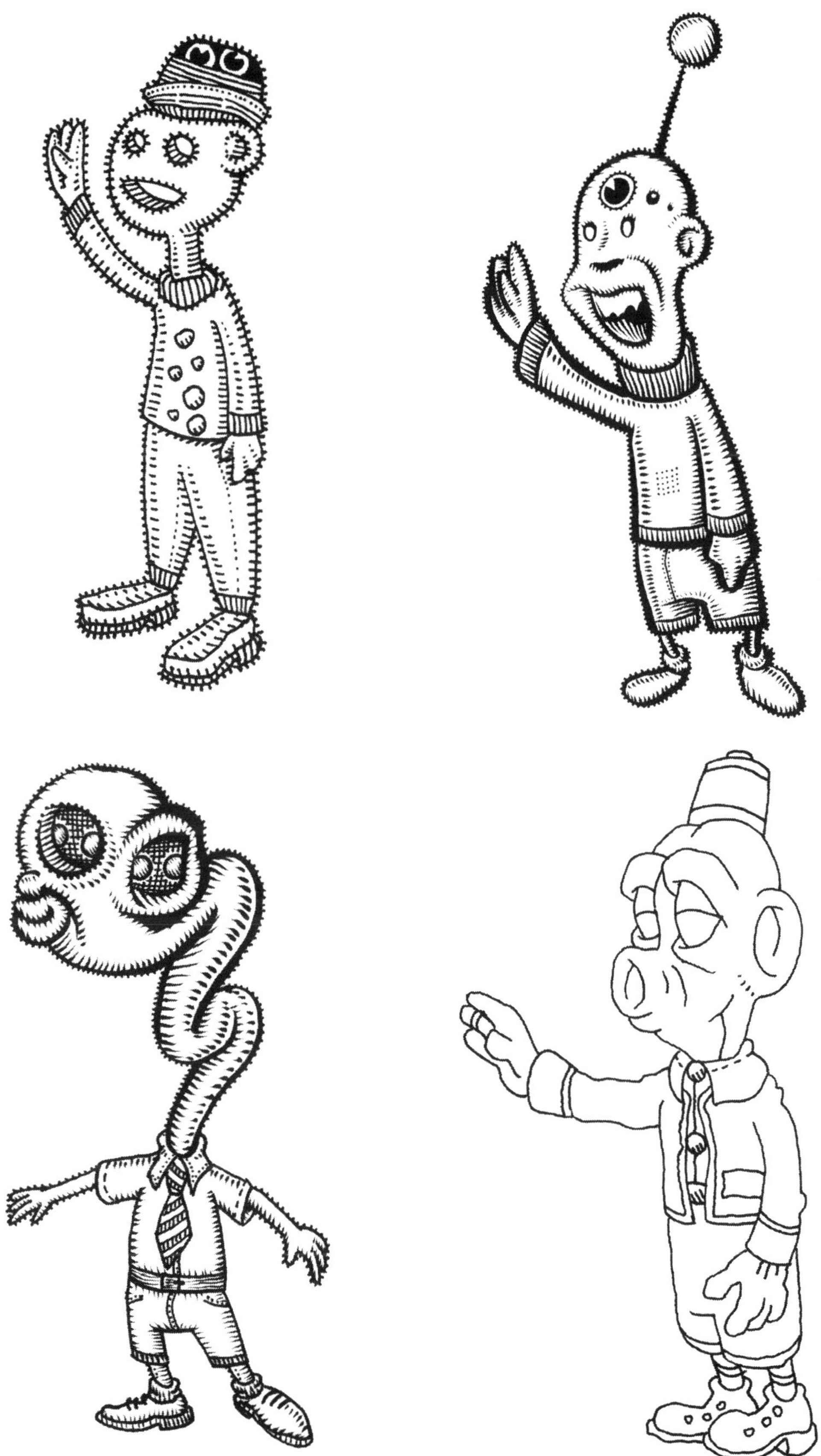

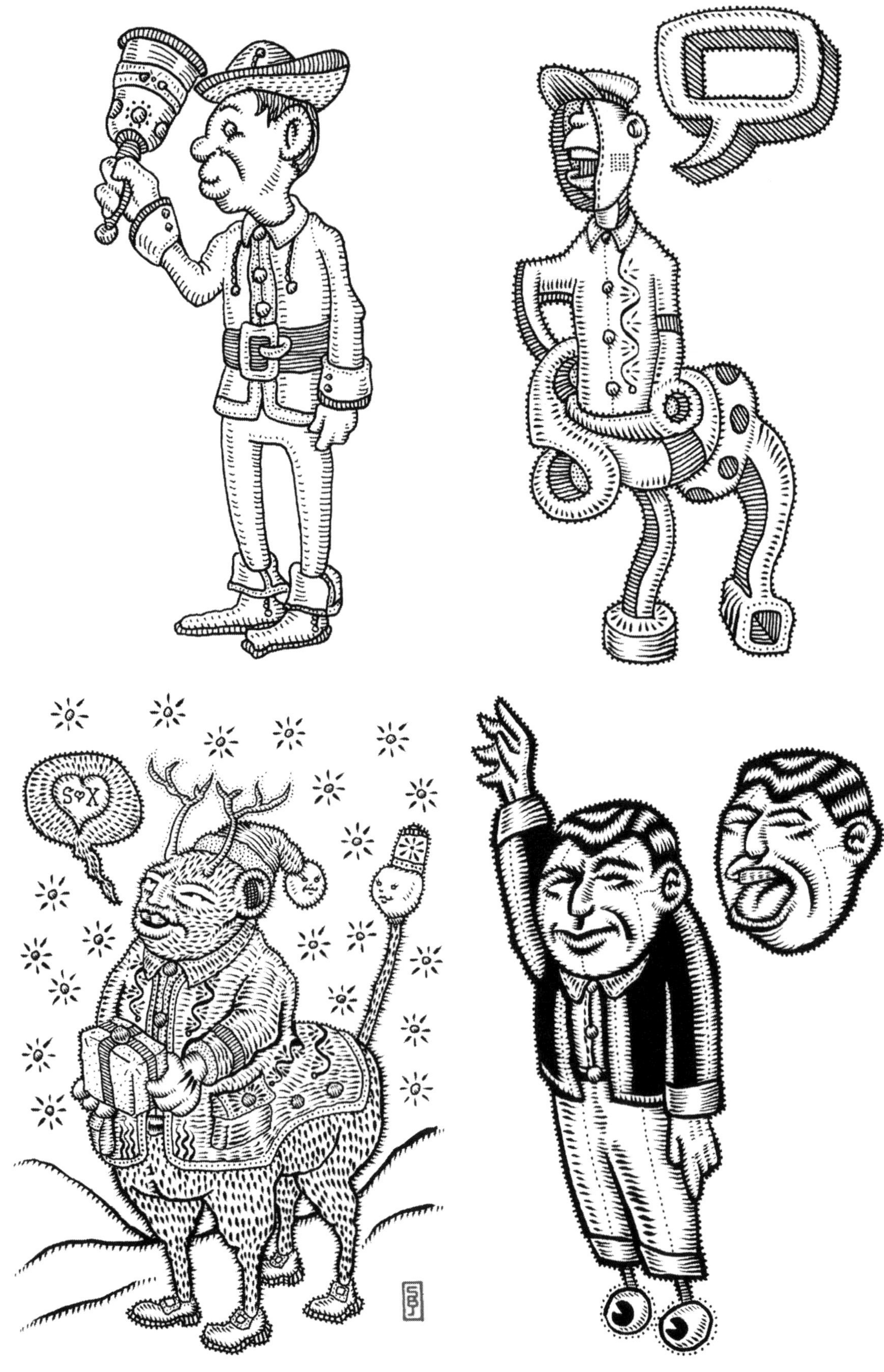
S♥X

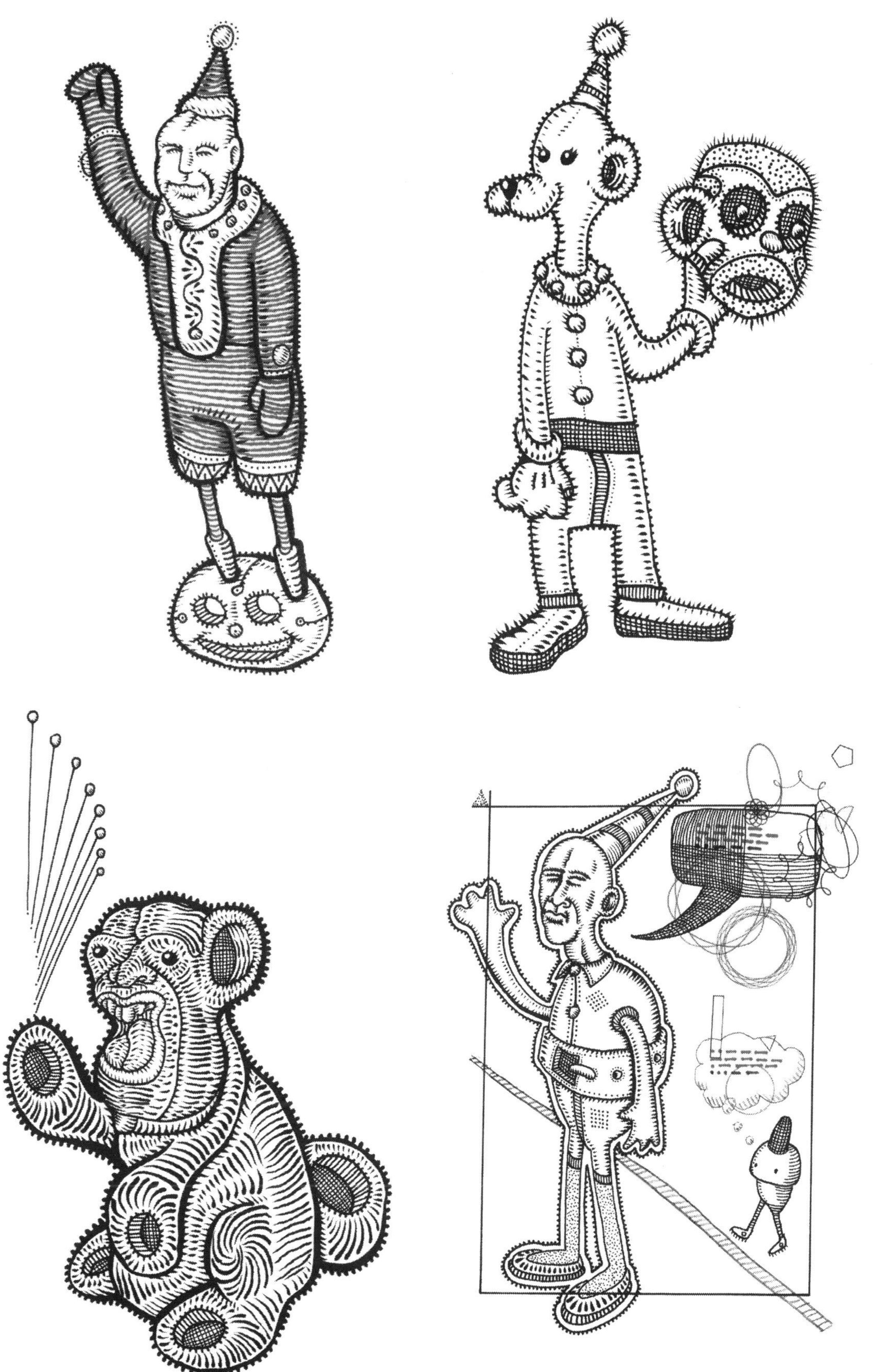

2013

JANUARY

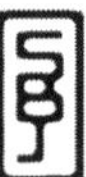

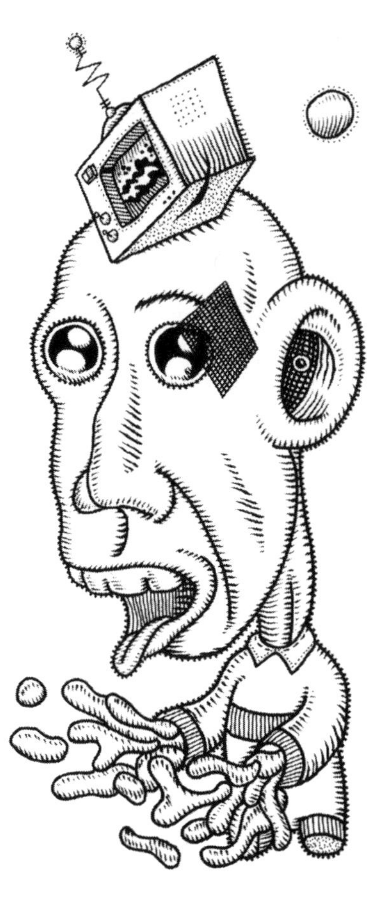

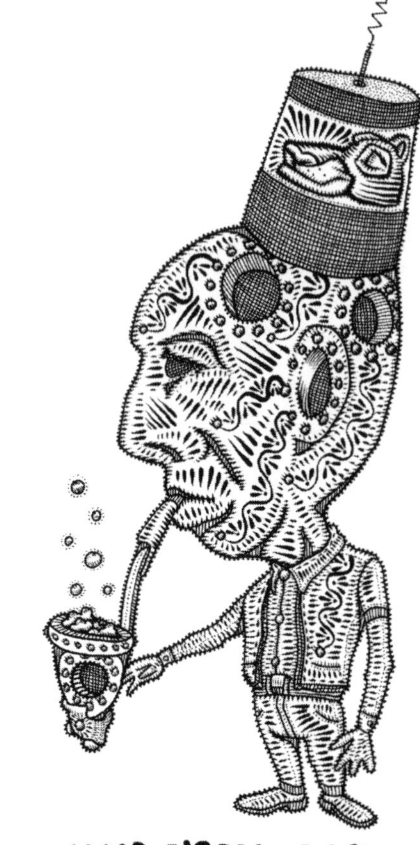

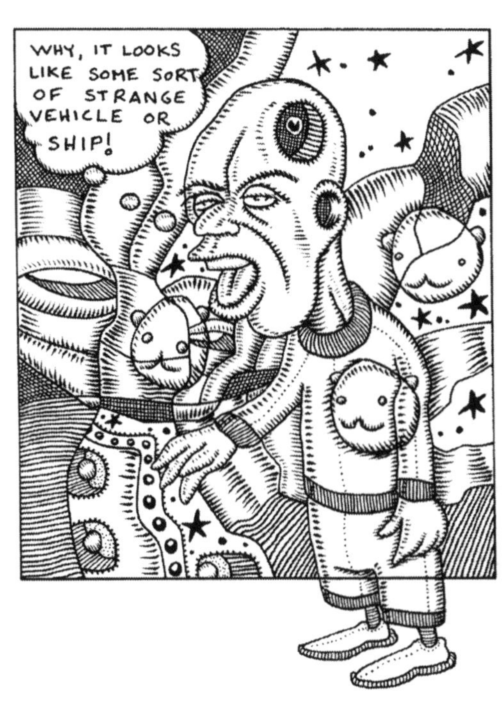
WHY, IT LOOKS LIKE SOME SORT OF STRANGE VEHICLE OR SHIP!

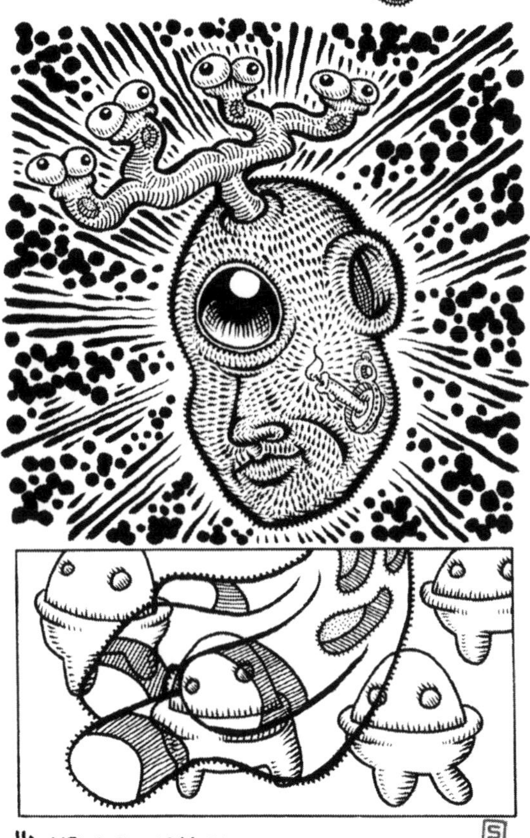
"A NEW STUDY SHOWS...
SBJ

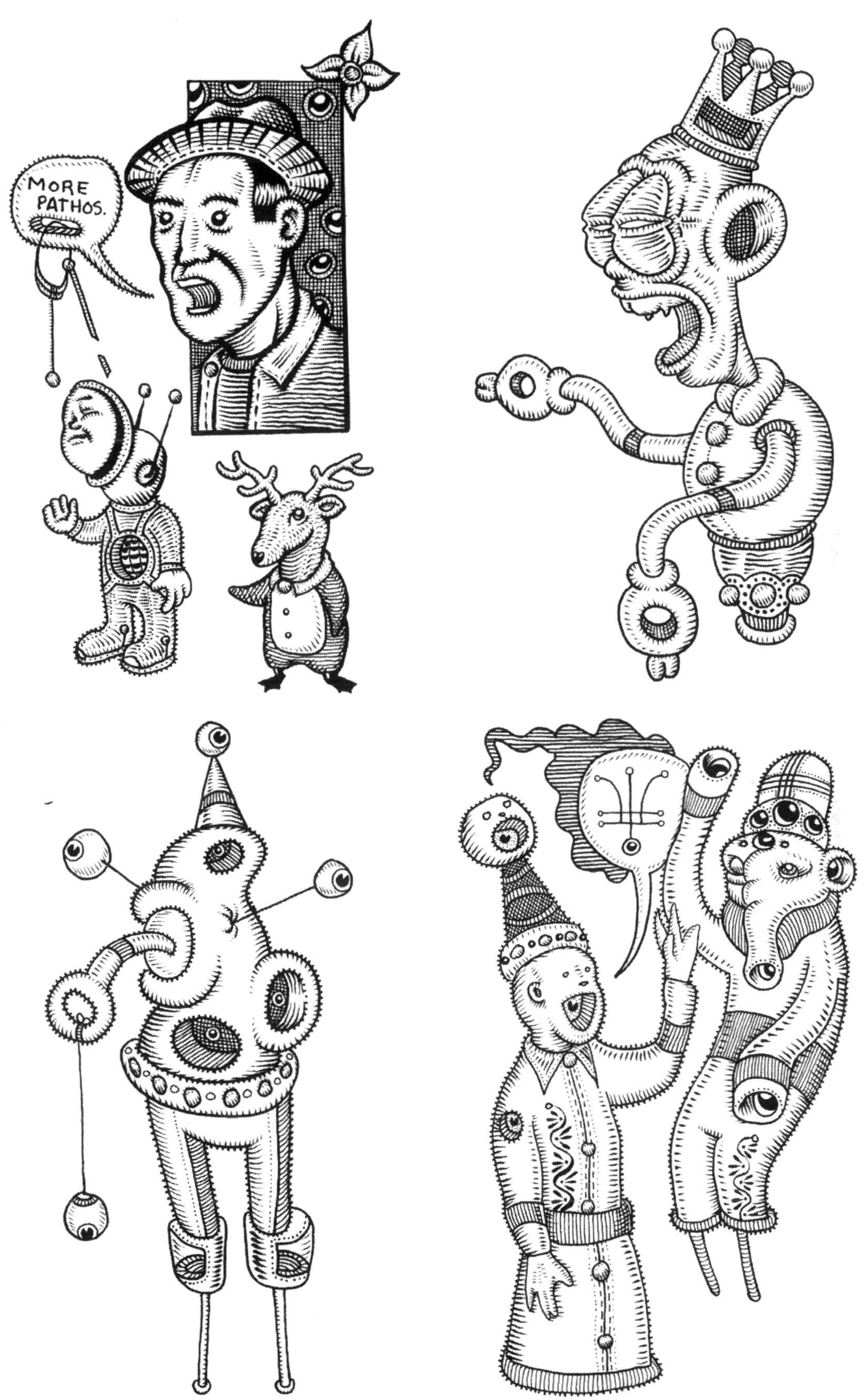
MORE PATHOS.

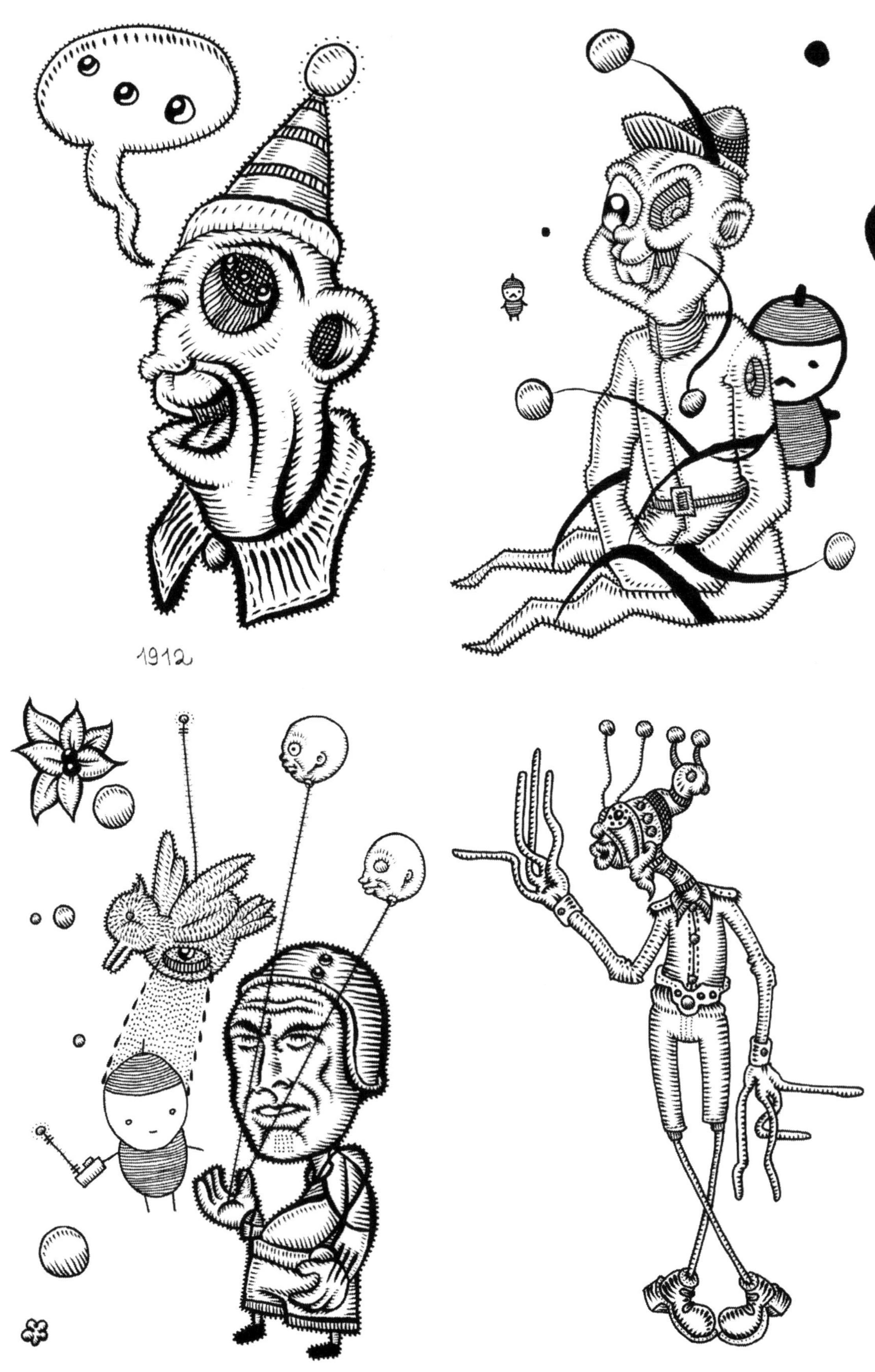
1912

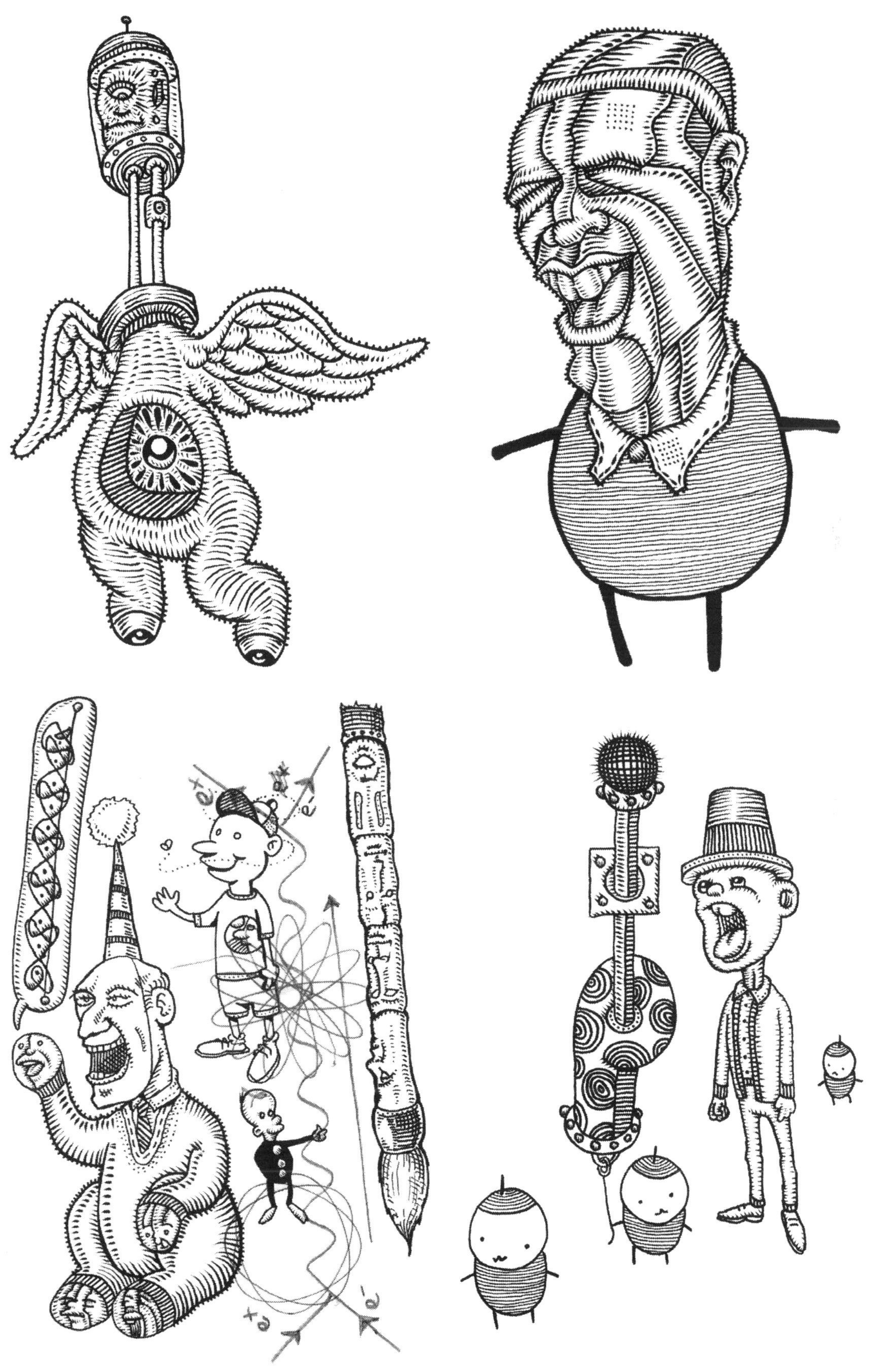

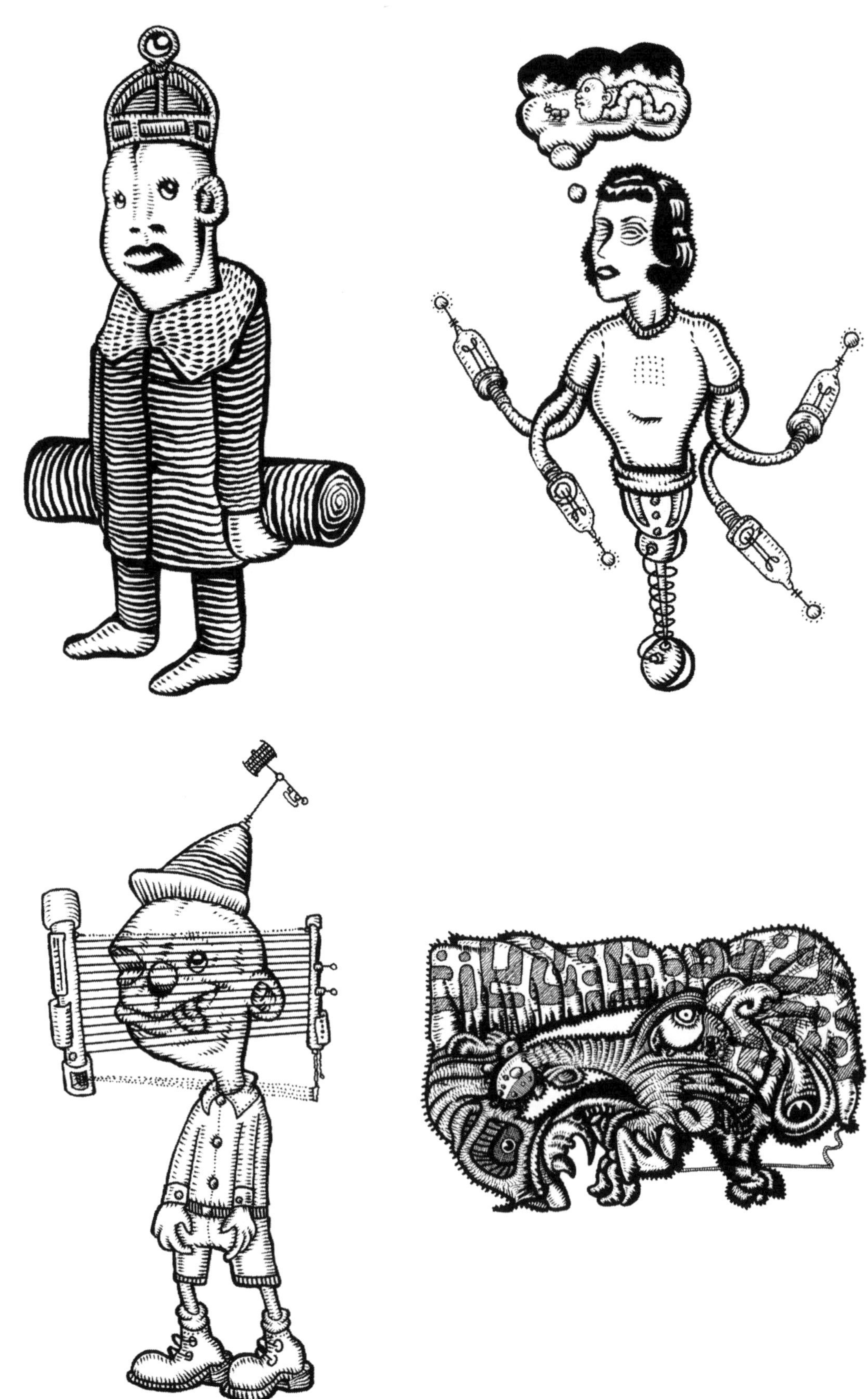

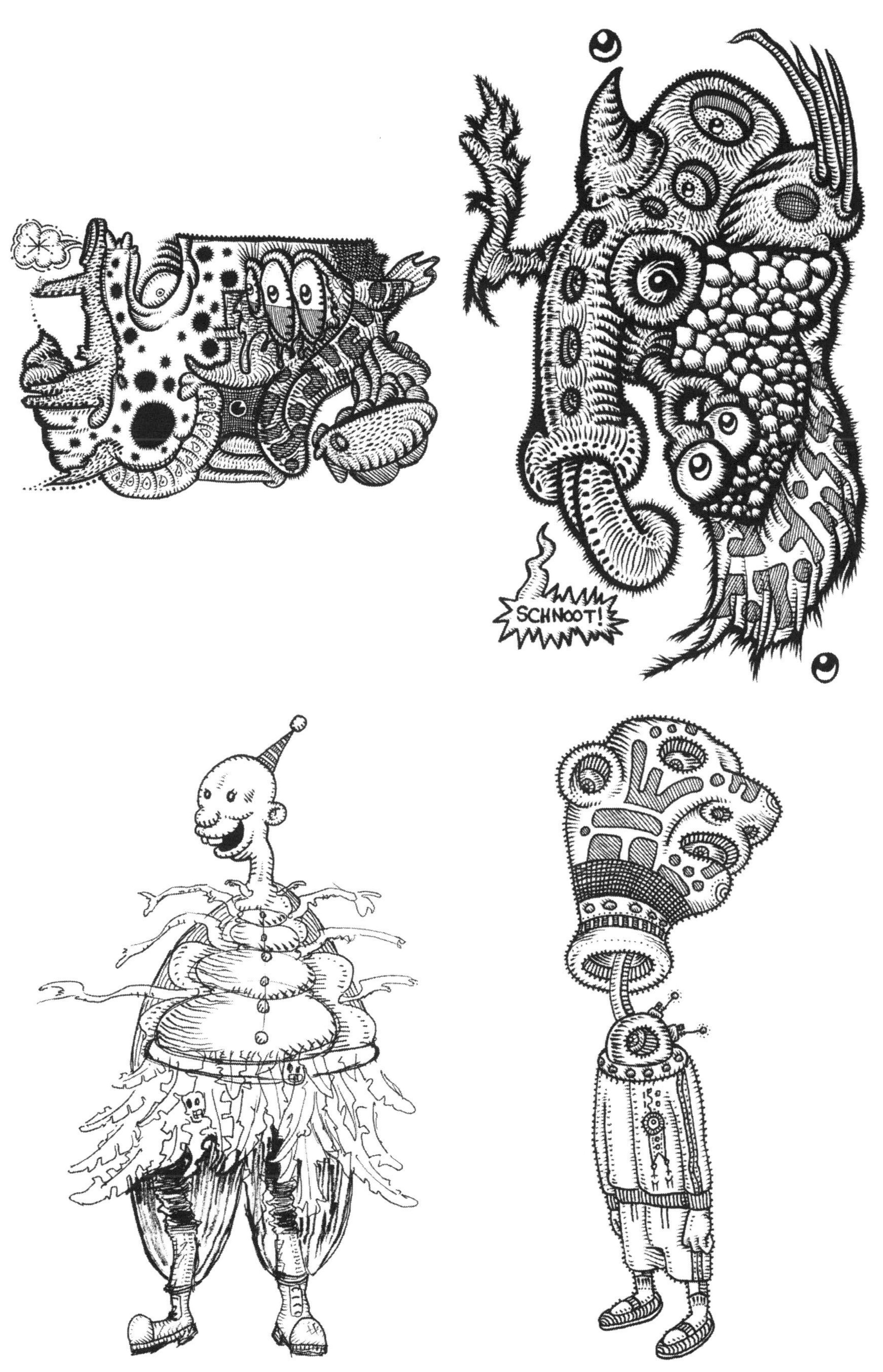
SCHNOOT!

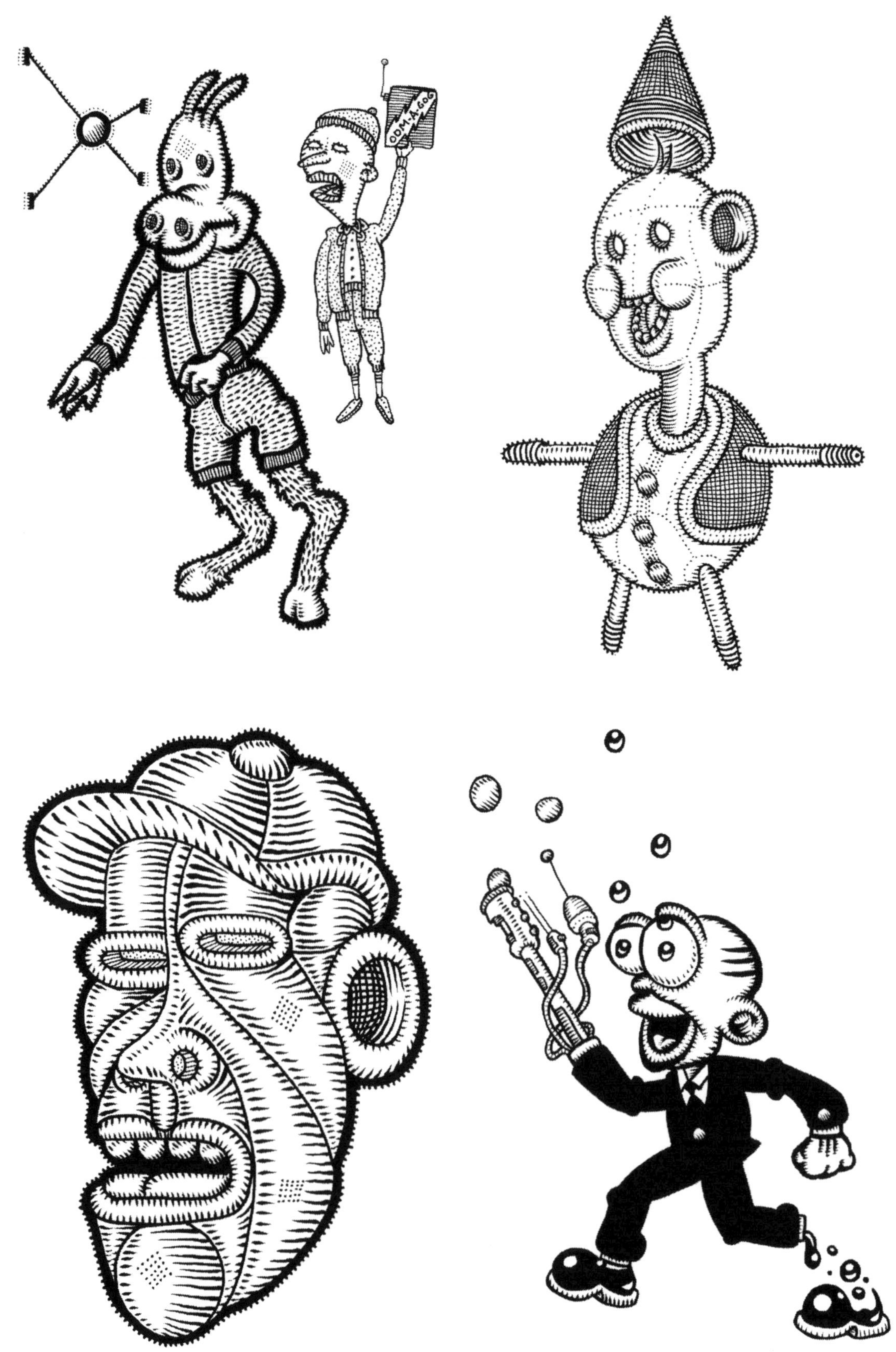
ODM-A-GOG

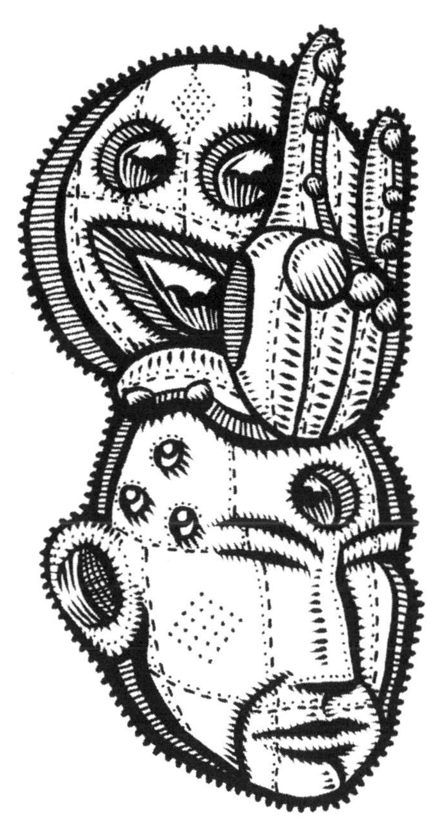

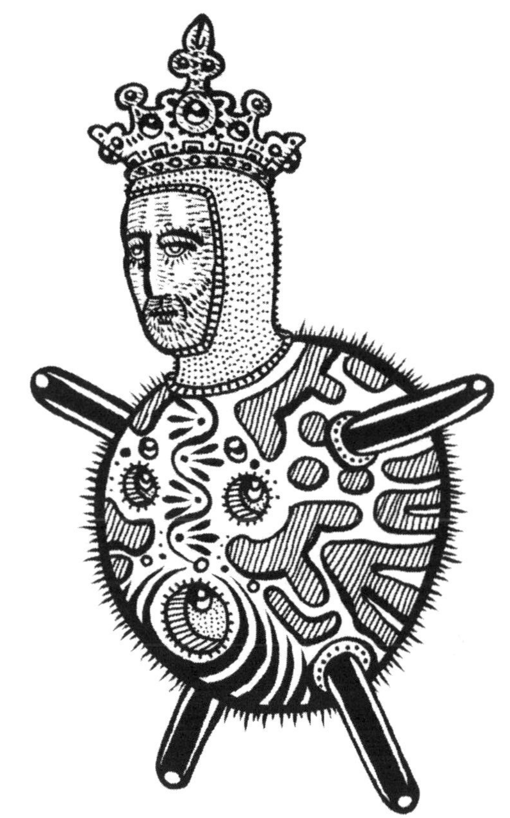

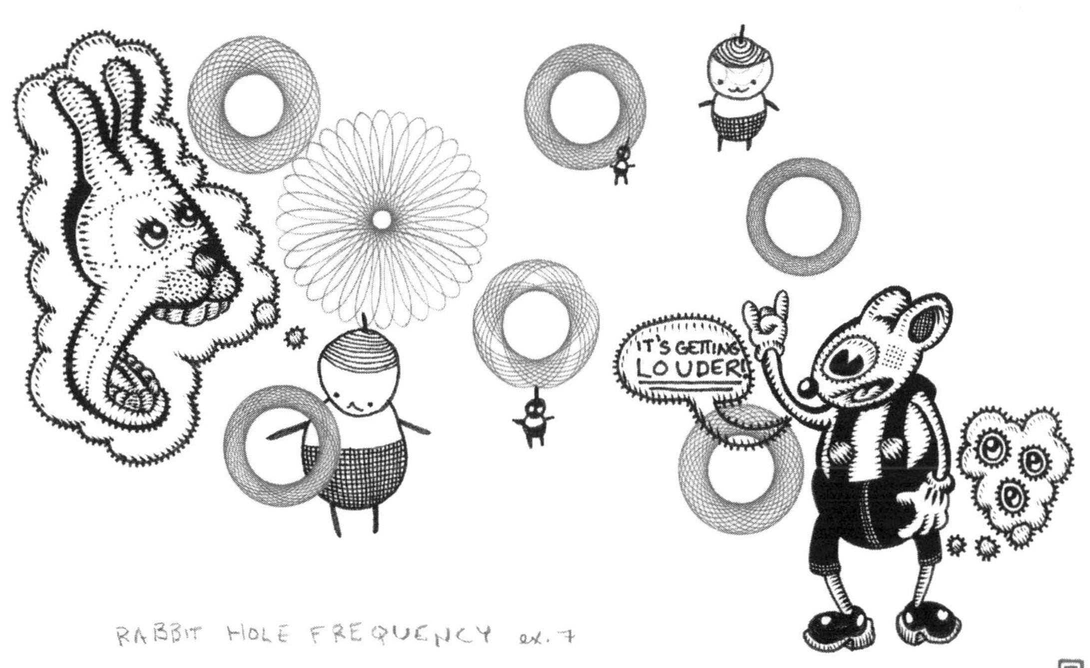
IT'S GETTING LOUDER!
RABBIT HOLE FREQUENCY ex. 7

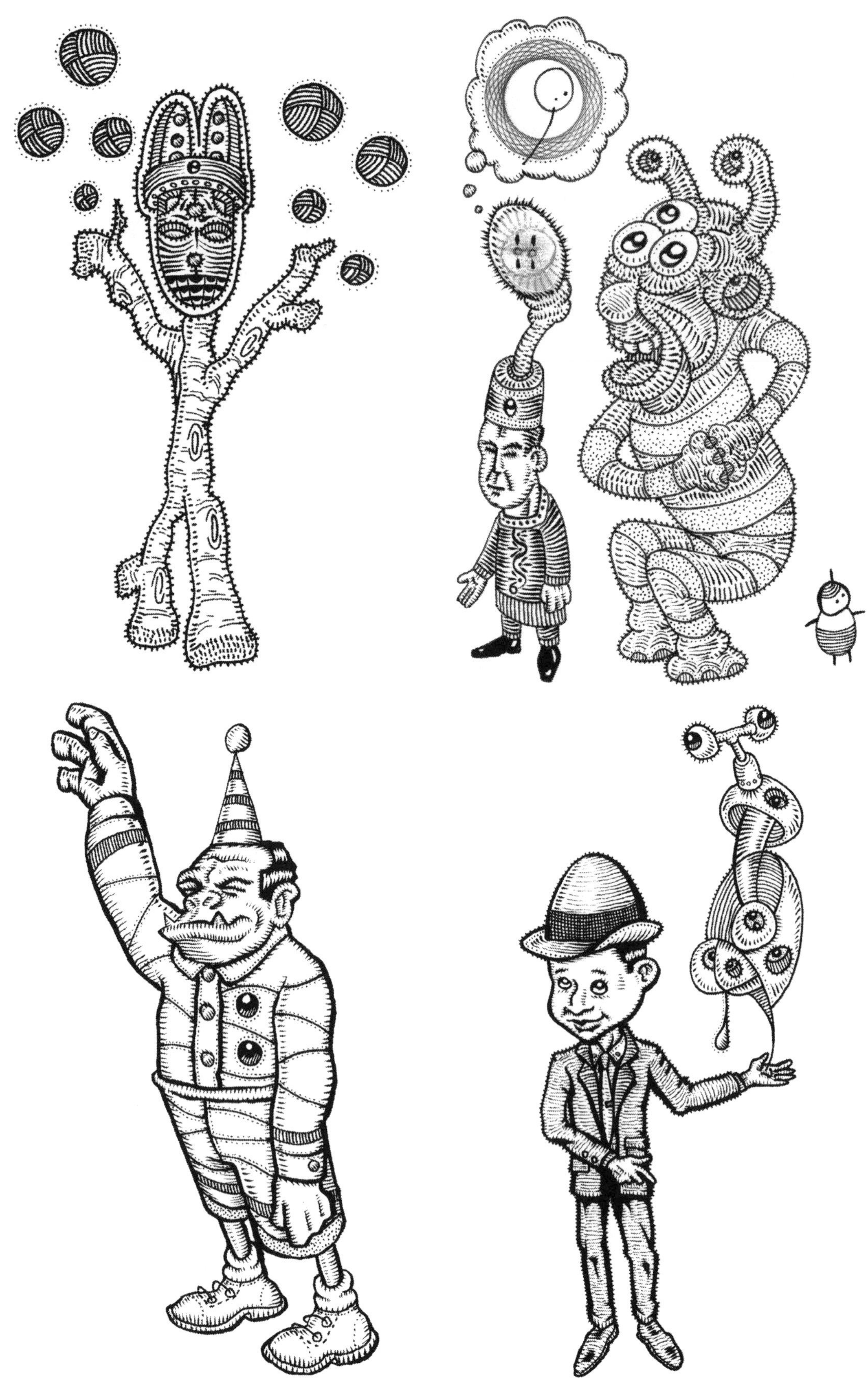

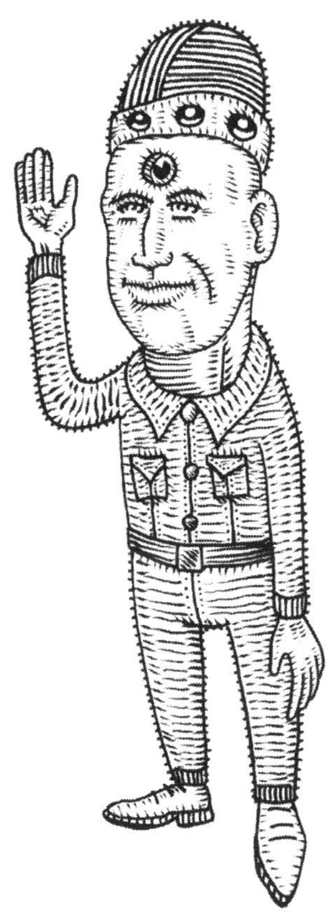

2013

FEBRUARY

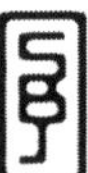

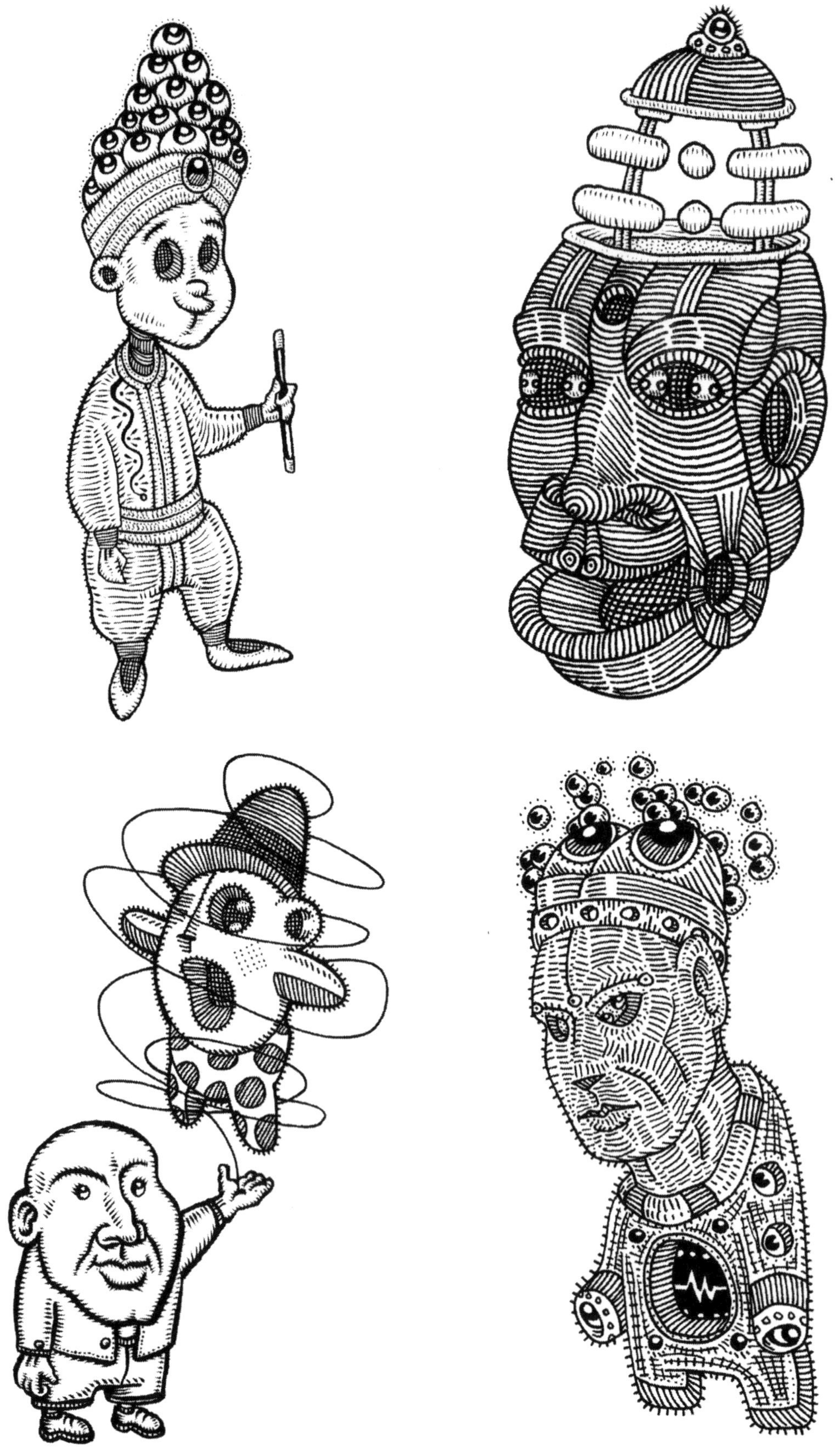

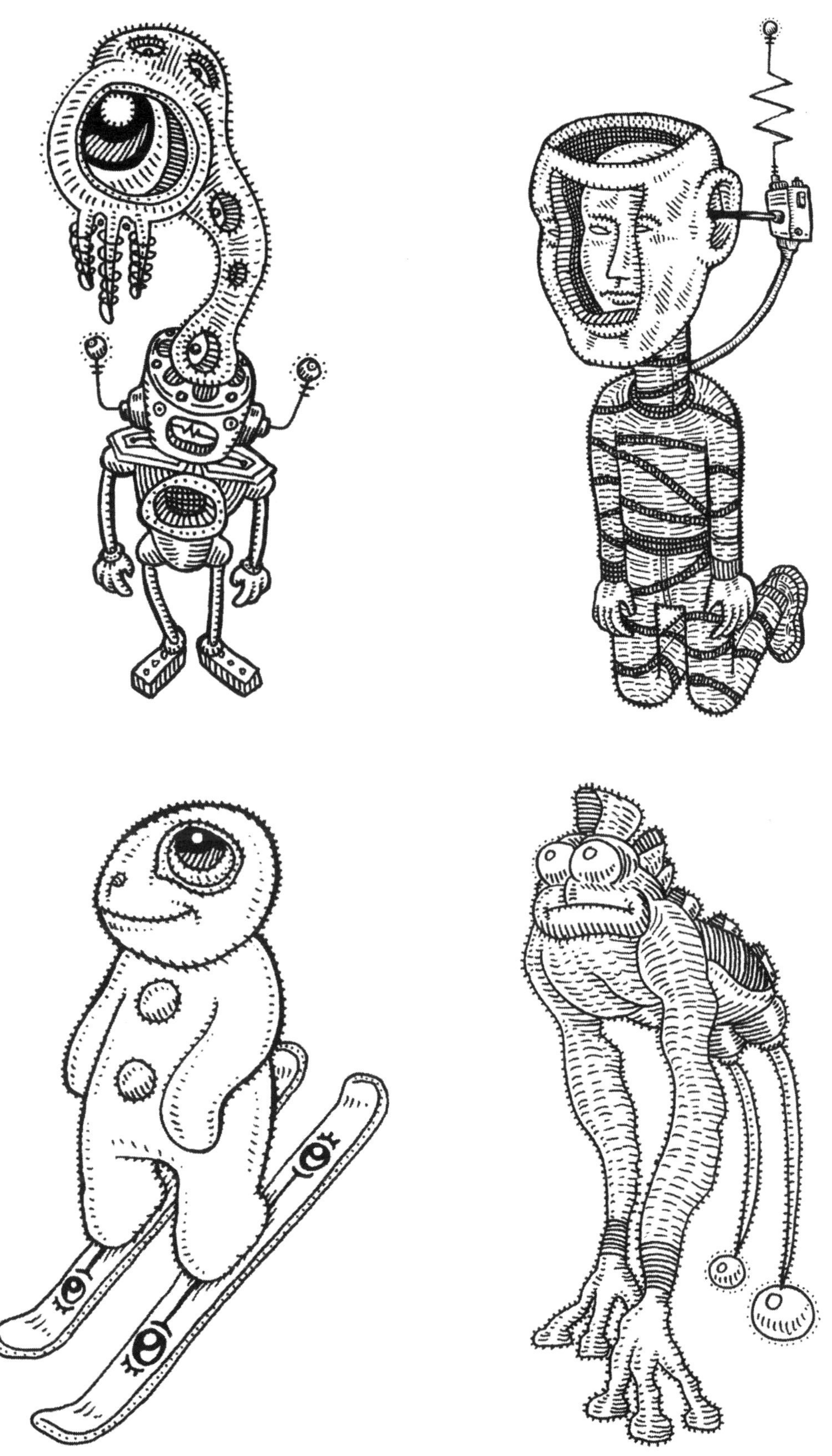

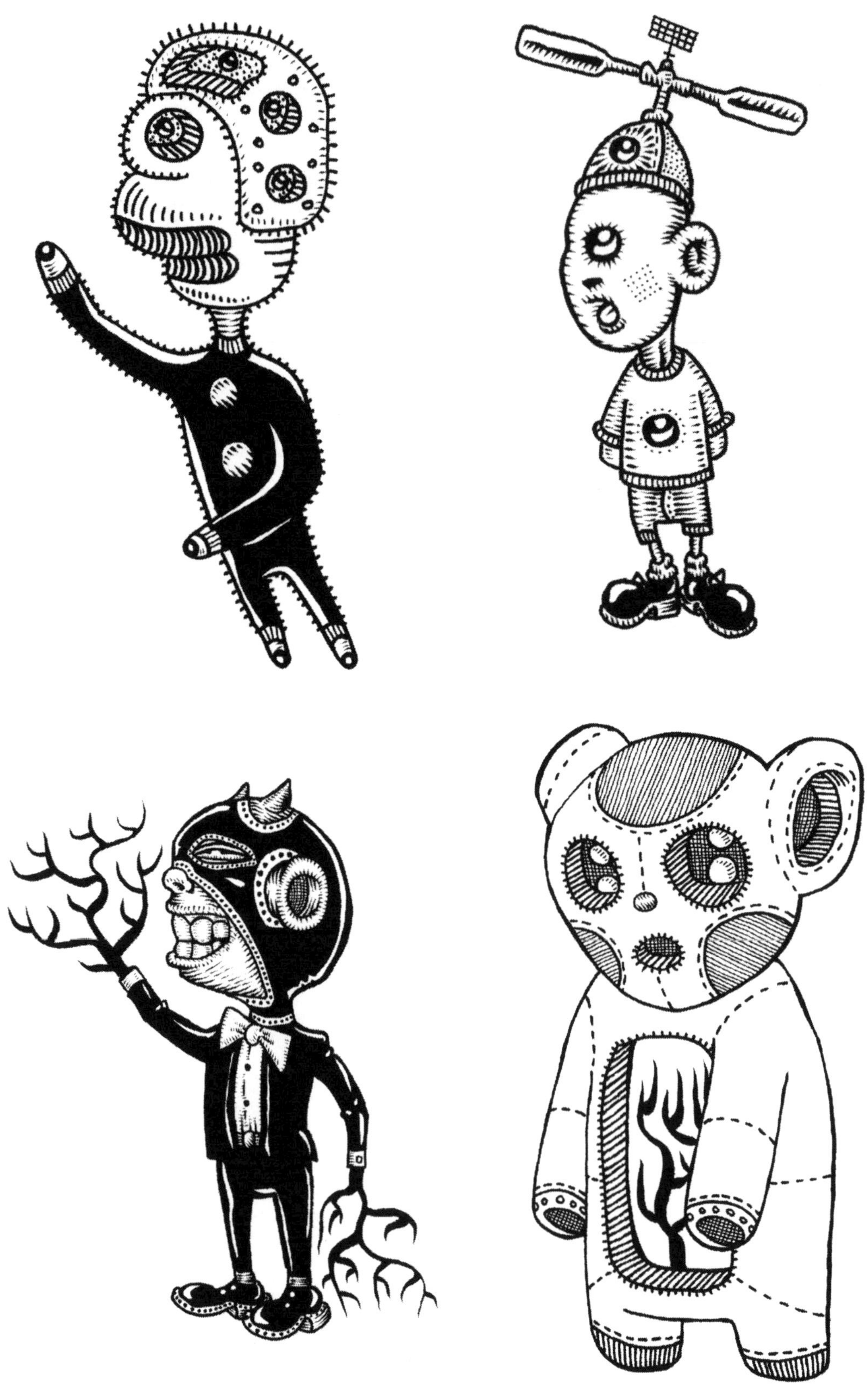

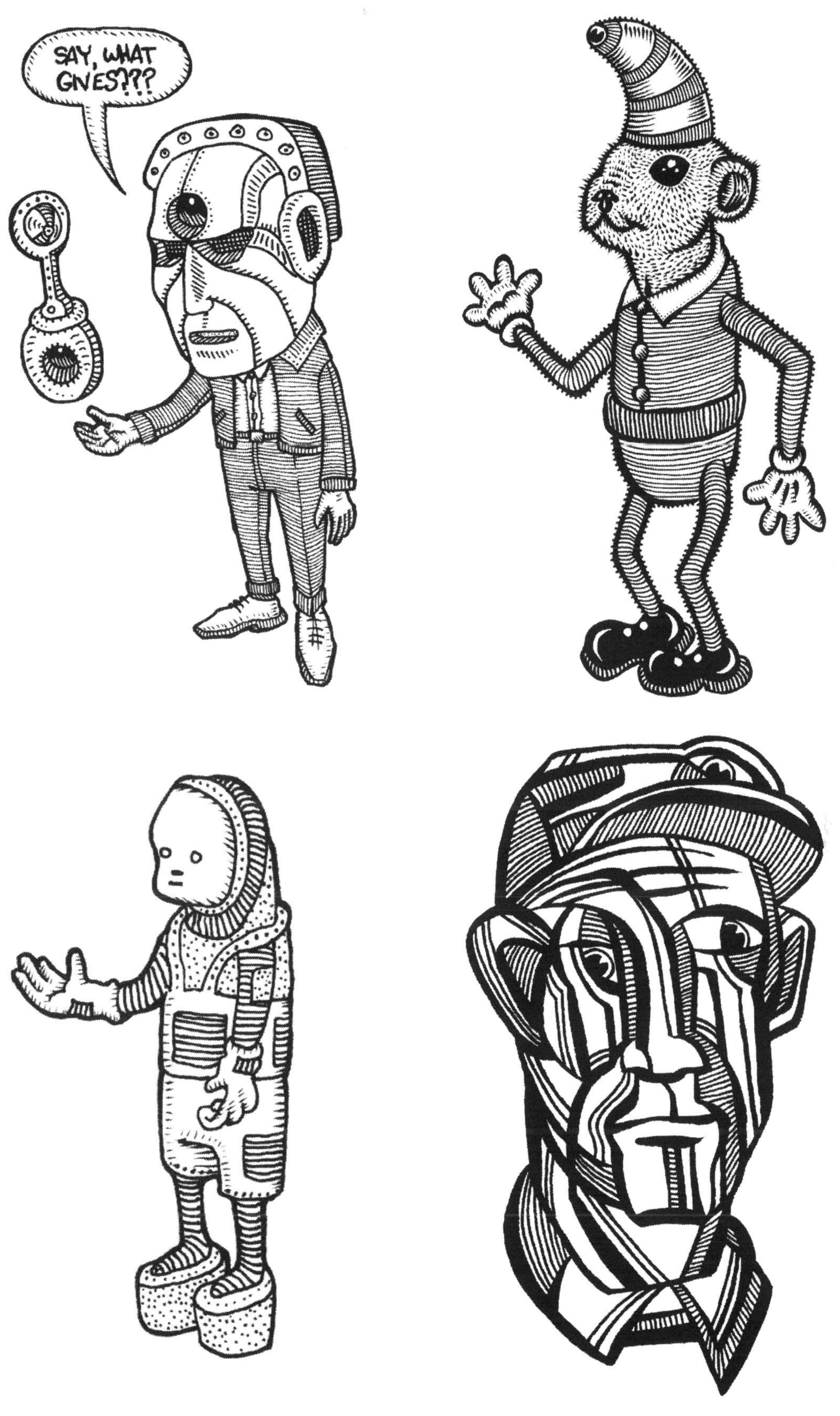
SAY, WHAT GIVES???

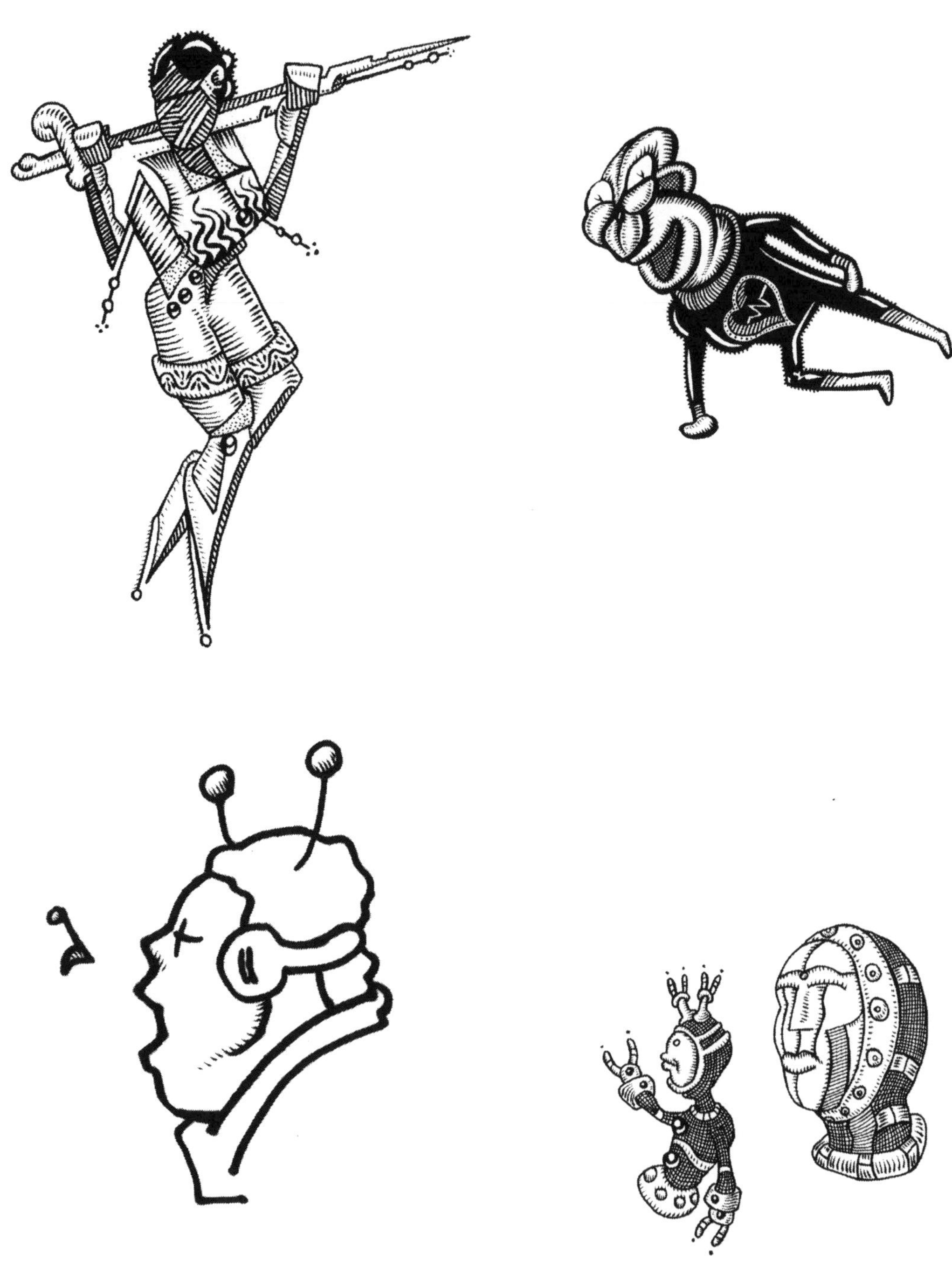

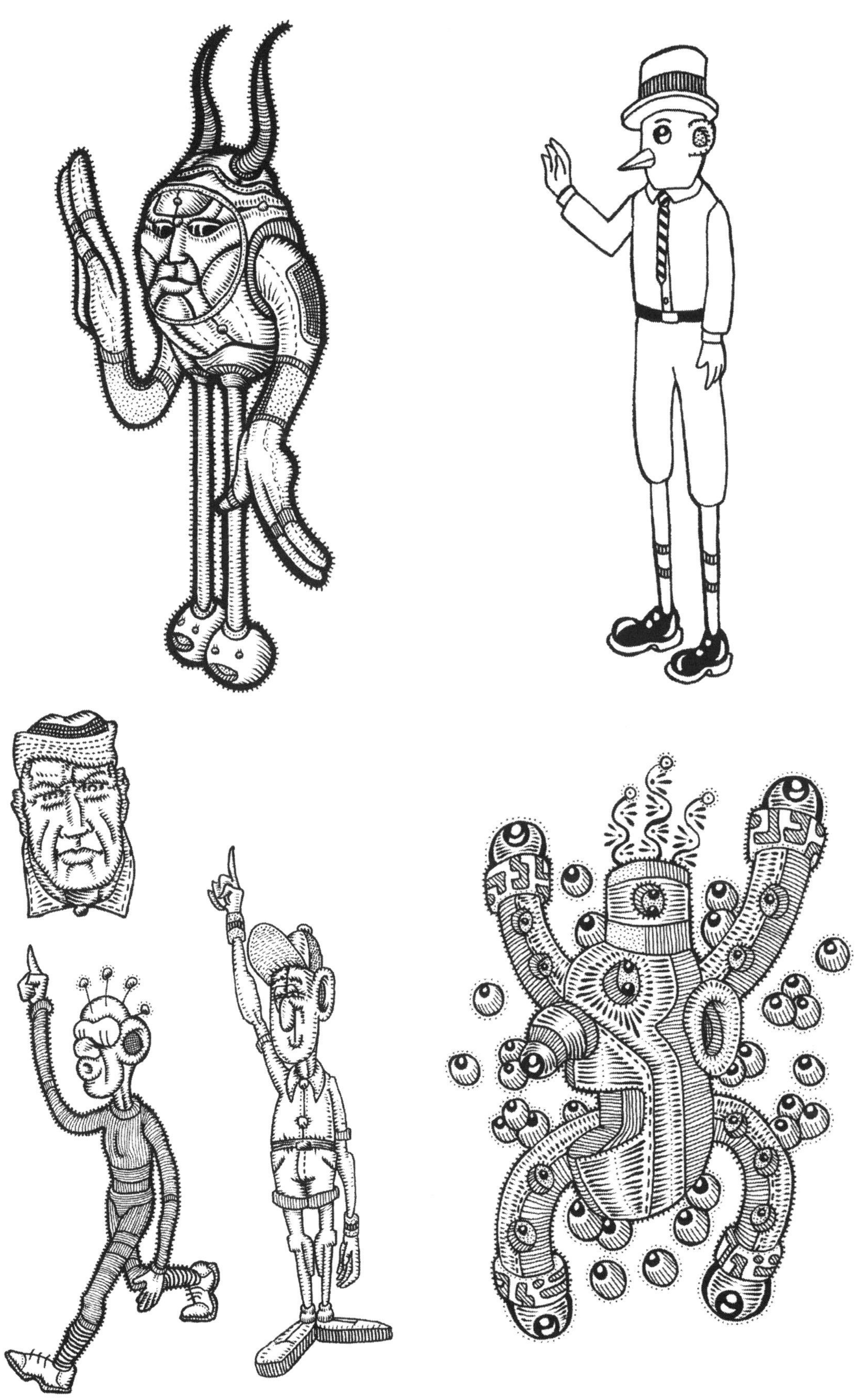

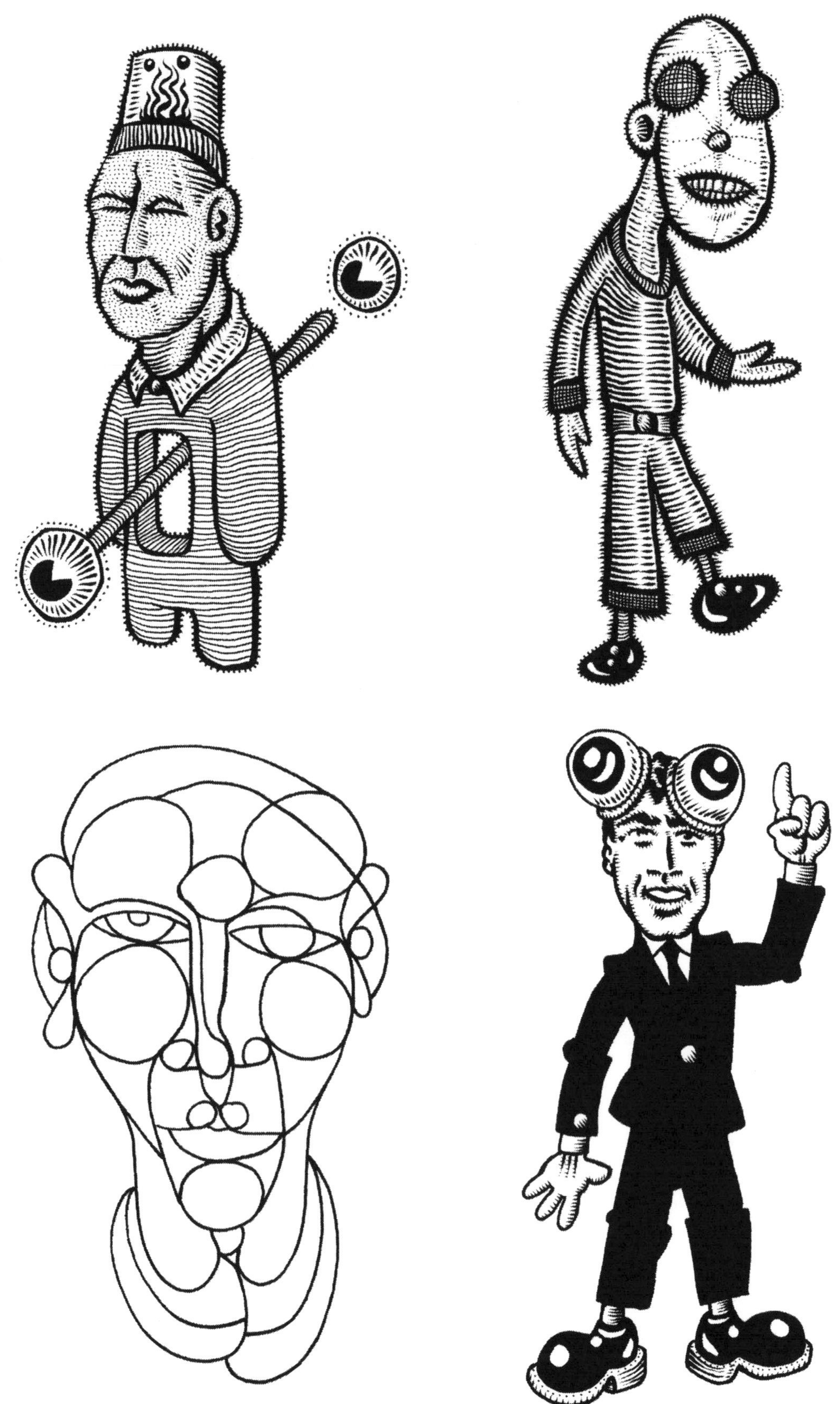

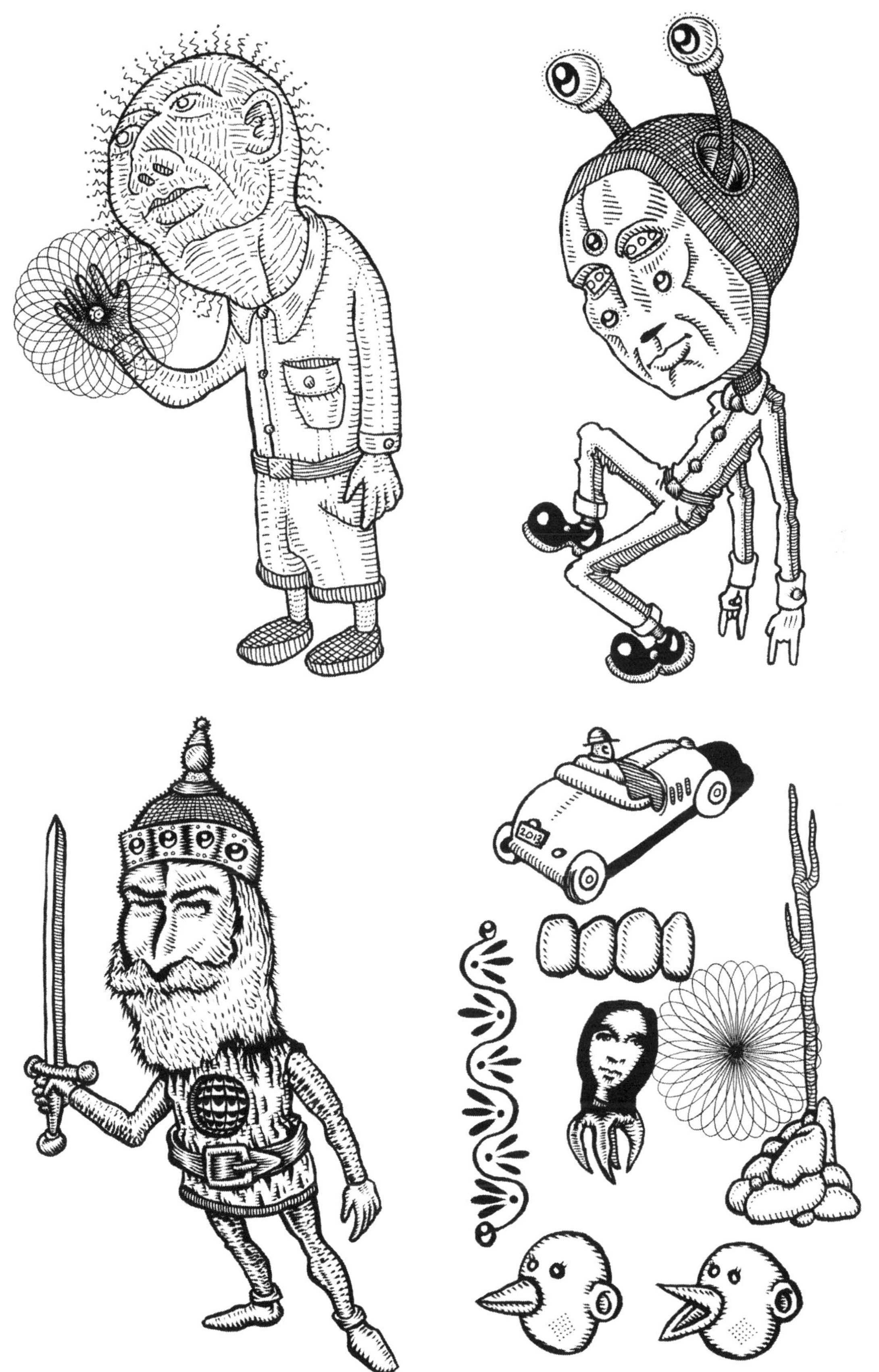
2013

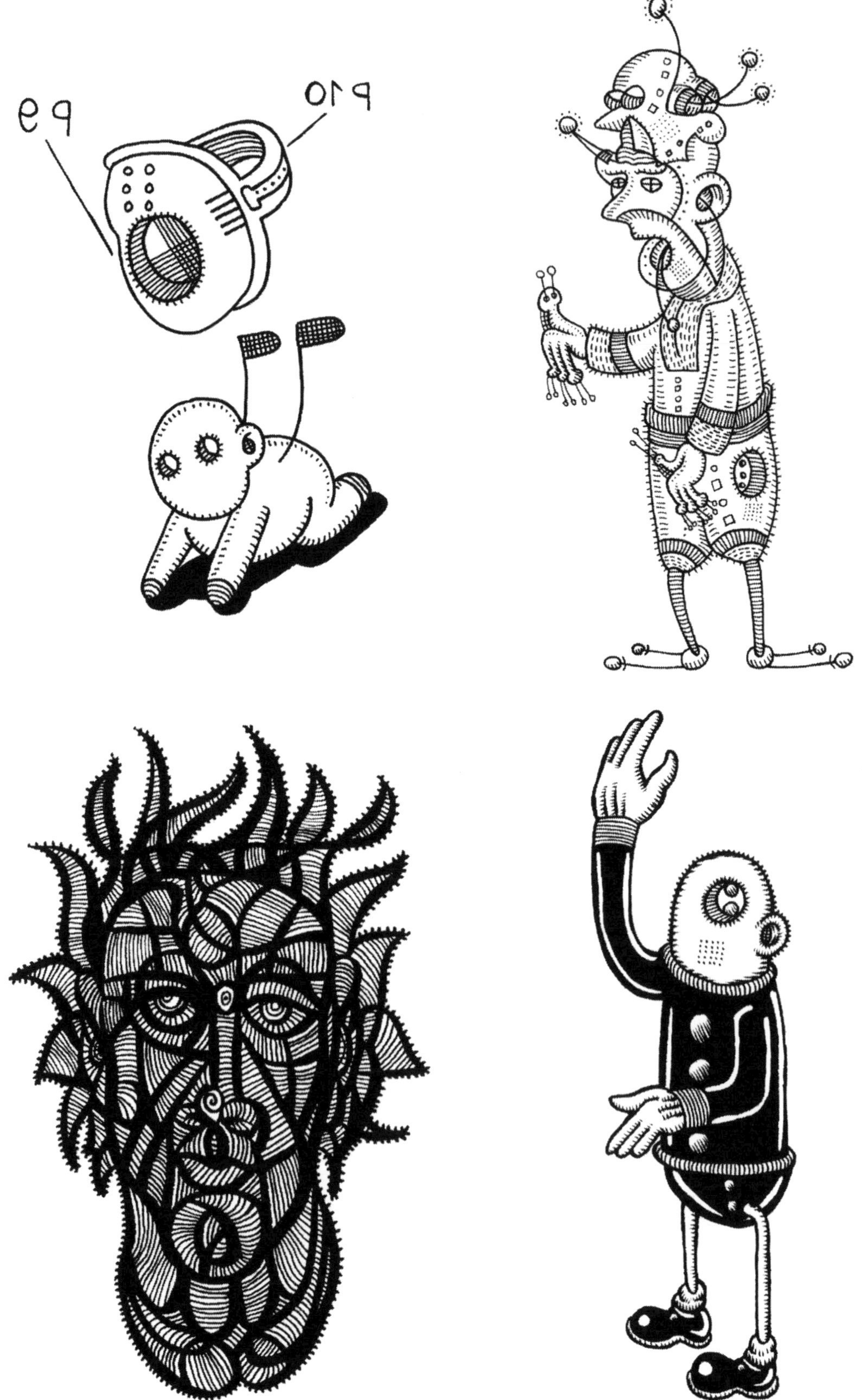
P9
P10

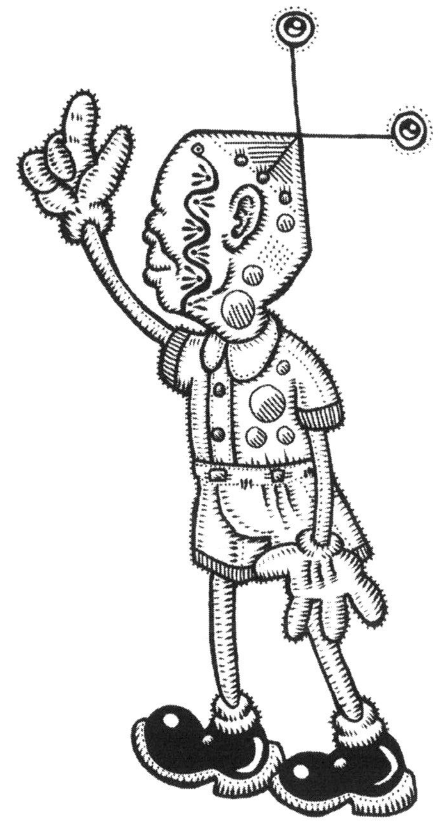

2013

MARCH

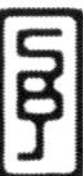

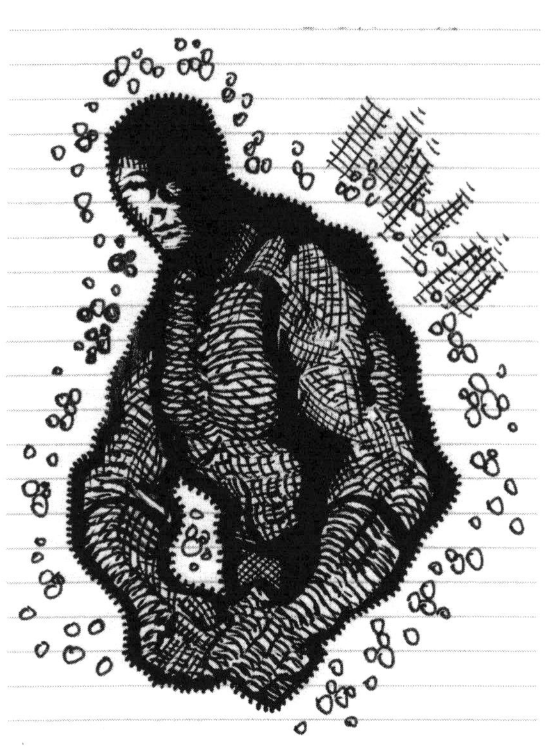

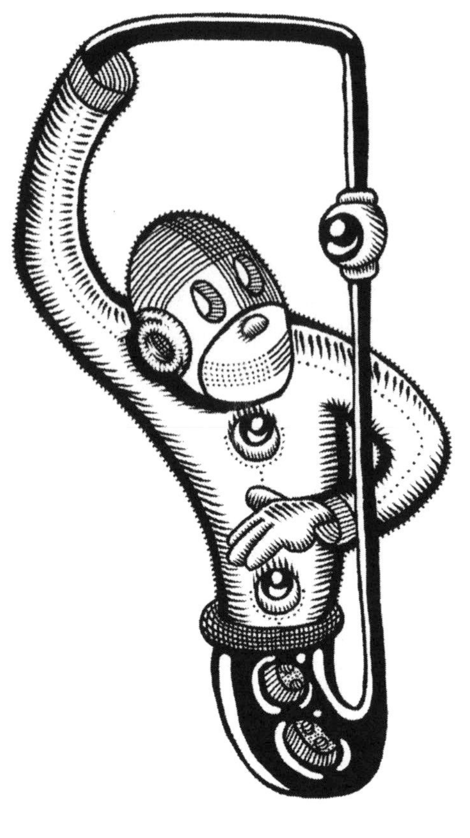

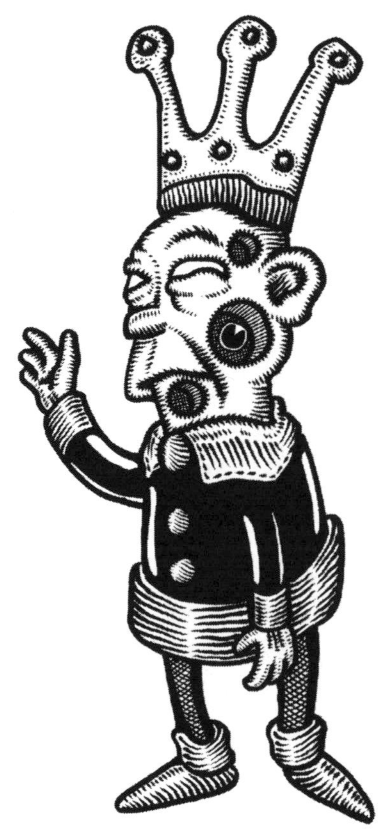

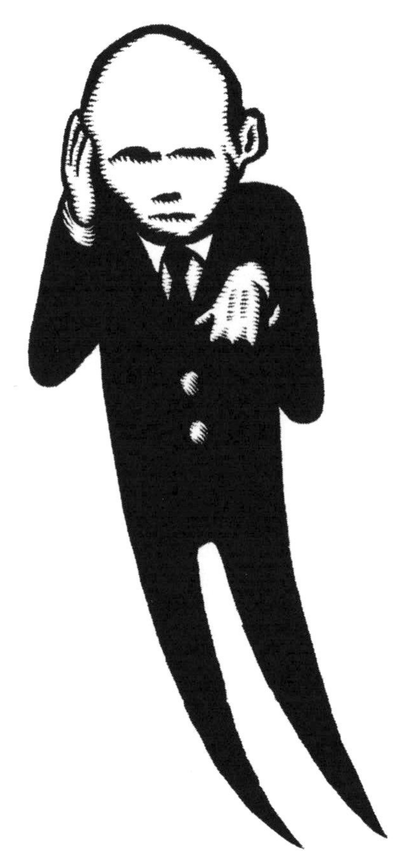

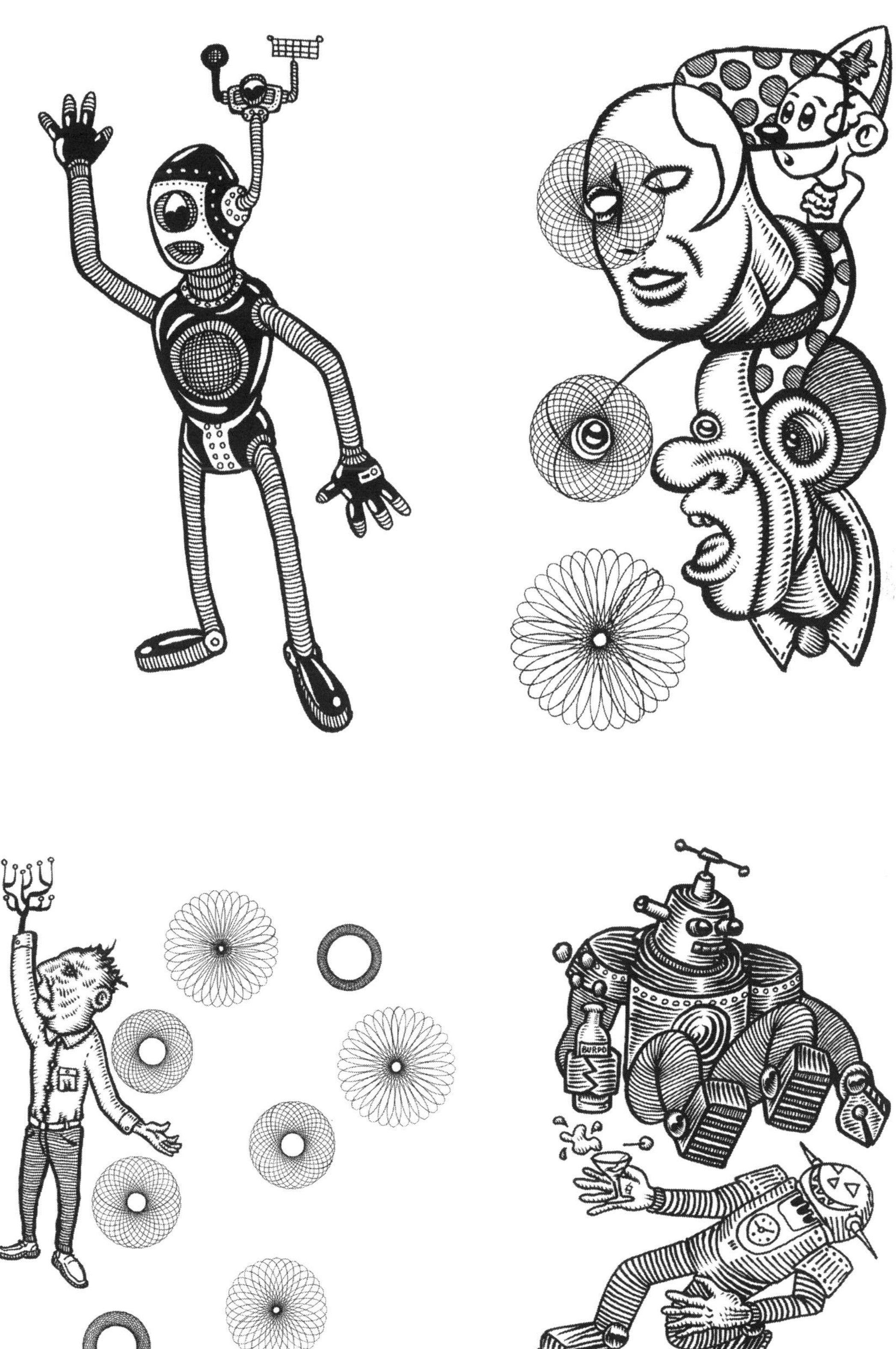
BURPO

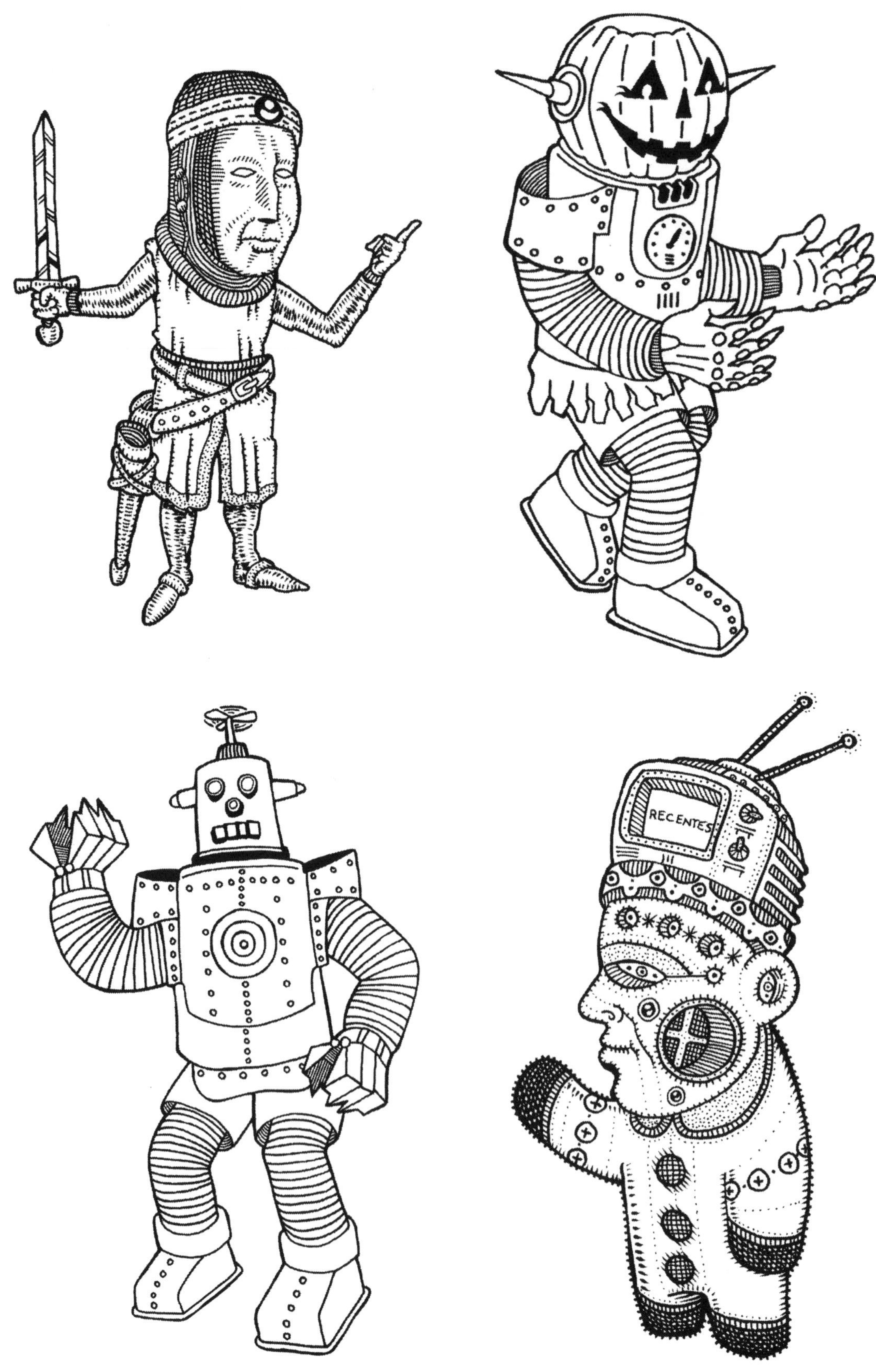
RECENTES

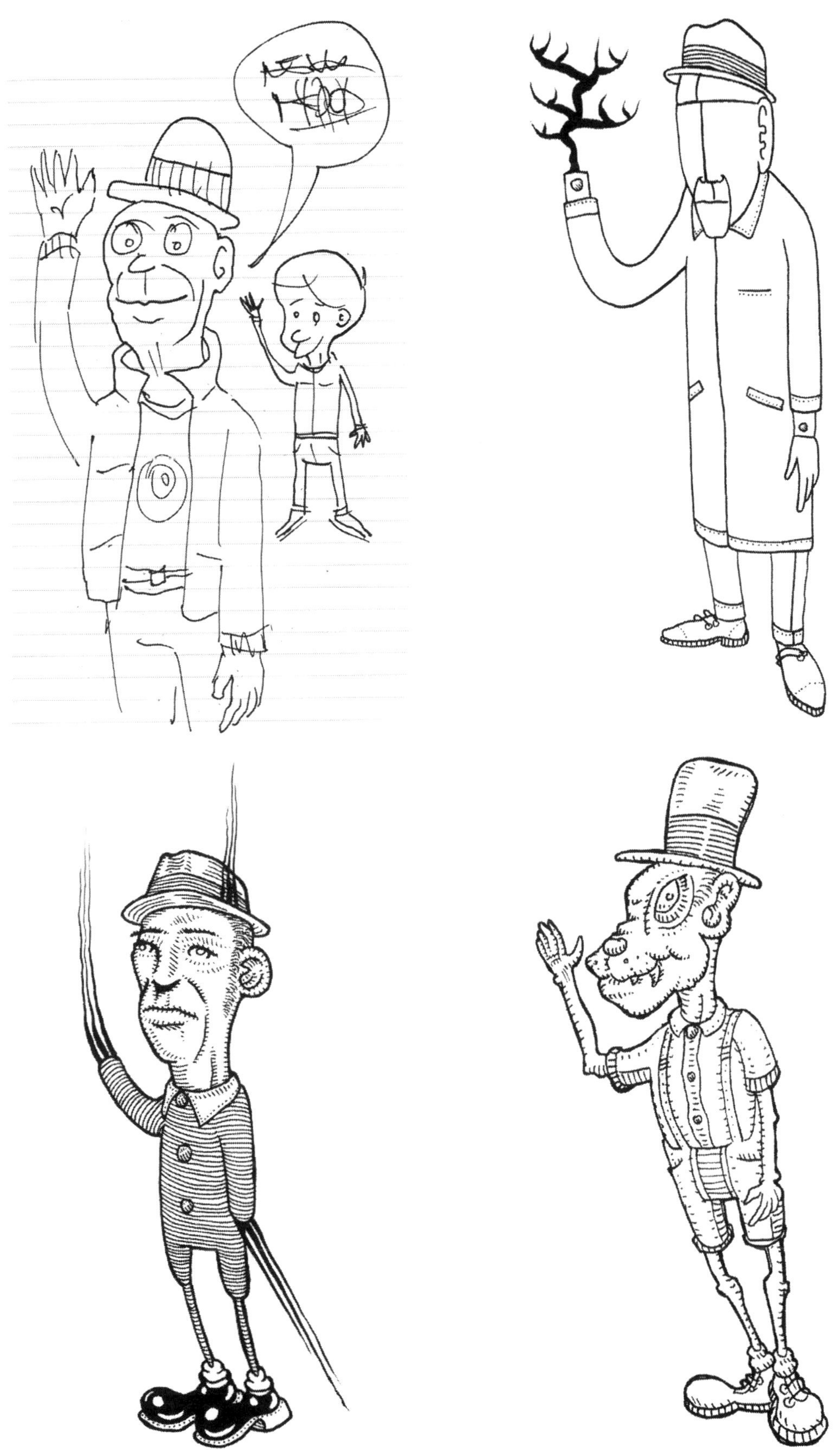

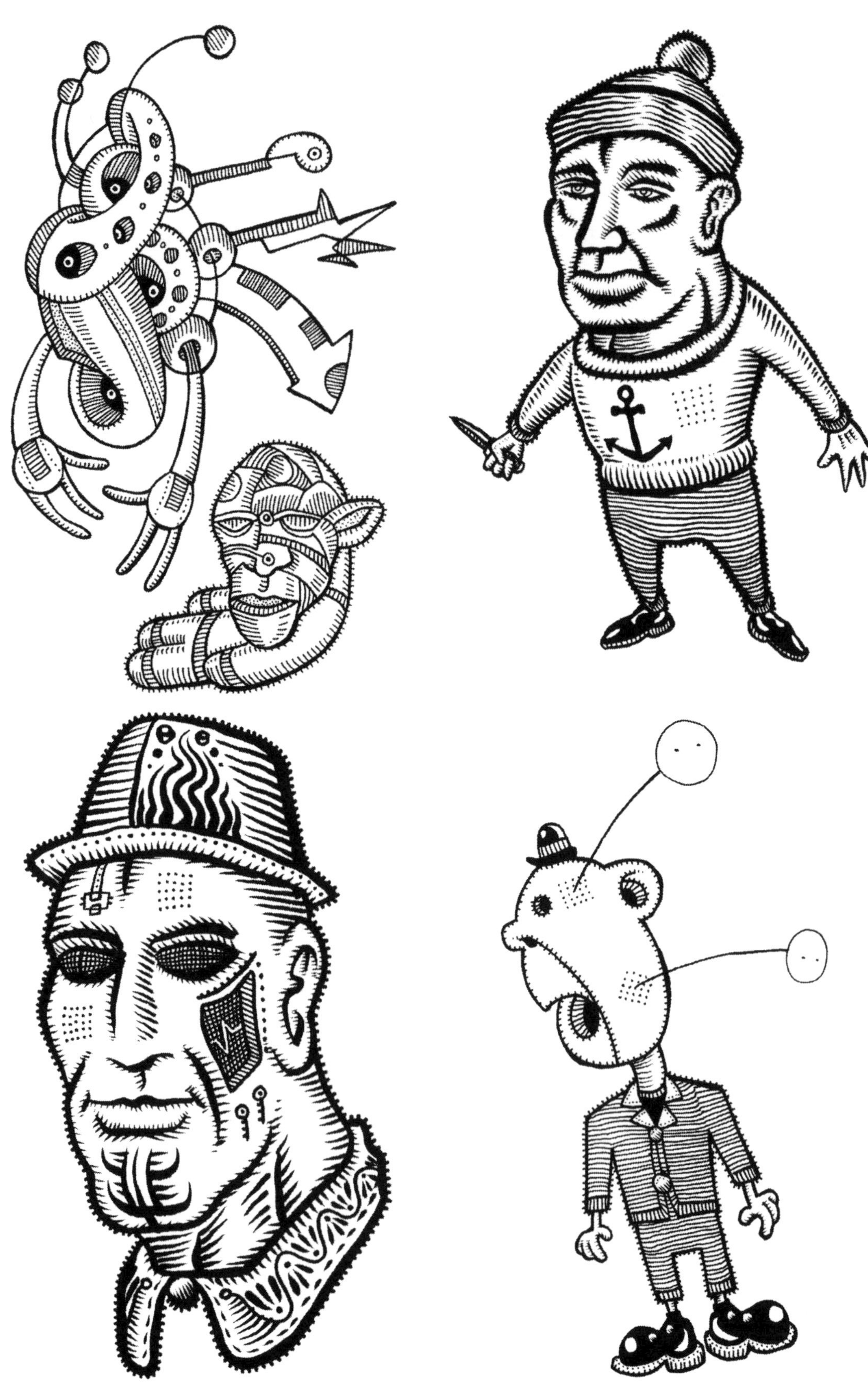

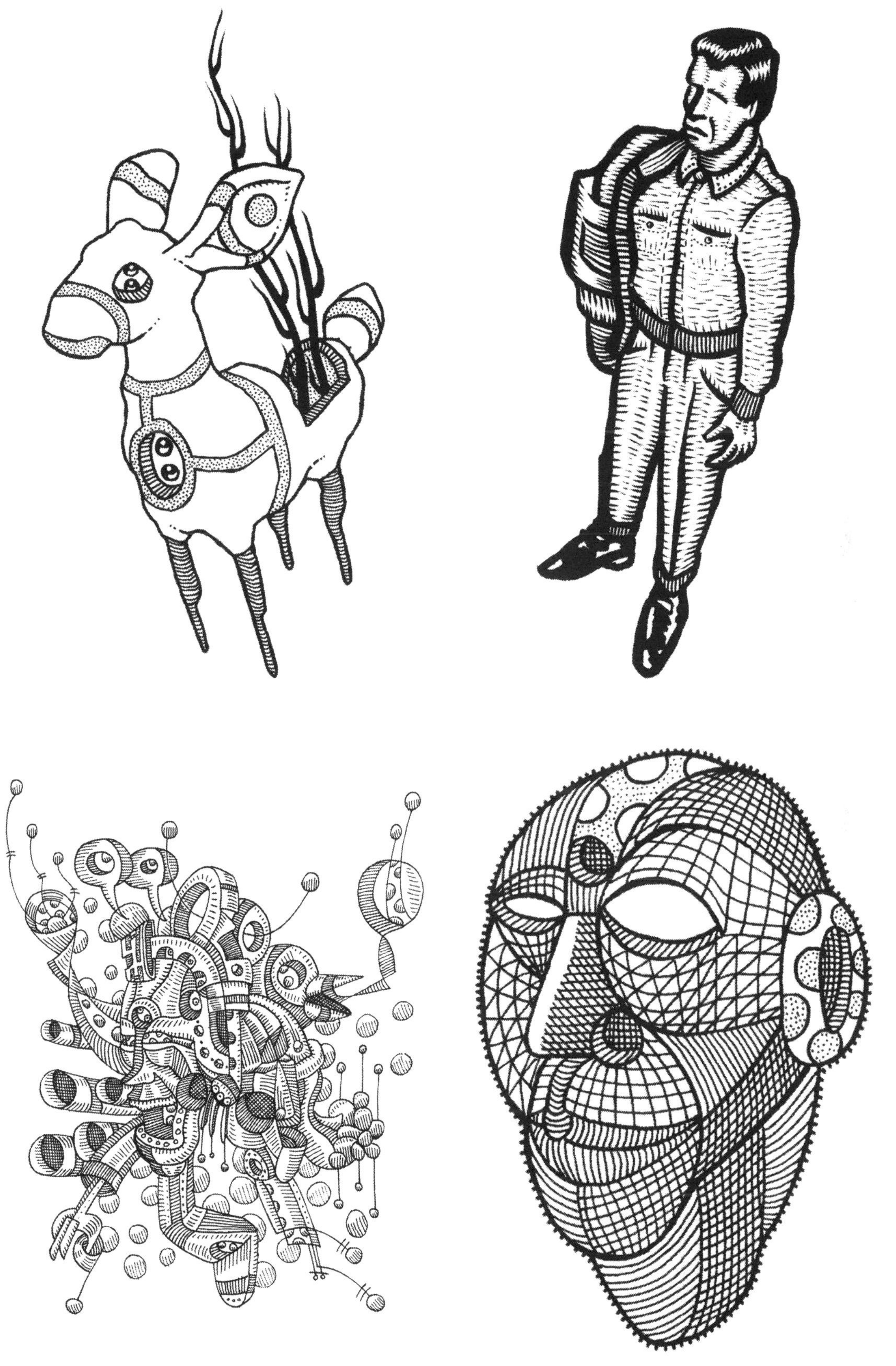

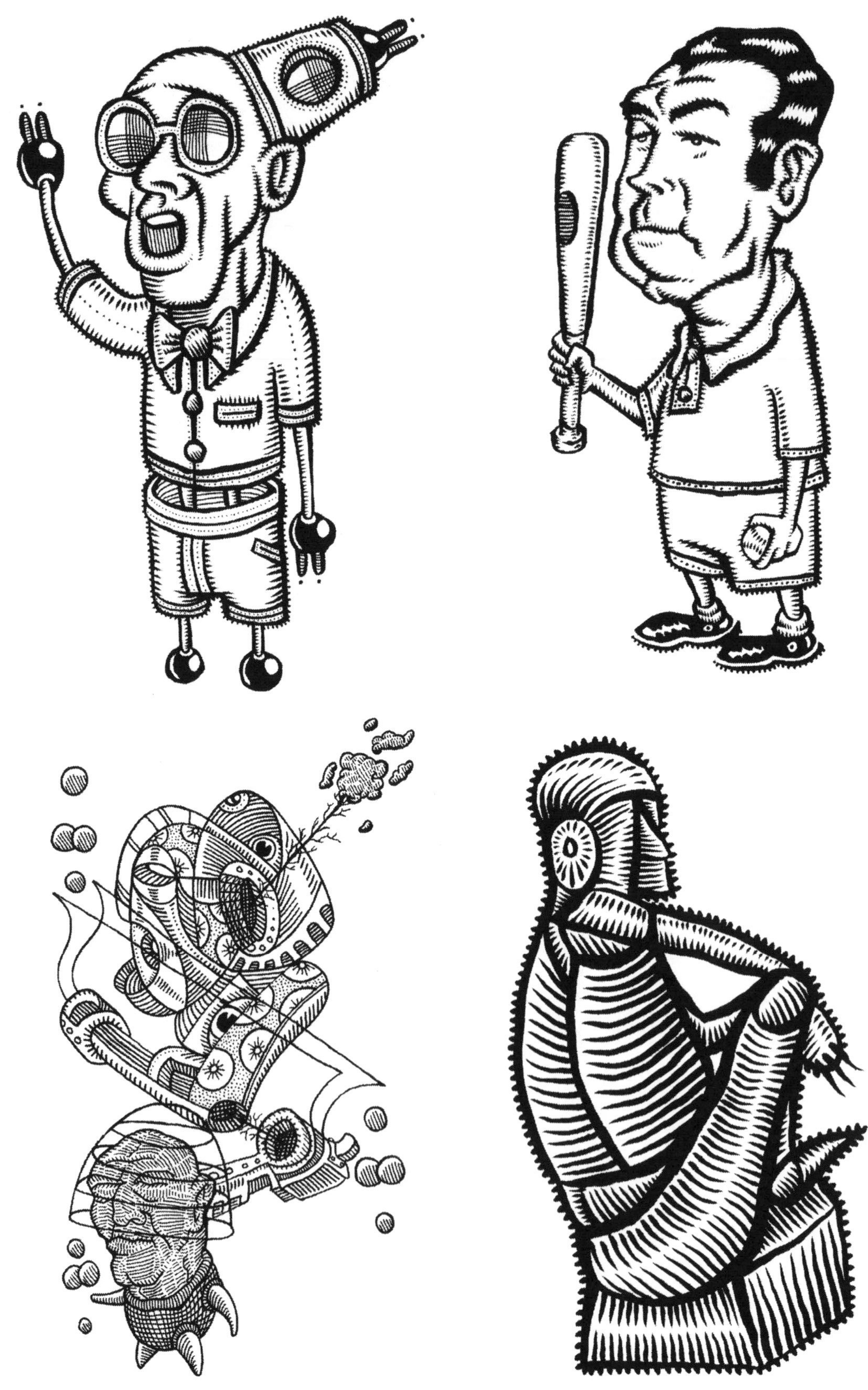

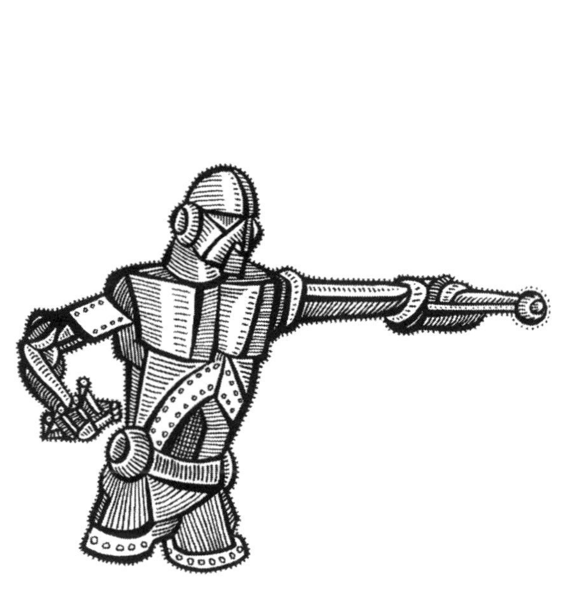

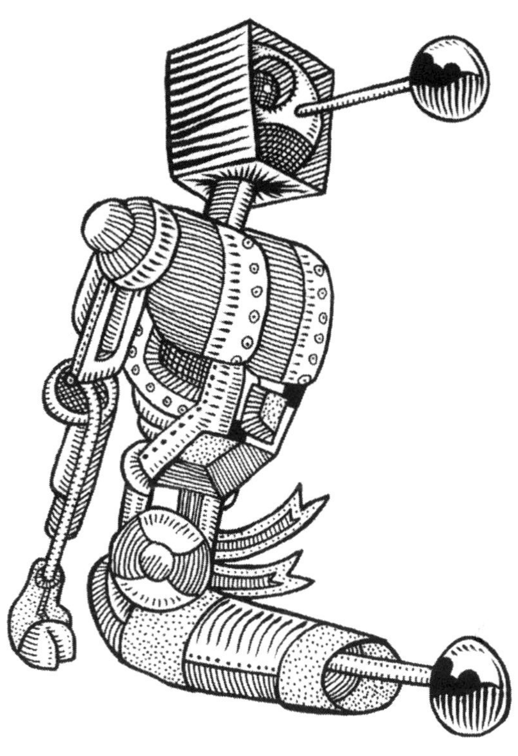

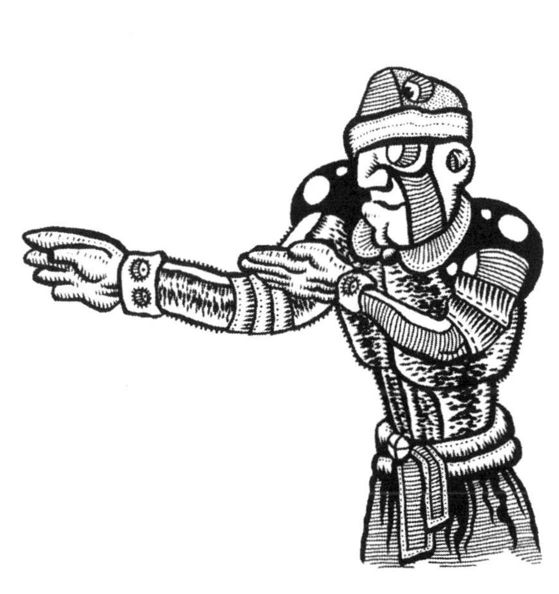

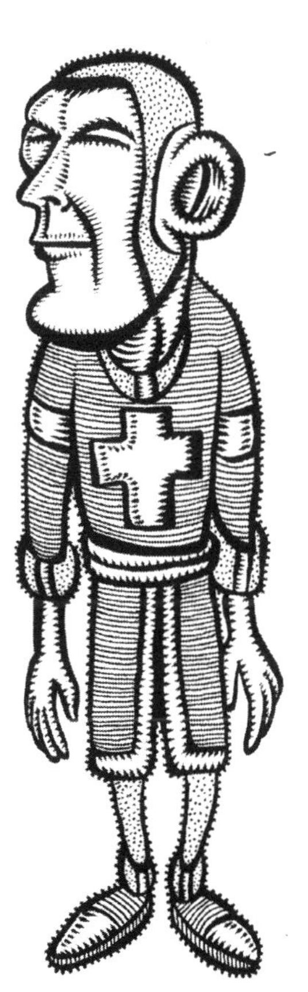

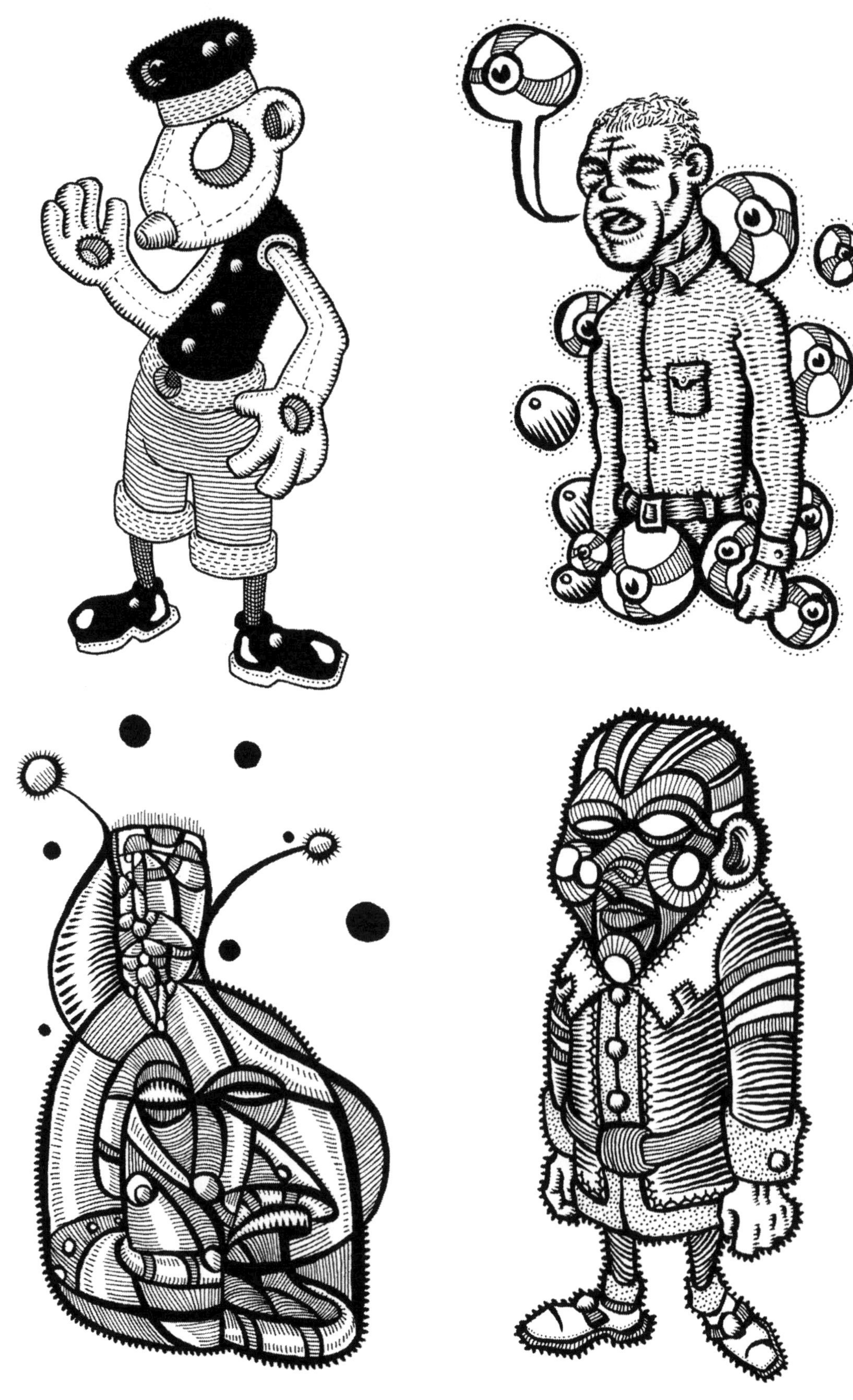

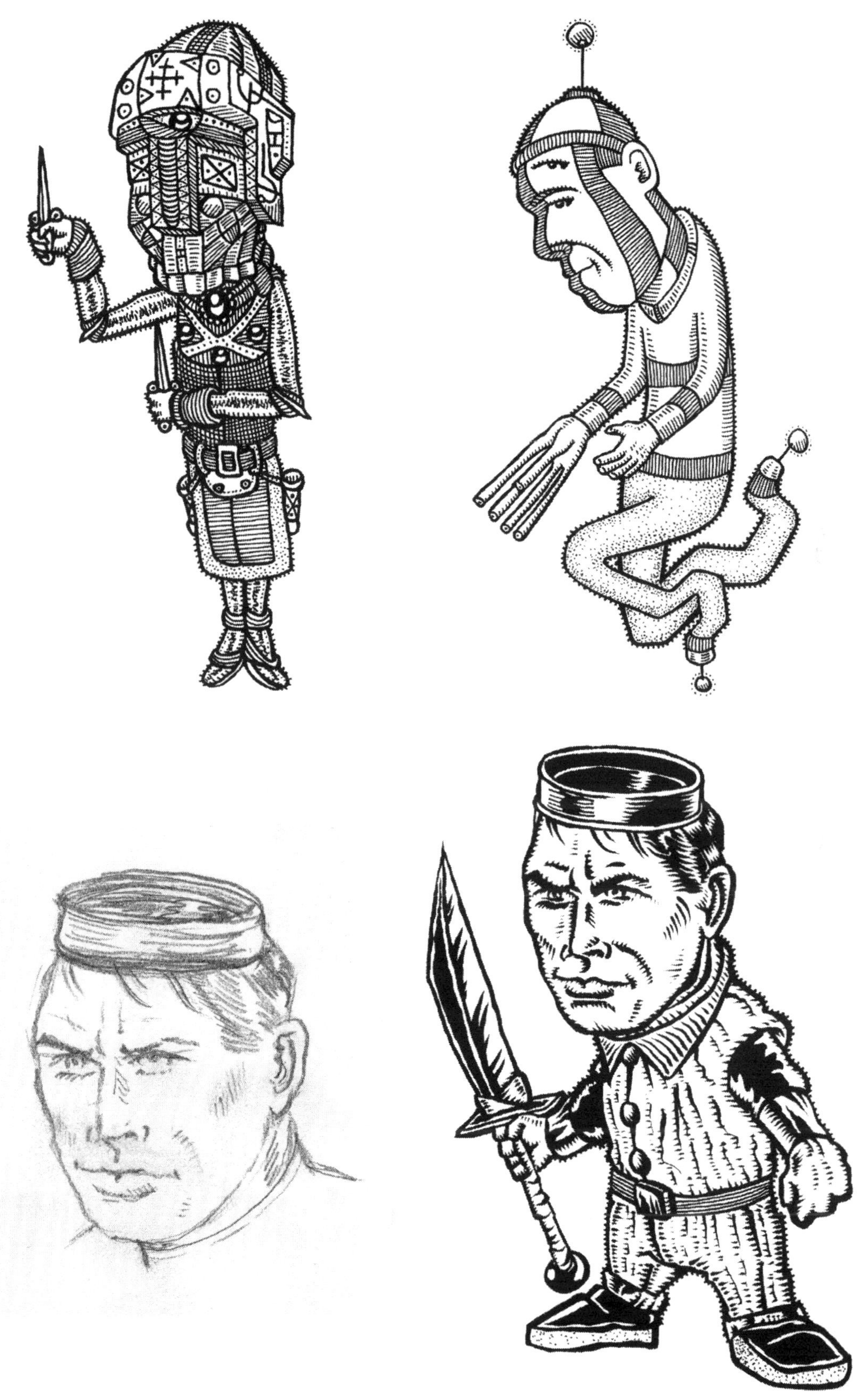

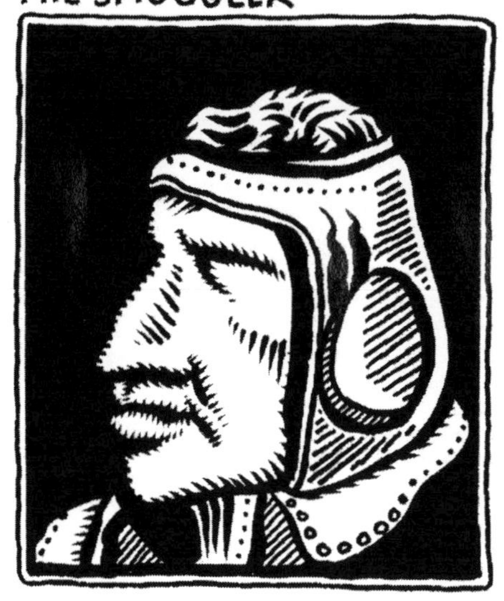
"THE SMUGGLER"

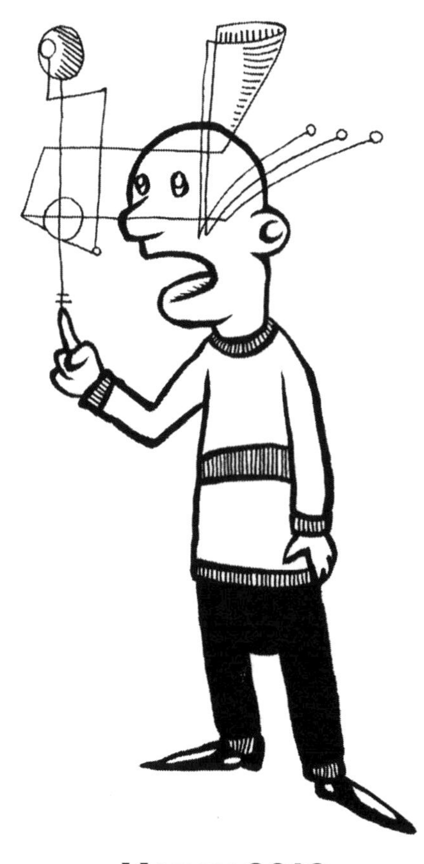

2013

April

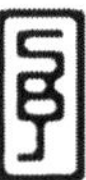

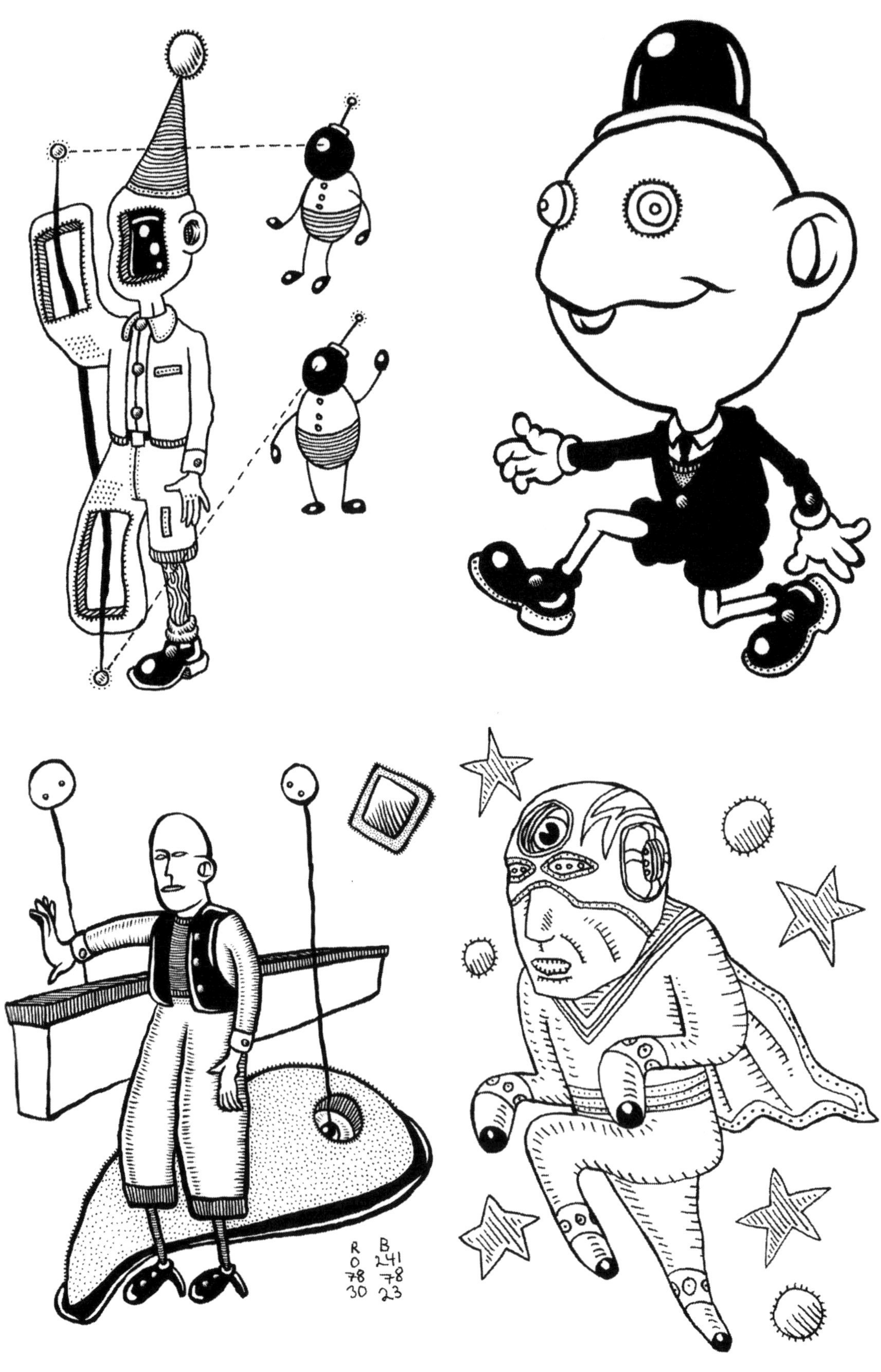
R B
0 241
78 78
30 23

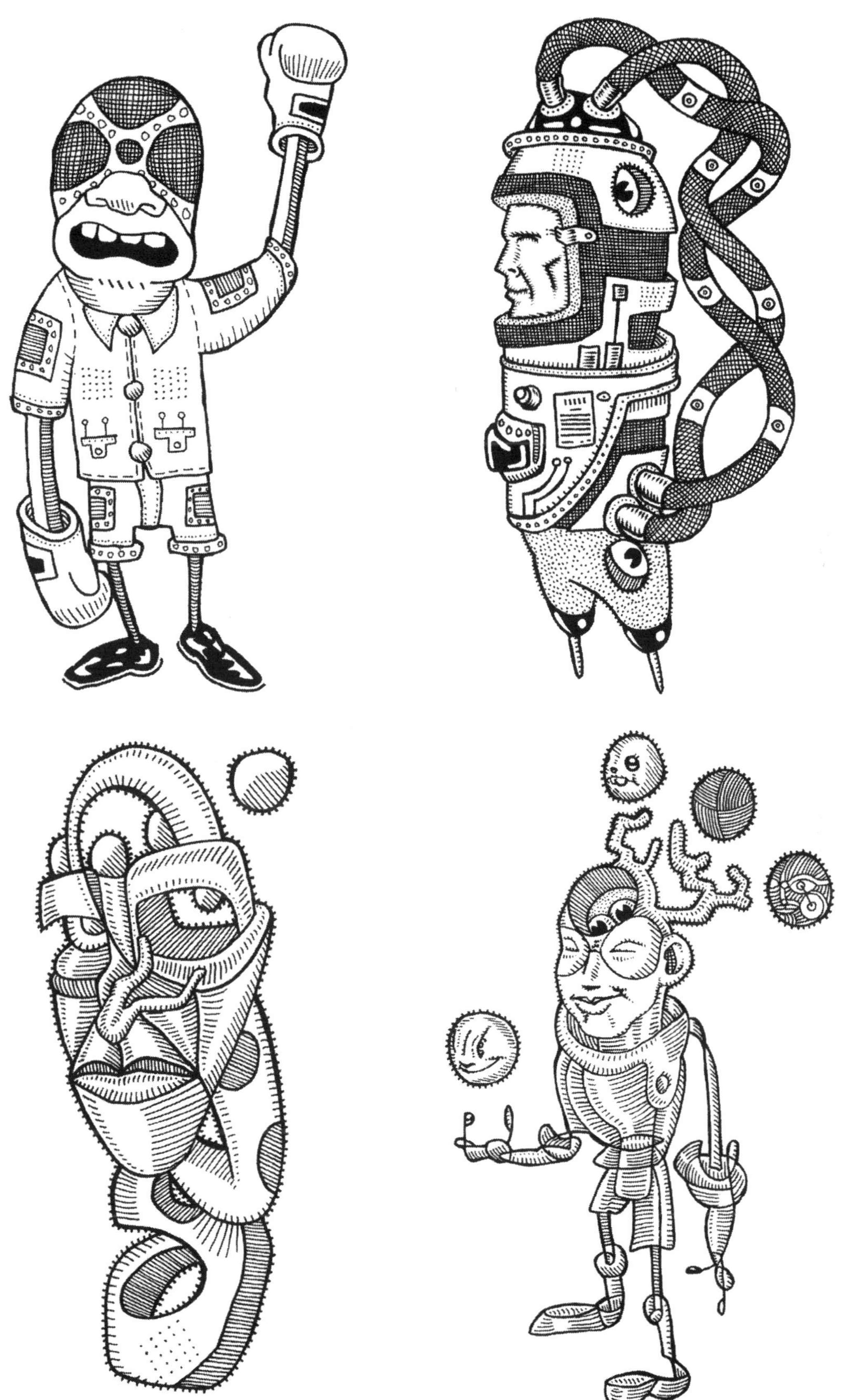

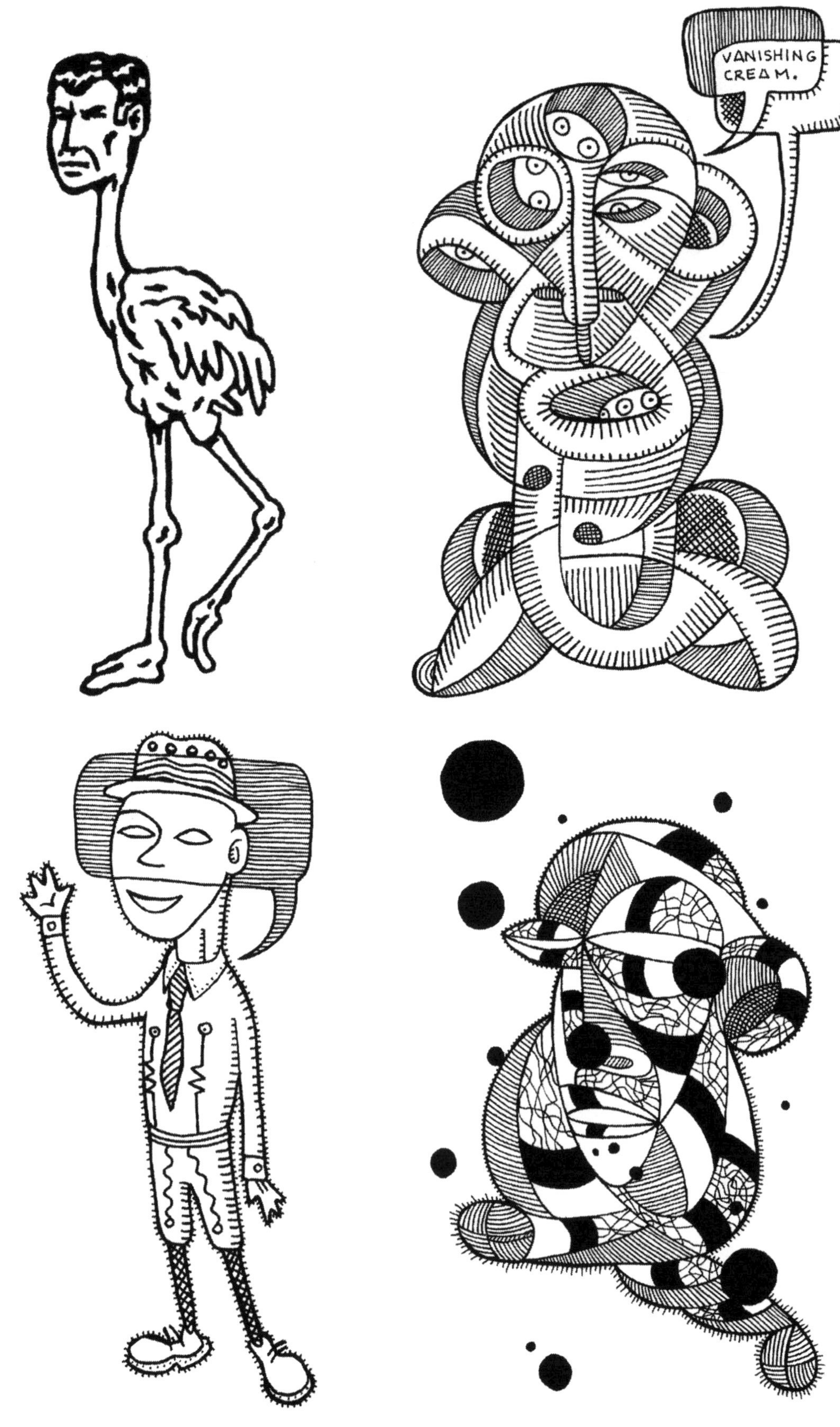
VANISHING CREAM.

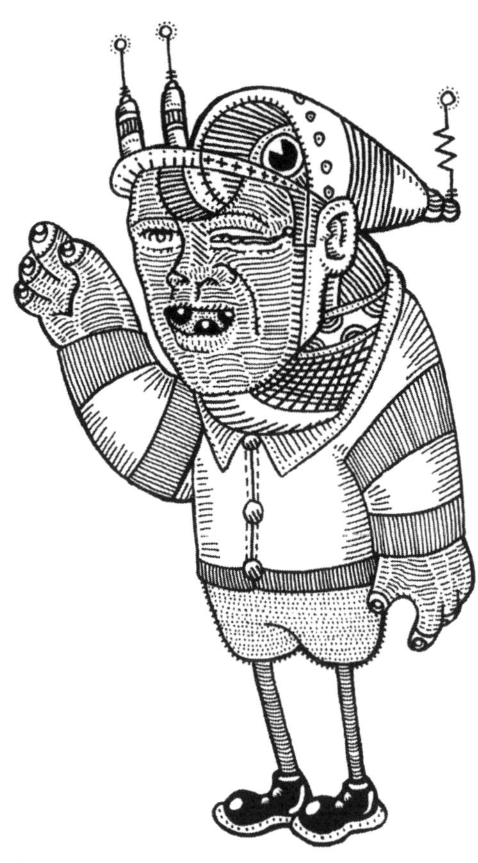

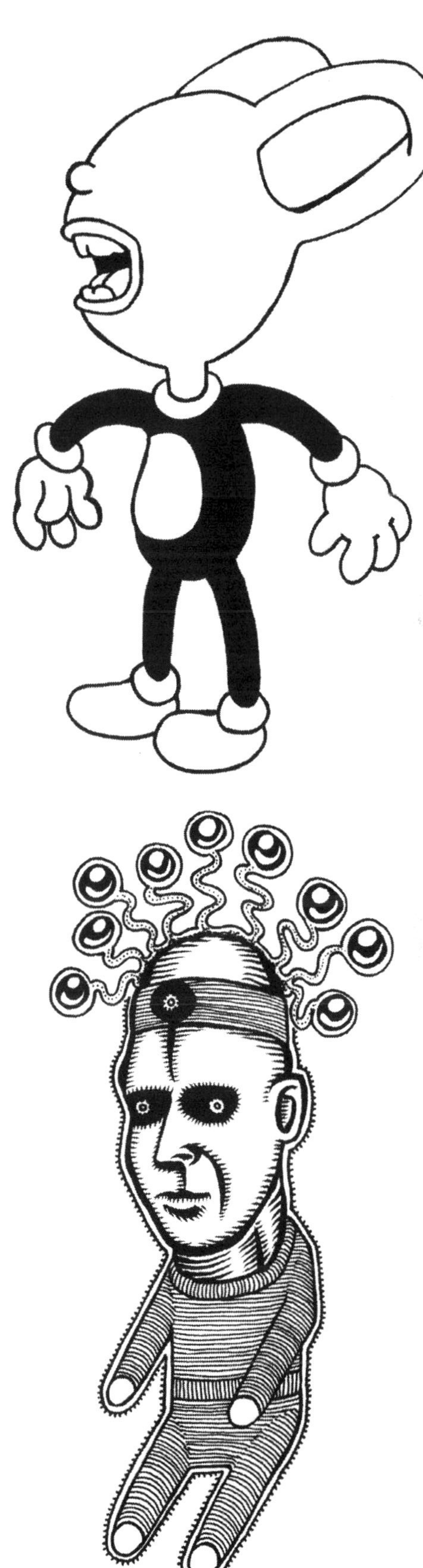

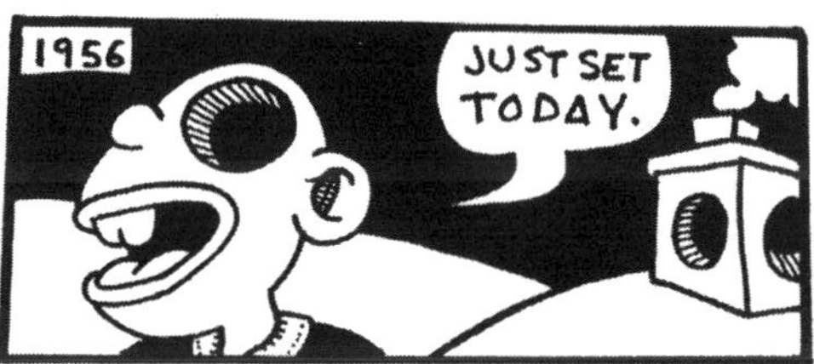

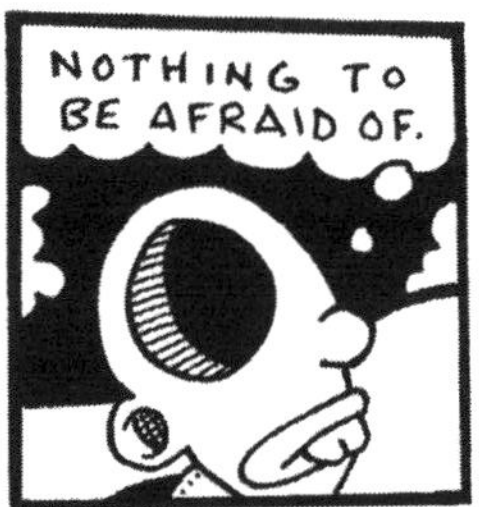

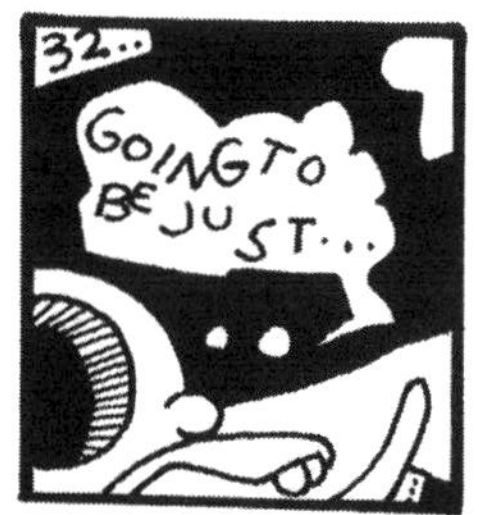

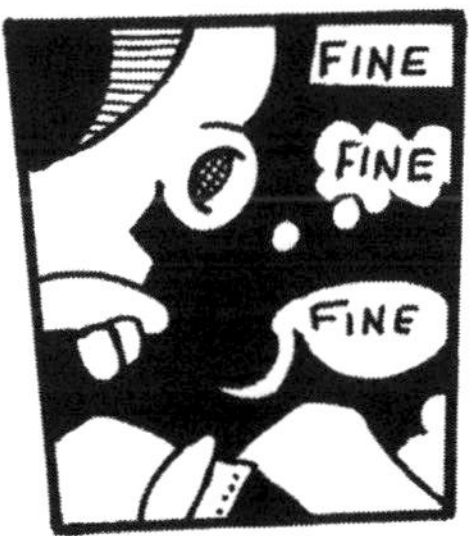

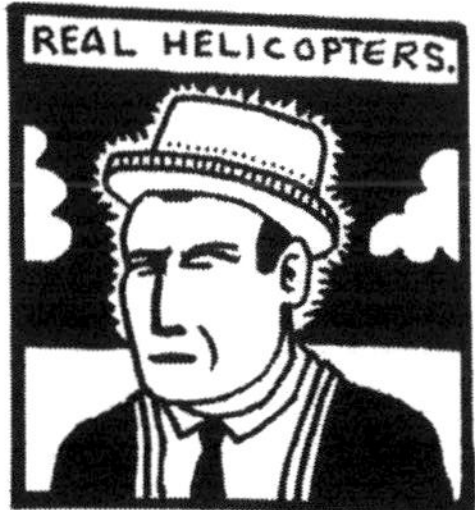

NEXT TIME: STARING IN A PORTA-POTTY THAT READS "OCCUPIED".

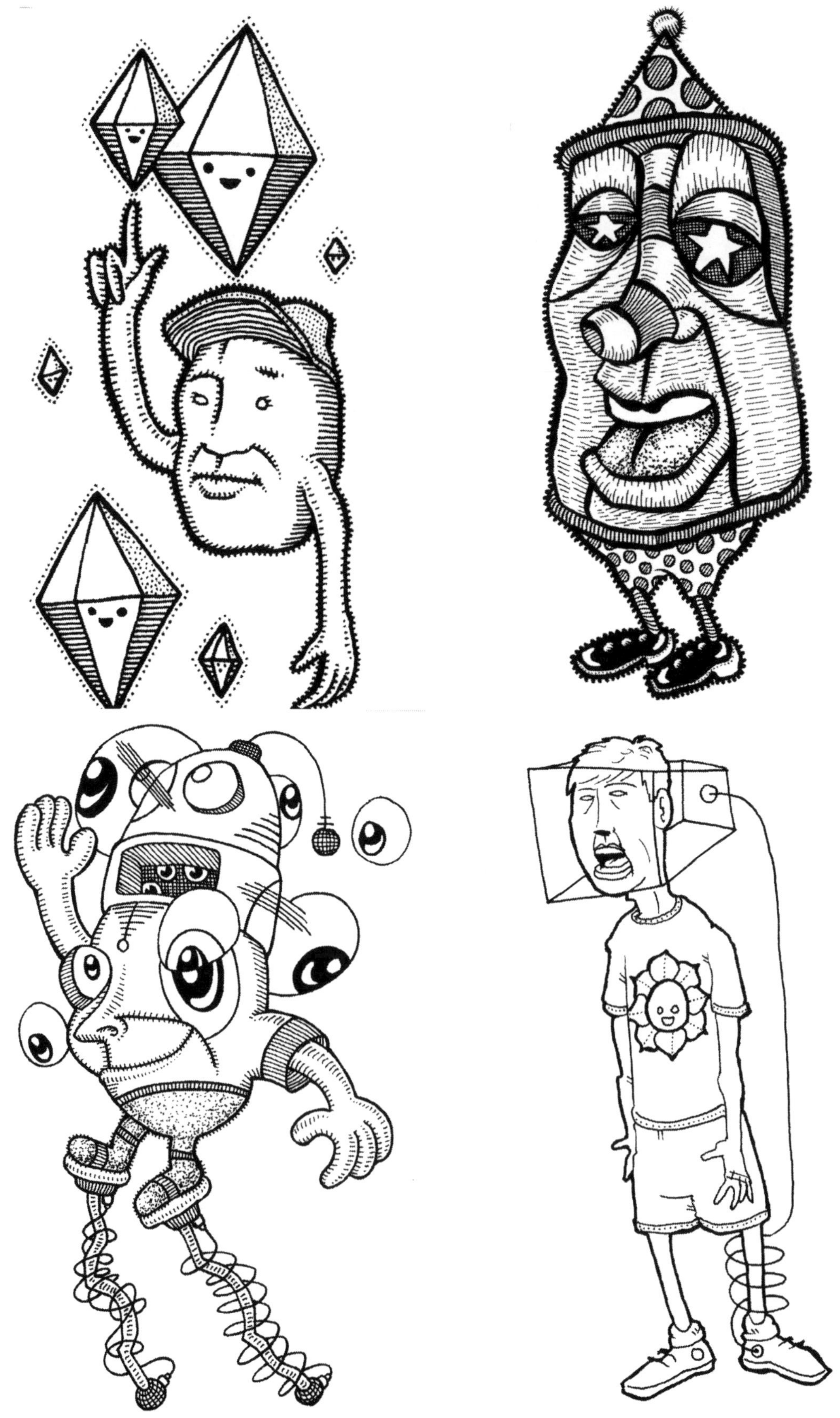

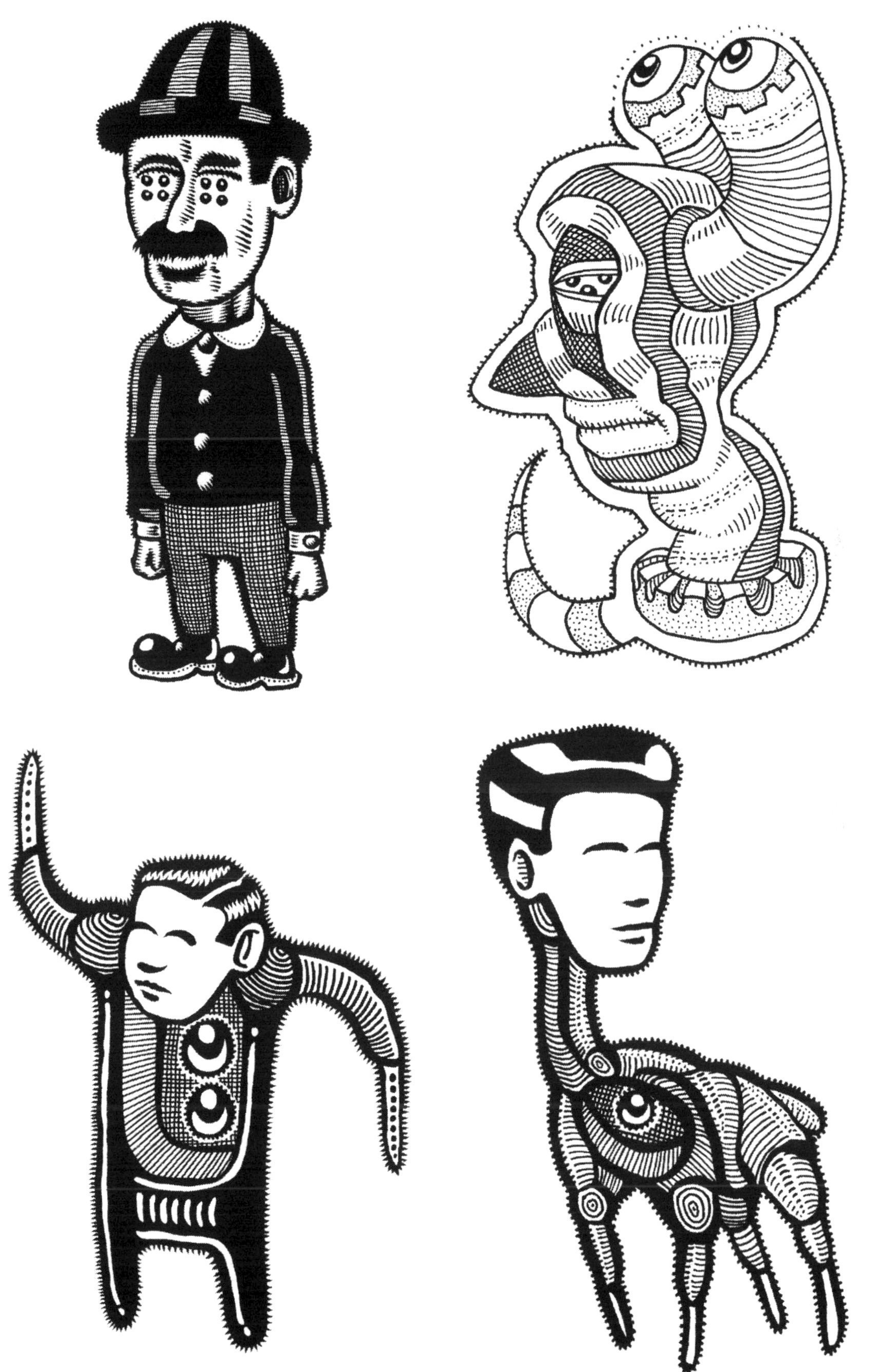

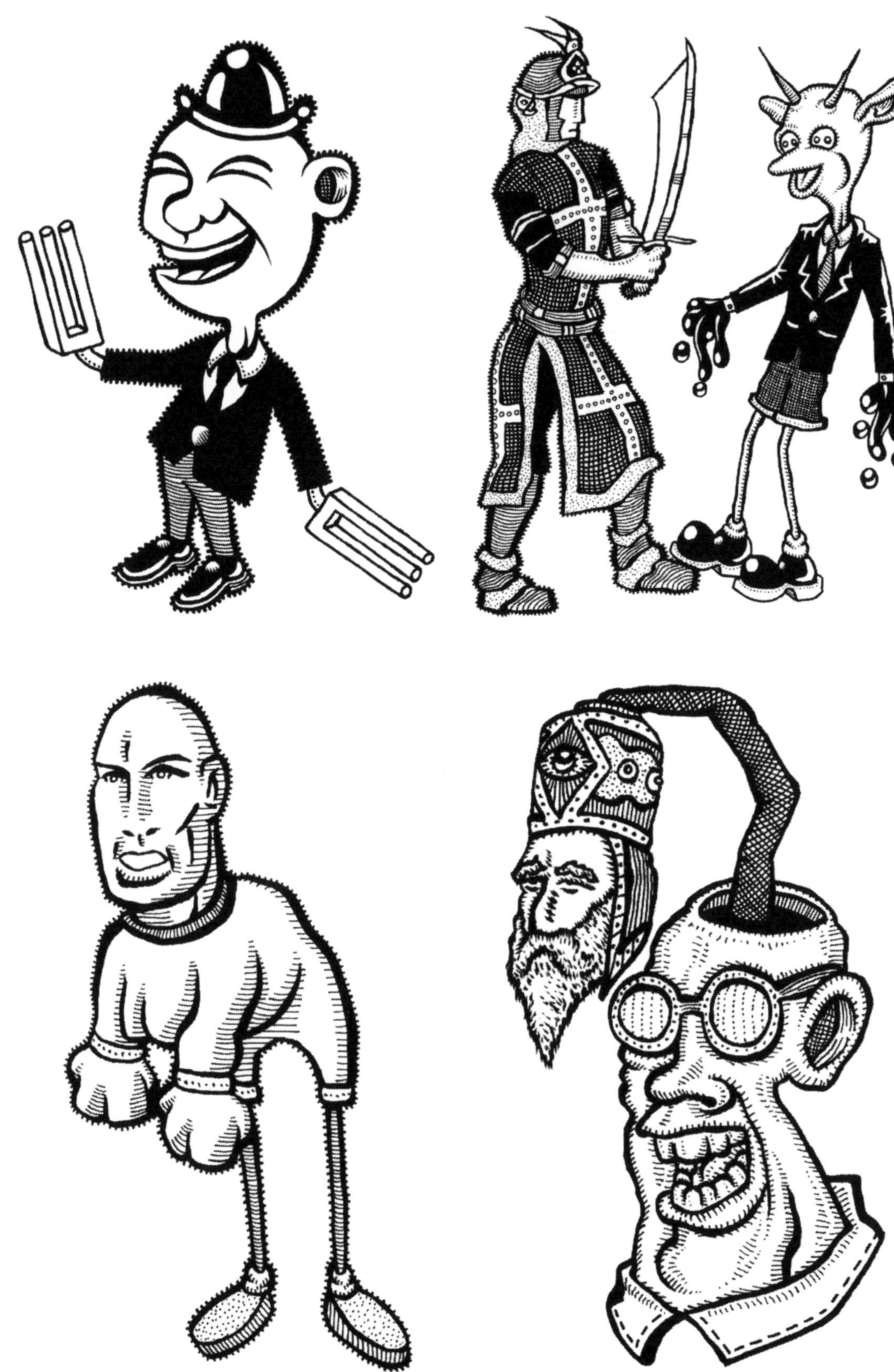

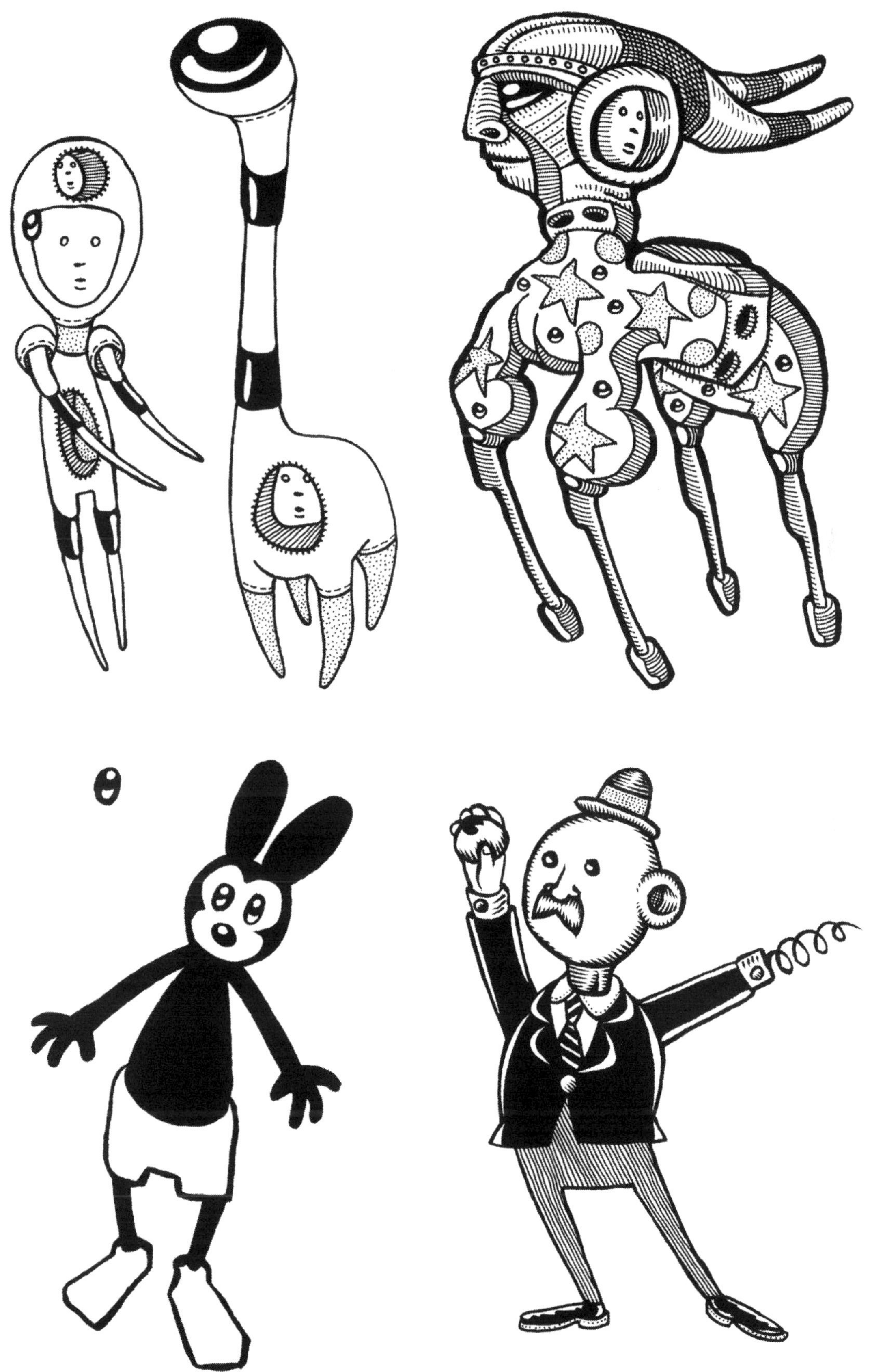

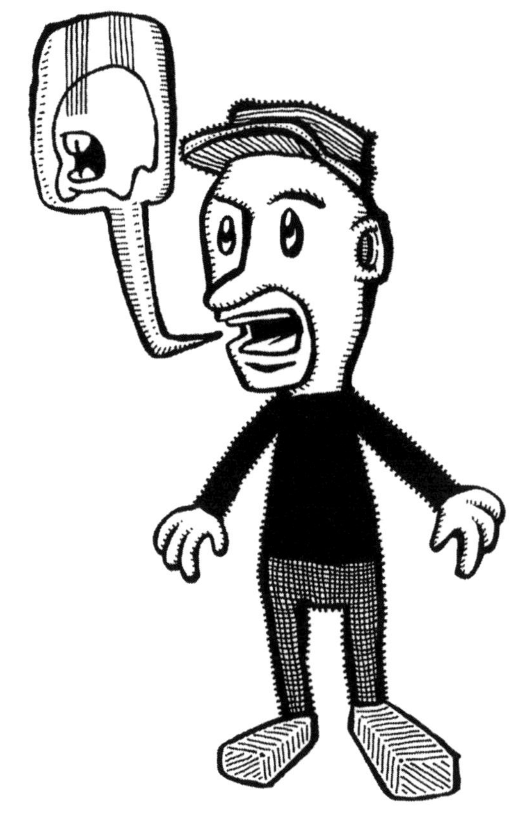

2013

May

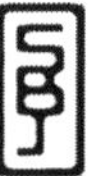

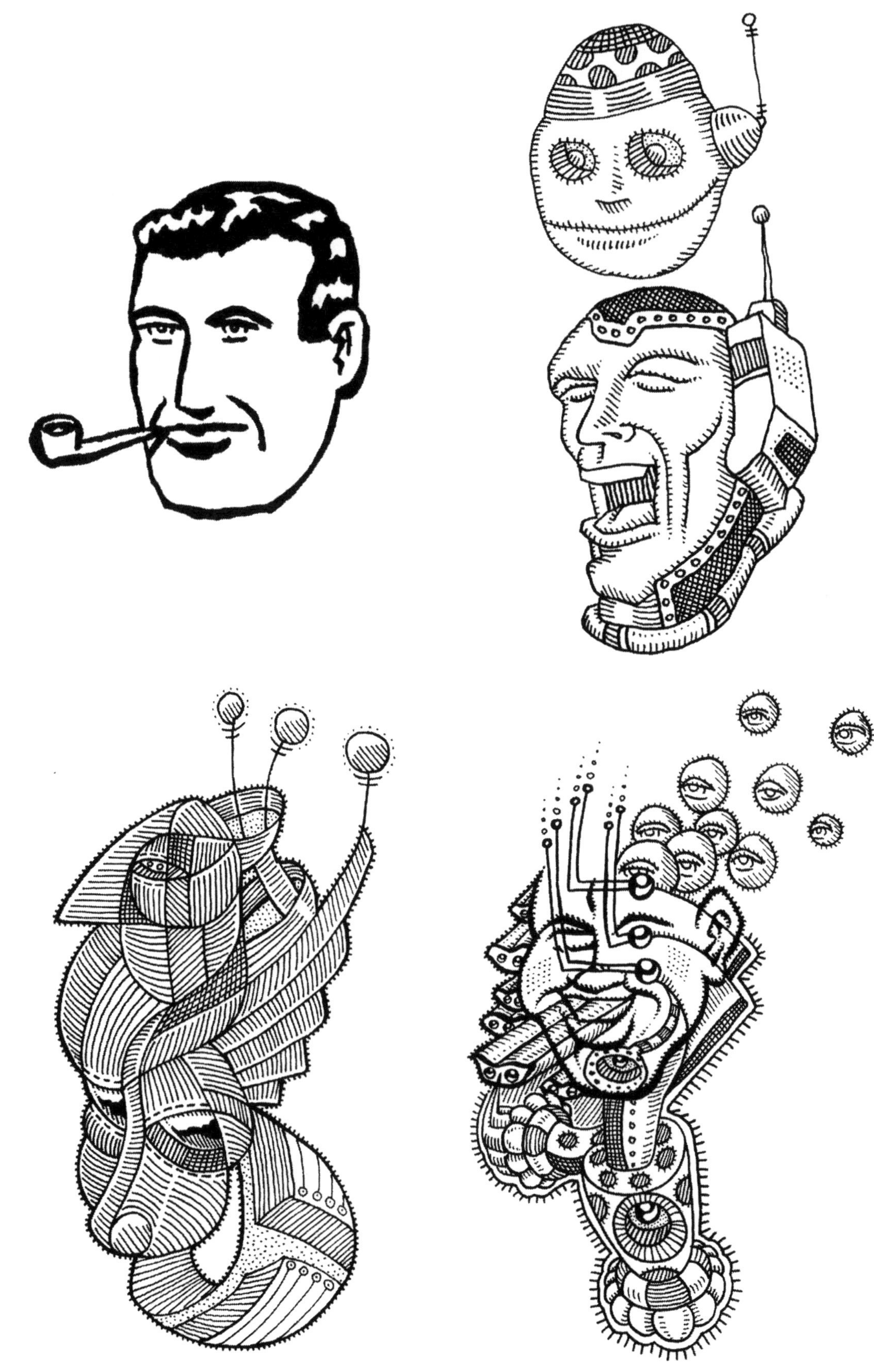

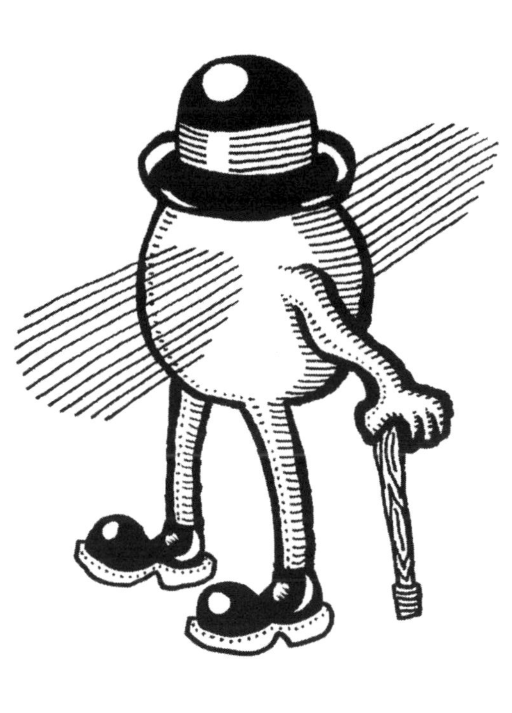

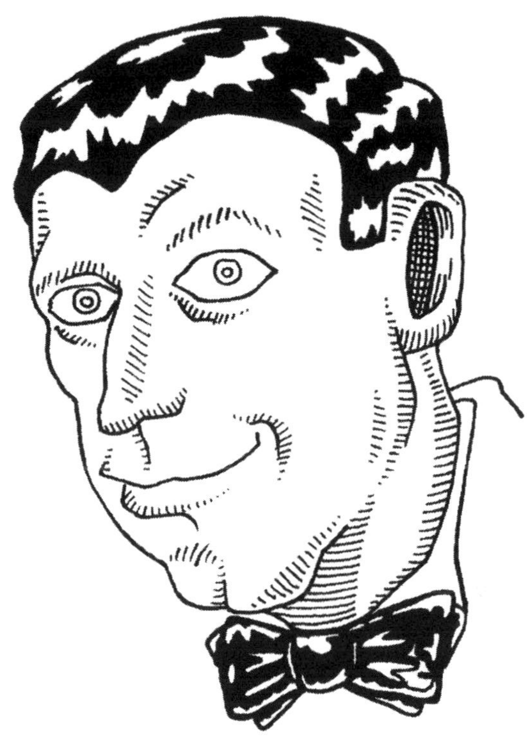

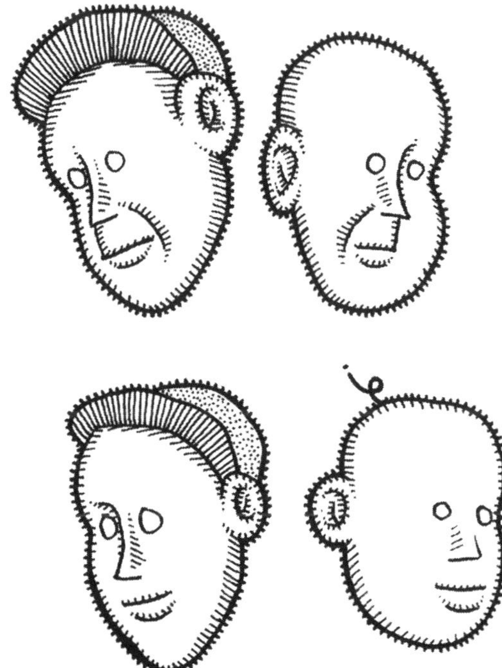

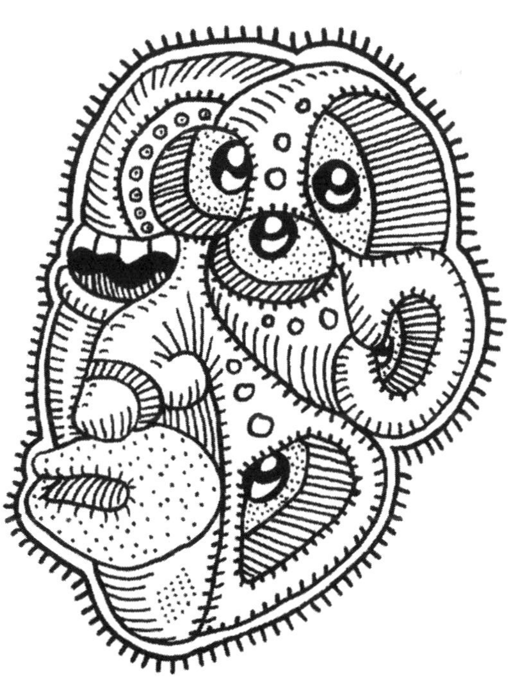

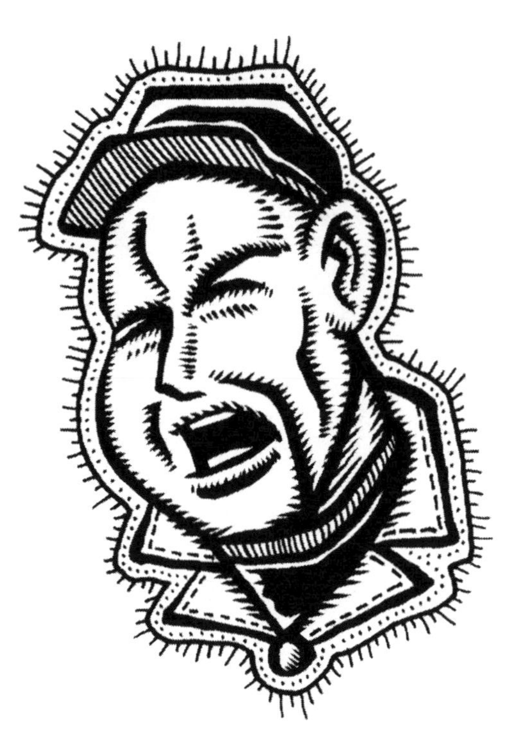

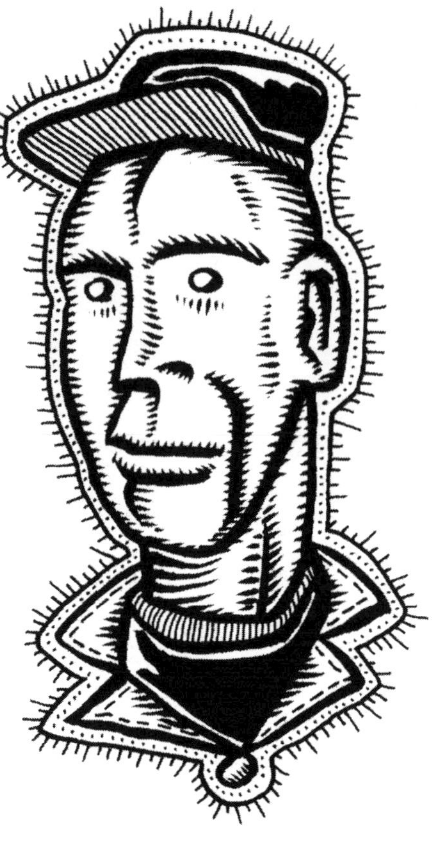

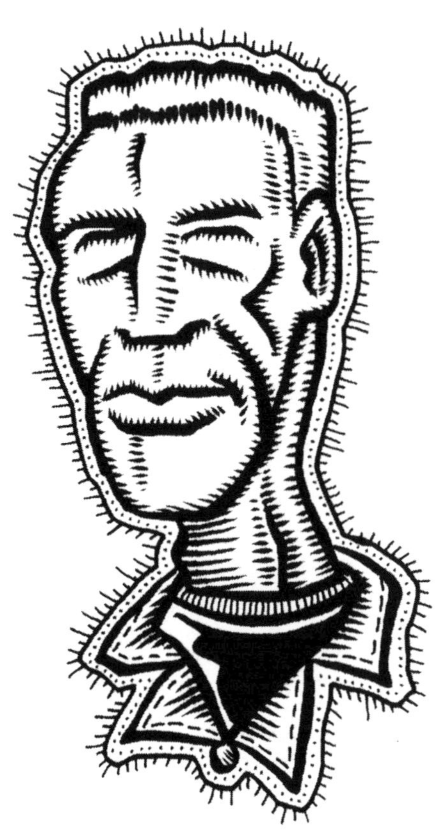

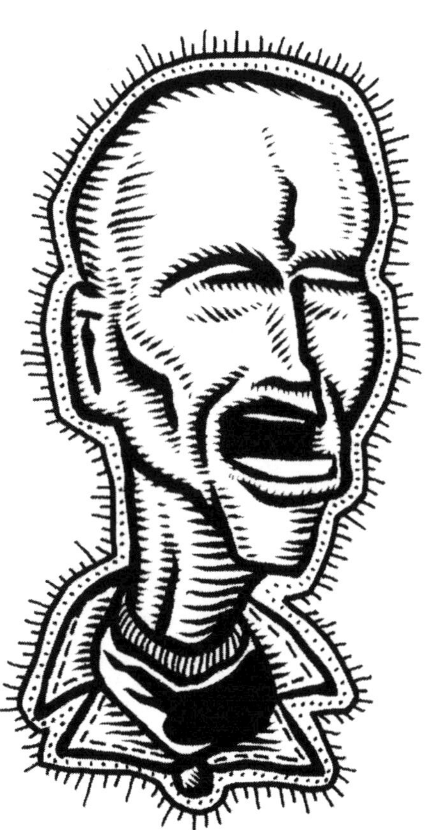

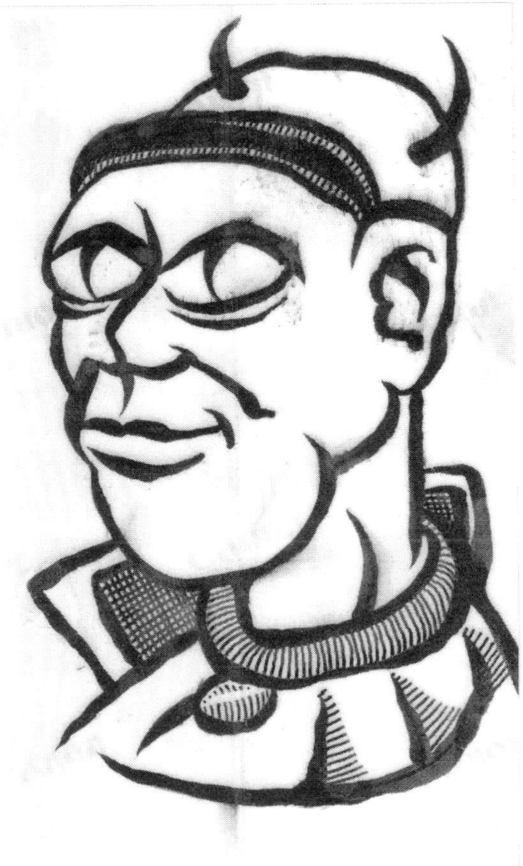

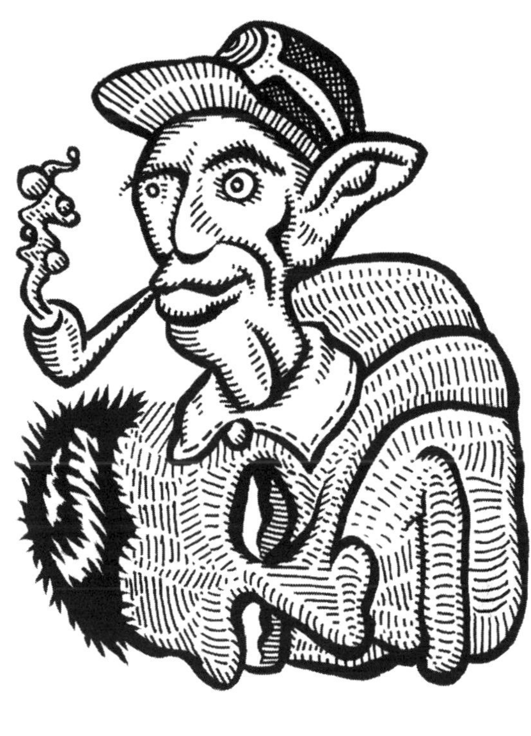

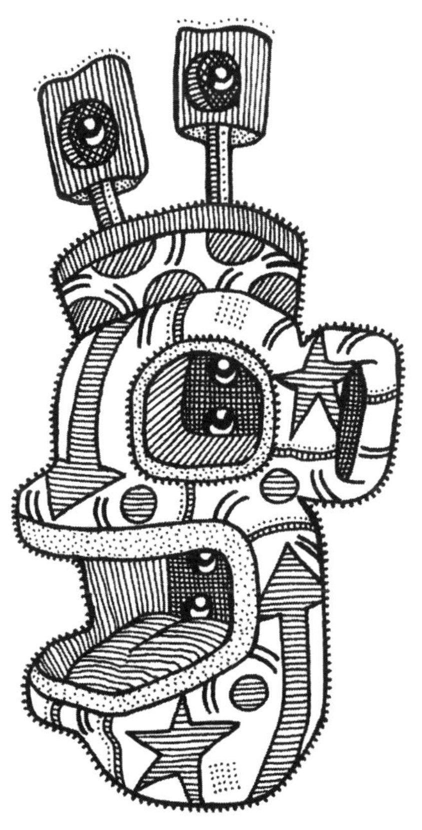

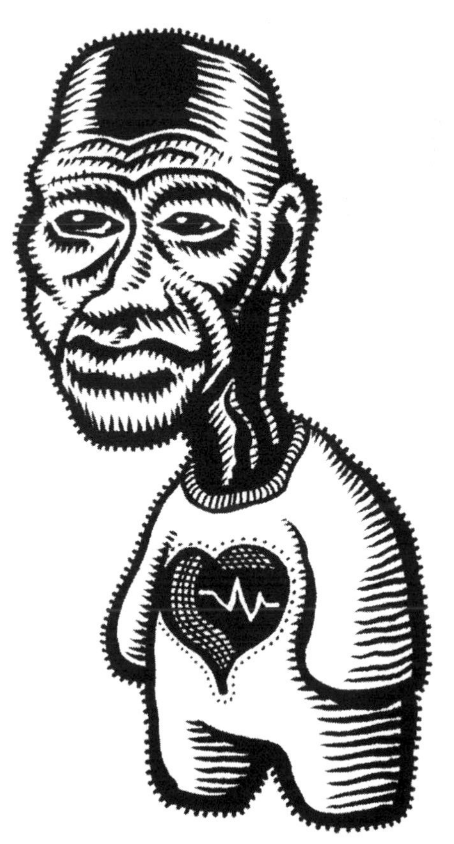

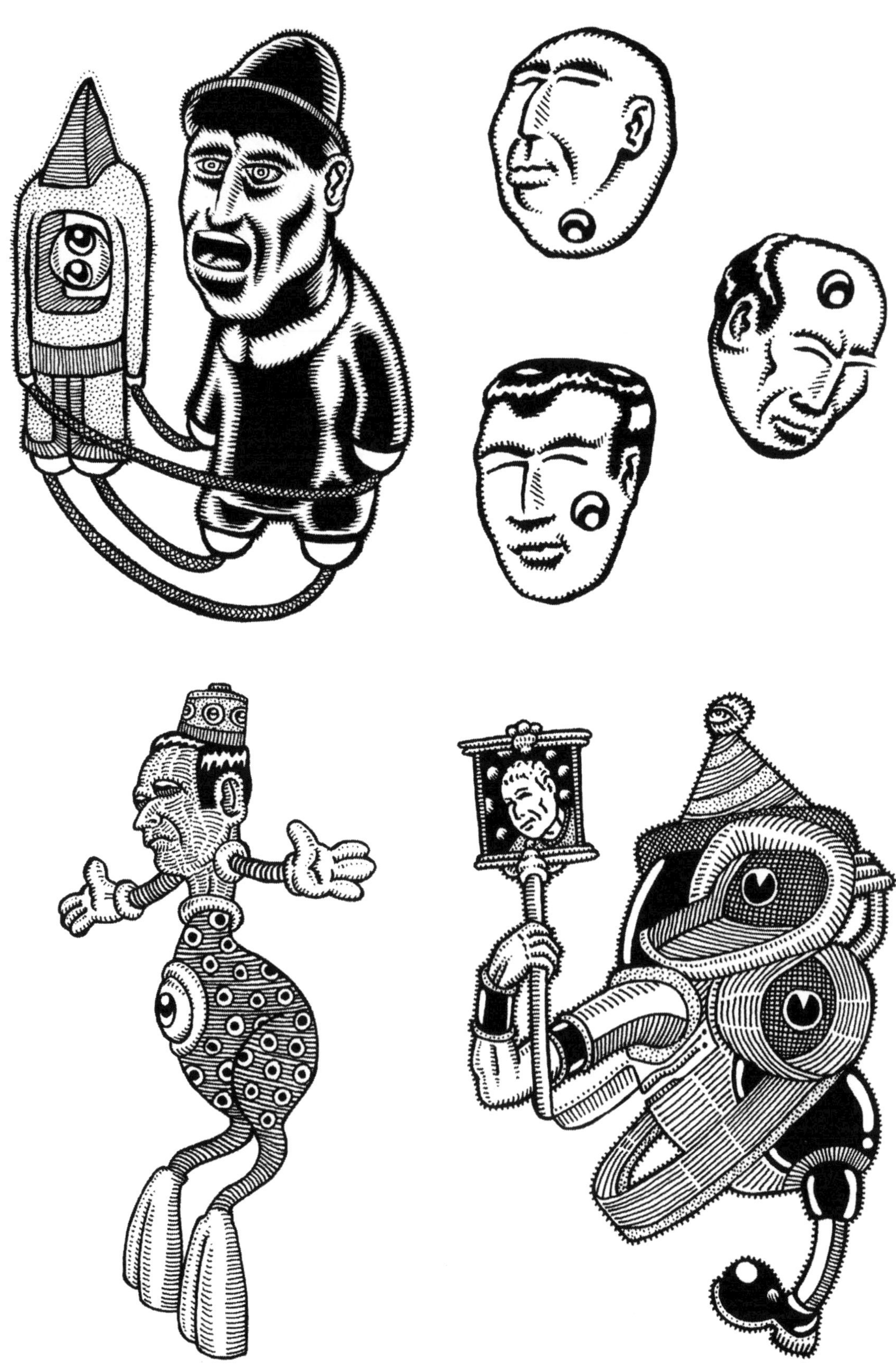

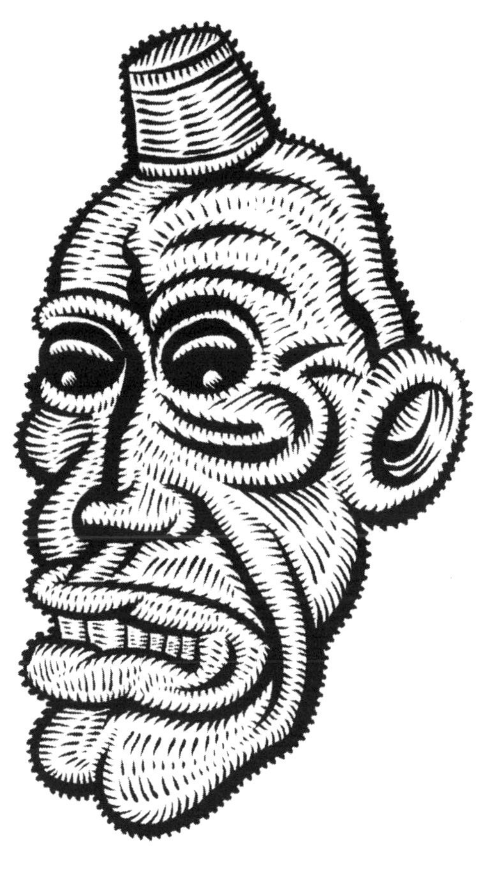

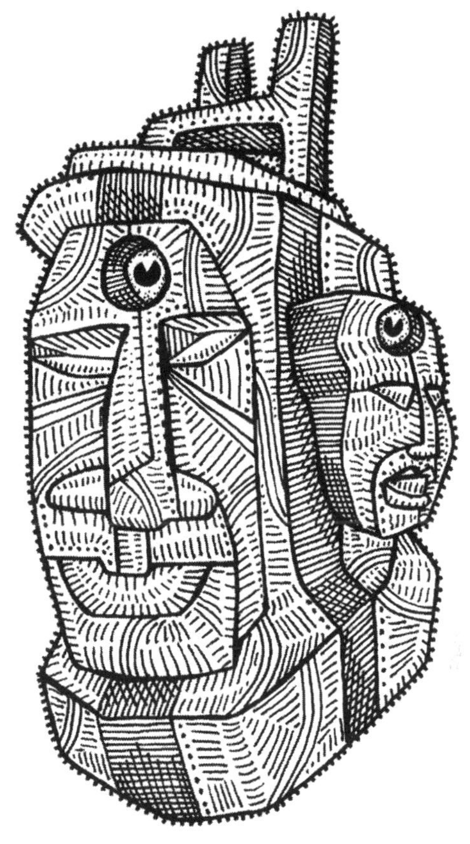

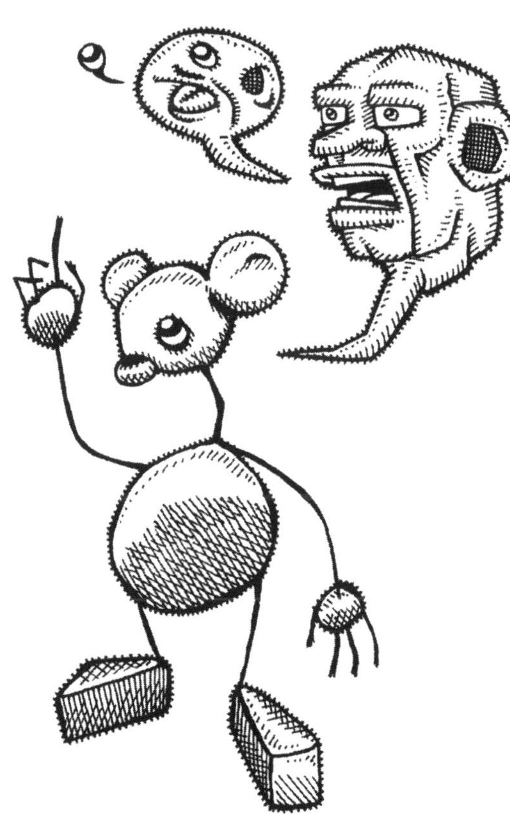

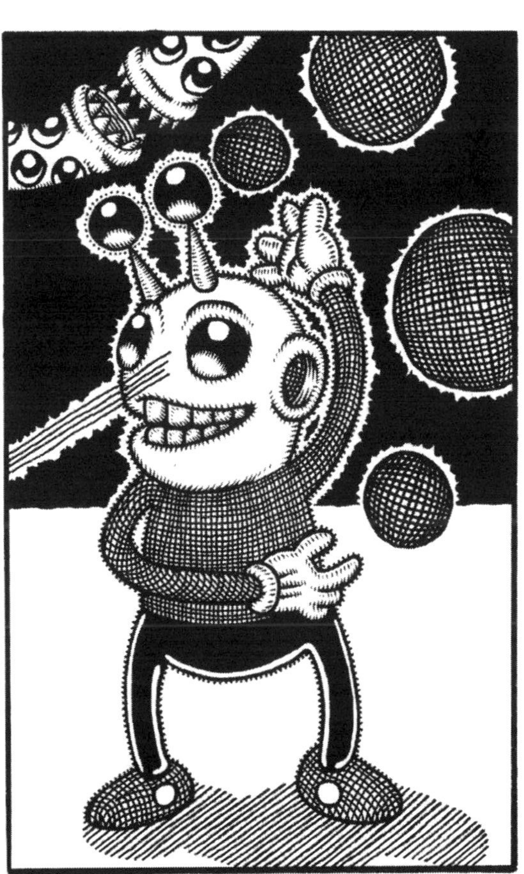

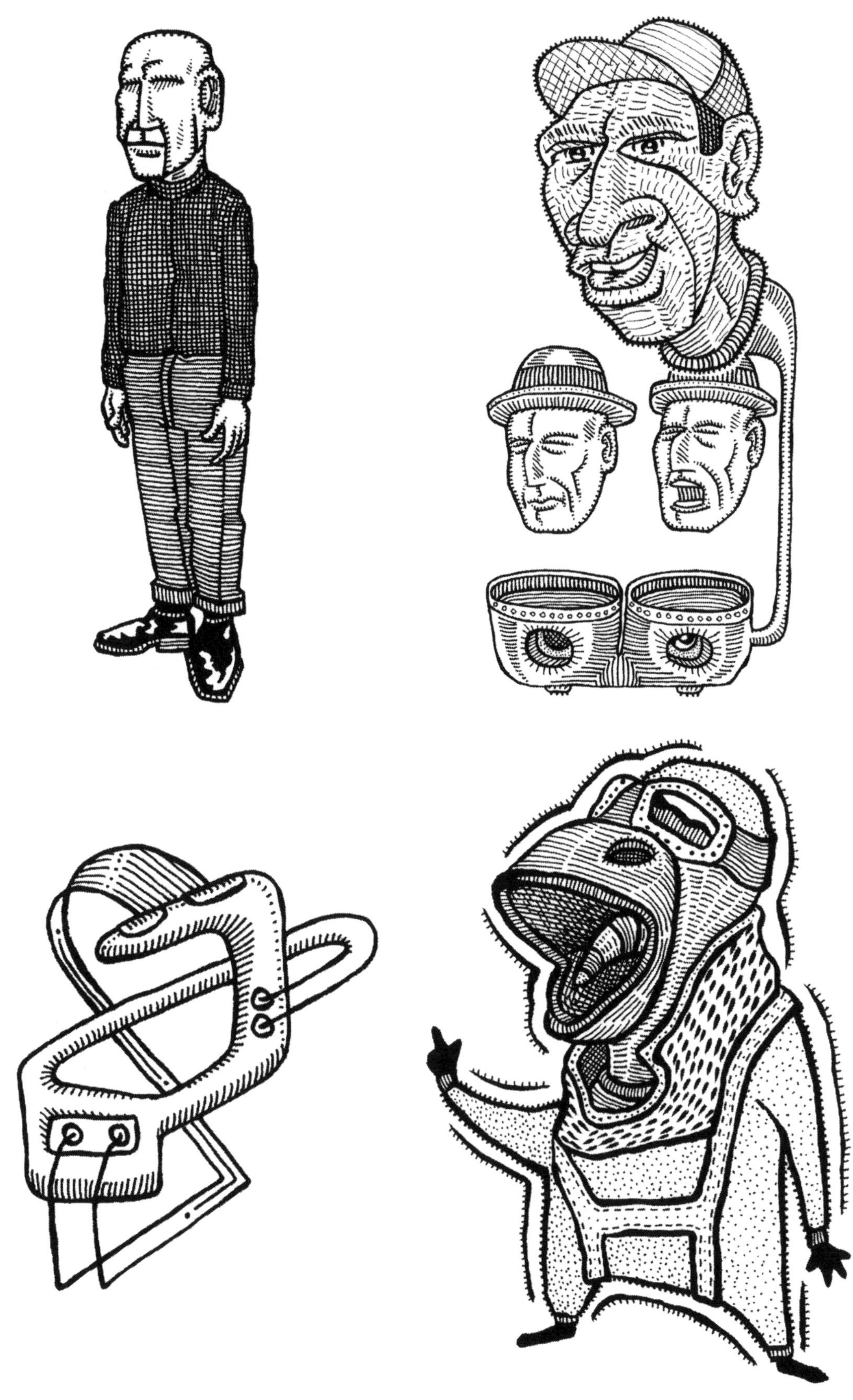

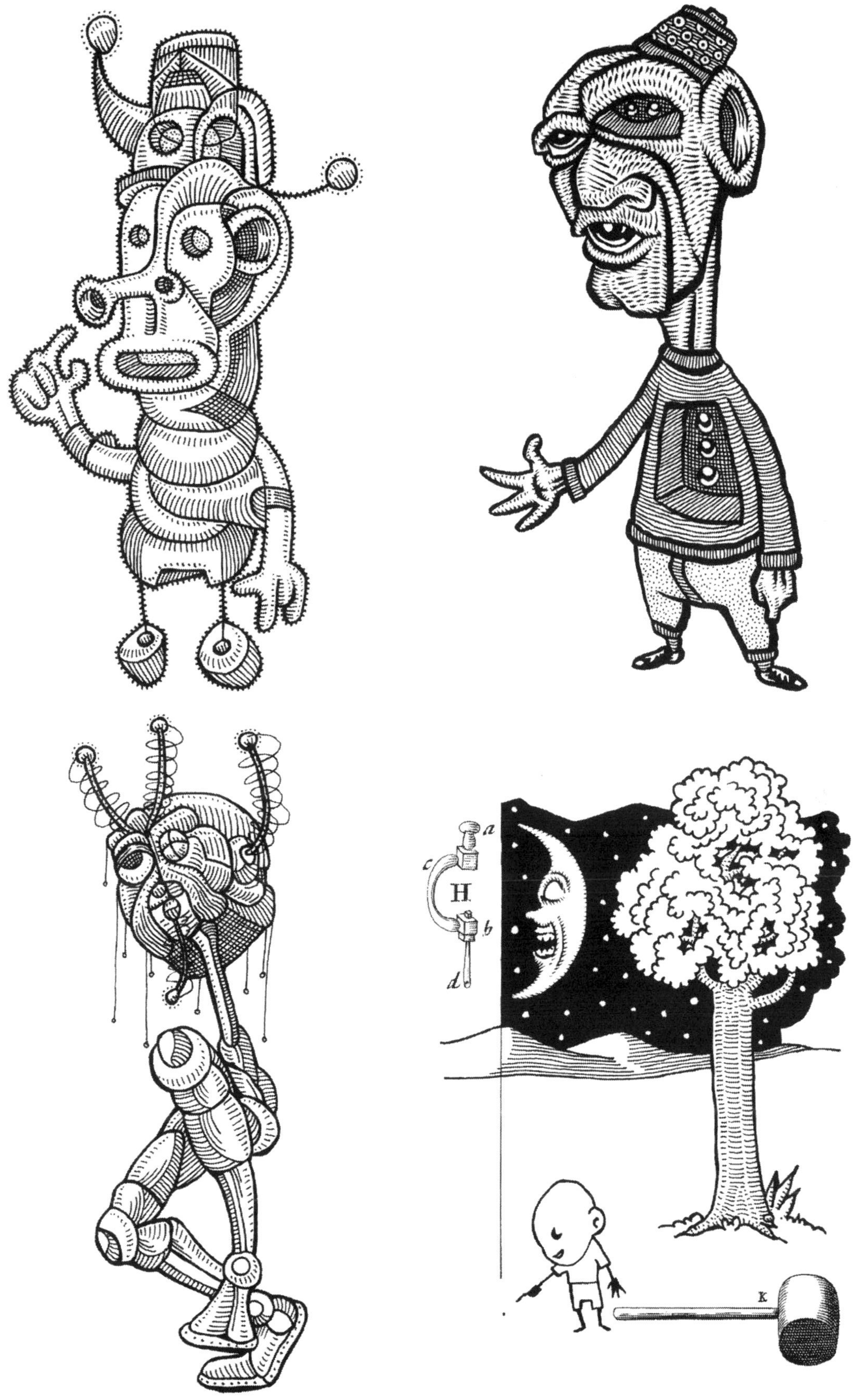
a
c
H
b
d
K

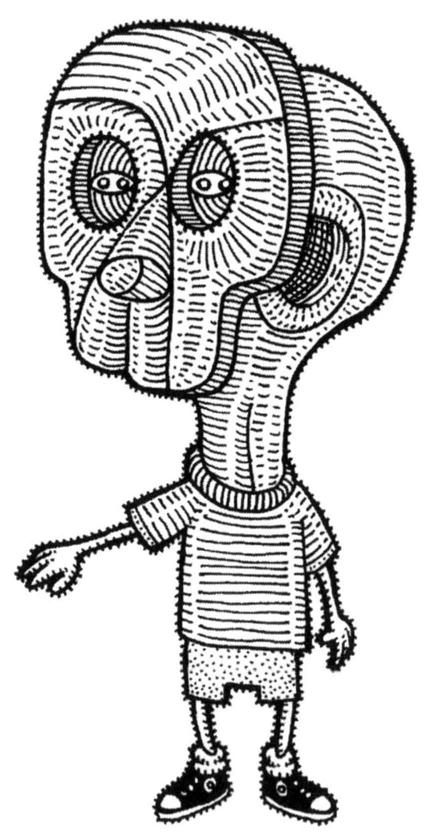

2013

June

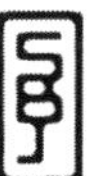

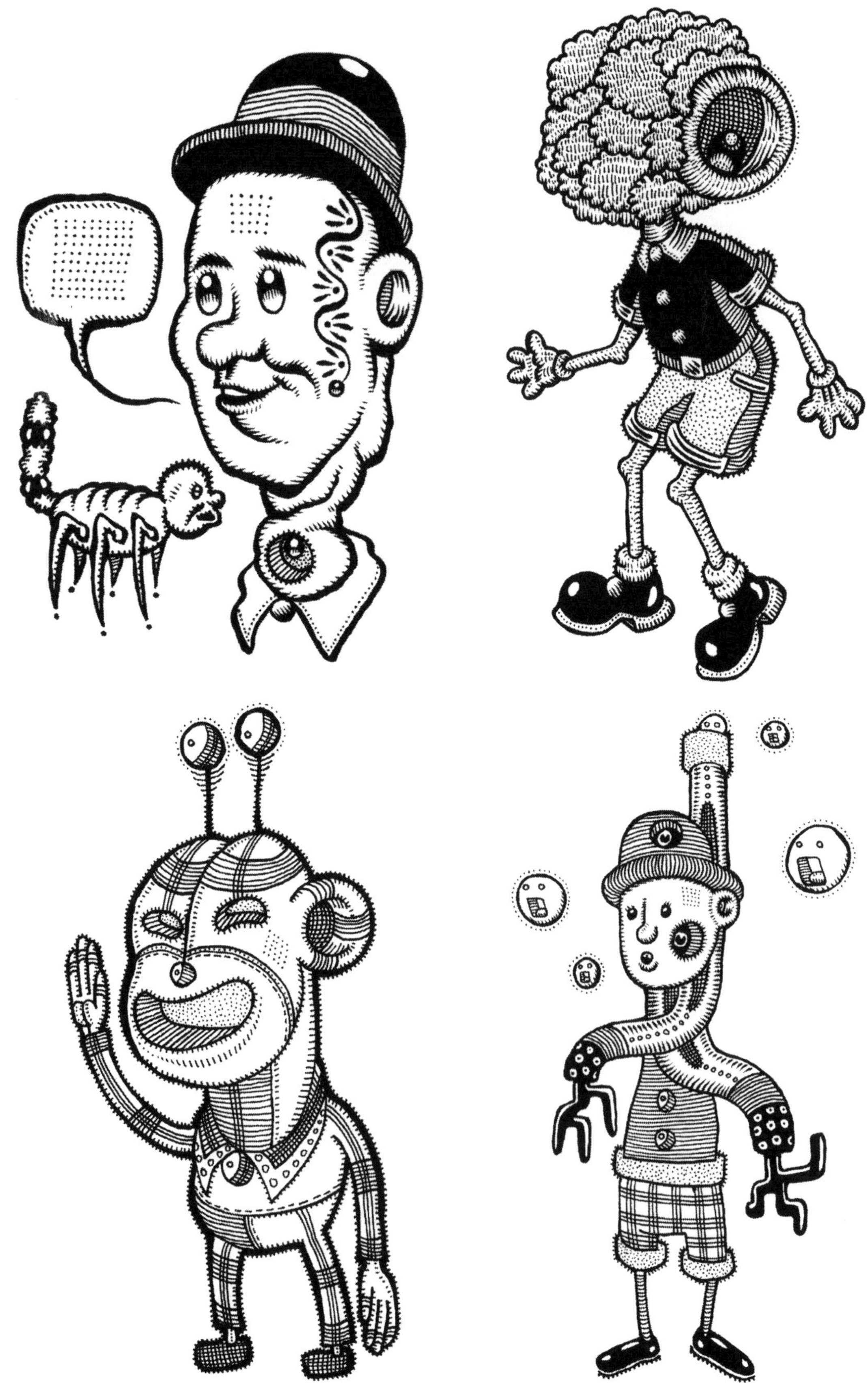

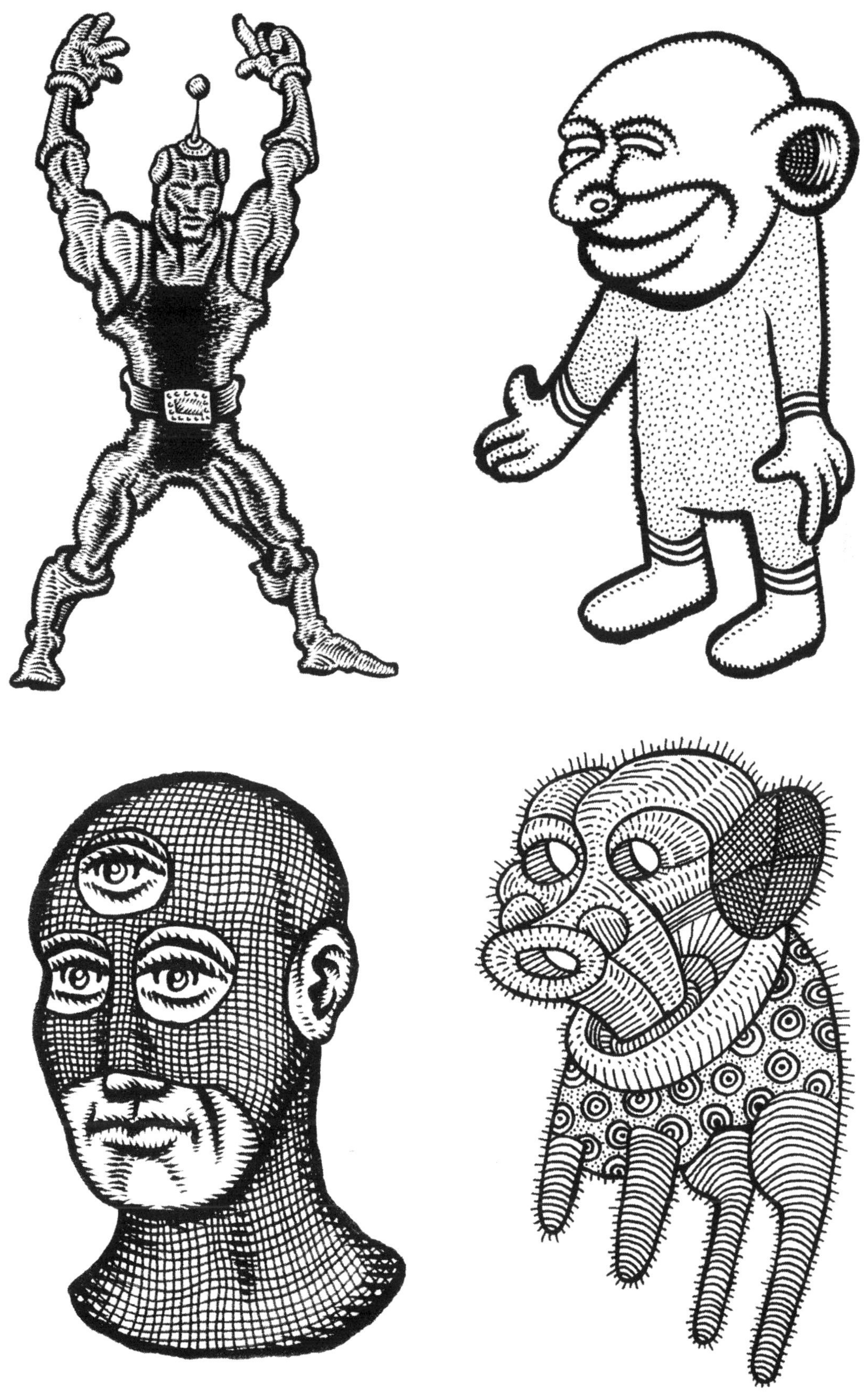

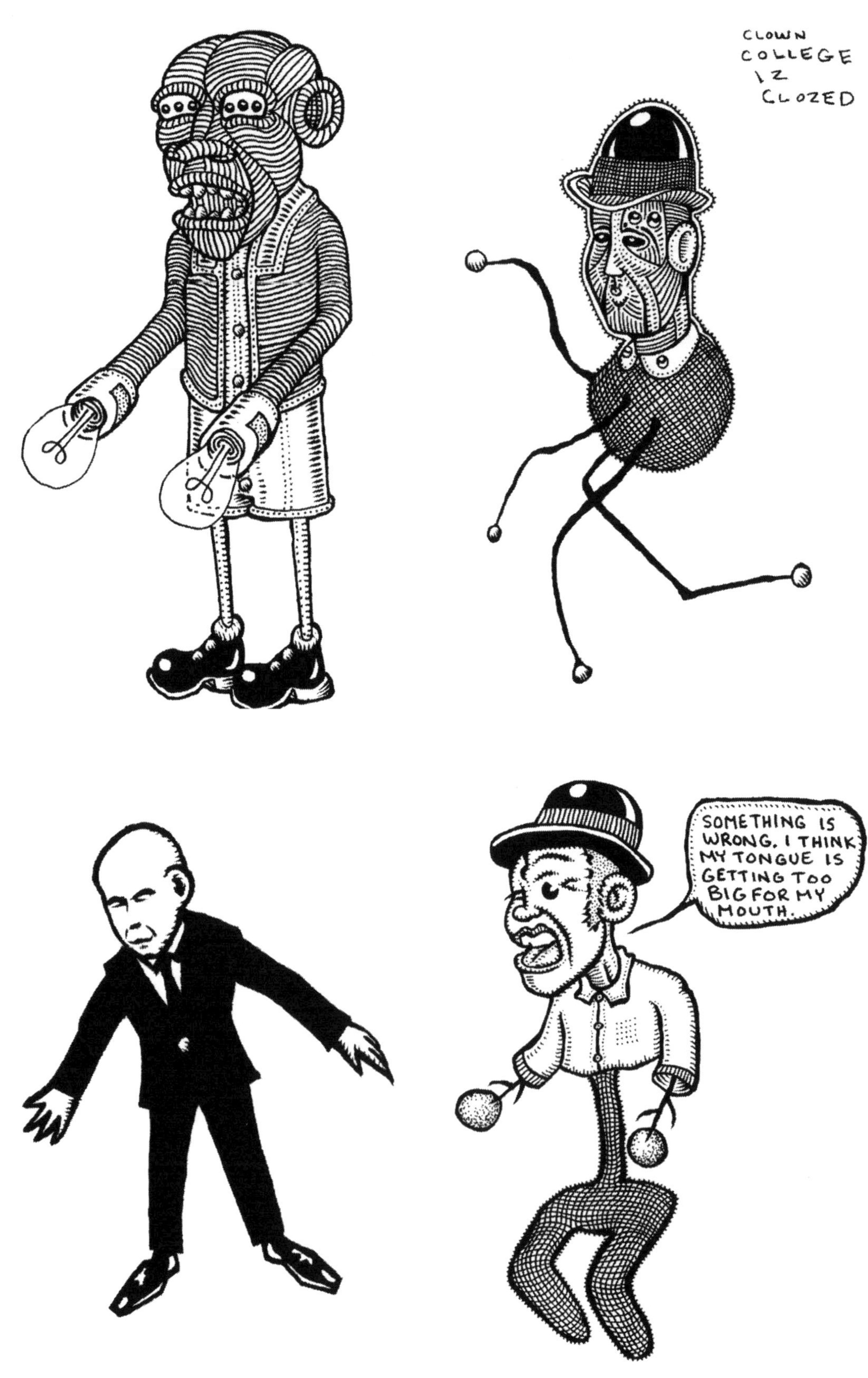
CLOWN COLLEGE IZ CLOZED
SOMETHING IS WRONG. I THINK MY TONGUE IS GETTING TOO BIG FOR MY MOUTH.

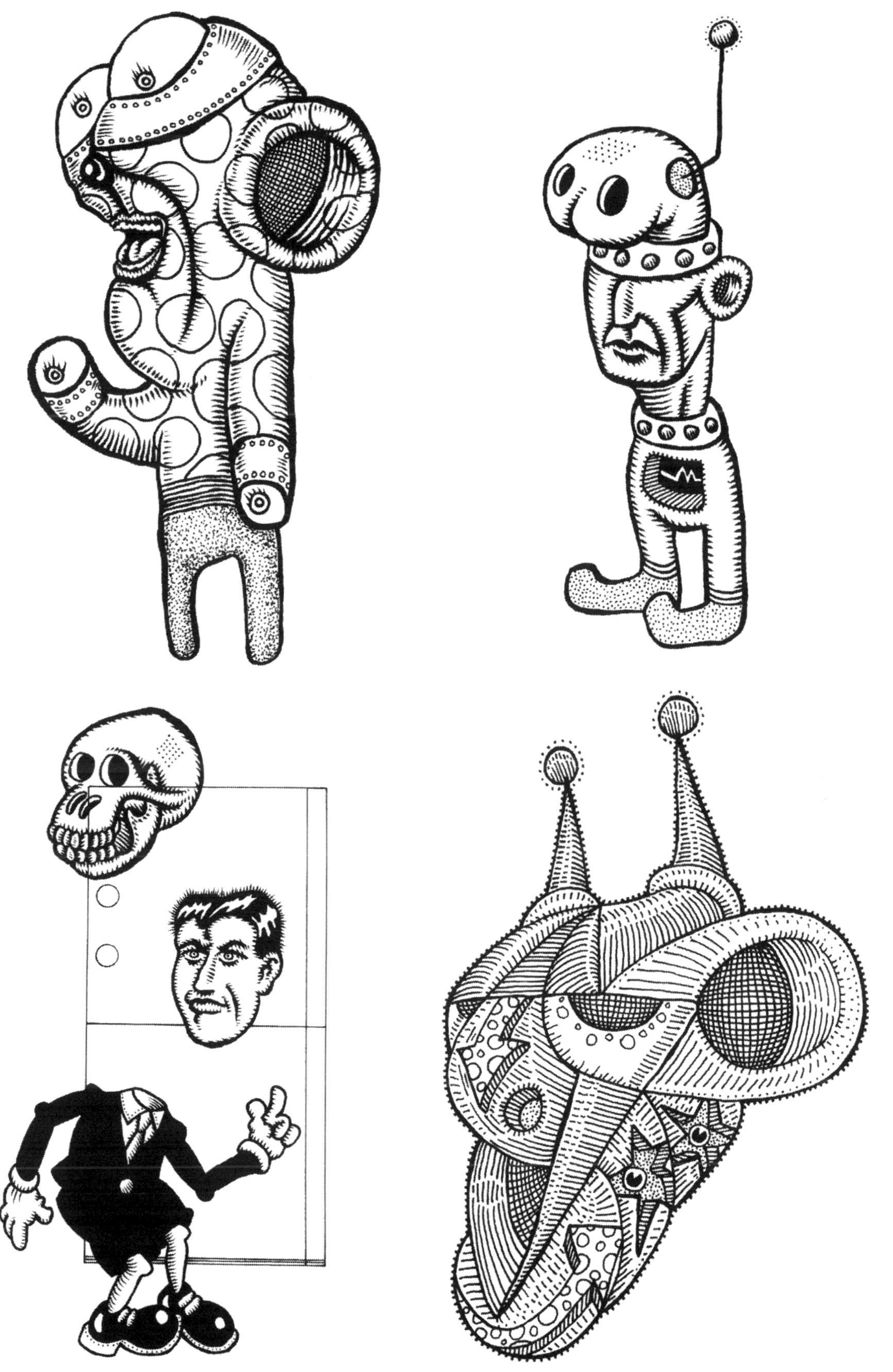

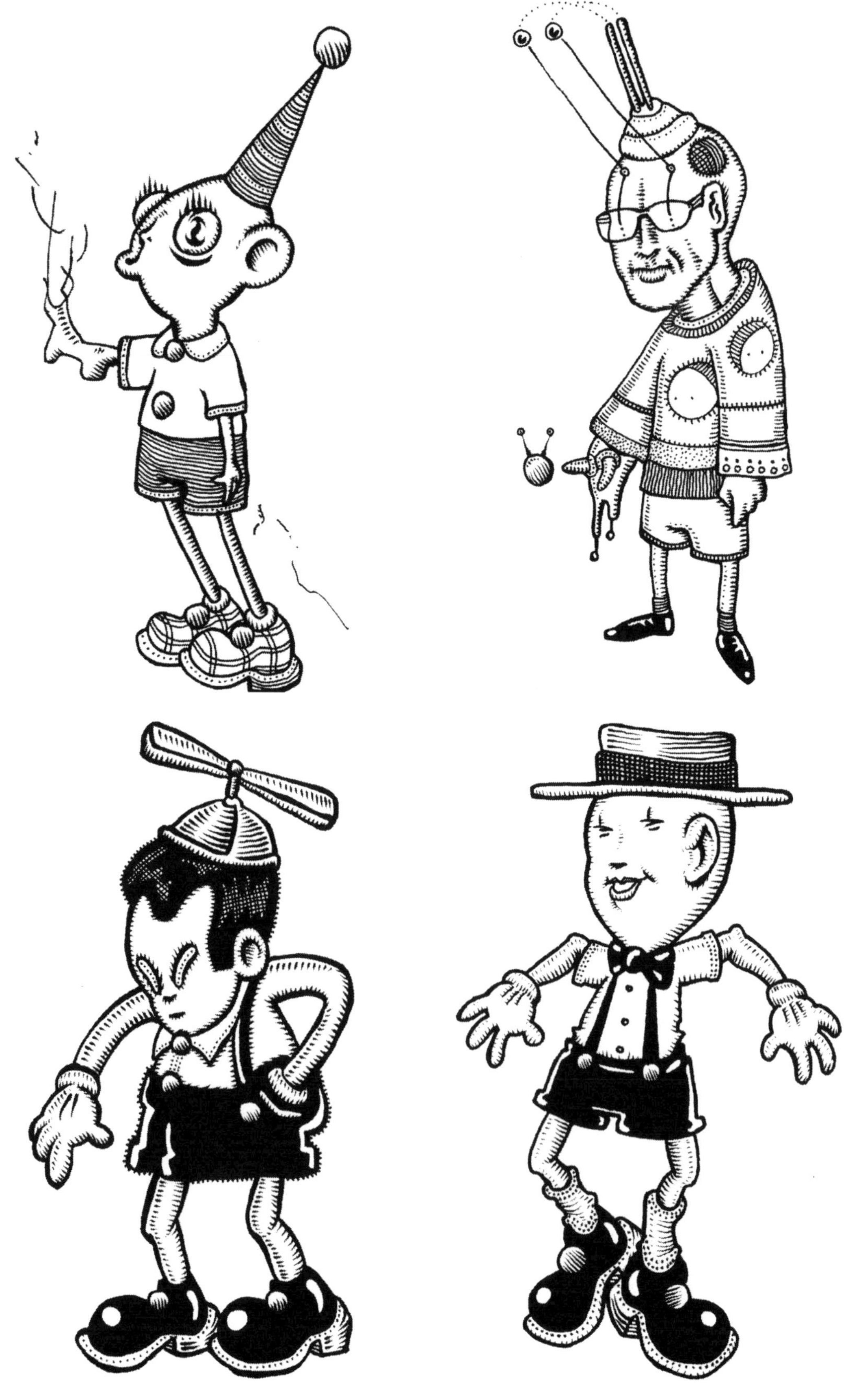

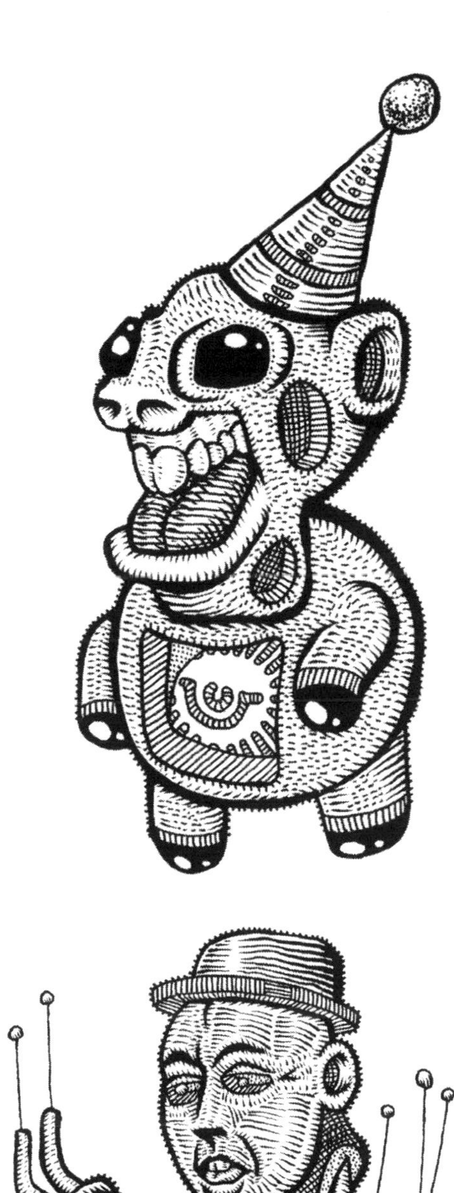

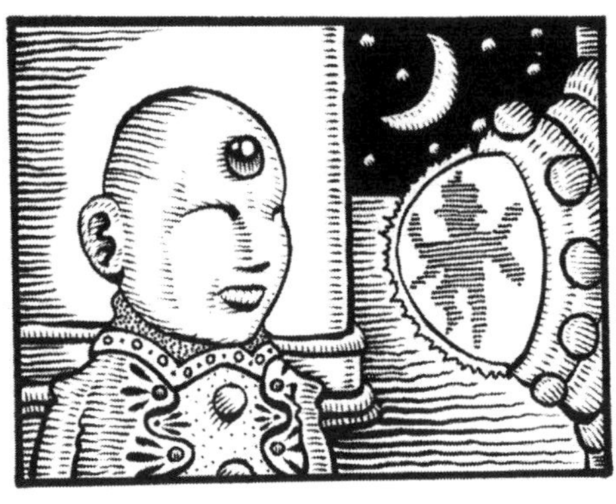

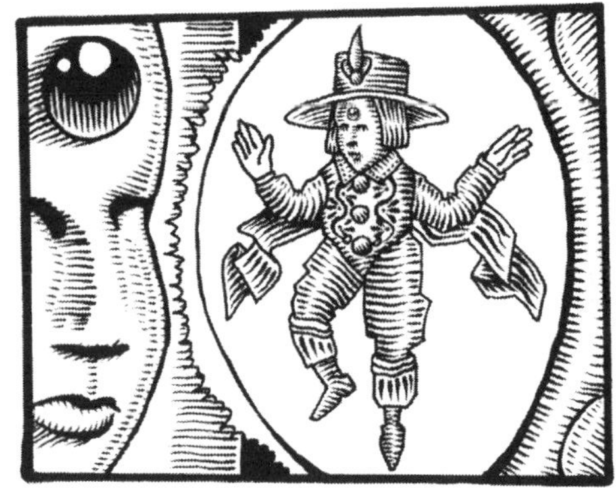

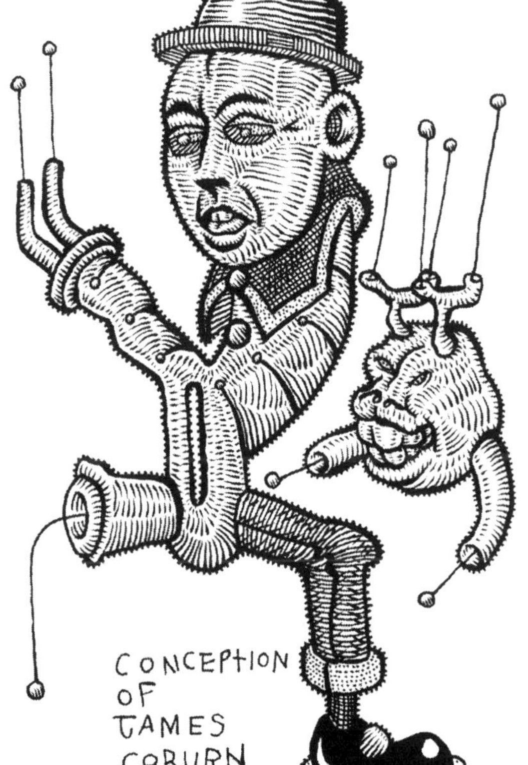
CONCEPtION
OF
JAMES
COBURN

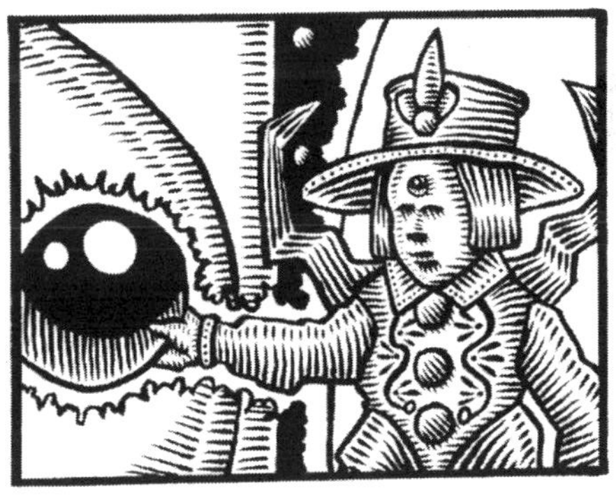

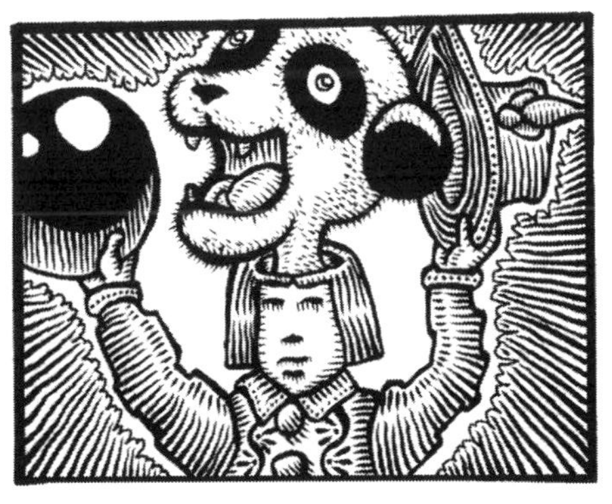

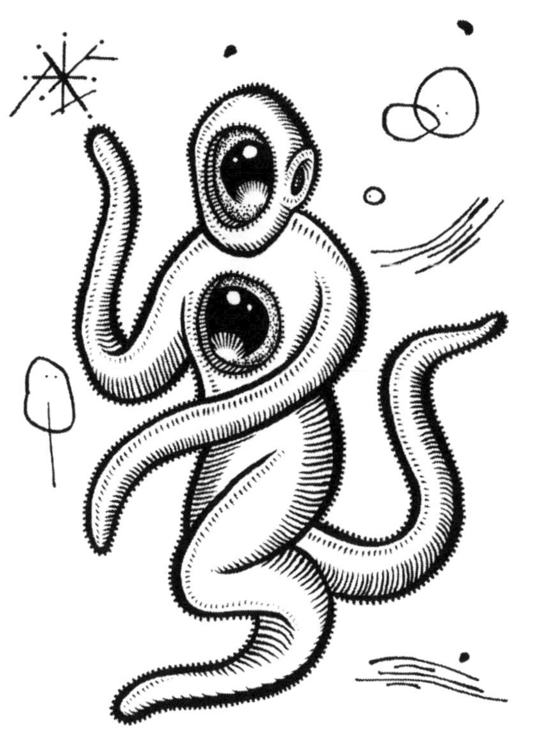

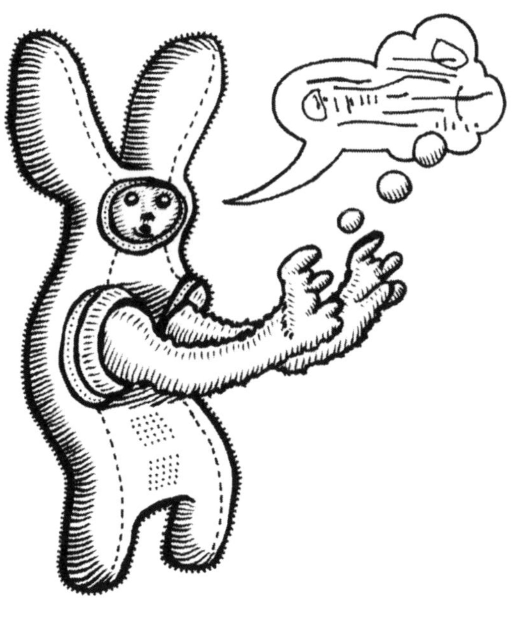

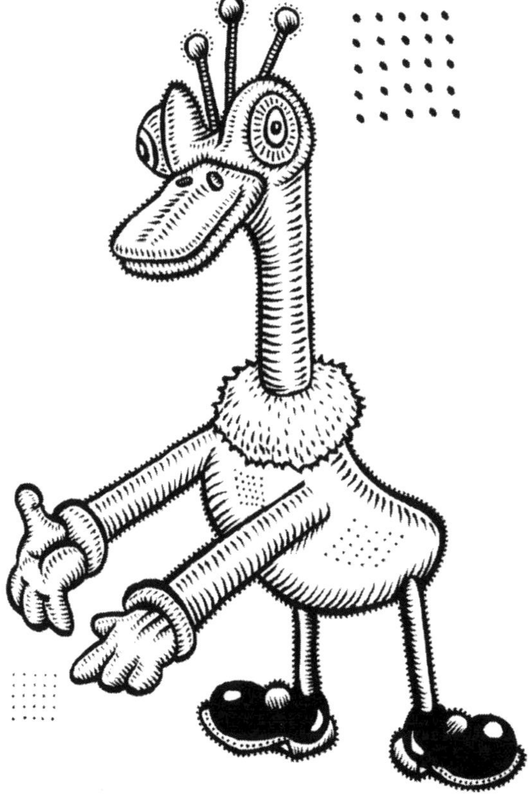

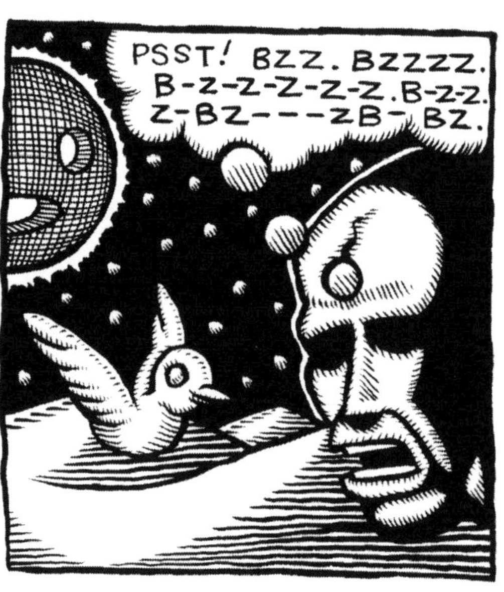
PSST! BZZ. BZZZZ.
B-Z-Z-Z-Z-Z.B-Z-Z.
Z-BZ---ZB-BZ.

2013

July

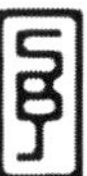

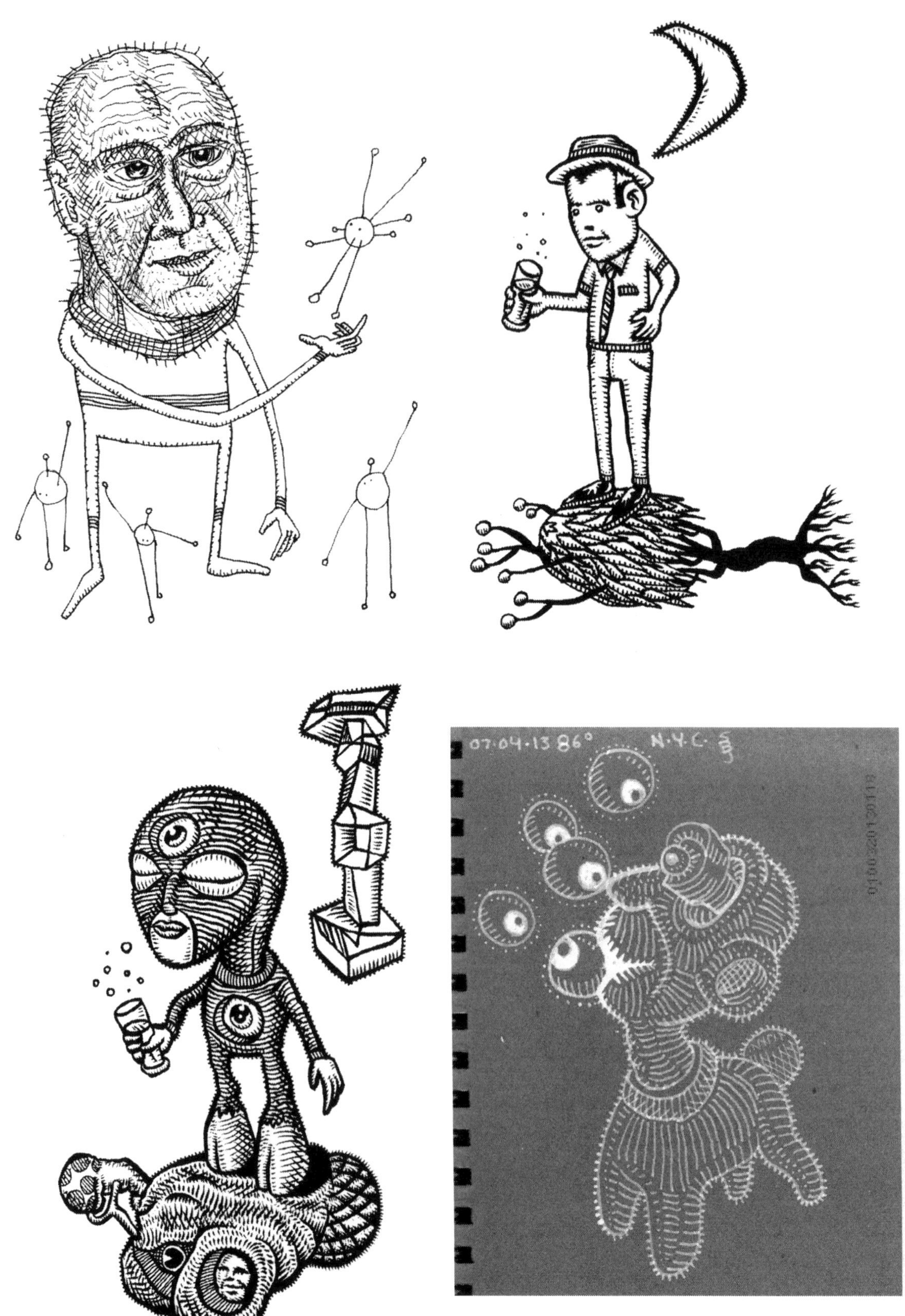
07·04·13 86°
N·Y·C·

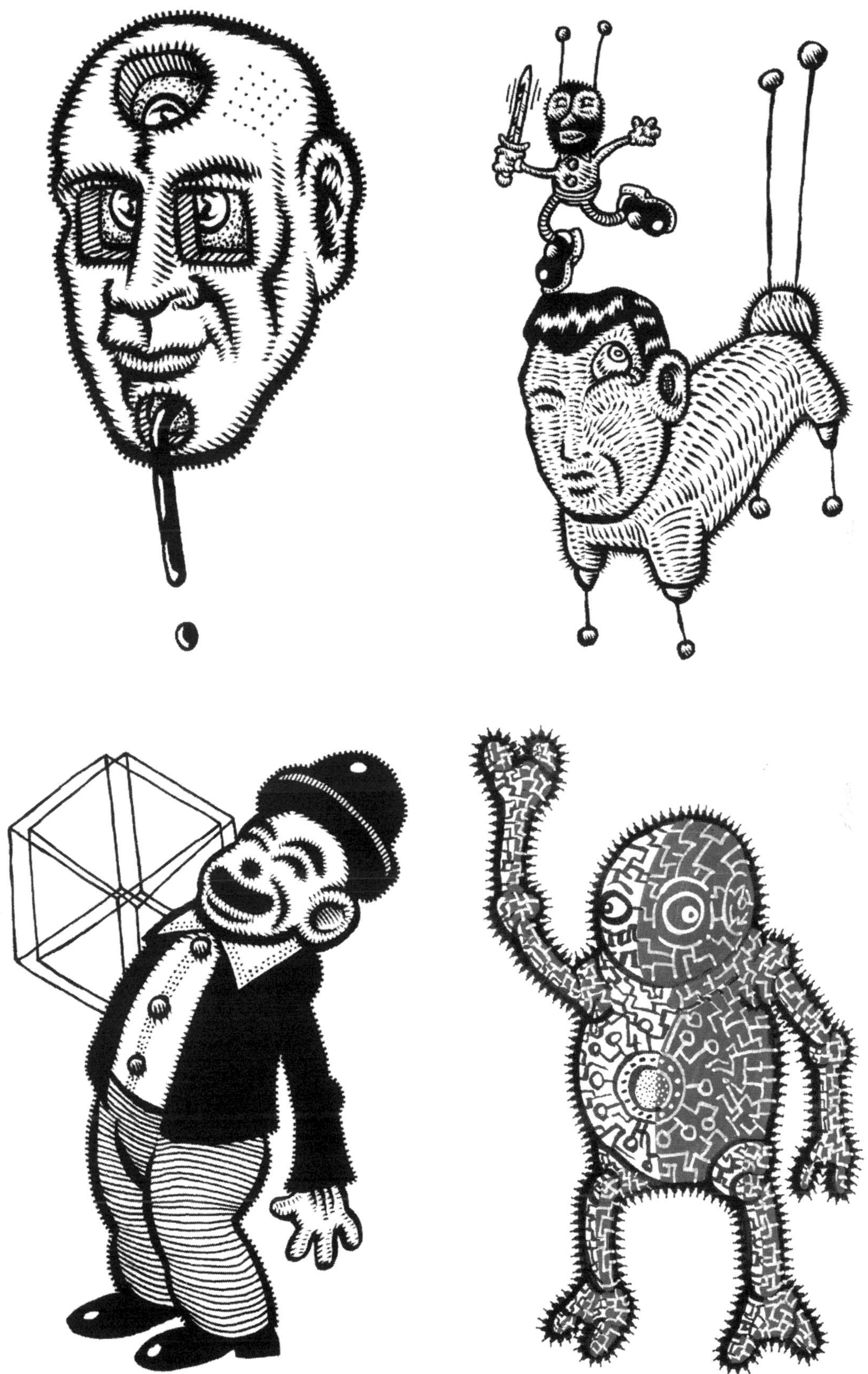

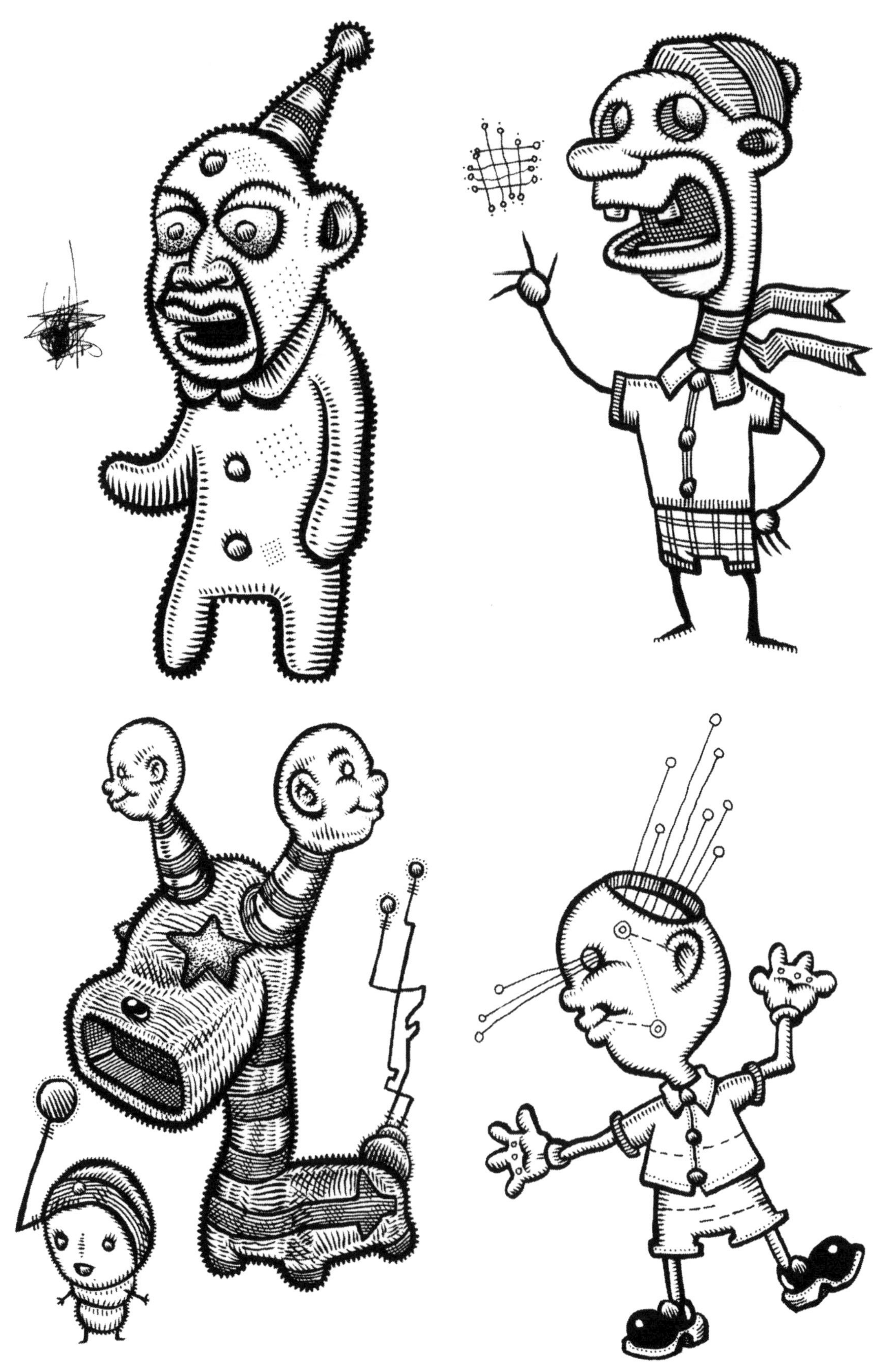

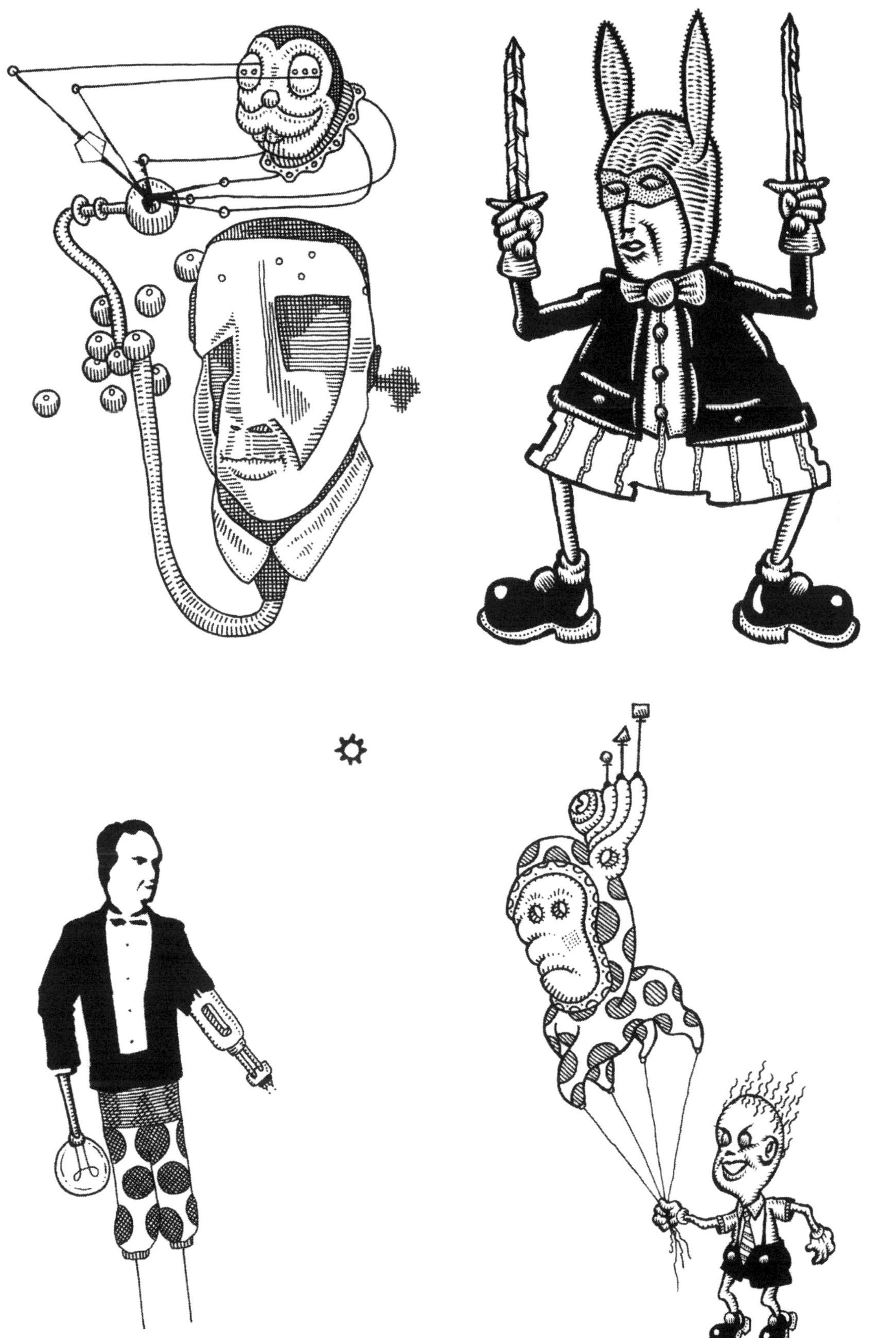

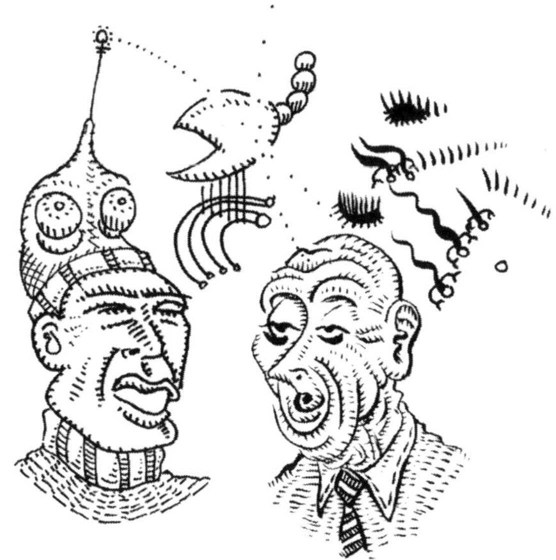

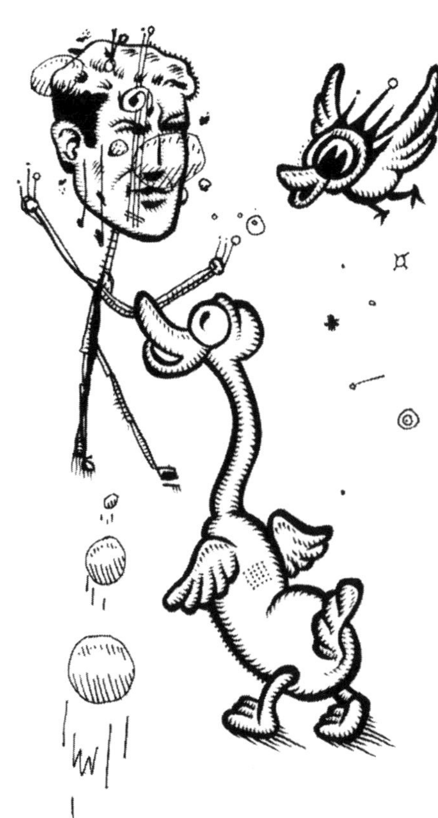

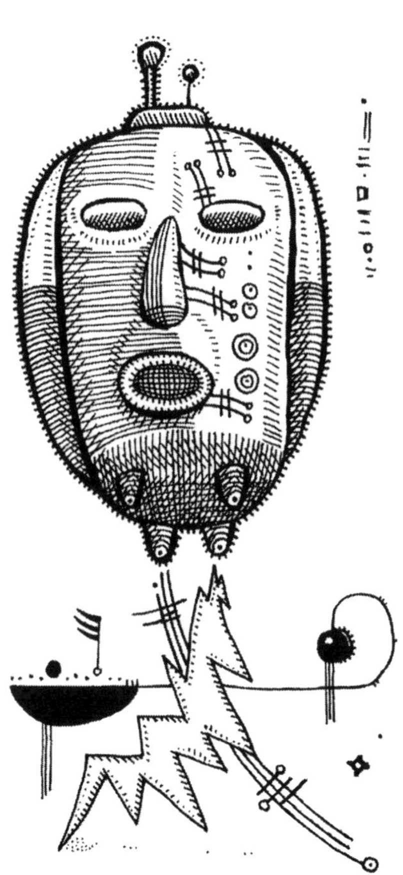

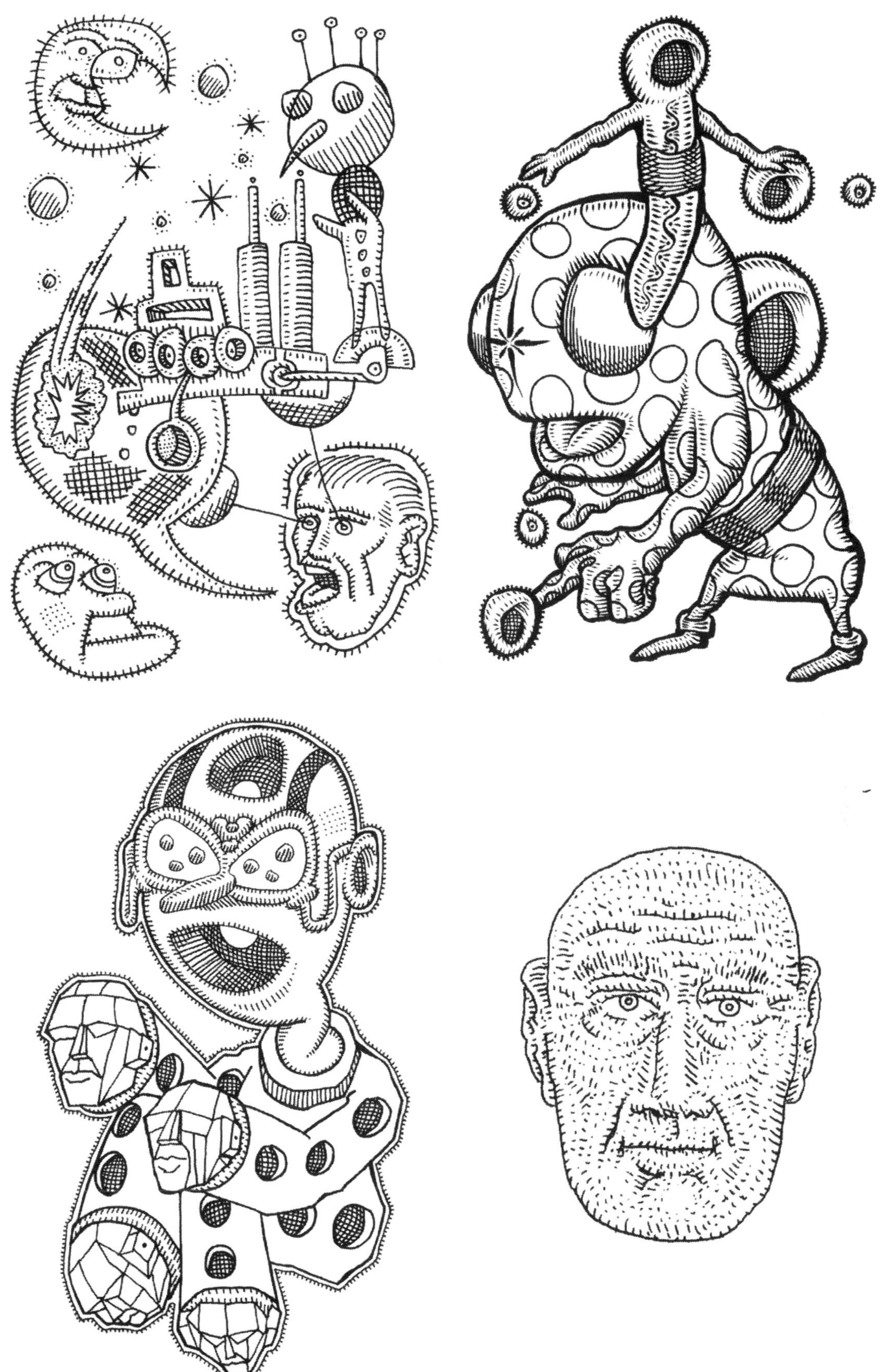

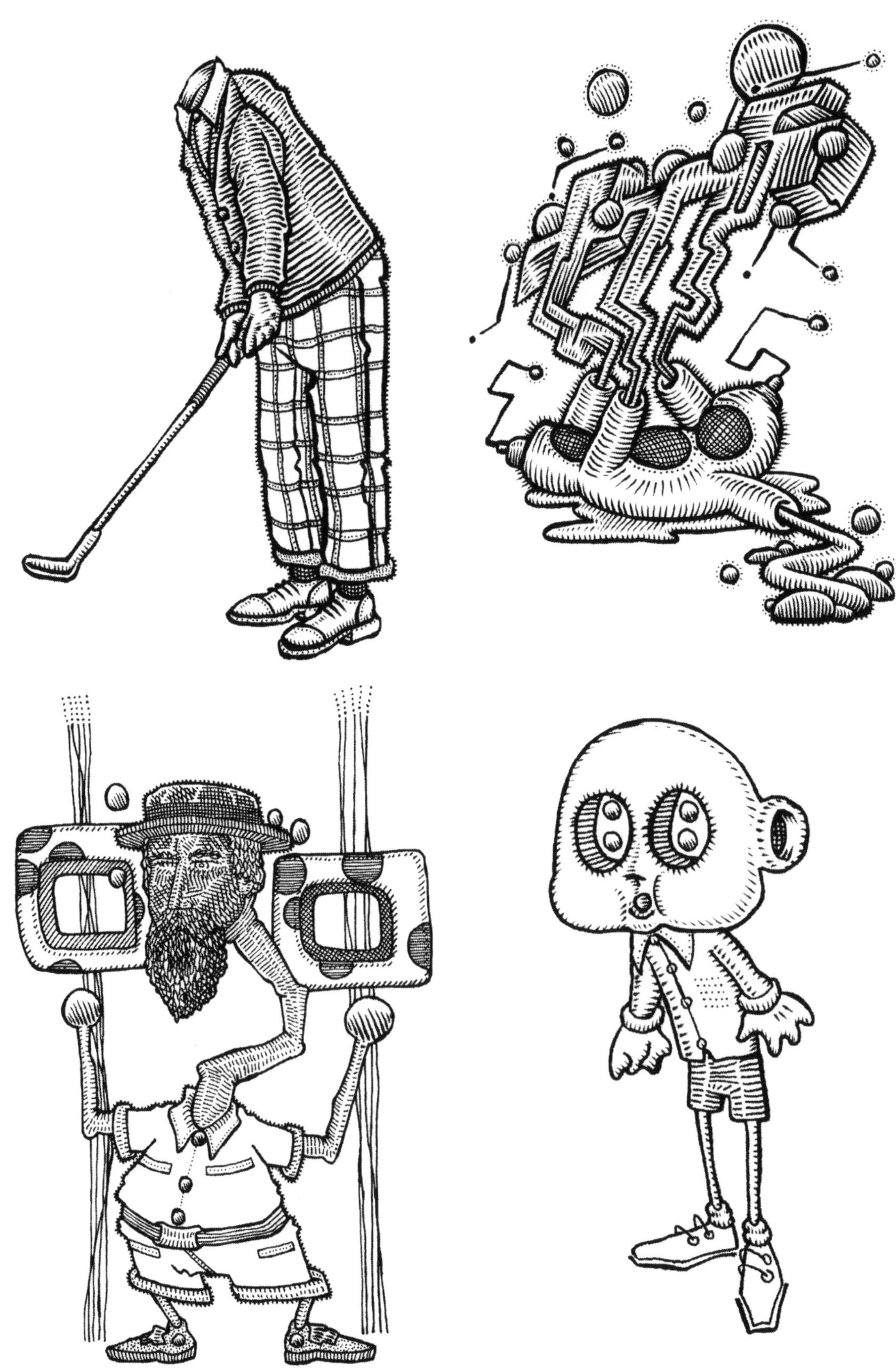

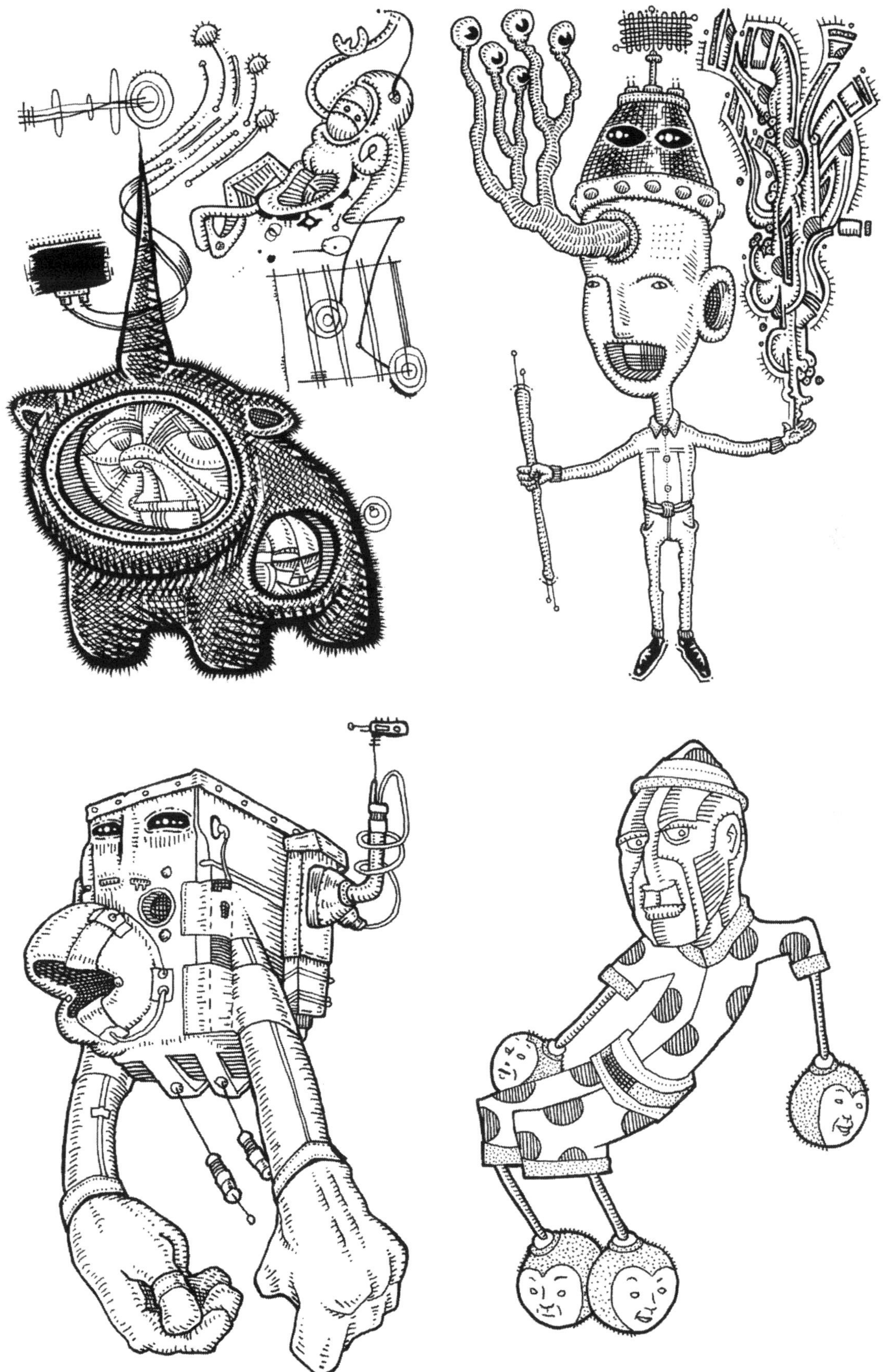

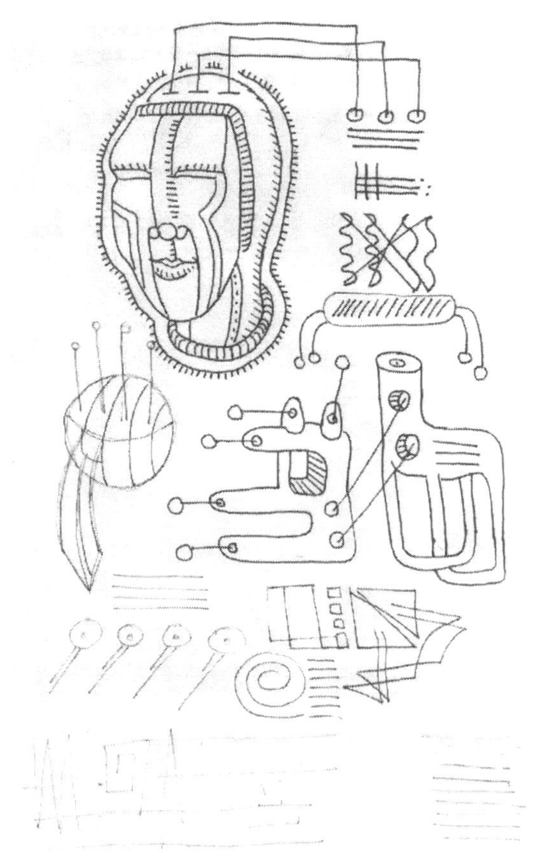

2013

August

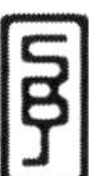

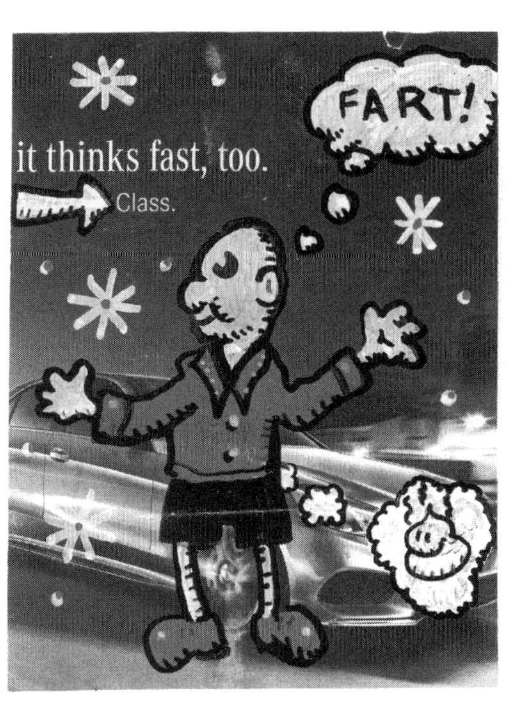
FART!
it thinks fast, too.
Class.

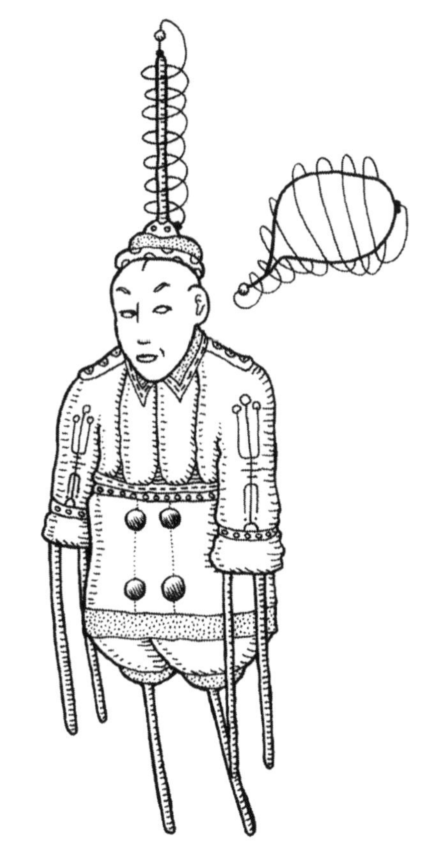

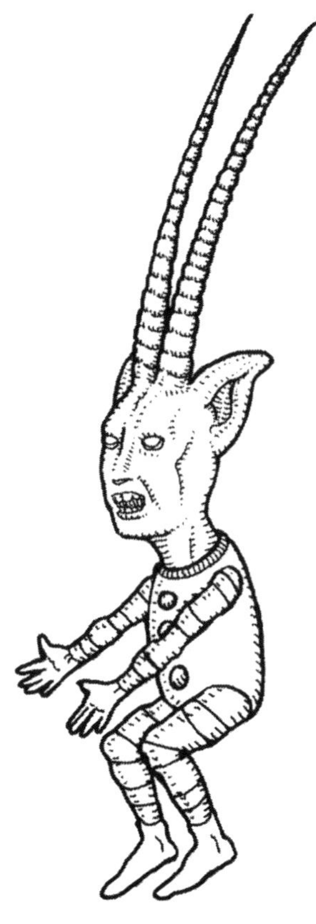

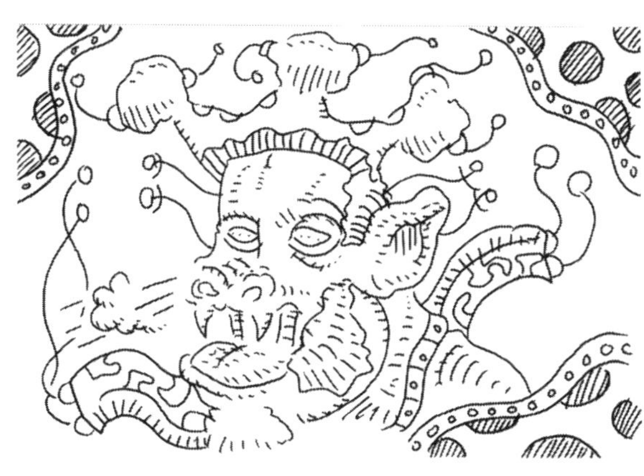

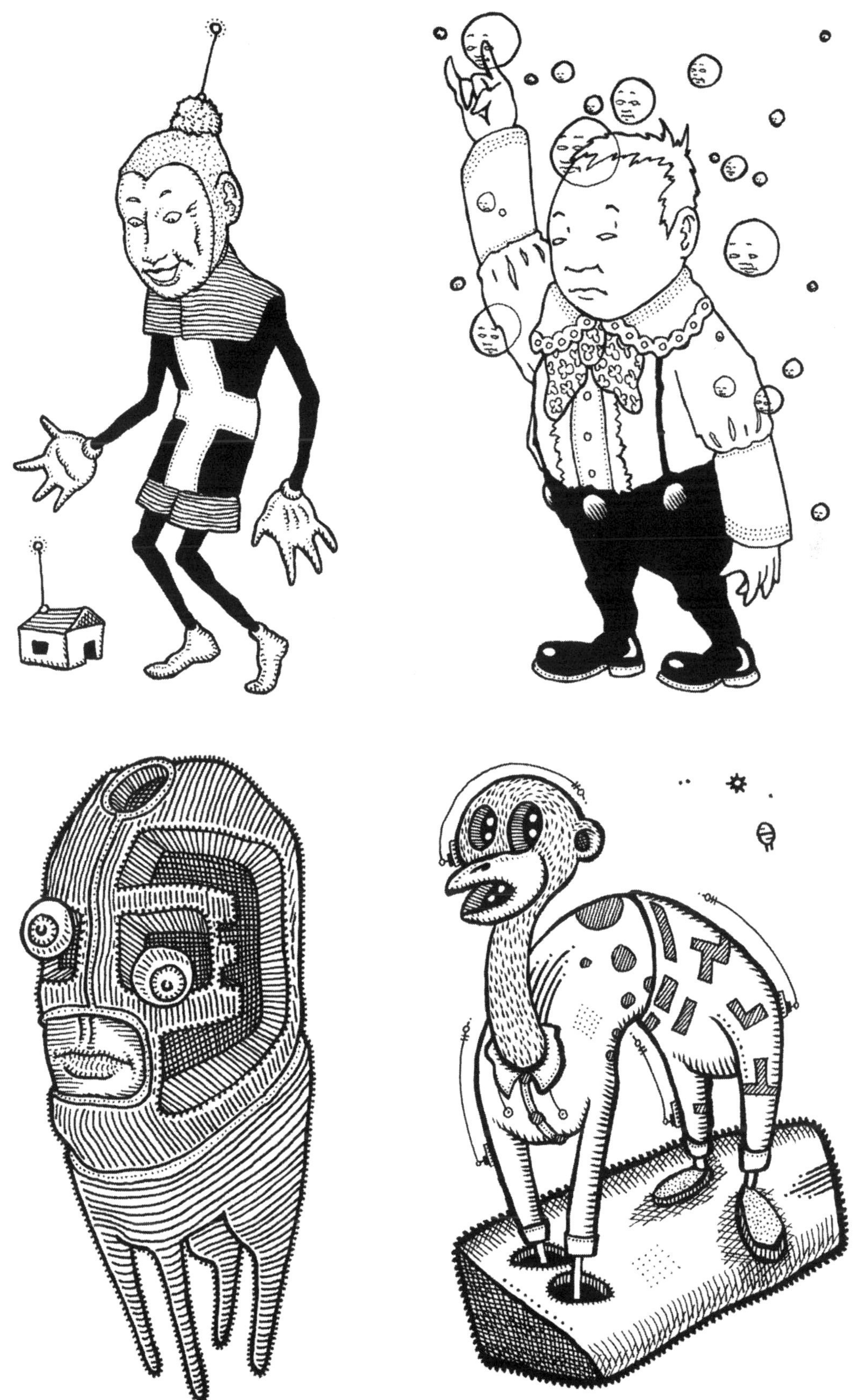

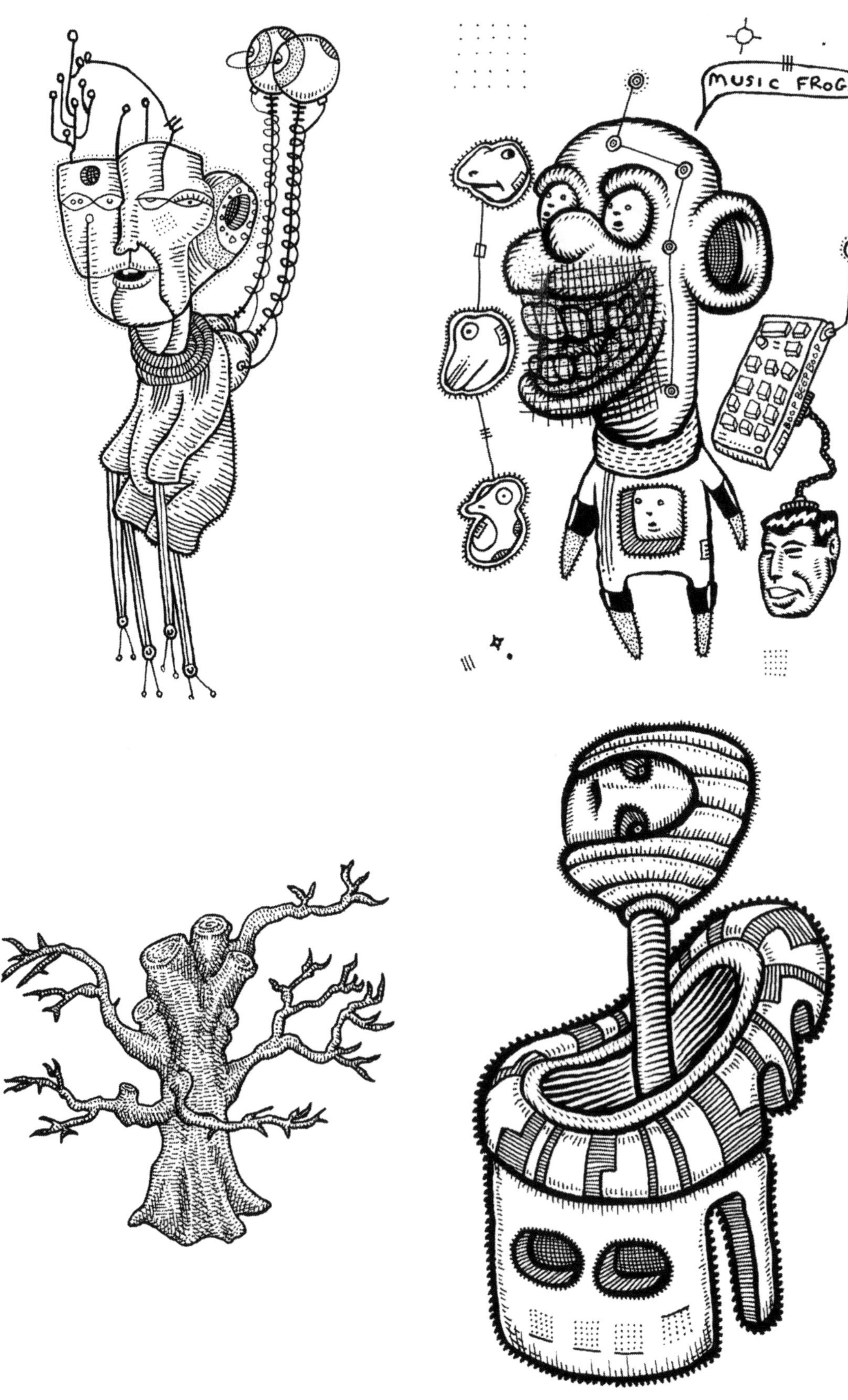
MUSIC FROGS.
BOOP BEEP BOOP

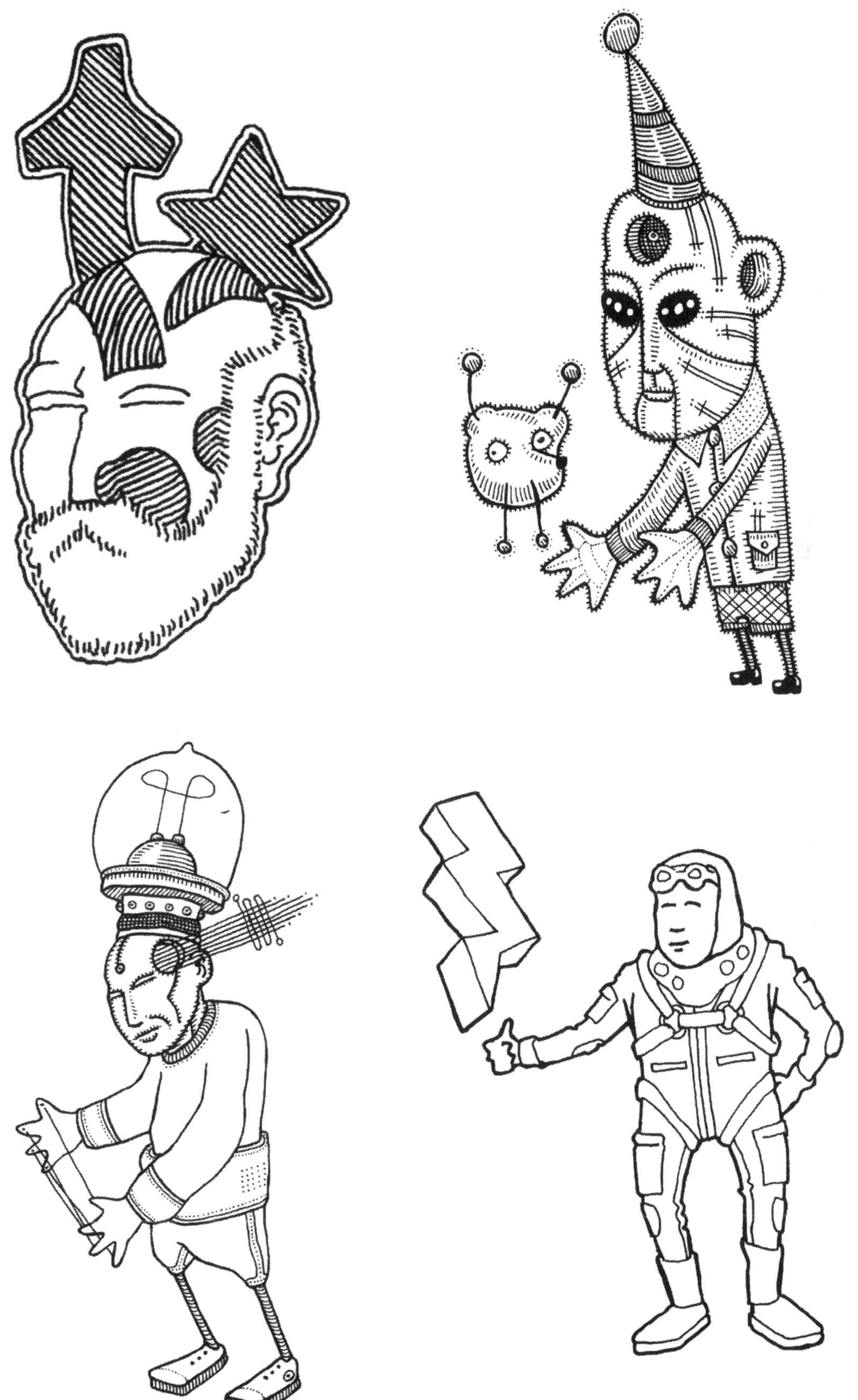

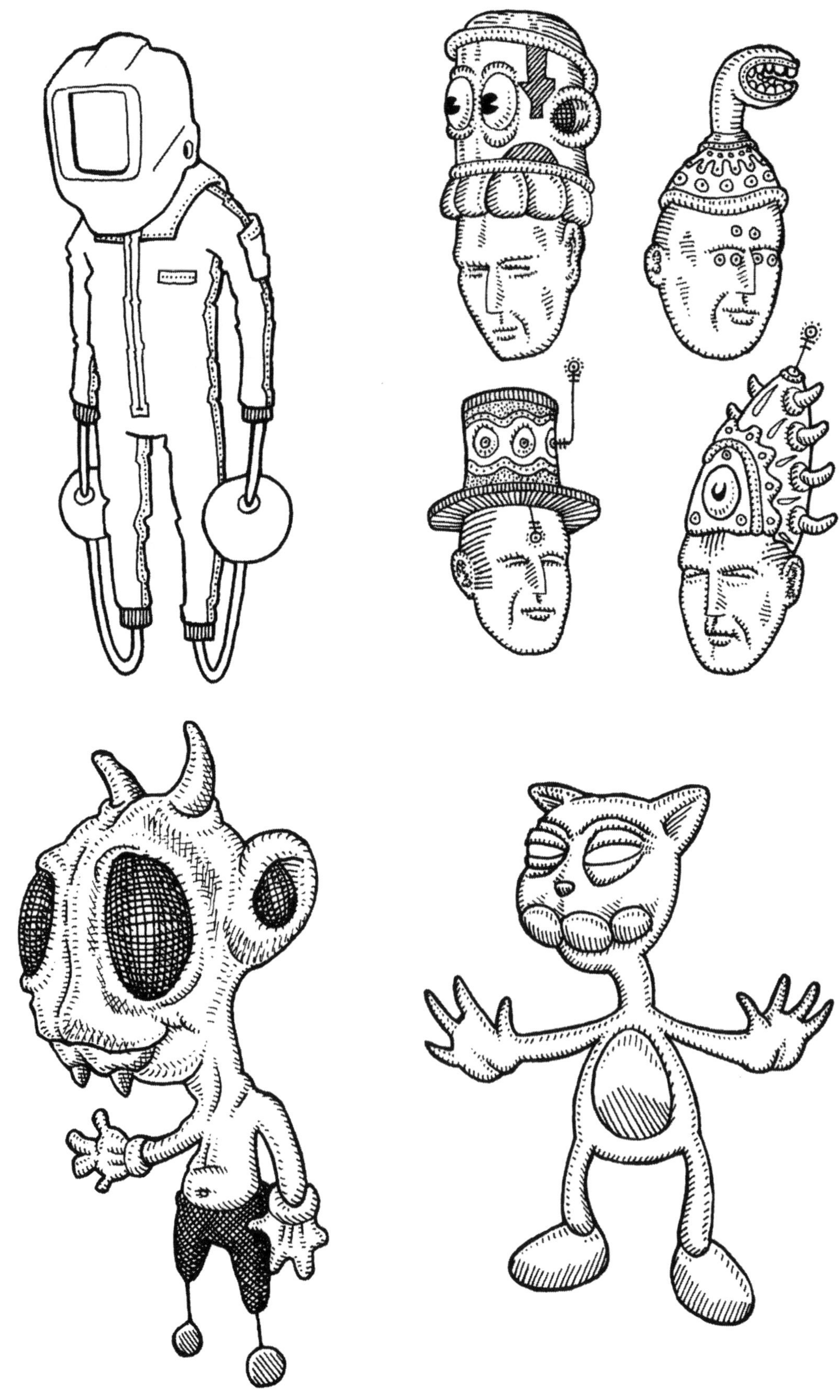

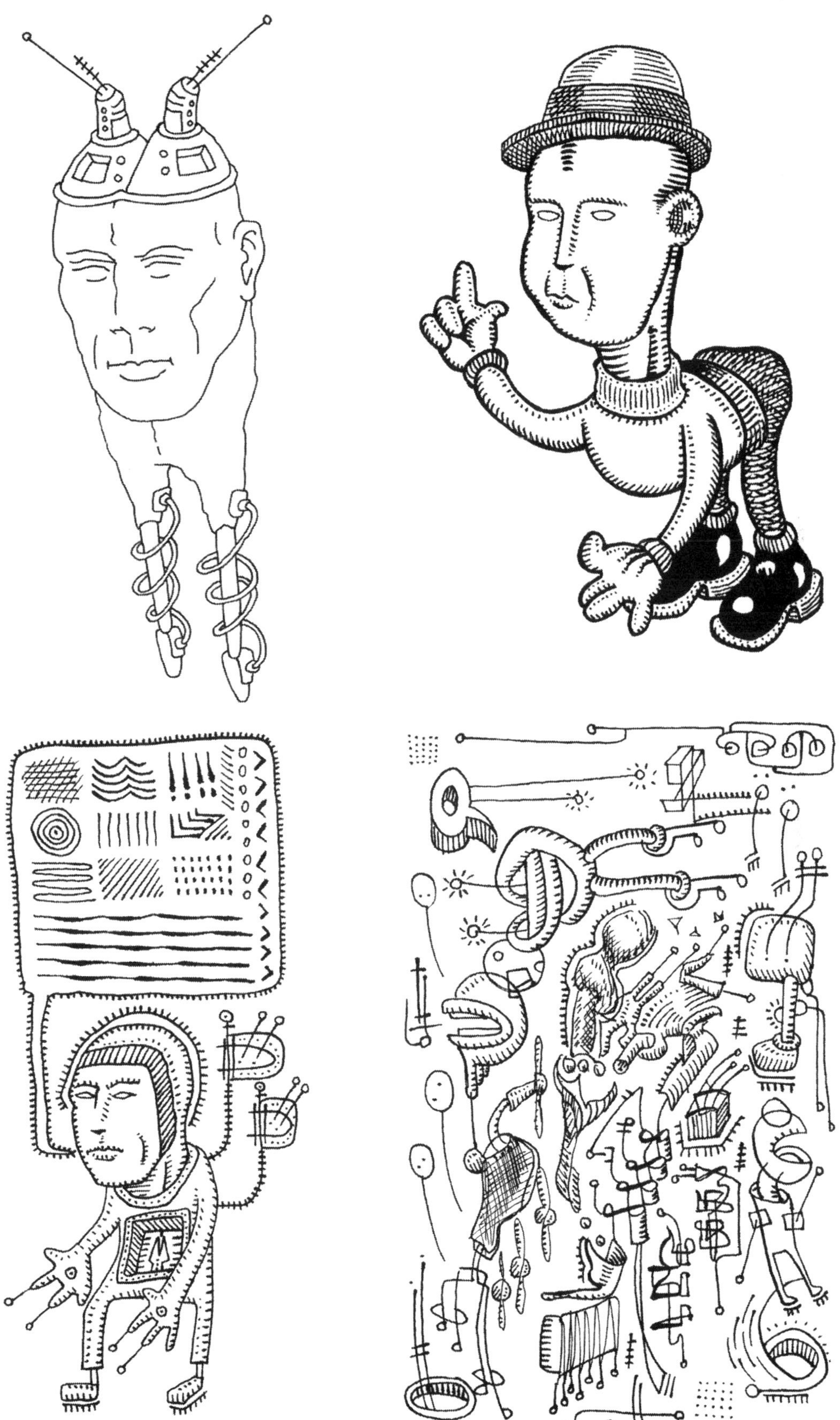

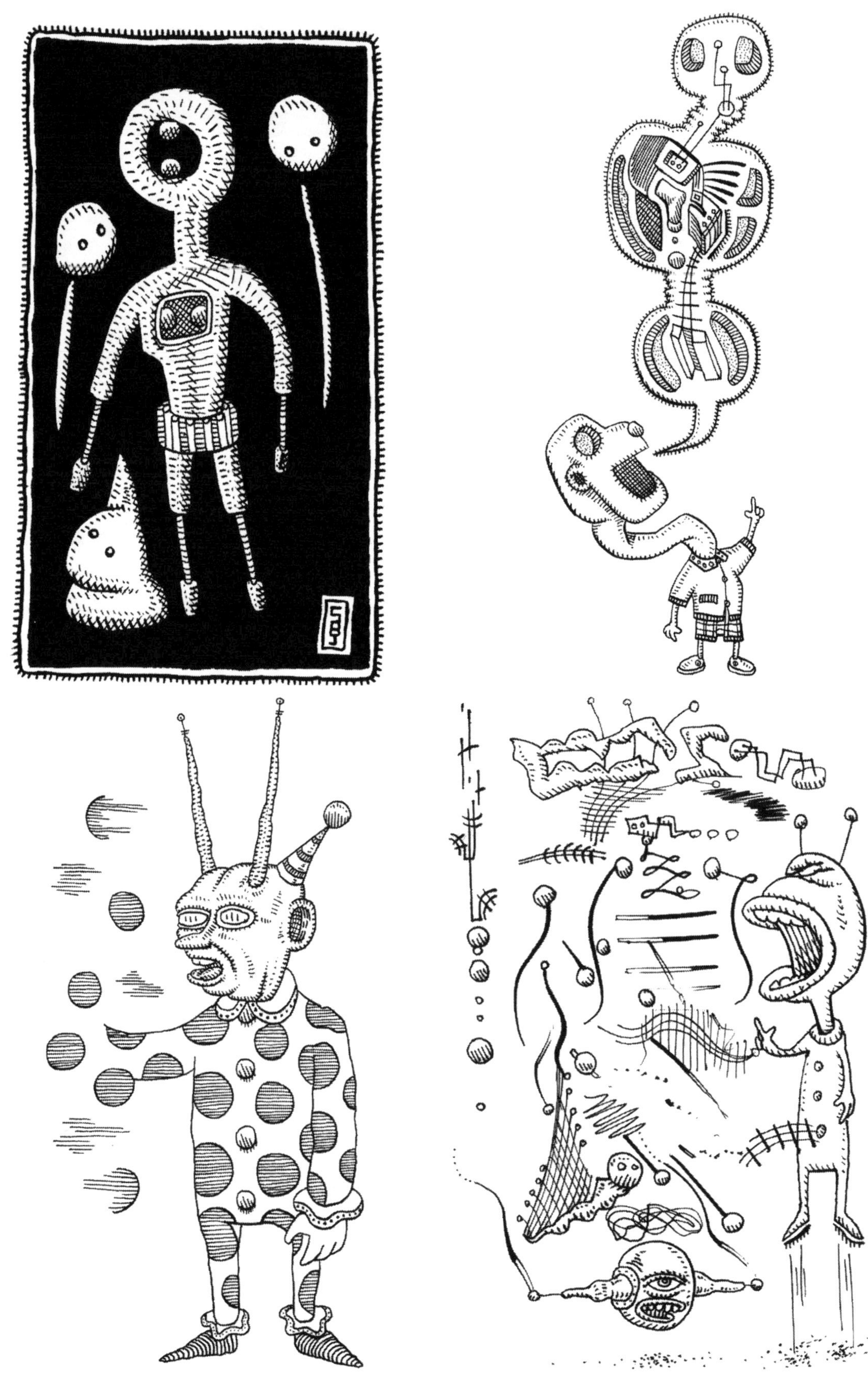

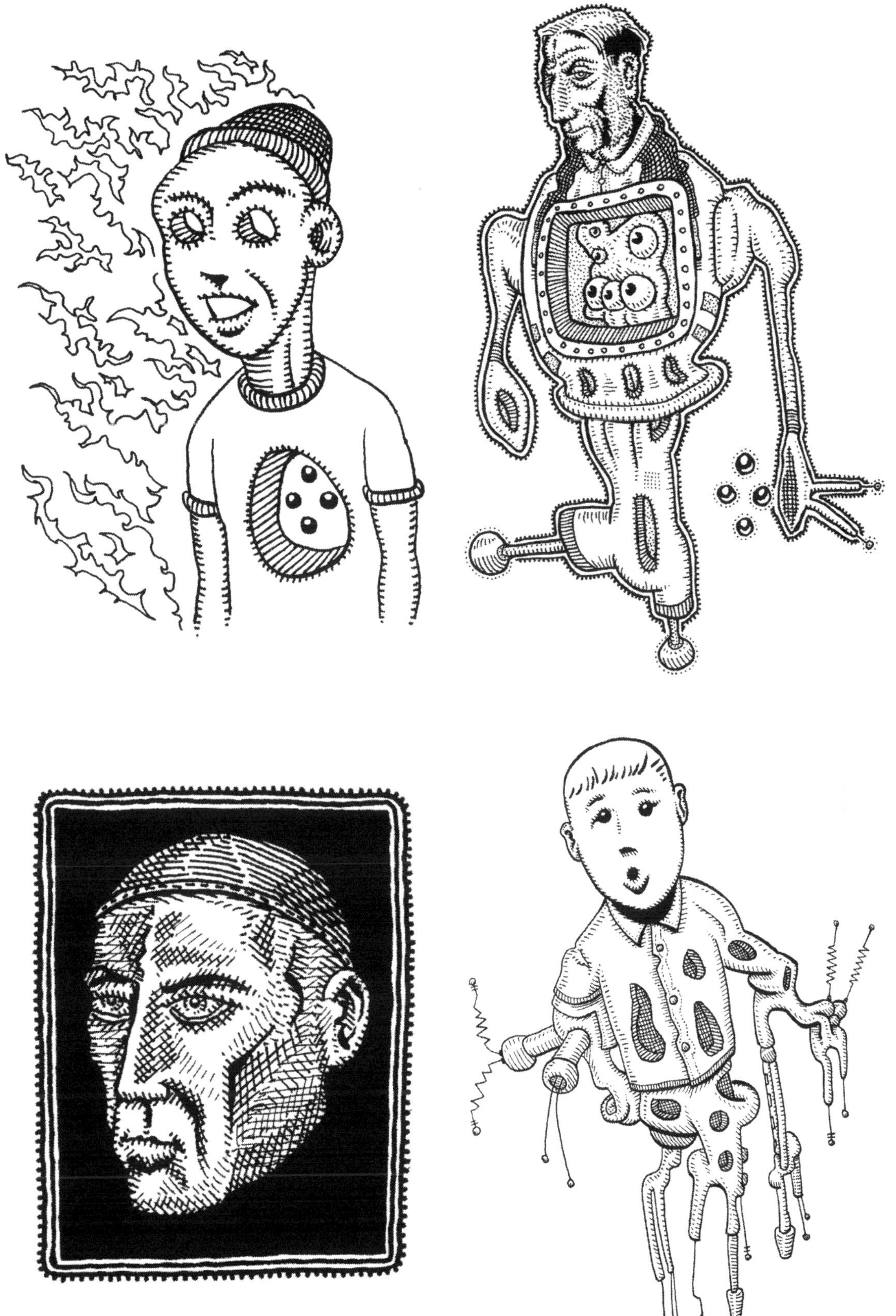

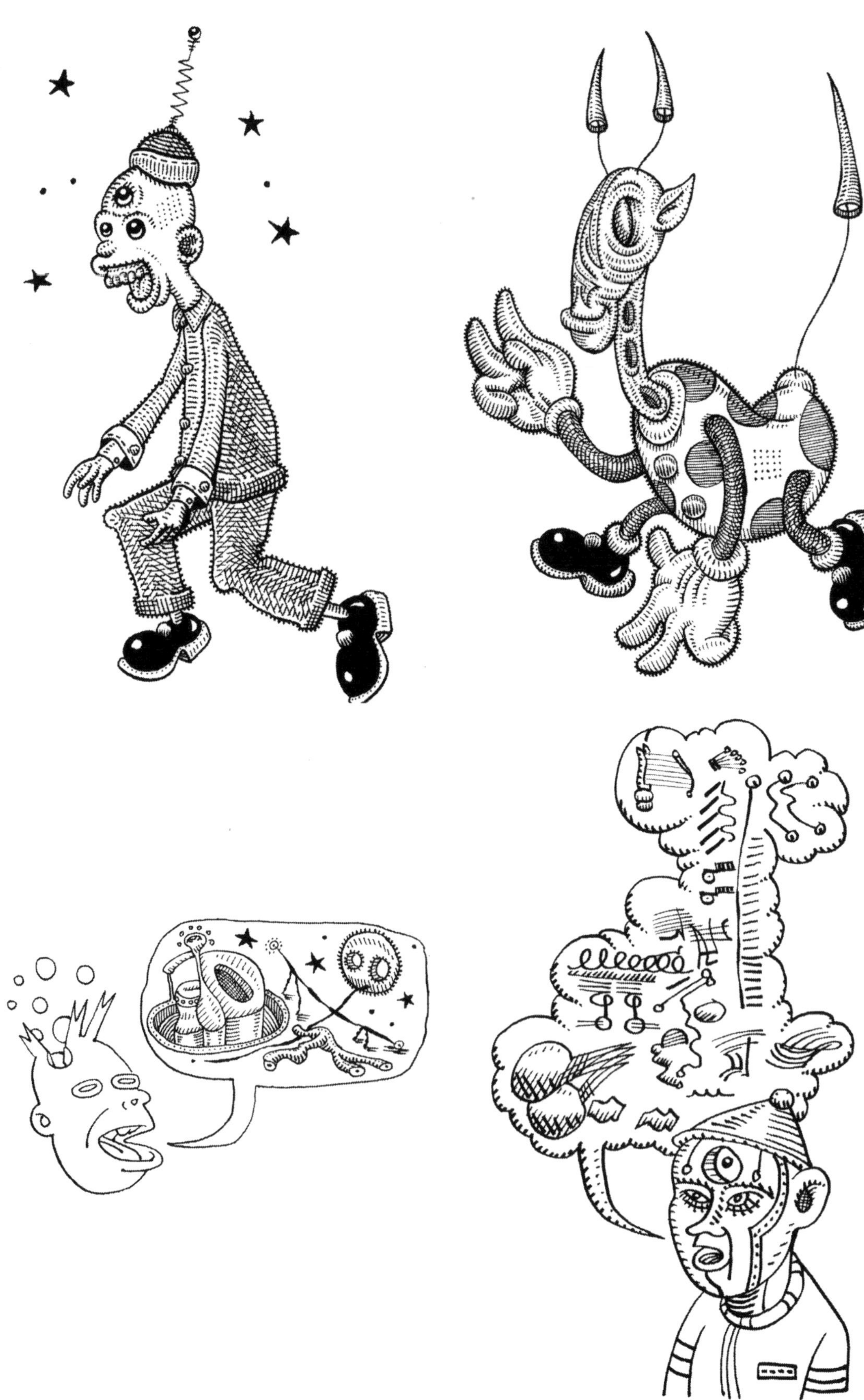

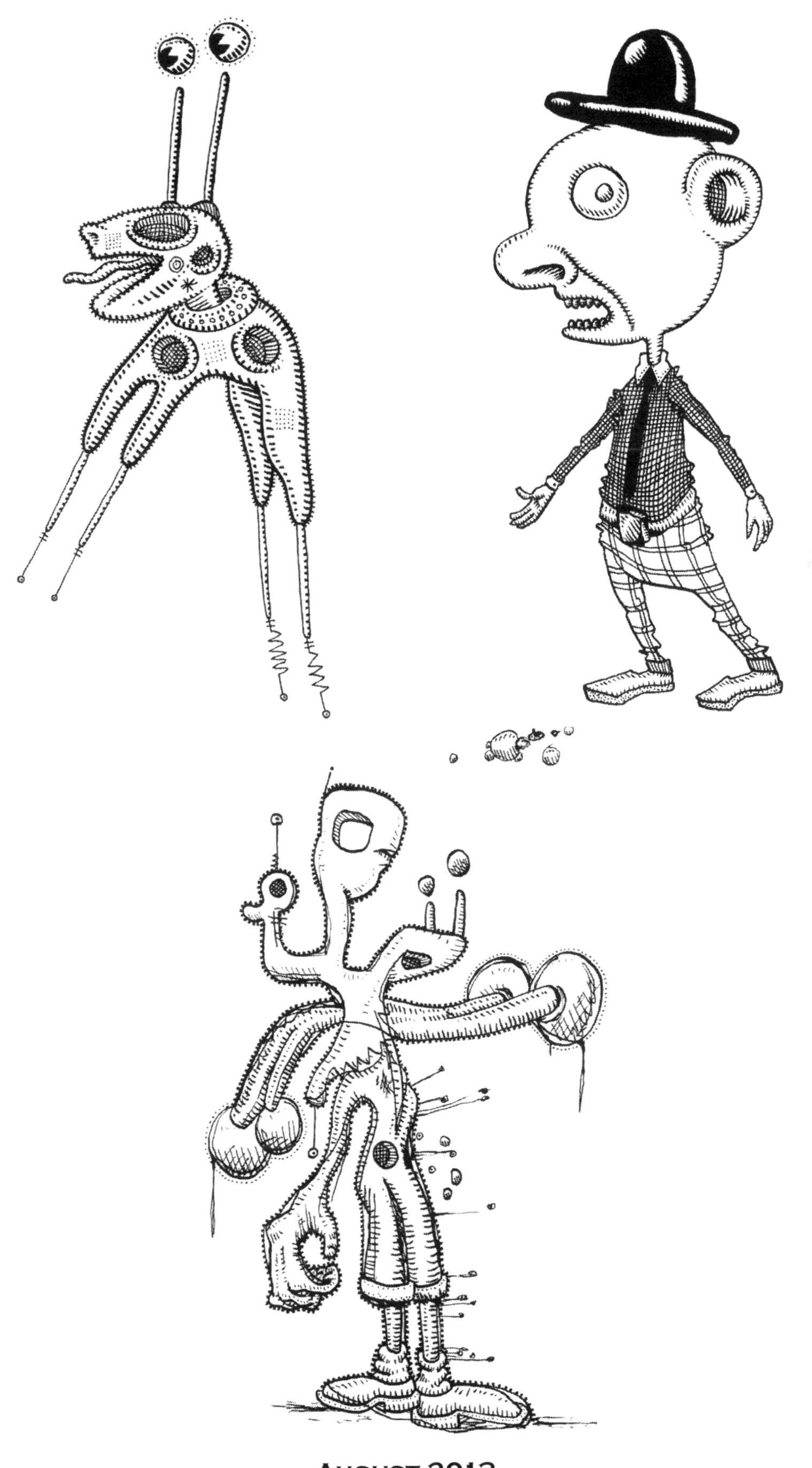

2013

September

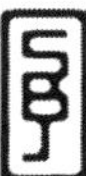

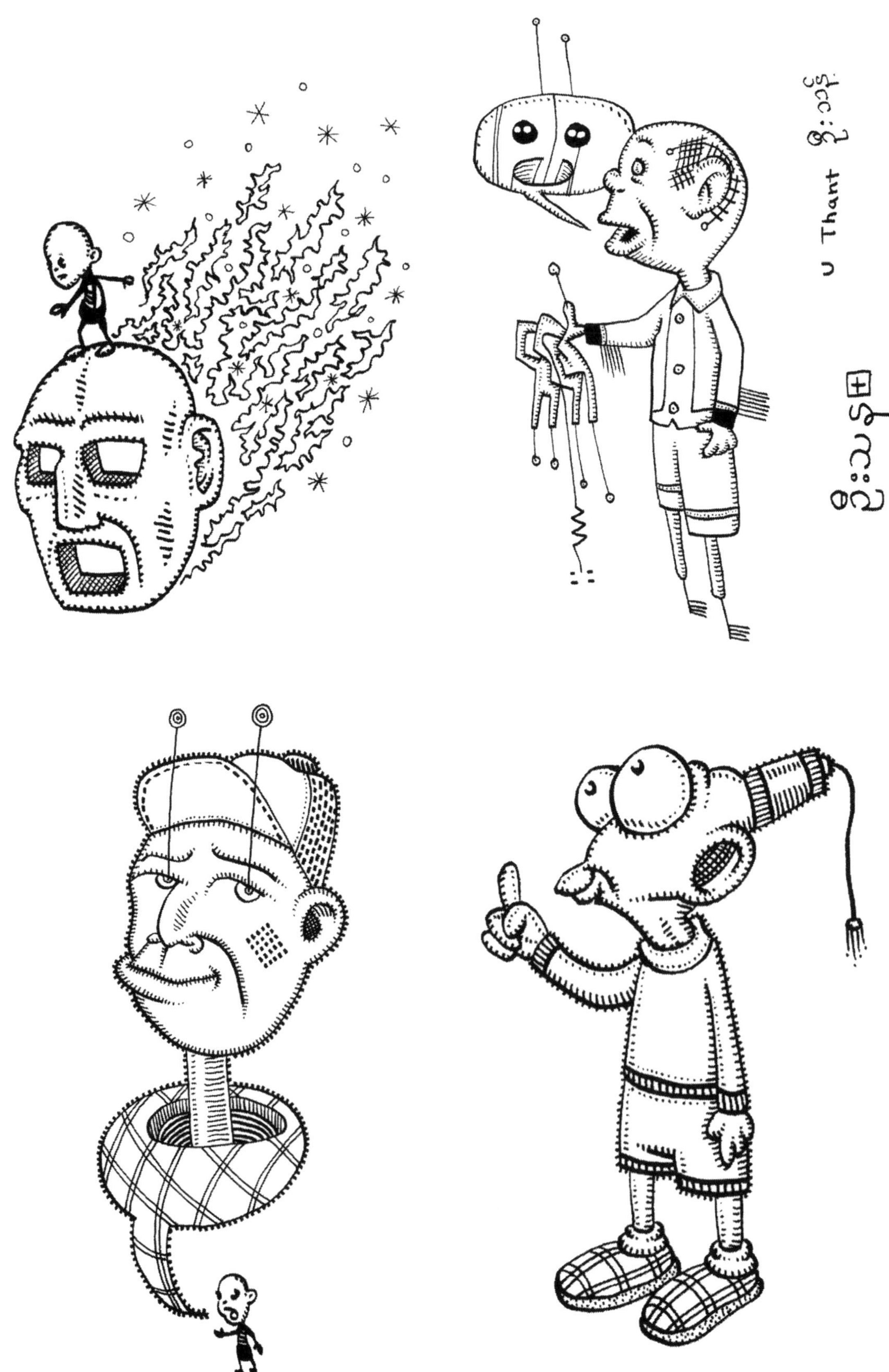
U Thant

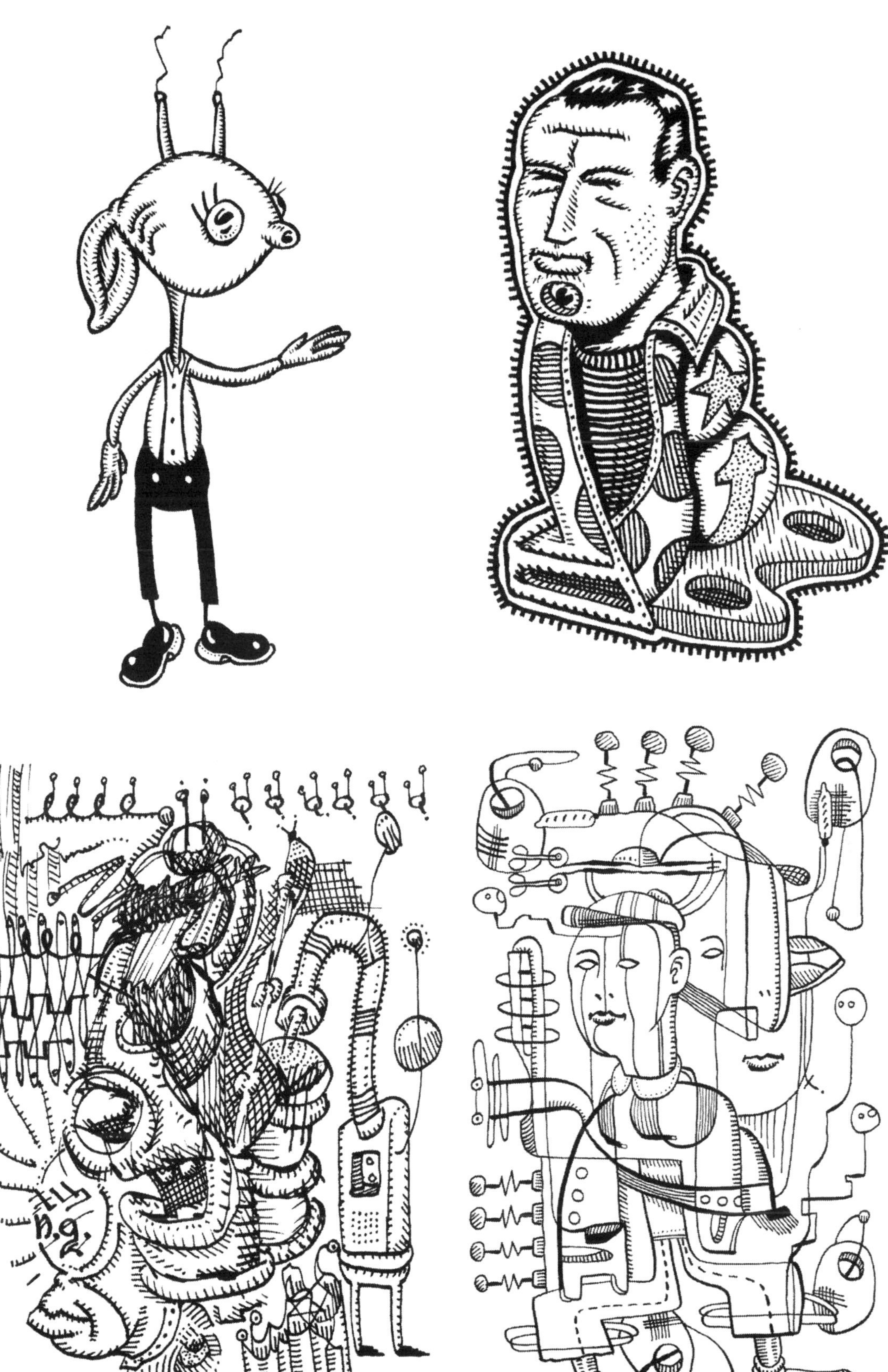

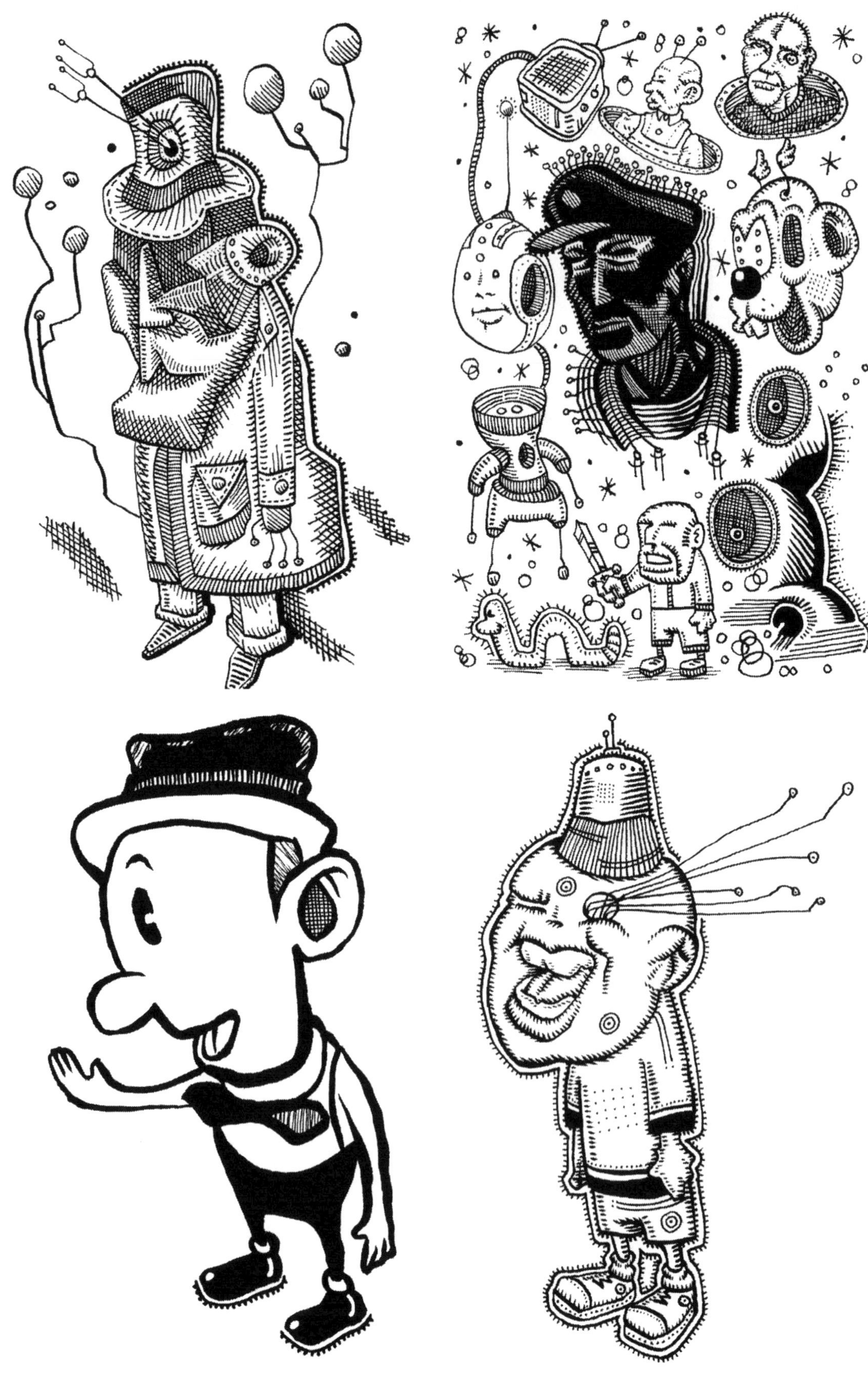

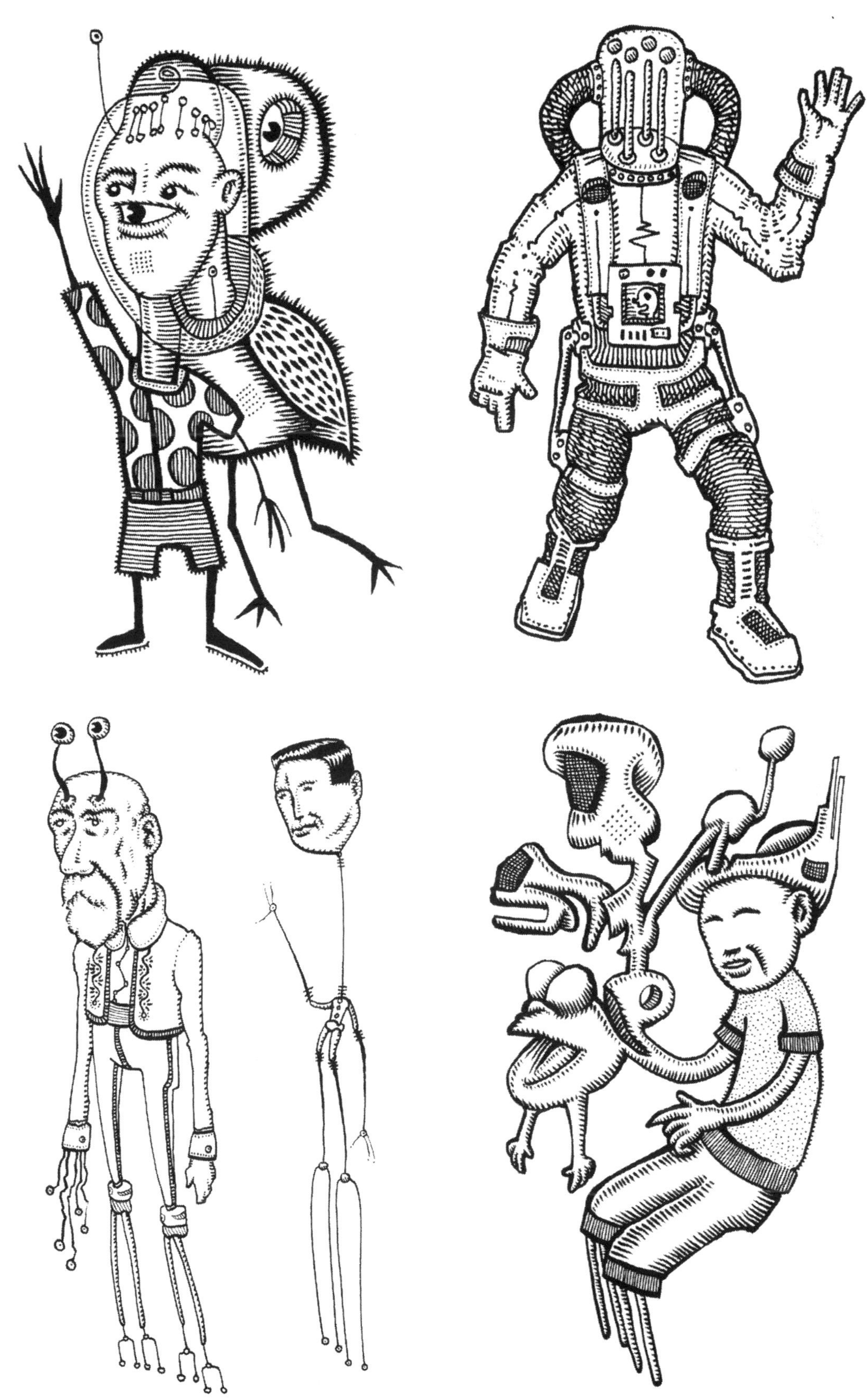

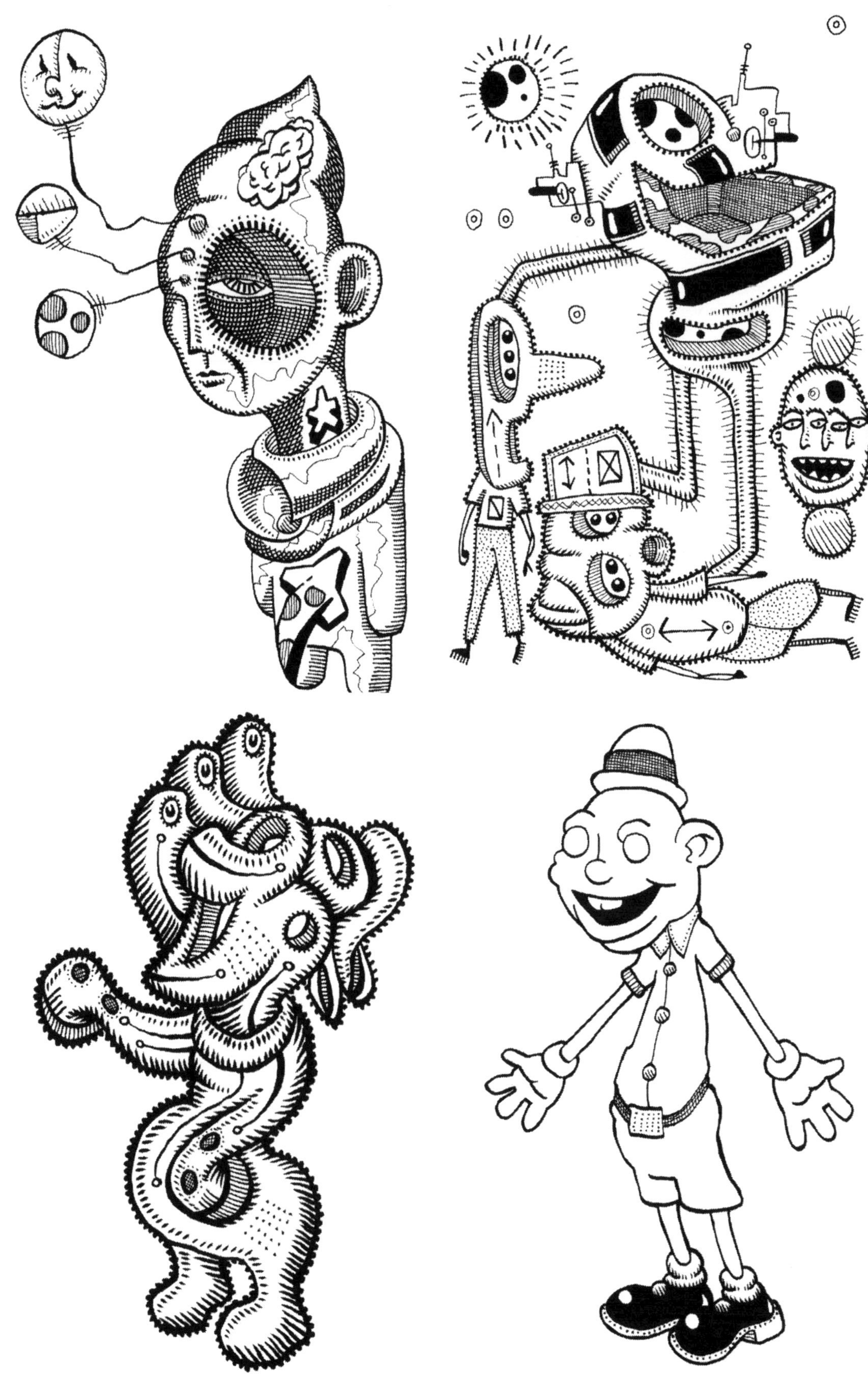

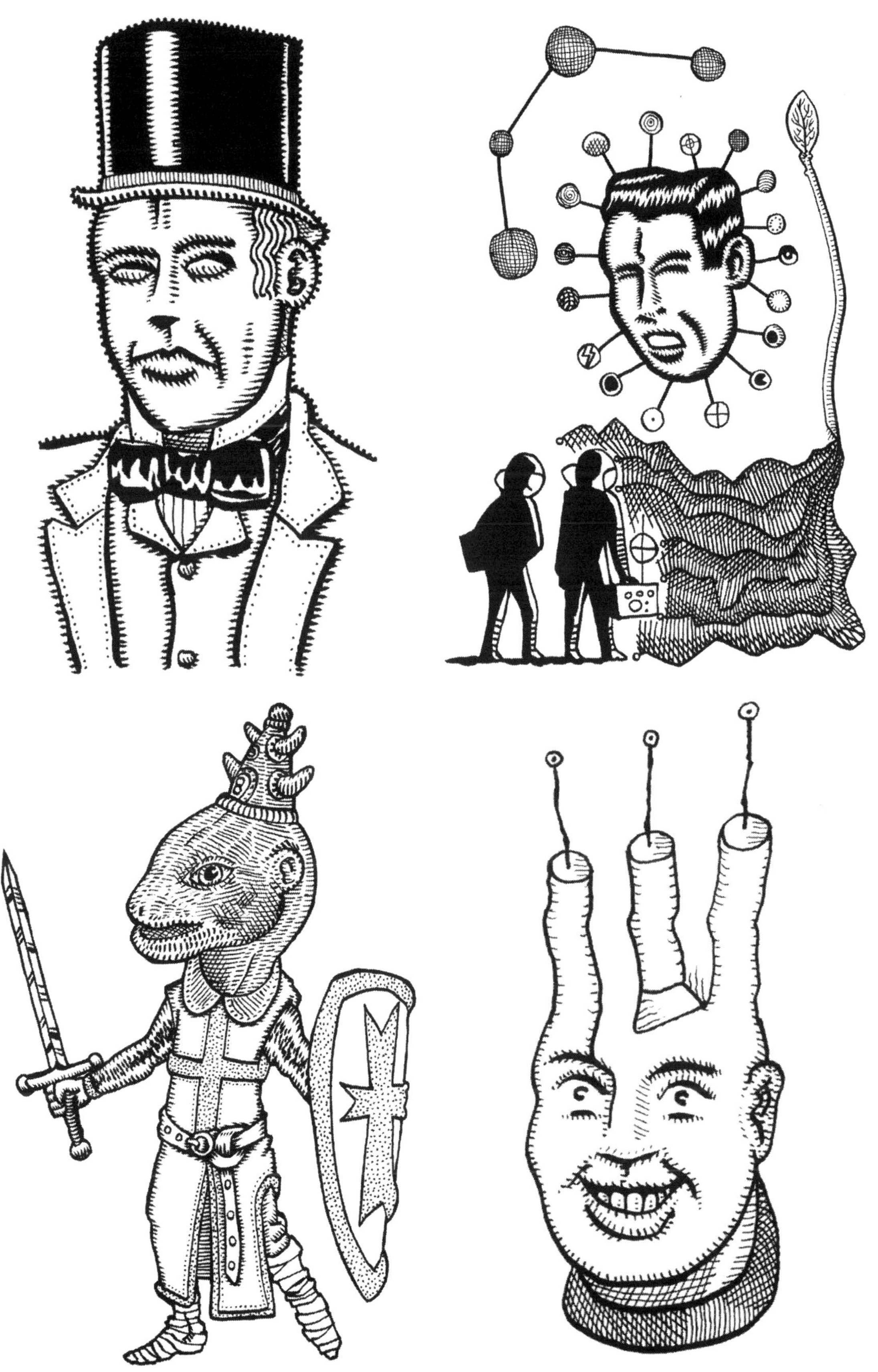

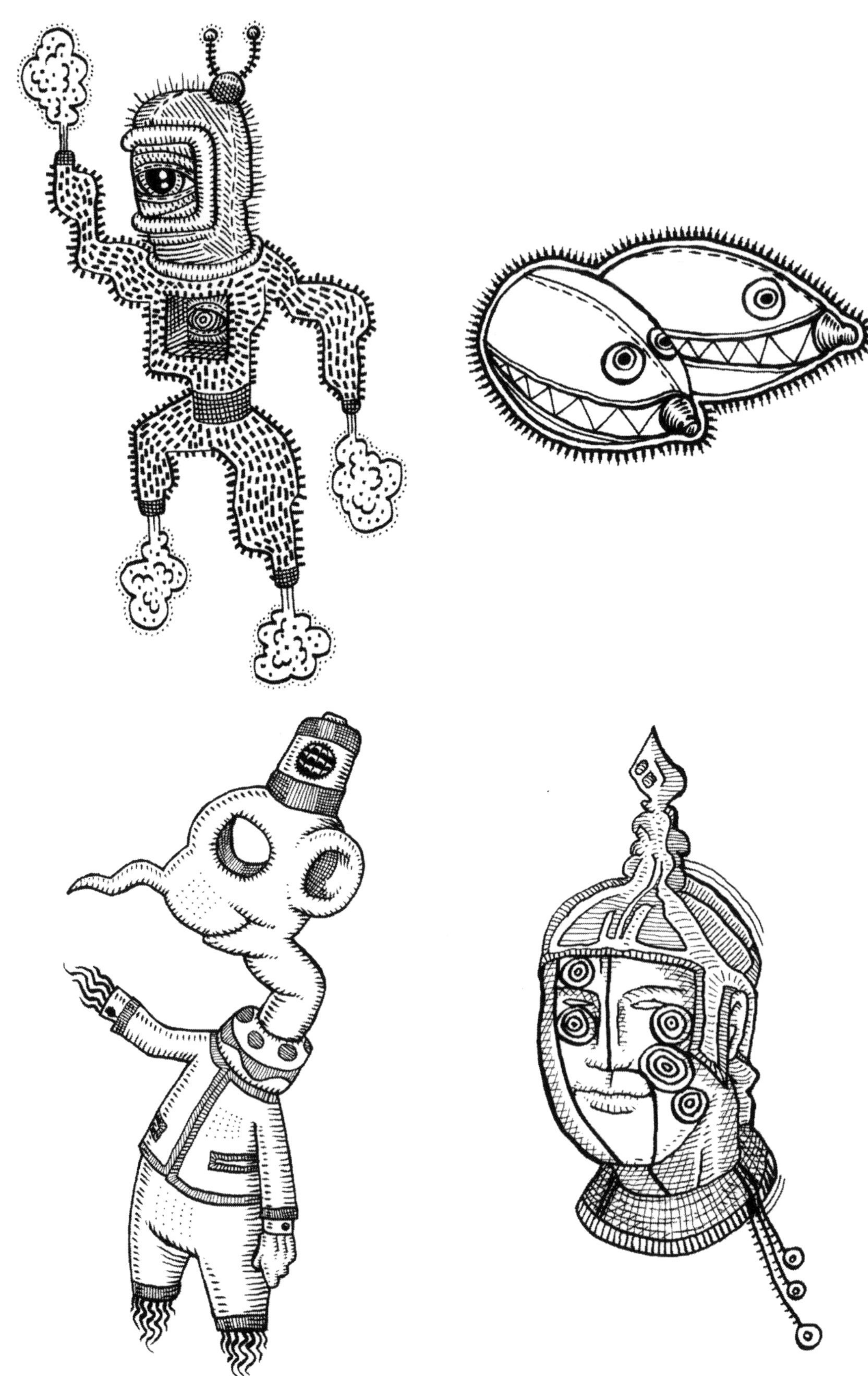

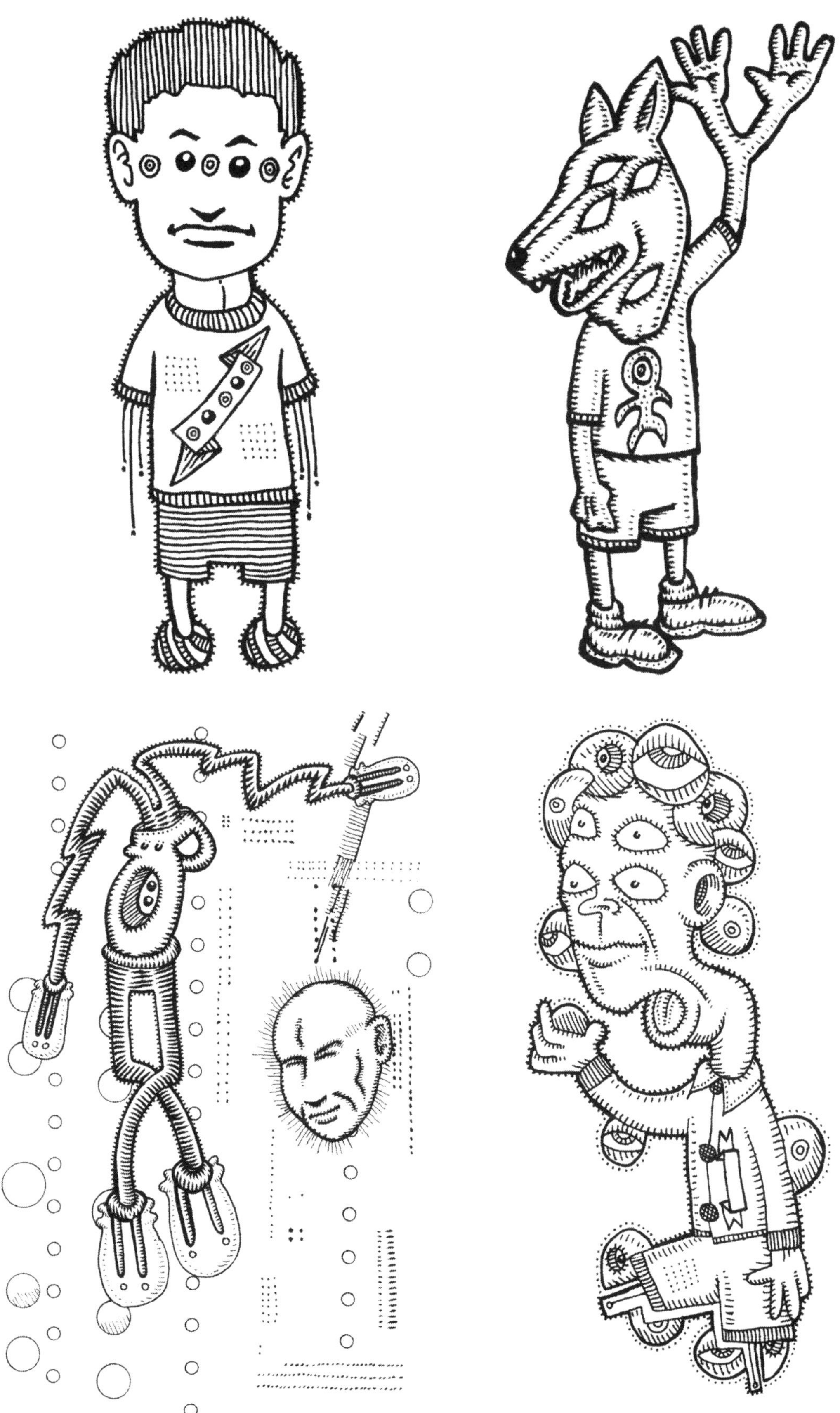

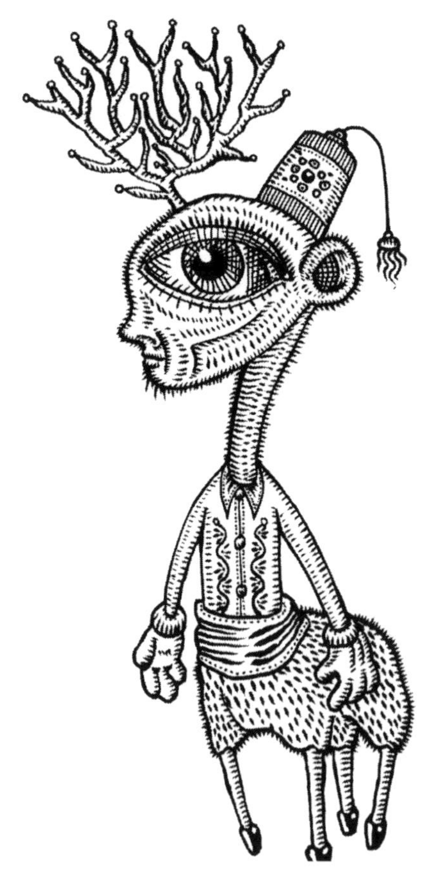

2013

October

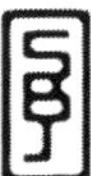

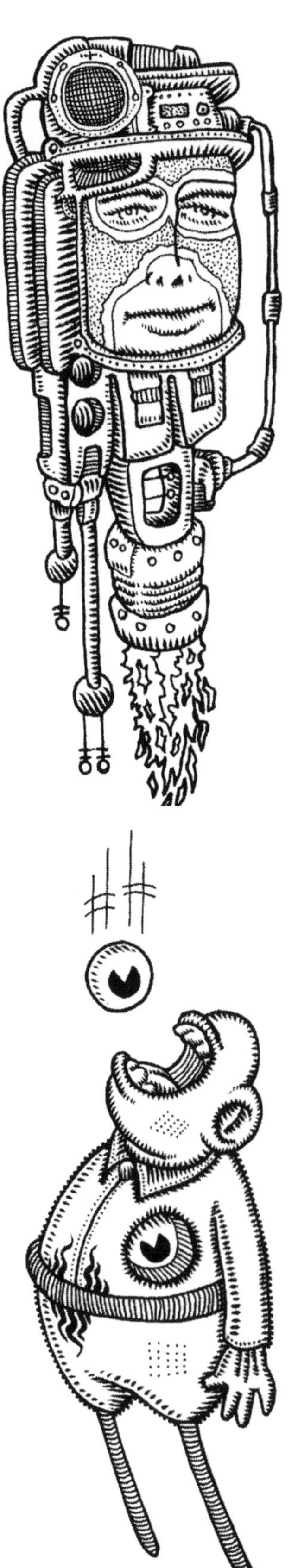

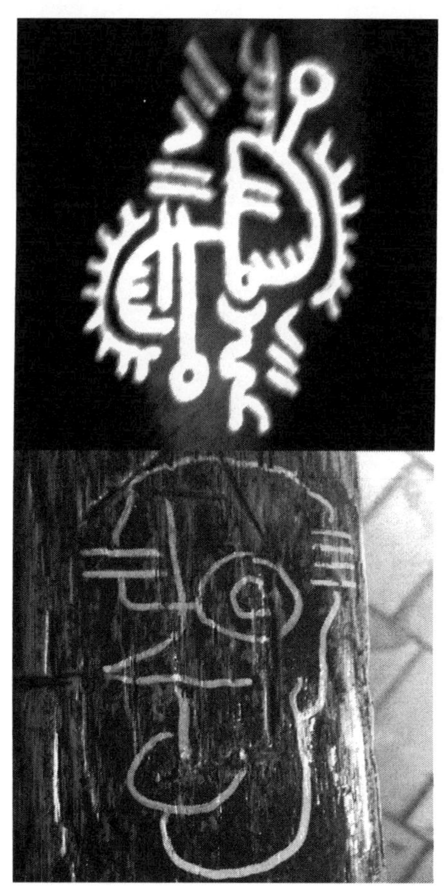

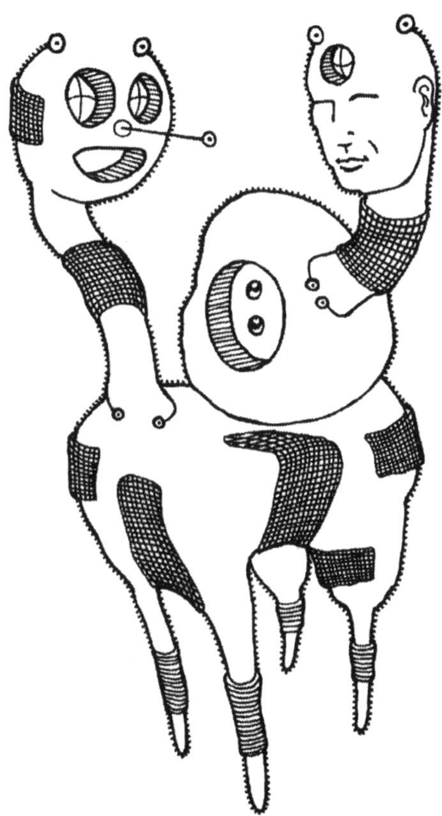

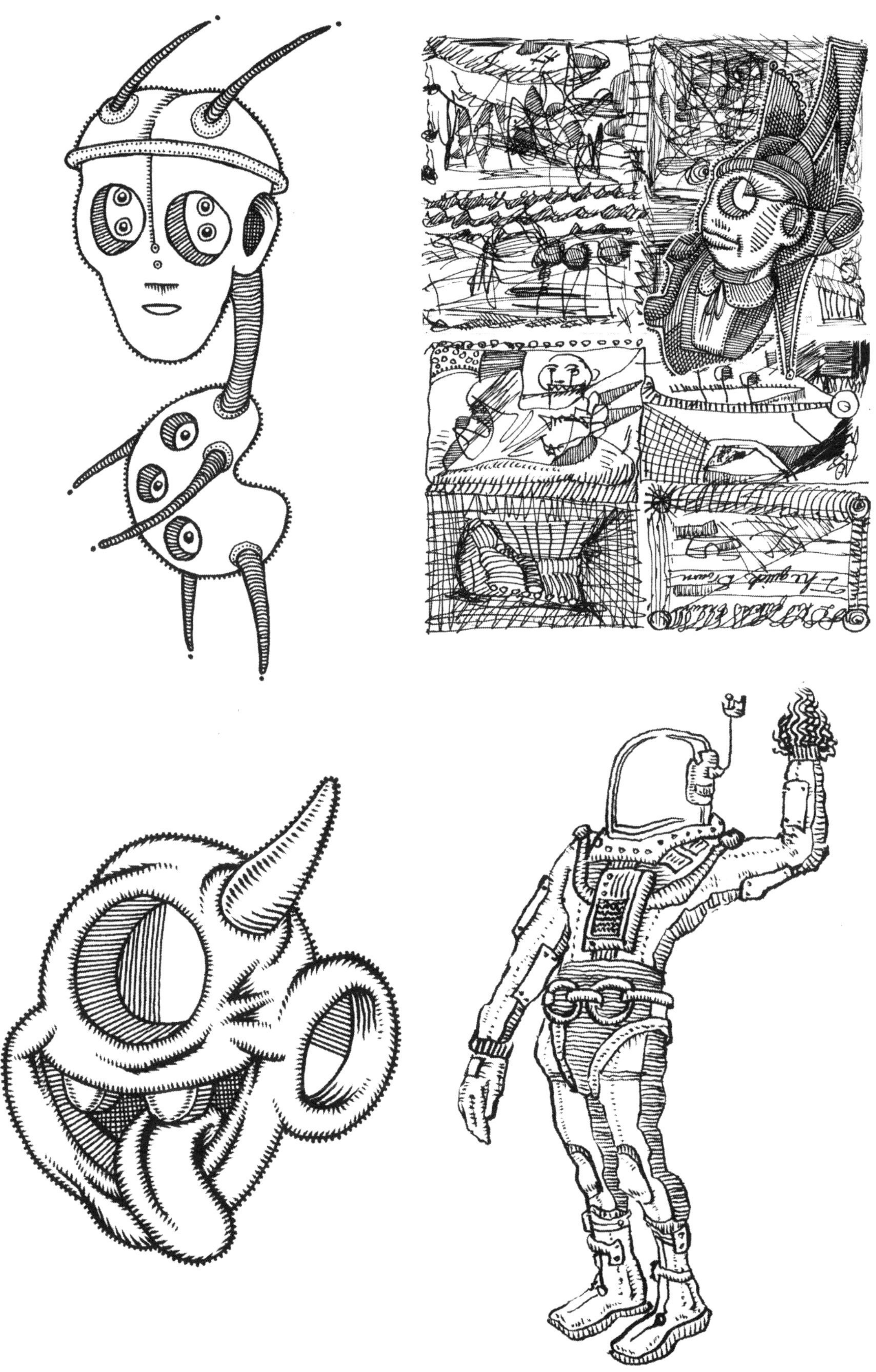

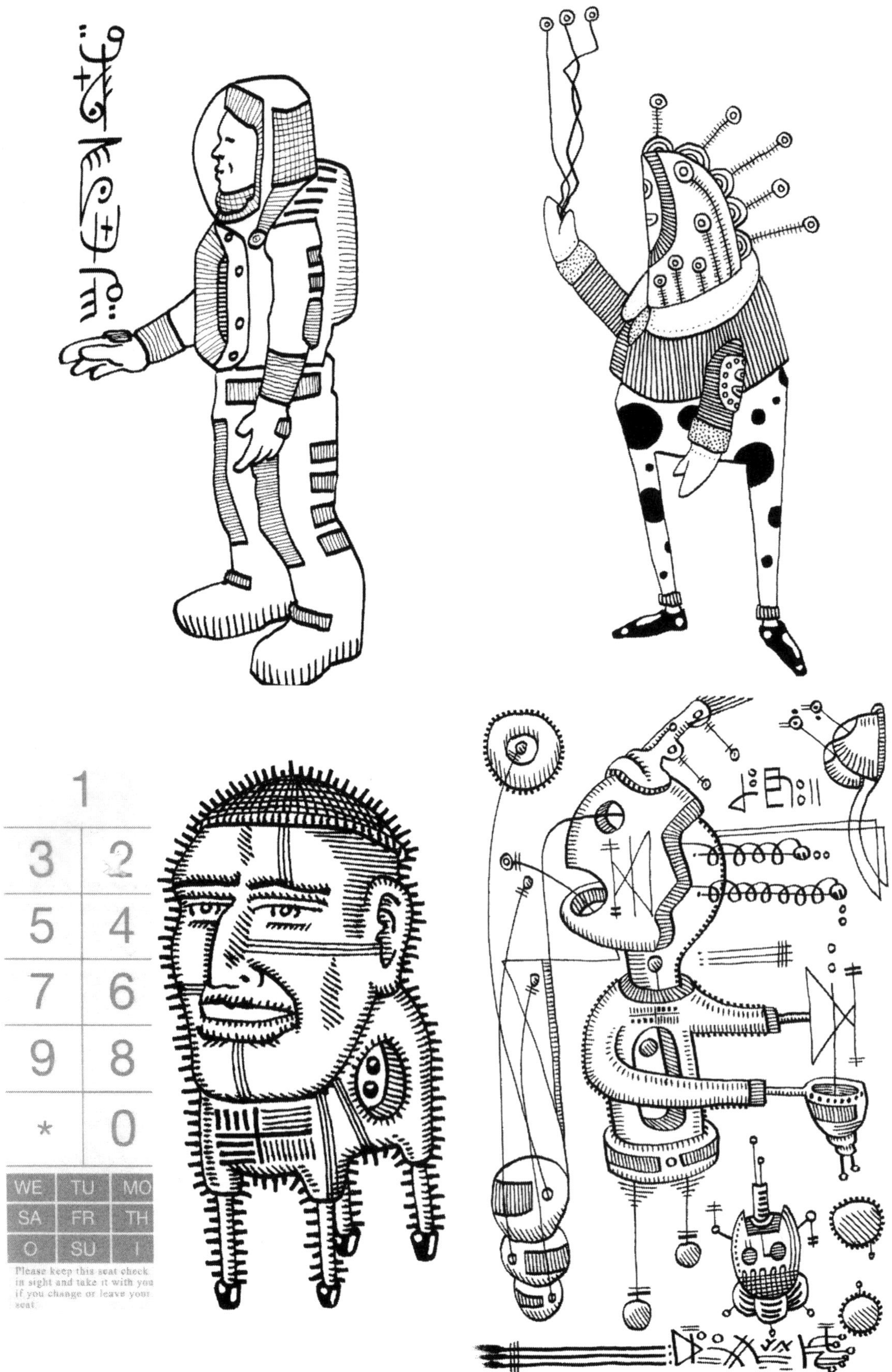
1
3 2
5 4
7 6
9 8
* 0
WE TU MO
SA FR TH
O SU I
Please keep this seat check in sight and take it with you if you change or leave your seat.

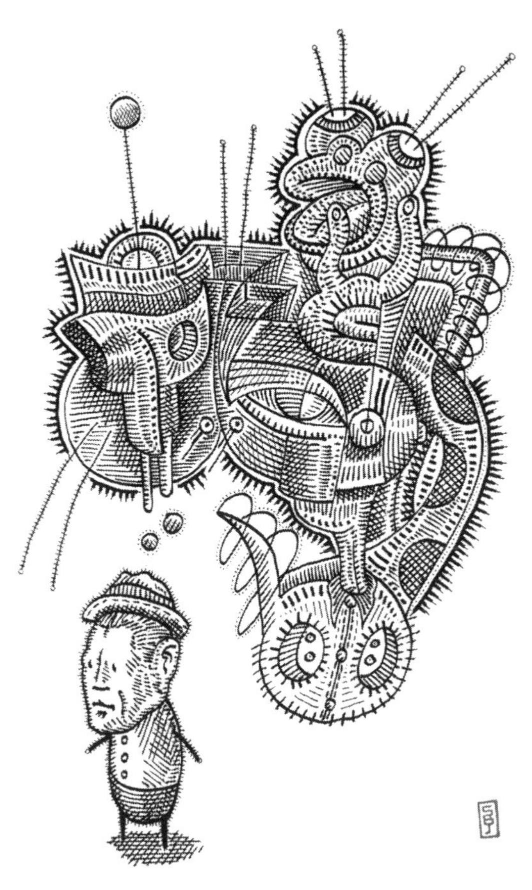

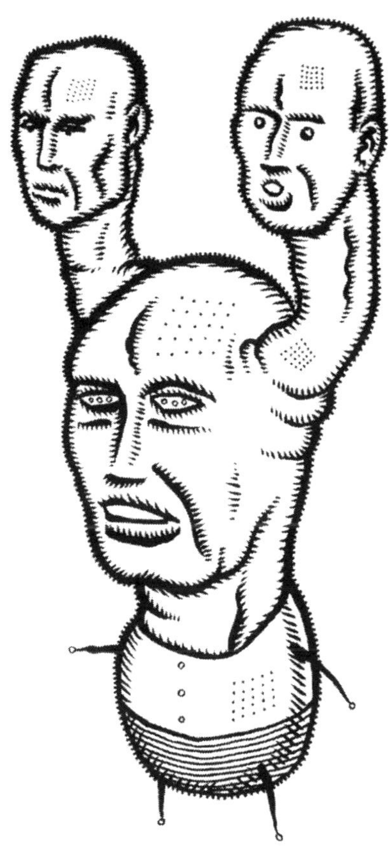

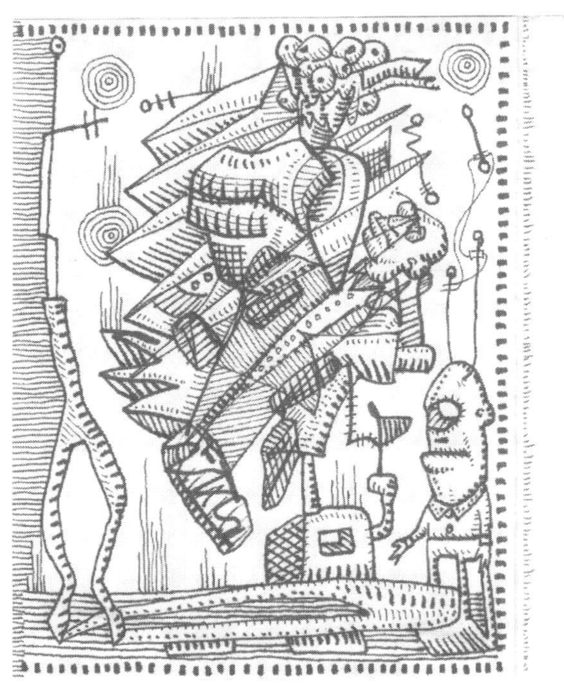

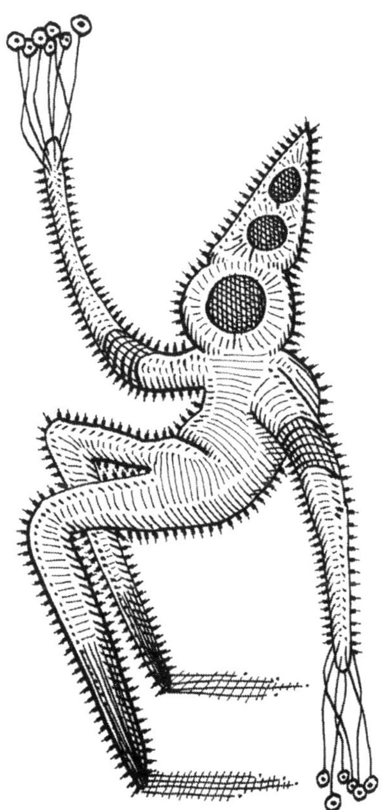

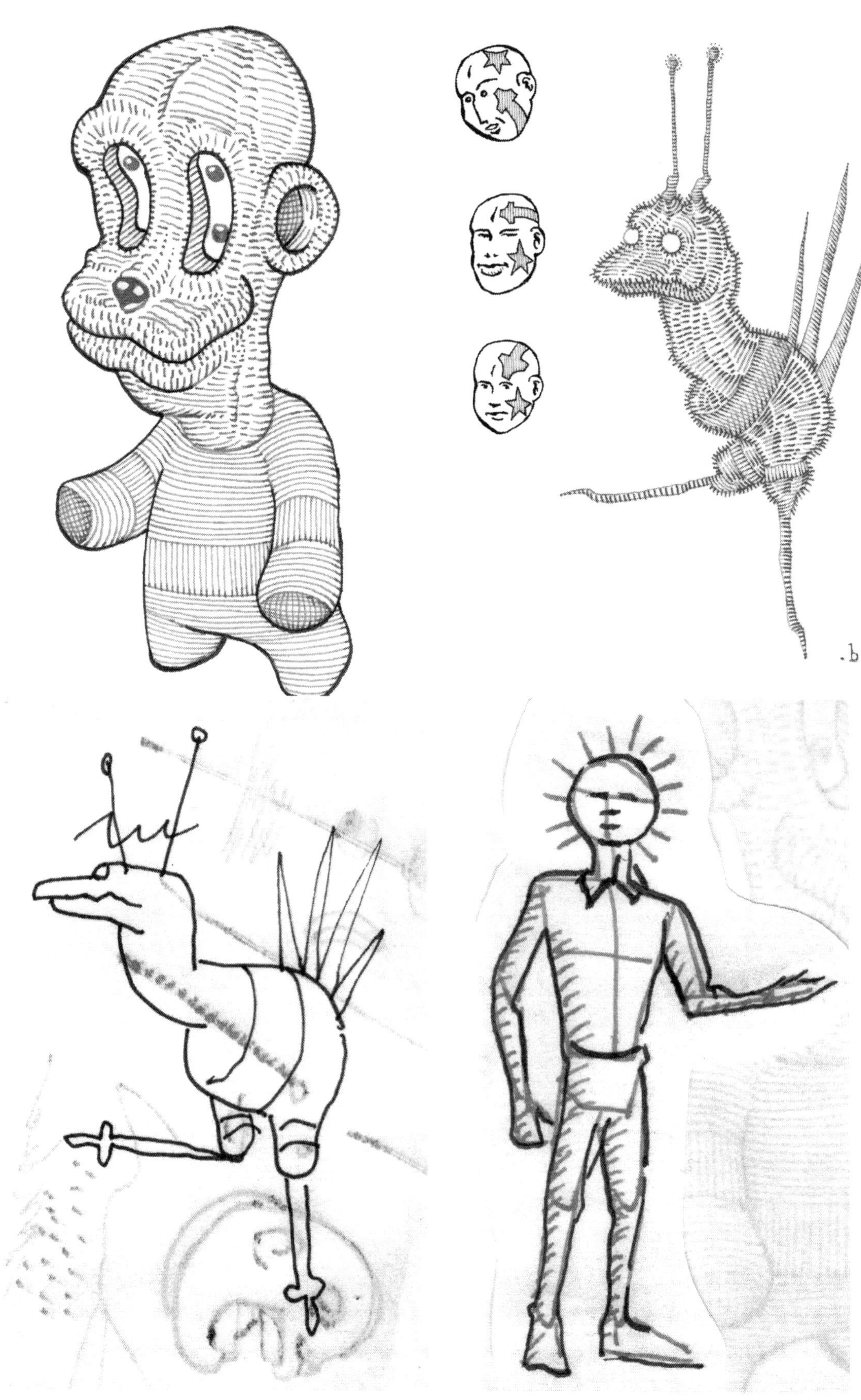

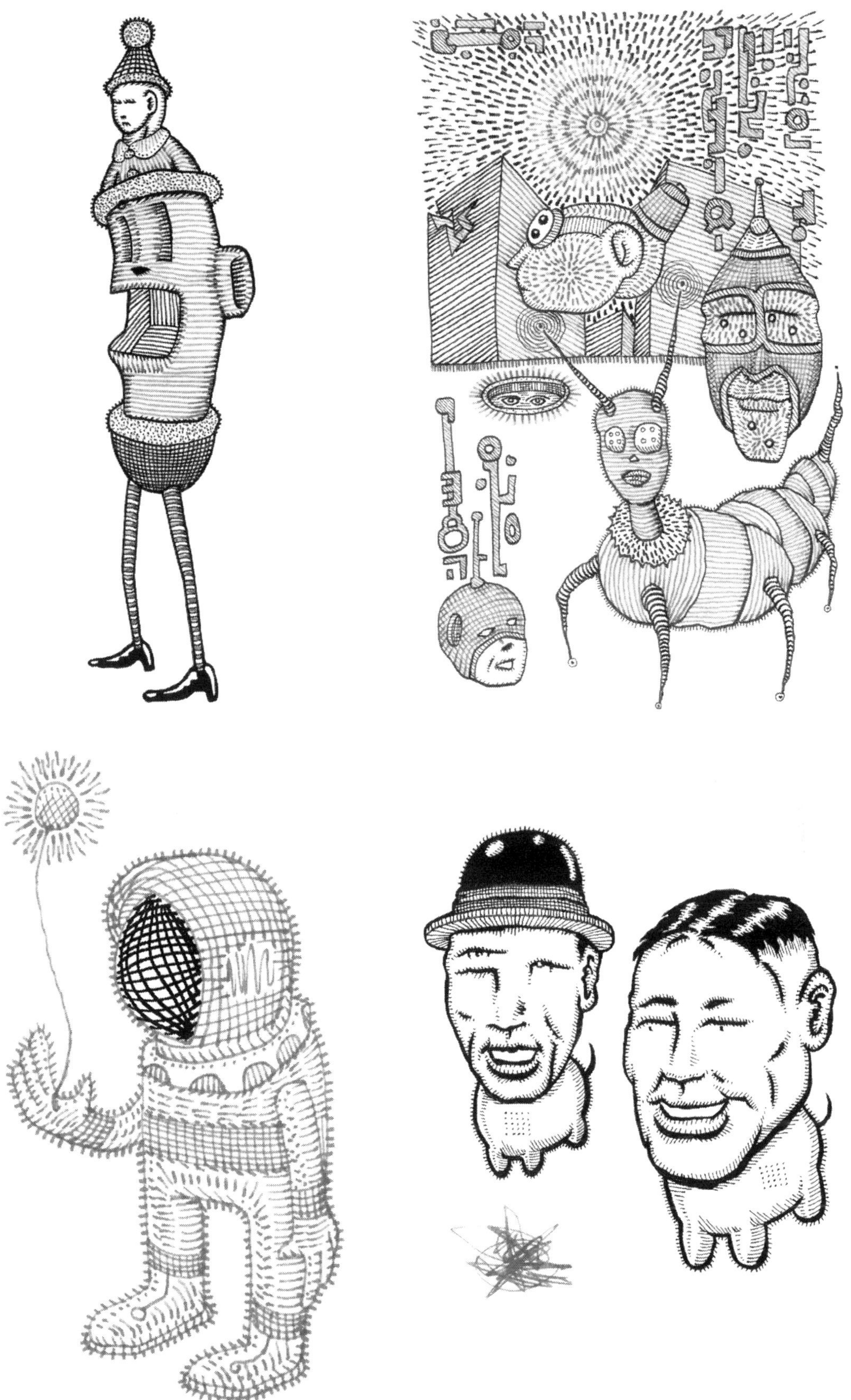

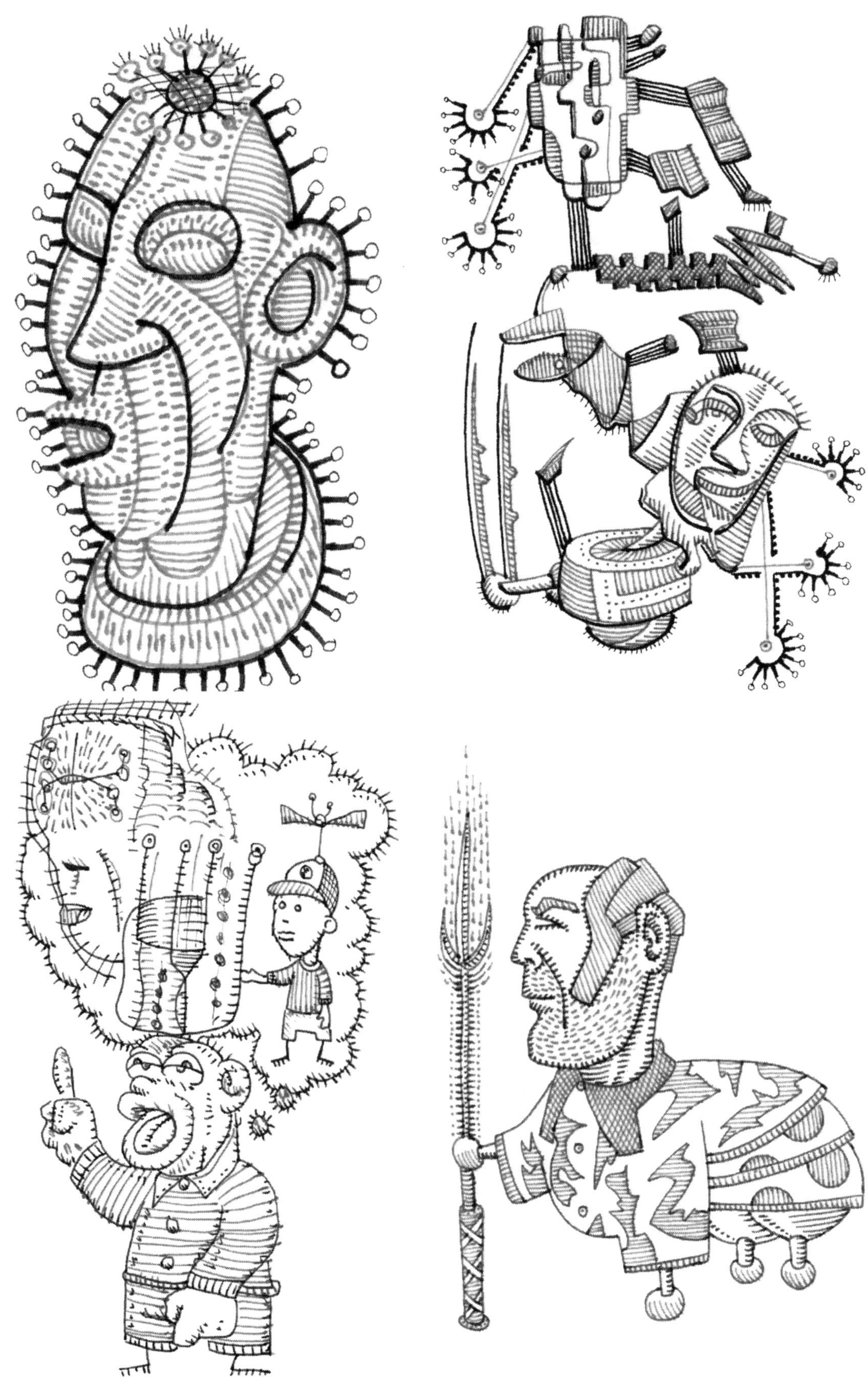

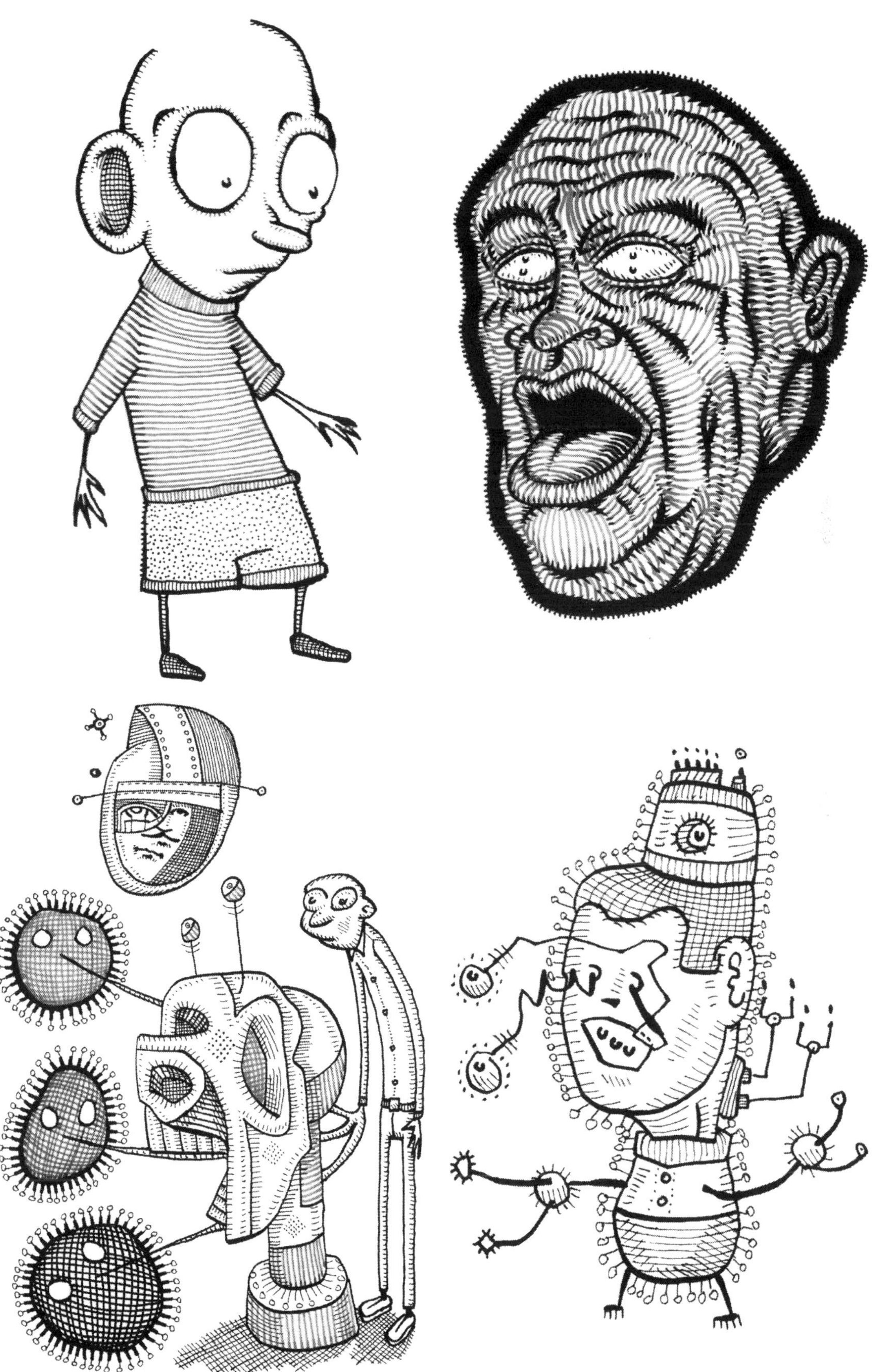

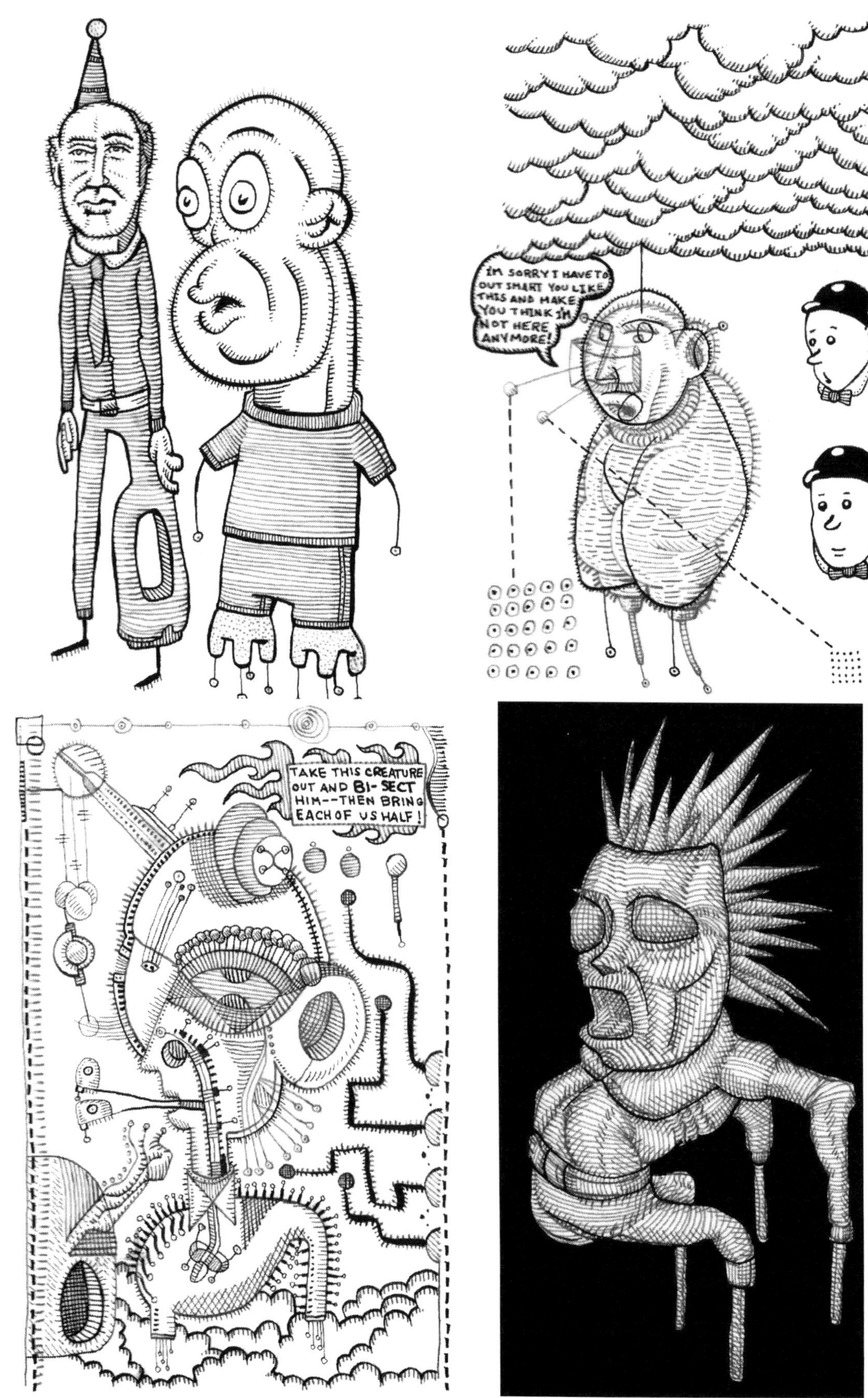
I'M SORRY I HAVE TO OUTSMART YOU LIKE THIS AND MAKE YOU THINK I'M NOT HERE ANYMORE!
TAKE THIS CREATURE OUT AND BI-SECT HIM--THEN BRING EACH OF US HALF!

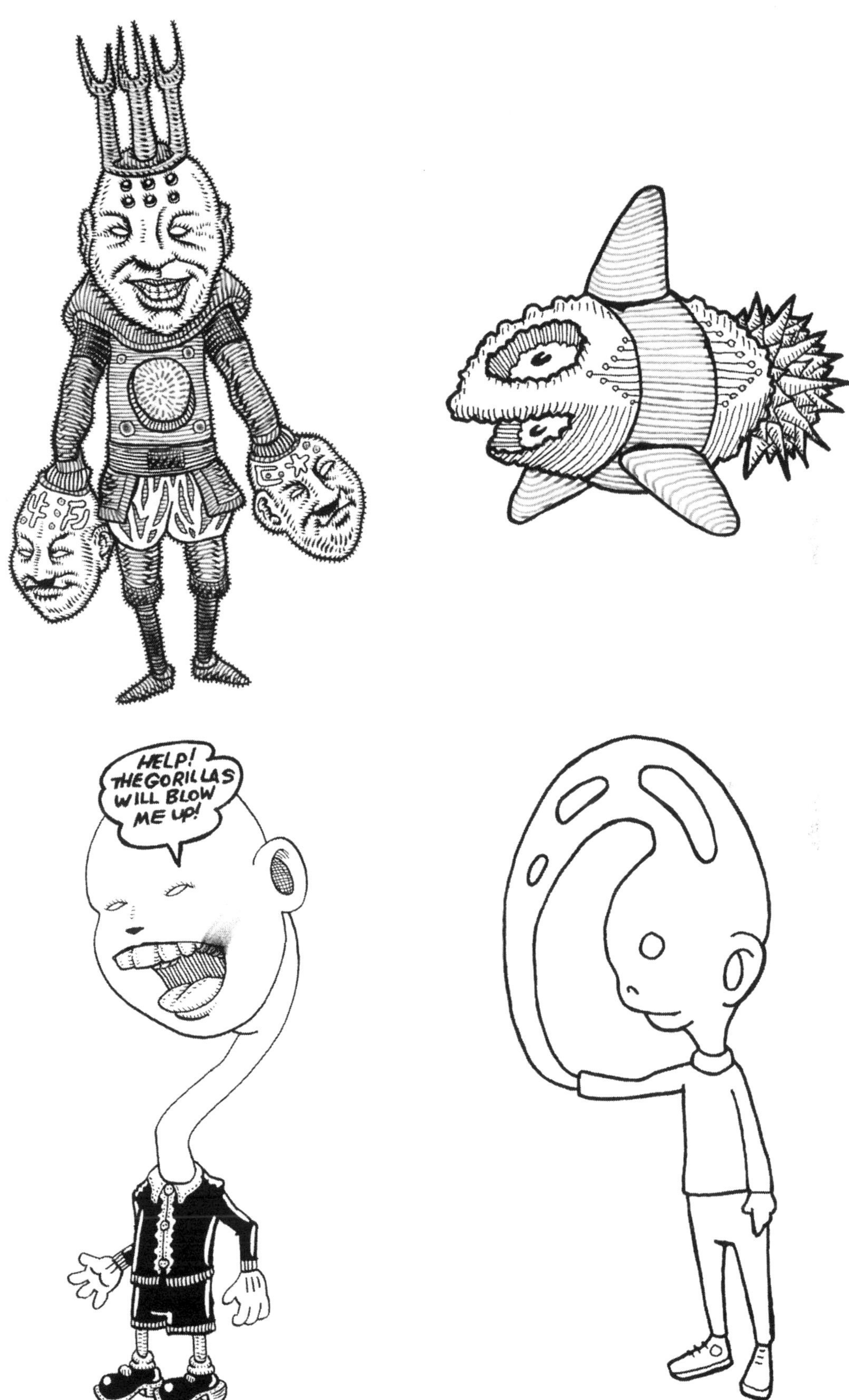
HELP! THEGORILLAS WILL BLOW ME UP!

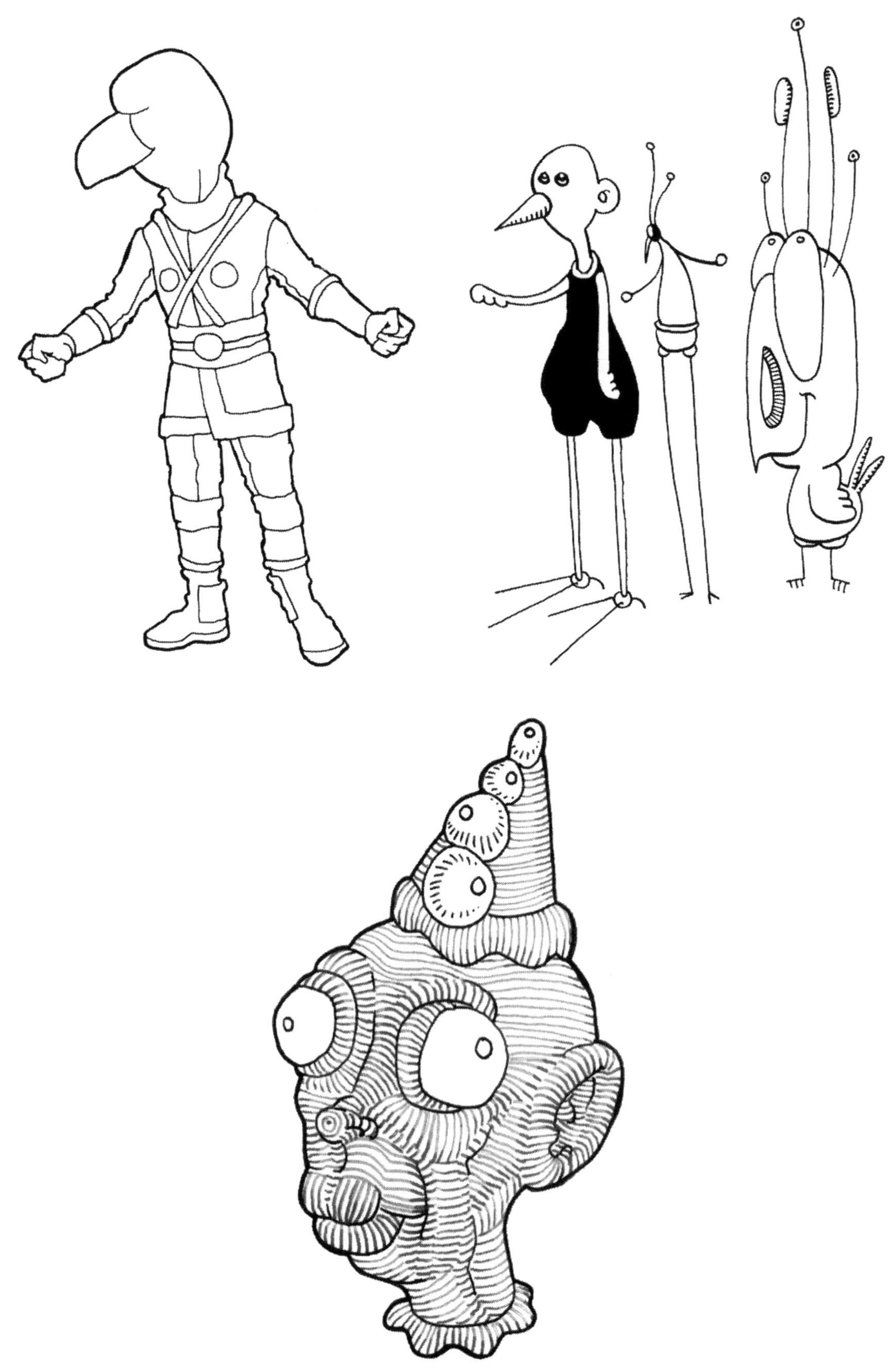

2013

November

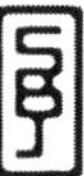

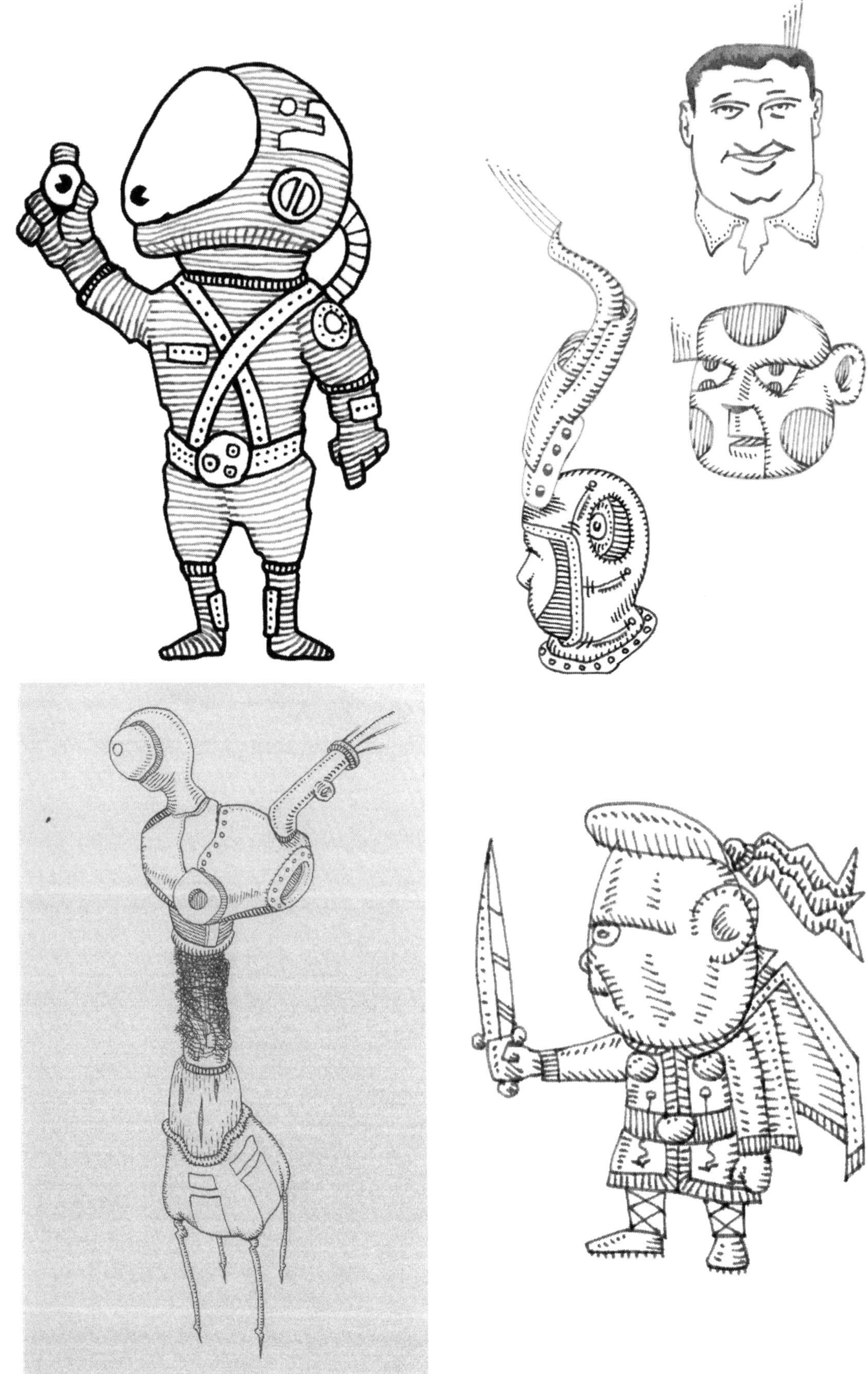

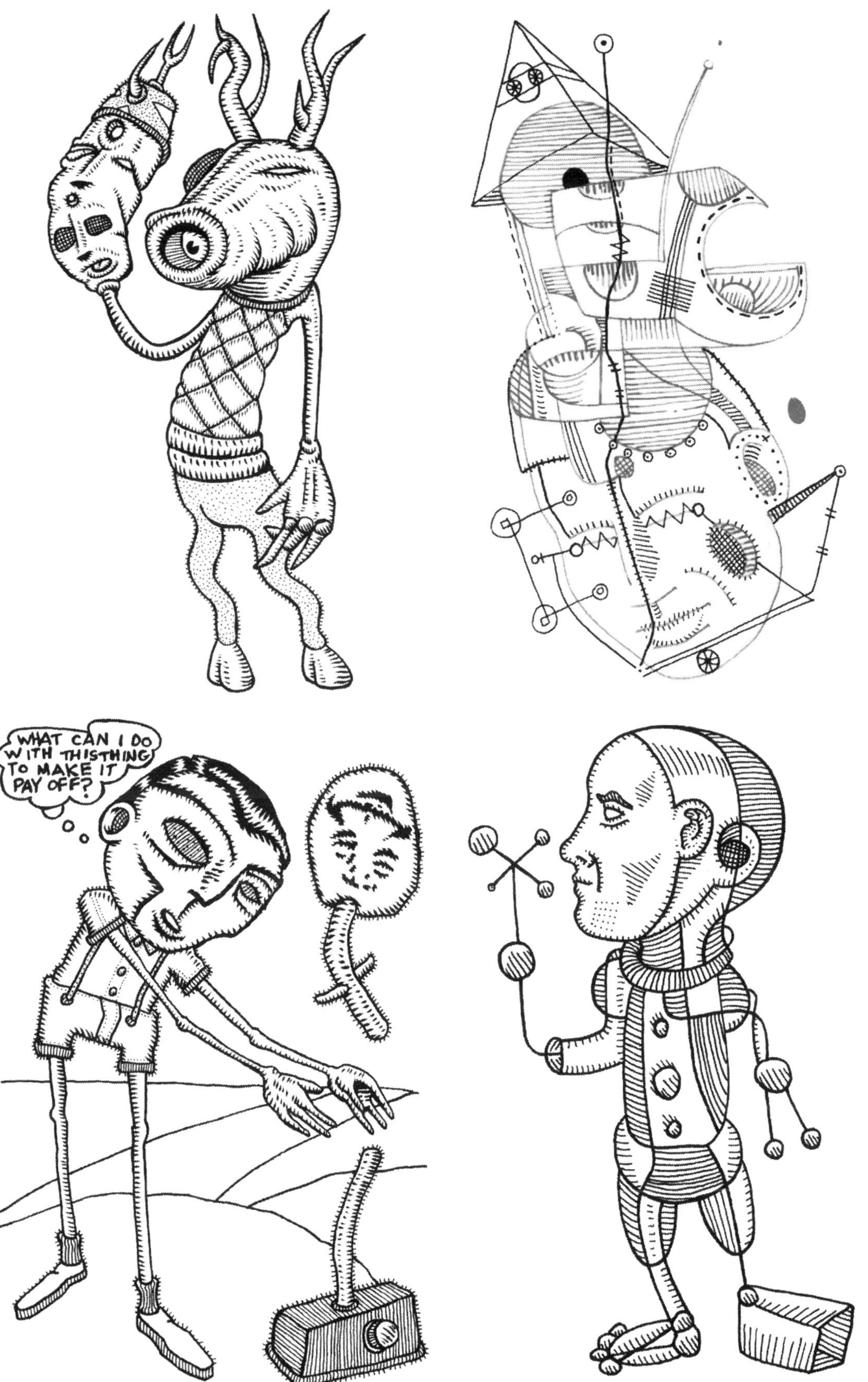
WHAT CAN I DO WITH THISTHING TO MAKE IT PAY OFF?

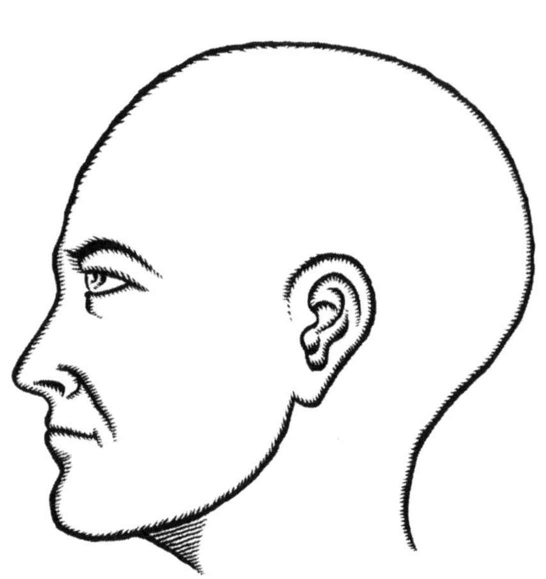
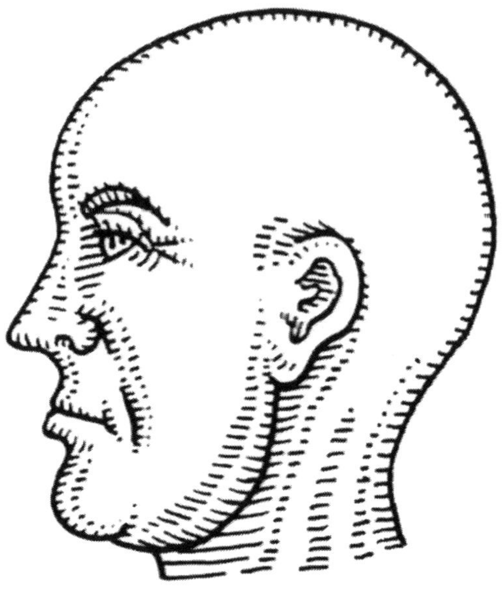
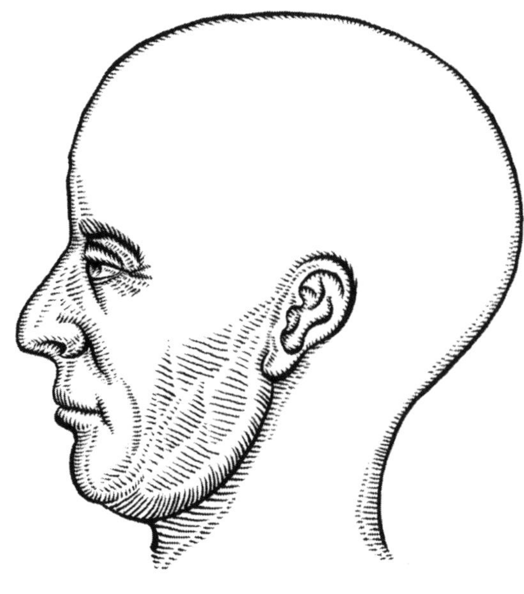
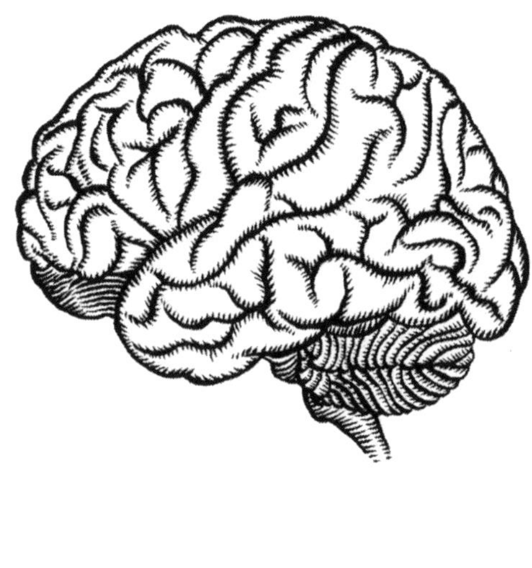

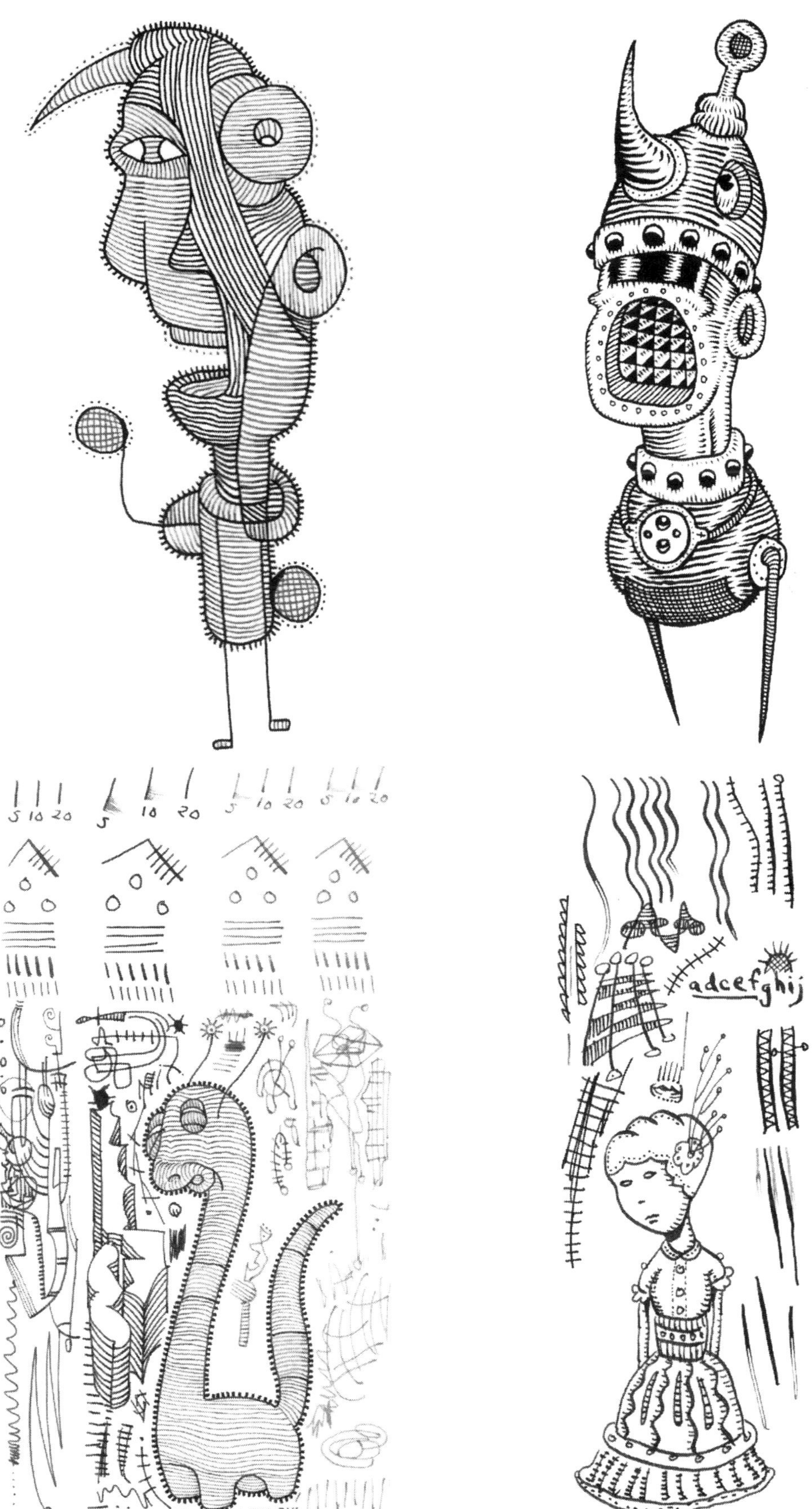
5 10 20
5 10 20
5 10 20
5 10 20
adcefghij

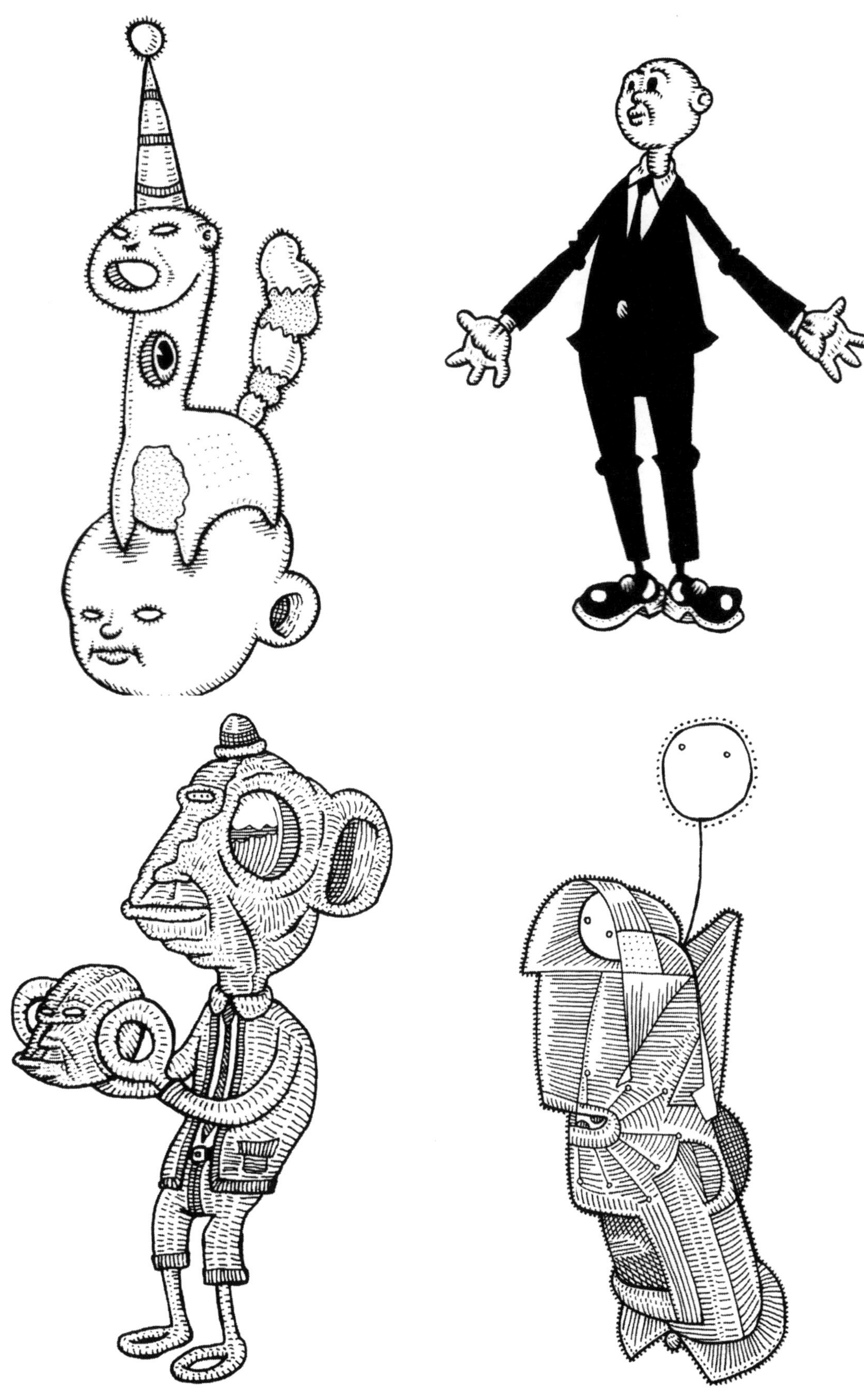

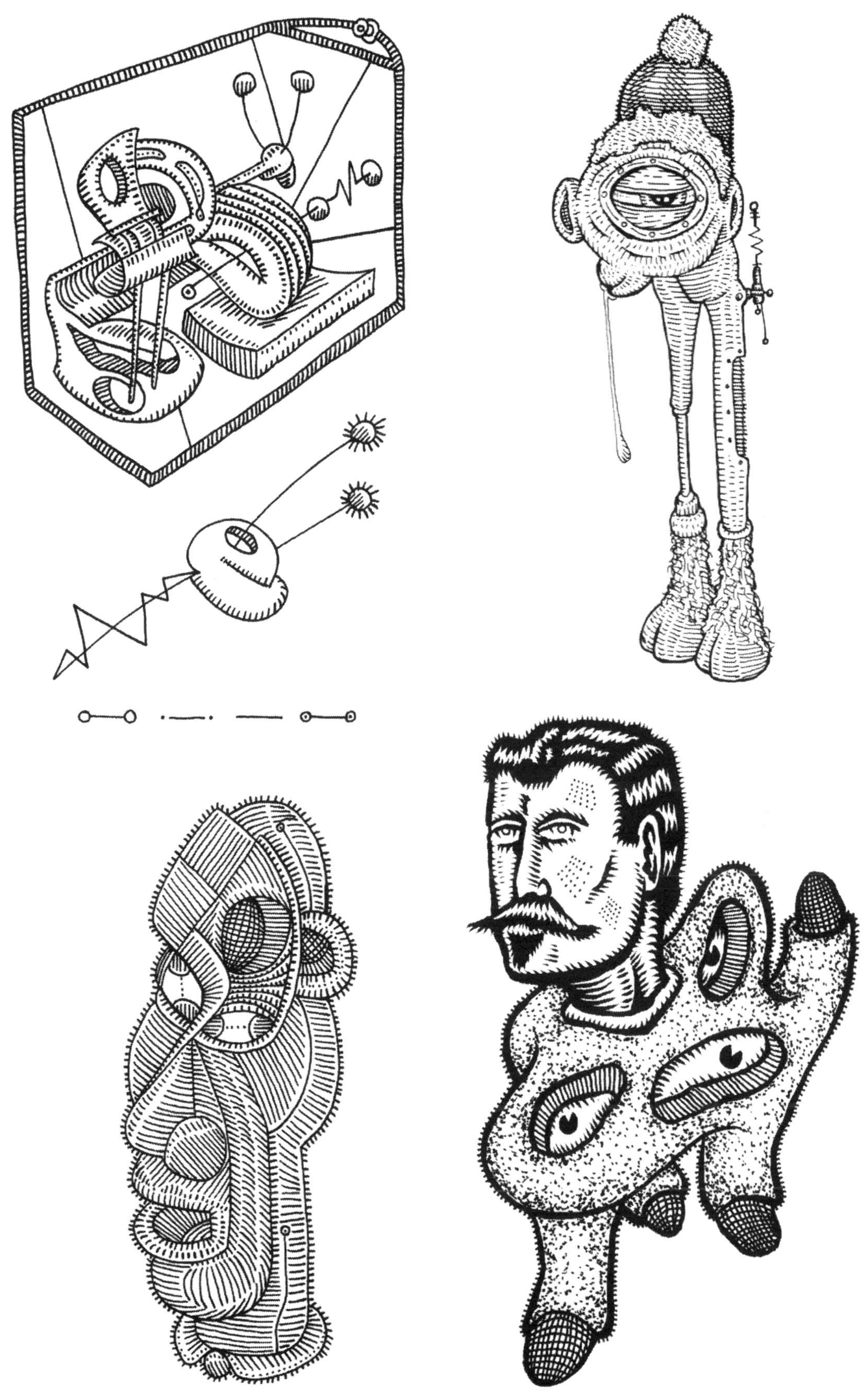

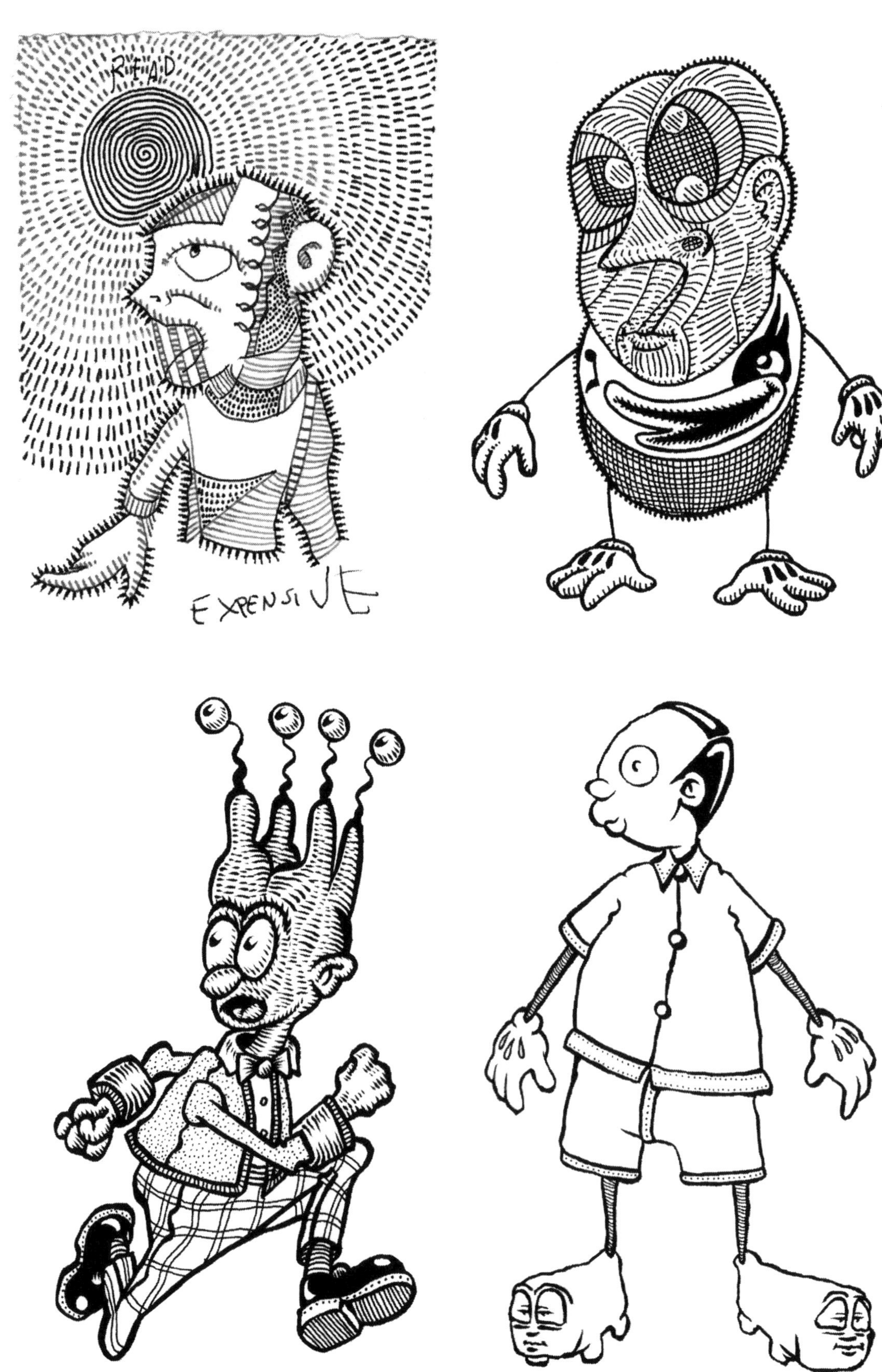
READ
EXPENSIVE

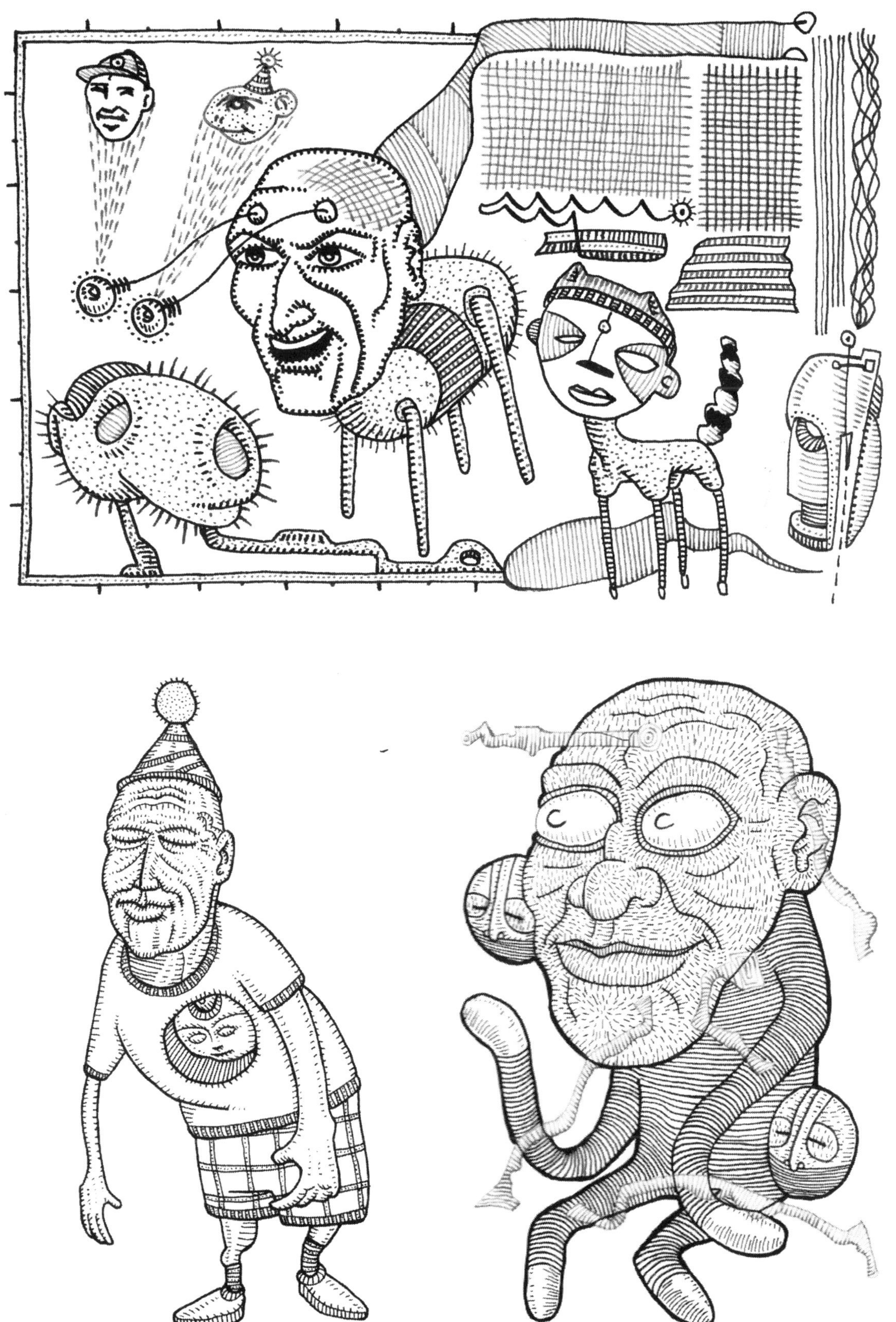

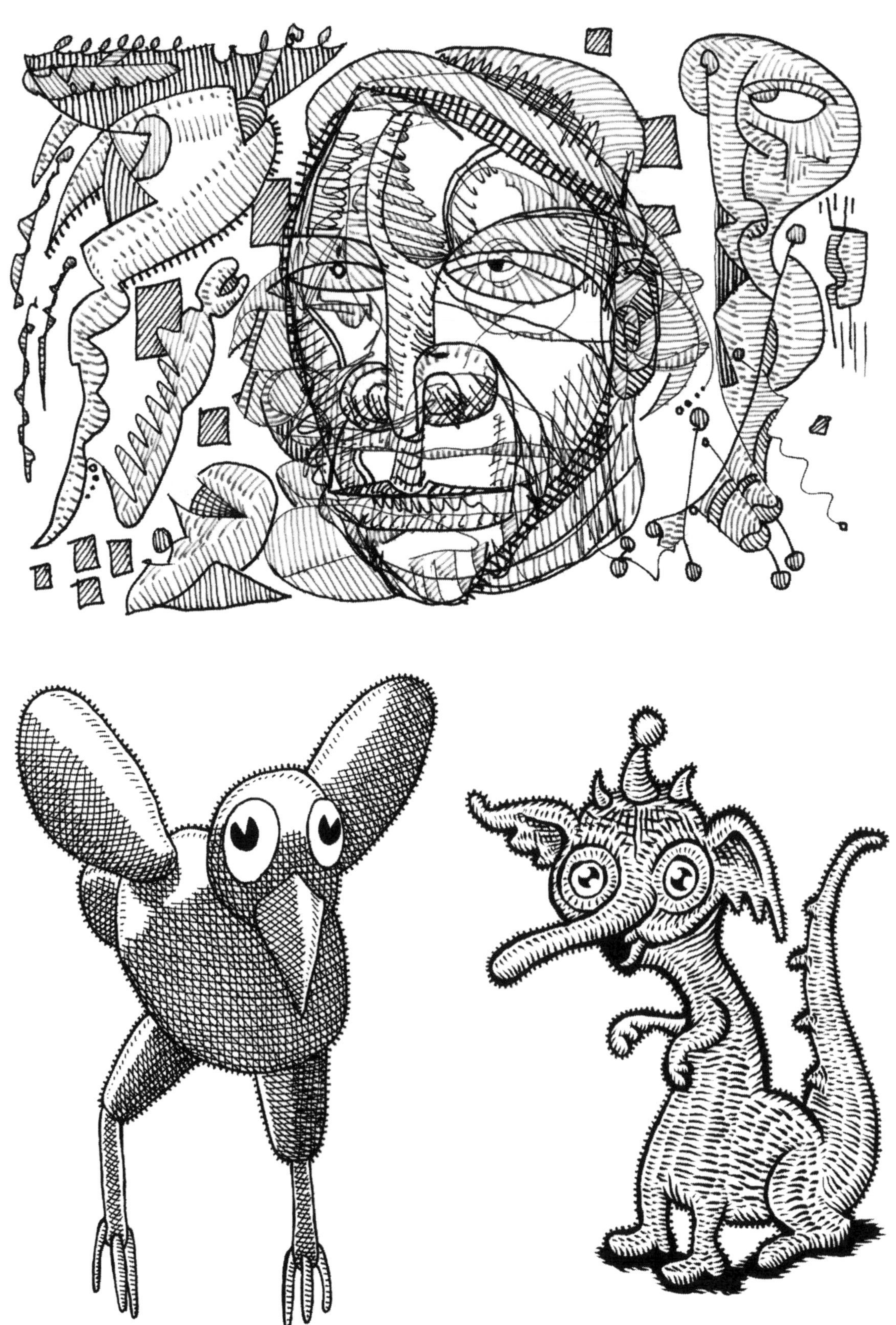

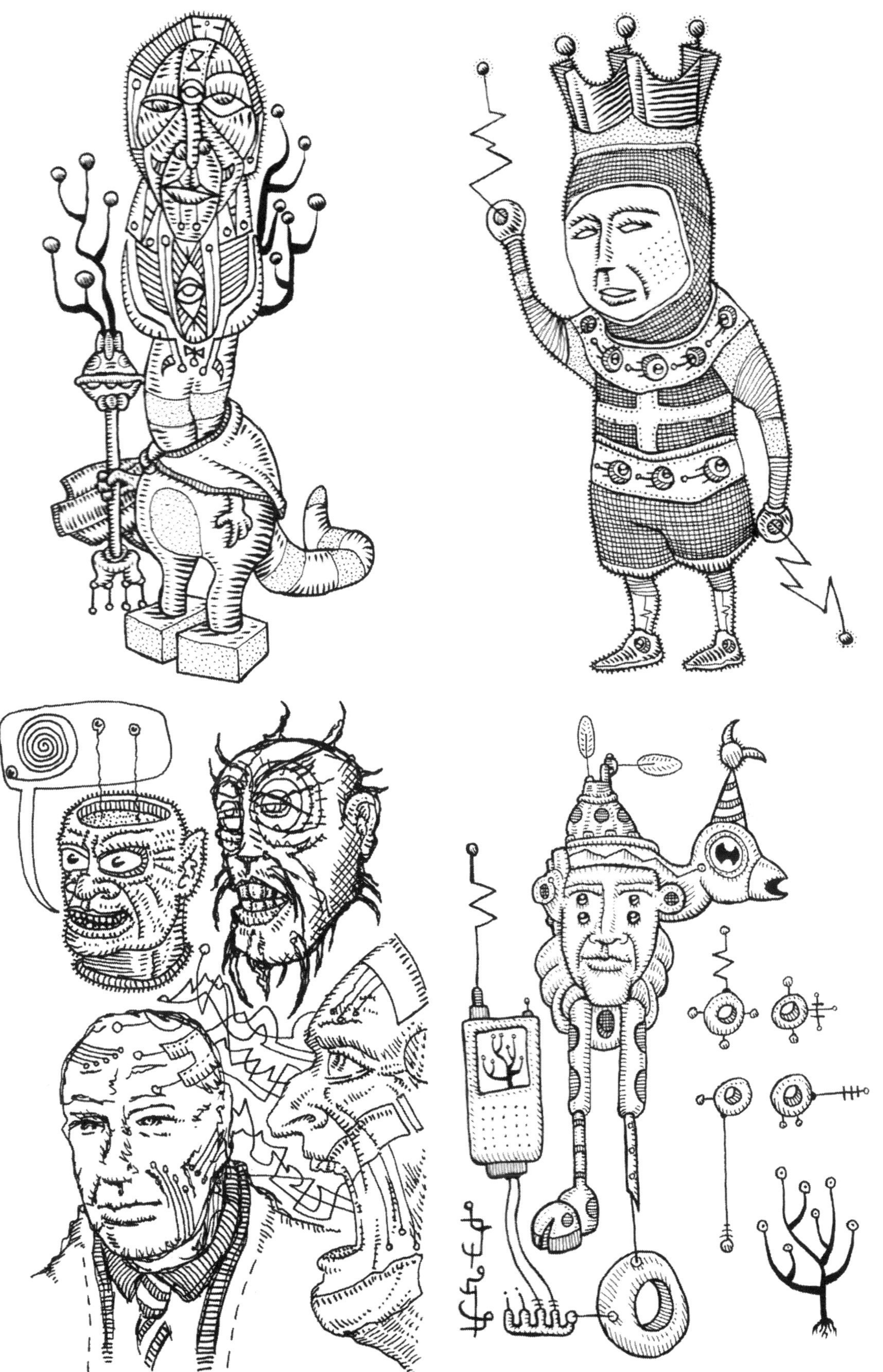

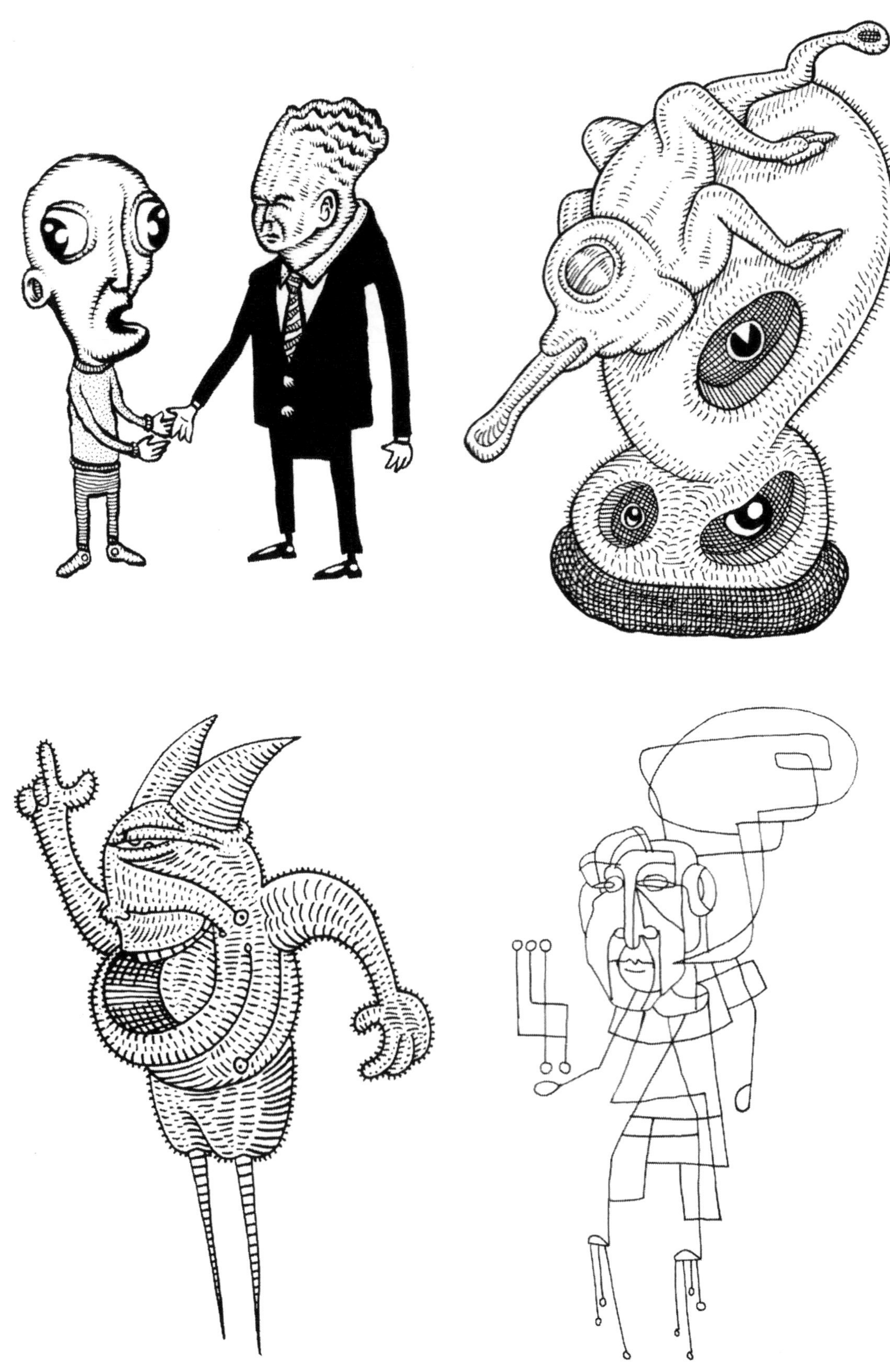

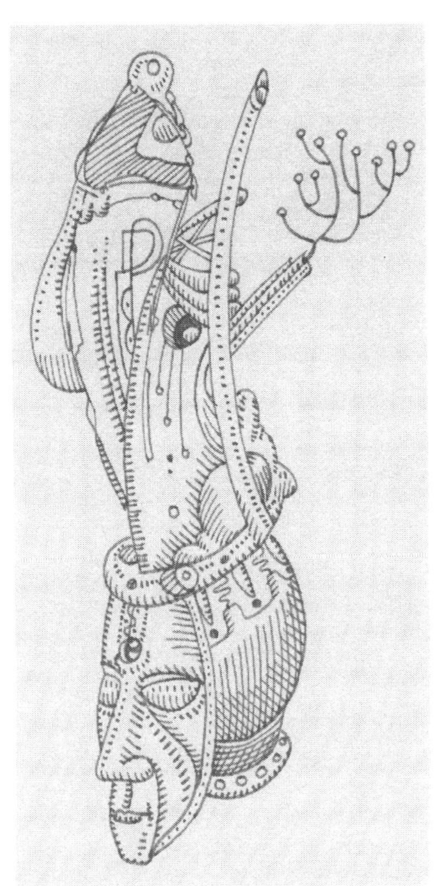

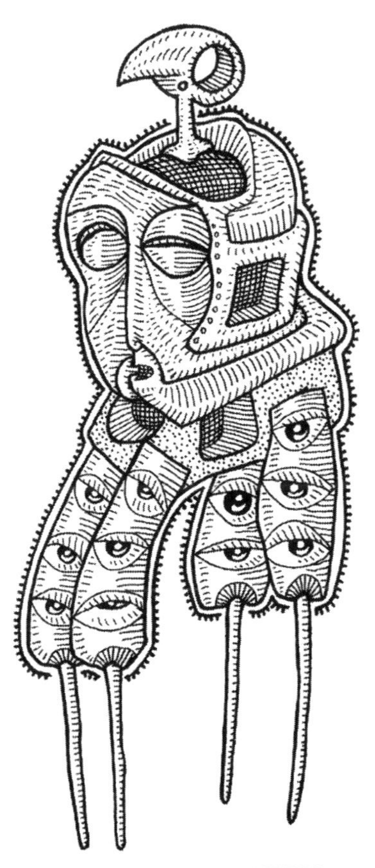

2013

December

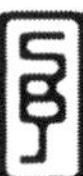

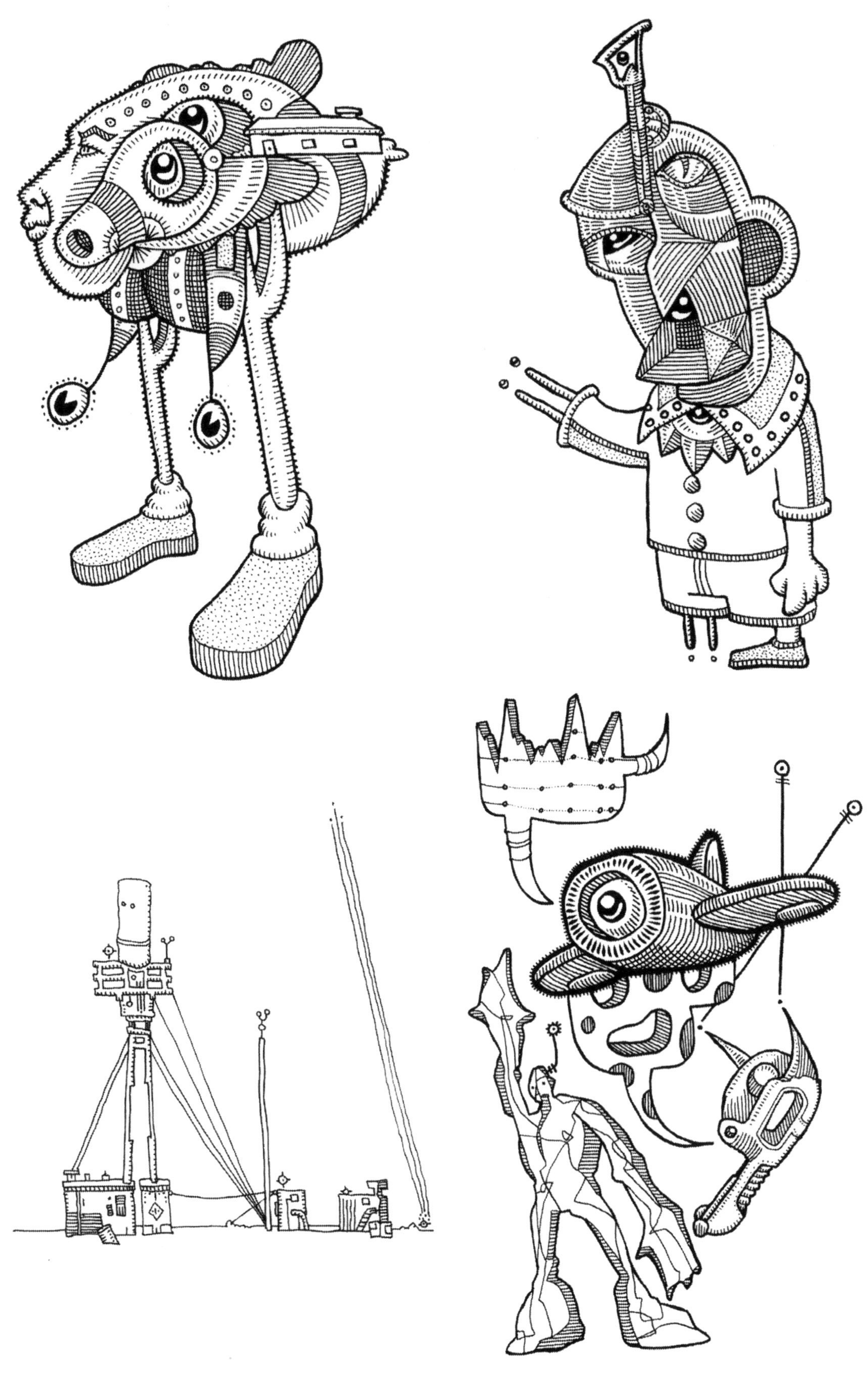

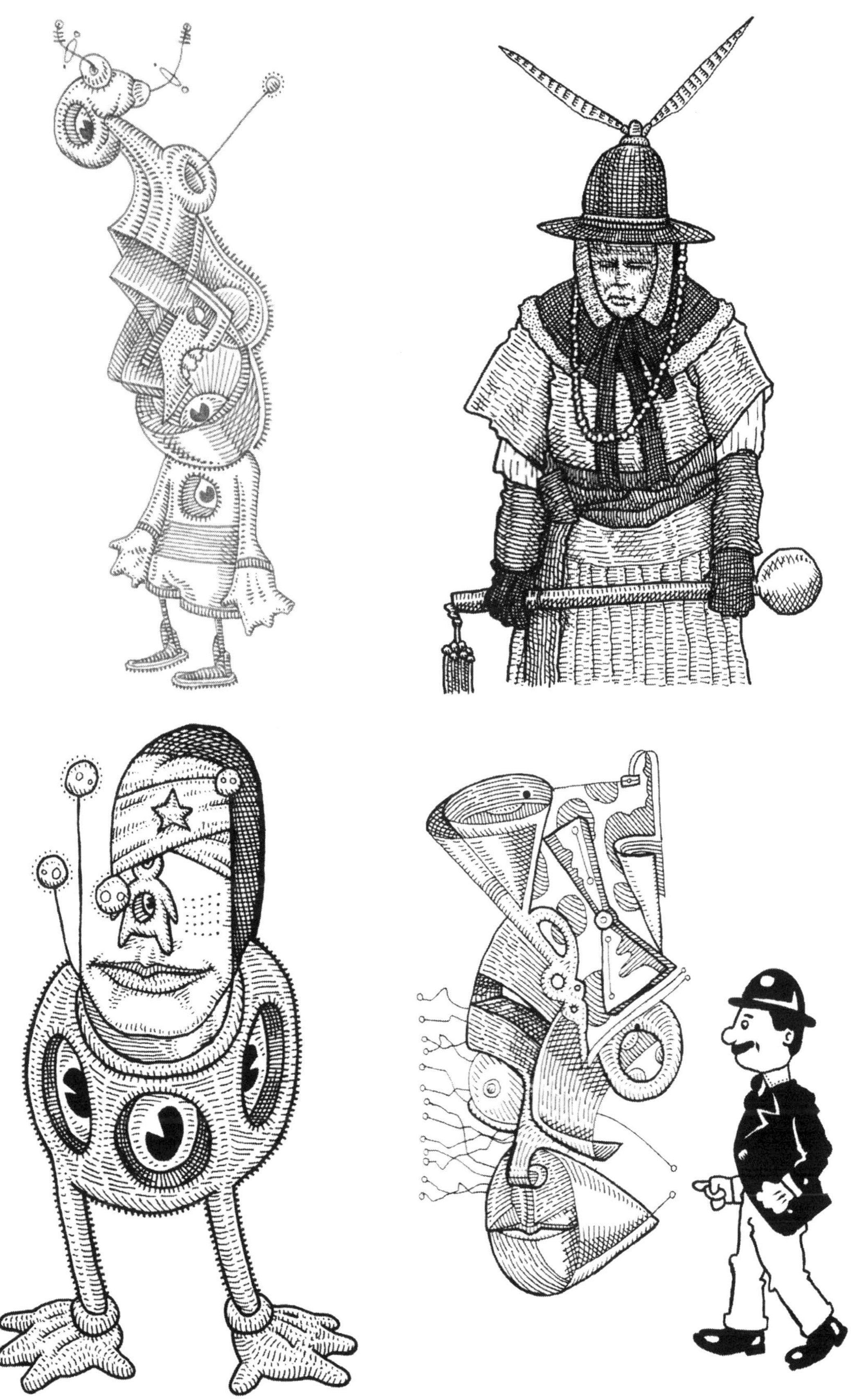

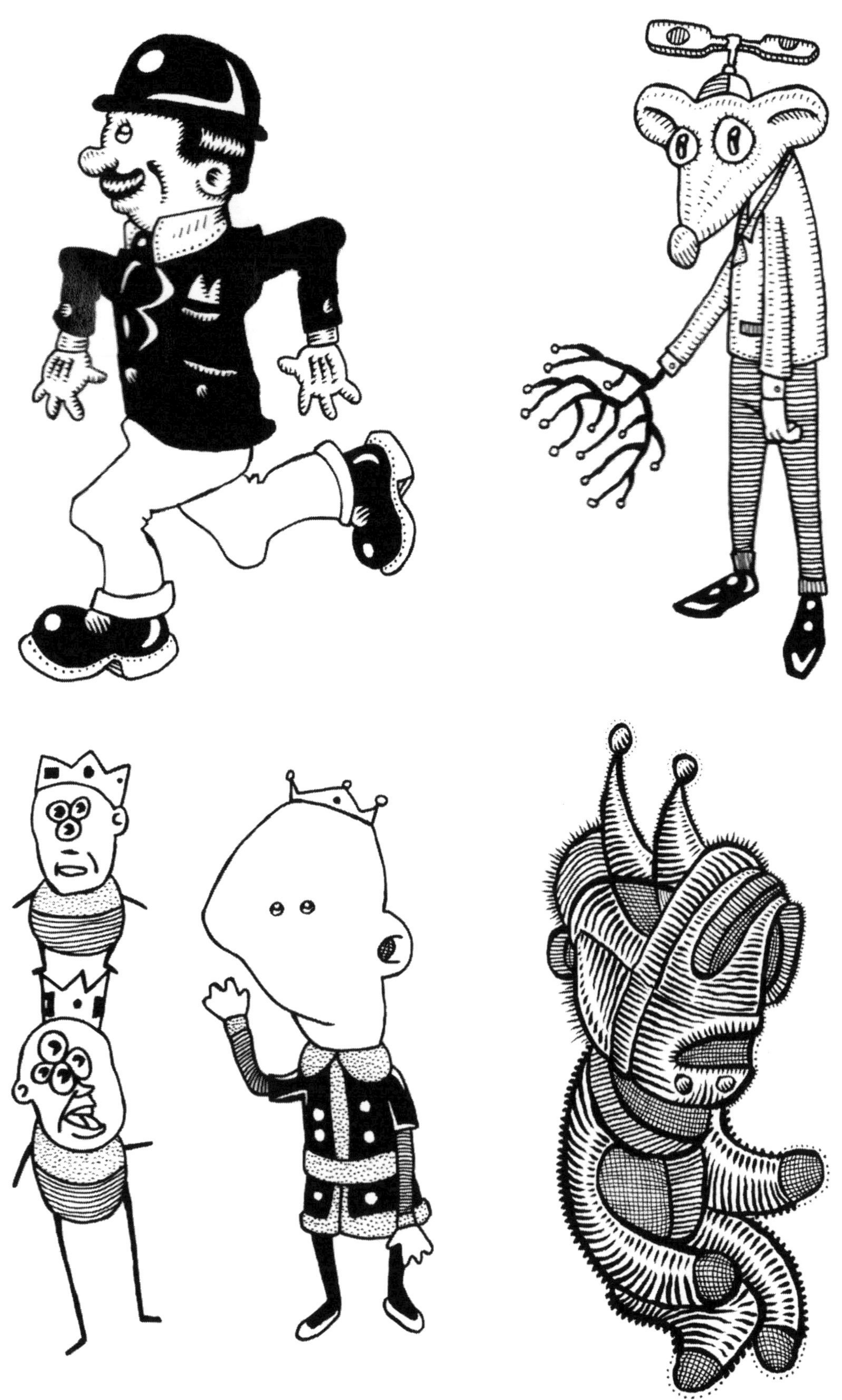

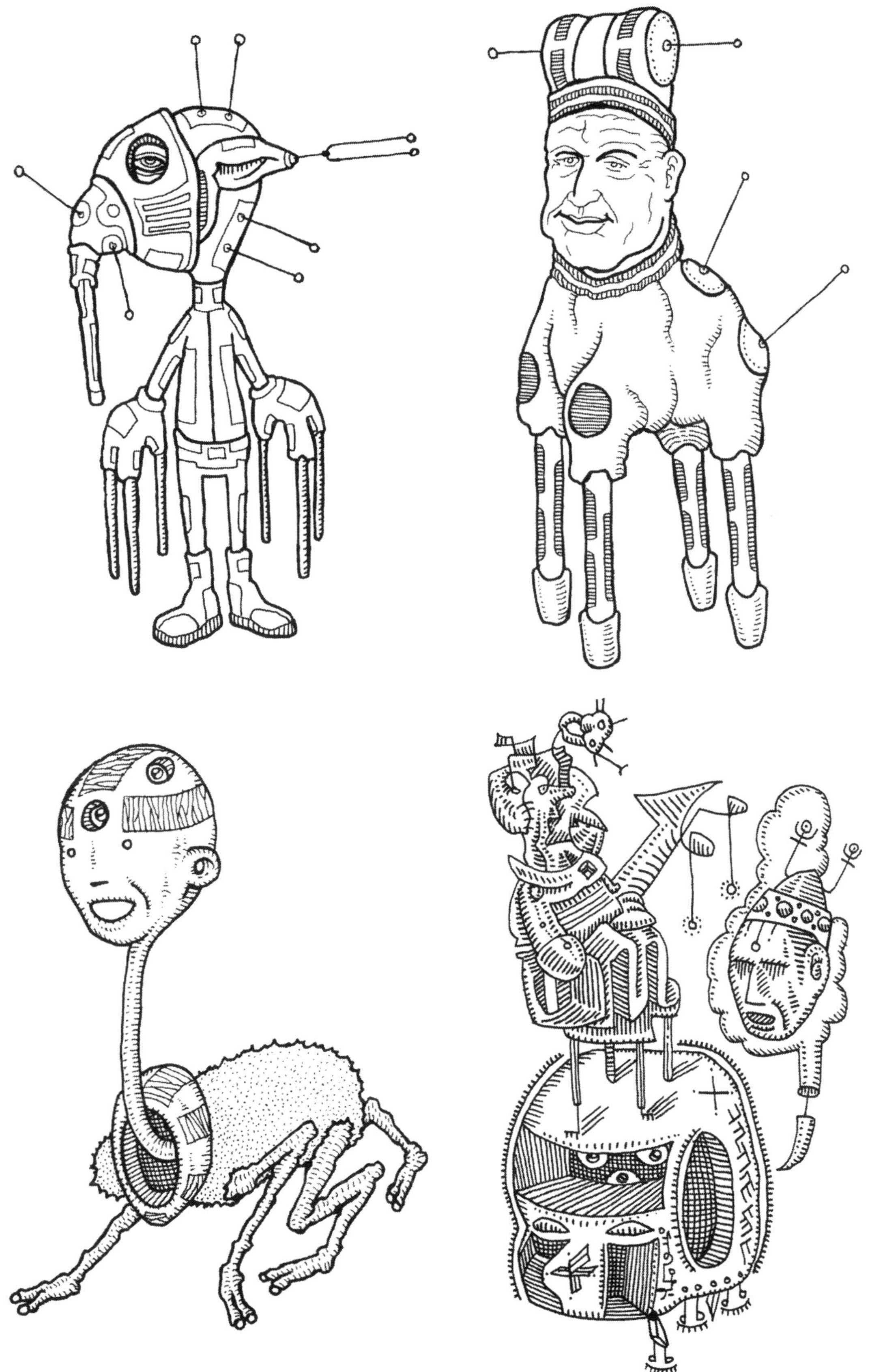

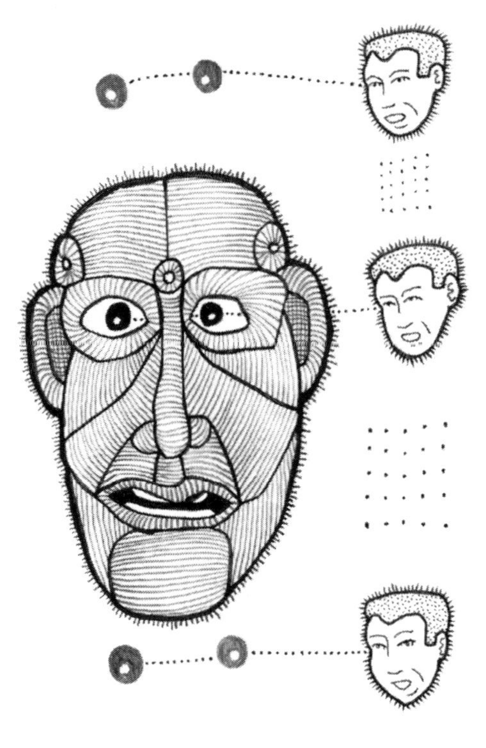

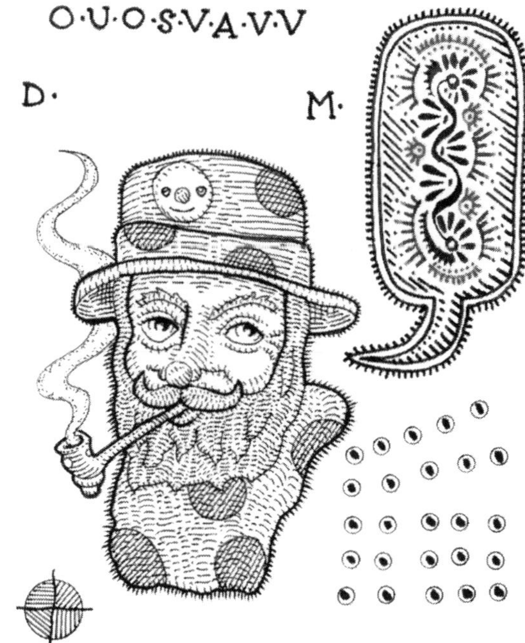
O·U·O·S·V·A·V·V
D·
M·

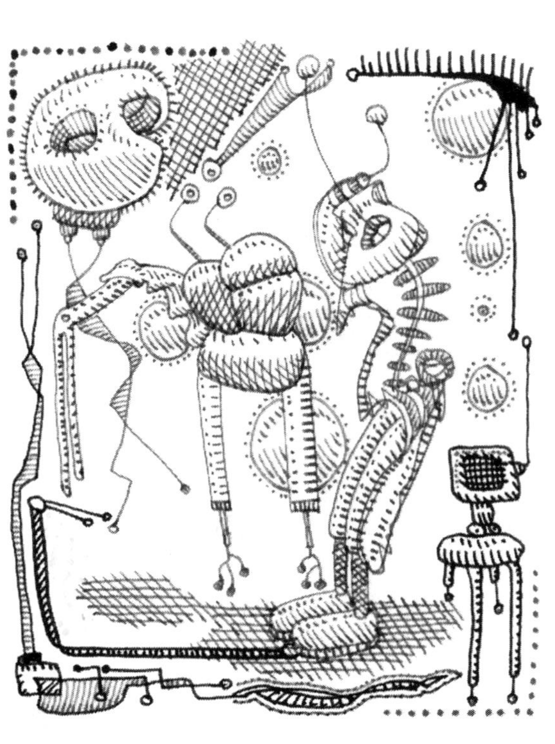

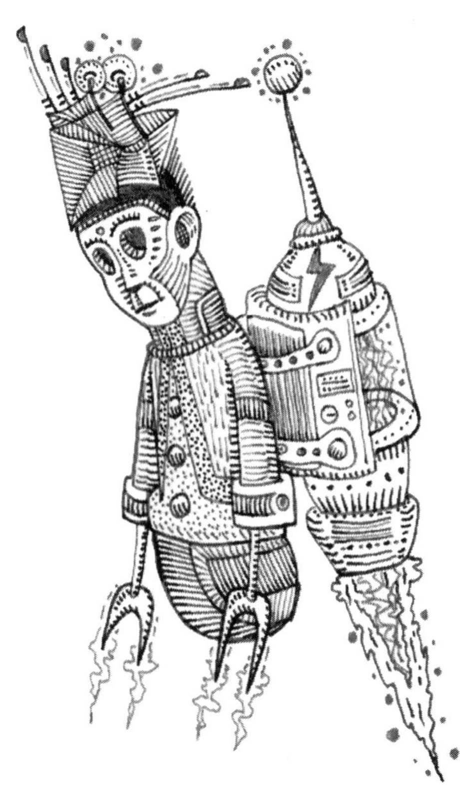

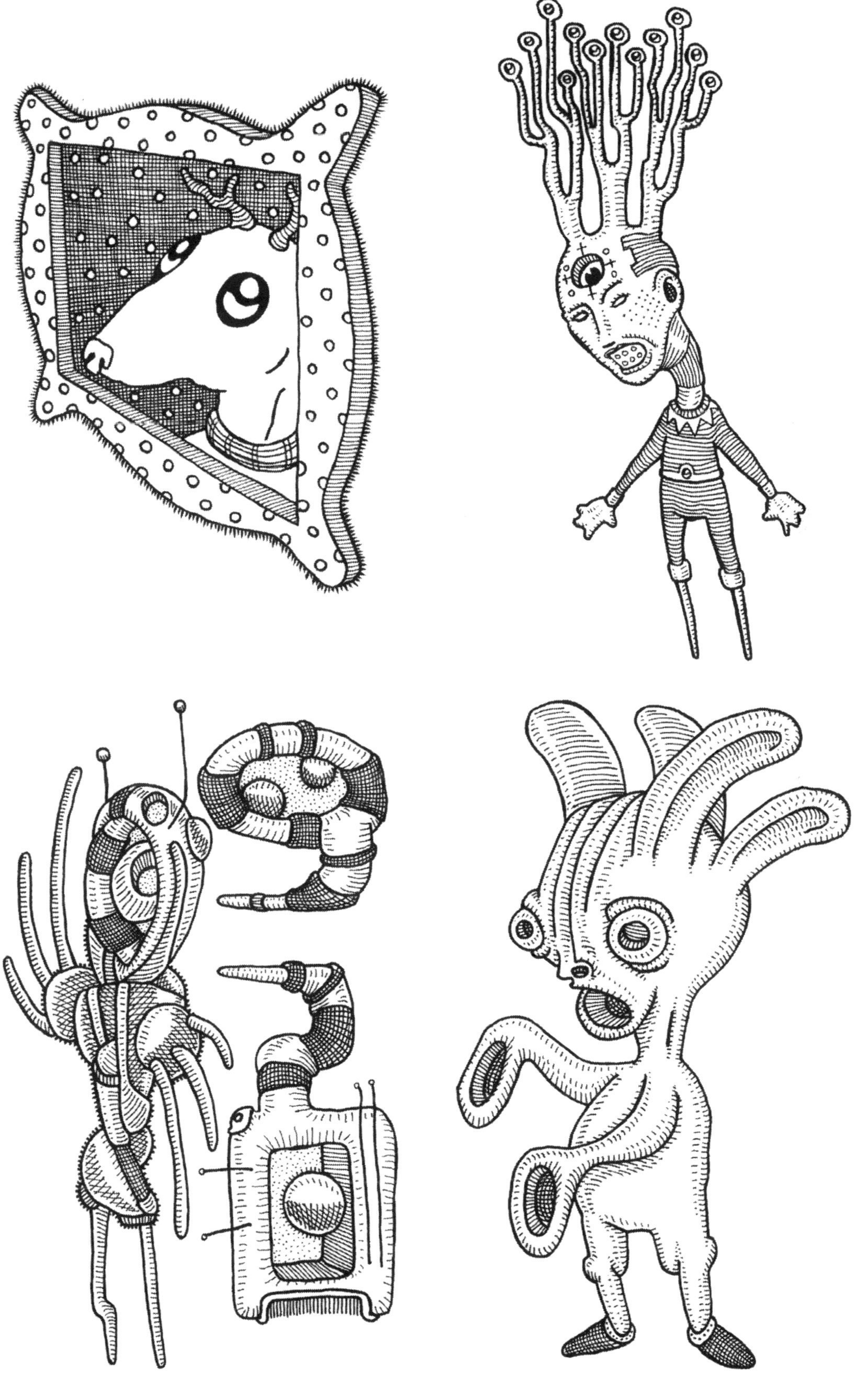

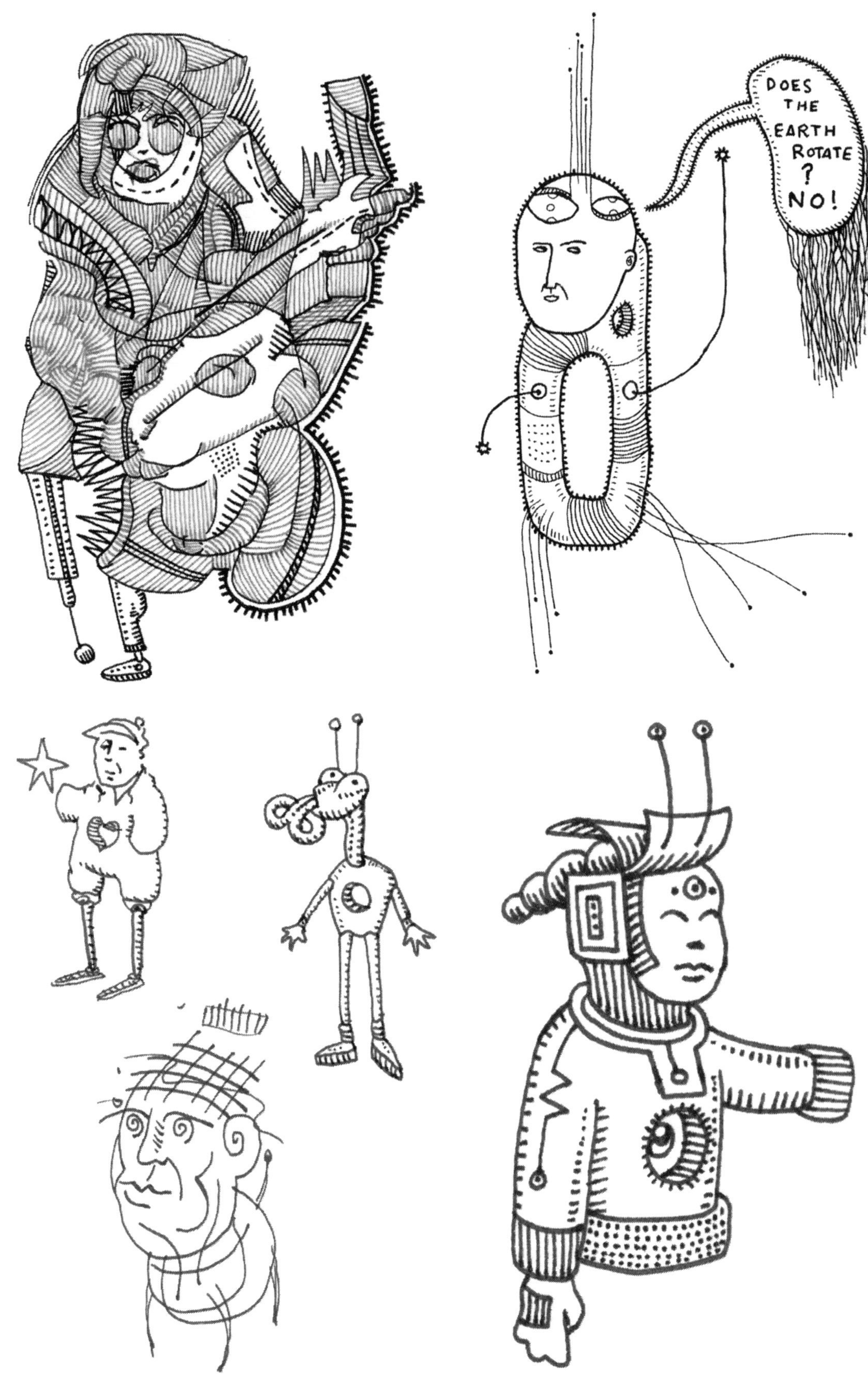
DOES THE EARTH ROTATE ? NO!

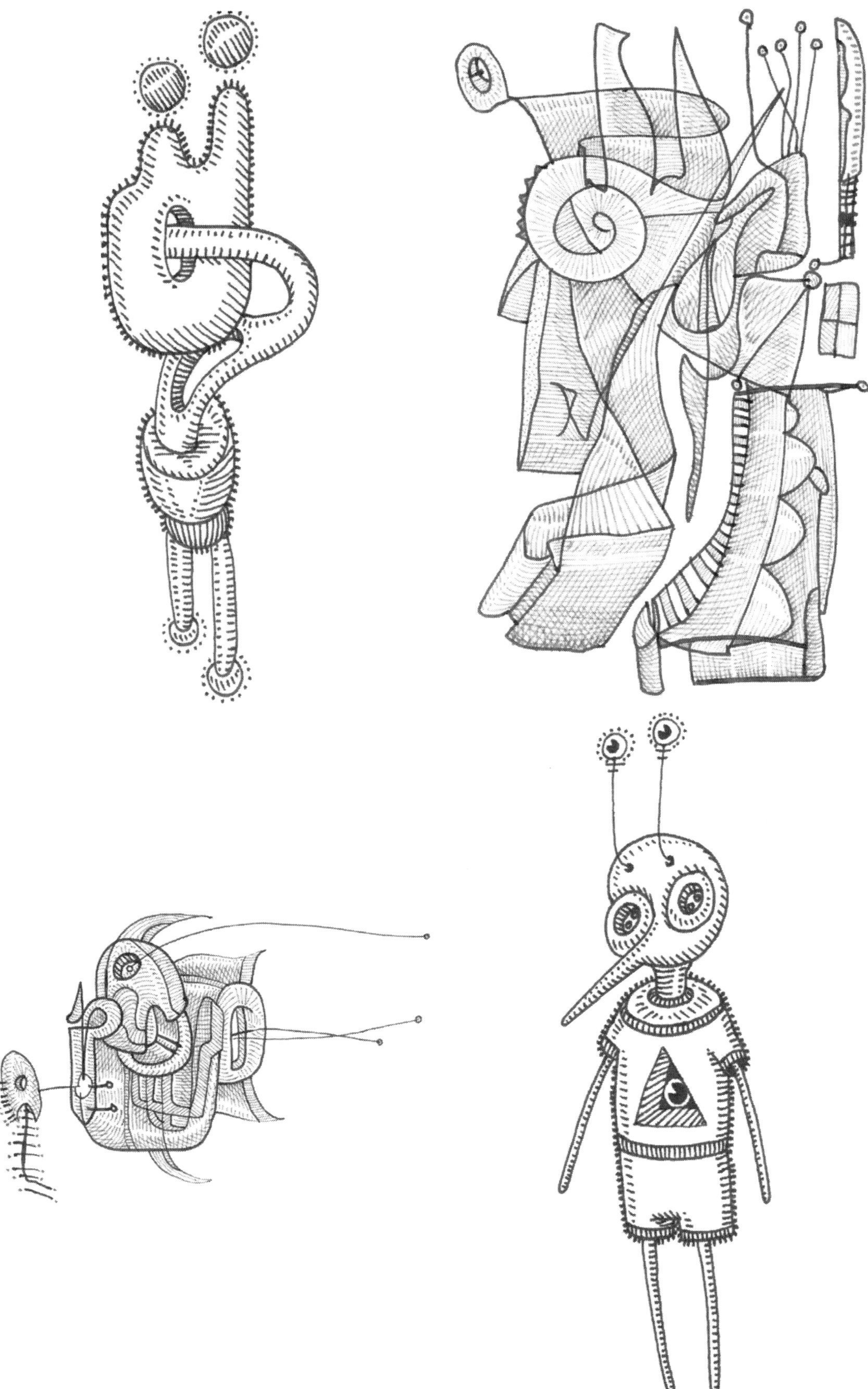

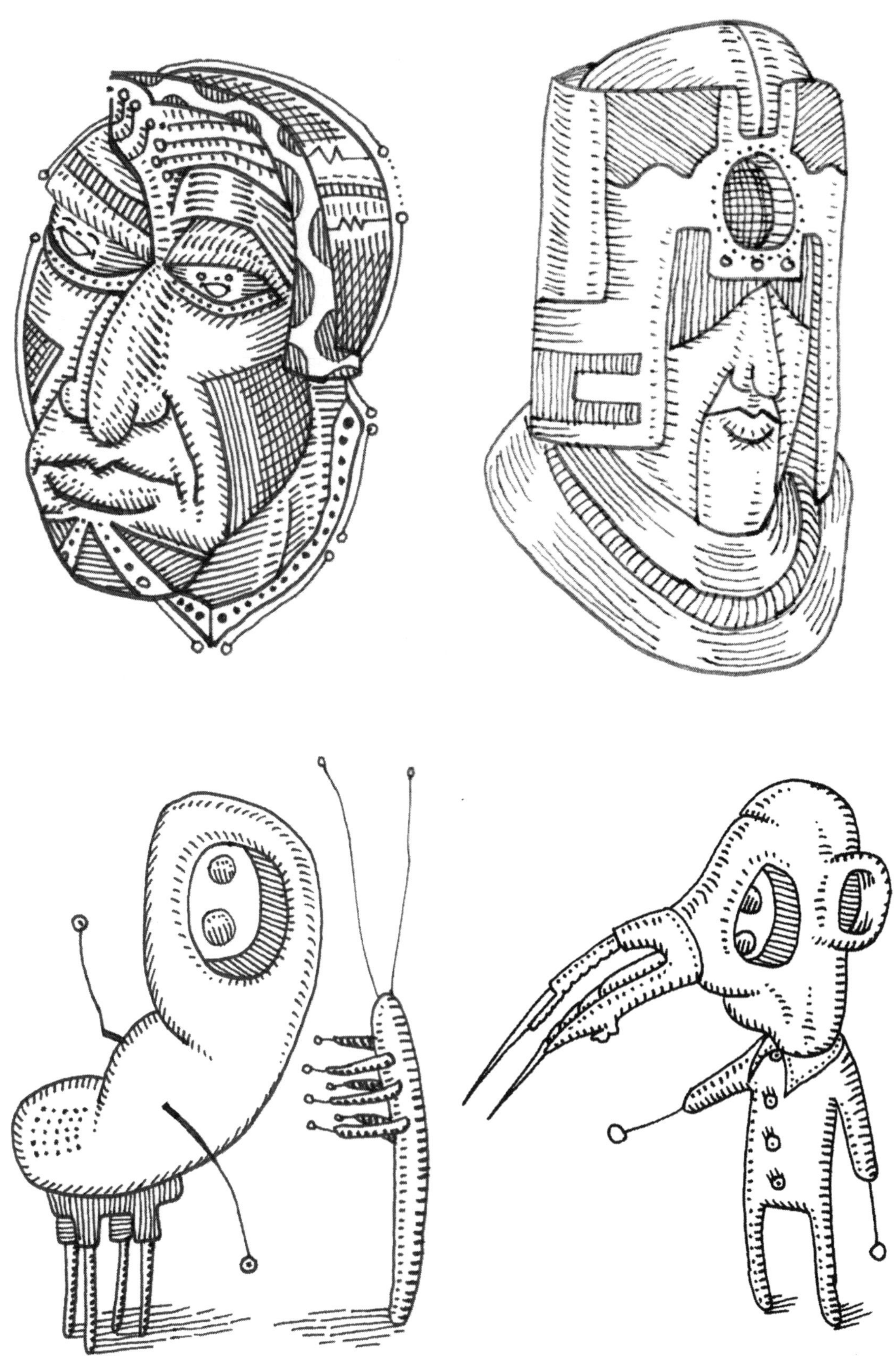

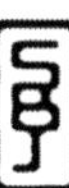

Made in the USA
Monee, IL
06 October 2024

66594567R00219